W9-BKD-395

The Essay Connection

Readings for Writers

Ninth Edition

Lynn Z. Bloom
The University of Connecticut

Australia • Brazil • Japan • Korea • Mexico • Singapore • Spain • United Kingdom • United States

The Essay Connection, Ninth Edition

Lynn Z. Bloom

Senior Publisher: Lyn Uhl

Acquisitions Editor: Kate Derrick

Development Editor: Amy Gibbons

Senior Assistant Editor: Kelli Strieby

Marketing Manager: Jenn Zourdos

Marketing Coordinator: Ryan Ahern

Marketing Communications Manager: Stacey Purviance Taylor

Associate Content Project Manager: Anne Finley

Senior Art Director: Jill Ort

Print Buyer: Marcia Locke

Permissions Editor: Katie Huha

Production Service: Elm Street Publishing Services

Photo Manager: Jennifer Meyer Dare

Photo Researcher: Bruce Carson

Cover Designer: Wing Ngan

Cover Image: © Luis Veiga/ The Image Bank, Getty Images

Compositor: Integra Software Services Pvt. Ltd.

© 2010, 2007 Wadsworth, Cengage Learning

ALL RIGHTS RESERVED. No part of this work covered by the copyright herein may be reproduced, transmitted, stored, or used in any form or by any means graphic, electronic, or mechanical, including but not limited to photocopying, recording, scanning, digitizing, taping, Web distribution, information networks, or information storage and retrieval systems, except as permitted under Section 107 or 108 of the 1976 United States Copyright Act, without the prior written permission of the publisher.

For product information and technology assistance, contact us at **Cengage Learning Academic Resource Center, 1-800-423-0563**

For permission to use material from this text or product, submit all requests online at **www.cengage.com/permissions.** Further permissions questions can be e-mailed to **permissionrequest@cengage.com.**

Library of Congress Control Number: 2008941713

ISBN-13: 978-0-547-19077-8

ISBN-10: 0-547-19077-8

Wadsworth
20 Channel Center St.
Boston, MA 02210
USA

Cengage Learning products are represented in Canada by Nelson Education, Ltd.

For your course and learning solutions, visit **www.cengage.com.**

Purchase any of our products at your local college store or at our preferred online store **www.ichapters.com.**

Printed in the United States of America
1 2 3 4 5 6 7 13 12 11 10 09

Contents

Topical Table of Contents *xiv*

Preface *xxi*

PART I *ON WRITING* 1

1. Writers in Process: Speaking, Reading, Imagining 1

AMY TAN, "Mother Tongue" 12

"I spend a great deal of my time thinking about the power of language—the way it can evoke an emotion, a visual image, a complex idea, or a simple truth. Language is the tool of my trade. And I use them all—all the Englishes I grew up with."

Reading Icons 19

RODIN, "The Thinker" (PHOTO) 19

MIKE PETERS, "Mother Goose and Grimm" (CARTOON) 19

MIKE D'ANGELO, "Do-It-Yourself Emoticons" 20

ELIE WIESEL, "Why I Write: Making No Become Yes" 21

"But for the survivor, writing is not a profession, but an occupation, a duty. Camus calls it 'an honor.' . . . Not to transmit an experience is to betray it. . . . [I write] to help the dead vanquish death."

JOAN DIDION, "Life Changes Fast" 28

"Life changes fast. Life changes in the instant. You sit down to dinner and life as you know it ends."

2. The Writing Process: Warmup, Vision, Re-Vision 33

STEPHEN KING, "A door . . . you are willing to shut" 39

"If possible, there should be no telephone in your writing room, certainly no TV or videogames for you to fool around with. . . . When you write, you want to get rid of the world, do you not? . . . When you're writing, you're creating your own worlds."

ORHAN PAMUK, "My Father's Suitcase" 42

"My real fear, the crucial thing that I did not wish to know or discover, was the possibility that my father might be a good writer. I couldn't open my

✧ Student writings.

father's suitcase [which held his manuscripts] because I feared this. Even worse, I couldn't even admit this to myself openly."

WILLIAM LEAST HEAT-MOON, "A List of Nothing in Particular" 48

"To say nothing is out here is incorrect; to say the desert is stingy with everything except space and light, stone and earth is closer to the truth."

DONALD M. MURRAY, "The Maker's Eye: Revising Your Own Manuscripts" 53

"When students complete a first draft, they consider the job of writing done . . . When professional writers complete the first draft, they usually feel they are at the start of the writing process. When a draft is completed, the job of writing can begin."

College Admissions Essays 63

RACHEL TOOR, "Which of These Essay Questions Is the Real Thing?" 63

"Please tell us what you do in your free time."
"If you were a vegetable, which vegetable would you be?"
"Please tell us why you want to attend Fancy Pants University."

✧ **ALEXANDER J. G. SCHNEIDER,** "What I Really Wanted to Write in My Admissions Essays" 66

"Essay 1: Explain . . . what you would like to do in college. What I wanted to say: ' . . . Are you delusional enough to actually believe you're going to get one honest heartfelt answer to this question?' "

PART II *DETERMINING IDEAS IN A SEQUENCE* 70

3. Narration 70

TIM O'BRIEN, "How to Tell a True War Story" (SHORT STORY) 76

"A true war story is never moral. It does not instruct, nor encourage virtue, nor suggest models of proper human behavior. . . . If a story seems moral, do not believe it."

SHERMAN ALEXIE, "What Sacagawea Means to Me" 84

"In the future, every U.S. citizen will get to be Sacagawea for fifteen minutes. For the low price of admission, every American, regardless of race, religion, gender, and age, will climb through the portal into Sacagawea's Shoshone Indian brain."

FREDERICK DOUGLASS, "Resurrection" 88

"You have seen how a man was made a slave; you shall see how a slave was made a man."

ART SPIEGELMAN, "Mein Kampf (My Struggle)" (GRAPHIC ESSAY) 95

"It's all a matter of record: I made a comic book about it . . . you know . . . the one with Jewish mice and Nazi cats. . . . You've gotta boil everything down to its essence in comix . . . "

LINDA HOGAN, "Waking" 98

"I was a sleeper for three weeks [after a car accident] and sometimes still. . . . Something else owns this mind, this awakening, and it is a mystery, as if the soul lives larger than the human knows or thinks. Morning after morning has been my world . . . everything newly seen."

ANNE FADIMAN, "Under Water" 102

On a summer wilderness program, the students in canoes on the Green River "saw the standing wave bend Gary's body forward at the waist, push his face underwater, stretch his arms in front of him, and slip his orange life jacket off his shoulders."

✧ **JASON VERGE,** "The Habs" 107

"I have spent so many years devoted to my Habs [the Montreal Canadiens] that it has become a religion to me. . . . How could I not love a sport that combines the gracefulness of ice skating and the brutality of football?"

4. Process Analysis 115

MEREDITH HALL, "Killing Chickens" (CREATIVE NONFICTION) 120

"I was killing chickens. It was my 38th birthday. My best friend, Ashley, had chosen that morning to tell me that my husband had slept with her a year before."

JOSEPH R. DiFRANZA, "Hooked from the First Cigarette" 124

"My research supports a new hypothesis asserting that limited exposure to nicotine—as little as one cigarette—can change the brain, modifying its neurons in a way that stimulates the craving to smoke."

SCOTT McCLOUD, "Character Design" (GRAPHIC ESSAY) 134

"There are three qualities that no great comics character can do without. An inner life—a unique history, world view and desires. Visual distinction—a distinct and memorable body, face and wardrobe. Expressive traits—traits of speech and behavior associated with that character."

SCOTT RUSSELL SANDERS, "The Inheritance of Tools" 143

"A house will stand, a table will bear weight, the sides of a box will hold together, only if the joints are square and the members upright. When the bubble is lined up between two marks etched in the glass tube of a level, you have aligned yourself with the forces that hold the universe together."

JAMES FALLOWS, "Tinfoil Underwear" 151

"How concerned . . . should ordinary computer users be about the evidence we leave behind when we browse, shop, communicate, and amuse ourselves on the Internet?"

NTOZAKE SHANGE, "What Is It We Really Harvestin' Here?" 158

"We got a sayin', 'The blacker the berry, the sweeter the juice,' which is usually meant as a compliment. To my mind, it also refers to the delectable treats we as a people harvested for our owners and for our own selves all these many years, slave or free."

✧ **NING YU,** "Red and Black, or One English Major's Beginning" 165

"In the late 1960s the [Communist] Revolution defined 'intellectual' as 'subversive.' So my father, a university professor . . . was regarded as a 'black' element, an enemy of the people. In 1967, our family was driven out of our university faculty apartment, and I found myself in a ghetto middle school, an undeserving pupil of the red expert Comrade Chang."

5. Cause and Effect 179

MARY OLIVER, "August" (POEM) 183

"When the blackberries hang swollen in the woods, in the brambles nobody owns, I spend all day . . . "

ZITKALA-SA, from *The School Days of an Indian Girl* 184

"I was . . . neither a wild Indian nor a tame one. This deplorable situation was the effect of my brief course in the East [four years in a boarding school run by whites]."

SCOTT RUSSELL SANDERS, "Under the Influence: Paying the Price of My Father's Booze" 192

"I am only trying to understand the corrosive mixture of helplessness, responsibility, and shame that I learned to feel as the son of an alcoholic."

ATUL GAWANDE, "On Washing Hands" 205

"The hardest part of the infection-control team's job . . . is not coping with the variety of contagions they encounter. . . . Instead, their greatest difficulty is getting clinicians like me to do the one thing that consistently halts the spread of infections: wash our hands."

CLIMATE CHANGE 214

WILLIAM COLLINS, ROBERT COLMAN, JAMES HAYWOOD, MARTIN R. MANNING, AND PHILIP MOTE, "The Physical Science behind Climate Change" 214

"Over the past 20 years, evidence that humans are affecting the climate has accumulated inexorably, and with it has come ever greater certainty across the scientific community . . . [of] the potential for much greater change in the future."

VACLAV HAVEL, "Our Moral Footprint" 226

"We can't endlessly fool ourselves that nothing is wrong and that we can go on cheerfully pursuing our wasteful lifestyles, ignoring the climate threats and postponing a solution."

✧ **MEGAN McGUIRE,** "Wake Up Call" 230

"Mom shows me the jeans she bought. I think about the pair I've been industriously saving for every week by cleaning an old lady's house; four floors for $13.50. I wonder how much hers cost."

PART III *CLARIFYING IDEAS* 240

6. Description 240

✧ **AMANDA N. CAGLE,** "On the Banks of the Bogue Chitto" (CREATIVE NONFICTION) 245

"This river is all the truth I've ever needed. It's where most of my family was born, where we were named, where we've found our food, where two of us have since chosen to die."

LINDA VILLAROSA, "How Much of the Body Is Replaceable?" (GRAPHIC ESSAY) 249

"From the top of the head to the tips of the toes, nearly every part of the body can be replaced by transplanting organs and tissues from one person to the next or substituting artificial parts for weakened or damaged tissue."

MARK TWAIN, "Uncle John's Farm" 252

"It was a heavenly place for a boy, that farm of my uncle John's. . . . I can see the farm yet, with perfect clearness. I can see all its belongings, all its details . . . "

MICHAEL POLLAN, "The Meal" 261

"The meal at the end of the industrial food chain that begins in an Iowa cornfield is prepared by McDonald's and eaten in a moving car."

KIM WARP, "Rising Sea Levels—An Alternative Theory" (CARTOON) 269

MARION NESTLE, "Eating Made Simple" 269

"Yes, nutrition advice seems endlessly mired in scientific argument, the self-interest of food companies and compromises by government regulators. Nevertheless, basic dietary principles are not in dispute: eat less; move more; eat fruits, vegetables and whole grains; and avoid too much junk food."

SUZANNE BRITT, "That Lean and Hungry Look" 281

"Thin people turn surly, mean and hard at a young age because they never learn the value of a hot-fudge sundae for easing tension."

ISTVAN BANYAI, "Inflation" (CARTOON) 285

✧ **MATT NOCTON,** "Harvest of Gold, Harvest of Shame" 285

"When [the tobacco harvester] gets off the bus he will find a pick-up truck parked nearby full of burlap and twine. He must tie this burlap around his waist as a source of protection against the dirt and rocks that he will be dragging himself through for the next eight hours."

7. Division and Classification 294

✧ **JENNY SPINNER,** "Together in the Old Square Print, 1976" (POEM) 299

"In just one hour, we will be led into different classrooms, our first separation since birth."

NATALIE ANGIER, "Why Men Don't Last: Self-Destruction as a Way of Life" 301

"[Men] are at least twice as likely as women to be alcoholics and three times more likely to be drug addicts. They have an eightfold greater chance than women do of ending up in prison. . . . [But] there is not a single, glib, overarching explanation for [these] sex-specific patterns . . . "

DEBORAH TANNEN, "Fast Forward: Technologically Enhanced Aggression" 307

"At the same time that technologically enhanced communication enables previously impossible loving contact, it also enhances hostile and distressing communication."

DAVID SEDARIS, "Make That a Double" 317

"Of all the stumbling blocks inherent in learning [French], the greatest for me is the principle that each noun has a corresponding sex that affects both its articles and its adjectives. Because it is a female and lays eggs, a chicken is masculine."

RICHARD RODRIGUEZ, "Family Values" 321

"I am sitting alone in my car, in front of my parents' house—a middle-aged man with a boy's secret to tell. . . . I hate the word gay *. . . I am happier with the less polite* queer*."*

GELAREH ASAYESH, "Shrouded in Contradiction" 329

"Even for a woman like me, who wears it with a hint of rebellion, hijab *is just not that big a deal. Except when it is."*

✧ **SUMBUL KHAN,** "Mirror, Mirror on the Wall, Who's the Fairest of Them All?" 332

"The hejaab *[used to be] for the woman and now it is the very thing our men strangle us with!"*

8. Definition 341

V. PENELOPE PELIZZON, "Clever and Poor" (POEM) 346

"She has always been clever and poor, . . . Clever are the six handkerchiefs stitched to the size of a scarf and knotted at her throat. Poor is the thin coat . . . "

NATALIE ANGIER, "A Supple Casing, Prone to Damage" 347

"You can no more survive without your skin than you can without your lungs. . . . Skin keeps the outside out . . . the inside in. With its rich array

of sensory receptors, skin is the bridge between private and public, wary self and beckoning other."

HOWARD GARDNER, "Who Owns Intelligence?" 350

"What is intelligence? How ought it to be assessed? And how do our notions of intelligence fit with what we value about human beings?" By proposing many intelligences—including moral intelligence—"experts are competing for the 'ownership' of intelligence in the next century."

JOHN HOCKENBERRY, from *Moving Violations* 364

"I am a gimp, crip, physically challenged, differently abled, paralyzed. I am a T-5 para. I am sick. I am well."

BRIAN DOYLE, "Joyas Voladoras" 372

"So much held in a heart in a lifetime. So much held in a heart in a day, an hour, a moment. We are utterly open with no one, in the end—not mother and father, not wife or husband, not lover, not child, not friend. We open windows to each but we live alone in the house of the heart."

LYNDA BARRY, "Common Scents" (GRAPHIC ESSAY) 375

"I have always noticed the smell of other people's houses, but when I was a kid I was fascinated by it. No two houses ever smelled alike, even if the people used the same air freshener."

✧ **CHRISTOPHER LaCASSE,** "Hegemony" 387

"The [Iraqi] child, stone in hand, cocked back and ready to fire, his knuckles white with a tight grip. . . . Other children—swimming around him, their chants a maddening blur: a dream sequence—a mob scene. Jeff, spinning, turning: the big gun tilted toward the crowd."

9. Comparison and Contrast 396

ELIZABETH TALLENT, "No One's a Mystery" (FICTION) 400

"Like I know what you'll be writing in that diary. . . . Tonight you'll write, 'I love Jack.' . . . In two years you'll write, 'I wonder what that old guy's name was, the one with . . . the filthy dirty pickup truck and time on his hands.'"

DEBORAH TANNEN, "Communication Styles" 402

"Women who go to single-sex schools do better in later life, and . . . when young women sit next to young men in classrooms, the males talk more."

ROZ CHAST, "An Excerpt from Men Are from Belgium, Women Are from New Brunswick" (GRAPHIC ESSAY) 408

When men say "Did you use a recipe?" they actually mean "Did you just throw all this stuff together randomly, or what?"

SHERRY TURKLE, "How Computers Change the Way We Think" 411

"The tools we use to think change the ways in which we think. . . . we are all computer people now."

BEN STEIN, "Connected, Yes, But Hermetically Sealed" 418

"All kinds of devices, like the BlackBerry, the iPhone and the Voyager . . . are the chains with which we have bound ourselves, losing much of our solitude and our ability to see the world around and inside us. . . . The cellphone and the P.D.A. have basically replaced thought."

CHARLES C. MANN, "Forever Young" 421

"In the past century U.S. life expectancy has climbed from forty-seven to seventy-seven, increasing by nearly two thirds. . . . [The likely result will be] a tripartite society: the very old and very rich on top . . . a mass of the ordinary old . . . and the diminishingly influential young."

✧ **MICHAEL BENEDETTO,** "Home Away from Home" 436

"Working the night shift was a challenge. . . . You have to make the transition to this vampire lifestyle, sleeping with the shades drawn all day, being removed from the rest of regular society."

PART IV *ARGUING DIRECTLY AND INDIRECTLY* 442

10. Appealing to Reason: Deductive and Inductive Arguments 442

MARILYN NELSON, "Friends in the Klan" (POEM) 448

" . . . the Veterans' Administration, to save face, opened in Tuskegee a brand-new hospital, for Negroes only. Under white control."

THOMAS JEFFERSON, "The Declaration of Independence" 450

" . . . to secure these rights [Life, Liberty and the pursuit of Happiness], Governments are instituted among Men deriving their just powers from the consent of the governed."

MARTIN LUTHER KING, JR. "Letter from Birmingham Jail" 455

"Injustice anywhere is a threat to justice everywhere. We are caught in an inescapable network of mutuality, tied in a single garment of destiny. Whatever affects one directly, affects all indirectly."

JARED DIAMOND, "The World as a Polder" 472

"Our world society is presently on a non-sustainable course," facing twelve major and interrelated problems that "are like time bombs with fuses of less than 50 years."

Cartoon Arguments 485

EVAN EISENBERG, "Dialogue Boxes You Should Have Read More Carefully" (GRAPHIC ESSAY) 485

"Are you sure you want to restart your computer now? If you do, all open applications will be closed and the Windows operating system will be bundled with the genetic code of your future offspring."

MARISA ACOCELLA MARCHETTO, "Why Haven't We Won the War on Cancer?" (OP ART) 487

Whereas cancer research is funded at $11.5 billion, Americans spend "$68 billion on sodas that make us fat. Money is so tight that only 18% of government grant applications . . . get funded."

ROBERT REICH, "The Global Elite" 489

" . . . the top fifth of working Americans [takes] home more money than the other four-fifths put together. . . . The fortunate fifth is quietly seceding from the rest of the nation."

✧ **MATTHEW ALLEN,** "The Rhetorical Situation of the Scientific Paper and the 'Appearance' of Objectivity" 500

" . . . the writer [of the scientific paper] persuades his or her audience largely through the appearance of objectivity."

11. Appealing to Emotion and Ethics 513

SEAMUS HEANEY, "Horace and the Thunder" (POEM) 517

"Anything can happen, the tallest things Be overturned, those in high places daunted, Those overlooked regarded."

ABRAHAM LINCOLN, "The Gettysburg Address" 518

"Four score and seven years ago our fathers brought forth on this continent, a new nation, conceived in liberty, and dedicated to the proposition that all men are created equal."

SOJOURNER TRUTH, "Ain't I a Woman?" 520

"I have ploughed and planted, and gathered into barns, and no man could head me! And ain't I a woman? I could work as much and eat as much as a man—when I could get it—and bear the lash as well! And ain't I a woman?"

JONATHAN SWIFT, "A Modest Proposal" 522

"I have been assured . . . that a young healthy child well nursed is at a year old the most delicious, nourishing, and wholesome food, whether stewed, roasted, baked, or boiled . . . "

Ethical Arguments: Visual Versions 532

OPEN, "Introducing NEW GoValue!™ Service" (OP ART) 532

"Do flight attendants bug you during a flight? Well, we got rid of them."

GARRY TRUDEAU, "Doonesbury" (CARTOON) 533

"[Our founder] foresaw a time when students wouldn't just need Sunday off . . . but would start partying on Wednesday night."

PETER SINGER, "The Singer Solution to World Poverty" 534

"Whatever money you're spending on luxuries, not necessities, should be given away [to the poor]. . . . If we don't do [this] . . . we are failing to live a morally decent life . . . "

✧ **SHERYL KENNEDY,** "About Suffering" 542

The young Staff Sergeant, one leg amputated, "wanted me to make sure that people knew that he is one of roughly twenty thousand men and women maimed by the [Iraq] war thus far [2006]."

PART V CONTROVERSY IN CONTEXT 551

12. Identity 551

JUDITH HALL, "Perilous Riddle" (POEM) 557

"If I am a riddle, I am not a man. If I am a man, I am not a riddle."

E. B. WHITE, "Democracy" 558

"Democracy is the recurrent suspicion that more than half of the people are right more than half of the time."

BARACK OBAMA, "To Form a More Perfect Union" 559

"We may have different stories, but we hold common hopes . . . we may not look the same and we may not have come from the same place, but we all want to move in the same direction—towards a better future for our children and our grandchildren."

BILL McKIBBEN, "Designer Genes" 571

"'Suppose parents could add thirty points to their child's IQ? . . . Wouldn't you want to do it?' . . . Deciding not to soup them up . . . well, it could come to seem like child abuse."

PHOTO ESSAY: THE ENVIRONMENT: SAVE IT OR LOSE IT

VIRGINIA POSTREL, "The Truth About Beauty" 583

"Dove is peddling the crowd-pleasing notions that beauty is a media creation, that recognizing plural forms of beauty is the same as declaring every woman beautiful, and that self-esteem means ignoring imperfections."

ERIC LIU, "Notes of a Native Speaker" 589

"I was keenly aware of the unflattering mythologies that attach to Asian Americans. . . . The irony is that in working so duteously to defy stereotype, I became a slave to it."

MICHAEL J. BUGEJA, "Facing the Facebook" 600

"Increasingly . . . our networks are being used to entertain members of 'the Facebook Generation' who text-message during class, talk on their cellphones during labs, and listen to iPods rather than guest speakers in the wireless lecture hall."

✧ **ZARA RIX,** "Corporality" 605

"I use my body to map who I am."

13. World Peace: Nobel Peace Prize Speeches 616

AL GORE, "A Planetary Emergency" (2007) 618

"So today, we dumped another 70 million tons of global-warming pollution into the thin shell of atmosphere surrounding our planet, as if it were an open sewer. . . . As a result, the earth has a fever. And the fever is rising. . . . We are what is wrong, and we must make it right."

WANGARI MAATHAI, "The Green Belt Movement" (2004) 620

"As we progressively understood the causes of environmental degradation, we saw the need for good governance. Indeed, the state of any country's environment is a reflection of the kind of governance in place, and without good governance there can be no peace."

KOFI ANNAN, "The United Nations in the 21st Century" (2001) 625

The United Nations, "founded on the principle of the equal worth of every human being," has "three key priorities for the future: eradicating poverty, preventing conflict, and promoting democracy."

NELSON MANDELA AND FREDERIK WILLEM DE KLERK, "The End of Apartheid" and "Reformation and Reconciliation in South Africa" (1993) 629

" . . . we shall, together, rejoice in a common victory over racism, apartheid and white minority rule."

"The road ahead is still full of obstacles and, therefore, dangerous. There is, however, no question of turning back."

AUNG SAN SUU KYI, "The Revolution of Spirit" (1991) 634

"To live the full life . . . one must have the courage to bear the responsibility of the needs of others . . . one must want to bear this responsibility."

RIGOBERTA MENCHÚ TUM, "Five Hundred Years of Mayan Oppression" (1992) 638

"Who can predict what other great scientific conquests and developments these [Mayan] people could have achieved, if they had not been . . . subjected to an ethnocide that affected nearly 50 million people in the course of 500 years."

THE 14TH DALAI LAMA (TENZIN GYATSO), "Inner Peace and Human Rights" (1989) 641

"Peace . . . starts with each one of us. When we have inner peace, we can be at peace with those around us. When our community is in a state of peace, it can share that peace with neighbouring communities . . . "

Glossary 648

Credits 658

Topical Table of Contents

IDENTITY

AMY TAN, "Mother Tongue" 12
✧ **RACHEL TOOR,** "Which One of These Essay Questions Is the Real Thing?" 63
✧ **ALEXANDER J. G. SCHNEIDER,** "What I Really Wanted to Write in My Admissions Essays" 66
SHERMAN ALEXIE, "What Sacagawea Means to Me" 84
FREDERICK DOUGLASS, "Resurrection" 88
JAMES FALLOWS, "Tinfoil Underwear" 151
✧ **NTOZAKE SHANGE,** "What Is It We Really Harvestin' Here?" 158
✧ **NING YU,** "Red and Black, or One English Major's Beginning" 165
ZITKALA-SA, from *The School Days of an Indian Girl* 184
✧ **AMANDA N. CAGLE,** "On the Banks of the Bogue Chitto" 245
LINDA VILLAROSA, "How Much of the Body Is Replaceable?" 249
SUZANNE BRITT, "That Lean and Hungry Look" 281
NATALIE ANGIER, "Why Men Don't Last: Self-Destruction as a Way of Life" 301
RICHARD RODRIGUEZ, "Family Values" 321
GELAREH ASAYESH, "Shrouded in Contradiction" 329
✧ **SUMBUL KHAN,** "Mirror, Mirror on the Wall, Who's the Fairest of Them All?" 332
V. PENELOPE PELIZZON, "Clever and Poor" 346
HOWARD GARDNER, "Who Owns Intelligence?" 350
JOHN HOCKENBERRY, from *Moving Violations* 364
LYNDA BARRY, "Common Scents" 375
DEBORAH TANNEN, "Communication Styles" 402
ROZ CHAST, "An Excerpt from Men Are from Belgium, Women Are from New Brunswick" 408
SHERRY TURKLE, "How Computers Change the Way We Think" 411
BEN STEIN, "Connected, Yes, But Hermetically Sealed" 418
CHARLES C. MANN, "Forever Young" 421
MARTIN LUTHER KING, JR., "Letter from Birmingham Jail" 455
SOJOURNER TRUTH, "Ain't I a Woman?" 520
JONATHAN SWIFT, "A Modest Proposal" 522
✧ **SHERYL KENNEDY,** "About Suffering" 542
JUDITH HALL, "Perilous Riddle" 557
E. B. WHITE, "Democracy" 558
BARACK OBAMA, "To Form a More Perfect Union" 559
BILL McKIBBEN, "Designer Genes" 571
VIRGINIA POSTREL, "The Truth About Beauty" 583
ERIC LIU, "Notes of a Native Speaker" 589
MICHAEL J. BUGEJA, "Facing the Facebook" 600
WANGARI MAATHAI, "The Green Belt Movement" 620
RIGOBERTA MENCHÚ TUM, "Five Hundred Years of Mayan Oppression" 638

✧ Student writings.

GROWING UP/FAMILIES/HERITAGE

AMY TAN, "Mother Tongue" 12
ELIE WIESEL, "Why I Write: Making No Become Yes" 21
ORHAN PAMUK, "My Father's Suitcase" 42
SHERMAN ALEXIE, "What Sacagawea Means to Me" 84
FREDERICK DOUGLASS, "Resurrection" 88
ART SPIEGELMAN, "Mein Kampf (My Struggle)" 95
ANNE FADIMAN, "Under Water" 102
✧ **JASON VERGE,** "The Habs" 107
SCOTT RUSSELL SANDERS, "The Inheritance of Tools" 143
NTOZAKE SHANGE, "What Is It We Really Harvestin' Here?" 158
✧ **NING YU,** "Red and Black, or One English Major's Beginning" 165
ZITKALA-SA, from *The School Days of an Indian Girl* 184
SCOTT RUSSELL SANDERS, "Under the Influence: Paying the Price of My Father's Booze" 192
✧ **MEGAN McGUIRE,** "Wake Up Call" 230
✧ **AMANDA N. CAGLE,** "On the Banks of the Bogue Chitto" 245
MARK TWAIN, "Uncle John's Farm" 252
✧ **JENNY SPINNER,** "Together in the Old Square Print, 1976" 299
RICHARD RODRIGUEZ, "Family Values" 321
GELAREH ASAYESH, "Shrouded in Contradiction" 329
✧ **SUMBUL KHAN,** "Mirror, Mirror on the Wall, Who's the Fairest of Them All?" 332
V. PENELOPE PELIZZON, "Clever and Poor" 346
JOHN HOCKENBERRY, from *Moving Violations* 364
LYNDA BARRY, "Common Scents" 375
ELIZABETH TALLENT, "No One's a Mystery" 400
CHARLES C. MANN, "Forever Young" 421
BARACK OBAMA, "To Form a More Perfect Union" 559
BILL McKIBBEN, "Designer Genes" 571
VIRGINIA POSTREL, "The Truth About Beauty" 583
ERIC LIU, "Notes of a Native Speaker" 589
✧ **ZARA RIX,** "Corporality" 605

WORK AND PLAY

ELIE WIESEL, "Why I Write: Making No Become Yes" 21
JOAN DIDION, "Life Changes Fast" 28
ORHAN PAMUK, "My Father's Suitcase" 42
ANNE FADIMAN, "Under Water" 102
✧ **JASON VERGE,** "The Habs" 107
SCOTT McCLOUD, "Character Design" 134
SCOTT RUSSELL SANDERS, "The Inheritance of Tools" 143
NTOZAKE SHANGE, "What Is It We Really Harvestin' Here?" 158
ATUL GAWANDE, "On Washing Hands" 205
✧ **AMANDA N. CAGLE,** "On the Banks of the Bogue Chitto" 245
MARK TWAIN, "Uncle John's Farm" 252
✧ **MATT NOCTON,** "Harvest of Gold, Harvest of Shame" 285
DAVID SEDARIS, "Make That a Double" 317
BRIAN DOYLE, "Joyas Voladoras" 372
LYNDA BARRY, "Common Scents" 375

✧ **CHRISTOPHER LaCASSE,** "Hegemony" 387
BEN STEIN, "Connected, Yes, But Hermetically Sealed" 418
✧ **MICHAEL BENEDETTO,** "Home Away from Home" 436
SOJOURNER TRUTH, "Ain't I a Woman?" 520
GARRY TRUDEAU, "Doonesbury" 533

TURNING POINTS/WATERSHED EXPERIENCES

ELIE WIESEL, "Why I Write: Making No Become Yes" 21
JOAN DIDION, "Life Changes Fast" 28
TIM O'BRIEN, "How to Tell a True War Story" 76
FREDERICK DOUGLASS, "Resurrection" 88
LINDA HOGAN, "Waking" 98
ANNE FADIMAN, "Under Water" 102
MEREDITH HALL, "Killing Chickens" 120
JOSEPH R. DiFRANZA, "Hooked from the First Cigarette" 124
SCOTT RUSSELL SANDERS, "The Inheritance of Tools" 143
✧ **NING YU,** "Red and Black, or One English Major's Beginning" 165
ZITKALA-SA, from *The School Days of an Indian Girl* 184
✧ **MEGAN McGUIRE,** "Wake Up Call" 230
✧ **AMANDA N. CAGLE,** "On the Banks of the Bogue Chitto" 245
✧ **MATT NOCTON,** "Harvest of Gold, Harvest of Shame" 285
✧ **JENNY SPINNER,** "Together in the Old Square Print, 1976" 299
RICHARD RODRIGUEZ, "Family Values" 321
✧ **SUMBUL KHAN,** "Mirror, Mirror on the Wall, Who's the Fairest of Them All?" 332
V. PENELOPE PELIZZON, "Clever and Poor" 346
JOHN HOCKENBERRY, from *Moving Violations* 364
BRIAN DOYLE, "Joyas Voladoras" 372
✧ **CHRISTOPHER LaCASSE,** "Hegemony" 387
SHERRY TURKLE, "How Computers Change the Way We Think" 411
THOMAS JEFFERSON, "The Declaration of Independence" 450
MARTIN LUTHER KING, JR., "Letter from Birmingham Jail" 455
SEAMUS HEANEY, "Horace and the Thunder" 517
ABRAHAM LINCOLN, "The Gettysburg Address" 518
JONATHAN SWIFT, "A Modest Proposal" 522
✧ **SHERYL KENNEDY,** "About Suffering" 542
BARACK OBAMA, "To Form a More Perfect Union" 559
BILL McKIBBEN, "Designer Genes" 571
AL GORE, "A Planetary Emergency" 618
NELSON MANDELA AND FREDERIK WILLEM DE KLERK, "The End of Apartheid" and "Reformation and Reconciliation in South Africa" 629
RIGOBERTA MENCHÚ TUM, "Five Hundred Years of Mayan Oppression" 638

THE NATURAL WORLD/ECOLOGY

WILLIAM LEAST HEAT-MOON, "A List of Nothing in Particular" 48
ANNE FADIMAN, "Under Water" 102
NTOZAKE SHANGE, "What Is It We Really Harvestin' Here?" 158
MARY OLIVER, "August" 183
ZITKALA-SA, from *The School Days of an Indian Girl* 184
ATUL GAWANDE, "On Washing Hands" 205
WILLIAM COLLINS ET AL., "The Physical Science behind Climate Change" 214

VACLAV HAVEL, "Our Moral Footprint" 226
✧ **AMANDA N. CAGLE,** "On the Banks of the Bogue Chitto" 245
LINDA VILLAROSA, "How Much of the Body Is Replaceable?" 249
MARK TWAIN, "Uncle John's Farm" 252
MICHAEL POLLAN, "The Meal" 261
MARION NESTLE, "Eating Made Simple" 269
✧ **MATT NOCTON,** "Harvest of Gold, Harvest of Shame" 285
NATALIE ANGIER, "A Supple Casing, Prone to Damage" 347
HOWARD GARDNER, "Who Owns Intelligence?" 350
BRIAN DOYLE, "Joyas Voladoras" 372
CHARLES C. MANN, "Forever Young" 421
JARED DIAMOND, "The World as a Polder" 472
BILL McKIBBEN, "Designer Genes" 571
AL GORE, "A Planetary Emergency" 618
WANGARI MAATHAI, "The Green Belt Movement" 620

SCIENCE AND TECHNOLOGY

JOSEPH R. DiFRANZA, "Hooked from the First Cigarette" 124
JAMES FALLOWS, "Tinfoil Underwear" 151
ATUL GAWANDE, "On Washing Hands" 205
WILLIAM COLLINS ET AL., "The Physical Science behind Climate Change" 214
LINDA VILLAROSA, "How Much of the Body Is Replaceable?" 249
MICHAEL POLLAN, "The Meal" 261
MARION NESTLE, "Eating Made Simple" 269
DEBORAH TANNEN, "Fast Forward: Technologically Enhanced Aggression" 307
NATALIE ANGIER, "A Supple Casing, Prone to Damage" 347
HOWARD GARDNER, "Who Owns Intelligence?" 350
JOHN HOCKENBERRY, from *Moving Violations* 364
✧ **CHRISTOPHER LaCASSE,** "Hegemony" 387
SHERRY TURKLE, "How Computers Change the Way We Think" 411
CHARLES C. MANN, "Forever Young" 421
JARED DIAMOND, "The World as a Polder" 472
EVAN EISENBERG, "Dialogue Boxes You Should Have Read More Carefully" 485
MARISA ACOCELLA MARCHETTO, "Why Haven't We Won the War on Cancer?" 487
ROBERT REICH, "The Global Elite" 489
✧ **MATTHEW ALLEN,** "The Rhetorical Situation of the Scientific Paper and the 'Appearance' of Objectivity" 500
✧ **SHERYL KENNEDY,** "About Suffering" 542
BILL McKIBBEN, "Designer Genes" 571
VIRGINIA POSTREL, "The Truth About Beauty" 583
MICHAEL J. BUGEJA, "Facing the Facebook" 600
AL GORE, "A Planetary Emergency" 618

EDUCATION

AMY TAN, "Mother Tongue" 12
JOAN DIDION, "Life Changes Fast" 28
ORHAN PAMUK, "My Father's Suitcase" 42
✧ **ALEXANDER J. G. SCHNEIDER,** "What I Really Wanted to Write in My Admissions Essays" 66
RACHEL TOOR, "Which One of These Essay Questions Is the Real Thing?" 63

SHERMAN ALEXIE, "What Sacagawea Means to Me" 84
ANNE FADIMAN, "Under Water" 102
SCOTT RUSSELL SANDERS, "The Inheritance of Tools" 143
✧ **NING YU,** "Red and Black, or One English Major's Beginning" 165
ZITKALA-SA, from *The School Days of an Indian Girl* 184
ATUL GAWANDE, "On Washing Hands" 205
✧ **JENNY SPINNER,** "Together in the Old Square Print, 1976" 299
DAVID SEDARIS, "Make That a Double" 317
RICHARD RODRIGUEZ, "Family Values" 321
HOWARD GARDNER, "Who Owns Intelligence?" 350
LYNDA BARRY, "Common Scents" 375
ELIZABETH TALLENT, "No One's a Mystery" 400
DEBORAH TANNEN, "Communication Styles" 402
SHERRY TURKLE, "How Computers Change the Way We Think" 411
BEN STEIN, "Connected, Yes, But Hermetically Sealed" 418
MARISA ACOCELLA MARCHETTO, "Why Haven't We Won the War on Cancer?" 487
GARRY TRUDEAU, "Doonesbury" 533
✧ **SHERYL KENNEDY,** "About Suffering" 542
BILL McKIBBEN, "Designer Genes" 571
ERIC LIU, "Notes of a Native Speaker" 589
MICHAEL J. BUGEJA, "Facing the Facebook" 600

LANGUAGE, LITERATURE, AND THE ARTS

AMY TAN, "Mother Tongue" 12
ELIE WIESEL, "Why I Write: Making No Become Yes" 21
JOAN DIDION, "Life Changes Fast" 28
STEPHEN KING, "A door . . . you are willing to shut" 39
ORHAN PAMUK, "My Father's Suitcase" 42
WILLIAM LEAST HEAT-MOON, "A List of Nothing in Particular" 48
DONALD M. MURRAY, "The Maker's Eye: Revising Your Own Manuscripts" 53
TIM O'BRIEN, "How to Tell a True War Story" 76
LINDA HOGAN, "Waking" 98
SCOTT McCLOUD, "Character Design" 134
SCOTT RUSSELL SANDERS, "The Inheritance of Tools" 143
NTOZAKE SHANGE, "What Is It We Really Harvestin' Here?" 158
DAVID SEDARIS, "Make That a Double" 317
HOWARD GARDNER, "Who Owns Intelligence?" 350
DEBORAH TANNEN, "Communication Styles" 402
ROZ CHAST, "An Excerpt from Men Are from Belgium, Women Are from New Brunswick" 408
SHERRY TURKLE, "How Computers Change the Way We Think" 411
EVAN EISENBERG, "Dialogue Boxes You Should Have Read More Carefully" 485
✧ **MATTHEW ALLEN,** "The Rhetorical Situation of the Scientific Paper and the 'Appearance' of Objectivity" 500
SEAMUS HEANEY, "Horace and the Thunder" 517

HUMOR AND SATIRE

AMY TAN, "Mother Tongue" 12
MIKE PETERS, "Mother Goose and Grimm" 19
MIKE D'ANGELO, "Do-It-Yourself Emoticons" 20

WILLIAM LEAST HEAT-MOON, "A List of Nothing in Particular" 48
RACHEL TOOR, "Which One of These Essay Questions Is the Real Thing?" 63
✧ **ALEXANDER J. G. SCHNEIDER,** "What I Really Wanted to Write in My Admissions Essays" 66
SHERMAN ALEXIE, "What Sacagawea Means to Me" 84
ART SPIEGELMAN, "Mein Kampf (My Struggle)" 95
✧ **JASON VERGE,** "The Habs" 107
SCOTT McCLOUD, "Character Design" 134
NTOZAKE SHANGE, "What Is It We Really Harvestin' Here?" 158
MARK TWAIN, "Uncle John's Farm" 252
SUZANNE BRITT, "That Lean and Hungry Look" 281
ISTVAN BANYAI, "Inflation" 285
DAVID SEDARIS, "Make That a Double" 317
JOHN HOCKENBERRY, from *Moving Violations* 364
LYNDA BARRY, "Common Scents" 375
ELIZABETH TALLENT, "No One's a Mystery" 400
ROZ CHAST, "An Excerpt from Men Are from Belgium, Women Are from New Brunswick" 408
✧ **MICHAEL BENEDETTO,** "Home Away from Home" 436
MARILYN NELSON, "Friends in the Klan" 448
EVAN EISENBERG, "Dialogue Boxes You Should Have Read More Carefully" 485
SOJOURNER TRUTH, "Ain't I a Woman?" 520
JONATHAN SWIFT, "A Modest Proposal" 522
OPEN, "Introducing NEW GoValue!™ Service" 532
GARRY TRUDEAU, "Doonesbury" 533

CREATIVE WRITING/GRAPHIC ESSAYS

Graphic Essays/Graphic Argument

ART SPIEGELMAN, "Mein Kampf (My Struggle)" 95
SCOTT McCLOUD, "Character Design" 134
LINDA VILLAROSA, "How Much of the Body Is Replaceable?" 249
KIM WARP, "Rising Sea Levels—An Alternative Theory" 269
ISTVAN BANYAI, "Inflation" 285
LYNDA BARRY, "Common Scents" 375
ROZ CHAST, "An Excerpt from Men Are from Belgium, Women Are from New Brunswick" 408
EVAN EISENBERG, "Dialogue Boxes You Should Have Read More Carefully" 485
MARISA ACOCELLA MARCHETTO, "Why Haven't We Won the War on Cancer?" 487
OPEN, "Introducing NEW GoValue!™ Service" 532
GARRY TRUDEAU, "Doonesbury" 533

Creative Nonfiction

MEREDITH HALL, "Killing Chickens" 120
✧ **AMANDA N. CAGLE,** "On the Banks of the Bogue Chitto" 245

Fiction

TIM O'BRIEN, "How to Tell a True War Story" 76
ELIZABETH TALLENT, "No One's a Mystery" 400

Poetry

MARY OLIVER, "August" 183
✧ **JENNY SPINNER,** "Together in the Old Square Print, 1976" 299
V. PENELOPE PELIZZON, "Clever and Poor" 346
MARILYN NELSON, "Friends in the Klan" 448
SEAMUS HEANEY, "Horace and the Thunder" 517
JUDITH HALL, "Perilous Riddle" 557

Preface: Transforming a Textbook for a Transformed World

Like the symbolic bridge on the cover of this book, *The Essay Connection* attempts to span the distance between reading and writing and bring the two activities closer together. To read, to write is to be human, to find the voice, the power, and the authority to communicate. As we become immersed in a new century, the importance of communication—clear, elegant, to the point—has never been more important.

"Writing," observes Toni Morrison, "is discovery; it's talking deep within myself." In *The Essay Connection,* the voices in this conversation are many and varied—professional writers, experts in a variety of fields, and students with their own abilities and experiences, side by side. Their good writing is good reading in itself, provocative, elegant, engaging, sometimes incendiary. This writing is also a stimulus to critical thinking, ethical reflection, social and political analysis, humorous commentary—and decision-making, on how to live in the present and make meaningful contributions to life in the ever-changing yet uncertain future. These are among the many possibilities when students write essays of their own. This Ninth Edition is designed not only to keep up with major changes but also to anticipate them.

What's Familiar, What's New

In the spirit of renovating an elegant building, the changes made to this edition of *The Essay Connection* retain the fundamental character of its distinguished architecture while bringing the work fully into the present.

Reading Images

Photographs, illustrations, cartoons, and other graphics often travel in the company of words, and so they do in highly significant ways in the revised *Essay Connection,* holding up their share of the dialogue. This edition features more—and more diverse—visual elements than ever before, with more photographs accompanying individual essays, more visual arguments, and a brand new full color insert on ecological issues.

Graphic Essays, Cartoons, and Op-art Graphic essays are demanding and often more complicated than they appear to be at first glance. They tell a story, make a point—or more stories with more points—sometimes with no words at all, as in the cartoon narratives of Lynda Barry's "Common Scents," Art Spiegelman's "Mein Kampf," Roz Chast's "An Excerpt from Men Are from Belgium, Women Are from New Brunswick."

Some clusters of graphic works are chosen to reflect and refract on one another, forming a visual commentary in juxtaposition. Thus the cluster "Reading Icons" incorporates a photograph of sculptor Auguste Rodin's famous statue, the massive "Thinker," bent and brooding, with Mike Peters's good-natured cartoon sequence of three alternatives, "The Nail Biter," "The Thumb Sucker," and "The Nose Picker"—its meaning, and humor, dependent on the viewer's knowledge of the original. Another pair of brief graphic essays, Evan Eisenberg's "Dialogue Boxes You Should Have Read More Carefully" and Marisa Acocella Marchetto's "Why Haven't We Won the War on Cancer?," depict conflicts between ethical and economic perspectives on computer software monopolies and on medical research. Other cartoon sequences in juxtaposition offer ethical critiques: Open's op-art depiction of worsening constraints on air travel ("We've eliminated all cargo compartments . . ."), and Garry Trudeau's satire on student partying, now starting "on Wednesday night."

Photographs As Arguments, As Advocacy The diverse photographs in the Ninth Edition range from the historical (the escort of black children to a newly integrated school during the Civil Rights era) to the timeless (school children posing for a class photo) to the contemporary (a firefighter drinking from a hydrant in front of the collapsing World Trade Center; beachgoers sunbathing near a makeshift memorial to the Iraq War dead). No photograph, like no essay, is innocent: How do we read the T-shirt that declares "Nobody knows I'm gay"? All of the pictures in *The Essay Connection* can be interpreted literally but also gain meaning from their contexts. Thus Dorothea Lange's haunting photograph of the beautiful "Migrant Mother" surrounded by her children echoes scores of classical iconic Madonna-and-child paintings, transmuted into the harsh 1930s Depression era. Although questions and commentary accompany each image, readers are encouraged to bring their own understanding to the stories they tell.

Color Photo Essay The eight color photographs in the photo essay, *The Environment: Save It or Lose It*, illustrate the worldwide significance of ecological issues. The Grand Tetons reflected in a pristine lake look stunningly beautiful, as does an illuminated globe photographed from outer space, until we realize that its brightness comes from lights in heavily populated areas such as the one epitomized in the photograph of "Seven Million Londoners" at Oxford Circus. The insert shows that the term **ecology** itself is no longer value-free. For the other photographs illuminate the detrimental effects of contemporary civilization on the environment: adjacent sections of Haiti and the Dominican Republic, brown versus green; overcrowding at Yellowstone National Park that requires buffalo to cross the road, halting a line of tourists' cars; a mountain of wrecked cars—what will become of them? What, in fact, will become of

Earth itself, as the glaciers melt, the Amazon burns? These photographs ask the questions; international cooperation (or the lack thereof) will furnish the answers.

Other Readings

The readings in the Ninth Edition of *The Essay Connection* are a lively, varied, timely, and provocative blend of favorite essays, modern and contemporary works, and new selections by a wide range of writers in a wide range of genres, including creative nonfiction and poetry. The first two chapters address aspects of the writing process—"Writers in Process: Speaking, Reading, Imagining"—and the writing process itself—"Warmup, Vision, Re-Vision." The next nine are organized according to familiar rhetorical principles: *narration, process analysis, cause and effect, description, division and classification, definition, comparison and contrast,* and *argument* (which is covered in two separate chapters, dealing first with deductive and inductive arguments and then with emotional and ethical appeals). The last two chapters are mini-casebooks, brief collections of thematically related essays on *identity* and *world peace.*

New and Familiar Authors Among the essays new to this edition of *The Essay Connection* are those by Joan Didion, Atul Gawande, Al Gore, Vaclav Havel, Linda Hogan, Scott McCloud, Barack Obama, Michael Pollan, and Sojourner Truth. Significant representations of women, cultures, and writers who address issues of class, race, ethnicity, and disability have been retained; new are considerations of beauty, age, the environment, and health. Many favorite essays have been retained from the previous edition. Although humorous works by authors such as Mark Twain, Ntozake Shange, and David Sedaris signal the book's upbeat tone, they do not diminish the seriousness of its essential concerns or its underlying ethical stance.

Creative Nonfiction The label *creative nonfiction* makes explicit in this edition of *The Essay Connection* what real writers have known all along, that many writers use the techniques of fiction to tell true stories. As two distinguished pieces, student Amanda N. Cagle's "On the Banks of the Bogue Chitto" and Meredith Hall's "Killing Chickens" reveal, these techniques include a narrator or narrative voice, plot, characters, dialogue, and setting. Other autobiographical essays use these techniques to provide social commentary and critique with a human face, a human voice—Richard Rodriguez's "Family Values," Scott Russell Sanders's "Under the Influence: Paying the Price of My Father's Booze," and Dr. Martin Luther King, Jr.'s "Letter from Birmingham Jail."

Fiction There are two works of fiction in this edition of *The Essay Connection*: Elizabeth Tallent's "No One's a Mystery" and Tim O'Brien's

"How to Tell a True War Story," a chapter of his Vietnam War novel *The Things They Carried*. Readers believe that the creative nonfiction works by Cagle and Hall are true because the authors say so, even though these works read like stories. Fiction writers send the same signals: they use character, plot, dialogue, settings, and symbols to explore multiple themes in works we are not expected to regard as literally true, even though we may well have met characters like Tallent's nameless romantic teenage girl and joyriding Jack, her transient lover. Yet even while O'Brien is giving us advice on "How to Tell a True War Story," he is pointing out the ambiguity of the truth, the blurred line between fact and fiction, which concurrently compels our belief—and calls it into question.

Poetry The six poems in this new edition of *The Essay Connection* provide powerful, condensed, forthright commentary on the rhetorical theme of the chapters they begin, and on the topics discussed in the essays they accompany. All are by distinguished contemporary writers: Nobel Laureate Seamus Heaney's "Horace and the Thunder," commemorating 9/11; Mary Oliver's "August," about a happy immersion in summer's bounty; V. Penelope Pelizzon's "Clever and Poor," the story of her parents' deceptive courtship, cleverness concealing poverty; Judith Hall's "Perilous Riddle," on the ambiguous nature of identity; Marilyn Nelson's "Friends in the Klan," from a biographical series on George Washington Carver; and student Jenny Spinner's "Together in the Old Square Print, 1976," depicting her first day of school and first separation from her identical twin sister.

Mini-Casebooks Chapter 12 addresses "Identity": international, national, and individual. Who we are, as individuals, students, members of families, ethnicities, citizens of a particular place and of the world, comprises an identity that is ever changing as the world's values, priorities, and very survival are in flux. Chapter 13, on "World Peace," is composed of excerpts from Nobel Peace Prize acceptance speeches by men and women of global distinction who form an international spectrum of the brave, the bold, the morally beautiful. Their talks, like their works, are beacons of faith, hope, goodwill, and moral courage. Intended to provoke discussion and debate on substantial issues, the essays in these chapters reflect not only on one another, but also on many other essays throughout this book and on the illustrations as well, including those that comprise the color photo essay.

Student Authors Eleven essays, one creative nonfiction piece, and a poem are by students. Although all the works were written when the students were enrolled in American universities, the students themselves come from all over the United States and the world at large. They discuss a variety of compelling subjects: coming to terms with oneself; with one's parents—whether known or unknown, living, or dead—with one's ethnic, political, or religious background—African-American, Asian, Chinese, Jewish, Muslim, Native American—and with one's social and economic class. All provide examples of excellent writing that other students should find meaningful as models in form, technique, and substance.

Support for Critical Thinking, Reading, and Writing

The essays are placed in a context of materials designed to encourage reading, critical thinking, and good writing. The following materials reinforce *The Essay Connection's* pervasive emphasis on the process(es) of writing.

- **Topical Clusters.** Many readings are clustered thematically within the chapters to encourage dialogue and debate among authors, and among student readers and writers. For example, Chapter 5, "Cause and Effect," has a trio of essays on the problematic effects of adults imposing their wills and harsh behavior on young children: the whites who separated Zitkala-Sa and other Indian children from their homes and culture; Scott Russell Sanders's alcoholic father intermittently terrorizing his family; Megan McGuire's dual life with divorced parents, one responsible, though disabled, the other able-bodied but selfish and irresponsible. Chapter 6, "Description," pairs essays by Nestle and Pollan describing "Eating Made Simple" (and bad for you) with Britt's and Banyai's humorous commentaries on the bloated consequences. Other topics, reiterated and refracted in various chapters, include ecology, civil and human rights, war and peace, and—ever and always—how to read, write, and think with clarity, elegance, honesty.
- **Blended Essay Types.** It is essential to remember that because these are real essays by real writers, who use whatever writing techniques suit their purpose, there are very few "pure" types: they illustrate not only the rhetorical mode that is the focus of the chapter, but others as well. For instance, Scott Russell Sanders's "Under the Influence: Paying the Price of My Father's Booze," in the *cause and effect* chapter, also incorporates *descriptions* of his alcoholic father's behavior, an *explanation* and *analysis* of "the family secret," and a discussion of the *causes and effects* of his father's problem on his own life. That most essays are a mixture of types and techniques is reflected in the new category of questions incorporated into many of the study questions, *Mixed Modes*. Throughout the book, *Mixed Modes* should serve as a realistic reminder of the nature and the complexity of the works at hand.
- **Tables of Contents.** The main Table of Contents reflects the book's organization, by types of writing. The Topical Table of Contents offers an alternative organization by subject to provide numerous other possibilities for discussion and writing.

- **Chapter introductions.** These define the particular type of writing in the chapter and identify its purposes (descriptions, process analysis, etc.), uses, and typical forms. They also discuss the rhetorical strategies authors typically use in that type of writing (for instance, how to structure an argument to engage a hostile audience), illustrated with reference to essays in the chapter, summarized in a concluding checklist.
- **Author biographies.** These capsule biographies are intended to transform the writers from names into real people, focusing on how, why, and what the authors write.
- **Study questions.** These follow the essays and are intended to encourage thoughtful discussion and writing about *Content*, rhetorical *Strategies/Structures/Language*, and larger concerns. These are addressed by a series of new writing and discussion prompts: "Journal Writing"; "Dialogues," which call attention to similar themes or literary devices in the essay just read and one or more others; "Mixed Modes," which help students consider the diverse rhetorical concepts embedded in a single essay; and "Second Look," which put the focus on how the photographs, cartoons, and other visual elements in the book relate to the text selections and encourage students to analyze them as they would a written text.
- **Suggestions for Writing.** Each set of study questions ends with *Suggestions for Writing* pertinent to a given work. Most chapters end with a longer list of *Additional Topics for Writing* that encourage dialogue and debate about essays related in theme, technique, or mode. Often these incorporate **multiple strategies for writing in a given mode** and ways to avoid potential pitfalls.
- **Glossary.** The Glossary defines terms useful in discussing writing (analogy, argument, voice) with illustrations from the essays.

Companion Website for *The Essay Connection*, 9th Edition
www.cengage.com/english/bloomEC9e
The Essay Connection's companion website offers additional resources for writing and research, including author web links; visual literacy activities; an annotated student essay; interactive flashcards of glossary terms; and practice quizzes that test reading comprehension. Instructors are also able to access an online Instructor's Resource Manual and sample syllabi.

English21 for Composition
ISBN-10: 0495800392 | ISBN-13: 9780495800392 (2-Semester Printed Access Card)
ISBN-10: 0495800406 | ISBN-13: 9780495800408 (2-Semester Instant Access Code)
The largest compilation of online resources ever organized for composition and literature courses, **English21** is a complete online support system that weaves robust, self-paced instruction with interactive assignments.

English21 supports students through every step of the writing process, from assignment to final draft. It includes carefully crafted multimedia projects; a full interactive handbook including hundreds of animations, exercises, and activities; a complete research guide with animated tutorials and a link to Gale's InfoTrac® database; and a rich multimedia library with images, audio clips, video clips, stories, poems and plays. Access to **Personal Tutor**, an easy-access online environment with one-on-one tutoring and on-demand assignment help, is included with English21. To learn more, visit www.cengage.com/english21.

English21 Plus for Composition
ISBN-10: 0495800414 | ISBN-13: 9780495800415 (2-Semester Printed Access Card)
ISBN-10: 0495800422 | ISBN-13: 9780495800422 (2-Semester Instant Access Code)
Access to **English21 Plus** is available for a nominal fee when packaged with new copies of the text. **English21 Plus** includes all of the features mentioned above plus access to Wadsworth's **InSite for Writing and Research™** (described below). To learn more, visit www.cengage.com/english21.

Infotrac® College Edition with InfoMarks™
ISBN-10: 0534558534 | ISBN-13: 9780534558536
InfoTrac® College Edition, an online research and learning center, offers over 20 million full-text articles from nearly 6,000 scholarly and popular periodicals. The articles cover a broad spectrum of disciplines and topics—ideal for every type of researcher.

Wadsworth's InSite for Writing and Research™
ISBN-10: 1413009212 | ISBN-13: 9781413009217
This online writing and research tool includes electronic peer review, an originality checker, an assignment library, help with common grammar and writing errors, and access to InfoTrac® College Edition. Portfolio management gives you the ability to grade papers, run originality reports, and offer feedback in an easy-to-use online course management system. Using InSite's peer review feature, students can easily review and respond to their classmates' work. Other features include fully integrated discussion boards, streamlined assignment creation, and more. Visit www.cengage.com/insite to view a demonstration.

Turnitin® Originality Checker
ISBN-10: 1413030181 | ISBN-13: 9781413030181
This proven online plagiarism-prevention software promotes fairness in the classroom by helping students learn to correctly cite sources and allowing instructors to check for originality before reading and grading papers. Visit www.cengage.com/turnitin for more information.

Acknowledgments

The Essay Connection has, in various ways, been in the making for the past forty years, and I am particularly indebted to the candid commentaries of multitudes of writing teachers and students over the years whose preferences and perplexities have so significantly influenced both the shape and emphasis of this volume, and the process-oriented style of teaching that it reflects.

I am also indebted to the reviewers who contributed to the development of the Ninth Edition of *The Essay Connection*: Clair Berry, Southwest Tennessee Community College; Joseph Campbell, East Carolina University; Elizabeth D. Gruber, Lock Haven University of Pennsylvania; Rita Kranidis, Montgomery College–Takoma Park; Daniel Olson, North Harris College; and Scott D. Yarbrough, Charleston Southern University.

Their work has been supplemented by a series of superb research assistants: Denise M. Lovett, co-author of the Instructor's Guide; Kathrine Aydelott; Sarah Aguiar; Matthew Simpson; Laura Tharp; Ning Yu; and Valerie M. Smith. Lori Corsini-Nelson, office manager, cheerfully handled the paper flow. Former Houghton Mifflin editor Lisa Kimball and Cengage Learning editors Lyn Uhl, publisher; Kate Derrick, sponsoring editor; Amy Gibbons, development editor; and Anne Finley, associate content project manager, have aided the creation of this edition with goodwill, good humor, and good sense.

When the first edition of *The Essay Connection* was in process, my sons, Laird and Bard, were in high school. Over the intervening years they've earned doctorates (in biology and computer science), have married inspiring women, Sara (a U.S. attorney) and Vicki (a food scientist), and parented joyous children, Paul, Beth, and Rhys. An ever-active participant in the protracted process of making *The Essay Connection* more friendly to readers has been my writer-friendly husband, Martin Bloom, social psychologist, professor, world traveler, fellow author, and most recently, artist. He has provided a retentive memory for titles and key words that I've called out from an adjacent lane during our daily lap swims, homemade apple pies at bedtime, and all the comforts in between. My whole family keeps me cheerful; every day is a gift.

Lynn Z. Bloom

PART I: ON WRITING

Writers in Process: Speaking, Reading, Imagining

On Reading

Writing is a complicated process that involves reading—immersing oneself in others' ideas—whether you're reading a hardcopy book or a computer screen; whether you're looking at words or visual images such as photographs, cartoons, or graphic novels. Part of this intellectual context of reading involves evoking what you already know about the subject—from firsthand experience, hearsay, media presentations, or other reading. Reading also involves immersing yourself in the conventions of the genre: we read poetry, short stories, and creative nonfiction somewhat differently from the way we read essays. As you read, consider the following questions to get the most from the experience.

Who Is the Author?

- When did the author live? Where? Is the author's class, ethnic origin, gender or sexual preference, or regional or national background relevant to understanding this essay?
- What is the author's educational background? Job experience? Do these or other significant life experiences make him or her an authority on the subject of the essay?
- Does the author have political, religious, economic, cultural, or other biases that affect the essay's treatment of the subject? The author's credibility? The author's choice of language?

What Are the Context and Audience of the Essay?

- When was the essay first published? Is it dated, or is it still relevant?
- Where (in what magazine, professional journal, book, or website, if at all) was the essay first published?
- For what audience was the essay originally intended? How much did the author expect the original readers to know about the subject?

To what extent did the author expect the original readers to share his or her point of view? To resist that view?
- Why would the original audience have read this essay? What ideas on the subject were current at the time?
- What similarities and differences exist between the essay's original audience and the student audience now reading it?
- What am I as a student reader expected to bring to my reading of this essay? My own or others' beliefs, values, past history, personal experience? Other reading? My own writing, previous or in an essay I will write in response to the essay(s) I am reading?

What Are the Purposes of the Essay?

- Why did the author write the essay? To inform, entertain, describe, define, explain, argue, or for some other reason or combination of reasons?
- Is the purpose explicitly stated anywhere in the essay? If so, where? Is this the thesis of the essay? Or is the thesis different?
- If the purpose is not stated explicitly, how can I tell what the purpose is? Through examples? Emphasis? Tone? Other means?
- Does the form of the essay suit the purpose? Would other forms or combinations of forms have been more appropriate?

What Are the Strategies of the Essay?

- What does the author do to make the essay interesting? Is he or she successful?
- What organizational pattern (and subpatterns, if any) does the author use? How do these patterns fit the subject? The author's purpose?
- What emphasis do the organization and proportioning provide to reinforce the author's purpose?
- What evidence, arguments, and illustrations, verbal or graphic, does the author employ to illustrate or demonstrate the thesis?
- On what level of language (formal, informal, slangy) and in what tone (serious, satiric, sincere, etc.) does the author write?
- Have I enjoyed the essay or found it stimulating or otherwise provocative? Why or why not?
- If I disagree with the author's thesis or am not convinced by or attracted to the author's evidence, illustrations, or use of language, am I nevertheless impelled to continue reading? If so, why? If not, why not?

The ways we read and write, and how we think about the ways we read and write, have been dramatically altered in the past thirty years. The New Critics, whose views dominated the teaching of reading and writing during the early and mid-twentieth century, promoted a sense of the text as a static, often enigmatic entity, whose sleeping secrets awaited a master critic or brilliant teacher to arrive, like Prince Charming on a white horse, and awaken their meaning. The numerous courses and textbooks encouraging students to read for experience, information, ideas, understanding, and appreciation reflect that view.

Yet contemporary literary theory encourages the sense of collaboration among author, text, and readers to make meaning. How we interpret any written material, whether a recipe, computer manual, love letter, or Martin Luther King, Jr.'s "Letter from Birmingham Jail" (456–70) depends, in part, on our prior knowledge of the subject, our opinion of the author, our experience with other works of the genre under consideration (what other recipes, or love letters, have we known?), and the context in which we're reading. We read Dr. King's "Letter" differently today than when he wrote it, jailed in Birmingham in 1963 for civil rights protests; liberals read it differently than conservatives; African Americans may read it differently than whites, Southern or Northern. Where readers encounter a piece of writing greatly influences their interpretation, as well. Readers might read Dr. King's "Letter" as a document of news, history, social protest, argument, literary style—or some combination of these—depending on whether they encounter it in a newspaper of the time, in a history of the United States or of the civil rights movement, or in *The Essay Connection*.

A variety of critical theories reinforce the view that a work invites multiple readings, claiming that strong readers indeed bring powerful meanings to the texts they read. The pieces collected in *The Essay Connection*, supplemented by photographs, cartoons, and visual essays by Art Spiegelman (96–97), Linda Villarosa (250–51), and Lynda Barry (376–85), open up a world of possibilities in interpreting not only what's on the page, but also what is *not* on the page. What's there for the writer, as for the reader, is not just another story but an assemblage of stories, all that has occurred in one's life and thought, waiting to bleed through and into the paper on which these stories, in all their variations, will be told. Readers and writers alike are always in process, always in flux, no matter what their sources of inspiration or places to think.

There are many ways to learn a language and to learn to read, determined by age, culture, and physical and intellectual circumstances. Amy Tan's mother ("Mother Tongue" 13–17), Ning Yu ("Red and Black, or One English Major's Beginning" 166–74), and David Sedaris ("Make That a Double" 318–20) deal with issues and difficulties of learning to speak a new language and learning to "read" the culture embodied in that language. Sherman Alexie, in "What Sacagawea Means to Me" (85–87)—like Tan and Sedaris and a host of other writers throughout *The Essay Connection*—demonstrates the influences of our cultural heritage on providing not only the words but also our understanding of both the language and its cultural connotations. Writers, in any language, any culture are looking for ideal readers, people who share the author's attitude toward the subject and love the style, readers who, as novelist Eudora Welty says of her mother, "read Dickens in the spirit in which she would have eloped with him." Yet most writers can't count on such automatic adoration or agreement. So they load their work with information, evidence, appeals to ethics, the senses, the imagination (see Chapters 10 and 11) to win readers to their point of view.

Working with the conventions of a genre will soon become as automatic for experienced readers as working with the conventions of reading are for new readers. In English, these familiar conventions include reading from left to right, with pauses dictated, in part, by punctuation: short ones for commas, slightly longer ones for periods, perhaps a bit more time out at the end of the paragraph.

When several (or more) readers share a background, common values, and a common language, they may be considered a *discourse community*. In "Mother Tongue" (13–17), Amy Tan explores how her writing reflects her Chinese-American discourse community. She understands, and uses, "all the Englishes I grew up with"—one for formal writing, another for intimate conversation with Chinese family members, and a combination of public and private languages for storytelling. Tan also understands, very well, the conventions of a professional American discourse community. When she speaks to her mother's stockbroker (¶s 10–12) or hospital personnel (¶ 14), she knows that her impeccable standard English will get the respect—and results—that prejudice denies to her mother's Chinese-accented English.

What Is an Essay?

What do we talk about when we talk about essays? Just what are we reading and writing? As a rule, in both college and high school, we're writing either literary nonfiction or a more academic essay. Both do the following:

- Essays are *prose*—they may lack poetic meter and usually don't rhyme, but the sentences, paragraphs, and whole work flow from beginning to end.
- Essays usually focus on a central *theme* or *subject*.
- Essays are *short*, ranging from a single paragraph to a book chapter.
- Essays are *true*—hence the term "nonfiction." Essayists claim and readers believe that what they're reading is the truth.
- Thus essays *present evidence from real life or research* that either the author or the readers can verify.
- Essays are *organized into recognizable patterns*, such as definition, comparison and contrast, argument; *most of the time these patterns appear in combination and serve multiple purposes*. Thus Suzanne Britt's "That Lean and Hungry Look" (281–83) *describes* thin and fat people

through *comparison and contrast*, thereby *defining* each type as a way to *argue* that the fat are decidedly superior to the thin.

- The *essay's author has a point of view*, either expressed or implied, even if the author is unobtrusive or not identifiable as a character in the work (known as an authorial persona). This viewpoint governs the choice of evidence (and counterevidence), organization, and language. In general, the author is asking the reader to, in the words of Joan Didion, *"Listen to me, see it my way, change your mind."*

As later chapters will illustrate, much of your writing in college will be articles in the language and conventions of the particular subjects you study—critical interpretations of literature, position papers in philosophy or political science, interpretive presentations of information in history, case histories in psychology, business, or law, explanations of processes in computer science, psychology, or climate change. For instance, in "The Physical Science Behind Climate Change" (214–26) William Collins and his coauthors explain the numerous causes of climate change, both natural and human. Dr. Martin Luther King, Jr., in "Letter from Birmingham Jail" (456–70) uses evidence from world religions, his own life experience and that of numerous other African Americans, theology, history, and the law to make the case for civil disobedience. And in "Hooked from the First Cigarette" (124–33), Joseph R. DiFranza challenges common beliefs about nicotine addiction—the first puff leads immediately to addiction.

Articles such as these do not have to be dry or devoid of a point of view. For instance, the science writings of Atul Gawande (206–12), Natalie Angier (347–49), Sherry Turkle (411–17), and Bill McKibben (572–82) are known for their reader-friendly clarity as well as their absolute accuracy. We can count on them to have a point of view—Angier invariably favors what is moderate and healthful. Gawande writes to take the mystery out of medicine and to dispel its myths, as well as to provide commonsense solutions to familiar problems—such as in "On Washing Hands" (206–12): to prevent the spread of disease and infection, in hospitals and out, *wash your hands*! Even academic essays don't have to be deadly serious (or dull), plodding along under the weight of obscure jargon, as all of these essays indicate.

Why a person writes often determines his or her point of view on a particular subject. George Orwell claims that people write for four main reasons: "sheer egoism," "esthetic enthusiasm," "historical impulse," and—his primary motive—"political purpose, the desire to push the world in a certain direction."

In "Why I Write: Making No Become Yes" (22–27), Elie Wiesel interprets *"see it my way"* as the role of the writer as witness. The survivor of imprisonment in several Nazi concentration camps, Wiesel explains, "I was duty-bound to give meaning to my survival, to justify each moment of my life." In this eloquent essay Wiesel, winner of the 1986 Nobel Peace Prize, demonstrates his continuing commitment to make survivors, the entire world, continually remember the meaning of the Holocaust: "Why do I write? To wrench those victims from oblivion. To help the dead vanquish death." This purpose is also served by the photograph of the burning village in Darfur (see photo on 23).

In addition to articles, *The Essay Connection* includes many types of essays that include elements of creative nonfiction. These include *memoir* and *partial autobiography*, such as Scott Russell Sanders's "The Inheritance of Tools" (143–50); *character sketches*, like Amy Tan's "Mother Tongue" (13–17); *descriptions of a place*, as in William Least Heat-Moon's "A List of Nothing in Particular" (49–51), or of *an experience*, such as the excerpts from Zitkala-Sa's *The School Days of an Indian Girl* (184–90); *narratives of events*, including Frederick Douglass's account of how he stood up to his cruel overseer ("You have seen how a man was made a slave; you shall see how a slave was made a man.") (89–93); *interpretations of phenomena*, such as Scott Russell Sanders's "Under the Influence: Paying the Price of My Father's Booze" (192–203); and *social commentary*, such as Richard Rodriguez's "Family Values" (321–28) and Charles Mann's "Forever Young" (422–33).

Creative Nonfiction

Creative nonfiction (sometimes called literary nonfiction) does everything that essays in general do, but in ways that make the writing look like fiction. Creative nonfiction speaks through a human face, a human voice, and has the following characteristics:

- A conspicuous, individual recognizable *voice*—usually the voice of the *narrator or the central character*, who is often a conspicuous commentator or actor in the narrative. Sometimes more than one voice speaks—for example, when there are several characters or the narrator is at different stages of life, as in autobiographies.
- A *plot*, a causal relationship among events that tells a story, usually with a beginning; a middle that may lead to a climax in the action or a profound (or less earthshaking) understanding of events or phenomena; and an ending.
- *Dialogue*. Sometimes, not always.
- *Shifting time*, departures from logical or chronological order; events may be narrated through flashback or flashforward.
- *Setting*—usually a place or combination of places, or an interior, a mental landscape.
- *Symbolism*—any character and anything in the environment may stand for something larger than itself, as well as for its intrinsic qualities.
- An *argument that is implied*, rather than stated explicitly, if in fact an argument is presented at all. This is made more often through indirect or emotional means than through evidence from research or

scientific investigation. "Show, don't tell" is the advice that creative writers follow.

Each of these characteristics may appear in more academic essays. Anthropologist Clifford Geertz refers to "blurred genres," in which documentaries "read like true confessions," and scientific discussions contain novelistic elements. Every writer in *The Essay Connection*, for instance, has a distinctive voice, a recognizable style. But not every essayist combines most of these techniques in a single work unless he or she is writing creative nonfiction. *The Essay Connection* highlights two creative nonfiction essays. In "On the Banks of the Bogue Chitto" (245–49), student Amanda Cagle presents an evocative portrait of her beloved Choctaw father, his many strengths ultimately unable to overcome the difficulties of poverty and racism in Louisiana bayou country. In "Killing Chickens" (120–23), Meredith Hall tells the story of the day when paradise is lost, as the inevitability of divorce snaps into sharp focus for a young mother and her two children. The experience of reading—and writing—a piece of creative nonfiction is very much like that of reading a short story: we respond to the characters in the narrative as we would to people we know; we may identify with them or be repelled by their fully human experiences. But because we believe in the truth of the creative nonfiction, if the tale is well told, we will not only care deeply about the characters, but we will want to know how their fate extends beyond the narrative.

Creative Nonfiction and Short Stories

The main difference between reading and writing creative nonfiction, as opposed to a short story, is the unspoken pact between writer and reader.

- In creative nonfiction, the writer claims to be telling a true story, whether literally or psychologically true, or both.
- The reader accepts the work as true and responds to it as to other real-world events as capable of external verification.

Fiction—including the short stories in *The Essay Connection*—employs the same techniques as creative nonfiction: characters, narrative voice(s), plot, dialogue, shifts of time, settings, symbols, and implied argument or message. But these are the main difference between creative nonfiction and fiction, whether short story or novel.

- Fiction is not expected to be true. The narrator, even one who claims to be telling a true story—as does Robinson Crusoe or Ishmael, the narrator of *Moby Dick*—is conceived of as the author's invented creation. Most authors and readers agree on this point.
- Thus events, even true ones, like the Vietnam War, can be altered to make a point or a "good story" in fiction. They do not require

external corroboration, though internal consistency provides a coherence that helps readers' interpretations.

Readers of stories (and novels) accept their characters and events as fictional, even if they seem to be slightly changed versions of reality. The reader of fiction exercises a "willing suspension of disbelief," plunges into the story, and—if it's a good one—for the duration of its reading, enters the world of the narrative—down the rabbit hole of *Alice in Wonderland*, up in the hot air balloon of *Around the World in 80 Days*, cast away on Robinson Crusoe's desert island. The title of Elizabeth Tallent's "No One's A Mystery" (400–02) comes from the lyrics of a Rosanne Cash song and conveys to readers country music's eternal theme of love, betrayal, and heartbreak. We are not surprised to learn—in two brief pages of dialogue—that the anonymous, eighteen-year-old narrator's view of her future differs considerably from that of her lover, an older man who is currently cheating on his wife as the couple speeds down the road at "eighty miles an hour" in a dirty pickup, smoking cigarettes and drinking tequila to the pulsating beat of country music on the radio. Whereas she creates a romantic scenario of her marriage ("grandmother's linen and her old silver") and two darling children born within three years, Jack predicts that "in two years you'll write, 'I wonder what that old guy's name was, the one with the curly hair and the filthy dirty pickup truck and time on his hands.'" Whether readers are world-weary cynics or not, we know whose version we'll believe—clued in by the story's first "fact": Jack's birthday gift of a "five-year diary" with a broken lock. It doesn't matter to us whether these specific characters ever existed in real life; what we see and hear and smell in that pickup (note the pun on the style of that truck) is enough.

Tim O'Brien's "How to Tell a True War Story" (77–84) (from *The Things They Carried*, a collection of narratives about the Vietnam War) intermingles good advice on writing a war story that rings true with characters—soldiers in the Vietnam war—and events presented as fiction. Whether or not the characters are real people, or are even based on real people, or whether or not the events actually happened, they illustrate O'Brien's points about true war stories because the reader will check the truth of O'Brien's advice against his or her own understanding of reality: "In any [true] war story . . . it's difficult to separate what happened from what seemed to happen. What seems to happen becomes its own happening and has to be told that way. The angles of vision are skewed" (79). If we haven't been in a war—although the events of 9/11 brought war into our very homes—we can check its truth against what we already know is plausible in war and also against the fictional evidence O'Brien gives us: "And in the end, of course, a true war story is never about war. It's about sunlight . . . It's about love and memory. It's about sorrow. It's about sisters who never write back and people who never listen" (84). In this work, which O'Brien calls fiction despite its compelling re-creation of characters in a grimly surreal Vietnam jungle setting, factual truth doesn't matter. But O'Brien's kind of truth matters greatly: "You can tell a true war story by the questions you ask. Somebody tells a story, let's say, and afterward you ask, 'Is it true?' and if the answer matters, you've got your answer" (82).

Poetry

Poetry has conventions of its own; its meaning is compact, compressed. Whether or not it rhymes—and lots of poems don't—a poem is held together by its metrical pattern (rhythm), sounds, and often a dominating image or emotion. The poems in *The Essay Connection* are short and sufficiently straightforward so readers can understand them without a lot of outside explanation. These poems usually depict a character (V. Penelope Pelizzon's "Clever and Poor" 346–47), relationship (Jenny Spinner's "Together in the Old Square Print, 1976" 300–01), emotion (Mary Oliver's "August" 183), event (Seamus Heaney's "Horace and the Thunder" 517), or social principle (Marilyn Nelson's "Friends in the Klan" 449).

Children who are reared on Dr. Seuss and nursery rhymes learn to love poetry at an early age. Too often, however, as they proceed through school, they learn to dislike it in formal contexts (say, textbooks) while nevertheless responding informally to the lyrics of rap, reggae, hip-hop, rhythm and blues, and rock music. Whereas memorizing and reciting poetry may become an embarrassment in the elementary grades, there are at least thirty-five high school Precision Poetry Drill Teams who compete and award school letters. In and out of college, poetry readings, poetry slams, and online poetry sources abound. A Google search for "poetry" on April 23, 2008 (Shakespeare's birthday!) listed 133,000,000 hits—a lively subject indeed. Thus one aspect of a college education is to reintroduce students as adults to poetry—in case you might have tuned out the more literary versions while tuning in on your iPod.

The Glossary contains terminology useful for discussing poetry: rhyme, meter, stanzaic form, imagery, and more (648). Some of your concerns as a reader surface whether you're reading any genre, in prose or in poetry.

- Who is the *author*? When did she or he write the poem?
- Who is the *speaker* in the poem? Unlike essays, where the speaker or narrative voice is usually the author, this is not necessarily the case in poetry.
- What is *the poem about*? What is its point? Try paraphrasing it, perhaps line by line or sentence by sentence. What evidence in the poem itself supports your interpretation? Does any evidence contradict your interpretation? If so, reread the poem to accommodate as much evidence as possible.
- What does the *title* signify?

- What is the prevailing *tone*? What does this tell you about the author's attitude toward the subject?

Because poetry is concentrated, often allusive, some additional considerations can help you as you read.

- Read the poem more than once, more than twice—give it a chance for the meaning to sink in.
- Read the poem aloud. Try this, listening to its sounds, and to the sounds of silence.
- Read the poem according to the punctuation, rather than according to the end of the line. Poetic sentences don't necessarily end at the line ends.
- Read the poem according to the meter but with gentle grace to convey its subtle heartbeat—though not the force of a heart attack.
- Many poems are full of ambiguity. If you've caught some of the meanings and have arrived at an interpretation that satisfies you, be prepared to enjoy what you've discovered—and to argue your case with people whose interpretations differ from your own.

Indeed, the best advice for all readers, and for all writers, is to enjoy yourself. As long as you're in the right ballpark, don't worry about touching all the bases. There's more than one way to play the game, more than one way to read the essays and the creative nonfiction, the stories and the poems. And don't forget the pictures, cartoons, and graphic essays.

Illustrations

"Reading" a photograph or cartoon involves many of the same considerations you bring to poetry. You look at it, once, twice, several times, sort of like watching a polaroid develop, and the meaning gradually becomes clear. In many cases, the longer you look or the more often you revisit the picture, multiple meanings emerge.

- *Subject*. What's in the picture? What's missing from it that the viewer would ordinarily expect to find and have to supply? In a joke, for instance, as in Istvan Banyai's "Inflation" (285) what changes—in the figure and in the cost of the postage stamp—occur in the successive panels?
- *Artist's attitude toward the subject*. What is the point? How do you know? Does the artist tell a story in a single illustration or in a sequence? See Scott McCloud's "Character Design" (135–42) for additional illumination. Does the cartoon or cartoon sequence incorporate an argument? See, for instance, Roz Chast's "Men Are from Belgium, Women Are from New Brunswick" (409) and Marisa Acocella Marchetto's "Why Haven't We Won the War on Cancer?" (488).

- If there are *captions* or *dialogue blocks,* what is the relation of these to the visual art? How can you tell when these are straightforward, as in Linda Villarosa's "How Much of the Body Is Replaceable?" (250–51) or satiric, as in Evan Eisenberg's "Dialogue Boxes You Should Have Read More Carefully" (486)?
- *Context.* If you can tell, where did the illustrations originally appear? How large were they? Full page? Small boxes? Are they free-standing or intended to accompany a written text? When there is a cartoon sequence, as in Lynda Barry's graphic narrative "Common Scents" (376–85), what story do the pictures, speech balloons, and captions tell?
- *Design*—overall visual sense. How does the artist's use of color, light and dark, sunshine and shadows, balance, and general layout affect your interpretation?
- *Ambiguities, uncertainties.* How can you be certain that your interpretation of the figures, ground, context is accurate? Do you need any additional information to understand what you're seeing?

There is no single right way to view an illustration, just as there is no single way to write about it. Indeed, there are as many ways to write as there are writers, for style is as individual as a fingerprint, and just as distinctive, as we'll see in the chapters that follow.

© Royalty-Free/Corbis

What clues in this photograph signify the type of writing in progress? Is this a student writer at work? Might she also be a creative writer? Given that she's writing on a laptop, why is she also holding a pencil between her teeth? Does the writer look comfortable? Is her work going well? Where is this writing taking place? By day or by night?

AMY TAN

Amy Tan was born in Oakland, California, in 1952. Fascinated with language, she earned a BA in English (1972) and an MA in linguistics (1973) from San Jose State University. As a language development specialist working with disabled children, Tan's sensitivity to languages both spoken (conversation) and unspoken (behavior) was translated into the stories of complex relationships between Chinese-born mothers and their American-born daughters that comprise *The Joy Luck Club*, whose publication in 1989 brought her immediate fame, fortune, and critical esteem.

Tan followed this book with the equally successful *The Kitchen God's Wife* (1991), a novel modeled on her mother's traumatic life in China before she emigrated to the United States after World War II; *The Hundred Secret Senses* (1995); *The Bonesetter's Daughter* (2001); and *The Opposite of Fate* (2003). Indeed, as Tan explains in the essay "Mother Tongue," originally published in *Threepenny Review* in 1990, her ideal reader became her mother, "because these were stories about mothers." Tan wrote "using all the Englishes [she] grew up with"—the "simple" English she used when speaking to her mother, the "broken" English her mother used when speaking to her, her "watered down" translation of her mother's Chinese, and her mother's passionate, rhythmic "internal language." Her mother paid the book the ultimate compliment: "So easy to read." Hearing these multiple languages by reading the essay aloud weds the words and the music.

Mother Tongue

I am not a scholar of English or literature. I cannot give you much more 1
than personal opinions on the English language and its variations in this country or others.

I am a writer. And by that definition, I am someone who has always 2
loved language. I am fascinated by language in daily life. I spend a great deal of my time thinking about the power of language—the way it can evoke an emotion, a visual image, a complex idea, or a simple truth. Language is the tool of my trade. And I use them all—all the Englishes I grew up with.

Recently, I was made keenly aware of the different Englishes I do 3
use. I was giving a talk to a large group of people, the same talk I had already given to half a dozen other groups. The nature of the talk was about my writing, my life, and my book, *The Joy Luck Club*. The talk was going along well enough, until I remembered one major difference that made the whole talk sound wrong. My mother was in the room. And it was perhaps the first time she had heard me give a lengthy speech, using the kind of English I have never used with her. I was saying things like, "The intersection of memory upon imagination" and "There is an aspect of my fiction that relates to thus-and-thus"—a speech filled with carefully wrought grammatical phrases, burdened, it suddenly seemed to me, with nominalized forms, past perfect tenses, conditional phrases, all the forms of standard English that I had learned in school and through books, the forms of English I did not use at home with my mother.

Just last week, I was walking down the street with my mother, and 4
I again found myself conscious of the English I was using, the English I do use with her. We were talking about the price of new and used furniture and I heard myself saying this: "Not waste money that way." My husband was with us as well, and he didn't notice any switch in my English. And then I realized why. It's because over the twenty years we've been together I've often used that same kind of English with him, and sometimes he even uses it with me. It has become our language of intimacy, a different sort of English that relates to family talk, the language I grew up with.

So you'll have some idea of what this family talk I heard sounds 5
like, I'll quote what my mother said during a recent conversation which I videotaped and then transcribed. During this conversation, my mother was talking about a political gangster in Shanghai who had the same last name as her family's, Du, and how the gangster in his early years wanted to be adopted by her family, which was rich by comparison. Later, the gangster became more powerful, far richer than my mother's family, and one day showed up at my mother's wedding to pay his respects. Here's what she said in part:

6 "Du Yusong having business like fruit stand. Like off the street kind. He is Du like Du Zong—but not Tsung-ming Island people. The local people call putong, the river east side, he belong to that side local people. That man want to ask Du Zong father take him in like become own family. Du Zong father wasn't look down on him, but didn't take seriously, until that man big like become a mafia. Now important person, very hard to inviting him. Chinese way, came only to show respect, don't stay for dinner. Respect for making big celebration, he shows up. Mean give lots of respect. Chinese custom. Chinese social life that way. If too important won't have to stay too long. He come to my wedding. I didn't see, I heard it. I gone to boy's side, they have YMCA dinner. Chinese age I was nineteen."

7 You should know that my mother's expressive command of English belies how much she actually understands. She reads the *Forbes* report, listens to *Wall Street Week*, converses daily with her stockbroker, reads all of Shirley MacLaine's books with ease—all kinds of things I can't begin to understand. Yet some of my friends tell me they understand 50 percent of what my mother says. Some say they understand 80 to 90 percent. Some say they understand none of it, as if she were speaking pure Chinese. But to me, my mother's English is perfectly clear, perfectly natural. It's my mother tongue. Her language, as I hear it, is vivid, direct, full of observation and imagery. That was the language that helped shape the way I saw things, expressed things, made sense of the world.

8 Lately, I've been giving more thought to the kind of English my mother speaks. Like others, I have described it to people as "broken" or "fractured" English. But I wince when I say that. It has always bothered me that I can think of no way to describe it other than "broken," as if it were damaged and needed to be fixed, as if it lacked a certain wholeness and soundness. I've heard other terms used, "limited English," for example. But they seem just as bad, as if everything is limited, including people's perceptions of the limited English speaker.

9 I know this for a fact, because when I was growing up, my mother's "limited" English limited *my* perception of her. I was ashamed of her English. I believed that her English reflected the quality of what she had to say. That is, because she expressed them imperfectly her thoughts were imperfect. And I had plenty of empirical evidence to support me: the fact that people in department stores, at banks, and at restaurants did not take her seriously, did not give her good service, pretended not to understand her, or even acted as if they did not hear her.

10 My mother has long realized the limitations of her English as well. When I was fifteen, she used to have me call people on the phone to pretend I was she. In this guise, I was forced to ask for information or even to complain and yell at people who had been rude to her. One time it was a call to her stockbroker in New York. She had cashed out her small

portfolio and it just happened we were going to go to New York the next week, our very first trip outside California. I had to get on the phone and say in an adolescent voice that was not very convincing, "This is Mrs. Tan."

And my mother was standing in the back whispering loudly, "Why 11
he don't send me check, already two weeks late. So mad he lie to me, losing me money."

And then I said in perfect English, "Yes, I'm getting rather con- 12
cerned. You had agreed to send the check two weeks ago, but it hasn't arrived."

Then she began to talk more loudly. "What he want, I come to 13
New York tell him front of his boss, you cheating me?" And I was trying to calm her down, make her be quiet, while telling the stockbroker, "I can't tolerate any more excuses. If I don't receive the check immediately, I am going to have to speak to your manager when I'm in New York next week." And sure enough, the following week there we were in front of this astonished stockbroker, and I was sitting there red-faced and quiet, and my mother, the real Mrs. Tan, was shouting at his boss in her impeccable broken English.

We used a similar routine just five days ago, for a situation that was 14
far less humorous. My mother had gone to the hospital for an appointment, to find out about a benign brain tumor a CAT scan had revealed a month ago. She said she had spoken very good English, her best English, no mistakes. Still, she said, the hospital did not apologize when they said they had lost the CAT scan and she had come for nothing. She said they did not seem to have any sympathy when she told them she was anxious to know the exact diagnosis, since her husband and son had both died of brain tumors. She said they would not give her any more information until the next time and she would have to make another appointment for that. So she said she would not leave until the doctor called her daughter. She wouldn't budge. And when the doctor finally called her daughter, me, who spoke in perfect English—lo and behold—we had assurances the CAT scan would be found, promises that a conference call on Monday would be held, and apologies for any suffering my mother had gone through for a most regrettable mistake.

I think my mother's English almost had an effect on limiting my 15
possibilities in life as well. Sociologists and linguists probably will tell you that a person's developing language skills are more influenced by peers. But I do think that the language spoken in the family, especially in immigrant families which are more insular, plays a large role in shaping the language of the child. And I believe that it affected my results on achievement tests, IQ tests, and the SAT. While my English skills were never judged as poor, compared to math, English could not be considered my strong suit. In grade school I did moderately well, getting perhaps B's, sometimes B-pluses, in English and scoring perhaps in the sixtieth

or seventieth percentile on achievement tests. But those scores were not good enough to override the opinion that my true abilities lay in math and science, because in those areas I achieved A's and scored in the ninetieth percentile or higher.

16 This was understandable. Math is precise; there is only one correct answer. Whereas, for me at least, the answers on English tests were always a judgment call, a matter of opinion and personal experience. Those tests were constructed around items like fill-in-the-blank sentence completion, such as, "Even though Tom was ________, Mary thought he was ________." And the correct answer always seemed to be the most bland combinations of thoughts, for example "Even though Tom was shy, Mary thought he was charming," with the grammatical structure "even though" limiting the correct answer to some sort of semantic opposites, so you wouldn't get answers like, "Even though Tom was foolish, Mary thought he was ridiculous." Well, according to my mother, there were very few limitations as to what Tom could have been and what Mary might have thought of him. So I never did well on tests like that.

17 The same was true with word analogies, pairs of words in which you were supposed to find some sort of logical, semantic relationship—for example, "*Sunset* is to *nightfall* as ________ is to ________." And here you would be presented with a list of four possible pairs, one of which showed the same kind of relationship: *red* is to *spotlight, bus* is to *arrival, chills* is to *fever, yawn* is to *boring*. Well, I could never think that way. I knew what the tests were asking, but I could not block out of my mind the images already created by the first pair, "*sunset* is to *nightfall*"—and I would see a burst of colors against a darkening sky, the moon rising, the lowering of a curtain of stars. And all the other pairs of words—red, bus, spotlight, boring—just threw up a mass of confusing images, making it impossible for me to sort out something as logical as saying: "A sunset precedes nightfall" is the same as "a chill precedes a fever." The only way I would have gotten that answer right would have been to imagine an associative situation, for example, my being disobedient and staying out past sunset, catching a chill at night, which turns into feverish pneumonia as punishment, which indeed did happen to me.

18 I have been thinking about all this lately, about my mother's English, about achievement tests. Because lately I've been asked as a writer, why there are not more Asian Americans represented in American literature. Why are there few Asian Americans enrolled in creative writing programs? Why do so many Chinese students go into engineering? Well, these are broad sociological questions I can't begin to answer. But I have noticed in surveys—in fact, just last week—that Asian students, as a whole, always do significantly better on math achievement tests than in English. And this makes me think that there are other Asian-American students whose

English spoken in the home might also be described as "broken" or "limited." And perhaps they also have teachers who are steering them away from writing and into math and science, which is what happened to me.

Fortunately, I happen to be rebellious in nature and enjoy the chal- 19
lenge of disproving assumptions made about me. I became an English major my first year in college, after being enrolled as pre-med. I started writing nonfiction as a freelancer the week after I was told by my former boss that writing was my worst skill and I should hone my talents toward account management.

But it wasn't until 1985 that I finally began to write fiction. And at 20
first I wrote using what I thought to be wittily crafted sentences, sentences that would finally prove I had mastery over the English language. Here's an example from the first draft of a story that later made its way into *The Joy Luck Club*, but without this line: "That was my mental quandary in its nascent state." A terrible line, which I can barely pronounce.

Fortunately, for reasons I won't get into today, I later decided 21
I should envision a reader for the stories I would write. And the reader I decided upon was my mother, because these were stories about mothers. So with this reader in mind—and in fact she did read my early drafts—I began to write stories using all the Englishes I grew up with: the English I spoke to my mother, which for lack of a better term might be described as "simple"; the English she used with me, which for lack of a better term might be described as "broken"; my translation of her Chinese, which could certainly be described as "watered down"; and what I imagined to be her translation of her Chinese if she could speak in perfect English, her internal language, and for that I sought to preserve the essence, but neither an English nor a Chinese structure. I wanted to capture what language ability tests can never reveal: her intent, her passion, her imagery, the rhythms of her speech and the nature of her thoughts.

Apart from what any critic had to say about my writing, I knew I 22
had succeeded where it counted when my mother finished reading my book and gave me her verdict: "So easy to read."

Content

1. What connections does Tan make throughout the essay between speaking and writing? In what English has Tan written "Mother Tongue"? Why?
2. What is Tan's relationship with her mother? How can you tell?
3. What problems does Mrs. Tan experience as a result of not speaking standard English? Are her problems typical of other speakers of "limited" English?
4. Do you agree with Tan that "math is precise" but that English is "always a judgment call, a matter of opinion and personal experience" (¶ 16)? Why or why not? If English is so subjective, how is it possible to write anything that is clear, "so easy to read" (¶ 22)?

Strategies/Structures/Language

5. Tan uses illustrative examples: a story told in her mother's speech (¶ 6), her mother's altercation with the stockbroker (¶s 10–13), her mother's encounter with rude and indifferent hospital workers who lost her CAT scan (¶ 14). What is the point of each example? Does Tan have to explain them? Why or why not?

6. How do the "Englishes" that Tan and her mother use convey their characters, personalities, intelligence? In what ways are mother and daughter similar? Different?

For Writing

7. ***Journal Writing.*** We all make judgments of people based on their accent, vocabulary, grammar, intonation, pace, and characteristic expressions. What judgments do you think people make of you based on the way you talk? Are these likely to change once they get to know you?

8. ***Dialogues.*** How is the narrator's use of language designed to appeal to the English-speaking reader in Zitkala-Sa's "The School Days of an Indian Girl" (Chapter 5) and Ning Yu's "Red and Black, or One English Major's Beginning" (Chapter 4)? Do you find that forms of electronic social networking such as *Facebook* encourage people to present themselves as products (see Michael J. Bugeja's "Facing the Facebook," Chapter 12)?

9. Consider a situation in which you have had to communicate with someone whose native language or dialect was different from yours. Tell the story of your experience in order to explain the ways that you communicated. As part of your narrative, describe the setting of your experience so that your reader can see it through your eyes.

10. ***Second Look.*** What does the photograph in this essay suggest about the different aspects of the writing process? How do different technologies of writing, the environment, and literacy interact in the production of writing?

11. How many Englishes have you grown up with? Were these variations of English or another language? Identify the circumstances under which you use each of them—perhaps at home or in conversation with friends. Consider such features as vocabulary (including slang and specialized words), sentence length, and the simplicity or complexity of what you're trying to say. Do you write papers for English classes in a different language than papers for some of your other courses?

12. Present to an audience of college-educated readers an argument for or against the necessity of speaking in standard English for general, all-purpose communication. Are there any exceptions to your position?

Reading Icons

RODIN, *The Thinker*

Iris and B. Gerald Cantor Foundation

Auguste Rodin made the original cast of his iconic sculpture, "The Thinker," in 1880. It was cast as a large bronze in 1902. During his lifetime Rodin authorized the production of as many casts of each of his sculptures as the market would bear, in various sizes; there were, for instance, 319 casts of "The Kiss." Thus, if you have seen one you have not seen them all, although since 1956 French law has limited the production of casts to twelve of each sculpture. The small bronze depicted here is owned by the Iris and Gerald B. Cantor Foundation, which since 1945 has collected, lent, and sold some 750 of Rodin's works to museums and universities. Does the ubiquity of this sculpture detract from its significance? Would you prefer to think of any given work of art as unique, even though many reproductions of beloved works are available?

MIKE PETERS, *Mother Goose and Grimm*

MOTHER GOOSE & GRIMM-(NEW) © GRIMMY, INC. KING FEATURES SYNDICATE

To be famous is to provoke imitation and satire, even if the original object, work, or person is beloved. Even if viewers don't have a photograph of Rodin's original "The Thinker" at hand, the cartoonist, Mike Peters, is counting on them to recognize the model for his spinoffs. Does the fact that we're expected to laugh at the cartoon affect the way we view the original? Why or why not? Does the juxtaposition of the sculpture and the cartoon create a resonance of the way we read each work that wouldn't exist if we read each in isolation?

MIKE D'ANGELO, *Do-It-Yourself Emoticons*

Obvious	More Nuanced	Sophisticated, Subtle
;-) wink	O+ female	~:-) baby
:-(sad	O-> male	,,–,,/"> dog
:-< really sad	8-I nerd	**,,–,,/"> French poodle
:-I bored	*:-I thinking	:-I:-I deja vu
:-\ undecided	:-# don't tell anyone	(::O::) bandaid; offering help
}{ face to face	:-$ embarrassed	=):-)= Uncle Sam

The potential for passion lies in your very fingertips as they tippy-tap over your computer keys. We've all used some of those naked icons of emotion—the smiley face :-), the laugh :-D, and others such as those identified in the "Obvious" column above. Advanced communicators may have tried "More Nuanced" versions in the middle column, or perhaps ^5 (high five) or :^D ("Great!", or "I like it"). With a little practice, you too can create your own emoticons, as seen in the "Sophisticated, Subtle" column. Once you've seen "dog" and "French poodle," you could move on to ~~,,----,,/"> (skunk); to get a snake, you might have to tilt the screen. If you've laid down I**-------I (bed and pillow), you can put someone in it: I**O–/-----/I.

Content

1. Rodin's figure *The Thinker* has become an iconic symbol of intellectual activity. Why is Peters's rendering of other, less cerebral but equally solitary activities humorous? Can you translate the visual joke into words? In what ways do the figures' facial expressions contribute to the viewer's understanding of the joke?
2. *The Thinker* suggests that thinking is a physical activity separate from writing. How do Peters's labels contribute to the humor of the image? Wouldn't the activity of each sculpture be obvious without the label? What is the significance of the position of each figure's head and the expression on each figure's face?
3. The sculptor is not dressed as Rodin, an early twentieth-century sculptor, might have been. What image of the sculptor does the cartoon convey? What does the cartoonist's rendering of the artist and the museum's representative suggest about the cartoonist's image of himself? What does the cartoon suggest about our culture's perception of thinking and of art?
4. How does emoticon, a form of graphic art that transforms text into images, fill in the gaps in textual electronic communications? Why might the adult reader find emoticon a foreign concept?

Strategies/Structures/Language

5. Describe the process of reading a cartoon. What information do you need to bring to Peters's cartoon to understand its humor?

6. To learn to read and write a series of emoticon symbols would be like learning another language. Is this practical? Why use emoticon? Under what circumstances? Are emoticon symbols here to stay?
7. What is the point of the increasing complexity of the emoticon symbols? How does D'Angelo's arrangement of the symbols ask the reader to participate in the construction of meaning?

For Writing

8. ***Journal Writing.*** Find a cartoon or a short comic strip, perhaps on the Internet, that you find particularly interesting. What information does the cartoon or comic ask you to contribute in order to understand it? How does language help the image create meaning for the viewer? What does the image and/or language leave unstated? Compare the cartoon or comic strip you have chosen with Kim Warp's "Rising Sea Levels—An Alternative Theory" (Chapter 6). What knowledge does each image ask you to supply? How does Warp's rendering of her characters add to the humor of the cartoon? Alternatively, compare your cartoon or comic strip to Lynda Barry's "Common Scents" (Chapter 8). How do Barry's characters' physiognomy, physique, and speech expand and develop the narrator's commentary?
9. ***Dialogues.*** In "Character Design" (Chapter 4), Scott McCloud writes that a great comic character needs "an inner life," "visual distinction," and "expressive traits" (panels 4–6). How does the viewer deduce these qualities of the artist and the museum representative in Peters's cartoon?

ELIE WIESEL

Elie Wiesel, born in 1928 and a survivor of the Holocaust, explains, "For me, literature abolishes the gap between [childhood and death]. . . . Auschwitz marks the decisive, ultimate turning point . . . of the human adventure. Nothing will ever again be as it was. Thousands and thousands of deaths weigh upon every word. How speak of redemption after Treblinka? and how speak of anything else?" As a survivor, he became a writer in order to become a witness: "I believed that, having survived by chance . . . I knew the story had to be told. Not to transmit an experience is to betray it." Wiesel has developed a literary style that reflects the distilled experience of concentration camps, in which "a sentence is worth a page, a word is worth a sentence. The unspoken weighs heavier than the spoken. . . . Say only the essential—say only what no other would say . . . a style sharp, hard, strong, in a word, pared. . . . Speak as a witness on the stand speaks. With no indulgence to others or oneself."

In May 1944, when he was fifteen, Wiesel was forcibly removed from his native town of Sighet, Hungary ("which no longer exists," he says, "except in the memory of those it expelled"), to the first of several concentration camps. Although six million Jews died in the camps, including members of his family, Wiesel was liberated from Buchenwald in April 1945 and sent to Paris, where he studied philosophy. For twenty years he worked as a journalist for Jewish newspapers, but the turning point in his career as a writer came in 1954 when he met novelist François Mauriac, who urged him to speak on behalf of the children in concentration camps. This encouraged Wiesel (who has lived in New York since 1956) to write some forty books of fiction, nonfiction, poetry, and drama, starting in 1958 with *Night*, which opens, "In the beginning was faith, confidence, illusion." He published his memoirs *All the Rivers Run to the Sea* in 1996, and *And the Sea Is Never Full* in 1999. Wiesel, true citizen of the world, named Jewish "Humanitarian of the Century," received the Nobel Peace Prize in 1986 for his efforts epitomized in "Why I Write: Making No Become Yes," originally published in the *New York Times Book Review*, April 14, 1986.

Why I Write: Making No Become Yes

1 Why do I write?

2 Perhaps in order not to go mad. Or, on the contrary, to touch the bottom of madness. Like Samuel Beckett, the survivor expresses himself "en désepoir de cause"—out of desperation.

3 Speaking of the solitude of the survivor, the great Yiddish and Hebrew poet and thinker Aaron Zeitlin addresses those—his father, his brother, his friends—who have died and left him: "You have abandoned me," he says to them. "You are together, without me. I am here. Alone. And I make words."

4 So do I, just like him. I also say words, write words, reluctantly.

5 There are easier occupations, far more pleasant ones. But for the survivor, writing is not a profession, but an occupation, a duty. Camus calls it "an honor." As he puts it: "I entered literature through worship." Other writers have said they did so through anger, through love. Speaking for myself, I would say—through silence.

6 It was by seeking, by probing silence that I began to discover the perils and power of the word. I never intended to be a philosopher, or a theologian. The only role I sought was that of witness. I believed that, having survived by chance, I was duty-bound to give meaning to my survival, to justify each moment of my life. I knew the story had to be told. Not to transmit an experience is to betray it. This is what Jewish tradition teaches us. But how to do this? "When Israel is in exile, so is the word," says the Zohar. The word has deserted the meaning it was intended to convey—impossible to make them coincide. The displacement, the shift, is irrevocable.

© Brian Steidle

The United States Holocaust Memorial Museum provides ongoing exhibits of "man's inhumanity to man" wherever, whenever it occurs in the world. These exhibits serve as witnesses to genocide, through photographs; sound and text; background information; and suggestions about how people worldwide can help the living victims, and "help the dead vanquish death," as Wiesel explains. Brian Steidle's photograph from the exhibit "In Darfur my camera was not nearly enough," shows the beginning of the burning of the village of Um Zeifa, Darfur, Sudan in 2004, after being looted and attacked by the Janjaweed. This government-supported militia, along with Sudanese government soldiers, has waged ethnic war—murdering tens of thousands of African ethnic groups, raping thousands of women, and driving over 1.5 million civilians from their homes, torching their villages and looting their property. What is the point, the hope, the expectation of exposing audiences in America—including yourselves as students—to such pictures?

This was never more true than right after the upheaval. We all knew 7
that we could never, never say what had to be said, that we could never express in words, coherent, intelligible words, our experience of madness on an absolute scale. The walk through flaming night, the silence before and after the selection, the monotonous praying of the condemned, the Kaddish of the dying, the fear and hunger of the sick, the shame and suffering, the haunted eyes, the demented stares. I thought that I would never be able to speak of them. All words seemed inadequate, worn, foolish, lifeless, whereas I wanted them to be searing.

Where was I to discover a fresh vocabulary, a primeval language? 8
The language of night was not human, it was primitive, almost animal—hoarse shouting, screams, muffled moaning, savage howling, the sound of beating. A brute strikes out wildly, a body falls. An officer raises his arm

and a whole community walks toward a common grave. A soldier shrugs his shoulders, and a thousand families are torn apart, to be reunited only by death. This was the concentration camp language. It negated all other language and took its place. Rather than a link, it became a wall. Could it be surmounted? Could the reader be brought to the other side? I knew the answer was negative, and yet I knew that "no" had to become "yes." It was the last wish of the dead.

9 The fear of forgetting remains the main obsession of all those who have passed through the universe of the damned. The enemy counted on people's incredulity and forgetfulness. How could one foil this plot? And if memory grew hollow, empty of substance, what would happen to all we had accumulated along the way? Remember, said the father to his son, and the son to his friend. Gather the names, the faces, the tears. We had all taken an oath: "If, by some miracle, I emerge alive, I will devote my life to testifying on behalf of those whose shadow will fall on mine forever and ever."

10 That is why I write certain things rather than others—to remain faithful.

11 Of course, there are times of doubt for the survivor, times when one gives in to weakness, or longs for comfort. I hear a voice within me telling me to stop mourning the past. I too want to sing of love and of its magic. I too want to celebrate the sun, and the dawn that heralds the sun. I would like to shout, and shout loudly: "Listen, listen well! I too am capable of victory, do you hear? I too am open to laughter and joy! I want to stride, head high, my face unguarded, without having to point to the ashes over there on the horizon, without having to tamper with facts to hide their tragic ugliness. For a man born blind, God himself is blind, but look, I see, I am not blind." One feels like shouting this, but the shout changes to a murmur. One must make a choice; one must remain faithful. A big word, I know. Nevertheless, I use it, it suits me. Having written the things I have written, I feel I can afford no longer to play with words. If I say that the writer in me wants to remain loyal, it is because it is true. This sentiment moves all survivors; they owe nothing to anyone, but everything to the dead.

12 I owe them my roots and my memory. I am duty-bound to serve as their emissary, transmitting the history of their disappearance, even if it disturbs, even if it brings pain. Not to do so would be to betray them, and thus myself. And since I am incapable of communicating their cry by shouting, I simply look at them. I see them and I write.

13 While writing, I question them as I question myself. I believe I have said it before, elsewhere. I write to understand as much as to be understood. Will I succeed one day? Wherever one starts, one reaches darkness. God? He remains the God of darkness. Man? The source of darkness. The killers' derision, their victims' tears, the onlookers' indifference, their complicity and complacency—the divine role in all that I do not understand. A million children massacred—I shall never understand.

Jewish children—they haunt my writings. I see them again and again. I shall always see them. Hounded, humiliated, bent like the old men who surround them as though to protect them, unable to do so. They are thirsty, the children, and there is no one to give them water. They are hungry, but there is no one to give them a crust of bread. They are afraid, and there is no one to reassure them. 14

They walk in the middle of the road, like vagabonds. They are on the way to the station, and they will never return. In sealed cars, without air or food, they travel toward another world. They guess where they are going, they know it, and they keep silent. Tense, thoughtful, they listen to the wind, the call of death in the distance. 15

All these children, these old people, I see them. I never stop seeing them. I belong to them. 16

But they, to whom do they belong? 17

People tend to think that a murderer weakens when facing a child. The child reawakens the killer's lost humanity. The killer can no longer kill the child before him, the child inside him. 18

But with us it happened differently. Our Jewish children had no effect upon the killers. Nor upon the world. Nor upon God. 19

I think of them, I think of their childhood. Their childhood is a small Jewish town, and this town is no more. They frighten me; they reflect an image of myself, one that I pursue and run from at the same time—the image of a Jewish adolescent who knew no fear, except the fear of God, whose faith was whole, comforting, and not marked by anxiety. 20

No, I do not understand. And if I write, it is to warn the reader that he will not understand either. "You will not understand, you will never understand," were the words heard everywhere during the reign of night. I can only echo them. You, who never lived under a sky of blood, will never know what it was like. Even if you read all the books ever written, even if you listen to all the testimonies ever given, you will remain on this side of the wall, you will view the agony and death of a people from afar, through the screen of a memory that is not your own. 21

An admission of impotence and guilt? I do not know. All I know is that Treblinka and Auschwitz cannot be told. And yet I have tried. God knows I have tried. 22

Have I attempted too much or not enough? Among some twenty-five volumes, only three or four penetrate the phantasmagoric realm of the dead. In my other books, through my other books, I have tried to follow other roads. For it is dangerous to linger among the dead, they hold on to you and you run the risk of speaking only to them. And so I have forced myself to turn away from them and study other periods, explore other destinies and teach other tales—the Bible and the Talmud, Hasidism and its fervor, the shtetl and its songs, Jerusalem and its echoes, the Russian Jews and their anguish, their awakening, their courage. At times, it has seemed to me that I was speaking of other 23 things with the sole purpose of keeping the essential—the personal experience—unspoken. At times I have wondered: And what if I was wrong? Perhaps I should not have heeded my own advice and stayed in my own world with the dead.

24 But then, I have not forgotten the dead. They have their rightful place even in the works about the Hasidic capitals Ruzhany and Korets, and Jerusalem. Even in my biblical and Midrashic tales, I pursue their presence, mute and motionless. The presence of the dead then beckons in such tangible ways that it affects even the most removed characters. Thus they appear on Mount Moriah, where Abraham is about to sacrifice his son, a burnt offering to their common God. They appear on Mount Nebo, where Moses enters solitude and death. They appear in Hasidic and Talmudic legends in which victims forever need defending against forces that would crush them. Technically, so to speak, they are of course elsewhere, in time and space, but on a deeper, truer plane, the dead are part of every story, of every scene.

25 "But what is the connection?" you will ask. Believe me, there is one. After Auschwitz everything brings us back to Auschwitz. When I speak of Abraham, Isaac and Jacob, when I invoke Rabbi Yohanan ben Zakkai and Rabbi Akiba, it is the better to understand them in the light of Auschwitz. As for the Maggid of Mezeritch and his disciples, it is in order to encounter the followers of their followers that I reconstruct their spellbound, spellbinding universe. I like to imagine them alive, exuberant, celebrating life and hope. Their happiness is as necessary to me as it was once to themselves.

26 And yet—how did they manage to keep their faith intact? How did they manage to sing as they went to meet the Angel of Death? I know Hasidim who never vacillated—I respect their strength. I know others who chose rebellion, protest, rage—I respect their courage. For there comes a time when only those who do not believe in God will not cry out to him in wrath and anguish.

27 Do not judge either group. Even the heroes perished as martyrs, even the martyrs died as heroes. Who would dare oppose knives to prayers? The faith of some matters as much as the strength of others. It is not ours to judge, it is only ours to tell the tale.

28 But where is one to begin? Whom is one to include? One meets a Hasid in all my novels. And a child. And an old man. And a beggar. And a madman. They are all part of my inner landscape. The reason why? Pursued and persecuted by the killers, I offer them shelter. The enemy wanted to create a society purged of their presence, and I have brought some of them back. The world denied them, repudiated them, so I let them live at least within the feverish dreams of my characters.

29 It is for them that I write, and yet the survivor may experience remorse. He has tried to bear witness; it was all in vain.

After the liberation, we had illusions. We were convinced that a new world would be built upon the ruins of Europe. A new civilization would see the light. No more wars, no more hate, no more intolerance, no fanaticism. And all this because the witnesses would speak. And speak they did, to no avail. 30

They will continue, for they cannot do otherwise. When man, in his grief, falls silent, Goethe says, then God gives him the strength to sing his sorrows. From that moment on, he may no longer choose not to sing, whether his song is heard or not. What matters is to struggle against silence with words, or through another form of silence. What matters is to gather a smile here and there, a tear here and there, a word here and there, and thus justify the faith placed in you, a long time ago, by so many victims. 31

Why do I write? To wrench those victims from oblivion. To help the dead vanquish death. 32

(*Translated from the French by Rosette C. Lamont*)

Content

1. Wiesel says, "The only role I sought [as a writer] was that of witness" (¶ 6). What does he mean by "witness"? Find examples of this role throughout the essay.
2. What does Wiesel mean by "not to transmit an experience is to betray it" (¶ 6)? What experience does his writing transmit? Why is this important to Wiesel? To humanity? Does "Why I Write" fulfill Wiesel's commitment to "make no become yes" (¶ 8)? Explain.

Strategies/Structures/Language

3. Identify some of Wiesel's major ethical appeals in this essay. Does he want to move his readers to action as well as to thought?
4. Why would Wiesel use paradoxes in an effort to explain and clarify? Explain the meaning of the following paradoxes:

   a. "No, I do not understand. And if I write, it is to warn the reader that he will not understand either" (¶ 21).
   b. I write "to help the dead vanquish death" (¶ 32).

5. For what audience does Wiesel want to explain "Why I Write"? What understanding of Judaism does Wiesel expect his readers to have? Of World War II? Of the operation of concentration camps? Why does he expect his reasons to matter to these readers, whether or not they have extensive knowledge of any of them?
6. Does Wiesel's style here fulfill his goals of a style that is "sharp, hard, strong, pared"? Why is such a style appropriate to the subject?
7. Explain the meaning of "concentration camp language" (¶ 8). Why did it negate all other language and take its place (¶ 8)?

For Writing

8. ***Journal Writing.*** Make a list of reasons to write. Which reasons appeal to you the most? Why? Is the form of writing (electronic, pen, or pencil) important to you? Do you find certain occasions more conducive to writing? What sources of inspiration do you find most powerful?

9. ***Dialogues.*** Elie Wiesel's motive for writing comes from a sense of duty: "to give meaning to my survival" (¶ 6). Compare this reason to write with Joan Didion's "attempt to make sense of the period that followed" her husband's death while her daughter was in a coma (30, ¶ 11) and with Orhan Pamuk's characterization of the writer's life as "listening only to the voice of his own conscience," thereby developing "his own thoughts, and his own world" (Chapter 2, ¶ 11). How do these motives differ? Does the quality of the writing depend on the writer's motives? Is all writing in a sense personal? Is all writing in a sense moral?

10. Consider Wiesel's descriptions of Jewish children's experience of persecution and impending death during the Holocaust (¶s 14–20). Compare Wiesel's choice of descriptive language with Suzanne Britt's in "That Lean and Hungry Look" (Chapter 6) and with Martin Luther King, Jr.'s description of the social condition of African Americans in "Letter from Birmingham Jail" (Chapter 10, ¶ 14). How does each author use specific language to generalize about the condition of a group of people? How does each author's choice of language shape the reader's perception of that group?

11. ***Second Look.*** How might the scope and arrangement of Brian Steidle's photograph in this essay illustrate Wiesel's question, "Have I attempted too much or not enough?" (¶ 23)?

12. What experiences, in your view, call out to be transmitted? Do such experiences require what Wiesel calls "a fresh vocabulary" (¶ 8)? Do you find that language is inadequate to the task of conveying a particularly painful or joyful experience? How might you supplement word choice to allow a reader to understand a particularly significant experience?

JOAN DIDION

Joan Didion (born 1934 in Sacramento, California) is known for her distinctive, highly polished style and her incisive social commentary. Didion's essays have been collected in *Slouching Towards Bethlehem* (1968), *The White Album* (1979), and *After Henry* (1992). Her nonfiction includes *Salvador* (1982), *Miami* (1987), *Political Fictions* (2001), and a memoir, *Where I Was From* (2003). She has also written novels (*Run River*, 1963; *Play It as It Lays*, 1970; *A Book of Common Prayer*, 1977; *Democracy*, 1984; and *The Last Thing He Wanted*, 1996), and, with her husband, John Gregory Dunne, the screenplays *Panic in Needle Park* (1971), *A Star is Born* (1976), *True Confessions* (1981), and *Up Close and Personal* (1996). "Life Changes Fast" is excerpted from Didion's memoir *The Year of Magical Thinking* (2005), the story of her husband's fatal heart attack during her daughter Quintana's serious and ultimately fatal illness. The memoir is a testament to writing as a way of reconstructing—and hence understanding—significant relationships, as well as trying to come to terms with trauma and grief. Recipient of a National Book Award in 2005, *The Year of Magical Thinking* was adapted as a one-woman show that played on Broadway in 2007.

Life Changes Fast

Life changes fast. 1
Life changes in the instant.
You sit down to dinner and life as you know it ends.
The question of self-pity.

Those were the first words I wrote after it happened. The computer dating on the Microsoft Word file ("Notes on change.doc") reads "May 20, 2004, 11:11 p.m.," but that would have been a case of my opening the file and reflexively pressing save when I closed it. I had made no changes to that file in May. I had made no changes to that file since I wrote the words, in January 2004, a day or two or three after the fact. 2

For a long time I wrote nothing else. 3

Life changes in the instant.
The ordinary instant.

At some point, in the interest of remembering what seemed most striking about what had happened, I considered adding those words, "the ordinary instant." I saw immediately that there would be no need to add the word "ordinary," because there would be no forgetting it: the word never left my mind. It was in fact the ordinary nature of everything preceding the event that prevented me from truly believing it had happened, absorbing it, incorporating it, getting past it. I recognize now that there was nothing unusual in this: confronted with sudden disaster we all focus on how unremarkable the circumstances were in which the unthinkable occurred, the clear blue sky from which the plane fell, the routine errand that ended on the shoulder with the car in flames, the swings where the children were playing as usual when the rattlesnake struck from the ivy. "He was on his way home from work—happy, successful, healthy—and then, gone," I read in the account of a psychiatric nurse whose husband was killed in a highway accident. In 1966 I happened to interview many people who had been living in Honolulu on the morning of December 7, 1941; without exception, these people began their accounts of Pearl Harbor by telling me what an "ordinary Sunday morning" it had been. "It was just an ordinary beautiful September day," people still say when asked to describe the morning in New York when American Airlines 11 4 and United Airlines 175 got flown into the World Trade towers. Even the report of the 9/11 Commission opened on this insistently premonitory and yet still dumbstruck narrative note: "Tuesday, September 11, 2001, dawned temperate and nearly cloudless in the eastern United States."

5 "And then—gone." *In the midst of life we are in death,* Episcopalians say at the graveside. Later I realized that I must have repeated the details of what happened to everyone who came to the house in those first weeks, all those friends and relatives who brought food and made drinks and laid out plates on the dining room table for however many people were around at lunch or dinner time, all those who picked up the plates and froze the leftovers and ran the dishwasher and filled our (I could not yet think *my*) otherwise empty house even after I had gone into the bedroom (our bedroom, the one in which there still lay on a sofa a faded terrycloth XL robe bought in the 1970s at Richard Carroll in Beverly Hills) and shut the door. Those moments when I was abruptly overtaken by exhaustion are what I remember most clearly about the first days and weeks. I have no memory of telling anyone the details, but I must have done so, because everyone seemed to know them. At one point I considered the possibility that they had picked up the details of the story from one another, but immediately rejected it: the story they had was in each instance too accurate to have been passed from hand to hand. It had come from me.

6 Another reason I knew that the story had come from me was that no version I heard included the details I could not yet face, for example the blood on the living room floor that stayed there until José came in the next morning and cleaned it up.

7 José. Who was part of our household. Who was supposed to be flying to Las Vegas later that day, December 31, but never went. José was crying that morning as he cleaned up the blood. When I first told him what had happened he had not understood. Clearly I was not the ideal teller of this story, something about my version had been at once too offhand and too elliptical, something in my tone had failed to convey the central fact in the situation (I would encounter the same failure later when I had to tell Quintana), but by the time José saw the blood he understood.

8 I had picked up the abandoned syringes and ECG electrodes before he came in that morning but I could not face the blood.

9 In outline.

10 It is now, as I begin to write this, the afternoon of October 4, 2004.

11 Nine months and five days ago, at approximately nine o'clock on the evening of December 30, 2003, my husband, John Gregory Dunne, appeared to (or did) experience, at the table where he and I had just sat down to dinner in the living room of our apartment in New York, a sudden massive coronary event that caused his death. Our only child, Quintana, had been for the previous five nights unconscious in an intensive care unit at Beth Israel Medical Center's Singer Division, at that time a hospital on East End Avenue (it closed in August 2004) more commonly

known as "Beth Israel North" or "the old Doctors' Hospital," where what had seemed a case of December flu sufficiently severe to take her to an emergency room on Christmas morning had exploded into pneumonia and septic shock. This is my attempt to make sense of the period that followed, weeks and then months that cut loose any fixed idea I had ever had about death, about illness, about probability and luck, about good fortune and bad, about marriage and children and memory, about grief, about the ways in which people do and do not deal with the fact that life ends, about the shallowness of sanity, about life itself. I have been a writer my entire life. As a writer, even as a child, long before what I wrote began to be published, I developed a sense that meaning itself was resident in the rhythms of words and sentences and paragraphs, a technique for withholding whatever it was I thought or believed behind an increasingly impenetrable polish. The way I write is who I am, or have become, yet this is a case in which I wish I had instead of words and their rhythms a cutting room, equipped with an Avid, a digital editing system on which I could touch a key and collapse the sequence of time, show you simultaneously all the frames of memory that come to me now, let you pick the takes, the marginally different expressions, the variant readings of the same lines. This is a case in which I need more than words to find the meaning. This is a case in which I need whatever it is I think or believe to be penetrable, if only for myself.

Content

1. How does Didion account for the human tendency to recall "the ordinary nature of everything" that precedes "the unthinkable" (¶ 4) when looking back on catastrophic or traumatic events? What is the effect on the reader of Didion's comparison of the loss of a loved one with the experiences of those who lived through Pearl Harbor and 9/11?

2. Didion writes that she has developed "a technique for withholding whatever it was I thought or believed behind an increasingly impenetrable polish" (¶ 11). Why does she wish, in the case of telling the story of husband's death, that she could "show you simultaneously all the frames of memory" so that the reader might "pick the takes" (¶ 11)? How does the conflict between writing with "polish" and playing back unedited memory illustrate the conflict between her desire to convey lived experience and her desire to write a coherent narrative? In your opinion, does a writer's stylistic "polish" create or hinder a sense of lived experience?

Strategies/Structures/Language

3. In the first section of this piece, Didion analyzes the language she, and other storytellers, use to describe a "sudden disaster" (¶ 4). In the second section, she begins with an "outline" (¶ 9) of the night of her husband's death. How does each section tell a different story? Why, in your opinion, did Didion choose this structure?

4. Which details does the narrator provide and withhold about her husband's death? For example, Didion mentions "the blood on the living room floor" (¶ 6), but does not mention the immediate aftermath of her husband's death. How does this, and other omissions, shape the narrative?

For Writing

5. ***Journal Writing.*** Reconstruct an important event in your life or your memory of an event in history, such as 9/11. As you write, observe how your experience has, as Didion writes, "cut loose any fixed idea" you might have had about "probability and luck, about good fortune and bad" (¶ 11). How did the event change your perceptions of your life and of your ability to predict your future?
6. ***Dialogues.*** Didion describes her husband's death by beginning with the first words she wrote on her computer "after it happened" (¶ 1). Compare her approach to that used by Scott Russell Sanders in "The Inheritance of Tools" (Chapter 4) in which he describes his father's death in the context of smashing his thumb with his father's hammer. How does each writer's focus on a particular action frame the story? Are there similarities as well as differences in each writer's approach to a narrative of the death of a loved one?
7. What does Didion's statement "I need more than words to find the meaning" of her experience (¶ 11) suggest to the reader about the path the rest of her narrative might take? What does it suggest about the purpose of her narrative? Does her statement "I was not the ideal teller of this story" (¶ 7) imply that such an ideal storyteller exists? How does her approach differ from a narrative in which the experience appears to be fully described by an objective viewer?

The Writing Process: Warmup, Vision, Re-Vision

Warmup: Getting Started

To expect some people to learn to write by showing them a published essay or book is like expecting novice bakers to learn to make a wedding cake from looking at the completed confection, resplendent with icing and decorations. Indeed, the completed product in each case offers a model of what the finished work of art should look like—in concept, organization, shape, and style. Careful examination of the text exposes the intricacies of the finished sentences, paragraphs, logic, illustrative examples, and nuances of style. The text likewise provides cues about the context (intellectual, political, aesthetic . . .) in which it originated, its purpose, and its intended audience. But no matter how hard you look, it's almost impossible to detect in a completed, professionally polished work much about the process by which it was composed—the numerous visions and revisions of ideas and expression; the effort, frustration, even exhilaration; whether the author was composing in bed, at a desk, or at a computer terminal. Blood, sweat, and tears don't belong on the printed page any more than they belong in the gymnast's flawless public performance on the balance beam. The audience wants not to agonize over the production but to enjoy the result.

Becoming a Writer

For better and for worse, computers and other manifestations of electronic technology influence the ways we think, read, and write. (For more extensive analyses of their effects, see the essays by Deborah Tannen [308–15] and Sherry Turkle [411–17].) Growing up surrounded by sounds—from iPods, computers, and cell phones—may provide an electronic wall between the listener and the rest of the world, including other sounds natural and human. Confronting electronic screens—of computers, television, even automobile GPSs day in and night out—imposes other people's configurations of reality on one's own view of the world, just as an orientation to books and newspapers did for earlier generations. Through the media and reading, we see the world through others' eyes; and the broader and more diverse these sources of vision, the more points of view the thoughtful person has available to ponder, accept, reject, ignore, or file away for future reference.

For college students, writing provides innumerable opportunities for both processing what you've already been exposed to and escaping from it. You can help yourself focus if you shut out the distractions—other people's words arriving by screen, headphones, or live conversation or music, and colors and images moving in and through your peripheral vision.

As you start to work, urges Stephen King in "A door . . . you are willing to shut" (39–41), find a private writing space, keeping people and other distractions out and yourself in. "The closed door is your way of telling the world and yourself that you mean business; you have made a serious commitment to write. . . ." King suggests you settle on a "daily writing goal" and get to work.

For many people, the most difficult part of writing is getting started. It's hard to begin if you don't know what to write about. Sometimes people make lists, to generate and sort out ideas. Making "A List of Nothing in Particular" (49–51), as William Least Heat-Moon did when he drove his van through the "barren waste" of west Texas on a circuit of the country, can enable one to extract some meaning, some significance even out of a territory where "'there's nothing out there.'" Least Heat-Moon's list has an eclectic span, seemingly random until it snaps into focus, ranging from "mockingbird" to "jackrabbit (chewed on cactus)" to "wind (always)." Talking with others, making an "idea tree," brainstorming, reading, thinking—even dreaming or daydreaming—all of these can provide you with something to write about, if you remain receptive to the possibilities.

You may end up writing a piece—preferably short—composed entirely of lists. Even if you simply go somewhere and take notes on what you see, once you've organized them into categories that make logical or artistic sense, you've got the start—if not the finish—of a paper.

Writers' Notebooks

Keeping a writer's diary or notebook, whether you do it with pencil, pen, word processor, or even cell phone, can be a good way to get started—and even to keep going. Writing regularly—and better yet, at a regular time of the day or week—in a notebook or its electronic equivalent, can give you a lot to think about while you're writing, and a lot to expand on later. You could keep an account of what you do every day (6:30–7:30, swimming laps, shower; 7:30–8:15, breakfast—toasted English muffin, orange juice, raspberry yogurt . . .), but if your life is routine, that might get monotonous.

A provocative and potentially useful writer's notebook might contain any or all of the following types of writing, and more:

- Reactions to one's reading.
- Provocative quotations—invented, read, or overheard; appealing figures of speech; dialogue, dialect.
- Lists—including sights, sounds, scents.
- Memorable details—of clothing, animals, objects, settings, phenomena, processes.
- Personal aspirations, fears, joy, anger.

- Sketches of people, either intrinsically interesting or engaged in intriguing activities, whether novel or familiar.
- Analyses of friendships, family relationships.
- Commentary on notable events, current or past, national or more immediate.
- Possibilities for adventure, exploration, conflict.
- Jokes, anecdotes, and humorous situations, characters, comic mannerisms, punch lines, provocative settings.

You'll need to put enough explanatory details in your notebook to remind yourself three weeks—or three years—later what something meant when you wrote it down. In a writer's notebook you can be most candid, most off guard, for there you're writing primarily for yourself. You're also writing for yourself when you're freewriting—writing rapidly, with or without a particular subject, without editing, while you're in the process of generating ideas. As you freewrite you can free-associate, thinking of connections among like and unlike things or ideas, exploring their implications. Anything goes into the notebook, but not everything stays in later drafts if you decide to turn some of your most focused discussion into an essay. If you get into the habit of writing regularly on paper, you may find that you're also hearing the "voices in your head" that professional writers often experience. As humorist James Thurber explained to an interviewer, "I never quite know when I'm not writing. Sometimes my wife comes up to me at a party and says, 'Dammit, Thurber, stop writing.' Or my daughter will look up from the dinner table and ask, 'Is he sick?' 'No,' my wife says, 'he's writing something.'"

Playing around with words and ideas in a notebook or in your head can also lead to an entire essay: a narrative, character sketch, reminiscence, discussion of how to do it, an argument, review, or some other form suitable for an extended piece of writing.

No matter what you write about, rereading a notebook entry or a freewriting can provide some material to start with. Ask yourself, "What do I want to write about?" "What makes me particularly happy—or angry?" Don't write about something that seems bland, like a cookie without sugar. If it doesn't appeal to you, it won't attract your readers either. As you write you will almost automatically be using description, narration, comparison and contrast, and other rhetorical techniques to express yourself, even if you don't attach labels to them.

Re-Vision and Revision*

The pun is intentional. *Re-vision* and *revision* both mean, literally, "to see again." Donald M. Murray's example of revision, "The Maker's Eye: Revising Your Own Manuscripts" (54–62), reveals the passionate commitment writers

---

* Note: Some material on pages 35–38 is adapted from Lynn Z. Bloom, *Fact and Artifact: Writing Nonfiction*, 2nd ed. (Englewood Cliffs, N.J.: Blair Press [Prentice Hall], 1994), 51–53.

make to their work. Because they are fully invested in their writing, mind, heart, and spirit, they care enough about it to be willing to rewrite again and again and again until they get it right—in subject and substance, structure and style.

Of course, this example is meant to inspire you, as well, to be willing "to see again." When you take a second, careful look at what you wrote as a freewriting or a first draft, chances are you'll decide to change it. If and when you do, you're approaching the process that most professional writers use—and your own work will be one step closer to professional. As playwright Neil Simon says, "Rewriting is when writing really gets to be fun. . . . In baseball you only get three swings and you're out. In rewriting, you get almost as many swings as you want and you know, sooner or later, you'll hit the ball."

Some people think that revision means correcting the spelling and punctuation of a first—and only—draft. Writers who care about their work know that such changes, though necessary, are editorial matters remote from the heart of real revising. For to revise is to rewrite. And rewrite again, though not in the spirit that Calvin tells Hobbes in the cartoon (61), making bad writing incomprehensible. Novelist Toni Morrison affirms, "The best part of all, the absolutely most delicious part, is finishing it and then doing it over. . . . I rewrite a lot, over and over again, so that it looks like I never did. I try to make it look like I never touched it, and that takes a lot of time and a lot of sweat."

When you rewrite, you're doing what computer language identifies as *insert, delete, cut and paste* (reorganize), and *edit*. The concept of "draft" may have become elusive for people writing on a computer; one part of a given document may have been revised extensively, other parts may be in various stages of development, while still others have yet to be written. For simplicity's sake, we'll use the term *draft* throughout *The Essay Connection* to refer to one particular version of a given essay (whether the writer considers it finished or not), as opposed to other versions of that same document. Even if you're only making a grocery list, you might add and subtract material, or change the organization. If your original list identified the items in the order they occurred to you, as lists often do, you could regroup them according to your route through the supermarket by categories of similar items: produce, staples, meat, dairy products, providing extra details when necessary—"a pound of Milagro super-hot green chilies" and "a half gallon of Death by Chocolate ice cream."

Some writers compose essentially in their minds. They work through their first drafts in their heads, over and over, before putting much—if anything—down on paper. As Joyce Carol Oates says, "If you are a writer, you locate yourself behind a wall of silence and no matter what you are doing, driving a car or walking or doing housework . . . you can still be writing." There's a lot of revising going on, but it's mostly mental. What appears on the paper the first time is what stays on the paper, with occasional minor changes. This writing process appears to work best with short pieces that can easily be held in the mind—a poem, a writing with a fixed and conventional format (such as a lab report), a short essay with a single central point, a narrative in which each point in the sequence reminds the writer of what comes next, logically, chronologically, psychologically. If you write that way, then what we say about revising on paper should apply to your mental revising, as well.

Other writers use a first draft, and sometimes a second, and a third, and more, to enable themselves to think on paper. Novelist E. M. Forster observed, "How do I know what I think until I see what I say?" How you wrote the first draft may provide cues about what will need special attention when you revise. If you use a first draft to generate ideas, in revising you'll want to prune and shape to arrive at a precise subject and focus and an organization that reinforces your emphasis. Or your first draft may be a sketch, little more than an outline in paragraph form, just to get down the basic ideas. In revising you'd aim to flesh out this bare-bones discussion by elaborating on these essential points, supplying illustrations, or consulting references that you didn't want to look up the first time around. On the other hand, you may typically write a great deal more than you need, just to be sure of capturing random and stray ideas that may prove useful. Your revising of such an ample draft might consist in part of deleting irrelevant ideas and redundant illustrations.

Donald M. Murray suggests a three-stage revising process that you might find helpful in general, whether or not you've settled on your own particular style of revising:

1. A quick first reading "to make sure that there is a single dominant meaning" and enough information to support that meaning.
2. A second quick reading, only slightly slower than the first, to focus on the overall structure and pace.
3. A third reading, "slow, careful, line-by-line editing of the text . . . here the reader cuts, adds, and reorders, paragraph by paragraph, sentence by sentence, word by word" (*Write to Learn*, Fort Worth, TX: Harcourt, 1993, 167).

First you look at the forest, then at the shape and pattern of the individual trees, then close up, at the branches and leaves. Although this may sound slow and cumbersome, if you try it, you'll find that it's actually faster and easier than trying to catch everything in one laborious reading, alternating between panoramic views and close-ups. Murray expands on these ideas in "The Maker's Eye: Revising Your Own Manuscripts" (54–62).

John Trimble, in *Writing with Style* (Englewood Cliffs, N.J.: Prentice Hall, 1975), offers a number of suggestions for writing in a very readable style that work equally well for first drafts as well as for revision. Trimble's cardinal principles are these: (1) Write as if your reader is a "companionable friend" who appreciates straightforwardness and has a sense of humor. (2) Write as if you were "talking to that friend," but had enough time to express your thoughts in a concise and interesting manner. He also suggests that if you've written three long sentences in a row, make the fourth sentence short. Even very short. Use contractions. Reinforce abstract discussions with "graphic illustrations, analogies, apt quotations, and concrete details." To achieve continuity, he advises, make sure each sentence is connected with those preceding and following it. And, most important: "Read your prose aloud. *Always* read your prose aloud. If it sounds as if it's come out of a machine or a social scientist's report . . . spare your reader and rewrite it."

Ernest Hemingway has said that he "rewrote the ending of *A Farewell to Arms*, the last page of it, thirty-nine times before I was satisfied"—which means a great deal of rewriting, even if you don't think he kept exact count.

"Was there some technical problem?" asked an interviewer. "What had you stumped?"

"Getting the words right," said Hemingway.

That is the essence of revision.

Strategies for Revising

1. Does my draft have a *thesis*, a focal point? Does the thesis cover the entire essay, and convey my attitude toward the subject?
2. Does my draft contain sufficient *information, evidence* to support that meaning? Is the writing developed sufficiently, or do I need to provide additional information, steps in an argument, illustrations, or analysis of what I've already said?
3. Who is my intended *audience*? Will they understand what I've said? Do I need to supply any background information? Will I meet my readers as friends, antagonists, or on neutral ground? How will this relationship determine what I say, the order in which I say it, and the language I use?
4. Do the *form* and *structure* of my writing suit the subject? (For instance, would a commentary on fast-food restaurants be more effective in an essay or description, comparison and contrast, analysis, some combination of the three—or as a narrative or satire?) Does the *proportioning* reinforce my emphasis (in other words, do the most important points get the most space)? Or do I need to expand some aspects and condense others?
5. Is the writing recognizably mine in *style, voice,* and *point of view*? Is the body of my prose like that of an experienced runner: tight and taut, vigorous, self-contained, and supple? Do I like what I've said? If not, am I willing to change it?

STEPHEN KING

"People want to be scared," says Stephen King (born 1947, a.k.a. Richard Bachman and John Swithen), but "beneath its fangs and fright wig," horror fiction is quite conservative, for readers understand that "the evildoers will almost certainly be punished." After working as a janitor, mill hand, and laundry laborer, he graduated from the University of Maine (BA, 1970) and taught high school English briefly while writing his enormously popular first novel, *Carrie* (1974). This inaugurated a career-long series of bestsellers, from *The Shining* (1977) to *From a Buick 8* (2002) and *Lisey's Story* (2006), as well as short stories, film, and video scripts characterized by a mix of horror, fantasy, science fiction, and humor. In June 1999 he was hit by a car while taking his habitual walk along a Maine highway. During his long recuperation from serious injuries he wrote *On Writing: A Memoir of the Craft* (2000), in which "A door . . . you are willing to shut" appears.

"Once I start to work on a project," explains King, "I don't stop and I don't slow down. . . . I write every day, workaholic dweeb or not. That includes Christmas, the Fourth [of July], and my birthday." Not working, he says, "is the real work. When I'm writing, it's all the playground, and the worst three hours I ever spent there were still pretty damn good." The work starts, he says, by finding "a door ... you are willing to shut," avoiding distractions such as telephones and video games. "Put your desk in the corner, and every time you sit down there to write, remind yourself of why it isn't in the middle of the room. Life isn't a support-system for art. It's the other way around."

"A door . . . you are willing to shut" *

You can read anywhere, almost, but when it comes to writing, library carrels, park benches, and rented flats should be courts of last resort—Truman Capote said he did his best work in motel rooms, but he is an exception; most of us do our best in a place of our own. Until you get one, you'll find your new resolution to write a lot hard to take seriously. 1

Your writing room doesn't have to sport a Playboy Philosophy decor, and you don't need an Early American rolltop desk in which to house your writing implements. I wrote my first two published novels, *Carrie* and *'Salem's Lot*, in the laundry room of a doublewide trailer, pounding away on my wife's portable Olivetti typewriter and balancing a child's desk on my thighs; John Cheever reputedly wrote in the basement of his Park Avenue apartment building, near the furnace. The space can 2

* Reprinted with the permission of Scribner, an imprint of Simon & Schuster Adult Publishing Group, from ON WRITING: A MEMOIR OF THE CRAFT. Copyright © 2000 by Stephen King. All rights reserved.

be humble (probably *should* be, as I think I have already suggested), and it really needs only one thing: a door which you are willing to shut. The closed door is your way of telling the world and yourself that you mean business; you have made a serious commitment to write and intend to walk the walk as well as talk the talk.

3 By the time you step into your new writing space and close the door, you should have settled on a daily writing goal. As with physical exercise, it would be best to set this goal low at first, to avoid discouragement. I suggest a thousand words a day, and because I'm feeling magnanimous, I'll also suggest that you can take one day a week off, at least to begin with. No more; you'll lose the urgency and immediacy of your story if you do. With that goal set, resolve to yourself that the door stays closed until that goal is met. Get busy putting those thousand words on paper or on a floppy disk. In an early interview (this was to promote *Carrie*, I think), a radio talk-show host asked me how I wrote. My reply—"One word at a time"—seemingly left him without a reply. I think he was trying to decide whether or not I was joking. I wasn't. In the end, it's always that simple. Whether it's a vignette of a single page or an epic trilogy like *The Lord of the Rings*, the work is always accomplished one word at a time. The door closes the rest of the world out; it also serves to close you in and keep you focused on the job at hand.

4 If possible, there should be no telephone in your writing room, certainly no TV or videogames for you to fool around with. If there's a window, draw the curtains or pull down the shades unless it looks out at a blank wall. For any writer, but for the beginning writer in particular, it's wise to eliminate every possible distraction. If you continue to write, you will begin to filter out these distractions naturally, but at the start it's best to try and take care of them before you write. I work to loud music—hard-rock stuff like AC/DC, Guns 'n Roses, and Metallica have always been particular favorites—but for me the music is just another way of shutting the door. It surrounds me, keeps the mundane world out. When you write, you want to get rid of the world, do you not? Of course you do. When you're writing, you're creating your own worlds.

5 I think we're actually talking about creative sleep. Like your bedroom, your writing room should be private, a place where you go to dream. Your schedule—in at about the same time every day, out when your thousand words are on paper or disk—exists in order to habituate yourself, to make yourself ready to dream just as you make yourself ready to sleep by going to bed at roughly the same time each night and following the same ritual as you go. In both writing and sleeping, we learn to be physically still at the same time we are encouraging our minds to unlock from the humdrum rational thinking of our daytime lives. And as your mind and body grow accustomed to a certain amount of sleep each night—six hours, seven, maybe the recommended eight—so can you train your waking mind to sleep creatively and work out the vividly imagined waking dreams which are successful works of fiction.

But you need the room, you need the door, and you need the determination to shut the door. You need a concrete goal, as well. The longer you keep to these basics, the easier the act of writing will become. Don't wait for the muse. As I've said, he's a hardheaded guy who's not susceptible to a lot of creative fluttering. This isn't the Ouija board or the spirit-world we're talking about here, but just another job like laying pipe or driving long-haul trucks. Your job is to make sure the muse knows where you're going to be every day from nine 'til noon or seven 'til three. If he does know, I assure you that sooner or later he'll start showing up, chomping his cigar and making his magic. 6

Content

1. Why are "the basics" King identifies—"the room," "the door," "the determination to shut the door," and "a concrete goal"—so important for writing? In your own experience, is each of equal importance? Do you share King's preference for writing with the shades drawn to "loud music—hard-rock stuff"? What is your ideal writing environment? How can you or do you control it?
2. King characterizes the act of "creating your own worlds" as "creative sleep" (¶s 3–4). Does King's view of writing pertain to nonfiction writing? How might you apply his advice to autobiographical writing or a paper on an academic subject?

Strategies/Structures/Language

3. Advice givers often preach. And readers often resent being preached at. King delivers his advice very emphatically. Is he preaching? If he doesn't offend you, will you take his advice?
4. King alludes to the muse of creativity—traditionally considered a beautiful woman playing alluring music—as a male, "chomping his cigar and making his magic" (¶ 6). Why does King choose such a macho muse instead of a more traditional figure? How does this muse relate to King's writing—his subjects and his style?
5. "A door which you are willing to shut" (¶ 2) works on both the literal and metaphorical levels. Explain why this is a good way to get double mileage out of your language.

For Writing

6. ***Journal Writing.*** Take King's advice and find a private writing space to which you can retreat daily. Write one page (around 250 words) a day for a full week. As the week goes on, try changing some of the features in your environment (write at different times of the day or night, let people or pets in or keep them out, turn the music or TV on or off) and record the effect each of these changes.
7. ***Dialogues.*** King emphasizes that discipline ("you need the determination to shut the door" [¶ 6]) is a prerequisite for writing successfully: "make sure the muse knows where you're going to be" (¶ 6). In contrast, Orhan Pamuk ("My Father's Suitcase" 42–47) emphasizes, among other things, the writer's development through reading "other people's stories, other people's books, other people's words, the thing we call tradition" (¶ 12). How does each writer's

definition of the work of writing suggest his motive for writing? If you have read any of King's fiction, discuss how he might have applied his reading of literature generally, of science fiction in particular, and perhaps knowledge he has acquired through reading other types of texts to the work of creating his fictional worlds.

8. ***Mixed Modes.*** Write an essay that describes the process of how you learned the basics of some activity that you now know how to do well. What did you have to learn first? How did you then build on that skill or knowledge? Where did you go astray? How did you finally achieve the desired result? Compare your description of this process with Donald M. Murray's analysis of writing in "The Maker's Eye: Revising Your Own Manuscripts" (54–62). Do you see any analogies between the process you describe and that of writing? Does writing about the process you have described clarify how you learned from your successes and failures?

9. ***Second Look.*** The photograph staged by Franz Boas and George Hunt on 86 reminds us that stories represent the selective vision or purposeful arrangement of their creators. Compare your reading of this photograph with King's commitment to "get rid of the world" in order to create "your own worlds" (¶ 4). What kinds of artistic and moral choices does a writer or a photographer face in selectively representing his or her material? What kinds of choices imply a compromise of the artist's integrity?

ORHAN PAMUK

Orhan Pamuk (born in Istanbul in 1952) is an internationally renowned novelist, journalist, and commentator on political and cultural affairs. His novels include *Cevdet Bey and His Sons* (1982), *The Silent House* (1983), *The White Castle* (1985), *The Black Book* (1990), *The New Life* (1994), *My Name is Red* (1998), and *Snow* (2002). His journalism and essays on literature and culture have been collected in *Other Colours* (2007). *Istanbul: Memories and the City* (2005) is a poetical work that combines memoir with essay, photographs, and paintings. Pamuk's critical comments on the Armenian and Kurdish genocides provoked criminal charges that fueled an international outcry in his support and were eventually dropped. Pamuk has been a visiting scholar at Columbia University. He has won multiple national and international literary awards, including the 2006 Nobel Prize in Literature. "My Father's Suitcase," excerpted from his Nobel lecture, draws on the image of his father's "small, black, leather suitcase" to explore the complex relationship between the solitary work of imaginative creation, the literary traditions the writer draws on, and the "great faith in humanity" that sustains him.

My Father's Suitcase

1 Two years before his death, my father gave me a small suitcase filled with his writings, manuscripts and notebooks. Assuming his usual joking, mocking air, he told me he wanted me to read them after he was gone, by which he meant after he died.

"Just take a look," he said, looking slightly embarrassed. "See if 2
there's anything inside that you can use. Maybe after I'm gone you can make a selection and publish it."

We were in my study, surrounded by books. My father was searching 3
for a place to set down the suitcase, wandering back and forth like a man who wished to rid himself of a painful burden. In the end, he deposited it quietly in an unobtrusive corner. It was a shaming moment that neither of us ever forgot, but once it had passed and we had gone back into our usual roles, taking life lightly, our joking, mocking personas took over and we relaxed. We talked as we always did, about the trivial things of everyday life, and Turkey's neverending political troubles, and my father's mostly failed business ventures, without feeling too much sorrow.

I remember that after my father left, I spent several days walking back 4
and forth past the suitcase without once touching it. I was already familiar with this small, black, leather suitcase, and its lock, and its rounded corners. My father would take it with him on short trips and sometimes use it to carry documents to work. I remembered that when I was a child, and my father came home from a trip, I would open this little suitcase and rummage through his things, savouring the scent of cologne and foreign countries. This suitcase was a familiar friend, a powerful reminder of my childhood, my past, but now I couldn't even touch it. Why? No doubt it was because of the mysterious weight of its contents.

I am now going to speak of this weight's meaning. It is what a person 5
creates when he shuts himself up in a room, sits down at a table, and retires to a corner to express his thoughts—that is, the meaning of literature.

When I did touch my father's suitcase, I still could not bring myself 6
to open it, but I did know what was inside some of those notebooks. I had seen my father writing things in a few of them. This was not the first time I had heard of the heavy load inside the suitcase. My father had a large library; in his youth, in the late 1940s, he had wanted to be an Istanbul poet, and had translated Valéry into Turkish, but he had not wanted to live the sort of life that came with writing poetry in a poor country with few readers. My father's father—my grandfather—had been a wealthy business man; my father had led a comfortable life as a child and a young man, and he had no wish to endure hardship for the sake of literature, for writing. He loved life with all its beauties—this I understood.

The first thing that kept me distant from the contents of my father's 7
suitcase was, of course, the fear that I might not like what I read. Because my father knew this, he had taken the precaution of acting as if he did not take its contents seriously. After working as a writer for 25 years, it pained me to see this. But I did not even want to be angry at my father for failing to take literature seriously enough . . . My real fear, the crucial thing that I did not wish to know or discover, was the possibility that my father might be a good writer. I couldn't open my father's suitcase because I feared this. Even worse, I couldn't even admit this myself openly. If true

and great literature emerged from my father's suitcase, I would have to acknowledge that inside my father there existed an entirely different man. This was a frightening possibility. Because even at my advanced age I wanted my father to be only my father—not a writer.

8 A writer is someone who spends years patiently trying to discover the second being inside him, and the world that makes him who he is: when I speak of writing, what comes first to my mind is not a novel, a poem, or literary tradition, it is a person who shuts himself up in a room, sits down at a table, and alone, turns inward; amid its shadows, he builds a new world with words. This man—or this woman—may use a typewriter, profit from the ease of a computer, or write with a pen on paper, as I have done for 30 years. As he writes, he can drink tea or coffee, or smoke cigarettes. From time to time he may rise from his table to look out through the window at the children playing in the street, and, if he is lucky, at trees and a view, or he can gaze out at a black wall. He can write poems, plays, or novels, as I do. All these differences come after the crucial task of sitting down at the table and patiently turning inwards. To write is to turn this inward gaze into words, to study the world into which that person passes when he retires into himself, and to do so with patience, obstinacy, and joy. As I sit at my table, for days, months, years, slowly adding new words to the empty page, I feel as if I am creating a new world, as if I am bringing into being that other person inside me, in the same way someone might build a bridge or a dome, stone by stone. The stones we writers use are words. As we hold them in our hands, sensing the ways in which each of them is connected to the others, looking at them sometimes from afar, sometimes almost caressing them with our fingers and the tips of our pens, weighing them, moving them around, year in and year out, patiently and hopefully, we create new worlds.

9 The writer's secret is not inspiration—for it is never clear where it comes from—it is his stubbornness, his patience. That lovely Turkish saying—to dig a well with a needle—seems to me to have been said with writers in mind. In the old stories, I love the patience of Ferhat, who digs through mountains for his love—and I understand it, too. In my novel, *My Name is Red*, when I wrote about the old Persian miniaturists who had drawn the same horse with the same passion for so many years, memorising each stroke, that they could recreate that beautiful horse even with their eyes closed, I knew I was talking about the writing profession, and my own life. If a writer is to tell his own story—tell it slowly, and as if it were a story about other people—if he is to feel the power of the story rise up inside him, if he is to sit down at a table and patiently give himself over to this art—this craft—he must first have been given some hope. The angel of inspiration (who pays regular visits to some and rarely calls on others) favours the hopeful and the confident, and it is when a writer feels most lonely, when he feels most doubtful about his efforts, his dreams, and the value of his writing—when he thinks his story is only his story—it is at

such moments that the angel chooses to reveal to him stories, images and dreams that will draw out the world he wishes to build. If I think back on the books to which I have devoted my entire life, I am most surprised by those moments when I have felt as if the sentences, dreams, and pages that have made me so ecstatically happy have not come from my own imagination—that another power has found them and generously presented them to me.

10 I was afraid of opening my father's suitcase and reading his notebooks because I knew that he would not tolerate the difficulties I had endured, that it was not solitude he loved but mixing with friends, crowds, salons, jokes, company. But later my thoughts took a different turn. These thoughts, these dreams of renunciation and patience, were prejudices I had derived from my own life and my own experience as a writer. There were plenty of brilliant writers who wrote surrounded by crowds and family life, in the glow of company and happy chatter. . . .

11 But as I gazed so anxiously at the suitcase my father had bequeathed me, I also felt that this was the very thing I would not be able to do. My father would sometimes stretch out on the divan in front of his books, abandon the book in his hand, or the magazine and drift off into a dream, lose himself for the longest time in his thoughts. When I saw on his face an expression so very different from the one he wore amid the joking, teasing, and bickering of family life—when I saw the first signs of an inward gaze—I would, especially during my childhood and my early youth, understand, with trepidation, that he was discontent. Now, so many years later, I know that this discontent is the basic trait that turns a person into a writer. To become a writer, patience and toil are not enough: we must first feel compelled to escape crowds, company, the stuff of ordinary, everyday life, and shut ourselves up in a room. We wish for patience and hope so that we can create a deep world in our writing. But the desire to shut oneself up in a room is what pushes us into action. The precursor of this sort of independent writer—who reads his books to his heart's content, and who, by listening only to the voice of his own conscience, disputes with other's words, who, by entering into conversation with his books develops his own thoughts, and his own world—was most certainly Montaigne, in the earliest days of modern literature. Montaigne was a writer to whom my father returned often, a writer he recommended to me. I would like to see myself as belonging to the tradition of writers who—wherever they are in the world, in the East or in the West—cut themselves off from society, and shut themselves up with their books in their room. The starting point of true literature is the man who shuts himself up in his room with his books.

12 But once we shut ourselves away, we soon discover that we are not as alone as we thought. We are in the company of the words of those who came before us, of other people's stories, other people's books, other people's words, the thing we call tradition. I believe literature to be the

most valuable hoard that humanity has gathered in its quest to understand itself. Societies, tribes, and peoples grow more intelligent, richer, and more advanced as they pay attention to the troubled words of their authors, and, as we all know, the burning of books and the denigration of writers are both signals that dark and improvident times are upon us. But literature is never just a national concern. The writer who shuts himself up in a room and first goes on a journey inside himself will, over the years, discover literature's eternal rule: he must have the artistry to tell his own stories as if they were other people's stories, and to tell other people's stories as if they were his own, for this is what literature is. But we must first travel through other people's stories and books. . . .

13 A writer talks of things that everyone knows but does not know they know. To explore this knowledge, and to watch it grow, is a pleasurable thing; the reader is visiting a world at once familiar and miraculous. When a writer shuts himself up in a room for years on end to hone his craft—to create a world—if he uses his secret wounds as his starting point, he is, whether he knows it or not, putting a great faith in humanity. My confidence comes from the belief that all human beings resemble each other, that others carry wounds like mine—that they will therefore understand. All true literature rises from this childish, hopeful certainty that all people resemble each other. When a writer shuts himself up in a room for years on end, with this gesture he suggests a single humanity, a world without a centre.

14 But as can be seen from my father's suitcase and the pale colours of our lives in Istanbul, the world did have a centre, and it was far away from us. In my books I have described in some detail how this basic fact evoked a Checkovian sense of provinciality, and how, by another route, it led to my questioning my authenticity. I know from experience that the great majority of people on this earth live with these same feelings, and that many suffer from an even deeper sense of insufficiency, lack of security and sense of degradation, than I do. Yes, the greatest dilemmas facing humanity are still landlessness, homelessness, and hunger . . . But today our televisions and newspapers tell us about these fundamental problems more quickly and more simply than literature can ever do. What literature needs most to tell and investigate today are humanity's basic fears: the fear of being left outside, and the fear of counting for nothing, and the feelings of worthlessness that come with such fears; the collective humiliations, vulnerabilities, slights, grievances, sensitivities, and imagined insults, and the nationalist boasts and inflations that are their next of kind . . . Whenever I am confronted by such sentiments, and by the irrational, overstated language in which they are usually expressed, I know they touch on a darkness inside me. We have often witnessed peoples, societies and nations outside the Western world—and I can identify with them easily—succumbing to fears that sometimes lead them to commit stupidities, all because of their fears of humiliation and their sensitivities. I also know that in the West—a world with which I can identify with the

same ease—nations and peoples taking an excessive pride in their wealth, and in their having brought us the Renaissance, the Enlightenment, and Modernism, have, from time to time, succumbed to a self-satisfaction that is almost as stupid.

This means that my father was not the only one, that we all give too 15
much importance to the idea of a world with a centre. Whereas the thing that compels us to shut ourselves up to write in our rooms for years on end is a faith in the opposite; the belief that one day our writings will be read and understood, because people all the world over resemble each other. . . .

Let me change the mood with a few sweet words that will, I hope, 16
serve as well as that music. As you know, the question we writers are asked most often, the favourite question, is; why do you write? I write because I have an innate need to write! I write because I can't do normal work like other people. I write because I want to read books like the ones I write. I write because I am angry at all of you, angry at everyone. I write because I love sitting in a room all day writing. I write because I can only partake in real life by changing it. I write because I want others, all of us, the whole world, to know what sort of life we lived, and continue to live, in Istanbul, in Turkey. I write because I love the smell of paper, pen, and ink. I write because I believe in literature, in the art of the novel, more than I believe in anything else. I write because it is a habit, a passion. I write because I am afraid of being forgotten. I write because I like the glory and interest that writing brings. I write to be alone. Perhaps I write because I hope to understand why I am so very, very angry at all of you, so very, very angry at everyone. I write because I like to be read. I write because once I have begun a novel, an essay, a page, I want to finish it. I write because everyone expects me to write. I write because I have a childish belief in the immortality of libraries, and in the way my books sit on the shelf. I write because it is exciting to turn all of life's beauties and riches into words. I write not to tell a story, but to compose a story. I write because I wish to escape from the foreboding that there is a place I must go but—just as in a dream—I can't quite get there. I write because I have never managed to be happy. I write to be happy. . . .

(Translation from Turkish by Maureen Freely)

Content

1. Why does the suitcase appear to Pamuk as his father's "painful burden" (¶ 3)? How does Pamuk characterize his father's relationship to writing? What are the reasons Pamuk gives for refusing to open his father's suitcase? What do those reasons suggest about his relationship with his father?
2. How does Pamuk describe the life of the writer? How does his discussion of his work as a writer lead him to reevaluate his feelings about his father's suitcase and the notebooks it contains?

3. Why does the act of writing for Pamuk suggest "a single humanity, a world without a centre" (¶ 13)? How does Pamuk reconcile the importance of the writer's seclusion and solitude and the writer's fundamental need to speak to an audience, to "to tell his own stories as if they were other people's stories" (¶ 12)? What role does literary tradition play for him as a writer?

Strategies/Structures/Language

4. Pamuk uses the descriptive phrase "the heavy load inside the suitcase" (¶ 6) to refer to both books and, metaphorically, to his father's memories, aspirations, and dreams. Identify other ways that Pamuk uses descriptive language to characterize the life and work of the writer. For example, Pamuk writes "the stones we writers use are words" (¶ 8). What does this language suggest about the narrator's view of his writing?

5. Pamuk likens the work of the writer to "old Persian miniaturists who had drawn the same horse with the same passion for so many years" (¶ 9). How does this comparison illustrate his feelings about his father's suitcase?

For Writing

6. ***Journal Writing.*** Do you agree with Pamuk that the role of literature today is "to tell and investigate . . . humanity's basic fears" (¶ 14)? How does this work differ from that of television, print, and Internet journalism?

7. ***Dialogues.*** Compare what writing and literacy represent to Pamuk's father with what they represent to Ning Yu's father in "Red and Black" (Chapter 4). What kind of legacy does each father leave to his son?

8. ***Second Look.*** How does the photograph of the child reading and writing (Chapter 4) illustrate the connection Pamuk draws between the writer's travels "through other people's stories and books" (¶ 12)? Does a writer inevitably convey his or her own experience through the lens of others' stories?

WILLIAM LEAST HEAT-MOON

William Least Heat-Moon (born 1939), as William Trogdon renamed himself to acknowledge his Osage Indian ancestry, earned four degrees from the University of Missouri–Columbia, including a BA in photojournalism (1978) and a PhD in literature (1973). His books include *PrairyErth* (1991) and *River-Horse* (1992). On one cold day in February 1979, "a day of canceled expectations," Least Heat-Moon lost both his wife ("the Cherokee") and his part-time job teaching English at a Missouri college.

True to the American tradition, to escape he took to the road, the "blue highways"—back roads on the old road maps—in the van that would be home as he circled the United States clockwise "in search of places where change did not mean ruin and where time and men and deeds connected." His account of his trip, *Blue Highways* (1982), is an intimate exploration of America's small towns, "Remote, Oregon; Simplicity, Virginia; New Freedom, Pennsylvania; New Hope, Tennessee; Why, Arizona; Whynot, Mississippi; Igo, California (just down the road from Ono). . . . " Though he tried to lose himself as a stranger in a strange land, as he came to know and appreciate the country through its back roads and small towns, Least Heat-Moon came inevitably to know and come to terms with himself. "The mere listing of details meaningless in themselves, at once provides them with significance which one denies in vain," says novelist Steven Millhauser. "The beauty of irrelevance fades away, accident darkens into design." Consequently, traveling—moving along a linear route—lends itself to list making, a good way to impose design on happenstance, to remember where you're going, where you've been, whom you've met, what you've seen or done.

A List of Nothing in Particular

Straight as a chief's countenance, the road lay ahead, curves so long 1
and gradual as to be imperceptible except on the map. For nearly a hundred miles due west of Eldorado, not a single town. It was the Texas some people see as barren waste when they cross it, the part they later describe at the motel bar as "nothing." They say, "There's nothing out there."

Driving through the miles of nothing, I decided to test the hypoth- 2
esis and stopped somewhere in western Crockett County on the top of a broad mesa, just off Texas 29. At a distance, the land looked so rocky and dry, a religious man could believe that the First Hand never got around to the creation in here. Still, somebody had decided to string barbed wire around it.

No plant grew higher than my head. For a while, I heard only miles 3
of wind against the Ghost; but after the ringing in my ears stopped, I heard myself breathing, then a bird note, an answering call, another kind of birdsong, and another: mockingbird, mourning dove, an enigma. I heard the high zizz of flies the color of gray flannel and the deep buzz of a blue bumblebee. I made a list of nothing in particular:

1. mockingbird
2. mourning dove
3. enigma bird (heard not saw)
4. gray flies
5. blue bumblebee
6. two circling buzzards (not yet, boys)
7. orange ants
8. black ants
9. orange-black ants (what's been going on?)
10. three species of spiders

11. opossum skull
12. jackrabbit (chewed on cactus)
13. deer (left scat)
14. coyote (left tracks)
15. small rodent (den full of seed hulls under rock)
16. snake (skin hooked on cactus spine)
17. prickly pear cactus (yellow blossoms)
18. hedgehog cactus (orange blossoms)
19. barrel cactus (red blossoms)
20. devil's pincushion (no blossoms)
21. catclaw (no better name)
22. two species of grass (neither green, both alive)
23. yellow flowers (blossoms smaller than peppercorns)
24. sage (indicates alkali-free soil)
25. mesquite (three-foot plants with eighty-foot roots to reach water that fell as rain two thousand years ago)
26. greasewood (oh, yes)
27. joint fir (steeped stems make Brigham Young tea)
28. earth
29. sky
30. wind (always)

That was all the nothing I could identify then, but had I waited until dark when the desert really comes to life, I could have done better. To say nothing is out here is incorrect; to say the desert is stingy with everything except space and light, stone and earth is closer to the truth.

4 I drove on. The low sun turned the mesa rimrock to silhouettes, angular and weird and unearthly; had someone said the far side of Saturn looked just like this, I would have believed him. The road dropped to the Pecos River, now dammed to such docility I couldn't imagine it formerly demarking the western edge of a rudimentary white civilization. Even the old wagonmen felt the unease of isolation when they crossed the Pecos, a small but once serious river that has had many names: Rio de las Vacas (River of Cows—perhaps a reference to bison), Rio Salado (Salty River), Rio Puerco (Dirty River).

5 West of the Pecos, a strangely truncated cone rose from the valley. In the oblique evening light, its silhouette looked like a Mayan temple, so perfect was its symmetry. I stopped again, started climbing, stirring a panic of lizards on the way up. From the top, the rubbled land below—veined with the highway and arroyos, topographical relief absorbed in the dusk—looked like a roadmap.

6 The desert, more than any other terrain, shows its age, shows time because so little vegetation covers the ancient erosions of wind and storm. What appears is tawny grit once stone and stone crumbling to grit. Everywhere rock, earth's oldest thing. Even desert creatures come from a time older than the woodland animals, and they, in answer to the arduousness,

have retained prehistoric coverings of chitin and lapped scale and primitive defenses of spine and stinger, fang and poison, shell and claw.

The night, taking up the shadows and details, wiped the face of the desert into a simple, uncluttered blackness until there were only three things: land, wind, stars. I was there too, but my presence I felt more than saw. It was as if I had been reduced to mind, to an edge of consciousness. Men, ascetics, in all eras have gone into deserts to lose themselves—Jesus, Saint Anthony, Saint Basil, and numberless medicine men—maybe because such a losing happens almost as a matter of course here if you avail yourself. The Sioux once chanted, "All over the sky a sacred voice is calling." 7

Back to the highway, on with the headlamps, down Six Shooter Draw. In the darkness, deer, just shadows in the lights, began moving toward the desert willows in the wet bottoms. Stephen Vincent Benét: 8

When Daniel Boone goes by, at night,
The phantom deer arise
And all lost, wild America
Is burning in their eyes.

From the top of another high mesa: twelve miles west in the flat valley floor, the lights of Fort Stockton blinked white, blue, red, and yellow in the heat like a mirage. How is it that desert towns look so fine and big at night? It must be that little is hidden. The glistening ahead could have been a golden city of Cibola. But the reality of Fort Stockton was plywood and concrete block and the plastic signs of Holiday Inn and Mobil Oil. 9

The desert had given me an appetite that would have made carrion crow stuffed with saltbush taste good. I found a Mexican cafe of adobe, with a whitewashed log ceiling, creekstone fireplace, and jukebox pumping out mariachi music. It was like a bunk house. I ate burritos, chile rellenos, and pinto beans, all ladled over with a fine, incendiary sauce the color of sludge from an old steel drum. At the next table sat three big, round men: an Indian wearing a silver headband, a Chicano in a droopy Pancho Villa mustache, and a Negro in faded overalls. I thought what a litany of grievances that table could recite. But the more I looked, the more I believed they were someone's vision of the West, maybe someone making ads for Levy's bread, the ads that used to begin "You don't have to be Jewish." 10

Content

1. What details of the desert landscape does Least Heat-Moon use to describe it? How clearly can you visualize this place? Although this desert can be precisely located on a highway map, do you need to know its exact location in order to imagine it?
2. Travel writer Paul Theroux says, "The journey, not the arrival, matters." Is that true for Least Heat-Moon? Explain your answer.

Strategies/Structures/Language

3. Least Heat-Moon structures this chapter from *Blue Highways* according to time (daylight to night) and distance. How does the structure relate to the subject matter?
4. What is the effect of ending this trip through the desert with the image of "three big, round men"—an Indian, a Chicano, and a black (¶ 10)? Does the reference to Levy's Jewish rye bread in the last sentence trivialize this example?
5. What kind of character does Least Heat-Moon play in his own narrative? Is this character identical to the author who is writing the essay?
6. Least Heat-Moon includes many place names. With what effect? Do you need to read the essay with a map in hand?
7. Why are the parenthetical remarks in the list? Why do they appear beside some items and not others?

For Writing

8. ***Journal Writing.*** Make a list of "nothing in particular" that you observe in a place so familiar that you take its distinguishing features for granted: your yard, your refrigerator, your clothes closet, your desk, a supermarket or other store, a library, or any other ordinary place. Write down as many specific details as you can, in whatever order you see them. (Use parenthetical remarks, too, if you wish.) Then, organize them according to some logical or psychologically relevant pattern (such as closet to farthest away, most to least dominant impression, largest to smallest, whatever) and put them into a larger context. For instance, how does the closet or the refrigerator relate to the rest of your house? Does organizing the list stimulate you to include even more details? What can you do to keep your essay from sounding like a collection of miscellaneous trivia? Add drawings, photographs, or diagrams as desired.
9. ***Journal Writing.*** Least Heat-Moon writes of his experience in the desert, "my presence I felt more than saw. It was as if I had been reduced to mind, to an edge of consciousness" (¶ 7). Explore a journey or experience in which a similar sense of liberation allowed you to become more fully aware of and alive to the world around you.
10. Write about some portion of a trip you have taken, where you have been a stranger in a strange land. Characterize yourself as a traveler, possibly an outsider, with a particular relationship to this place (enjoyment, curiosity, boredom, loneliness, fear, fatigue, a desire to move on, or any combination of emotions you want to acknowledge). Illustrate with maps, photographs, or travel documents, if you wish.
11. ***Dialogues.*** Least Heat-Moon's list draws the reader's attention to the vibrant life of the desert. Compare his list to Jonathan Swift's in "A Modest Proposal," which highlights the plight of the starving Irish by enumerating the advantages of eating Irish babies (Chapter 11, ¶s 21–26), and Thomas Jefferson's list of grievances against the English king in the Declaration of Independence (Chapter 10, ¶s 3–29). What do these lists have in common? How do these lists serve each writer's distinct purpose?
12. ***Second Look.*** How might the photograph of the Chinese schoolgirl (Chapter 11) illustrate Least Heat-Moon's objective of pointing out what a casual observer might easily pass over? How does the angle of the photo contribute to such an interpretation?

DONALD M. MURRAY

Donald M. Murray (1924–2006) was a successful writer long before he began teaching others to write. He wrote editorials for the *Boston Herald,* (1948–1954), for which he won a Pulitzer Prize in 1954; in retirement, he wrote "Reflections," an award-winning column for the *Boston Globe*. During his quarter-century of teaching at the University of New Hampshire, Murray wrote poetry; a novel, *The Man Who Had Everything* (1964); and his most influential work, *A Writer Teaches Writing* (1964; rev. 1985). In this writer-friendly book, he explained how people really write—as opposed to how the rule books say they should—thereby persuading generations of writing teachers to focus on the process of writing, rather than on the finished product.

Revision, in Murray's view, is central to the writing process: "Good writing is essentially rewriting," by making changes—in content, in form and in proportion, and finally in voice and word choice—that will substantially improve their work, even though "the words on a page are never finished." Indeed, Murray completely rewrote this essay twice before it was first published in *The Writer* in 1973. Then, for an anthology, Murray "re-edited, re-revised, re-read, re-re-edited" it again. A draft of the first twelve paragraphs of the "re-edited, revised" version, with numerous changes is reprinted below. As you examine both versions, note that many changes appear in the final ("re-re-edited") version that are not in the "revised" draft.

*THE MAKER'S EYE: REVISING YOUR OWN MANUSCRIPTS** by DONALD M. MURRAY

1 When ~~the beginning writer~~ *students* complete~~s~~ ~~his~~ *a* first draft, ~~he usually reads it through to correct typographical errors and~~ *they* consider~~s~~ the job of writing done *-- and their teachers too often agree.* When ~~the~~ professional writer*s* complete~~s~~ ~~his~~ *the* first draft, ~~he~~ *they* usually feel~~s~~ ~~he is~~ *they are* at the start of the writing process. ~~Now that he has~~ *When* a draft *is completed, the job of* ~~he can begin~~ writing *can begin.*

2 That difference in attitude is the difference between amateur and professional, inexperience and experience, journeyman and craftsman. Peter F. Dru~~k~~*c*ker, the prolific business writer, for example, calls his first draft "the zero draft"--after that he can start cou~~t~~*n*ting. Most ~~productive~~ writers share the feeling ~~that~~ the first draft*,* and ~~most of those~~ *all* which follow*,* ~~is an~~ *are* opportunit~~y~~*ies* to discover what they have to say and how they can best say it.

~~Detachment and caring~~

3 To produce a progression of drafts, each of which says more and says it better, the writer has to develop a special *kind of* reading skill. In school we are taught to ~~read~~ *decode* what ~~is~~ *appears* on the page *as finished writing.* ~~We try to comprehend what the author has said, what he meant and what are the implications of his words.~~ *Writers, however, face a different category of possibility and responsibility. To them, the words are never finished on the page. Each can be changed, rearranged, set off a chain reaction of confusion or clarified meaning. This is a different kind of reading, possibly more difficult and certainly more exciting.*

*A different version of this article was published in *The Writer,* October 1973.

~~The~~ writers ~~of such drafts~~ must learn to be ~~his~~ their own best enemy. 4
~~He~~ Writers must accept the criticism of others -- especially teachers -- and be suspicious of
it; ~~he~~ they must accept the praise of others -- especially teachers -- and be even more
suspicious of it. ~~He~~ Writers cannot depend on others. ~~He~~ They must
detach ~~himself~~ themselves from ~~his~~ their own pages so that ~~he~~ they can apply both
~~his~~ their caring and ~~his~~ their craft to ~~his~~ their own work.

Detachment is not easy. Science fiction writer Ray 5
Bradbury supposedly puts each manuscript away for a year and
then rereads it as a stranger. Not many writers can afford
the time to do this. We must read when our judgment may be
at its worst, when we are close to the euphoric moment of
creation. The writer "should be critical of everything that
seems to him most delightful in his style," advises novelist
Nancy Hale. "He should excise what he most admires, because
he wouldn't thus admire it if he weren't . . . in a sense
protecting it from criticism."

~~The writer must learn to protect himself from his own~~ 6
~~ego, when it takes the form of uncritical pride or~~
~~uncritical self-destruction.~~ ¶ ~~As~~ Poet John Ciardi points
out, ". . . the last act of the writing must be to become
one's own reader. It is, I suppose, a schizophrenic
process, to begin passionately and to end critically, to
begin hot and to end cold; and, more important, to be
passion-hot and critic-cold at the same time."

~~Just as~~ ~~dangerous~~ unproductive ~~as the protective writer is the~~
~~despairing one, who thinks everything he does is terrible,~~
~~dreadful, awful. If he is to publish, he must save what is~~
~~effective on his page while he cuts away what doesn't work.~~
[~~The writer must hear and respect his own voice.~~]

7 Remember ~~how each~~ how the craftsm~~a~~en you have seen--the carpenter ~~eyeing the level~~ looking at the lie of a shelf, the mechanic listening to the motor--takes the instinctive step back. This is what ~~the~~ writers ~~has to~~ have to do when ~~he~~ they read~~s~~ ~~his~~ their own work. "The writer must survey his work critically, coolly, and as though he were a stranger to it," says children's book writer Eleanor Estes. "He must be willing to prune, expertly and hard-heartedly. At the end of each revision, a manuscript may look like a battered old hive, worked over, torn apart, pinned together, added to, deleted from, words changed and words changed back. Yet the book must maintain its original freshness and spontaneity."

8 ¶ We are aware of ~~the~~ writers who think everything they have written is literature but a more ~~serious~~ frequent and serious problem ~~is the~~ are writers ~~is~~ who are ~~overly~~ overly critical of each page, tear~~s~~ up each page and never complete~~s~~ a draft. The ~~cut~~ writer must cut what is bad to ~~save~~ reveal what is good.

9 ~~It is far easier for most beginning writers to understand the need for rereading and rewriting than it is to understand how to go about it. The publishing writer doesn't necessarily break down the various stages of rewriting and editing; he just goes ahead and does it.~~ ¶ one of our most prolific ~~fiction~~ writers in the English-speaking world, Anthony Burgess, says, "I might revise a page twenty times." Short story and children's writer Roald Dahl states, "By the time I'm nearing the end of a story, the first part will have been reread and altered and corrected at least 150 times. . . . Good writing is essentially rewriting. I am positive of this."

~~There is nothing virtuous in~~ *itself about* the rewriting process *isn't virtuous*. It is simply an essential condition of life for most writers. There are *a few* writers who do very little rewriting, mostly because they have the capacity and experience to create and review a large number of invisible drafts in their minds before they get to the page. And ~~many~~ *some* writers *who slowly produce finished pages, performing* ~~perform~~ all ~~of~~ the tasks of revision simultaneously, page by page, rather than draft by draft. But it is still possible to break down the process of rereading one's own work into the sequence most published writers follow *most of the time.* ~~as he studies his own page.~~ 10

~~Seven elements~~

Many writers ~~at first just~~ scan their manuscript, reading as quickly as possible ~~for~~ *to catch the larger* problems of subject and form. *They take the craftsman's step back* ~~In this way, they stand back~~ from the more ~~technical~~ *superficial* details of language so they can spot ~~any weaknesses in content or in organization.~~ *the larger problems in writing.* *Then as they reread—and reread and* ~~the reader~~ *reread—they* ~~When the writer reads his manuscript, he is usually looking~~ *move in closer in a logical sequence which usually* ~~must~~ *involves,* ~~for~~ seven elements. 11

The first is subject. ~~As a writer~~ ~~Do you have anything to say? If you are lucky, you will~~ *Sometimes writers are lucky, they* find ~~that~~ indeed ~~you do~~ *that they* have something to say, perhaps a little more than you expected. *Writers look first to discover if they have said anything* ~~anything to say~~ If the subject is not clear, or if it is not yet limited or defined enough for you to handle, don't go on. What you have to say is always more important than how you say it. *writers know they can't write nothing,* *SAVE* 12

Novelist Elizabeth Janeway says, "I think there's a nice cooking word ~~which~~ *that explains a little of what happens while (the manuscript is) standing. It clarifies, like a consommé perhaps."*

The Maker's Eye: Revising Your Own Manuscripts

1 When students complete a first draft, they consider the job of writing done—and their teachers too often agree. When professional writers complete the first draft, they usually feel they are at the start of the writing process. When a draft is completed, the job of writing can begin.

2 That difference in attitude is the difference between amateur and professional, inexperience and experience, journeyman and craftsman. Peter F. Drucker, the prolific business writer, calls his first draft "the zero draft"—after that he can start counting. Most writers share the feeling the first draft, and all which follow, are opportunities to discover what they have to say and how they can best say it.

3 To produce a progression of drafts, each of which says more and says it more clearly, the writer has to develop a special kind of reading skill. In school we are taught to decode what appears on the page as finished writing. Writers, however, face a different category of possibility and responsibility when they read their own drafts. To them the words on the page are never finished. Each can be changed and rearranged, can set off a chain reaction of confusion or clarified meaning. This is a different kind of reading which is possibly more difficult and certainly more exciting.

4 Writers must learn to be their own best enemy. They must accept the criticism of others and be suspicious of it; they must accept the praise of others and be even more suspicious of it. Writers cannot depend on others. They must detach themselves from their own pages so that they can apply both their caring and their craft to their own work.

5 Such detachment is not easy. Science fiction writer Ray Bradbury supposedly puts each manuscript away for a year to the day and then rereads it as a stranger. Not many writers have the discipline or the time to do this. We must read when our judgment may be at its worst, when we are close to the euphoric moment of creation.

6 Then the writer, counsels novelist Nancy Hale, "should be critical of everything that seems to him most delightful in his style. He should excise what he most admires, because he wouldn't thus admire it if he weren't . . . in a sense protecting it from criticism." John Ciardi, the poet, adds, "The last act of the writing must be to become one's own reader. It is, I suppose, a schizophrenic process, to begin passionately and to end critically, to begin hot and to end cold; and, more important, to be passion-hot and critic-cold at the same time."

7 Most people think that the principal problem is that writers are too proud of what they have written. Actually, a greater problem for most professional writers is one shared by the majority of students. They are

overly critical, think everything is dreadful, tear up page after page, never complete a draft, see the task as hopeless.

The writer must learn to read critically but constructively, to cut 8
what is bad, to reveal what is good. Eleanor Estes, the children's book author, explains: "The writer must survey his work critically, coolly, as though he were a stranger to it. He must be willing to prune, expertly and hard-heartedly. At the end of each revision, a manuscript may look . . . worked over, torn apart, pinned together, added to, deleted from, words changed and words changed back. Yet the book must maintain its original freshness and spontaneity."

Most readers underestimate the amount of rewriting it usually 9
takes to produce spontaneous reading. This is a great disadvantage to the student writer, who sees only a finished product and never watches the craftsman who takes the necessary step back, studies the work carefully, returns to the task, steps back, returns, steps back, again and again. Anthony Burgess, one of the most prolific writers in the English-speaking world, admits, "I might revise a page twenty times." Roald Dahl, the popular children's writer, states, "By the time I'm nearing the end of a story, the first part will have been reread and altered and corrected at least 150 times. . . . Good writing is essentially rewriting. I am positive of this."

Rewriting isn't virtuous. It isn't something that ought to be done. It is 10
simply something that most writers find they have to do to discover what they have to say and how to say it. It is a condition of the writer's life.

There are, however, a few writers who do little formal rewriting, 11
primarily because they have the capacity and experience to create and review a large number of invisible drafts in their minds before they approach the page. And some writers slowly produce finished pages, performing all the tasks of revision simultaneously, page by page, rather than draft by draft. But it is still possible to see the sequence followed by most writers most of the time in rereading their own work.

Most writers scan their drafts first, reading as quickly as possible to 12
catch the larger problems of subject and form, then move in closer and closer as they read and write, reread and rewrite.

The first thing writers look for in their drafts is *information*. They 13
know that a good piece of writing is built from specific, accurate, and interesting information. The writer must have an abundance of information from which to construct a readable piece of writing.

Next writers look for *meaning* in the information. The specifics must 14
build to a pattern of significance. Each piece of specific information must carry the reader toward meaning.

Writers reading their own drafts are aware of *audience*. They put 15
themselves in the reader's situation and make sure that they deliver information which a reader wants to know or needs to know in a manner which is easily digested. Writers try to be sure that they anticipate and answer the questions a critical reader will ask when reading the piece of writing.

16 Writers make sure that the *form* is appropriate to the subject and the audience. Form, or genre, is the vehicle which carries meaning to the reader, but form cannot be selected until the writer has adequate information to discover its significance and an audience which needs or wants that meaning.

17 Once writers are sure the form is appropriate, they must then look at the *structure*, the order of what they have written. Good writing is built on a solid framework of logic, argument, narrative, or motivation which runs through the entire piece of writing and holds it together. This is the time when many writers find it most effective to outline as a way of visualizing the hidden spine by which the piece of writing is supported.

18 The element on which writers may spend a majority of their time is *development*. Each section of a piece of writing must be adequately developed. It must give readers enough information so that they are satisfied. How much information is enough? That's as difficult as asking how much garlic belongs in a salad. It must be done to taste, but most beginning writers underdevelop, underestimating the reader's hunger for information.

19 As writers solve development problems, they often have to consider questions of *dimension*. There must be a pleasing and effective proportion among all the parts of the piece of writing. There is a continual process of subtracting and adding to keep the piece of writing in balance.

20 Finally, writers have to listen to their own voices. *Voice* is the force which drives a piece of writing forward. It is an expression of the writer's authority and concern. It is what is between the words on the page, what glues the piece of writing together. A good piece of writing is always marked by a consistent, individual voice.

21 As writers read and reread, write and rewrite, they move closer and closer to the page until they are doing line-by-line editing. Writers read their own pages with infinite care. Each sentence, each line, each clause, each phrase, each word, each mark of punctuation, each section of white space between the type has to contribute to the clarification of meaning.

22 Slowly the writer moves from word to word, looking through language to see the subject. As a word is changed, cut, or added, as a construction is rearranged, all the words used before that moment and all those that follow that moment must be considered and reconsidered.

23 Writers often read aloud at this stage of the editing process, muttering or whispering to themselves, calling on the ear's experience with language. Does this sound right—or that? Writers edit, shifting back and forth from eye to page to ear to page. I find I must do this careful editing in short runs, no more than fifteen to twenty minutes at a stretch, or I become too kind with myself. I begin to see what I hope is on the page, not what actually is on the page.

24 This sounds tedious if you haven't done it, but actually it is fun. Making something right is immensely satisfying, for writers begin to

CALVIN AND HOBBES © 1993 Watterson. Distributed by Universal Press Syndicate. Reprinted with permission. All rights reserved.

"I used to hate writing assignments, but now I enjoy them," Calvin observes. "With a little practice, writing can be an intimidating and impenetrable fog." Are readers meant to take him seriously? How can you tell? Judging from the advice of authors in this book, particularly in the pieces on writing, what is the ideal style—or range of styles—of writing for college essays?

learn what they are writing about by writing. Language leads them to meaning, and there is the joy of discovery, of understanding, of making meaning clear as the writer employs the technical skills of language.

Words have double meanings, even triple and quadruple meanings. 25
Each word has its own potential for connotation and denotation. And when writers rub one word against the other, they are often rewarded with a sudden insight, an unexpected clarification.

The maker's eye moves back and forth from word to phrase to 26
sentence to paragraph to sentence to phrase to word. The maker's eye sees the need for variety and balance, for a firmer structure, for a more appropriate form. It peers into the interior of the paragraph, looking for coherence, unity, and emphasis, which make meaning clear.

I learned something about this process when my first bifocals were 27
prescribed. I had ordered a larger section of the reading portion of the glass because of my work, but even so, I could not contain my eyes with this new limit of vision. And I still find myself taking off my glasses and bending my nose towards the page, for my eyes unconsciously flick back and forth across the page, back to another page, forward to still another, as I try to see each evolving line in relation to every other line.

When does this process end? Most writers agree with the great 28
Russian writer Tolstoy, who said, "I scarcely ever reread my published writings, if by chance I come across a page, it always strikes me: all this must be rewritten; this is how I should have written it."

The maker's eye is never satisfied, for each word has the potential 29
to ignite the new meaning. This article has been twice written all the way through the writing process, and it was published four years ago. Now it is to be republished in a book. The editors made a few small suggestions, and then I read it with my maker's eye. Now it has been re-edited, re-revised, re-read, re-re-edited, for each piece of writing to the writer is full of potential and alternatives.

30 A piece of writing is never finished. It is delivered to a deadline, torn out of the typewriter on demand, sent off with a sense of accomplishment and shame and pride and frustration. If only there were a couple more days, time for just another run at it, perhaps then. . . .

Content

1. Why does Murray say that when a first "draft is completed, the job of writing can begin" (¶ 1)? If you thought before you read the essay that one draft was enough, has Murray's essay convinced you otherwise?
2. How does Murray explain John Ciardi's analysis of the "schizophrenic process" of becoming one's own reader, "to be passion-hot and critic-cold at the same time" (¶ 6)? Why is it important for writers to be both?
3. What are writers looking for when they revise? How can writers be sure that their "maker's eye" accurately sees in revision the "need for variety and balance, for a firmer structure, for a more appropriate form" and "for coherence, unity, and emphasis" (¶ 26)? How do you know whether your writing is good or not?

Strategies/Structures/Language

4. Murray revises for conciseness. For example, the first sentence of paragraph 11 initially read, "There is nothing virtuous in the rewriting process." Murray then revised it to "The rewriting process isn't virtuous." The published version says, "Rewriting isn't virtuous." What are the effects of these successive changes and of other comparable changes?
5. Compare and contrast the deleted paragraph 8 of the original version and the rewritten paragraphs 7 and 8 of the typescript with paragraphs 7 and 8 in the printed version. Why did Murray delete the original paragraph 8? Which ideas did he salvage? Why did he delete the first two sentences of the original paragraph 8? Are the longer paragraphs of the printed version preferable to the shorter paragraphs of the original?
6. In many places in the revision typescript (see ¶s 1, 4) Murray has changed masculine pronouns (he, his) to the plural (they, their). What is the effect of these changes? What occurred in America between 1973, when the essay was first written, and 1980, when it was again revised, to affect this usage?
7. In the typescript Murray has added references to students and teachers which were not in the original published version. For whom was the original version intended? What do the additions reveal about the intended readers of the revision?

For Writing

8. Prepare a checklist of the points Murray says that writers look for in revising a manuscript: information, meaning, audience, form, structure, development, dimension, voice (¶s 13–20). Add others appropriate to your writing, and use the checklist as a guide in revising your own papers. Which of these aspects do you find the

most difficult to look for in your own writing? Which do you find the easiest? How do you know whether your writing is good or not? Add other points to Murray's checklist that are appropriate to your own writing, and use the checklist to revise a paper you are currently working on. How effective was using your list?

9. ***Journal Writing.*** Explore an athletic or creative activity you enjoy in which you must "be passion-hot and critic-cold at the same time" (¶ 6). How do you maintain a critical but constructive perspective on your performance or creative work? Does this experience offer you any insights on the process of writing?

10. ***Dialogues.*** How does Murray's emphasis on rewriting as "a condition of the writer's life" (¶ 10) differ from or resemble Pamuk's (42–47) description of the writer who "by listening only to the voice of his own conscience, disputes with other's words" (¶ 11)? How might revision help a writer discover an authentic voice?

COLLEGE ADMISSIONS ESSAYS

RACHEL TOOR

Rachel Toor (born 1962 in Pennsylvania) wrote *Admissions Confidential: An Insider's Account of the Elite College Selection Process* (2001) after working in the Office of Undergraduate Admissions at Duke University. She is also the author of *The Pig and I: How I Learned to Love Men (Almost) as Much as I Love My Pets* (2005) and *Personal Record: A Love Affair with Running* (2008). Toor writes a monthly column in *The Chronicle of Higher Education* and is a Senior Writer for *Running Times* magazine. She is Assistant Professor of Creative Writing at the Inland Northwest Center for Writers in Spokane, Washington, the graduate writing program of Eastern Washington University. "Which One of These Essay Questions Is the Real Thing?" first appeared in *The Chronicle of Higher Education* (2007). Toor's mock admissions essays capture the spontaneity of personal writing, even as they are carefully crafted to convey the (often unintended) irony, humor, self-embellishment, and flashes of candor that the college admissions process can elicit from applicants.

Which of These Essay Questions Is the Real Thing?

Please tell us what you do in your free time. (No more than 500 words.)

When I was 12 years old, I got the international record for my age group for the marathon. After that I moved up to running longer races, and regularly compete in 100-milers. I run eight miles before 1 school (I get up at 3 a.m.) and on some days do 12 to 15 miles after school. I am a member of the Future Farmers of America and a nationally ranked cheese taster. I go to Dairy Products contests and Agriscience Fairs at the local, regional, state, and national levels. In order to fully appreciate the process of making cheeses, I have purchased a cow, a goat, and a sheep.

2 I work part time as an auto mechanic. Mostly I rebuild engines and program automobile computer equipment. When I saw the photos on the wall at Pete's (where I work), I began thinking of earning extra money that I need through modeling. Now I do runway shows for Victoria's Secret and Frederick's of Hollywood.

3 At school this year, I am taking eight AP classes, and because I have maxed out the math and science curriculum, I am auditing classes in topology, geophysics, and nonlinear dynamics at our community college. I have written a play that will be produced at the local rep company, and my self-titled debut CD will be released next fall.

4 I am president of the National Honor Society, the Speech and Debate Club, the Pro-Life Club, the Gay/Straight Alliance, and the Unwed Mothers on Crack Club. I am treasurer of Key Club, Habitat for Humanity, Teens for a Drug-Free America, and the Legalize Cannabis Club. I participate in French Club, Latin Club, Multicultural Club, the Aryan Youth Nation, Kids on Prozac, the Anime Society, Parent Management Group, and the Knitting Bee.

5 I am captain of the field-hockey, soccer, and bingo teams. I am a cheerleader for boys' water polo, and occasionally I join the Polar Bear Club for a dip.

6 I attend meetings of NYLC, AIME, SADD, FBLA, ASB, JROTC, JSA, YCC, FCA, Al-Anon, and BYOB.

7 I go to Chinese school and Hebrew school, and participate in our church youth group.

8 I am certified as a PADI scuba diver and am currently licensed to fly a plane, give manicures, and do Reiki massage therapy.

9 I have more than 30,000 friends on MySpace.

10 Please forgive me, but I do not understand the question.

What is the most important social problem currently facing society?

11 The most important social problem currently facing society is homelessness. There are more homeless people today than ever before in history! Many people do not have homes and are living on the street, and this is not a good thing. Something must be done about homelessness!

12 Every day on my way to soccer practice, I see homeless people. They've got grocery carts they steal and use to carry their crud around. They use cardboard boxes like blankets. Sometimes they write crazy stuff on the boxes, like "Out of Work Vet." I mean, if you're a vet, there

are plenty of sick animals that could use your services. Get a job! Other people do.

When I had to do my court-ordered community service, I got sent 13
to work in the homeless shelter. These people smelled bad! It's like they didn't know the first thing about personal hygiene. I was wearing a nice pair of Abercrombie khakis and an Izod shirt and they called me "rich boy"! My Beemer is two years old!

In conclusion, homelessness is a big problem. 14

If you were a vegetable, which vegetable would you be?

If I were a member of the vegetable kingdom, I would be an artichoke. 15

First, I am unique. I am not like the cookie-cutter cucumbers, all 16
long and cylindrical and boring. I am not one of those oddly formed root vegetables—you know the way sweet potatoes can go all twisted and weird, with fat middles and pointy ends? I am unique, but not weird. I have more substance than the leafy greens, more heft than an herb. No anorexic carrot am I. I am neither miniature, like a brussels sprout, nor overgrown, like a squash. I don't have the flashiness of eggplant, nor the dirtiness of a potato.

It is true, my edges are sharp. (It's not easy being green.) On the 17
outside I can be incisive to the point of drawing blood, especially if you rub me the wrong way. I'm not shiny and polished, but rather a bit gruff and gritty. But that tough, sturdy, complex protective covering is there for one reason.

My outer shell is a coat of armor. While some people may find 18
me off-putting and different, when you peel away the many layers and get to know me, you realize that at the core, I am all heart, soft and fuzzy.

I am an artichoke. Not your average vegetable, but one that stands 19
out from the crowded produce shelf.

Please tell us why you want to attend Fancy Pants University.

Fancy Pants University is an excellent school, with excellent teachers 20
and excellent students. Fancy Pants University has a beautiful campus, with nice buildings and big trees and very green grass. The food at Fancy Pants is delicious and nutritious. The sports teams always win and the parties are always fun. Everyone I met while visiting was friendly and welcoming. My tour guide was extremely intelligent *and* hot. I have wanted to go to Fancy Pants since before I could talk. Everyone I know who went there is really, really smart and got really well educated. I like that the classes are smaller than at State U., and that there is an honor code and a club for left-handed origamists as well as a support group for perfectionists. Plus my parents say I need to be able to get a high-paying job after college, and they think the Fancy Pants name will help. Those are some of the many reasons I really want to attend Different Name University.

ALEXANDER J. G. SCHNEIDER

In the twelfth grade, Alexander Schneider (born 1988) was assigned to write a satire and he composed this essay in the throes of the college admissions process. He is currently a psychology major at George Washington University. He told the *Chronicle of Higher Education*, where this essay was initially published, in April, 2007, "I am definitely happy with my college choice."

✧ *What I Really Wanted to Write in My Admissions Essays*

1 Right now I'm in the process of applying to college. Besides filling out the Common Application, I have to write lots of supplemental essays to prove to the admissions officers that I'm a literate person and that I really want to go to their college because I'm bothering to answer their annoying questions. What I hate about the supplemental essays is that they force me to suck up to an institution. Sometimes I'd like to answer the questions honestly because the essay subjects just get me so annoyed. I wonder how those answers would compare to my real answers.

2 **Essay 1**: Explain your academic interests and what you would like to do in college.

3 *What I said:* As far back as I can remember I have been interested in history and politics. I have enjoyed studying both of these subjects for one reason: As long as you can support your arguments with evidence, you can come to any conclusion you desire. I enjoy being able to argue, defend, refute, and occasionally change my ideas based on discussion and reading, rather than simply memorizing a series of equations or scientific laws. In college I would like to take my study of these two fields outside the classroom through internships and political activism.

4 *What I wanted to say:* I'm not a very academic person. I do like some stuff in my history and English classes, but basically I'm not a big fan of "academic" activities. I like to read, but frequently I don't have time to read what I'd like because I spend too much time doing homework. The effect of spending my time doing what my school wants me to do and not what I want to do is that I've become an angry person. My only "academic interests" nowadays are doing well enough in high school to get into college and filling out college forms. But now let me ask you some questions. What 17- or 18-year-old is going to know his or her academic interests at this stage in life? Most people don't really know what

they're interested in studying until they're halfway through college, so expecting me to know what I want to do is stupid. Are you delusional enough to actually believe you're going to get one honest heartfelt answer to this question? If so, you're too out of touch with youth to educate them; now I'm not sure if I'm going to apply here.

What I'd actually like to do in college is enjoy myself. I'll be free of 5
my parents' watchful eyes, so I'd definitely go to a lot of parties and clubs. Eventually I'll get tired of kicking it, and I'll begin to take my classes more seriously. I'll worry about the actual learning stuff once I'm done having fun, so I can't really say what else I'd like to do.

Essay 2: What unique qualities could you bring to College X [a small 6
liberal arts college]?

What I said: College X is a school that emphasizes small classes and 7
discussions as a way to learn. This works to my benefit because all through high school, class discussions have helped me grasp the material best. Discussions force me to see the viewpoints of others and to question my own beliefs. My strongest ability, as far as discussions go, is being able to empathize with both sides of an argument, which lets me fully understand an issue. This has contributed to my other talent, writing. Throughout high school my best classes have been writing-based, and I would continue to work on my writing at College X. I could enrich the community by being active in the classroom and by contributing to campus publications.

What I wanted to say: When I took a tour of College X, all the people 8
I saw were weird hippies. The thing I don't get is that if you asked all of these people what makes them unique, and since they all seem fairly similar, they probably answered the question in the same way, so it doesn't look like you're trying to find any unique people; you're trying to keep the college filled with hippies. Now the problem is: Do I tell you that I'm a kid from [name of major city] and not a hippie? Or do I lie and pretend to be a hippie? If I go with Option 1, I come across as unique, but I don't fit any "prospective student profile" that you might have. If I go with Option 2, I do come across as a good prospective student, but then not only am I not unique, I'm also lying. This is a real Catch-22.

Essay 3: Why is College X a good match for you? 9

What I said: College X's interdisciplinary style of teaching matches 10
the way I have learned throughout high school. Next semester I am taking a course on both the history and American literature of Paris during the 1920s. I enjoy the combination and overlap of many disciplines because the world does not exist in exact disciplines. One of my personal goals is to become a "world citizen." I think it is important for people to expose themselves to different cultures and ways of living in order to become more aware of the world around them. College X's study-abroad programs will add cultural immersion to my list of college and personal experiences.

11 *What I wanted to say:* The truth is, my mom picked out College X, signed me up for a tour and interview, and made me apply. You might actually want to ask my mom why College X meets my academic and personal goals. In actuality I was looking for a large urban college, so I'm not completely sure why I'm applying here. I think this is one of the places that my mom classified as a "safety school" even though it's pretty hard to get into. Let me clear this one up with my mom and I'll get back to you.

12 **Essay 4:** What sets College X apart from other colleges?

13 *What I said:* A relative mentioned the excellent history and film programs at College X, and I visited and from that point on my interest in attending has only increased. I was impressed with the values of the college. My tour guide told me that the professors care so much about students that they will send you an e-mail asking why you missed a class and will meet with you often to make sure you stay on track. The students I spoke to explained how the faculty are involved with students in the formation of a strong learning community on the campus.

14 Another thing that sets College X apart from many of the other schools I visited is the commitment to community service. During high school I participated in many community-service activities, and I have looked for colleges with a strong commitment to community service, but few have service directly in their mission statement, as College X does.

15 *What I wanted to say:* You and I both know that probably half the applicants are applying because College X is located in [name of major city], and I'm definitely part of that half. The truth is, if it weren't in [name of major city] I wouldn't be applying.

16 **Essay 5:** Is there anything else you would like us to know about you?

17 *What I said*: I didn't answer this one.

18 *What I wanted to say:* Ask me what I thought of the new Wu-Tang Clan album or about the best hosts for *Saturday Night Live*. Ask why Menace II Society keeps it real. Don't ask me about what I'd like to see myself doing in college, because I'm not actually there yet to figure it out. What I'm basically trying to say is: You never actually asked me about who I am, and if you ever decided to write a new application, please, cut the crap.

Content

1. What kind of "prospective student profile" do Schneider's "*What I said*" answers suggest? What type of profile do his "*What I wanted to say*" answers suggest?
2. Why does Schneider object to the questions asked on the Common Application? What does he expect from college? Can you distinguish between his reactions to the questions and his genuine expectations of the college experience?

3. What do Toor's mock answers to essay questions suggest about student admission essays? How is your perception of these essays influenced by knowing that the writer is not a student, but faculty?

4. Do Schneider and Toor expect students, college faculty and administrators, or parents to read these pieces? What does their publication in the *Chronicle of Higher Education* imply about their intended audience? How might a student's reactions to these texts differ from an admissions officer's or a parent's?

Strategies/Structures/Language

5. Toor's humor employs hyperbole (exaggeration), irony (an expression contrary to intended meaning), and pleonasm (superfluous words). Find an example of each and explain why the effect is humorous.

6. Compare and characterize Schneider's tone in his "*What I said*" and "*What I wanted to say*" essays. How do his word choices and sentence structure achieve these changes in tone?

7. Schneider only mentions popular culture in Essay 5. Why?

For Writing

8. ***Journal Writing.*** Do you agree with Schneider that "most people don't really know what they're interested in studying until they're halfway through college" (¶ 4)? Compare your expectations of college with your experience of it thus far. Have your experiences changed your view of the value of a college education?

9. ***Second Look.*** The photograph of three students on National Coming Out Day (Chapter 7) reminds us that political activity can be an important part of the experience of higher education. If college is a time of exploration, how can the college application process give the candidate room to express his or her need for self-discovery without sounding aimless?

10. Do these satirical treatments of the college application essay suggest that the process should be reformed? If so, in what ways? Would a change in the application process help students choose a more appropriate institution? How does the application process shape student expectations of what college will be like as well as their actual experience of college? In what respects have your early college experiences fulfilled or disappointed your expectations?

PART II: *DETERMINING IDEAS IN A SEQUENCE*

Narration

Western culture is embedded in narrative: what happened then, and then, and after that, with causation and consequences strung together like beads along a timeline necklace. Analyses of processes (Chapter 4), cause-and-effect relationships (Chapter 5), some descriptions (Chapter 6), and many arguments (Chapters 10 and 11) are based on narrative, stated directly or implied. Research proposals in the social, physical, and natural sciences, in medicine and business, require narrative interpretations: if we do this, we expect these events or phenomena to follow and to yield the following results.

Most commonly, we think of narration as telling a story, true or invented, or containing some mixture of each. Narration is a particularly attractive mode of writing, and ours is a storytelling culture. It is as old as Indian legends, Br'er Rabbit, Grimm's fairy tales, and the stories of Edgar Allan Poe. It is as new as speakers' warm-up jokes ("A funny thing happened on my way to . . .") and anecdotal leads to otherwise impersonal news stories. Narration can be as profound as the story of a life, the chronicle of a discovery, the history of a nation, or the account of one single, intense moment. Consider how Don DeLillo begins a brief story:

> Ash was spattering the windows, Karen was half dressed, grabbing the kids and trying to put on some clothes and talking with her husband and scooping things to take out to the corridor, and they looked at her, twin girls, as if she had fourteen heads.
>
> They stayed in the corridor for a while, thinking there might be secondary explosions. They waited, and began to feel safer, and went back to the apartment.
>
> At the next impact, Marc knew in the sheerest second before the shock wave broadsided their building that it was a second plane, impossible, striking the second tower. Their building was two blocks away, and he'd thought the first crash was an accident.

This excerpt from DeLillo's essay "In the Ruins of the Future" (*Harper's*, December 2001, 33) contains the major elements of a narrative.

1. *Characters:* Karen, Marc (whom we later learn is DeLillo's nephew), their twin daughters, and unidentified antagonists who are crashing planes into the World Trade Center
2. *Setting:* an apartment two blocks away from the World Trade Center
3. *Conflict:* terrorists versus New York's peaceful civilian population
4. *Plot*—beginning to unfold: Will this family survive? Will more attacks occur? What will be the consequences?
5. *Motives:* although the attackers' motives are murky, the victims' are clear—safety for themselves and their children
6. *Point of view:* a third-person account by an omniscient narrator who understands what the characters are thinking

It is unnecessary to specify the date, indelibly engraved on the minds of the readers as well as the participants. Only *dialogue* is missing; actions and eloquent silence say what is necessary. All these features make the incident or any vivid narrative a particularly easy form of writing for readers to remember. As this narration reveals, a narrative does *not* necessarily have to be a personal essay.

Narratives can be whole novels, stories, creative nonfiction essays, poems, or segments of other types of writings. They can be as long and as complicated as Charles Dickens's novels or an account of the events leading up to 9/11 and its aftermath, including the war in Iraq and a host of unforeseen consequences (see Chapter 13). Or they can be short and to the point, as in V. Penelope Pelizzon's elliptical interpretation of her parents' courtship in "Clever and Poor" (346–47). This evocative poem (yes, poems can and do tell stories) offers revealing, snapshot-like glimpses of two people [*characters*], both clever and heartbreakingly poor—the woman "here off the Yugoslav train" [*setting*], arriving to meet the "newspaper-man who liked her in the picture." The primary *purpose* of the meeting is matrimony. But the woman's expectations of escaping poverty [the immediate *motivation* for her journey] are immediately undercut by "what is poor is what she sees" in the dispiriting station [*setting*] at which she arrives, with its cracked clock and girls selling "candle grease"—a poor offering indeed, reflected, perhaps literally, in the poverty of her husband-to-be, "his shined shoes tied with twine." How the *plot* will unfold is implied by the clever deceptions already accomplished by the cape "hiding her waist" as her presumably out-of-wedlock baby is "left with the nuns" and the valiant attempts of each of the characters to hide their poverty—a condition evident to the sympathetic narrator [*point of view*], the daughter who wrote the poem, and the readers, as well.

A narrative need not be fictional, as the above examples and the essays in this section indicate. When you're writing a narrative based on real people and actual incidents, you shape the material to emphasize the *point of view, sequence of action* (a chase, an exploration), a *theme* (greed, pleasure), a *particular relationship between characters* (love, antagonism), or the *personalities of the people involved* (vigorous, passive). This shaping—supplying information or other specific details where necessary, deleting trivial or irrelevant material—is essential in transforming skeletal notes or diary entries into three-dimensional configurations.

A narrative can *exist for its own sake,* as does "Clever and Poor." As sixteenth-century poet and courtier Sir Philip Sidney observed, such writing can attract "children from play and old men from the chimney corner." Through a narrative you can also *illustrate or explore a personality or an idea,* as in the photograph of the slave's scarred back on 90, a silent but articulate protest.

In "The Inheritance of Tools" (143–50), Scott Russell Sanders uses a comparable narrative technique to interpret the character of his father. As Sanders's essay becomes a tribute to his father, and to the extended family of which his father was a member, Sanders describes his legacy, the carpenters' tools ("the hammer [that] had belonged to him, and to his father before him") and the knowledge of how to use them, transmitted through years of patient teaching and an insistence on high-quality work, "making sure before I drove the first nail that every line was square and true." This type of description consists of stories embedded within stories: how Sanders's father taught him to use the hammer (¶s 6, 9), the saw (¶s 10, 12), the square (¶s 14–16). Still more stories incorporate the current use to which Sanders puts this knowledge (he's building a bedroom in the basement), the incident of the gerbil escaping behind the new bedroom wall (¶s 17, 22), learning of his father's death (¶s 26, 28)—all embedded in the matrix of the stories of four generations of the Sanders family.

If you wish to write a personal narrative you can *present a whole or partial biography or autobiography,* as does Frederick Douglass in "Resurrection" (89–93), an excerpt from his *Life and Times* that recounts a single narrative incident in the life of a slave. Here Douglass tells the story of how he defied—in a two-hour fistfight—a Simon Legree–like overseer who had determined to break his spirit through repeated beatings. This, explains Douglass, was "the turning-point in my career as a slave. . . . It recalled the departed self-confidence, and inspired me again with a determination to be free. . . . It was a glorious resurrection, from the tomb of slavery, to the heaven of freedom." The photograph on 90 corroborates Douglass's story with a story of its own.

Through narration you can *impart information* or *an account of historical events*, from either an impartial or—more likely—an engaged eyewitness point of view. The resulting narrative is always an interpretation, whether of an individual, a group, or a historical or contemporary event. Jason Verge's "The Habs" (107–11) presents a comical account of his lifelong love for his favorite hockey team, the Montreal Canadiens, as well as a facetious self-portrait: "If you had to give up either me or hockey, which would you choose?'" asks his girlfriend. If she has to ask, we know the answer. Self-mockery is a convincing stance for any sports fan to adopt, since not everyone reading the narrative is guaranteed to love the home team—whatever that team may be—as much as the author does. Verge writes to entertain readers, partly at his own expense.

At other times, the narrative point of view can be satiric and highly critical of causes, unfolding events, outcomes, or all three. Sherman Alexie's satiric "What Sacagawea Means to Me" (85–87) is a critical commentary on white America's appropriation and exploitation of the historical Sacagawea, transformed into an icon ("our mother") in the process. Alexie tells only fragments of Sacagawea's story—that she accompanied Lewis and Clark on their "immigrant" expedition to spread the colonizing virus amongst the Indians; that she carried her first child, baby "Jean-Baptiste," with her on the journey; that she "died of some mysterious illness when she was only in her twenties." Sacagawea's biography—whether actual or imaginative, literal or symbolic—is composed of many contradictions embedded in the question "Why wouldn't she ask her brother and her tribe to take revenge against the men who had enslaved her?" Indeed, they are asked by the narrator, a Native American who himself is "a contradiction; I am Sacagawea."

Art Spiegelman's "Mein Kampf (My Struggle)" (96–97), with its embedded story of the Nazi death camps of the Holocaust, signals satire in its very title—also the title of Adolf Hitler's autobiography. In a mere sixteen cartoon panels we are invited to "read" the author's multigenerational life story and to interpret this through the split perspective of his critical eyes and our own. Thus we understand the Cave of Memory to be full of the memories identified by the signs on the labeled doors—"repressed memories," memories erotic and neurotic, intrauterine memories and childhood memories. His childhood memories are augmented by two photographs: one of Spiegelman as a child in a Cisco Kid outfit and one of his small son, Dashiell, in a Superman costume—both prepared to hold their own, if not to conquer their own corners of the world. The antihero cartoonist renders his life, the memories of his parents who "survived Auschwitz," and the image of his own child to comment on the need for struggle and survival against evil.

Fables, parables, and other *morality* or *cautionary tales* are as old as Aesop, as familiar as the Old and New Testaments of the Bible, as contemporary as Anne Fadiman's "Under Water" (102–05), a cautionary tale whose sunny beginning belies its complex moral undertow, which the narrator does not fully acknowledge until the passage of slow time for reflection, twenty-seven years after she was eighteen and "wanted to hurry through life as fast as I could." Although Fadiman focuses on telling the story and what it means to her, she expects the readers to apply to their own lives the moral understanding gained from reading about her experience of pleasure transformed, over time, to shame. The photograph on 103 captures the event, but does it convey the spirit and tone of Fadiman's essay?

Must a story have a happy ending? This is guaranteed only in some versions of some fairy tales, and then only after great suffering. Douglass's victory over the vicious slave overseer, Covey, strengthened him to defy other oppressors and eventually to escape to freedom, where he found life difficult as well. Fadiman survives her teenage companion's death by drowning, but lives for years with the guilt. Although the desperately hopeful couple in Pelizzon's poem may marry, their beginning does not augur well for their future.

To write a narrative you can ask, What do I want to demonstrate? Through what characters, performing what actions or thinking what thoughts? In what setting and time frame? From what point of view do I want to tell the tale? Do I want to use a first-person involved narrator who may also be a character in the story, as are the narrators of all the essays in this section? Or would a third-person narrator be more effective, either on the scene or depending on the reports of other people, as in the account of terrorism quoted on 70–71? An easy way to remember these questions is to ask yourself:

1. *Who* participated?
2. *What* happened?
3. *Why* did this event/these phenomena happen?
4. *When* did it (or they) happen?
5. *Where* did it (or they) happen?
6. *How* did it (or they) happen? Under what circumstances?
7. Was the outcome expected, unexpected? With what consequences, actual or potential?

Narratives have as many purposes, as many plots, as many characters as there are people to write them. You have but to examine your life, your thoughts, your experiences, to find an unwritten library of narratives yet to tell. Therein lie a thousand tales. Or a thousand and one. . . .

Strategies for Writing: Narration

1. You'll need to consider, "What is the purpose of my narrative?" Am I telling the tale for its own sake, or am I using it to make a larger point?
2. For what audience am I writing this? What will they have experienced or be able to understand, and what will I need to explain? How do I want my audience to react?
3. What is the focus, the conflict of my narrative? How will it begin? Gain momentum and develop to a climax? End? What emphasis will I give each part, or separate scenes or incidents within each part?
4. Will I write from a first- or third-person point of view? Will I be a major character in my narrative? As a participant or as an observer? Or both, if my present self is observing my past self?
5. What is my attitude toward my material? What tone do I want to use? Will it be consistent throughout, or will it change during the course of events?

TIM O'BRIEN

Tim O'Brien's "striking sequence of stories," *The Things They Carried* (1990), is told by a character named—surprise!—Tim O'Brien. Says this narrator, "In June of 1968, a month after graduating from Macalester College [in Minnesota, where the author grew up], I was drafted to fight a war I hated. I was twenty-one years old." O'Brien the author (born 1947) first came to public notice with the anecdotal *If I Die in a Combat Zone, Box Me Up and Ship Me Home* (1973), followed by a number of other novels including *Northern Lights* (1975), *In the Lake of the Woods* (1994), and *Tomcat in Love* (1998). *Going after Cacciato* (1978) won the National Book Award. His most recent novel, *July, July* (2002), is a tale of disillusioned baby boomers—with the Vietnam War hovering in the background "like some unfinished business from the past." In response to an interviewer's query, "What can you teach people, just for having been in a war?," O'Brien said, "By 'teach,' I mean provide insight, philosophy. . . . and that means reading and hard thought. I didn't intend *If I Die* to stand as a profound statement, and it's not. Teaching is one thing and telling stories is another. I wanted to use stories to alert readers to the complexity and ambiguity of a set of moral issues—but without preaching a moral lesson."

Like all meaningful war fiction, *The Things They Carried* puts a human face on the faceless abstraction of war. It is the single book that many say gets closest to the truth of the Vietnam War. Indeed, although "How to Tell a True War Story" is the seventh chapter of a work that is nominally fiction, what O'Brien says about writing the truth is dead accurate, and it applies to all sorts of creative nonfiction and personal essays, as well as to fiction.

- "A true war story is never moral. It does not instruct, nor encourage virtue, nor suggest models of proper human behavior, nor restrain men from doing the things men have always done. If a story seems moral, do not believe it." (¶ 8)
- "You can tell a true war story if it embarrasses you. If you don't care for obscenity, you don't care for the truth. . . . " (¶ 9)
- "In any [true] war story . . . it's difficult to separate what happened from what seemed to happen. What seems to happen becomes its own happening and has to be told that way. The angles of vision are skewed." (¶ 18)
- "You can tell a true war story by the questions you ask. Somebody tells a story, let's say, and afterward you ask, 'Is it true?' and if the answer matters, you've got your answer." (¶ 51)
- "[Yet] absolute occurrence is irrelevant. A thing may happen and be a total lie; another thing may not happen and be truer than the truth." (¶ 55)
- "In war you lose your sense of the definite, hence your sense of the truth itself, and therefore it's safe to say that in a true war story nothing is ever absolutely true." (¶ 47)

- "It comes down to gut instinct. A true war story, if truly told, makes the stomach believe." (¶ 24)
- "Often in a true war story there is not even a point, or else that point doesn't hit you until twenty years later, in your sleep. . . ." (¶ 48)
- "In the end, of course, a true war story is never about war. It's about sunlight. . . . It's about love and memory. It's about sorrow. It's about sisters who never write back and people who never listen." (¶ 64)

How to Tell a True War Story

This is true. 1

I had a buddy in Vietnam. His name was Bob Kiley, but everybody called him Rat. 2

A friend of his gets killed, so about a week later Rat sits down and writes a letter to the guy's sister. Rat tells her what a great brother she had, how together the guy was, a number one pal and comrade. A real soldier's soldier, Rat says. Then he tells a few stories to make the point, how her brother would always volunteer for stuff nobody else would volunteer for in a million years, dangerous stuff, like doing recon or going out on these really badass night patrols. Stainless steel balls, Rat tells her. The guy was a little crazy, for sure, but crazy in a good way, a real daredevil, because he liked the challenge of it, he liked testing himself, just man against gook. A great, great guy, Rat says. 3

Anyway, it's a terrific letter, very personal and touching. Rat almost bawls writing it. He gets all teary telling about the good times they had together, how her brother made the war seem almost fun, always raising hell and lighting up villes and bringing smoke to bear every which way. A great sense of humor, too. Like the time at this river when he went fishing with a whole damn crate of hand grenades. Probably the funniest thing in world history, Rat says, all that gore, about twenty zillion dead gook fish. Her brother, he had the right attitude. He knew how to have a good time. On Halloween, this real hot spooky night, the dude paints up his body all different colors and puts on this weird mask and hikes over to a ville and goes trick-or-treating almost stark naked, just boots and balls and an M-16. A tremendous human being, Rat says. Pretty nutso sometimes, but you could trust him with your life. 4

And then the letter gets very sad and serious. Rat pours his heart out. He says he loved the guy. He says the guy was his best friend in the world. They were like soul mates, he says, like twins or something, they had a whole lot in common. He tells the guy's sister he'll look her up when the war's over. 5

6 So what happens?

7 Rat mails the letter. He waits two months. The dumb cooze never writes back.

8 A true war story is never moral. It does not instruct, nor encourage virtue, nor suggest models of proper human behavior, nor restrain men from doing the things men have always done. If a story seems moral, do not believe it. If at the end of a war story you feel uplifted, or if you feel that some small bit of rectitude has been salvaged from the larger waste, then you have been made the victim of a very old and terrible lie. There is no rectitude whatsoever. There is no virtue. As a first rule of thumb, therefore, you can tell a true war story by its absolute and uncompromising allegiance to obscenity and evil. Listen to Rat Kiley. Cooze, he says. He does not say bitch. He certainly does not say woman, or girl. He says cooze. Then he spits and stares. He's nineteen years old—it's too much for him—so he looks at you with those big sad gentle killer eyes and says *cooze*, because his friend is dead, and because it's so incredibly sad and true: she never wrote back.

9 You can tell a true war story if it embarrasses you. If you don't care for obscenity, you don't care for the truth; if you don't care for the truth, watch how you vote. Send guys to war, they come home talking dirty.

10 Listen to Rat: "Jesus Christ, man, I write this beautiful fuckin' letter, I slave over it, and what happens? The dumb cooze never writes back."

11 The dead guy's name was Curt Lemon. What happened was, we crossed a muddy river and marched west into the mountains, and on the third day we took a break along a trail junction in deep jungle. Right away, Lemon and Rat Kiley started goofing. They didn't understand about the spookiness. They were kids; they just didn't know. A nature hike, they thought, not even a war, so they went off into the shade of some giant trees—quadruple canopy, no sunlight at all—and they were giggling and calling each other yellow mother and playing a silly game they'd invented. The game involved smoke grenades, which were harmless unless you did stupid things, and what they did was pull out the pin and stand a few feet apart and play catch under the shade of those huge trees. Whoever chickened out was a yellow mother. And if nobody chickened out, the grenade would make a light popping sound and they'd be covered with smoke and they'd laugh and dance around and then do it again.

12 It's all exactly true.

13 It happened, to *me*, nearly twenty years ago, and I still remember that trail junction and those giant trees and a soft dripping sound somewhere beyond the trees. I remember the smell of moss. Up in the canopy there were tiny white blossoms, but no sunlight at all, and I remember the shadows spreading out under the trees where Curt Lemon and Rat Kiley were playing catch with smoke grenades. Mitchell Sanders sat flipping

his yo-yo. Norman Bowker and Kiowa and Dave Jensen were dozing, or half dozing, and all around us were those ragged green mountains.

Except for the laughter things were quiet. 14

At one point, I remember, Mitchell Sanders turned and looked at 15
me, not quite nodding, as if to warn me about something, as if he already *knew*, then after a while he rolled up his yo-yo and moved away.

It's hard to tell you what happened next. 16

They were just goofing. There was a noise, I suppose, which must've 17
been the detonator, so I glanced behind me and watched Lemon step from the shade into bright sunlight. His face was suddenly brown and shining. A handsome kid, really. Sharp gray eyes, lean and narrow-waisted, and when he died it was almost beautiful, the way the sunlight came around him and lifted him up and sucked him high into a tree full of moss and vines and white blossoms.

In any war story, but especially a true one, it's difficult to separate what 18
happened from what seemed to happen. What seems to happen becomes its own happening and has to be told that way. The angles of vision are skewed. When a booby trap explodes, you close your eyes and duck and float outside yourself. When a guy dies, like Curt Lemon, you look away and then look back for a moment and then look away again. The pictures get jumbled; you tend to miss a lot. And then afterward, when you go to tell about it, there is always that surreal seemingness, which makes the story seem untrue, but which in fact represents the hard and exact truth as it *seemed*.

In many cases a true war story cannot be believed. If you believe it, be skepti- 19
cal. It's a question of credibility. Often the crazy stuff is true and the normal stuff is necessary to make you believe the truly incredible craziness.

In other cases you can't even tell a true war story. Sometimes it's just 20
beyond telling. . . .

In a true war story, if there's a moral at all, it's like the thread that makes 21
the cloth. You can't extract the meaning without unraveling the deeper meaning. And in the end, really, there's nothing much to say about a true war story, except maybe "Oh."

True war stories do not generalize. They do not indulge in abstrac- 22
tion or analysis.

For example: War is hell. As a moral declaration the old truism 23
seems perfectly true, and yet because it abstracts, because it generalizes, I can't believe it with my stomach. Nothing turns inside.

It comes down to gut instinct. A true war story, if truly told, makes 24
the stomach believe.

This one does it for me. I've told it before—many times, many versions— 25
but here's what actually happened.

26 We crossed that river and marched west into the mountains. On the third day, Curt Lemon stepped on a booby-trapped 105 round. He was playing catch with Rat Kiley, laughing, and then he was dead. The trees were thick; it took nearly an hour to cut an LZ for the dustoff.

27 Later, higher in the mountains, we came across a baby VC water buffalo. What it was doing there I don't know—no farms or paddies—but we chased it down and got a rope around it and led it along to a deserted village where we set up for the night. After supper Rat Kiley went over and stroked its nose.

28 He opened up a can of C rations, pork and beans, but the baby buffalo wasn't interested.

29 Rat shrugged.

30 He stepped back and shot it through the right front knee. The animal did not make a sound. It went down hard, then got up again, and Rat took careful aim and shot off an ear. He shot it in the hindquarters and in the little hump at its back. He shot it twice in the flanks. It wasn't to kill; it was to hurt. He put the rifle muzzle up against the mouth and shot the mouth away. Nobody said much. The whole platoon stood there watching, feeling all kinds of things, but there wasn't a great deal of pity for the baby water buffalo. Curt Lemon was dead. Rat Kiley had lost his best friend in the world. Later in the week he would write a long personal letter to the guy's sister, who would not write back, but for now it was a question of pain. He shot off the tail. He shot away chunks of meat below the ribs. All around us there was the smell of smoke and filth and deep greenery, and the evening was humid and very hot. Rat went to automatic. He shot randomly, almost casually, quick little spurts in the belly and butt. Then he reloaded, squatted down, and shot it in the left front knee. Again the animal fell hard and tried to get up, but this time it couldn't quite make it. It wobbled and went down sideways. Rat shot it in the nose. He bent forward and whispered something, as if talking to a pet, then he shot it in the throat. All the while the baby buffalo was silent, or almost silent, just a light bubbling sound where the nose had been. It lay very still. Nothing moved except the eyes, which were enormous, the pupils shiny black and dumb.

31 Rat Kiley was crying. He tried to say something, but then cradled his rifle and went off by himself.

32 The rest of us stood in a ragged circle around the baby buffalo. For a time no one spoke. We had witnessed something essential, something brand-new and profound, a piece of the world so startling there was not yet a name for it.

33 Somebody kicked the baby buffalo.

34 It was still alive, though just barely, just in the eyes.

35 "Amazing," Dave Jensen said. "My whole life, I never seen anything like it."

36 "Never?"

37 "Not hardly. Not once."

Kiowa and Mitchell Sanders picked up the baby buffalo. They 38
hauled it across the open square, hoisted it up, and dumped it in the village well.

Afterward, we sat waiting for Rat to get himself together. 39

"Amazing," Dave Jensen kept saying. "A new wrinkle. I never seen 40
it before."

Mitchell Sanders took out his yo-yo. "Well, that's Nam," he said. 41
"Garden of Evil. Over here, man, every sin's real fresh and original."

How do you generalize? 42

War is hell, but that's not the half of it, because war is also mystery 43
and terror and adventure and courage and discovery and holiness and pity and despair and longing and love. War is nasty; war is fun. War is thrilling; war is drudgery. War makes you a man; war makes you dead.

The truths are contradictory. It can be argued, for instance, that 44
war is grotesque. But in truth war is also beauty. For all its horror, you can't help but gape at the awful majesty of combat. You stare out at tracer rounds unwinding through the dark like brilliant red ribbons. You crouch in ambush as a cool, impassive moon rises over the nighttime paddies. You admire the fluid symmetries of troops on the move, the harmonies of sound and shape and proportion, the great sheets of metal-fire streaming down from a gunship, the illumination rounds, the white phosphorus, the purply orange glow of napalm, the rocket's red glare. It's not pretty, exactly. It's astonishing. It fills the eye. It commands you. You hate it, yes, but your eyes do not. Like a killer forest fire, like cancer under a microscope, any battle or bombing raid or artillery barrage has the aesthetic purity of absolute moral indifference—a powerful, implacable beauty—and a true war story will tell the truth about this, though the truth is ugly.

To generalize about war is like generalizing about peace. Almost 45
everything is true. Almost nothing is true. At its core, perhaps, war is just another name for death, and yet any soldier will tell you, if he tells the truth, that proximity to death brings with it a corresponding proximity to life. After a firefight, there is always the immense pleasure of aliveness. The trees are alive. The grass, the soil—everything. All around you things are purely living, and you among them, and the aliveness makes you tremble. You feel an intense, out-of-the-skin awareness of your living self—your truest self, the human being you want to be and then become by the force of wanting it. In the midst of evil you want to be a good man. You want decency. You want justice and courtesy and human concord, things you never knew you wanted. There is a kind of largeness to it, a kind of godliness. Though it's odd, you're never more alive than when you're almost dead. You recognize what's valuable. Freshly, as if for the first time, you love what's best in

yourself and in the world, all that might be lost. At the hour of dusk you sit at your foxhole and look out on a wide river turning pinkish red, and at the mountains beyond, and although in the morning you must cross the river and go into the mountains and do terrible things and maybe die, even so, you find yourself studying the fine colors on the river, you feel wonder and awe at the setting of the sun, and you are filled with a hard, aching love for how the world could be and always should be, but now is not.

46 Mitchell Sanders was right. For the common soldier, at least, war has the feel—the spiritual texture—of a great ghostly fog, thick and permanent. There is no clarity. Everything swirls. The old rules are no longer binding, the old truths no longer true. Right spills over into wrong. Order blends into chaos, love into hate, ugliness into beauty, law into anarchy, civility into savagery. The vapors suck you in. You can't tell where you are, or why you're there, and the only certainty is overwhelming ambiguity.

47 In war you lose your sense of the definite, hence your sense of truth itself, and therefore it's safe to say that in a true war story nothing is ever absolutely true.

48 Often in a true war story there is not even a point, or else the point doesn't hit you until twenty years later, in your sleep, and you wake up and shake your wife and start telling the story to her, except when you get to the end you've forgotten the point again. And then for a long time you lie there watching the story happen in your head. You listen to your wife's breathing. The war's over. You close your eyes. You smile and think, Christ, what's the *point*?

49 This one wakes me up.

50 In the mountains that day, I watched Lemon turn sideways. He laughed and said something to Rat Kiley. Then he took a peculiar half step, moving from shade into bright sunlight, and the booby-trapped 105 round blew him into a tree. The parts were just hanging there, so Dave Jensen and I were ordered to shinny up and peel him off. I remember the white bone of an arm. I remember pieces of skin and something wet and yellow that must've been the intestines. The gore was horrible, and stays with me. But what wakes me up twenty years later is Dave Jensen singing "Lemon Tree" as we threw down the parts.

51 You can tell a true war story by the questions you ask. Somebody tells a story, let's say, and afterward you ask, "Is it true?" and if the answer matters, you've got your answer.

52 For example, we've all heard this one. Four guys go down a trail. A grenade sails out. One guy jumps on it and takes the blast and saves his three buddies.

53 Is it true?

The answer matters. 54

You'd feel cheated if it never happened. Without the grounding 55
reality, it's just a trite bit of puffery, pure Hollywood, untrue in the way all such stores are untrue. Yet even if it did happen—and maybe it did, anything's possible—even then you know it can't be true, because a true war story does not depend upon that kind of truth. Absolute occurrence is irrelevant. A thing may happen and be a total lie; another thing may not happen and be truer than the truth. For example: Four guys go down a trail. A grenade sails out. One guy jumps on it and takes the blast, but it's a killer grenade and everybody dies anyway. Before they die, though, one of the dead guy says, "The fuck you do *that* for?" and the jumper says, "Story of my life, man," and the other guy starts to smile but he's dead.

That's a true story that never happened. 56

Twenty years later, I can still see the sunlight on Lemon's face. I can see 57
him turning, looking back at Rat Kiley, then he laughed and took that curious half step from shade into sunlight, his face suddenly brown and shining, and when his foot touched down, in that instant, he must've thought it was the sunlight that was killing him. It was not the sunlight. It was a rigged 105 round. But if I could ever get the story right, how the sun seemed to gather around him and pick him up and lift him high into a tree, if I could somehow recreate the fatal whiteness of that light, the quick glare, the obvious cause and effect, then you would believe the last thing Curt Lemon believed, which for him must've been the final truth.

Now and then, when I tell this story, someone will come up to me 58
afterward and say she liked it. It's always a woman. Usually it's an older woman of kindly temperament and humane politics. She'll explain that as a rule she hates war stories; she can't understand why people want to wallow in all the blood and gore. But this one she liked. The poor baby buffalo, it made her sad. Sometimes, even, there are little tears. What I should do, she'll say, is put it all behind me. Find new stories to tell.

I won't say it but I'll think it. 59

I'll picture Rat Kiley's face, his grief, and I'll think, *You dumb cooze.* 60

Because she wasn't listening. 61

It *wasn't* a war story. It was a *love* story. 62

But you can't say that. All you can do is tell it one more time, 63
patiently, adding and subtracting, making up a few things to get at the real truth. No Mitchell Sanders, you tell her. No Lemon, no Rat Kiley. No trail junction. No baby buffalo. No vines or moss or white blossoms. Beginning to end, you tell her, it's all made up. Every goddamn detail—the mountains and the river and especially that poor dumb baby buffalo. None of it happened. *None* of it. And even if it did happen, it didn't happen in the mountains, it happened in this little village on the Batangan

Peninsula, and it was raining like crazy, and one night a guy named Stink Harris woke up screaming with a leech on his tongue. You can tell a true was story if you just keep on telling it.

64 And in the end, of course, a true war story is never about war. It's about sunlight. It's about the special way that dawn spreads out on a river when you know you must cross the river and march into the mountains and do things you are afraid to do. It's about love and memory. It's about sorrow. It's about sisters who never write back and people who never listen.

SHERMAN ALEXIE

Sherman Alexie (born 1966) is a Spokane/Coeur d'Alene Indian who grew up on the Spokane Indian Reservation in Wellpinit, Washington. By the time he earned his BA from the University of Washington (1995)—prognostic of his literary future—he had already published five volumes of poetry, a collection of short stories, and a novel, *Reservation Blues*. Indeed, the novel's title is the motif for much of Alexie's writing. His works include the films *Smoke Signals* (1998) and *The Business of Fancydancing* (2002), collections of stories such as *Ten Little Indians* (2003), and the novels *Indian Killer* (1996) and *The Absolutely True Diary of a Part-Time Indian*, the latter of which won the 2007 National Book Award for Young People's Literature. All present Alexie's characteristically ironic, humorous interpretations of three profound central questions: "What does it mean to live as an Indian in this time? As an Indian man? On an Indian reservation?" Alexie's Indians, laid-back, casual, comic, often drunk, are waging war on two fronts. They battle as colonized people must on reservations—against alcoholism, poverty, and cultural destruction; they can never be treated fairly—anywhere. They also battle the stereotyping of Indians, not only in the popular media (as in the iconic figures of Tonto and Sacagawea), but also in the "Mother Earth Father Sky" clichés promoted in the works of other Indians, such as N. Scott Momaday. Along with the publication of numerous books (sixteen to date, and counting) have come a host of awards.

Alexie says, "I think humor is the most effective political tool out there, because people will listen to anything if they're laughing. . . . There's nothing worse than earnest emotion and I never want to be earnest. I always want to be on the edge of offending somebody. . . . Humor is really just about questioning the status quo." "What Sacagawea Means to Me," first published in *Time* (June 30, 2002) offers a critique of the mythic, white version of the Lewis and Clark expedition, a "multicultural, trigenerational, bigendered, animal-friendly" exploration, through a counterinterpretation of their faithful companion and guide Sacagawea, the American Eve.

What Sacagawea Means to Me[*]

In the future, every U.S. citizen will get to be Sacagawea for fifteen minutes. For the low price of admission, every American, regardless of race, religion, gender, and age, will climb through the portal into Sacagawea's Shoshone Indian brain. In the multicultural theme park called Sacagawea Land, you will be kidnapped as a child by the Hidatsa tribe and sold to Toussaint Charbonneau, the French-Canadian trader who will take you as one of his wives and father two of your children. Your first child, Jean-Baptiste, will be only a few months old as you carry him during your long journey with Lewis and Clark. The two captains will lead the adventure, fighting rivers, animals, weather, and diseases for thousands of miles, and you will march right beside them. But you, the aboriginal multitasker, will also breastfeed. And at the end of your Sacagawea journey, you will be shown the exit and given a souvenir T-shirt that reads, IF THE U.S. IS EDEN, THEN SACAGAWEA IS EVE. 1

Sacagawea is our mother. She is the first gene pair of the American DNA. In the beginning, she was the word, and the word was possibility. I revel in the wondrous possibilities of Sacagawea. It is good to be joyous in the presence of her spirit, because I hope she had moments of joy in what must have been a grueling life. This much is true: Sacagawea died of some mysterious illness when she was only in her twenties. Most illnesses were mysterious in the nineteenth century, but I suspect that Sacagawea's indigenous immune system was defenseless against an immigrant virus. Perhaps Lewis and Clark infected Sacagawea. If that is true, then certain postcolonial historians would argue that she was murdered not by germs but by colonists who carried those germs. I don't know much about the science of disease and immunities, but I know enough poetry to recognize that individual human beings are invaded and colonized by foreign bodies, just as individual civilizations are invaded and colonized by foreign bodies. In that sense, colonization might be a natural process, tragic and violent to be sure, but predictable and ordinary as well, and possibly necessary for the advance, however constructive and destructive, of all civilizations. 2

After all, Lewis and Clark's story has never been just the triumphant tale of two white men, no matter what the white historians might need to believe. Sacagawea was not the primary hero of this story either, no matter what the Native American historians and I might want to believe. The story of Lewis and Clark is also the story of the approximately forty-five nameless and faceless first- and second-generation European Americans who joined the journey, then left or completed it, often without monetary or historical compensation. Considering the time and place, I imagine those forty-five were illiterate, low-skilled laborers subject to 3

* Copyright © 2002 *Time*, Inc., reprinted by permission.

Negative #11604 courtesy of the Library, American Museum of Natural History

We often forget that many—perhaps most—professional quality photographs are staged. This photograph was staged by anthropologist Franz Boas (left) and photographer George Hunt (right) during a late-nineteenth-century expedition to study indigenous cultures of the Pacific Northwest, which were becoming increasingly infiltrated by western "civilization." The creation of an artificial backdrop enables the Kwakiutl woman weaving cedar bark to appear more "authentic" than she would have if posed against the picket and stockade fences, or the building with columns and Romanesque arches, behind her. How do you "read" the photograph in front of the blanket background? How does the presence of the actual background influence your reading? In what ways does this photograph metaphorically capture the essence of "What Sacagawea Means to Me"? In what ways can a photograph of one century be used to comment on an essay written a century later?

managerial whims and nineteenth-century downsizing. And it is most certainly the story of the black slave York, who also cast votes during this allegedly democratic adventure. It's even the story of Seaman, the domesticated Newfoundland dog who must have been a welcome and friendly presence and who survived the risk of becoming supper during one lean time or another. The Lewis and Clark Expedition was exactly the kind of multicultural, trigenerational, bigendered, animal-friendly, government-supported, partly French-Canadian project that should rightly be celebrated by liberals and castigated by conservatives.

4 In the end, I wonder if colonization might somehow be magical. After all, Miles Davis is the direct descendant of slaves and slave owners. Hank Williams is the direct descendant of poor whites and poorer Indians. In 1876 Emily Dickinson was writing her poems in an Amherst attic while Crazy Horse was killing Custer on the banks of the Little Big

Horn. I remain stunned by these contradictions, by the successive generations of social, political, and artistic mutations that can be so beautiful and painful. How did we get from there to here? This country somehow gave life to Maria Tallchief and Ted Bundy, to Geronimo and Joe McCarthy, to Nathan Bedford Forrest and Toni Morrison, to the Declaration of Independence and Executive Order No. 1066, to Cesar Chavez and Richard Nixon, to theme parks and national parks, to smallpox and the vaccine for smallpox.

As a Native American, I want to hate this country and its contradic- 5
tions. I want to believe that Sacagawea hated this country and its contradictions. But this country exists, in whole and in part, because Sacagawea helped Lewis and Clark. In the land that came to be called Idaho, she acted as diplomat between her long-lost brother and the Lewis and Clark party. Why wouldn't she ask her brother and her tribe to take revenge against the men who had enslaved her? Sacagawea is a contradiction. Here in Seattle, I exist, in whole and in part, because a half-white man named James Cox fell in love with a Spokane Indian woman named Etta Adams and gave birth to my mother. I am a contradiction; I am Sacagawea.

Content

1. Alexie's short piece depends on readers to understand a host of common cultural references: Sacagawea as a cultural and historical figure; Lewis and Clark and the purpose(s) and nature of their expedition; other members of the expedition (including the Newfoundland dog); and all of the people and events referred to in ¶ 4: Miles Davis, Hank Williams, Emily Dickinson, Crazy Horse, and Custer. Do you recognize most of them? If you don't, can you still understand Alexie's general point and the means by which he's making it? Or is he too allusive? Explain.

2. Identify and amplify from your own knowledge of history the various roles in American history that Alexie attributes to Sacagawea whether she actually played them or not: Indian icon who helped Lewis and Clark on their expedition (a fact so well-known that Alexie does not fully articulate it in this essay); child kidnap victim; wife of a French-Canadian trader; mother of infant Jean-Baptiste, who accompanied her on the journey. He also calls her the mother of our nation, an undeserving victim of "immigrant" viruses, diplomat between her "long-lost brother and the Lewis and Clark party," a "contradiction" who lives on in subsequent Indian generations. Do you disagree with any of his interpretations? If so, explain why.

3. Why does Alexie say "Sacagawea was not the primary hero of [the Lewis and Clark story], no matter what the Native American historians and I might want to believe" (¶ 3). Who is the hero, if not Lewis and Clark or Sacagawea?

Strategies/Structures/Language

4. Why does Alexie set up Sacagawea's brain as a "multicultural theme park called Sacagawea Land," into which readers go for a "low price of admission" to allegedly recreate the Indian's experiences? What are readers expected to learn as a consequence of all the roles they'll play therein (see question 1)?

5. At what point in the essay do you recognize that Alexie is being sarcastic? Why did he title the piece "What Sacagawea Means to Me"?

For Writing

6. Write a short "true" story of some historical event—particularly one involving oppression of other groups or cultures—that you thought you understood but that a new rendering (perhaps as a new story rather than just a collection of facts) or new information reveals a new concept to you and to your readers. How much information will you have to supply? How much can you expect your readers to understand? If you can write with a partner who represents the other culture you're examining, so much the better.

7. ***Journal Writing.*** Choose a particular theme park and describe how it both represents and fails to represent American history, society, or culture. What myths about America does this theme park employ and promote? Do these myths necessarily mask contemporary social problems or realities?

8. ***Dialogues.*** Compare Alexie's view of American culture as the product of "successive generations of social, political, and artistic mutations that can be so beautiful and painful" (¶ 4) with Ntozake Shange's (Chapter 4) description of the culture that African descendants of the Diaspora have preserved in the form of knowledge of "the land, sensuality, rhythm and ourselves that has continued to elude our captors" (¶ 1). Alexie refers to colonization as a "tragic and violent . . . , but [also] predictable and ordinary" process (¶ 2). How does Shange illustrate American history in the same way? After reading both Alexie and Shange, do you believe that a cultural heritage can survive invasive colonization and assimilation? What reasons do Alexie and Shange provide, or allude to, in support of the idea that ethnic groups should preserve their history and culture?

9. ***Mixed Modes.*** Alexie redefines—implicitly or explicitly—concepts such as colonization, heroism, culture, and even the notion of story itself. How do these concepts support his conclusion that "I am Sacagawea" (¶ 5)? Does his definition of American culture as inherently contradictory suggest integration or conflict?

10. ***Second Look.*** In what ways does the photograph in this essay, of Franz Boas and George Hunt holding a backdrop behind a Kwakiutl woman, capture the essence of "What Sacagawea Means to Me"? How can this late-nineteenth-century photograph enrich our understanding of Alexie's essay?

FREDERICK DOUGLASS

Frederick Douglass (1817–1895) was born a slave in Talbot County, Maryland. Unlike many slaves, he learned to read, and the power of this accomplishment—coupled with an iron physique and the will to match—enabled him to escape to New York in 1838. For the next twenty-five years he toured the country as a powerful spokesperson for the abolitionist movement, serving as an adviser to Harriet Beecher Stowe, author of *Uncle Tom's Cabin*, and to President Lincoln, among others. After the war he campaigned for civil rights for African Americans and women. In 1890 his political significance was acknowledged in his appointment as minister to Haiti.

Slave narratives, written or dictated by the hundreds in the nineteenth century, provided memorable accounts of the physical, geographical, and psychological movement from captivity to freedom. Douglass's autobiography, an abolitionist document like many other slave narratives, is exceptional in its forthright language and absence of stereotyping of either white or black people; his people are multidimensional. Crisis points, and the insights and opportunities they provide, are natural topics for personal narratives. This episode, taken from the first version (of four) of *The Narrative of the Life of Frederick Douglass, an American Slave* (1845), explains the incident that was "the turning point in my career as a slave," for it enabled him to make the transformation from slave to independent human being.

Resurrection

I have already intimated that my condition was much worse, during the first six months of my stay at Mr. Covey's, than in the last six. The circumstances leading to the change in Mr. Covey's course toward me form an epoch in my humble history. You have seen how a man was made a slave; you shall see how a slave was made a man. On one of the hottest days of the month of August, 1833, Bill Smith, William Hughes, a slave named Eli, and myself, were engaged in fanning wheat. Hughes was clearing the fanned wheat from before the fan. Eli was turning, Smith was feeding, and I was carrying wheat to the fan. The work was simple, requiring strength rather than intellect; yet, to one entirely unused to such work, it came very hard. About three o'clock of that day, I broke down; my strength failed me; I was seized with a violent aching of the head, attended with extreme dizziness; I trembled in every limb. Finding what was coming, I nerved myself up, feeling it would never do to stop work. I stood as long as I could stagger to the hopper with grain. When I could stand no longer, I fell, and felt as if held down by an immense weight. The fan of course stopped; every one had his own work to do; and no one could do the work of the other, and have his own go on at the same time. 1

Mr. Covey was at the house, about one hundred yards from the treading-yard where we were fanning. On hearing the fan stop, he left immediately, and came to the spot where we were. He hastily inquired what the matter was. Bill answered that I was sick, and there was no one to bring wheat to the fan. I had by this time crawled away under the side of the post and rail-fence by which the yard was enclosed, hoping to find relief by getting out of the sun. He then asked where I was. He was told by one of the hands. He came to the spot, and, after looking at me awhile, 2

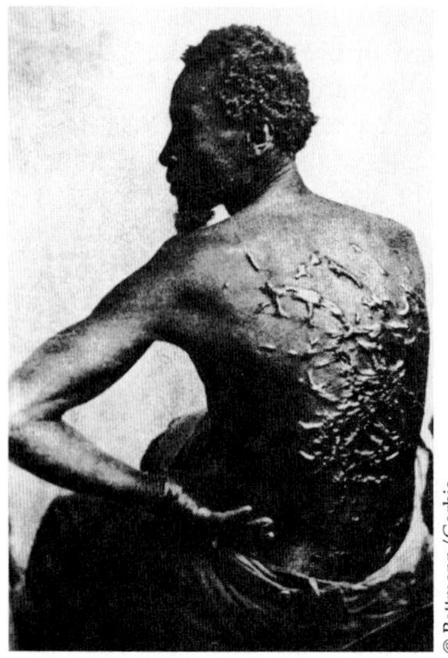

© Bettmann/Corbis

Interpret the pattern on the slave's back. What stories does this tell? Is there any ambiguity or uncertainty about their meaning? Do you need to know that this is a photograph of a slave to be able to understand the picture? Does it matter whether this picture was taken in the United States or somewhere else? (See also the discussion in Second Look, *following this essay.)*

asked me what was the matter. I told him as well as I could, for I scarce had strength to speak. He then gave me a savage kick in the side, and told me to get up. I tried to do so, but fell back in the attempt. He gave me another kick, and again told me to rise. I again tried, and succeeded in gaining my feet; but, stooping to get the tub with which I was feeding the fan, I again staggered and fell. While down in this situation, Mr. Covey took up the hickory slat with which Hughes had been striking off the half-bushel measure, and with it gave me a heavy blow upon the head, making a large wound, and the blood ran freely; and with this again told me to get up. I made no effort to comply, having now made up my mind to let him do his worst. In a short time after receiving this blow, my head grew better. Mr. Covey had now left me to my fate. At this moment I resolved, for the first time, to go to my master, enter a complaint, and ask his protection. In order to do this, I must that afternoon walk seven miles; and this, under the circumstances, was truly a severe undertaking. I was exceedingly feeble; made so as much by the kicks and blows which I received, as by the severe fit of sickness to which I had been subjected. I, however, watched my chance, while Covey was looking in an opposite direction, and started for St. Michael's: I succeeded in getting a considerable distance on my way to the woods, when Covey discovered me, and called after me to come back, threatening what he would do if I did not come. I disregarded both his calls and his threats, and made my way to the woods as fast as my feeble state would allow; and thinking I might be overhauled by him if I kept to the road, I walked through the woods, keeping far enough from the road to avoid detection, and near enough to prevent losing my way. I had not gone far before my little strength again failed me. I could go no farther. I fell down, and lay for a considerable time. The blood was yet oozing from the wound on my head. For a time I thought I should bleed to death; and think now that I should have done so, but that the blood so matted my hair as to stop the wound. After lying there about three quarters of an hour, I nerved myself up again, and started on my way, through bogs and briers, barefooted and bareheaded, tearing my feet sometimes at nearly every step; and after a journey of about seven miles, occupying some five hours to perform it, I arrived at master's store. I then presented an appearance enough to affect any but a heart of iron. From the crown of my head to my feet, I was covered with blood. My hair was all clotted with dust and blood; my shirt was stiff with blood. My legs and feet were torn in sundry places with briers and thorns, and were also covered in blood. I suppose I looked like a man who had escaped a den of wild beasts, and barely escaped them. In this state I appeared before my master, humbly entreating him to interpose his authority for my protection. I told him all the circumstances as well as I could, and it seemed, as I spoke, at times to affect him. He would then walk the floor, and seek to justify Covey by saying he expected I deserved it. He asked me what I wanted. I told him, to let me get a new home; that as sure as I lived with Mr. Covey again, I should live with but to die with him; that Covey would surely kill me; he was in a fair way for it. Master Thomas ridiculed the idea that there was any danger of Mr. Covey's killing me, and said that he knew Mr. Covey, that he was a good man, and that he could not think of taking me from him; that, should he do so, he would lose the whole year's wages; that I belonged to Mr. Covey for one year, and that I must go back to him, come what might; and that I must not trouble him with any more stories, or that he would himself *get hold of me*. After threatening me thus, he gave me a very large dose of salts, telling me that I might remain in St. Michael's that night, (it being quite late,) but that I must be off back to Mr. Covey's early in the morning; and that if I did not, he would *get hold of me*, which meant that he would whip me. I remained all night, and, according to his orders, I started off to Covey's in the morning, (Saturday morning,) wearied in body and broken in spirit. I got no supper that night, or breakfast that morning. I reached Covey's about nine o'clock; and just as I was getting over the fence that divided Mrs. Kemp's fields from ours, out ran Covey with his cowskin, to give me another whipping. Before he could reach me, I succeeded in getting to the cornfield; and as the corn was very high, it afforded me the means of hiding. He seemed very angry, and searched for me a long time. My behavior was altogether unaccountable. He finally gave up the chase, thinking, I suppose, that I must come home for something to eat; he would give himself no further trouble in looking for me. I spent that day mostly in the woods, having the alternative before me—to go home and be whipped to death, or stay in the woods and be starved to death. That night, I fell in with Sandy Jenkins, a slave with whom I was somewhat acquainted. Sandy had a free wife who lived about four miles from Mr. Covey's; and it being Saturday, he was on his way to see her. I told him my circumstances, and he very kindly invited me to go home with him. I went home with him, and talked this whole matter over, and got his advice as to what course it was best for me to pursue. I found Sandy an old adviser. He told me, with great solemnity, I must go back to Covey; but that before I went, I must go with him into another part of the woods, where there was a certain *root*, which, if I would take some of it with me, carrying it *always on my right side*, would render it impossible for Mr. Covey, or any other white man, to whip me. He said he had carried it for years; and since he had done so, he had never received a blow, and never expected to while he carried it. I at first rejected the idea, that the simple carrying of a root in my pocket would have any such effect as he had said, and was not disposed to take it; but Sandy impressed the necessity with much earnestness, telling me it could do no harm, if it did no good. To please him, I at length took the root, and, according to his direction, carried it upon my right side. This was Sunday morning. I immediately started for home; and upon entering the yard gate, out came Mr. Covey on his way to meeting. He spoke to me very kindly, bade me drive the pigs from a lot near by, and passed on towards the church. Now, this singular conduct of Mr. Covey really made me begin to think that there was something in the *root* which Sandy had given me; and had it been on any other day than Sunday, I could have attributed the conduct to no other cause than the influence of that root; and as it was, I was half inclined to think the *root* to be something more than I at first had taken it to be. All went well till Monday morning. On this morning, the virtue of the *root* was fully tested. Long before daylight, I was called to go and rub, curry, and feed, the horses. I obeyed, and was glad to obey. But whilst thus engaged, whilst in the act of throwing down some blades from the loft, Mr. Covey entered the stable with a long rope; and just as I was half out of the loft, he caught hold of my legs, and was about tying me. As soon as I found what he was up to, I gave a sudden spring, and as I did so, he holding to my legs, I was brought sprawling on the stable floor. Mr. Covey seemed now to think he had me, and could do what he pleased; but at this moment—from whence came the spirit I don't know—I resolved to fight; and, suiting my action to the resolution, I seized Covey hard by the throat; and as I did so, I rose. He held on to me, and I to him. My resistance was so entirely unexpected, that Covey seemed taken all aback. He trembled like a leaf. This gave me assurance, and I held him uneasy, causing the blood to run where I touched him with the ends of my fingers. Mr. Covey soon called out to Hughes for help. Hughes came, and while Covey held me, attempted to tie my right hand. While he was in the act of doing so, I watched my chance, and gave him a heavy kick close under the ribs. This kick fairly sickened Hughes, so that he left me in the hands of Mr. Covey. This kick had the effect of not only weakening Hughes, but Covey also. When he saw Hughes bending over with pain, his courage quailed. He asked me if

I meant to persist in my resistance. I told him I did, come what might; that he had used me like a brute for six months, and that I was determined to be used so no longer. With that, he strove to drag me to a stick that was lying just out of the stable door. He meant to knock me down. But just as he was leaning over to get the stick, I seized him with both hands by his collar, and brought him by a sudden snatch to the ground. By this time, Bill came. Covey called upon him for assistance. Bill wanted to know what he could do. Covey said, "Take hold of him, take hold of him!" Bill said his master hired him out to work, and not to help whip me; so he left Covey and myself to fight our own battle out. We were at it for nearly two hours. Covey at length let me go, puffing and blowing at a great rate, saying that if I had not resisted, he would not have whipped me half so much. The truth was, that he had not whipped me at all. I considered him as getting entirely the worst end of the bargain; for he had drawn no blood from me, but I had from him. The whole six months afterwards, that I spent with Mr. Covey, he never laid the weight of his finger upon me in anger. He would occasionally say, he didn't want to get hold of me again. "No," thought I, "you need not; for you will come off worse than you did before."

This battle with Mr. Covey was the turning-point in my career as a 3
slave. It rekindled the few expiring embers of freedom, and revived within me a sense of my own manhood. It recalled the departed self-confidence, and inspired me again with a determination to be free. The gratification afforded by the triumph was a full compensation for whatever else might follow, even death itself. He only can understand the deep satisfaction which I experienced, who has himself repelled by force the bloody arm of slavery. I felt as I never felt before. It was a glorious resurrection, from the tomb of slavery, to the heaven of freedom. My long-crushed spirit rose, cowardice departed, bold defiance took its place; and I now resolved that, however long I might remain a slave in form, the day had passed forever when I could be a slave in fact. I did not hesitate to let it be known of me, that the white man who expected to succeed in whipping, must also succeed in killing me.

Content

1. Twelve years after he successfully defied Mr. Covey, Douglass identified this incident as "the turning-point in my career as a slave" (¶ 3). Why? Would Douglass have been able to recognize its significance at the time or only in retrospect?
2. Would slave owners have been likely to read Douglass's autobiography? Why or why not? Would Douglass's emphasis have been likely to change for an audience of Northern post–Civil War blacks? Southern antebellum whites? What, if anything, does Douglass expect his audience—mostly white Northerners—to do about slavery, as a consequence of having read his narrative?

Strategies/Structures/Language

3. Douglass's account begins with Friday afternoon and ends with Monday morning, but some events receive considerable emphasis while others are scarcely mentioned. Which ones does he focus on? Why?

4. Why is paragraph 2 so long? Should it have been divided into shorter units, or is the longer unit preferable? Justify your answer.

5. Douglass provides considerable details about his appearance after his first beating by Covey (¶ 2), but scarcely any about the appearance of either Covey or Master Thomas. Why?

6. How sophisticated is Douglass's level of diction? Is it appropriate for the narrative he tells? How is this related to his self-characterization?

For Writing

7. Write a narrative in which you recount and explain the significance of an event in which you participated that provided you with an important change of status in the eyes of others. Provide enough specific details so readers unfamiliar with either you or the situation can experience it as you did.

8. ***Dialogues.*** Tim O'Brien (77–84) writes that a "true war story is never moral . . . If at the end of a war story you feel uplifted, or if you feel that some small bit of rectitude has been salvaged from a larger waste, then you have been made the victim of a very old and terrible lie" (¶ 8). Is Douglass's "battle with Mr. Covey" (¶ 3) a war story? Does Douglass's narrative of moral and physical victory over his condition conceal some aspects of the "larger waste" of slavery? What aspects of Douglass's autobiography (88–89) support the idea that his narrative conceals some aspects of slavery in order to highlight other aspects?

9. Douglass's narrative uses Christian imagery to describe his battle with Covey, while Martin Luther King, Jr. (Chapter 10) appeals to the Christian ethics of his audience. Why does each writer pursue his particular strategy?

10. ***Mixed Modes.*** The sentence "You have seen how a man was made a slave; you shall see how a slave was made a man" (¶ 1) is an example of *metabasis*, a statement that summarizes what has been said and tells the reader what will follow. It is also an *antithesis*, or the juxtaposition of contrasting ideas, since it contrasts the state of slavery with the state of manhood, and a *chiasmus*, because the paired concepts in the first part of the sentence ("a man was made a slave") are reversed in the second part. How do these multiple functions—summary and preparation, contrast, and reversal—set the pattern and theme for the narrative of Douglass's battle with Covey? What does this statement suggest about Douglass's characterization of freedom and humanity?

11. ***Second Look.*** Douglass was concerned in his autobiography with illustrating the evils of slavery while excluding specific details of his escape to the North in order to protect those who had helped him. How does the photograph in this essay, particularly the anonymity of the scarred man and the plain background, articulate a similar concern? What kind of judgment does the photograph seem to ask of the viewer? How does the response the photograph appears to elicit differ from Douglass's appeal to his audience?

ART SPIEGELMAN

Art Spiegelman's innovative work *Maus, A Survivor's Tale* (two volumes: 1986 and 1992), a classic of Holocaust literature, is a sequentially illustrated narrative of genocide, survival, and family history. The idea of depicting Jews as mice and Nazis as persecutory cats came to Spiegelman when his college film professor compared cartoon cat-and-mouse chases to racist film stereotypes. Born to Holocaust survivors in Stockholm, Sweden (1948), Spiegelman grew up in Queens, New York City, in a neighborhood with many Jewish families. Influenced by popular cartoons and *Mad Magazine*, he made drawings for his junior high school newspaper, attended the famous public High School of Art and Design, and made it through three years at Harpur College in upstate New York before personal and family crises intervened. Spiegelman suffered a nervous breakdown and shortly afterward his mother committed suicide, partly out of depression after the loss of her brother in a car accident. In 1971 Spiegelman moved to San Francisco, where he joined the dynamic underground comic book scene and taught at the San Francisco Academy of Art. Returning to New York (1975), Spiegelman married, taught at the School of Visual Arts, and began researching *Maus* by journeying to Auschwitz in 1978 and again in 1986. Spiegelman received the Pulitzer prize in 1992. His recent work includes *In the Shadow of No Towers* (2004), about the September 11 attacks—seen from his perspective as a downtown New Yorker—and the geopolitical aftermath.

"Mein Kampf (My Struggle)," taken from the *New York Times Magazine* (1996), ironically bears the same title as Adolf Hitler's autobiography and manifesto of Nazi ideology. Spiegelman's struggle, however, concerns his artistic vision—specifically, how to find a new topic when a "5,000-pound mouse" is breathing down his neck.

Mein Kampf (My Struggle)

Art Spiegelman, "Mein Kampf (My Struggle)," from *Maus I: A Survivor's Tale/My Father Bleeds History*, by Art Spiegelman. First published in the *New York Times Magazine*, May 12, 1996. Copyright © 1996 by Art Spiegelman, reprinted with permission of The Wylie Agency LLC

Content

1. As "Mein Kampf" begins, we learn that Spiegelman's previous artistic creation, *Maus*, is overpowering and intimidating him; the rest of the narrative unfolds from that premise. What other problems is Spiegelman facing, and how does he attempt to solve them?

2. What is the message of the last few panels, in which the artist's son appears? What is resolved by the ending, or in what way is the reader perhaps left hanging? Explain why this ending is either effective or ineffective.

Strategies/Structures/Language

3. For some readers, comics are mainly associated with humor; yet in "Mein Kampf" Spiegelman uses the comic book form to handle serious themes such as his troubled past, his artistic self-doubts, and his lack of appropriate memories. In what ways do his comic book techniques especially reinforce his themes?

4. What is the irony in Spiegelman showing himself being chased by a gigantic mouse, given what you know about his two-volume series *Maus* (see the headnote for information). What are some of the other ways that "Mein Kampf" uses visual or verbal humor? For what purposes?

5. How does Spiegelman use line, texture, frame-to-frame pacing, and approach to the human figure to create a visual narrative? For example, is it appropriate to set the action in the "murky caverns" of his memory? In what other ways do the visuals support the topics and themes of "Mein Kampf"?

6. For many readers, comics—or "sequential art"—have an instant attraction. Why do you suppose this is so? What are your favorite comic strips or works of sequential art, and why do you enjoy them?

For Writing

7. If you had the talents of a comic strip artist, what story would you tell? Would you base your work on your life experience, or would you create fiction and fantasy? What characters would you create? What color themes and visual effects would you use? (See Scott McCloud, "Character Design," in Chapter 4.) Explore ideas for a work of sequential art, including a description of your topic, characters, and a sample story or episode. What are your artistic and literary goals, and how would the piece achieve them?

8. ***Dialogues.*** Compare the reasons Spiegelman includes his son in "Mein Kampf" with the roles Lynda Barry gives to her grandmother and husband in "Common Scents" (Chapter 8). How do these characters act as observers of American culture? What information do they provide the reader about the narrator? Do you see a parallel between the conflicts Barry and Spiegelman describe?

9. ***Mixed Modes.*** Write a panel-by-panel analysis of *how* "Mein Kampf" works as a narrative. What does the progression from one part of the sequence to the next tell you, aside from the information you get in the dialogue balloons? (See questions 3, 4, and 5 for ideas.) Consider details, such as the labels on the doors of Spiegelman's memories, as well as larger factors, such as his movements and facial expressions. Or compare Spiegelman's "Mein Kampf" with Lynda Barry's "Common Scents" (Chapter 8).

LINDA HOGAN

Linda Hogan (born in 1947 in Denver, Colorado) is a Chickasaw writer, essayist, playwright, environmental theorist, social and political commentator, and activist. Her poetry has been collected in *Calling Myself Home* (1978), *Daughters, I Love You* (1981), *Eclipse* (1983), *Seeing Through the Sun*

(1985), *Savings* (1988), and *Book of Medicines* (1993). She has also published a memoir (*The Woman Who Watches over the World: A Native Memoir*, 2001), essays (*Dwellings*, 1995), novels (*Mean Spirit*, 1990; *Solar Storms*, 1995, and *Power*, 1998), and short stories ("Aunt Moon's Young Man," in *The Best American Short Stories*, 1989). Her work voices her concerns with racism, poverty, ethno-history, eco-feminism, and spiritual environmentalism. Notable for her use of allegory and myth to explore humanity's—and especially women's—relationship to nature, Hogan locates spirituality in the natural world. Hogan has won multiple literary awards and edited anthologies on nature and spirituality. She currently teaches at the University of Colorado at Boulder.

Waking

Last night thunder and lightning opened the world. Hail beat down on 1
earth, drumming the roof. I watched the round layers of ice bounce off the ground. This morning I wake early to the sound of the young horse running, to the voices of magpies teaching their young to fly, the wings fluttering as they jump only from branch to branch, the parents hovering, urging, flying away, calling the young ones to them. A woodpecker hammers at a hole in the dead tree.

From the swaddling comfort of bed, I look out to watch such joy. It 2
is a new morning and beautiful and I rise with the beauty to a morning knowing more of my past has slipped away and that this night of storms, this morning of beauty may also disappear, so I write it down.

Time. I have lost it, and I think of my ancestors who tied knots in 3
ropes to keep track of it, or other tribes who painted events and each year revealed them, telling the stories.

Daily something is lost from me. It began with an accident I don't 4
remember, an impact to my head, a woman finding my body in the road. I do remember hearing once, as if in a very far distance, the sound of sirens, entrancing like the ones in the *Odyssey* calling me to an island and I surrendered and went to that island where I still live, never going back home, never returning to the same journey and at night there is the unraveling of memory that takes place and parts of my past disappear. Yet I am happy. I think, I have forgotten last month and it should matter, but it doesn't.

I remain on that island without intending it, but I am conscious. I can 5
recall many things: what I read, that I bought pillowcases. But not what someone said or a movie I saw. We laugh. I can see reruns and think they are new. And the shadows of words sometimes only float past. I try to recall them. I say, It is the thing with a handle. It is the thing that cleans the floor.

But I know there are rooms of jade. From the hospital bed there was 6
a great traveling and I was awake in other worlds. Not dreams, nothing even similar to dreams, but a new kind of waking. I traveled. I described

to my daughter and friend in great detail the jade carvings in China. I saw the carved jade and silk embroideries of another world. There were pale animals, beautifully polished, a horse, great detail in the carvings of a wall made of jade, entire vignettes of life carved by some artist of the past, a woman sitting and playing an instrument, trees trimmed to some notion of perfection. Jade, the stone of heaven, once carried from the White Jade River by camels. There were also the fabrics, silks and brocades with embroidery, some with gold stitches. I traveled maps with no roads, no towns, no named waters. The world was China, I suppose, and I was a child digging through earth to the other side and succeeding, through soil, stone, magma, through the darkness of unconsciousness to another kind of waking and seeing.

7 At the same time, others traveled toward me, passing through the walls. In the room with me were ancestors I hadn't seen, far ones, from before the Trail of Tears of Chickasaws to Oklahoma, a woman dressed in lavender and wearing a turban as our women did in the past. I wonder if she was my own blood. I remember my father's own recent awakening in bed before his death to the old ones, our people. He said the names of the grandmothers, some I'd never heard, as he looked up at them smiling, and then he introduced me, placing me in my line at the bottom of our world, the present, in my own place as a woman, a grandmother.

8 But for me, I was going to live, and live with memory loss. Important events vanished from my memory. Some didn't. It was random. I forgot neighbors' faces. I remembered some small detail of a poem. Rumi: *Break the wine glass and go toward the glassblower's breath.* The names of the wildflowers in bloom around my house would be gone. What I told someone I told again and again. What I asked, I repeated. Words were gone. I searched for them, coming up with things similar until someone guessed.

9 No one has ever seen an atom yet they believe it is there. No one has ever understood how the brain works. Who could think that love might be electrical, or that consciousness could be chemical? The brain is an organ. The mind is a transient. But the body, I find, is not the husk for the soul. It is knowing. It is consciousness. For a time I was a divine traveler through no will of my own, far beyond my world and its limits. It was a virginal state. While I slept, a restless spirit woke to travel another reality, another realm or layer of existence. But my body, even without words, knows this world, every morning the first morning. I watch the light move, lengthen. Daily there is beauty. The wildflowers still exist, even nameless. They know their own names and those are beyond human knowing. Ask me the name of the month and I could say October when it is June, but there is bread and butter. Pleasure. I listen to the thunder, look at the dew in the flowers. There is joy even in such vulnerability, such fragility. There is even happiness.

10 Awakening isn't always to a state of enlightenment. It isn't always a sudden change in consciousness. I can't say I know what it is. I can't say I understand the boundary, the skin, between the worlds we may journey or where I now live. Stirrings there I feel, but don't know.

Unconscious, a richness was there. Perhaps it is because I was missing. This is what is said about the self. That when you are given up, a whole cosmos opens. I remember Lakota Wallace Black Elk once saying about the space program, that we have always traveled through the universe. 11

I was a sleeper for three weeks and sometimes still. And yet something grows in it, something wakes. Something else owns this mind, this awakening, and it is a mystery, as if the soul lives larger than the human knows or thinks. Morning after morning has been my world, the sunrise always beautiful, everything newly seen. I am afraid to miss any of it. 12

It is an infant life, too soon to tell what it will become but I trust it is a sacred beginning like all beginnings. Sometimes you drink from an empty bowl thinking it is full and it is. Sometimes you open your empty palm and receive. The world is always fresh. Sometimes there is morning with birds and the sound of a running horse and you are awake. 13

Content

1. How does the narrator's loss of memory and time change her perceptions of her immediate surroundings? How does this loss paradoxically enhance her experience of the immediate present?
2. Identify and describe the various states of consciousness the narrator experiences. How does memory loss seem to give her access to these states? What imagery does the narrator use to describe these experiences?
3. "Waking" employs several *antitheses* (contrasting ideas) to describe the narrator's experience, including present/past, body/mind, awake/asleep, empty/full, self/cosmos. How does Hogan's use of names and her inability to remember names break down these distinctions? What is the significance of the narrator's use of the two meanings of the word *siren* (¶ 4)?

Strategies/Structures/Language

4. Why does the narrator begin and end her essay with images of nature and new life? How does the pattern of the text reflect its theme?
5. How does Hogan's use of visual imagery, such as "knots in ropes" to keep track of time (¶ 3), "the unraveling of memory" at night (¶ 4), and "maps with no roads, no towns, no named waters" (¶ 6) illustrate how she now perceives immediate experience (see question 2)?
6. The narrator's use of contrasting ideas (see question 3) leads to a paradox: memory loss brings knowledge. How do her allusions to the Greek poet Homer, Native American history and historical figures, and the mystic poet Rumi contribute to the idea that knowing is a process of the unconscious?

For Writing

7. ***Journal Writing.*** Describe the conscious and unconscious elements of an experience in which you struggled to understand something, such as an emotionally charged event or an intellectual problem. How did your unconscious processes,

perhaps while you dreamed or were immersed in some absorbing activity such as running or hiking, help you come to terms with the event or solve the problem?

8. ***Dialogues.*** Both Hogan and Brian Doyle (Chapter 8) employ images of nature to explore the human spirit. How does each writer characterize the human relationship to nature?

9. ***Second Look.*** "Waking" emphasizes the experience of the active consciousness while the body is at rest. Choose a photograph from *The Essay Connection* that seems to convey the same paradoxical sense of movement and stasis. Using your chosen photograph, explain Hogan's idea that the resting body "is knowing" and not simply "the husk for the soul" (¶ 9).

ANNE FADIMAN

Anne Fadiman was born (in 1953) to bookish parents, the noted writer/editor Clifton Fadiman and writer Annalee Fadiman. After graduating from Harvard (BA, 1975), Fadiman worked as an editor and staff writer for *Life* magazine, then as a columnist for *Civilization,* the now-defunct magazine of the Library of Congress. From 1998 to 2004 she was editor of the *American Scholar,* Phi Beta Kappa's national magazine, which published distinguished essays, including her award-winning commentary on "Mail," a learned romp that moves wittily from stagecoach delivery to e-mail. Her first book, *The Spirit Catches You and You Fall Down: A Hmong Child, Her American Doctors, and the Collision of Two Cultures* (1997), won a National Book Critics Circle Award for general nonfiction. She has published two collections of essays, *Ex Libris: Confessions of a Common Reader* (1998) and *At Large and At Small* (2007).

"Under Water" is the account of a happy summer wilderness expedition that turned into a tragedy. Fadiman is full of regret prompted by her inability not only to rescue her fellow student, but by her unworthy—though thoroughly human—thoughts during the futile rescue and ever since: "I find myself wanting to backferry, to hover midstream, suspended. I might then avoid many things: harsh words, foolish decisions, moments of inattention, regrets that wash over me, like water."

Under Water

1 When I was eighteen, I was a student on a month-long wilderness program in western Wyoming. On the third day, we went canoeing on the Green River, a tributary of the Colorado that begins in the glaciers of the Wind River Range and flows south across the sagebrush plains. Swollen by warm-weather runoff from an unusually deep snowpack, the Green was higher and swifter that month—June of 1972—than it had been in forty years. A river at flood stage can have strange currents. There is

Don Seabrook/The Wenatchee World/AP Images

What has happened in this picture? What is about to happen? With what consequences? How does Fadiman's story in "Under Water" influence the ways you "read" this picture? Would you "read" it differently if you saw it as an ad for a wilderness travel company? An adventure film?

not enough room in the channel for the water to move downstream in an orderly way, so it collides with itself and forms whirlpools and boils and souse holes. Our instructors decided to stick to their itinerary nevertheless, but they put in at a relatively easy section of the Green, one that the flood had merely upgraded, in the international system of white-water classification, from Class I to Class II. There are six levels of difficulty, and Class II was not an unreasonable challenge for novice paddlers.

The Green River did not seem dangerous to me. It seemed magnificently unobstructed. Impediments to progress—the rocks and stranded trees that under normal conditions would protrude above the surface—were mostly submerged. The river carried our aluminum canoe high and lightly, like a child on a broad pair of shoulders. We could rest our paddles on the gunwales and let the water do our work. The sun was bright and hot. Every few minutes, I dipped my bandanna in the river, draped it over my head, and let an ounce or two of melted glacier run down my neck. 2

I was in the bow of the third canoe. We rounded a bend and saw, fifty feet ahead, a standing wave in the wake of a large black boulder. The students in the lead canoe were backferrying, slipping crabwise across the current by angling their boat diagonally and stroking backward. Backferrying allows paddlers to hover midstream and carefully plan 3 their course instead of surrendering to the water's pace. But if they lean upstream—a natural inclination, for few people choose to lean toward the difficulties that lie ahead—the current can overflow the lowered gunwale and flip the boat. And that is what happened to the lead canoe.

4 I wasn't worried when I saw it go over. Knowing that we might capsize in the fast water, our instructors had arranged to have our gear trucked to our next campsite. The packs were all safe. The water was little more than waist-deep, and the paddlers were both wearing life jackets. They would be fine. One was already scrambling onto the right-hand bank.

5 But where was the second paddler? Gary, a local boy from Rawlins, a year or two younger than I, seemed to be hung up on something. He was standing at a strange angle in the middle of the river, just downstream from the boulder. Gary was the only student on the course who had not brought sneakers, and one of his mountaineering boots had become wedged between two rocks. The other canoes would come around the bend in a moment, and the instructors would pluck him out.

6 But they didn't come. The second canoe pulled over to the bank and ours followed. Thirty seconds passed, maybe a minute. Then we saw the standing wave bend Gary's body forward at the waist, push his face underwater, stretch his arms in front of him, and slip his orange life jacket off his shoulders. The life jacket lingered for a moment at his wrists before it floated downstream, its long white straps twisting in the current. His shirtless torso was pale and undulating, and it changed shape as hills and valleys of water flowed over him, altering the curve of the liquid lens through which we watched him. I thought, He looks like the flayed skin of St. Bartholomew in the Sistine Chapel. As soon as I had the thought, I knew that it was dishonorable. To think about anything outside the moment, outside Gary, was a crime of inattention. I swallowed a small, sour piece of self-knowledge: I was the sort of person who, instead of weeping or shouting or praying during a crisis, thought about something from a textbook (H. W. Janson's *History of Art*, page 360).

7 Once the flayed man had come, I could not stop the stream of images: Gary looked like a piece of seaweed, Gary looked like a waving handkerchief, Gary looked like a hula dancer. Each simile was a way to avoid thinking about what Gary was, a drowning boy. To remember these things is dishonorable, too, for I have long since forgotten Gary's last name and the color of his hair and the sound of his voice.

8 I do not remember a single word that anyone said. Somehow, we got into one of the canoes, all five of us, and tried to ferry the twenty feet or so to the middle of the river. The current was so strong, and we were so incompetent, that we never got close. Then we tried it on foot, linking arms to form a chain. The water was so cold that it stung. And it was noisy—not the roar and crash of white water but a groan, a terrible bass grumble, from the stones that were rolling and leaping down the

riverbed. When we got close to Gary, we couldn't see him; all we could see was the reflection of the sky. A couple of times, groping blindly, one of us touched him, but he was as slippery as soap. Then our knees buckled and our elbows unlocked, and we rolled downstream, like the stones. The river's rocky load, moving invisibly beneath its smooth surface, pounded and scraped us. Eventually, the current heaved us, blue-lipped and panting, onto the bank. In that other world above the water, the only sounds were the buzzing of bees and flies. Our wet sneakers kicked up red dust. The air smelled of sage and rabbitbrush and sunbaked earth.

We tried again and again, back and forth between the worlds. Wet, 9
dry, cold, hot, turbulent, still.

At first, I assumed that we would save him. He would lie on the bank 10
and the sun would warm him while we administered mouth-to-mouth resuscitation. If we couldn't get him out, we would hold him upright in the river; and maybe he could still breathe. But the Green River was flowing at nearly three thousand cubic feet—about ninety tons—per second. At that rate, water can wrap a canoe around a boulder like tinfoil. Water can uproot a tree. Water can squeeze the air out of a boy's lungs, undo knots, drag off a life jacket, lever a boot so tightly into the riverbed that even if we had had ropes—the ropes that were in the packs that were in the trucks—we could never have budged him.

We kept going in, not because we had any hope of rescuing Gary after 11
the first ten minutes, but because we had to save face. It would have been humiliating if the instructors came around the bend and found us sitting in the sagebrush, a docile row of five with no hypothermia and no skinned knees. Eventually, they did come. The boats had been delayed because one had nearly capsized, and the instructors had made the other students stop and practice backferrying until they learned not to lean upstream. Even though Gary had already drowned, the instructors did all the same things we had done, more competently but no more effectively, because they, too, would have been humiliated if they hadn't skinned their knees. Men in wet suits, belayed with ropes, pried the body out the next morning.

When I was eighteen, I wanted to hurry through life as fast as 12
I could. Twenty-seven years have passed, and my life now seems too fast. I find myself wanting to backferry, to hover midstream, suspended. I might then avoid many things: harsh words, foolish decisions, moments of inattention, regrets that wash over me, like water.

Content

1. From what point of view does Anne Fadiman narrate the events that take place in "Under Water"? In what ways does Fadiman as author prepare her readers to interpret Fadiman as a character in this tale? How does she want the readers to react to the circumstances she describes and to the others on this trip, including the instructors?

2. Anne Fadiman's statement "The Green River did not seem dangerous to me. . . . Impediments to progress—the rocks and stranded trees that under normal conditions would protrude above the surface—were mostly submerged" (¶ 2) is meant to be read literally. Why can we also say it possesses another level of meaning that transcends the literal?

Strategies/Structures/Language

3. Fadiman's tale unfolds chronologically, although she speaks in the present, merely remembering the past. How and why does she foreshadow the events that will occur with statements such as "Class II was not an unreasonable challenge for novice paddlers" (¶ 1)? At what point in the story is a reader likely to become aware of the inevitable outcome toward which the narrative is moving? Why not simply begin with the drowning of the young man?

4. Does Fadiman's tale contain all the major components of a narrative: characters, conflict, motives, plot, setting, point of view, and dialogue? Find examples from the text to illustrate which features are there. Since "Under Water" looks and reads like a short story, how do you know it's true?

5. Fadiman uses some extremely vivid description—for example, "Then we saw the standing wave bend Gary's body forward at the waist, push his face underwater, stretch his arms in front of him, and slip his orange life jacket off his shoulders" (¶ 6). What effect is such graphic representation likely to have on her readers?

For Writing

6. ***Journal Writing.*** Describe an incident you either witnessed or participated in that involved a serious error of judgment. This can be anything from a car accident to rejecting, insulting, discriminating against, or otherwise mistreating someone, to a benign event that turned serious and ugly. Explore how the story might be told from the point of view of another person involved in the incident. How does the shift in perspective change your implicit or explicit judgments of those involved?

7. ***Dialogues.*** Fadiman describes the students' and the instructors' hopeless efforts to rescue a drowned boy as saving face, and so suggests that others' perceptions play a major role in shaping our behavior. How does Peter Singer's "The Singer Solution to World Poverty" (Chapter 11) or Bill McKibben's "Designer Genes" (Chapter 12) suggest that human behavior can and should be shaped? How does each author express our ethical obligations to one another? In what situations is peer pressure appropriate and effective in promoting ethical behavior?

8. ***Mixed Modes.*** In the last paragraph, Fadiman's narrative becomes an analogy for her own life. Find the metaphors in the narrative that prepare the reader for this final paragraph. How do these metaphors and the structure of the essay serve Fadiman's larger purpose?

9. ***Second Look.*** Fadiman's essay describes several contrasts that incorporate the ideas of "wet, dry, cold, hot, turbulent, still" (¶ 9), as well as the contrast between her desire "to hurry through life" and then "wanting to backferry" (¶ 12). How does the photograph in this essay capture these contrasts?

10. Write a true story in which the setting, preferably a natural one, plays a major role in relation to the human participants. This role may be benign or malevolent, active or passive, but it should be important and the humans should be constantly aware of this role. Because you will need to pay close attention to the specific details of the setting, it should be a place you either know well or can revisit.

JASON VERGE

A Canadian who was born in Ottawa (1982) and grew up in Montreal, Jason Verge's first language was French. His earliest passion was for the Montreal Jason Canadiens, "The Habs," whose example encouraged him to play hockey as an adolescent. Then he "did what any die-hard hockey fan would do after graduating high school": he decided to attend college in Hawaii, where because of the time difference, he had to watch the games live at 9 A.M. Transferring to Marymount University, he completed his BA in English in 2005. Verge says he is "currently putting the finishing touches" on his first novel. Although he once owned a recording company, he decided he wasn't suited for the business world when he "accepted an 8-bit Nintendo in lieu of cash payment." He has now returned to writing.

He says of "The Habs," "my friends were tired of hearing me talk incessantly about hockey, so I decided to get it down on paper. It's a love letter to the sport and to the team, for the Habs are inextricably linked with the identities of myself and my family. I wanted the piece to be humorous without losing its honesty."

✧ *The Habs*

Game seven: the deciding game of the Stanley Cup finals. I was six, captured in old home movies running and screaming "By the power of Greyskull!" at the top of my lungs. It was the only phrase I knew how to say in English, learned from episodes of *He-man.* Earlier that night, my family had been embroiled in a heated political argument, as was the custom when we got together. Watching the Montreal Canadiens play hockey was the only viable reason to put political arguments on hiatus, and so we had. With the game on, the light conflict in the air turned to a deep sense of unity. My grandfather—usually a calm man—cheered like a rabid child during the games. For the length of three periods, all worries went away; there were no financial worries, there were no disagreements. The only thing that seemed to matter in the entire universe was the Montreal Canadiens, or "the Habs," as we called them. The Habs were in our blood. 1

2 Calling the team "Habs" started in the 1920s as a joke. The Canadiens logo has an "H" in the center of the "C," which initially stood for "Hockey" in "Club de hockey Canadien." Tex Rickard, an Anglophone from the Toronto Maple Leafs, asked a Montreal coach what it stood for, and the coach said "Habitants" to mess with him. ("Club de hockey Canadien" was plastered everywhere when Tex asked.) Somehow, the name stuck. The story is mostly ignored these days because it's completely inexplicable—to most people—why the guy lied and said "Habitants" instead of the plain truth. A Montreal fan, however, instantly knows why the coach lied: because the team and the city's culture are inextricably linked and because no Toronto Maple Leafs Fan is deserving of a straight answer.

3 The Island of Montreal in Quebec is an oddity of sorts; the population is bilingual, whereas the rest of Quebec is devoutly French. Quebec has always been the proverbial stepchild of Canada; they have a different culture than the rest of Canada and never quite fit in. Quebec is a province divided between those who wish to secede from Canada (the devout French) and those who wish to remain a part of the country. Referendums occur where they actually vote on this issue; the last decided by 1 percent to stay. Whereas Americans determined divisive issues through a bloody civil war, Canadians prefer to vote incessantly on something until people lose their passion. It's too cold outside to fight. The votes from Montreal always swing the decision toward staying a part of the country. Somewhere down the line, the Habs became intertwined with the political debate. Habs fans are loyal to Canada. When the Habs played the Quebec Nordiques, people would come out in full force, the Habs fans being loyalists and the Nordiques fans being separatists. A win on the ice was a political victory of sorts, a justification for a person's given side of the political debate. Not only is hockey a way of life in Canada, it's also used to make important political decisions. (A little known fact: Canada entered World War I because the Habs won the night the decision was made.)

4 I was too big for the team jerseys when I started playing hockey in a league. The jerseys they handed out were made for the typical twelve-year-old, and I was anything but. I was already well over six feet by that time. I tried to stuff myself into the assigned jersey and ended up looking like a giant marshmallow. Instead, they let me wear my bright red Canadiens jersey. I'd imagine myself playing for the Habs, my family proudly watching me on TV (I'd reserve my tickets to the game for groupies).

5 Since the leagues were organized by age, I ended up playing with people I towered over. Years later, my dad would tell me that a lot of the parents were upset that a kid my height was allowed to play in the league. My dad tells me that that kind of made him proud. I was a goaltender, so it's not as if my physical play was a big factor—though I'm pretty sure I still hold the record for most penalty minutes by a goaltender. I wasn't a mean kid; in fact, most of the penalty minutes were justified. The only

female player in the league was on my team, and I didn't take too kindly to watching her get roughed up. I was a big brother to her; if someone hurt her, I'd politely snatch their legs with my stick and trip them. It was nothing personal; it was all part of the game. Yep, I was a true gentleman.

Jacques Plante was the goalie for the Habs in the sixties. He was 6
the first goalie to wear a mask during play, but only after years of pucks hitting him in the face. He had a reputation of being fearless on the ice and a true gentleman off it. In one game a puck hit him in the face and tore it open; he went back to the trainers, received over thirty stitches near his eye, and was back on the ice the next period. He didn't complain to anyone. The cut was so bad that the swelling and blood almost completely blinded him, yet the tough bastard continued to play despite not being able to see. The coach eventually figured out that Plante couldn't see; when the coach asked him why he didn't say something, Plante said he didn't want to bother anyone. Jacques Plante was a true gentleman.

I did what any die-hard hockey fan would do after graduating high 7
school: I decided to attend university in Hawaii. Apparently I was too busy thinking about doing homework on a beach to think of the ramifications it would have on my hockey viewing. Fortunately, I brought a few hockey videos, which I rationed with more intensity than the people in the movie *Alive* rationed peanuts.

However, my roommate from France was able to get a constant flow 8
of soccer on the TV, feeding his addiction. His happiness made me sick. The soccer players, with the little shin guards and floppy hair, made me sick. Soccer was the bizzaro hockey; soccer blazed at the equivalent speed of a physics lecture. I began to lose my mind.

Luckily, salvation came in the form of the occasional game on 9
ESPN 43. Since Hawaii had a six-hour time difference, it meant watching hockey at an ungodly early hour, or watching the replay. Since I enjoyed the consumption of beer during a game, I opted for the replay. Getting drunk at noon didn't quite appeal to me. I was so excited for that first game that I shook. The puck dropped and a giant grin appeared on my face. Not two minutes into the first period, the sports ticker on the bottom of the screen revealed the final score of the very game I was watching. I'm pretty sure I snapped something internally. I wanted the world to feel my wrath; I wanted to stand outside the movie theater and tell everyone how their movie would end.

Two weeks later, I would get my second chance. I slapped duct tape 10
across the bottom of the screen so I wouldn't be able to see the ticker. During intermission, the nice people at ESPN told me the final score of the game once again. I screamed in such agony that Janine, a girl across the hall, came to see what was wrong. She got my mind off of the game with tales of her sexual exploits. I told her that I was a writer, and she responded by letting me read her diary. Based on what I read, I vowed never to touch Janine.

11 When my third attempt came around, I was emaciated and pale, despite the Hawaiian sun. Hadn't shaved. I was all set to turn off the TV when intermission began. I made it to the second period, and then I heard a knock on the door. It was Janine. I decided her tales of sexual exploits could wait: "Go away!" I yelled.

12 "What's wrong?"

13 "I'm not talking to anyone until the game's over."

14 "Your door's locked."

15 "Go away."

16 "Let me in, I saw the score and they lost."

17 From that point on, I disliked Janine. I began to wonder if I could get televised hockey in the mountains of Tibet. I also vowed to watch the next game live at—cringe—nine in the morning.

18 It took college to make me realize how counterproductive getting drunk at nine in the morning is. You'd think they'd cover it in high school, in health class or something. I found a friend who shared my enthusiasm for the sport, at least, so he claimed. I had a sneaking suspicion all he really wanted was an excuse to drink at nine in the morning. Through that experience, I learned that beer is not a proper substitute for milk in cereal (foams too much when you chew). Tuition put to good use.

19 After the first two meetings of the nine A.M. drinkers club, we disbanded. I was content simply watching hockey. The whole experience made me grateful for every minute of hockey I'd get to see.

20 Maurice "The Rocket" Richard played for the Habs back around the time my father was a kid. I see a twinkle in my dad's eye when he says Richard's name—I get the same twinkle these days. "The Rocket" was a quiet, humble man. In a way, I like to think of myself as having the same demeanor. On the ice, Richard became the most clutch player of all time. He received a concussion in a deciding playoff game against the Leafs one year and had to be carried off—he wobbled back on and scored the game-winning goal. When the reporters asked him about it later, he had no recollection. The following year, against the same team, he was evicted from the game and suspended for fighting back. After the announcer reported his fate, riots started. Police flooded the Montreal forum. The riots leaked out onto the street; the city shut down. Richard stood quiet despite the passion of his fans; he always felt weird talking about himself to the press. Despite his taciturn demeanor, he became a deity in Montreal. At his funeral, a decade ago, decades after he stopped playing, two hundred thousand people showed up.

21 I watched all but three of the eighty-two regular season Montreal games last year. My girlfriend at the time asked me, "If you had to give up either me or hockey, which would you choose?" I may be a man, but I'm not stupid. I told her I'd give up hockey. Then I told her never to ask me that question again—ever. After years of philosophy and ethics courses, I still have yet to encounter a bigger dilemma. After she left the

room, I rubbed my jersey on my face and assured it that I would never give it up.

I have spent so many years devoted to my Habs that it has become a religion to me. I've spent a small fortune on a piece of cardboard with a Habs player on it. I've missed a final because it clashed with a playoff game. How could I not love a sport that combines the gracefulness of ice skating and the brutality of football? It is a paradox; it is beautiful yet violent. I am a Canadian; I come from a culture where aggressions are played out on the ice and not off it. Hockey is the opiate of my people. 22

I call my dad during intermissions to talk about the game, much as he'd call his dad when he was younger. I once told my mom that I wanted my ashes dumped in the arena the Canadiens play in. She didn't like the idea. 23

(Update: Due to arbitration, the 2004 hockey season was officially canceled until further notice. The author is currently seeking out a local mental institution that will willingly let him pretend it is 1993, the last year the Canadiens won the Stanley Cup.) 24

Content

1. If you're an American reader, what do you find in "The Habs" that makes it distinctively Canadian? (If possible, discuss your views with a Canadian reader.) At the editor's suggestion, Verge added paragraph 2, explaining the origin of the term "the Habs." Would you have understood the meaning of the term without this explanation?
2. Are rabid hockey fans any different from enthusiasts of any other sport?
3. If Verge is such a proud Canadian citizen and "die-hard" Habs fan, why would he choose to go to college in Hawaii? Are his reasons self-evident, or don't they matter?

Strategies/Structures/Language

4. Why is this piece funny? Do readers need to know much—or anything—about hockey to appreciate the humor?
5. Like many comic writers, Verge characterizes himself in a variety of self-deprecations. Identify some. Are readers expected to take him at his word—that is, is he an utterly reliable narrator? Why or why not?

For Writing

6. Write an essay explaining your lifelong love for an activity (such as reading, cooking, driving, painting, playing or listening to music, shopping), an individual (running, fishing, boating) or team sport, or participation in a worthy cause whose purpose is to benefit others rather than yourself. At the outset, try writing comic and serious versions of the same subject until you find a mode and vocabulary that does justice to both the topic and your attitude toward it. Try out alternative versions on a reader to see how he or she reacts.

7. ***Journal Writing.*** Do you identify with a particular sport or team? What does your appreciation of that sport or team say about your political beliefs, background, or cultural identity? Explore the ways in which that identification liberates or restricts you in your personal development—or both.

8. ***Dialogues.*** O'Brien, Alexie, Spiegelman, Fadiman, and Verge use satire and irony to make their points—all of which are critical of either the author, the subject, or both. What clues do these authors provide to tell readers to read these figuratively, rather than literally?

9. ***Mixed Modes.*** Team sports often function as a metaphor for life. What other activities (e.g., creative, individual, or noncompetitive) allow people to express their desires, aggressions, and fears? Compare the kinds of ideals these activities encourage with those that team sports promote.

Additional Topics for Writing Narration

(For strategies for writing narration, see 75.)

Multiple Strategies for Writing: Narration

In writing on any of the narrative topics below, you'll find it useful to draw on a variety of strategies to help tell your story.

You may choose to write your narrative using elements of *creative nonfiction,* and thus to tell the story through:

- a *narrator* in the role of a storyteller or a character or both
- *dialogue*
- a *time sequence,* either in chronological order or with flashbacks or flash-forwards, which, in combination, will provide a *plot,* with beginning, middle, and end
- *setting(s)*
- *symbolism,* through characters, objects, events
- an *implied*—rather than an overt—point or argument

Through the preceding techniques, or in a more conventional essay form, narratives can employ:

- *character sketches: who* was involved
- *illustrations* and *examples: what* happened and *when*
- *process analysis: how* it happened
- *cause* and *effect: why* it happened, with *what consequences*

Feel free to experiment, to use what works and discard what doesn't—but save the rejects in a separate file; you may be able to use them somewhere else.

1. Write two versions of the earliest experience you can remember that involved some fright, danger, discovery, or excitement. Write the first version as the experience appeared to you at the time it happened. Then, write another version interpreting how the experience appears to you now.
2. Write a narrative of an experience you had that taught you a difficult lesson. (See Fadiman, "Under Water" 102–05; Yu, "Red and Black, or One English Major's Beginning" 166–74; and Nocton, "Harvest of Gold, Harvest of Shame" 286–90; and LaCasse, "Hegemony" 387–92.) You can either make explicit the point of the lesson or imply it through your reactions to the experience.
3. Sometimes a meaningful incident or significant relationship with someone can help us to mature, easily or painfully. Tell the story of such an incident or relationship in your own life or in the life of someone you know well. Douglass addresses this in "Resurrection" (89–93), Cagle in "On the Banks of the Bogue Chitto" (245–49), Sanders in "The Inheritance of Tools" (143–50) and "Under the Influence: Paying the Price of My Father's Booze" (192–203), and McGuire in "Wake Up Call" (230–36).

4. Have you ever witnessed an event important to history, sports, science, or some other field of endeavor? If so, tell the story either as an eyewitness or from the point of view of someone looking back on it and more aware now of its true meaning.

5. If you have ever been to a place that is particularly significant to you, narrate an incident to show its significance through specified details. (See Fadiman, "Under Water" 102–05; Twain, "Uncle John's Farm" 253–59; and Shange, "What Is It We Really Harvestin' Here?" 158–63.)

6. Have you ever worshipped someone as a hero or heroine or modeled yourself after someone? Or have you ever been treated as someone's particular favorite (or nemesis)? Tell the story of this special relationship you have (or had) with a parent or grandparent, brother or sister, friend or antagonist, spouse, employer, teacher. Through narrating one or two typical incidents to convey its essence, show why this relationship has been beneficial, harmful, or otherwise significant to you. Control your language carefully to control the mood and tone.

7. If you have had a "watershed experience"—made an important discovery, survived a major traumatic event, such as an automobile accident, a natural disaster, a flood, or a family breakup; met a person who has changed your life—that has changed your life or your thinking about life significantly, narrate the experience and analyze its effects, short- or long-term. You will need to explain or imply enough of what you were like beforehand so readers can recognize the effects of the experience. (See Wiesel, "Why I Write" 22–27; Douglass, "Resurrection" 89–93; or Hall, "Killing Chickens" 120–23.)

8. Explain what it's like to be a typical student or employee (on an assembly line, in a restaurant or store, or elsewhere) through an account of "A Day in the Life of. . . . " If you find that life to be boring or demeaning, your narrative might be an implied protest or an argument for change. (See Barry, "Common Scents" 376–85; Nocton, "Harvest of Shame" 286–90; and Benedetto, "Home Away from Home" 436–38.)

9. Write a fairy tale or fable, a story with a moral, or some other cautionary tale. Make it suitable for children (but don't talk down to them) or for people of your own age. (See Spiegelman, "Mein Kampf (My Struggle)" 96–97; Zitkala-Sa, "The School Days of an Indian Girl" 184–90; Gawande, "On Washing Hands" 206–12; and Doyle, "Joyas Voladoras" 372–74.)

10. Write a pseudo-diary, an imaginary account of how you would lead a day in your life if all your wishes were fulfilled—or if all your worst fears were realized.

11. Imagine that you're telling a major news event of the day (or of your lifetime) to someone fifty years from now. What details will you have to include and explain to make sure your reader understands it? (See O'Brien, "How to Tell a True War Story" 77–84.)

12. Using your own experiences or those of someone you know well, write an essay showing the truth or falsity of an adage about human nature, such as:

a. Quitters never win. Or do they?
b. Try hard and you'll succeed. Or will you?
c. It doesn't matter whether you win or lose, it's how you play the game.
d. Absence makes the heart grow fonder, or Out of sight, out of mind.

Process Analysis

Analysis involves dividing something into its component parts and explaining what they are, on the assumption that it is easier to consider and to understand the subject in smaller segments than in a large, complicated whole (see Chapter 7, "Division and Classification"). To analyze the human body, you could divide it into systems—skeletal, circulatory, respiratory, digestive, neurological—before identifying and defining the components of each. Of the digestive system, for instance, you would discuss the mouth, pharynx, esophagus, stomach, and large and small intestines. Scott McCloud's "Character Design" (135–42), from his comprehensive how-to book *Making Comics*, identifies the three essential qualities "that no great comics character can do without": "an inner life," consisting of "a unique history, world view and desires;" "visual distinction"—a "distinct and memorable body, face and wardrobe;" and "expressive traits—traits of speech and behavior associated with that character." In brief but densely packed illustrative pages, McCloud shows how aspiring cartoonists can create such memorable characters.

You can analyze a process in the same way, focusing on *how* rather than *what*, that will lead to a particular consequence, product, or result. Meredith Hall's true story, "Killing Chickens" (120–23), briefly narrates the events that led to the breakup of her marriage (her husband's affair with her best friend) embedded in the dual processes of killing chickens to make room for the incoming brood of new chicks and celebrating a birthday. Both are metaphorical activities frought with doom and disaster as they refract on a marriage in the process of shattering to pieces.

A *directive process analysis* identifies the steps in how to make or do something: how to sail a catamaran; how to get to Kuala Lumpur; how to make brownies; how to prevent the spread of germs (see Atul Gawande "On Washing Hands" 206–12). The Introduction to Chapter 1, for instance, explains the general processes embedded in reading and writing essays, poetry, stories, and creative nonfiction. One of the differences between an art and a science is that in the arts even those who follow a similar process will end up with qualitatively different results. For example, an accomplished singer's or writer's style is so markedly different from that of any other singer or writer that the individual performer is immediately recognized.

An *informative process analysis* can identify the stages by which something is created or formed, or how something is done. In "Hooked from the First Cigarette" (124–33), Joseph DiFranza explains the evidence for his hypothesis that "limited exposure to nicotine—as little as one cigarette—can change the brain, modifying its neurons in a way that stimulates the craving to smoke" using considerations of cause and effect incorporated with an analysis of the process by which the first cigarette leads to addiction. DiFranza's controversial research contradicts conventional claims that "people smoke primarily for pleasure," becoming psychologically and physically dependent on nicotine only as it builds up in their blood as they smoke more and more heavily.

In "Tinfoil Underwear" (151–57), James Fallows explains how computer users can try to protect their secrets, including the "evidence we leave behind when we browse, shop, communicate, and amuse ourselves on the Internet," using measures ranging from "tools of disguise" such as encryption software, to avoiding sending e-mails "they would not want to see broadly forwarded," to passing laws that would create a "privacy firewall." All—except the most extreme measure, "doing absolutely nothing"—involve a host of other processes.

A process analysis can incorporate an explanation and appreciation of a way of life, as implied in the photograph of the Mennonite carpenter (145), taken in 1999 but in many respects timeless. Ntozake Shange does this in "What Is It We Really Harvestin' Here?" (158–63). Shange explains how to grow potatoes, mustard greens, and watermelon, and how to cook "Mama's rice"; in the process, she offers a joyous interpretation not only of "'colored' cuisine," but of the people who cultivate, prepare, and eat this nourishment for the soul as well as the body. An analysis can also incorporate a critique of a process, sometimes as a way to advocate an alternative, as Scott Russell Sanders does in showing the deleterious effects of alcoholism on alcoholics' families in "Under the Influence: Paying the Price of My Father's Booze" (192–203). Matt Nocton's "Harvest of Gold, Harvest of Shame" (286–90) provides both an overt explanation of a process—how tobacco is harvested—and an implied critique of the exploitation of the migrant workers who do the backbreaking labor. Each worker must "must tie [a burlap sack] around his waist as a source of protection against the dirt and rocks that he will be dragging himself through for the next eight hours."

A process analysis can also embed a critique of the process it discusses. Ning Yu's "Red and Black, or One English Major's Beginning" (166–74) is an explanation of how he learned English from two sources: his father, a sophisticated professor of Chinese language and literature, and the anti-intellectual members of the People's Liberation Army, who expelled (and imprisoned) the intellectuals and took over the schools. Ning analyzes how the Reds taught: by lecturing and having the middle school pupils memorize verbal "hand grenades"—"Drop your guns! Down with U.S. Imperialism!"—which they didn't understand. Here Ning criticizes the teachers, the process, and the results: "books were dangerous," and ignorance prevailed. In contrast, Dr. Yu does it right, beginning with the alphabet, then on to the basics of grammar, and then the reading of short sentences and learning vocabulary, to provide his son with an adequate foundation for genuine reading and understanding—a particularly important heritage while Dr. Yu is imprisoned.

The following suggestions for writing an essay of process analysis are in themselves—you guessed it—a process analysis.

To write about a process, for whatever audience, you first have to *make sure you understand it yourself.* If it's a process you can perform, such as parallel parking or hitting a good tennis forehand, try it out before you begin to write, and note the steps and possible variations from start to finish.

Early on you'll need to *identify the purpose or function of the process and its likely outcome:* "How to lose twenty pounds in ten weeks." Then the steps or stages in the process occur in a given sequence; it's helpful to *list them in their logical or natural order* and to *provide time markers* so your readers will know what comes first, second, and thereafter. "First, have a physical exam. Next, work out a sensible diet, under medical supervision. Then. . . ."

If the process involves many simultaneous operations, for clarity you may need to *classify all aspects of the process and discuss each one separately,* as you might in explaining the photograph of what the Chinese boy is doing in order to learn to read and write his native language (169). For instance, since playing the violin requires bowing with the right hand and fingering with the left, it makes sense to consider each by itself. After you've done this, however, be sure to *indicate how all of the separate elements of the process fit together.* To play the violin successfully, the right hand does indeed have to know what the left hand is doing. If the process you're discussing is cyclic or circular—as in the life cycle of a plant, or the water cycle, involving evaporation, condensation, and precipitation—start with whatever seems to you most logical or most familiar to your readers.

If you're using specialized or technical language, *define your terms* unless you're writing for an audience of experts. You'll also need to *identify specialized equipment* and *be explicit about whatever techniques and measurements your readers need to know.* For example, an essay on how to throw a pot would need to tell a reader who had never potted what the proper consistency of the clay should be before one begins to wedge it or how to tell when all the air bubbles have been wedged out. But how complicated should an explanation be? The more your reader knows about your subject, the more sophisticated your analysis can be, with less emphasis, if any, on the basics. How thin can the pot's walls be without collapsing? Does the type of clay (white, red, with or without grog) make any difference? The reverse is true if you're writing for novices—keep it simple to start with.

If subprocesses are involved in the larger process, you can either *explain these where they would logically come in the sequence* or *consider them in footnotes or an appendix.* You don't want to sidetrack your reader from the main thrust. For instance, if you were to explain the process of Prank Day, an annual ritual at Cal Tech, you might begin with the time by which all seniors have to be out of their residence halls for the day: 8 a.m. You might then follow a typical prank from beginning to end: the selection of a senior's parked car to disassemble; the transportation of its parts to the victim's dorm room; the reassembling of the vehicle; the victim's consternation when he encounters it in his room with the motor running. If the focus is on the process of playing the prank, you probably wouldn't want to give directions on how to disassemble and reassemble the car; to do so would require a hefty manual. But you might want to supplement your discussion with helpful hints on how to pay (or avoid paying) for the damage.

After you've finished your essay, if it explains how to perform a process, ask a friend, preferably one who's unfamiliar with the subject, to try it out. (Even people who know how to tie shoelaces can get all tangled up in murky directions.) She can tell you what's unclear, what needs to be explained more fully—and even point out where you're belaboring the obvious. Ask your reader to tell you how well she understands what you've said. If, by the end, she's still asking you what the fundamental concept is, you'll know you've got to run the paper through your typewriter or computer once again.

Process analysis can serve as a vehicle for explaining personal relationships. For example, an analysis of the sequential process of performing some activity can serve as the framework for explaining a complicated relationship among the people involved in performing the same process or an analogous one. In such essays the relationship among the participants or the character of the person performing the process is more important than the process itself; whether or not the explanation is sufficient to enable the readers to actually perform the process is beside the point.

Scott Russell Sanders's "The Inheritance of Tools" (143–50) is typical of such writing. Although his father is showing Sanders, as a young child, how to pound nails and saw, the information is not sufficient in the text, even for such a simple process, to provide clear directions of how to do it. The real point of Sanders's commentary is not instructions in how to use tools, but in the relationship between the tender father and his admiring son. In contrast, even though Ntozake Shange's "What Is It We Really Harvestin' Here?" (158–63) is not intended as a cookbook, her freewheeling recipes offer enough directions on how to prepare the food.

Writing parodies of processes, particularly those that are complicated, mysterious, or done badly—may be the ideal revenge of the novice learner or the person obsessed with or defeated by a process. Parodies such as these may include a critique of the process, a satire of the novice or victim (often the author), or both.

Strategies for Writing: Process Analysis

1. Is the purpose of my essay to provide directions—a step-by-step explanation of how to do or make something? Or is the essay's purpose informative—to explain how something happens or works? Do I know my subject well enough to explain it clearly and accurately?
2. If I'm providing directions, how much does my audience already know about performing the process? Should I start with definitions of basic terms ("sauté," "dado") and explanations of subprocesses, or can I focus on the main process at hand? Should I simplify the process for a naive audience, or are my readers sophisticated enough to understand its complexities? Likewise, if I'm providing an informative explanation, where will I start? How complicated will my explanation become? The assumed expertise of my audience will help determine my answers.
3. Have I presented the process in logical or chronological sequence (first, second, third . . .)? Have I furnished an overview so that my readers will have the outcome (or desired results) and major aspects of the process in mind before they immerse themselves in the particulars of the individual steps?
4. Does my language fit both the subject, however general or technical, and the audience? Do I use technical terms when necessary? Which of these do I need to define or explain for my intended readers?
5. What tone will I use in my essay? A serious or matter-of-fact tone will indicate that I'm treating my subject "straight." An ironic, exaggerated, or understated tone will indicate that I'm treating it humorously.

MEREDITH HALL

Meredith Hall was born in 1949 and grew up in New Hampshire. She quit college at eighteen and returned only after "forced to" by divorce as the only fulltime nontraditional student at Bowdoin College. This experience ("my great intellectual hungers were fed"), enhanced by a full scholarship, changed her life and launched her career as a teacher and writer. Graduating at age forty-four, she earned an MA in writing from the University of New Hampshire (1995) and has taught there ever since. Her prize-winning essays have been published in *Creative Nonfiction*, in *The New York Times*, and in a collection titled *Without a Map* (2007). In 2005, she received the Gift of Freedom Award, a two-year writing grant from A Room of Her Own Foundation. She lives on the coast of Maine.

Of "Killing Chickens," Hall says, "The image of the soft, dusty light in the chicken coop and my little hens laid out one by one has come to embody for me the difficulties of our family breakup. Love and violence tangle in this essay. My children were unaware of what I was doing outside, of my first desperate efforts to take charge of my new life. Inside the house, they had already started their own young reckoning. That it was such a beautiful spring day, so full of promise, and my birthday, plays in my memory against the finality and trauma of the deaths and the impending divorce."

As you read this piece of creative nonfiction—a true story and so labeled—compare this with the fictional short stories you have read—or Elizabeth Tallent's "No One's a Mystery" (400–02). What, if any, aspects of "Killing Chickens" itself—events, characters, dialogue, setting, details of everyday life—tell you this is a true story rather than a work of fiction? Or does your understanding that this is a true story arise from the fact that the author identifies it as truth rather than fiction? Suppose Hall had called it "fiction." Would you have read it any differently?

Killing Chickens

1 I tucked her wings tight against her heaving body, crouched over her, and covered her flailing head with my gloved hand. Holding her neck hard against the floor of the coop, I took a breath, set something deep and hard inside my heart, and twisted her head. I heard her neck break with a crackle. Still she fought me, struggling to be free of my weight, my gloved hands, my need to kill her. Her shiny black beak opened and closed, opened and closely silently, as she gasped for air. I didn't know this would happen. I was undone by the flapping, the dust rising and choking me, the disbelieving little eye turned up to mine. I held her beak closed, covering that eye. Still she pushed, her reptile legs bracing against mine, her warmth, her heart beating fast with mine. I turned her head on her floppy neck again, and again, corkscrewing her breathing tube, struggling to end

the gasping. The eye, turned around and around, blinked and studied me. The early spring sun flowed onto us through a silver stream of dust, like a stage light, while we fought each other. I lifted my head and saw that the other birds were eating still, pecking their way around us for stray bits of corn. This one, this twisted and broken lump of gleaming black feathers, clawed hard at the floor, like a big stretch, and then deflated like a pierced ball. I waited, holding her tiny beak and broken neck with all my might.

I was killing chickens. It was my 38th birthday. My best friend, Ashley, had chosen that morning to tell me that my husband had slept with her a year before. I had absorbed the rumors and suspicions about other women for 10 years, but this one, I knew, was going to break us. When I roared upstairs and confronted John, he told me to go fuck myself, ran downstairs and jumped into the truck. Our sons, Sam and Ben, were making a surprise for me at the table; they stood behind me silently in the kitchen door while John gunned the truck out of the yard. "It's okay, guys," I said. "Mum and Dad just had a fight. You better go finish my surprise before I come peeking." 2

I carried Bertie's warm, limp body outside and laid her on the grass. Back inside the coop, I stalked my hens and came up with Tippy-Toes. I gathered her frantic wings and crouched over her. John was supposed to kill off our beautiful but tired old hens, no longer laying, last month to make way for the new chicks that were arriving tomorrow. But he was never around, and the job had not been done. I didn't know how to do this. But I was going to do it myself. This was just a little thing in all the things I was going to have to learn to do alone. 3

I had five more to go. Tippy-Toes tried to shriek behind my glove. I clamped my hand over her beak and gave her head a hard twist. I felt her body break deep inside my own chest. 4

Two down. I felt powerful, capable. I could handle whatever came to me. 5

But I needed a rest. I was tired, exhausted, with a heavy, muffled weight settling inside. "I'm coming in," I called in a false, singsong voice from the kitchen door. "Better hide my surprise." Ten and 7, the boys knew something was up, something bigger than the moody, dark days John brought home, bigger than the days-long silent treatment John imposed on me if I asked too many questions about where he had been and why. Sam and Ben were working quietly in the kitchen, not giggling and jostling the way they usually did. Their downy blond heads touched as they leaned over their projects. I felt a crush of sadness, of defeat. We were exploding into smithereens on this pretty March day, and we all knew it. 6

"I have to make a cake!" I sang from the doorway. "When are you guys going to be done in there?" 7

"Wait! Wait!" they squealed. It was an empty protest, their cheer as hollow as mine. 8

9 Our old house smelled good, of wood and the pancakes the three of us had eaten this morning, in that other world of hope and tight determination before Ashley's phone call. We lived on a ridge high over the mouth of the Damariscotta River on the coast of Maine. From our beds, we could all see out over Pemaquid Point, over Monhegan Island, over the ocean to the edge of the Old World. The rising sun burst into our sleep each morning. At night, before bed, we lay on my bed together—three of us—naming Orion and Leo and the Pleiades in whispers. Monhegan's distant light swept the walls of our rooms all night at 36-second intervals. Our little house creaked in the wind during February storms. Now spring had come, and the world had shifted.

10 "Help me make my cake," I said to the boys. They dragged their chairs to the counter.

11 "Mum, will Dad be home for your birthday tonight?" Sam asked. Both boys were so contained, so taut, so helpless. They leaned against me, quiet.

12 Guilt and fear tugged me like an undertow. I started to cry.

13 "I don't know, my loves. I think this is a really big one."

14 Bertie and Tippy-Toes lay side by side on the brown grass, their eyes open, necks bent. I closed the coop door behind me and lunged for the next hen.

15 "It's all right," I said softly. "It's all right. Everything's going to be all right. Shhh, Silly, shh." I crouched over her. Silly was the boys' favorite because she let them carry her around the yard. I hoped they would forget her when the box of peeping balls of fluff arrived tomorrow.

16 "It's okay, Silly," I said quietly, wrapping my gloved fingers around her hard little head. she was panting, her eyes wild, frantic, betrayed. I covered them with my fingers and twisted her neck hard. Her black wings, iridescent in the dusty sunlight, beat against my legs. I held her close to me while she scrabbled against my strong hands. I started to cry again.

17 When I went back up to the house, Bertie and Tippy-Toes and Silly and Mother Mabel lay on the grass outside the coop.

18 Benjamin came into the kitchen and leaned against my legs. "What are we going to do?" he asked.

19 "About what, Sweetheart?" I hoped he was not asking me about tomorrow. Or the next day.

20 "Nothing," he said, drifting off to play with Sam upstairs.

21 We frosted the cake blue, Ben's favorite color, and put it on the table next to their presents for me, wrapped in wallpaper. I wanted to call someone, to call my mother or my sister. Yesterday I would have called Ashley, my best friend, who had listened to me cry and rail about John again and again. Instead, I brought in three loads of wood and put them in the box John had left empty.

"Sam, will you lay up a fire for tonight? And Ben, go down to the 22
cellar and get a bunch of kindling wood."

Like serious little men, my children did what I asked. 23

"What are we going to make for my birthday supper?" 24

"I thought we were going to Uncle Stephen's and Aunt Ashley's" 25
Sam said.

"Know what?" I said. "Know what I want to do? Let's just stay here 26
and have our own private little party. Just us."

I felt marooned with my children. I sat at the table, watching while 27
they did their chores, then headed back out to finish mine.

Minnie Hen was next. She let me catch her and kill her without 28
much fight. I laid her next to the others in the cold grass.

Itty-Bit was last. She was my favorite. The others had chewed off her 29
toes, one by one, when she was a chick. I had made a separate box for her, a separate feeder, separate roost, and smeared antibiotic ointment four times a day on the weeping stubs. She survived, and ate from my hand after that. She had grown to be fierce with the other hens, never letting them too close to her, able to slip in, grab the best morsels and flee before they could peck her. I had come to admire her very much, my tough little biddie.

She cowered in the corner, alone. I sat next to her, and she let me pull 30
her up into my lap. I stroked her feathers smooth, stroke after stroke. Her comb was pale and shriveled, a sign of her age. I knew she hadn't laid an egg for months. She was shaking. I held her warmth against me, cooing to her, "It's all right, Itty-Bit. Everything's going to be all right. Don't be scared." My anger at John centered like a tornado on having to kill this hen. "You stupid, selfish son of a bitch," I said. I got up, crying again, holding Itty-Bit tight to me. I laid her gently on the floor and crouched over her. The sun filled the coop with thick light.

That night, after eating spaghetti and making a wish and blowing 31
out 38 candles and opening presents made by Sam and Benjamin—a mail holder made from wood slats, a sculpture of 2-by-4s and shells; after baths and reading stories in bed and our sweet, in-the-dark, whispered good nights; after saying "I don't know what is going to happen" to my scared children; after banking the fire and turning off the lights, I sat on the porch in the cold, trying to imagine what had to happen next. I could see the outline of the coop against the dark, milky sky. I touched my fingers, my hands, so familiar to me. Tonight they felt like someone else's. I wrapped my arms around myself—thin, tired—and wished it were yesterday.

Tomorrow morning, I thought, I have to turn over the garden and go 32
to the dump. Tomorrow morning, I have to call a lawyer. I have to figure out what to say to Sam and Benjamin. I have to put Ben's sculpture on the mantel and put some mail in Sam's holder on the desk. I have to clean out the coop and spread fresh shavings.

JOSEPH R. DiFRANZA

Joseph R. DiFranza (born in 1954 in Revere, Massachusetts) is a family physician and professor in the Department of Family Medicine and Community Health at the University of Massachusetts Medical School in Worcester, where he received his MD (1981). DiFranza serves on the board of the Tobacco Control Resource Center, which implements tobacco control projects in the interests of public health. He has published extensively on nicotine dependence; the effects of tobacco advertising; smoking among children, adolescents, and young adults; the effectiveness of laws banning tobacco sales to children; and maternal smoking and tobacco-related complications in pregnancy. In "Hooked from the First Cigarette," originally published in *Scientific American* (2008), DiFranza combines empirical observations of his patients' struggles with smoking with his own and colleagues' research to describe the development of a new theory of nicotine dependence, "that as little as one cigarette" can cause nicotine addiction. In combining his experiences as a family physician with the work of developing hypotheses and testing them, DiFranza links theoretical research with its applications, the prevention and cure of nicotine addiction.

*Hooked from the First Cigarette**

1 While I was training to become a family doctor, I learned the conventional wisdom about nicotine addiction. Physicians have long believed that people smoke primarily for pleasure and become psychologically dependent on that pleasure. Tolerance to the effects of nicotine prompts more frequent smoking; when the habit reaches a critical frequency—about five cigarettes per day—and nicotine is constantly present in the blood, physical dependence may begin, usually after thousands of cigarettes and years of smoking. Within hours of the last cigarette, the addicted smoker experiences the symptoms of nicotine withdrawal: restlessness, irritability, inability to concentrate, and so on. According to this understanding, those who smoke fewer than five cigarettes per day are not addicted.

2 I was armed with this knowledge when I encountered the proverbial patient who had not read the textbook. During a routine physical, an adolescent girl told me she was unable to quit smoking despite having started only two months before. I thought this patient must be an outlier, a rare exception to the rule that addiction takes years to develop. But my curiosity was piqued, so I went to the local high school to interview students about their smoking.

---

* Joseph R. DiFranza, "Hooked from the First Cigarette," SCIENTIFIC AMERICAN, May 2008. Reprinted with permission. Copyright © 2008 by SCIENTIFIC AMERICAN, Inc. All rights reserved.

There a 14-year-old girl told me that she had made two serious attempts to quit, failing both times. This was eyeopening because she had smoked only a few cigarettes a week for two months. When she described her withdrawal symptoms, her story sounded like the lament of one of my two-pack-a-day patients. The rapid onset of these symptoms in the absence of daily smoking contradicted most of what I thought I knew about nicotine addiction. And when I tracked that received wisdom back to its source, I found that everything I had learned was just a poor educated guess.

With funding from the National Cancer Institute and the National Institute on Drug Abuse (NIDA), I have spent the past decade exploring how nicotine addiction develops in novice smokers. I now know that the model of addiction described in the opening paragraph is fiction. My research supports a new hypothesis asserting that limited exposure to nicotine—as little as one cigarette—can change the brain, modifying its neurons in a way that stimulates the craving to smoke. This understanding, if proved correct, may someday provide researchers with promising avenues for developing new drugs and other therapies that could help people kick the habit. 3

A Loss of Autonomy

When I started this investigation in 1997 with my colleagues at the University of Massachusetts Medical School in Worcester, our first challenge was to develop a reliable tool to detect the first symptoms of addiction as they emerged. In my view, the defining feature of addiction is the loss of autonomy, when the smoker finds that quitting cigarettes requires an effort or involves discomfort. To detect this loss, I devised the Hooked on Nicotine Checklist (HONC); an answer of "yes" to any of the questions on the list indicates that addiction has begun [*see box on 129*]. Now in use in 13 languages, the HONC is the most thoroughly validated measure of nicotine addiction. (And the checklist could easily be adapted to the study of other drugs.) 4

We administered the HONC to hundreds of adolescents repeatedly over three years. It turned out that the rapid onset of addiction was quite common. The month after the first cigarette was by far the most likely time for addiction to begin; any of the HONC symptoms, including cravings for cigarettes and failed attempts at quitting, could appear within the first weeks of smoking. On average, the adolescents were smoking only two cigarettes a week when the first symptoms appeared. The data shattered the conventional wisdom and provided a wealth of insight into how addiction starts. But when I presented these findings in February 2000 and proclaimed that some youths had symptoms of addiction after smoking just one or two cigarettes, I was widely regarded as the professor who had not read his textbook correctly. 5

Many laypeople told me that they knew from experience that I was on the right track. But if any scientists believed me, they were not willing to risk their reputations by admitting it publicly. Skepticism was 6

QUICK ADDICTION

Researchers have proposed a new theory to explain how withdrawal symptoms can develop so quickly in novice smokers. Although this model is controversial, it may someday lead to a better understanding of cigarette addiction.

A HEALTHY BALANCE
In nonsmokers, the brain's systems for generating and inhibiting cravings are in balance. The craving-generation system triggers appetitive behavior (such as eating), and the craving-inhibition system stops the behavior when the individual is satiated (at the end of the meal).

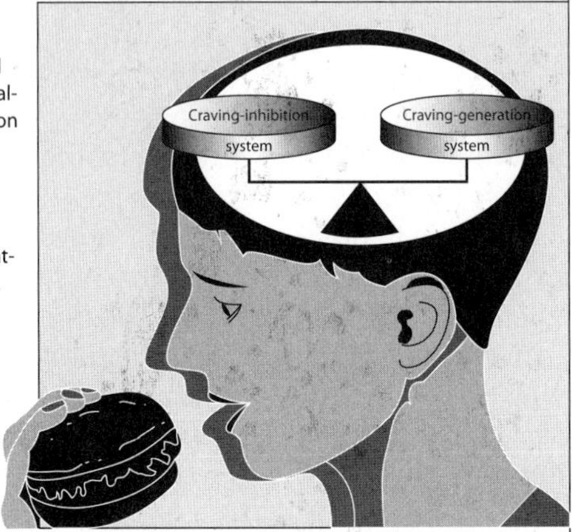

THE FIRST CIGARETTE
Nicotine stimulates the craving-inhibition system until its activity far exceeds that of the craving-generation system. The brain attempts to restore its balance by rapidly developing adaptations that boost the activity of the craving-generation system. (These changes are called withdrawal-related adaptations.)

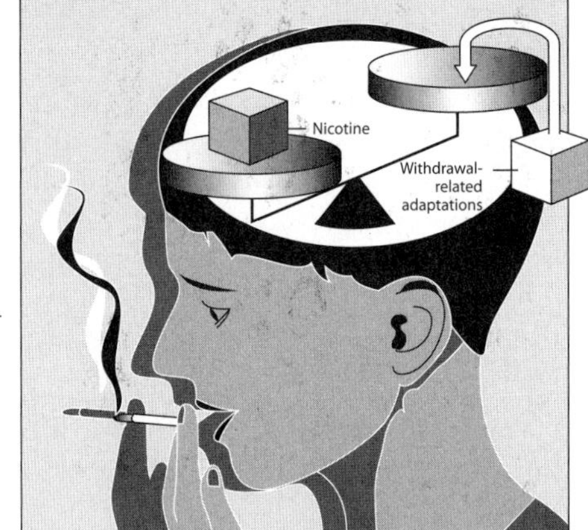

WITHDRAWAL
Once the effects of nicotine wear off, the craving-inhibition system is no longer stimulated and returns to a lower level of activity. But the craving-generation system, enhanced by the withdrawal-related adaptations, now throws the brain off-balance again, producing an intense desire for the one thing that can inhibit, the craving—another cigarette.

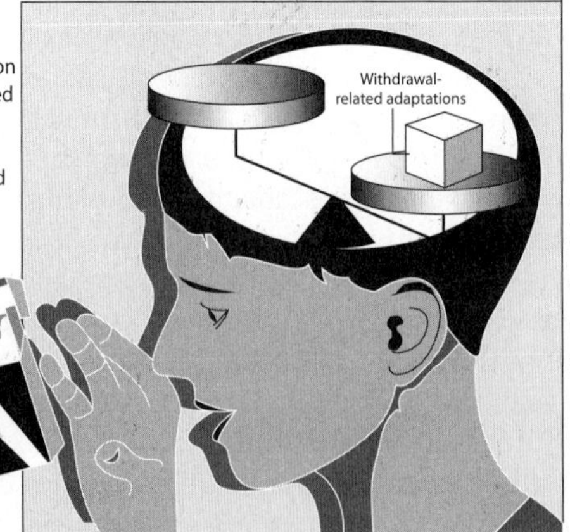

Artwork: Lisa Apfelbacher. Reprinted with permission.

widespread. How could addiction start so quickly? How could withdrawal symptoms be present in smokers who do not maintain constant blood levels of nicotine?

Vindication has come with time as teams of investigators led by 7
Jennifer O'Loughlin of McGill University, Denise Kandel of Columbia University and Robert Scragg of the University of Auckland in New Zealand replicated all of my discoveries. A dozen studies have now established that nicotine withdrawal is common among novice smokers. Of those who experience symptoms of addiction, 10 percent do so within two days of their first cigarette and 25 to 35 percent do so within a month. In a very large study of New Zealand youths, 25 percent had symptoms after smoking one to four cigarettes. And the early appearance of HONC symptoms increased the odds that the youths would progress to daily smoking by nearly 200-fold.

These results raise the question of how the nicotine from a single 8
cigarette could alter the brain enough to trigger the onset of addiction. Earlier research with laboratory animals has found that chronic high-dose exposure to nicotine—the equivalent of one to three packs a day—stimulates an increase in the number of neuron receptors that have a high affinity for nicotine. Autopsies of human smokers reveal 50 to 100 percent increases in the brain's frontal lobe, hippocampus and cerebellum.

I persuaded Theodore Slotkin of Duke University to determine the 9
minimum nicotine exposure needed to provoke this so-called up-regulation of receptors. On consecutive days his team administered small amounts of nicotine (equivalent to one to two cigarettes) to rats and found up-regulation in the hippocampus—which is involved in long-term memory—by the second day. Subsequently, Arthur Brody and his colleagues at the University of California, Los Angeles, discovered that the nicotine from one cigarette was sufficient to occupy 88 percent of the brain's nicotinic receptors. Although the role of receptor up-regulation in addiction is unknown, these studies make it physiologically plausible that adolescents could have withdrawal symptoms just two days after their first cigarette.

According to addiction researchers, withdrawal symptoms result 10
from drug-induced homeostatic adaptations—the body's attempts to keep its functions and chemicals in balance. For example, certain addictive drugs increase the production of neurotransmitters—chemicals that transmit signals among neurons—and in response the body develops adaptations that inhibit these chemicals. When the user stops taking the drug, however, the inhibition becomes excessive and withdrawal symptoms appear. We know that these withdrawal-related adaptations could develop rapidly after the first cigarette, because other addictive drugs such as morphine produce similar changes very quickly. But most longtime smokers find they can forgo cigarettes for only an hour or two before craving another, whereas novice smokers can go weeks without lighting up. Amazingly, in the early stages of addiction a single cigarette can suppress withdrawal symptoms for weeks, even though the nicotine is gone from the body within a day.

A Nicotine Glossary

Nicotine withdrawal: A cluster of symptoms that include craving, restlessness, nervousness, irritability, difficulty concentrating and difficulty sleeping.

Latency to withdrawal: The symptom-free interval between the last cigarette and the onset of withdrawal symptoms. It can shrink from weeks to minutes over many years of tobacco use.

Dependence-related tolerance: The mechanism that causes the latency to withdrawal to shrink gradually over time.

Abstinence-related adaptations: A mechanism that mimics the action of nicotine by inhibiting craving. It develops in ex-smokers to counter the enduring effects of dependence-related tolerance.

11 The explanation for this remarkable fact is that the consequences of flooding the brain with nicotine linger long after the event itself. Nicotine triggers brain circuits involving biochemical compounds such as acetylcholine, dopamine, GABA, glutamate, noradrenaline, opioid peptides and serotonin. In rats, a single dose of nicotine increases noradrenaline synthesis in the hippocampus for at least one month, and nicotine's effects on certain neurological and cognitive functions also persist for weeks. Although it is not known if any of these phenomena are related to withdrawal, they establish that the impact of nicotine far outlasts its presence in the brain.

12 The symptom-free interval between the last cigarette and the onset of withdrawal is called the latency to withdrawal (LTW). For novice smokers the LTW is long, and a cigarette every few weeks keeps withdrawal in check. With repeated use, however, tolerance develops and the impact of each cigarette diminishes; the LTW shortens, and cigarettes must be spaced at ever closer intervals to stave off withdrawal. This phenomenon of diminishing LTW is called dependence-related tolerance. Compared with the withdrawal-related adaptations that may appear overnight, dependence-related tolerance typically develops at a glacial pace. It may take years for the LTW to shrink enough to require someone to smoke five cigarettes a day. In reality, then, withdrawal symptoms are the cause of long-term heavy use, not the other way around as we had previously thought.

Time for a New Theory

13 I had always been skeptical of the notion that smokers were addicted to the pleasure of smoking, because some of my most addicted patients hated the habit. If the conventional thinking were correct, shouldn't the most addicted smokers enjoy it the most? Eric Moolchan of the NIDA demonstrated that although adolescents showed increasing levels of addiction over time, they reported decreasing pleasure from smoking. A new theory was needed to explain these discoveries.

While struggling to understand the rapid onset of nicotine addiction, a paradox occurred to me. The only action of nicotine that is obvious to the casual observer is that it provides a temporary suppression of craving for itself, yet only people previously exposed to nicotine crave it. How can one drug both create craving and suppress it? I began to speculate that the direct immediate action of nicotine is to suppress craving and that this action could become magnified to an extreme because subsequent doses of nicotine provoke greater responses than the first dose. (This phenomenon, common to all addictive drugs, is known as sensitization.) The brain might then quickly develop withdrawal-related adaptations to counter the action of nicotine, thereby restoring the homeostatic balance. But when the action of nicotine wore off, these adaptations would stimulate craving for another cigarette. 14

Under this sensitization-homeostasis theory, nicotine is addictive not because it produces pleasure but simply because it suppresses craving. Because nicotine stimulates neurons, I envisioned it activating the nerve cells in a craving-inhibition system in the brain. Activation of this hypothesized system would then suppress the activity in a complementary system for generating cravings. The natural role of the craving-generation system would be to receive sensory cues (such as sights and smells), compare them with memories of rewarding objects (such as food), and produce craving to motivate and direct appetitive behavior (such as eating). The role of the craving-inhibition system would be to signal satisfaction so that the animal would stop the appetitive behavior when it became appropriate to do so. 15

Because the body would try to keep these two systems in balance, the nicotine-induced suppression of the craving-generation system would 16

The Hooked on Nicotine Checklist

Researchers use the following questions to determine whether adolescent smokers are addicted. An answer of "yes" to any one of the questions indicates that addiction has begun:

1. Have you ever tried to quit smoking, but couldn't?
2. Do you smoke now because it is really hard to quit?
3. Have you ever felt like you were addicted to tobacco?
4. Do you ever have strong cravings to smoke?
5. Have you ever felt like you really needed a cigarette?
6. Is it hard to keep from smoking in places where you are not supposed to, like school?

When you tried to stop smoking (or, when you haven't used tobacco for a while):

7. Did you find it hard to concentrate because you couldn't smoke?
8. Did you feel more irritable because you couldn't smoke?
9. Did you feel a strong need or urge to smoke?
10. Did you feel nervous, restless or anxious because you couldn't smoke?

trigger the development of withdrawal-related adaptations that would boost the system's activity. During the withdrawal period, when the inhibitory effect of nicotine has worn off, the craving-generation system would be left in a state of excitement that would result in the excessive desire for another cigarette [*see box on 126*]. These shifts in brain activity would come about through rapid changes in the configurations of neuron receptors, which would explain why adolescents could start to crave cigarettes after smoking just once.

17 The first support for this model has come from the many functional magnetic resonance imaging (fMRI) studies of humans showing that cue-induced craving for nicotine, alcohol, cocaine, opiates and chocolate increases metabolic activity in the anterior cingulate gyrus and other frontal-lobe areas of the brain. This finding suggests the existence of a craving-generation system. And Hyun-Kook Lim and his colleagues at the Korea College of Medicine recently found evidence that nicotine suppresses this system. The researchers demonstrated that prior administration of the drug can block the pattern of regional brain activation that accompanies cue-induced craving in humans.

18 The sensitization-homeostasis model can also explain dependence-related tolerance. Repeated suppression of activity in the craving-generation system triggers another homeostatic adaptation that stimulates craving by shortening the duration of nicotine's inhibitory effects. As mentioned earlier, tolerance develops much more slowly than the withdrawal-related adaptations, but once it emerges tolerance becomes firmly entrenched. Although it usually takes two years or more before adolescents need to smoke five cigarettes a day, I noticed that when my patients quit smoking and then relapsed, it took them only a few days to return to their old frequency, even after a lengthy abstinence.

19 Along with Robert Wellman of Fitchburg State College, I investigated this phenomenon in a study that asked 2,000 smokers how much they smoked before quitting, how long they had remained abstinent and how much they smoked immediately after relapsing. Smokers who relapsed after an abstinence of three months resumed smoking at about 40 percent of their previous rate, indicating that their LTW had lengthened. We believe the craving-free interval between cigarettes increases because the withdrawal-related adaptations disappear during the first few weeks of abstinence. With the resumption of smoking, however, the withdrawal-related adaptations quickly redevelop, and over the next few weeks relapsed smokers find they must smoke just as often as they used to.

20 We also discovered, however, that abstinences greater than three months had almost no additional impact on the length of the LTW. Even after years of abstinence, smoking resumed at about 40 percent of the prior rate, typically six or seven cigarettes a day. This finding suggests that increases in tolerance are permanent; a relapsing smoker will never get as much suppression of craving from a single cigarette as a novice

smoker will. In other words, the brain of a smoker is never restored to its original state.

But if dependence-related tolerance stimulates the craving-generation system and never completely goes away, why don't former smokers continue hungering for cigarettes forever? Our research subjects could not tell us why their craving for nicotine eventually lessened, so I looked at what the sensitization-homeostasis theory would predict. I reasoned that former smokers must develop abstinence-related adaptations that mimic the action of nicotine, inhibiting the craving-generation system and restoring homeostasis. Smoking cessation would not result in a quiet return to normal brain function; rather it would trigger a dynamic period of neuroplasticity during which new adaptations would appear in the former smoker's brain. Because of these adaptations, the ex-smoker's brain would resemble neither that of the smoker nor of the nonsmoker. 21

To test this prediction, Slotkin and his colleagues examined the brains of rats before nicotine exposure, during exposure, during withdrawal and long after withdrawal. They found clear-cut evidence of changes in the functioning of neurons in the brain's cortex that employ acetylcholine and serotonin to transmit signals—changes that appeared only after the acute withdrawal period. As predicted, the brains of the "ex-smoker" rats showed unique adaptations that were not present in the "smokers" or "nonsmokers." And at the College of Medicine at the Catholic University of Korea, HeeJin Lim and colleagues found evidence of brain remodeling in humans who quit smoking by studying brain-derived neurotrophic factor, a stimulant of neuroplasticity. Levels of this factor in ex-smokers tripled after two months of abstinence. 22

Thus, abstinence-related adaptations seem to counter the tolerance-related adaptations by inhibiting the craving-generation system so that it eventually stops compelling the former smoker to light up. Smoking cues in the environment might still provoke craving, however, and if the long-abstinent smoker were to surrender to an urge to smoke just once, nicotine would again produce a profound suppression of activity in the craving-generation system. The abstinence-related adaptations would then make a bad situation worse. Because these adaptations mimic the effect of nicotine, they would need to be removed to restore homeostasis; when the effect of nicotine wears off, the tolerance-related adaptations would be left unopposed in stimulating the craving-generation system. Struck with a strong craving, the relapsing smoker would need to puff six or seven cigarettes a day to keep it under control. 23

New Hope for Smokers

This model of addiction by no means represents the prevailing opinion. In my view, addiction is an accident of physiology. Because so many careers have been built on the assumption that the roots of addiction lie 24

NICOTINE ON THE BRAIN

Recent studies have confirmed that nicotine evokes rapid changes in brain physiology. The author and Jean A. King of the Center for Comparative NeuroImaging at the University of Massachusetts Medical School used functional magnetic resonance imaging (fMRI) to measure levels of metabolic activity in the brains of rats given a dose of nicotine on five consecutive days. The response to the first dose was relatively limited, but brain activity was much more intense and widespread after the fifth dose. These findings indicate that the brain quickly becomes sensitized to nicotine, enabling addiction to appear after just a few doses.

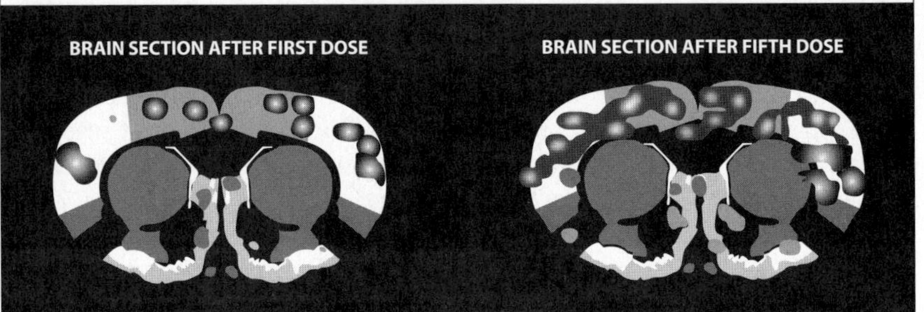

Images reprinted courtesy of UMASS Medical School.

in psychology rather than physiology, I did not expect my ideas to receive a warm welcome.

25 Whether or not the sensitization-homeostasis theory is correct, it is clear that the nicotine from the first cigarette is sufficient to trigger a remodeling of the brain. Although some may argue about what criteria should be used to render a proper diagnosis of addiction, it is now well established that adolescents have many symptoms of addiction very soon after they smoke their first cigarette. This finding underlines the importance of bolstering government funding for antismoking campaigns, which has fallen in recent years.

26 To fully test my theory, which has been simplified here, researchers need a reliable method to detect sensitization in humans. I have worked with Jean A. King and her colleagues at the Center for Comparative NeuroImaging to demonstrate nicotine sensitization in rats using fMRI. Images comparing brain responses to the first dose of nicotine and to the fifth dose given four days later illustrate the dramatic changes in brain function in areas such as the anterior cingulate gyrus and hippocampus. We have just received funding from the NIDA to use fMRI to visualize sensitization in smokers, with future plans to determine which brain regions are involved in the craving-inhibition and craving-generation systems.

27 Our long-term goal is to identify drugs that can manipulate these systems to treat or cure addiction. Although nicotine-replacement therapies may double the success rate for smoking cessation, failed attempts still far outnumber the successes. The sensitization-homeostasis theory suggests that what is needed is a therapy that will suppress craving without stimulating compensatory responses that only make the craving

worse in the long run. A better understanding of the addiction process may help researchers develop new treatments that can safely liberate smokers from nicotine's deadly pull.

Content

1. How did DiFranza's hypothesis that "limited exposure to nicotine—as little as one cigarette—can change the brain, modifying its neurons in a way that stimulates the craving to smoke" (¶ 3) challenge "conventional wisdom about nicotine addiction" (¶ 1)? What evidence does DiFranza provide that supports his hypothesis that a single cigarette can trigger the onset of addiction (¶s 8–11)?

2. How does diminishing "latency to withdrawal (LTW)," or "dependence-related tolerance," explain why withdrawal symptoms are the cause of, rather than the effect of, long-term, heavy smoking (¶ 12)?

3. What is "sensitization" (¶ 14)? How does this add to the concept of dependence-related tolerance in explaining the brain's craving for tobacco (¶ 15–18)? What evidence suggests that "the brain of a smoker is never restored to its original state" (¶ 20)?

4. What are "abstinence-related adaptations" (¶ 21)? How does the sensitization-homeostasis model explain why quitting smoking reduces the brain's craving for tobacco (¶ 22–23)?

Strategies/Structures/Language

5. DiFranza uses several examples of how his empirical observations about patients who smoke have led him to question conventional wisdom about smoking and conduct research (¶s 2, 6, 10, 13, 18). How do his observations help him explain and help the reader understand the complex research on the brain he describes?

6. DiFranza characterizes smoking as an addiction with a physiological basis and concludes that "the nicotine from the first cigarette is sufficient to trigger a remodeling of the brain" (¶ 25). Why does he then add that "some may argue about what criteria should be used to render a proper diagnosis of addiction" (¶ 25)? Is the evidence that links this remodeling with addiction tentative? For example, which studies does DiFranza cite that suggest that the susceptibility to addiction varies among individuals?

For Writing

7. ***Journal Writing.*** DiFranza has spoken out against the tobacco industry for marketing cigarettes to children, in particular against R. J. R. Nabisco's cartoon character Joe Camel. In "Why Men Don't Last" (Chapter 7), Natalie Angier alludes to the impact of advertisements on behavior: "the Marlboro Man who never even gasps for breath" portrays "the image of the dispassionate, resilient, action-oriented male" (¶ 20). Is the association of smoking with strength and fearlessness, or stylishness and sophistication, changing? Do you see a future in which smoking is obsolete? What would it take to convince children and teens not to smoke?

8. ***Dialogues.*** In "Under the Influence: Paying the Price of My Father's Booze" (Chapter 5), Scott Russell Sanders describes his family's understanding of his

father's alcoholism as "a moral weakness, a sin" (¶ 25) and yet his fear of becoming an alcoholic is rooted in his understanding of addiction as a physiological problem: he sips "warily," listening "for the turning of a key in my brain" (¶ 55). Does DiFranza's research suggest that views of addiction are likely to change? How does he suggest that society deals with addictive behaviors?

9. If you are a smoker, use your own experiences—with smoking and with trying to quit—as the basis for writing a reply to DiFranza in which you either corroborate or refute his research.

10. If you're not a smoker, why not? Write a paper based on your own experiences, offering guidelines to prevent teenagers from starting to smoke.

SCOTT McCLOUD

Scott McCloud (born in Boston in 1960) decided at the age of fifteen to become a professional comic book artist. He created the superhero story series *Zot!* (1984–1991) and is the author of *Understanding Comics* (1993), *Reinventing Comics* (2000), and *Making Comics: Storytelling Secrets of Comics, Manga and Graphic Novels* (2006), from which "Character Design" is taken. McCloud's focus on the art form of comics, from theory to mechanics, aims to challenge the cultural barrier between high and low culture. McCloud won the Quill Award in 2007 in the Graphic Novel category. His work has been translated into more than fifteen languages. In "Character Design," McCloud describes the process of creating graphic characters in accessible, practical language, and by using the graphic form to show as much as to tell. At the same time, he represents the process as fluid, leaving room for the magic, individuality, and discovery of the artist's work.

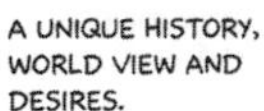

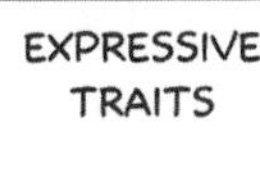

Specified panels from "Character Design," pages 63–70, from MAKING COMICS by SCOTT McCLOUD. Copyright © 2006 by Scott McCloud. Reprinted by permission of HarperCollins Publishers.

CREATING A COMPELLING INNER LIFE FOR YOUR CHARACTERS MAY BE THE MOST IMPORTANT, AND LEAST UNDERSTOOD, ASPECT OF CHARACTER CREATION.

BEGINNERS KNOW THAT EACH CHARACTER NEEDS A "PERSONALITY" --
WHO'S THE ONE ON THE FRIDGE, HONEY?
HE'S THE MEAN ONE!
-- BUT OFTEN THAT MEANS A LIST OF BEHAVIORAL TRAITS WITHOUT A SPECIFIC ORIGIN OR UNIFYING PURPOSE.

BY GOING DEEPER INTO CHARACTERS' MINDS, WE CAN LOOK FOR THOSE FACTORS THAT GIVE THEM A REASON FOR EVERYTHING THEY DO AND SAY --

-- AND HELP US PREDICT WHAT THEY'LL DO IN ANY GIVEN SITUATION --
Did Someone say Ice Cream?

-- TO SUCH AN EXTENT THAT THEY VIRTUALLY WRITE THEMSELVES!

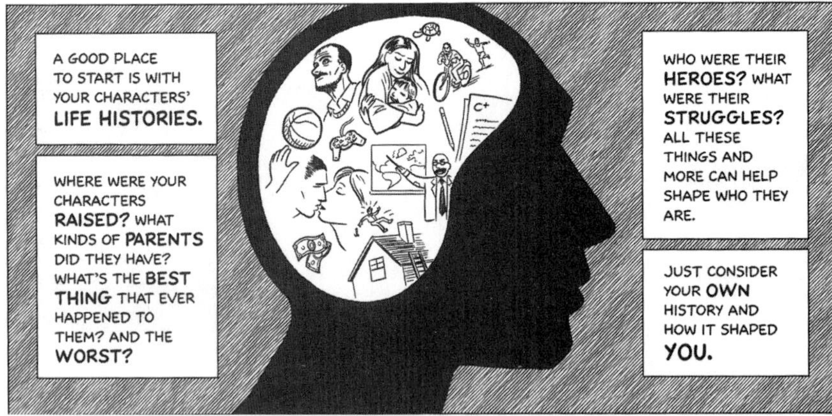
A GOOD PLACE TO START IS WITH YOUR CHARACTERS' LIFE HISTORIES.
WHERE WERE YOUR CHARACTERS RAISED? WHAT KINDS OF PARENTS DID THEY HAVE? WHAT'S THE BEST THING THAT EVER HAPPENED TO THEM? AND THE WORST?
C+
WHO WERE THEIR HEROES? WHAT WERE THEIR STRUGGLES? ALL THESE THINGS AND MORE CAN HELP SHAPE WHO THEY ARE.
JUST CONSIDER YOUR OWN HISTORY AND HOW IT SHAPED YOU.

FINDING COMMON GROUND BETWEEN THE EXPERIENCES OF YOUR CHARACTERS AND THOSE OF THE READER CAN HELP EMOTIONALLY CONNECT THEM --
-- WHILE THE DIFFERENCES IN LIFE EXPERIENCE BETWEEN ONE CHARACTER AND ANOTHER CAN TRIGGER MANY STORIES.

A CHARACTER RAISED IN POVERTY, FOR EXAMPLE, MAY HAVE TROUBLE RELATING TO A SHOPPING-ADDICTED HEIRESS.
STYLE

THE SON OF A FUNDAMENTALIST MINISTER MIGHT FIND ROMANCE PROBLEMATIC WITH THE DAUGHTER OF AN ANTHROPOLOGIST.
LEFT BEHIND
ORIGIN OF THE SPECIES

A RUNNER WHO'S BEEN ON THE WINNING SIDE ALL HIS LIFE MIGHT APPROACH A COMPETITION DIFFERENTLY FROM A RUNNER FIGHTING TO OVERCOME A LIFE FILLED WITH LOSSES.
57

THESE LIFE HISTORIES -- OR "BACKSTORIES" -- DON'T HAVE TO BE TOO ELABORATE, ESPECIALLY FOR MINOR CHARACTERS.
IN FACT, OBSESSING TOO MUCH OVER SUCH DETAILS IS A CLASSIC BEGINNER'S MISTAKE!

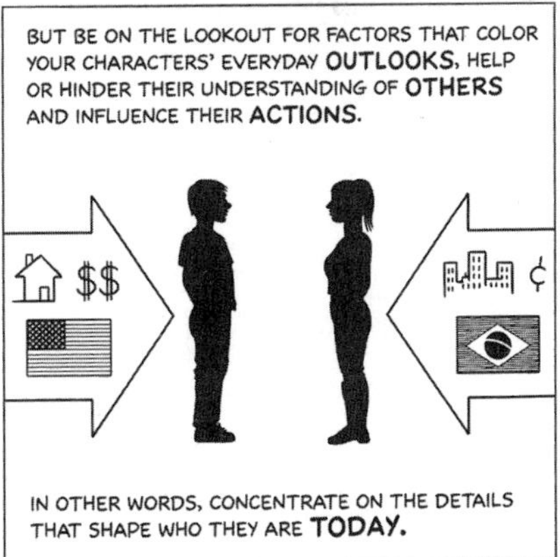
BUT BE ON THE LOOKOUT FOR FACTORS THAT COLOR YOUR CHARACTERS' EVERYDAY OUTLOOKS, HELP OR HINDER THEIR UNDERSTANDING OF OTHERS AND INFLUENCE THEIR ACTIONS.
¢
IN OTHER WORDS, CONCENTRATE ON THE DETAILS THAT SHAPE WHO THEY ARE TODAY.

* * *

OUR HISTORY AFFECTS HOW WE SEE THE WORLD.
HOW WE SEE THE WORLD AFFECTS WHAT WE WANT AND EXPECT FROM THE WORLD.

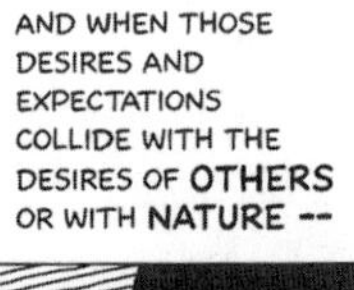
AND WHEN THOSE DESIRES AND EXPECTATIONS COLLIDE WITH THE DESIRES OF OTHERS OR WITH NATURE --

-- THAT'S THE SOURCE OF MANY OF THE BEST STORIES EVER TOLD,

IN SCHOOL, WE'RE TAUGHT THAT STORIES RELY ON "CONFLICT" AND THAT SOME CONFLICTS ARE INTERNAL WHILE SOME ARE EXTERNAL.
CONFLICT MEANS FIGHTING, RIGHT?
Conflict
WELL...

TRACK THEM TO THEIR SOURCE, THOUGH, AND NEARLY ALL CONFLICTS ARE INTERNAL --

-- BECAUSE THEY ALL START WITH SOMEONE, SOMEWHERE, WANTING SOMETHING.

WE CAN ADD TO A CHARACTER'S PERSONALITY ALL WE WANT -- MAKE THEM KIND-HEARTED OR WITTY OR SENTIMENTAL OR NEUROTIC --

-- BUT IT'S ONLY WHEN THEY START TO WANT SOMETHING THAT THOSE TRAITS ARE SET IN MOTION AND GIVEN A PURPOSE.

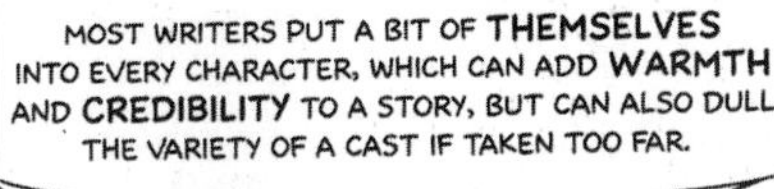

THAT'S WHAT I DID IN THE EARLY '80S WHEN I PARTIALLY MODELED THE FOUR MAIN CHARACTERS FOR MY FIRST COMIC BOOK SERIES *ZOT!* AFTER CARL JUNG'S FOUR PROPOSED TYPES OF HUMAN THOUGHT.

ZOT INTUITION
JENNY FEELING
PEABODY INTELLECT
BUTCH SENSATION

THE RELIANCE ON A SINGLE THEME FOR A CHARACTER'S INNER LIFE MAY SEEM TO RUN AGAINST THAT AMBITION --

-- AND IT CAN IF USING SUCH THEMES JUST PRODUCES CHARACTERS MIRED IN CLICHES AND STEREOTYPES --

* * *

THE IDEA ISN'T TO SIMPLIFY A CHARACTER AT ALL, BUT TO INSURE, BY WHATEVER MEANS, THAT YOUR CAST OF CHARACTERS REPRESENTS A FULL SPECTRUM OF APPROACHES TO LIFE --

ONE
OF THE REASONS
WE ALL LOVE
STORIES IS THAT THEY
OFFER PROPOSALS FOR
LIFE'S MEANING AND
PURPOSE.

BY PRESENTING
CHARACTERS WITH COMPETING
PHILOSOPHIES OF LIFE YOU CAN OFFER A
TRIANGULATED, FULLER PICTURE OF THE
WORLD YOUR CHARACTERS LIVE IN.

AND FOR ALL THE
BEAUTIFUL ART OR
WORDPLAY YOU MIGHT
DELIVER, IT'S THAT
PICTURE OF THE
WORLD THAT YOUR
READERS MAY
REMEMBER BEST.

OF COURSE, COMICS
IS A VISUAL
MEDIUM --

-- SO
THAT INTERNAL VARIETY OF
CHARACTER TYPES WILL NEED AN
OUTWARD VARIETY OF VISUAL
DESIGNS TO MATCH.

VARIETY AND
DISTINCTION IN
CHARACTER DESIGN
ARE IMPORTANT FOR
A FEW REASONS.

ON A PURELY PRACTICAL LEVEL, THEY HELP
THE READER KEEP TRACK OF WHO'S WHO.
A CAST OF CHARACTERS THAT ALL LOOK THE
SAME CAN BE CONFUSING.
I AM SPARTACUS!
I AM SPARTACUS!
I AM SPARTACUS!
YEAH, LIKE ANYONE CAN TELL THE DIFFERENCE...

AND EVEN IF DETAILS LIKE FACIAL HAIR AND
CLOTHING ARE THROWN IN TO DISTINGUISH
THEM, TOO MUCH SIMILARITY IN CHARACTERS'
UNDERLYING APPEARANCE CAN LEAD TO A
BLAND COOKIE-CUTTER LOOK.
NO! IT CAN'T BE TRUE!
NO, IT CAN'T BE TRUE!
NO, IT CAN'T BE TRUE!
NO, IT CAN'T BE TRUE!

* * *

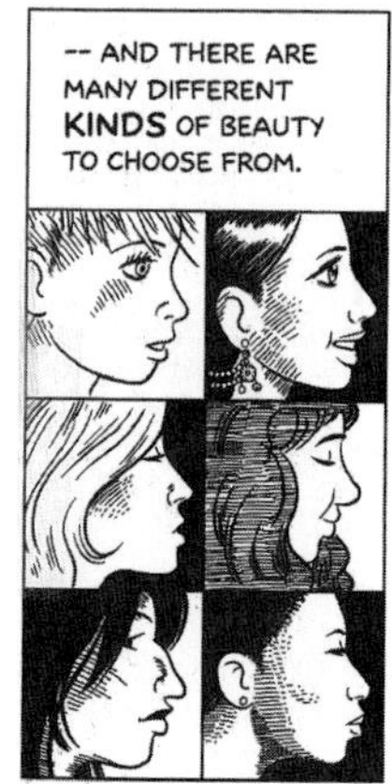

Content

1. Explain what McCloud means when he writes that a character's personality needs "a specific origin or unifying purpose." What are McCloud's reasons for arguing that creating "a compelling inner life" is the "most important" part of character creation?
2. According to McCloud, well developed characters "virtually write themselves." What does this suggest about his view of his artistry and of himself as an artist? How do McCloud's illustrations of himself with his characters support his view of his characters as autonomous creatures, ones that "don't see themselves as part of **your** story at all"?

Strategies/Structures/Language

3. How does McCloud visually represent abstract concepts such as *psyche, autonomy, conflict, obsession, worldview, purpose,* and *complexity*?
4. Does McCloud's audience consist solely of graphic artists? Is his process description also of interest to readers of comics? Writers of fiction or creative non-fiction? Why or why not?
5. Why does McCloud appear alone in some panels? What is the purpose of these panels?

For Writing

6. ***Journal Writing.*** Choose a comic strip that you currently enjoy or enjoyed as a child. Describe the characters' inner lives; origin and purpose; outlook and understanding of others; and internal and external conflicts. Why do these characters appeal to you? What aspects of the human condition do these characters seem to evoke? Do these characters' conflicts speak to your own personal development?

7. ***Dialogues.*** McCloud speaks to the reader as one artist speaking to another (potential) artist. Compare his role inside his panels to the role of the artist in Marchetto's "Why Haven't We Won the War on Cancer?" (Chapter 10). How, in each comic strip, does the mediation of the artist convey information to the reader? What would be the effect if, in McCloud's comic strip, the characters spoke for themselves and, in Marchetto's op-art, Dr. Larry Norton spoke without the artist's mediation?
8. ***Mixed Modes.*** McCloud organizes his approach to character development as an argument with a thesis ("There are three qualities that no great comics character can do without") and a step-by-step structure ("Let's take a closer look at each"). How does McCloud make this structure more interesting by using humor, exemplification, allusion, and variety in the scale and positioning of the images, the size of the panels, and the context of the characters and the artist?

SCOTT RUSSELL SANDERS

Scott Russell Sanders (born 1945) grew up in Ohio, earned a PhD in English from Cambridge University in 1971, and has taught ever since at Indiana University. His books include fiction, a biography of Audubon, and several essay collections. Among them, *In Limestone Country* (1985), *Staying Put* (1993), *Writing from the Center* (1995), and *Hunting for Hope* (1998) focus on living and writing in the Midwest. In his most recent books, *The Force of Spirit* (2000) and *A Private History of Awe* (2006), Sanders pursues his concerns with spirituality, nature, social justice, and community. "My writing . . . is bound together by a web of questions" concerning "the ways in which human beings come to terms with the practical problems of living on a small planet, in nature . . . and families and towns. . . ."

The elegiac "The Inheritance of Tools" appeared in the award-winning *The Paradise of Bombs* (1987), personal essays mainly about the American culture of violence. This essay reveals Sanders's concerns, as a writer and as a son, husband, and father, with the inheritance of skills and values through the generations. Here narration is explanation. Sanders shows how tools become not just extensions of the hand and brain, but of the human heart, as the knowledge of how to use and care for them is transmitted from grandfather to father to son to grandchildren.

The Inheritance of Tools

At just about the hour when my father died, soon after dawn one February morning when ice coated the windows like cataracts, I banged my thumb with a hammer. Naturally I swore at the hammer, the reckless thing, and in the moment of swearing I thought of what my father would say: "If you'd try hitting the nail it would go in a whole lot faster. Don't you know your thumb's not as hard as that hammer?" We both were 1 doing carpentry that day, but far apart. He was building cupboards at my brother's place in Oklahoma; I was at home in Indiana, putting up a wall in the basement to make a bedroom for my daughter. By the time my mother called with news of his death—the long distance wires whittling her voice until it seemed too thin to bear the weight of what she had to say—my thumb was swollen. A week or so later a white scar in the shape of a crescent moon began to show above the cuticle and month by month it rose across the pink sky of my thumbnail. It took the better part of a year for the scar to disappear, and every time I noticed it I thought of my father.

2 The hammer had belonged to him, and to his father before him. The three of us have used it to build houses and barns and chicken coops, to upholster chairs and crack walnuts, to make doll furniture and bookshelves and jewelry boxes. The head is scratched and pockmarked, like an old plowshare that has been working rocky fields, and it gives off the sort of dull sheen you see on fast creek water in the shade. It is a finishing hammer, about the weight of a bread loaf, too light, really, for framing walls, too heavy for cabinet work, with a curved claw for pulling nails, a rounded head for pounding, a fluted neck for looks, and a hickory handle for strength.

3 The present handle is my third one, bought from a lumberyard in Tennessee, down the road from where my brother and I were helping my father build his retirement house. I broke the previous one by trying to pull sixteen-penny nails out of floor joists—a foolish thing to do with a finishing hammer, as my father pointed out. "You ever hear of a crowbar?" he said. No telling how many handles he and my grandfather had gone through before me. My grandfather used to cut down hickory trees on his farm, saw them into slabs, cure the planks in his hayloft, and carve handles with a drawknife. The grain in hickory is crooked and knotty, and therefore tough, hard to split, like the grain in the two men who owned this hammer before me.

4 After proposing marriage to a neighbor girl, my grandfather used this hammer to build a house for his bride on a stretch of river bottom in northern Mississippi. The lumber for the place, like the hickory for the handle, was cut on his own land. By the day of the wedding he had not quite finished the house, and so right after the ceremony he took his wife home and put her to work. My grandmother had worn her Sunday dress for the wedding, with a fringe of lace tacked on around the hem in honor of the occasion. She removed this lace and folded it away before going out to help my grandfather nail siding on the house. "There she was in her good dress," he told me some fifty-odd years after that wedding day, "holding up them long pieces of clapboard while I hammered, and together we got the place covered up before dark." As the family grew to four, six, eight, and eventually thirteen, my grandfather used this hammer to enlarge his house room by room, like a chambered nautilus expanding its shell.

5 By and by the hammer was passed along to my father. One day he was up on the roof of our pony barn nailing shingles with it, when I stepped out the kitchen door to call him for supper. Before I could yell, something about the sight of him straddling the spine of that roof and

© Bojan Brecelj/Corbis

Despite the United States' diverse population—composed of significant numbers of Asians, Hispanics, African Americans, and others from around the world—Americans tend to regard with suspicion people from religious groups that are not mainstream, particularly if their clothing or hair styles are distinctive and separatist. What values and qualities emanate from the picture of the Mennonite carpenter above, taken by Bojan Brecelj? What is the man doing? With what tools? In what room are they? What is its condition? Do you assume the people in this picture are father and daughter? Why? Are they healthy? Clean? At ease? What distinctive clothing are they wearing? Why? Do you find them attractive? How does this photograph comment on Sanders's "The Inheritance of Tools"? What is the heritage of the little girl in this picture?

swinging the hammer caught my eye and made me hold my tongue. I was five or six years old, and the world's commonplaces were still news to me. He would pull a nail from the pouch at his waist, bring the hammer down, and a moment later the *thunk* of the blow would reach my ears. And that is what had stopped me in my tracks and stilled my tongue, that momentary gap between seeing and hearing the blow. Instead of yelling from the kitchen door, I ran to the barn and climbed two rungs up the ladder—as far as I was allowed to go—and spoke quietly to my father. On our walk to the house he explained that sound takes time to make its way through air. Suddenly the world seemed larger, the air more dense, if sound could be held back like any ordinary traveler.

By the time I started using this hammer, at about the age when I discovered the speed of sound, it already contained houses and mysteries for me. The smooth handle was one my grandfather had made. In those days I needed both hands to swing it. My father would start a nail in a scrap of wood, and I would pound away until I bent it over. 6

"Looks like you got ahold of some of those rubber nails," he would tell me. "Here, let me see if I can find you some stiff ones." And he would 7 rummage in a drawer until he came up with a fistful of more cooperative nails. "Look at the head," he would tell me. "Don't look at your hands, don't look at the hammer. Just look at the head of that nail and pretty soon you'll learn to hit it square."

8 Pretty soon I did learn. While he worked in the garage cutting dovetail joints for a drawer or skinning a deer or tuning an engine, I would hammer nails. I made innocent blocks of wood look like porcupines. He did not talk much in the midst of his tools, but he kept up a nearly ceaseless humming, slipping in and out of a dozen tunes in an afternoon, often running back over the same stretch of melody again and again, as if searching for a way out. When the humming did cease, I knew he was faced with a task requiring great delicacy or concentration, and I took care not to distract him.

9 He kept scraps of wood in a cardboard box—the ends of two-by-fours, slabs of shelving and plywood, odd pieces of molding—and everything in it was fair game. I nailed scraps together to fashion what I called boats or houses, but the results usually bore only faint resemblance to the visions I carried in my head. I would hold up these constructions to show my father, and he would turn them over in his hands admiringly, speculating about what they might be. My cobbled-together guitars might have been alien spaceships, my barns might have been models of Aztec temples, each wooden contraption might have been anything but what I had set out to make.

10 Now and again I would feel the need to have a chunk of wood shaped or shortened before I riddled it with nails, and I would clamp it in a vise and scrape at it with a handsaw. My father would let me lacerate the board until my arm gave out, and then he would wrap his hand around mine and help me finish the cut, showing me how to use my thumb to guide the blade, how to pull back on the saw to keep it from binding, how to let my shoulder do the work.

11 "Don't force it," he would say, "just drag it easy and give the teeth a chance to bite."

12 As the saw teeth bit down, the wood released its smell, each kind with its own fragrance, oak or walnut or cherry or pine—usually pine because it was the softest, easiest for a child to work. No matter how weathered and gray the board, no matter how warped and cracked, inside there was this smell waiting, as of something freshly baked. I gathered every smidgen of sawdust and stored it away in coffee cans, which I kept in a drawer of the workbench. When I did not feel like hammering nails, I would dump my sawdust on the concrete floor of the garage and landscape it into highways and farms and towns, running miniature cars and trucks along miniature roads. Looming as huge as a colossus, my father worked over and around me, now and again bending down to inspect my work, careful not to trample my creations. It was a landscape that smelled dizzyingly of wood. Even after a bath my skin would carry the smell, and so would my father's hair, when he lifted me for a bedtime hug.

I tell these things not only from memory but also from recent observation, 13 because my own son now turns blocks of wood into nailed porcupines, dumps cans full of sawdust at my feet and sculpts highways on the floor. He learns how to swing a hammer from the elbow instead of the wrist, how to lay his thumb beside the blade to guide a saw, how to tap a chisel with a wooden mallet, how to mark a hole with an awl before starting a drill bit. My daughter did the same before him, and even now, on the brink of teenage aloofness, she will occasionally drag out my box of wood scraps and carpenter something. So I have seen my apprenticeship to wood and tools reenacted in each of my children, as my father saw his own apprenticeship renewed in me.

The saw I use belonged to him, as did my level and both of my 14 squares, and all four tools had belonged to his father. The blade of the saw is the bluish color of gun barrels, and the maple handle, dark from the sweat of hands, is inscribed with curving leaf designs. The level is a shaft of walnut two feet long, edged with brass and pierced by three round windows in which air bubbles float in oil-filled tubes of glass. The middle window serves for testing if a surface is horizontal, the others for testing if a surface is plumb or vertical. My grandfather used to carry this level on the gun rack behind the seat in his pickup, and when I rode with him I would turn around to watch the bubbles dance. The larger of the two squares is called a framing square, a flat steel elbow, so beat up and tarnished you can barely make out the rows of numbers that show how to figure the cuts on rafters. The smaller one is called a try square, for marking right angles, with a blued steel blade for the shank and a brass-faced block of cherry for the head.

I was taught early on that a saw is not to be used apart from a 15 square: "If you're going to cut a piece of wood," my father insisted, "you owe it to the tree to cut it straight."

Long before studying geometry, I learned there is a mystical virtue 16 in right angles. There is an unspoken morality in seeking the level and the plumb. A house will stand, a table will bear weight, the sides of a box will hold together, only if the joints are square and the members upright. When the bubble is lined up between two marks etched in the glass tube of a level, you have aligned yourself with the forces that hold the universe together. When you miter the corners of a picture frame each angle must be exactly forty-five degrees, as they are in the perfect triangles of Pythagoras, not a degree more or less. Otherwise the frame will hang crookedly, as if ashamed of itself and of its maker. No matter if the joints you are cutting do not show. Even if you are butting two pieces of wood together inside a cabinet, where no one except a wrecking crew will ever see them, you must take pains to ensure that the ends are square and the studs are plumb.

I took pains over the wall I was building on the day my father died. 17 Not long after that wall was finished—paneled with tongue-and-groove boards of yellow pine, the nail holes filled with putty and the wood all stained and sealed—I came close to wrecking it one afternoon when my daughter ran howling up the stairs to announce that her gerbils had escaped from their cage and were hiding in my brand new wall. She could hear them scratching and squeaking behind her bed. Impossible! I said. How on earth could they get inside my drum-tight wall? Through the heating vent, she answered. I went downstairs, pressed my ear to the honey-colored wood, and heard the *scritch scritch* of tiny feet.

18 "What can we do?" my daughter wailed. "They'll starve to death, they'll die of thirst, they'll suffocate."

19 "Hold on," I soothed. "I'll think of something."

20 While I thought and she fretted, the radio on her bedside table delivered us the headlines: Several thousand people had died in a city in India from a poisonous cloud that had leaked overnight from a chemical plant. A nuclear-powered submarine had been launched. Rioting continued in South Africa. An airplane had been hijacked in the Mediterranean. Authorities calculated that several thousand homeless people slept on the streets within sight of the Washington Monument. I felt my usual helplessness in the face of all these calamities. But here was my daughter, weeping because her gerbils were holed up in a wall. This calamity I could handle.

21 "Don't worry," I told her. "We'll set food and water by the heating vent and lure them out. And if that doesn't do the trick, I'll tear the wall apart until we find them."

22 She stopped crying and gazed at me. "You'd really tear it apart? Just for my gerbils? The *wall?*" Astonishment slowed her down only for a second, however, before she ran to the workbench and began tugging at drawers, saying, "Let's see, what'll we need? Crowbar. Hammer. Chisels. I hope we don't have to use them—but just in case."

23 We didn't need the wrecking tools. I never had to assault my handsome wall, because the gerbils eventually came out to nibble at a dish of popcorn. But for several hours I studied the tongue-and-groove skin I had nailed up on the day of my father's death, considering where to begin prying. There were no gaps in that wall, no crooked joints.

24 I had botched a great many pieces of wood before I mastered the right angle with a saw, botched even more before I learned to miter a joint. The knowledge of these things resides in my hands and eyes and the webwork of muscles, not in the tools. There are machines for sale—powered miter boxes and radial-arm saws, for instance—that will enable any casual soul to cut proper angles in boards. The skill is invested in the gadget instead of the person who uses it, and this is what distinguishes a machine from a tool. If I had to earn my keep by making furniture or building houses, I suppose I would buy powered saws and pneumatic nailers; the need for speed would drive me to it. But since I carpenter only for my own pleasure or to help neighbors or to remake the house around the ears of my family, I stick with hand tools. Most of the ones I own were given to me by my father, who also taught me how to wield them. The tools in my workbench are a double inheritance, for each hammer and level and saw is wrapped in a cloud of knowing.

All of these tools are a pleasure to look at and to hold. Merchants would never paste NEW NEW NEW! signs on them in stores. Their designs are old because they work, because they serve their purpose well. Like folk songs and aphorisms and the grainy bits of language, these tools have been pared down to essentials. I look at my claw hammer, the distillation of a hundred generations of carpenters, and consider that it holds up well beside those other classics—Greek vases, Gregorian chants, *Don Quixote,* barbed fish hooks, candles, spoons. Knowledge of hammering stretches back to the earliest humans who squatted beside fires, chipping flints. Anthropologists have a lovely name for those unworked rocks that served as the earliest hammers. "Dawn stones," they are called. Their only qualification for the work, aside from hardness, is that they fit the hand. Our ancestors used them for grinding corn, tapping awls, smashing bones. From dawn stones to this claw hammer is a great leap in time, but no great distance in design or imagination. 25

On that iced-over February morning when I smashed my thumb with the hammer, I was down in the basement framing the wall that my daughter's gerbils would later hide in. I was thinking of my father, as I always did whenever I built anything, thinking how he would have gone about the work, hearing in memory what he would have said about the wisdom of hitting the nail instead of my thumb. I had the studs and plates nailed together all square and trim, and was lifting the wall into place when the phone rang upstairs. My wife answered, and in a moment she came to the basement door and called down softly to me. The stillness in her voice made me drop the framed wall and hurry upstairs. She told me my father was dead. Then I heard the details over the phone from my mother. Building a set of cupboards for my brother in Oklahoma, he had knocked off work early the previous afternoon because of cramps in his stomach. Early this morning, on his way into the kitchen of my brother's trailer, maybe going for a glass of water, so early that no one else was awake, he slumped down on the linoleum and his heart quit. 26

For several hours I paced around inside my house, upstairs and down, in and out of every room, looking for the right door to open and knowing there was no such door. My wife and children followed me and wrapped me in arms and backed away again, circling and staring as if I were on fire. Where was the door, the door, the door? I kept wondering. My smashed thumb turned purple and throbbed, making me furious. I wanted to cut it off and rush outside and scrape away at the snow and hack a hole in the frozen earth and bury the shameful thing. 27

I went down into the basement, opened a drawer in my workbench, and stared at the ranks of chisels and knives. Oiled and sharp, as my father would have kept them, they gleamed at me like teeth. I took up a clasp knife, pried out the longest blade, and tested the edge on the hair of my forearm. A tuft came away cleanly, and I saw my father testing the sharpness of tools on his own skin, the blades of axes and knives and gouges and hoes, saw the red hair shaved off in patches from his arms and the backs of his hands. 28

"That will cut bear," he would say. He never cut a bear with his blades, now my blades, but he cut deer, dirt, wood. I closed the knife and put it away. Then I took up the hammer and went back to work on my daughter's wall, snugging the bottom plate against a chalk line on the floor, shimming the top plate against the joists overhead, plumbing the studs with my level, making sure before I drove the first nail that every line was square and true.

Content

1. Sanders characterizes his father, and grandfather, and himself by showing how they used tools and transmitted this knowledge to their children. What characteristics do they have in common? Why does he omit any differences they might have, focusing on their similarities?
2. Sanders distinguishes between a machine and a tool, saying "The skill is invested in the gadget instead of the person who uses it" (¶ 24). Why does he favor tools over machines? Do you agree with his definition? With his preference?

Strategies/Structures/Language

3. What is the point of this essay? Why does Sanders begin and end with the relation between banging his thumb with a hammer and his father's death?
4. Why does Sanders include the vignette of his daughter and her gerbils, which escaped inside the "drum-tight wall" he had just built (¶s 17–23)? Would he really have wrecked the wall to get the gerbils out?
5. For what audience is Sanders writing? Does it matter whether or not his readers know how to use tools?
6. Show, through specific examples, how Sanders's language and quotations of his father's advice fits his subject, tools, and the people who use them. Consider phrases such as "ice coated the windows like cataracts" (¶ 1) and "making sure before I drove the first nail that every line was square and true" (¶ 28).

For Writing

7. Sanders defines the "inheritance" of tools as, "So I have seen my apprenticeship to wood and tools reenacted in each of my children, as my father saw his own apprenticeship renewed in me" (¶ 13). Tell the story of your own apprenticeship with a tool or collection of tools (kitchen utensils, art supplies, a sewing machine, computer, skis, or other equipment). The explanation of your increasing skill in learning to use it should be intertwined with your relationship with the person who taught you how to use it (not necessarily a family member) and the manner of the teaching—and of the learning.
8. ***Journal Writing.*** Identify an important skill or specific knowledge (which differs from learning to use a tool as in question 7) that you have learned from your parents or grandparents. How do you use this inheritance? What are some of the tangible ways people inherit values from older generations?
9. ***Dialogues.*** Sanders's father is the central figure in two essays in *The Essay Connection*, "The Inheritance of Tools" and "Under the Influence: Paying the Price of My Father's Booze" (192–203). Each uses a series of stories, narratives, to

characterize this significant figure in Sanders's life, yet the father of "Inheritance" is a very different character from the father of "Under the Influence." Write an essay in which you compare and contrast Sanders's portraits of his father to show the different ways of presenting the same person.

10. ***Mixed Modes.*** Write a description of someone you know well, or of a public figure you know a great deal about, using two or more significant stories that illustrate the contradictory sides of the same person.

11. ***Second Look.*** How does the photograph here illustrate a particular relationship between the man, his tools, and his workplace? Does the inclusion of the child influence your interpretation of the photograph? How does the photograph suggest movement? What does the arrangement of the two figures, window, wall of tools, and the object being crafted suggest about its focus?

JAMES FALLOWS

James Fallows (born in 1949 in Redlands, California) earned a BA at Harvard and studied economics at Oxford as a Rhodes Scholar (1970–72). His first book, *National Defense*, won the American Book Award in 1981. He is also the author of *Breaking the News: How the Media Undermine American Democracy* (1996), *Looking at the Sun* (1994), and *Blind into Baghdad: America's War in Iraq* (2006). An article he wrote in response to the 9/11 attacks, "The Fifty-first State?," won the National Magazine Award. He is also a software designer and instrument-rated pilot. Since 1979 he has served in various editorial capacities at *The Atlantic Monthly*, where he currently writes a technology column, including "Tinfoil Underwear," reprinted here from the March 2006 issue. Here, Fallows describes the way businesses compile personal information on computer users, the difficulties facing users who want to protect that information, and the choices that will increasingly face our online society.

*Tinfoil Underwear**

How concerned, really, should ordinary computer users be about the evidence we leave behind when we browse, shop, communicate, and amuse ourselves on the Internet? Early this year, as controversy built over the government's warrantless surveillance of telephone and computer messages, I asked a number of technology experts whether they were worried about their own privacy, and what steps, if any, they would 1

* Copyright © 2006 The Atlantic Monthly Group, as first published in THE ATLANTIC MONTHLY. Distributed by Tribune Media Services.

recommend to the nonexpert computing public. I found strong agreement among them about the scale and nature of the problem, and a surprising emphasis on the need and the right way to deal with it.

2 The main thing the experts said they know, and the public probably doesn't, is how completely modern life has shifted to an "on-the-record" basis. You can drop a letter in a mailbox without a return address and still expect to have it delivered. But that is about the only form of untraceable communication left. Most people understand this change to some degree. As long ago as the mid-1980s, a major twist in the plot of Scott Turow's *Presumed Innocent* involved computerized logs of calls made and received. Today a novel could be based on the details preserved in a single credit-card statement.

3 What most of us might not grasp is just how many activities can now be logged and stored. "To a large extent, we've willingly sacrificed our privacy for the conveniences of the Internet age," says Richard Forno, principal consultant with the information security firm KRvW Associates. OnStar and similar services keep track of locations from which customers make calls. This can be a lifesaver in an emergency, but it also creates a record. Amazon and other online retailers can refine their sense of what we're looking for by analyzing permanent records of past purchases. We avoid the nuisance of reregistering each time we visit favorite sites, notably newspaper sites, by permitting (even if inadvertently) our computers to store "cookies," the small files that are created by the site we've visited and identify us when we return.

4 "There are three big categories" of possible intrusions into people's online privacy, according to Kevin Bankston, a lawyer with the Electronic Frontier Foundation, or EFF, in San Francisco. These are "what you store on your own computer, what other people are storing about you, and what's actually being captured or overheard in real time, by surveillance."

5 The first problem—cookies, old files, unfortunate browsing histories, and other potentially compromising data left on a machine—is the easiest for users to control. Nicole Wong, an associate general counsel at Google, made me burst out laughing with her preposterously wholesome illustration of how awkward situations might arise. "Suppose a husband was shopping online for his wife's birthday present, and he didn't want to spoil the surprise by having her see the sites he had visited—" (When I interjected "Come on!" she replied, "I've been interviewed before.") For instance, Internet Explorer, Firefox, and other major browsers can be set up not to retain cookies, temporary files, or histories of sites visited. This solves the problem, of course, only for family members or others who might want to peruse the contents of your hard drive.

6 Most people I spoke with said that the third problem—the highly publicized threat of eavesdropping by a Big Brotherish state—might bother them as a policy matter, but was not an active personal worry. EFF's Kevin Bankston pointed out that users could go far toward protecting themselves by encrypting their communications with powerful, relatively easily installed utilities like PGP ("Pretty Good Privacy"),

a program that sells for $99 and up at pgp.com, and GPG, an open-source counterpart available for free at gnupg.org. "We don't know the [National Security Agency]'s code-breaking capabilities," Bankston said, "but [any sort of encryption] would certainly slow them down."

7 It was the second category—the inexorable pileup of information on a variety of Web sites—that all of the experts identified as the major long-term threat to a user's privacy. "Data is being collected that was never collected before, that should not be collected now, and that cannot be protected in the long run," says Marc Rotenberg, executive director of the Electronic Privacy Information Center, a civil-liberties advocacy group based in Washington. The technical developments that make this possible cannot easily be undone, but the business policies could be.

8 Nearly every interaction in today's digital life is traceable. Cell-phone calls are of course routed to and from particular handsets—actually, to unique Subscriber Identity Modules, or SIM cards, inside the handset, each associated with a particular customer. E-mail messages, Web search requests, music-download orders, and all other signals sent from a computer are marked with the "IP address," or Internet Protocol address, of the machine that sent them. This is a number something like "192.165.1.204" that identifies your particular computer amid the vastness of the Internet. IP addresses differ from phone numbers in many ways: some are permanently assigned to a given machine, some are reassigned session by session, some are shared on local networks. But in the end, their function is similar. They let other people reach you, and tell others who is trying to reach them.

9 Every query you send to Google contains both the terms you're looking for and the IP address of your machine. Every site you visit can register the fact that someone from your IP address was there. (You can delete the cookies placed by ViolentOverthrowOfTheGovernment.org on your machine; you can't do anything about the site's own logs.) Every time you choose a story to read on an online news site the story you read, and your IP address, can be recorded in the site's log. Every blog posting or comment, every email sent even under a fictitious account name, every item bid on through eBay or bought from an online merchant, every request for a map to be downloaded or a picture viewed—they all carry an IP address.

10 Like a phone number, an IP address is merely digits, without a person's name attached. But the connection between IP addresses and real people is almost as close as with telephone accounts. Anyone who pays for home Internet service, whether cable, DSL, or humble dial-up, has been assigned an IP address by a company that also knows the customer's name. Most for-pay WiFi hot spots also require customers to create accounts with a real name and billing address. You can still go online without revealing your identity, if you're willing to live like a fugitive: paying cash to use Internet cafés, sticking strictly to free, public WiFi spots, libraries, or schools. But for most people this is a chore.

11 The main privacy concerns about IP addresses stem from one business decision: the companies that collect and own the information traceable to them have decided to retain it more or less forever.

12 Why would Google, which receives hundreds of millions of search requests per day, warehouse every one of them, with IP address attached? Because it can. Disk storage has become essentially free. Also it wants to, because for Google and most other online firms, real-world transaction data is the most precious form of market intelligence. Nicole Wong, of Google, gave me the standard reasons why this ever-expanding hoard of data is best for the company and for its users as well. It may be retained to help firms investigate and remedy "click fraud," or invalid clicks on advertisements, in which it matters (for reasons not worth going into here) how many requests come from each unique address. It helps show the "geolocation" of all requests, "which lets us address a number of issues at a geographic level, such as where there might be too much latency [slowness in Google's response to a query], for example, in Africa."

13 The real reason, for firms from Google and Yahoo to Amazon, eBay, and Expedia, is that they are all in an endless struggle to entice more people to spend more time on their sites, so they can sell more advertising. This whole effort, they believe, depends crucially on their ability to "personalize" their services. "The information about you is gold, and it's used for ever more perfect marketing to you," Kevin Bankston told me. "Nothing will change that unless there is a law to force them to stop."

14 For users, "the fear is Panopticon," says Lawrence Lessig, of Stanford Law School, referring to the unseen but all-seeing observer in a prison watchtower once proposed by Jeremy Bentham. "The critical point to recognize is that there simply is no such thing as anonymity on the Internet. That is not because of its technical architecture. It is because of the business model of these companies, which depends on gathering and storing as much data about the customer as you possibly can."

15 What's the potential harm? Every person I spoke with gave an example. A few were political, but most concerned the drawbacks of life in which everyone is on the record, all the time. A spouse in a divorce case might ask for Web-browsing histories to show the other spouse's peccadilloes or peculiar interests. Vetting applicants for jobs—or nominees for official positions—could become even more intrusive than it is already, and even less forgiving of adventure or eccentricity, in an extension of today's "just Google him" effect.

16 No one suggests that an online firm will deliberately disgorge everything it knows about you. Technically, Google could list every IP address that has ever launched a search for "underaged hotties" or "how to make a bomb." Commercially, that would be suicide. Since the Googles and Yahoos need users' trust in order to keep getting data, they, like banks or credit-card companies, have a strong incentive to compete on trustworthiness. But

the long-run fear is that as unprecedented amounts of personal information pile up, all of it linked by IP addresses, more will ultimately be used.

So what are we supposed to do about it? The answers I got covered a very wide range, with one area of consensus that made me think differently about how hard individual users should—or should not—try to protect their own secrets. 17

At one extreme is the approach that Richard Forno describes as "wearing tinfoil underwear." Marvelous tools of disguise exist, starting with encryption software for e-mail. Perhaps the most powerful one, called Tor, can be found at the Electronic Frontier Foundation Web site, tor.eff.org. Originally funded by the Navy, the system effectively conceals a user's IP address by bouncing every Web query among routers around the world, making it harder to trace back to its origin. Tor is free but somewhat tricky to install (I have succeeded, but it took time), and it slows Web response time noticeably. I would use it only if I were working on a project I really wanted to keep under cover. 18

There are other, more modest protective measures. Politicians and CEOs should think twice about doing anything they wouldn't want to see on the front page of a newspaper. Everyone else should think twice before sending e-mail they would not want to see broadly forwarded. (I get and send more e-mail than ever for routine business, but stick to the phone or meetings for anything sensitive.) To keep your computer from piling up data you'd rather not have it store, you can configure your Web browser to reject all cookies, or to ask you before it accepts any. (In IE, you find this via Tools/Internet Settings/Privacy. In Firefox, via Tools/Options/Privacy/Cookies.) Doing without cookies means not being able to use some sites or services at all, for instance Gmail, plus manually logging into other sites every single time. A more moderate step is to have the browser accept cookies but purge them whenever you close the browser. 19

On the other extreme is the approach Lawrence Lessig takes. "I don't do anything" about privacy, he says. "I think there is no way to hide. I just live life thinking everything is in the open." Esther Dyson, of CNET, says something similar. "The short answer is: Nothing," she replied by e-mail when I asked what concealing steps she takes. "For a while I tried flagging every cookie I got, just for fun, but I let them all go through anyway, so eventually I stopped." 20

Mitchell Kapor, the founder of Lotus, who now directs the Open Source Applications Foundation, does take a few protective measures. When using an Internet café, he doesn't log on to PayPal, his credit-card account, or any other site that involves his finances, just in case some keystroke-capture program has been installed. He wasn't comfortable using Gmail as one of his personal e-mail accounts until he grilled Google officials and determined that they "took privacy and security seriously when they store mail." Kapor said that what changed his mind was evidence that Google understands how important a reputation for guarding 21 privacy is to the company's prospects. "They do take steps," he told me, "to make sure that Google employees don't just satisfy their curiosity by looking at people's e-mail, as well as making sure that if you delete the account, they clobber all copies everywhere, including the backups."

22 Between these alternatives—the hypercautious approach of encoding all e-mail and the fatalistic belief that Big Brother will see everything anyway—lay the surprise in what I heard from these informants. This was the idea that legislation—the intrusion of the stodgy old pre-digital government—offers modern computer users their best hope.

23 "When your choices are the tinfoil or doing nothing, that's not right," Lessig says. "I would rather think about how we could actually increase privacy without giving up the versatility of the Internet."

24 For instance, a future law might require Google and other companies to strip specific IP addresses from records of searching or browsing activity that they intended to store for more than a brief period. This would be a balancing act similar to the creation of the "do-not-call" list for telemarketers. It would preserve the legitimate commercial value of aggregate data about Internet use, while protecting individuals if the records were dredged up in legal proceedings—or simply lost, stolen, or exposed through negligence or incompetence. TiVo already applies such a policy. It keeps records of aggregate viewing patterns, which is how it knows that the Janet Jackson breast exposure, from the 2004 Super Bowl, is the most replayed event in TiVo history—but it removes all evidence of which specific customers have viewed or replayed which shows.

25 Nicole Wong unsurprisingly rejects the idea of controls on her own company. But she also suggests that the real privacy firewall, or at least wall, will be built through legislation, rather than ever warier behavior by individual users or more restraint by companies. "I don't think that the fix for user privacy is companies providing less service," she told me. "At the systemic level, the solution is to limit what personal data the government can ask for"—and by extension to limit what information banks, potential employers, divorcing spouses, and other potential snoops can find out.

26 "This is a big, macro public-policy issue about the design of our infrastructure," Marc Rotenberg, of EPIC, says. "It involves payment systems, communications networks, identification, transportation toll design. It's not something that will be solved by 'privacy survivalism'—anonymizers, dark glasses, people paying for everything in cash. Collective problems require collective solutions."

27 I feel worse than I did when I started this project, because I've realized how fully exposed my whole life is. I feel better when I think that companies could be required to purge data every so often, or to store data in a way that makes it hard to link one person's name and IP address to the details of what he or she has done online. Then I remember that

Congress would need to concentrate long enough to enact this change in a thoughtful, far-reaching way with minimal glitches, and I really start worrying.

Content

1. Why, according to Fallows, should individuals be concerned about privacy on the Internet? What types of information about an individual can others access? Which type of traceable information poses the greatest threat to privacy?
2. With the technology Fallows describes, what can Internet users do to protect their privacy?
3. Why do businesses collect and store transaction data from the Internet? How does data collection help users? How else might data collection be utilized?
4. Why might legislation be needed to protect users' privacy? According to Fallows, how might such legislation work? What are the alternatives to government regulation of data on the Internet?

Strategies/Structures/Language

5. Fallows elicits the reader's interest in his thesis by beginning his essay with a question: "How concerned, really, should ordinary computer users be about the evidence we leave behind when we browse, shop, communicate, and amuse ourselves on the Internet?" (¶ 1). Is this effective? How does his inclusion of the word "really" modify the meaning of the question?
6. Fallows uses his interview with Nicole Wong of Google three times in his article. How does each of these instances, including his quotes of Wong, support his argument?

For Writing

7. ***Journal Writing.*** Does the idea that there is no anonymity on the Internet and that your email, searches, downloads, and other activities are logged and stored worry you? Or, do you take the position that "there is no way to hide" (¶ 20)?
8. ***Dialogues.*** Sherry Turkle, in "How Computers Change the Way We Think" (Chapter 9), argues that contemporary college students are not interested in electronic surveillance and violations of privacy (¶ 10–11). Do you agree with Turkle that our society should promote "information-technology literacy" (¶ 29)? Is such literacy necessary in order to have a public debate on government regulations on data collection and storage?
9. ***Mixed Modes.*** Why does Fallows include in this article his own process of investigation of the privacy issues involved in data collection? Identify when he uses himself as a source that supports his argument, such as when he claims to have installed encryption software for email (¶ 18). Explain how this strategy engages the reader and effectively illustrates the dangers and difficulties the Internet presents to users. Why does Fallows end his article on a skeptical note?
10. If you (or someone you know well) have ever experienced identity theft or theft of credit card numbers or other personal information, describe your

experiences. What, if anything, could have been done to prevent this? Are there measures that can be taken to prevent such theft in the future?

11. Present your conclusions for question 10 in a ten-step list, "How to Avoid Identity Theft." Discuss these with a partner to make sure they are clear and, presumably, efficient and effective.

NTOZAKE SHANGE

In 1971, the year after she graduated from Barnard with a BA in American Studies, Paulette Williams (born 1948), daughter of a noted St. Louis surgeon and a social worker, adopted the Zulu name Ntozake Shange (en-toh-ZAH-kee SHAHN-gay), Ntozake meaning "she who comes with her own things" and Shange, "who walks like a lion." Within three years of earning an MA from the University of Southern California (1973), her first and most memorable play had been produced, *for colored girls who have considered suicide/when the rainbow is enuf.* It received an Obie award for the best play of 1977 and Tony and Grammy award nominations, and it established Shange as a writer as well as a dancer and an actress who performed in her own work.

Shange's works include over a dozen other plays and dramatic adaptations, ranging from *Boogie Woogie Landscapes* (1978) to an Obie award-winning adaptation of Bertolt Brecht's *Mother Courage and Her Children* (1981). She has written novels, including *Liliane: Resurrection of the Daughter* (1994); poetry, of which *Nappy Edges* (1978) is the best known; children's books, including *Ellington Was Not a Street* (2003); and numerous short stories and essays. "What Is It We Really Harvestin' Here?" published in *Creative Nonfiction* in 1998, is characteristic of Shange's free-flowing form and fast-paced conversational style, simultaneously lyrical, comical, and satiric. In the process of explaining how to garden, Shange incorporates African-American history, social commentary, autobiography, and recipes—American studies with attitude.

What Is It We Really Harvestin' Here?

1 We got a sayin', "The blacker the berry, the sweeter the juice," which is usually meant as a compliment. To my mind, it also refers to the delectable treats we as a people harvested for our owners and for our own selves all these many years, slave or free. In fact, we knew something about the land, sensuality, rhythm and ourselves that has continued to elude our captors—puttin' aside all our treasures in the basement of the British Museum, or the Met, for that matter. What am I talkin' about? A different approach to the force of gravity, to our bodies, and what we

produce: a reverence for the efforts of the group and the intimate couple. Harvest time and Christmas were prime occasions for courtin'. A famine, a drought, a flood or Lent do not serve as inspiration for couplin', you see.

The Juba, a dance of courtin' known in slave quarters of North 2
America and the Caribbean, is a phenomenon that stayed with us through the jitterbug, the wobble, the butterfly, as a means of courtin' that's apparently very colored, and very "African." In fact we still have it and we've never been so "integrated"—the *Soul Train* dancers aren't all black anymore, but the dynamic certainly is. A visitor to Cuba in Lynne Fauley Emery's "Dance Horizon Book" described the Juba as a series of challenges.

> A woman advances and commencing a slow dance, made up of shuffling of the feet and various contortions of the body, thus challenges a rival from among the men. One of these, bolder than the rest, after a while steps out, and the two then strive which shall tire the other; the woman performing many feats which the man attempts to rival, often excelling them, amid the shouts of the rest. A woman will sometimes drive two or three successive beaux from the ring, yielding her place at length to some impatient belle.

John Henry went up against a locomotive, but decades before 3
we simply were up against ourselves and the elements. And so we are performers in the fields, in the kitchens, by kilns, and for one another. Sterling Stuckey points out, in "Slave Culture," however, that by 1794 "it was illegal to allow slaves to dance and drink on the premises . . . without the written consent of their owners," the exceptions being Christmas and the burials, which are communal experiences. And what shall we plant and harvest, so that we might "Hab big times duh fus hahves, and duh fus ting wut growed we take tuh duh church so as ebrybody could hab a pieces ub it. We pray over it and shout. Wen we hab a dance, we use tuh shout in a rinig. We ain't have wutyuh call a propuh dance tuday."

Say we've gone about our owners' business. Planted and harvested his 4
crop of sugar cane, remembering that the "ratio of slaves/sugar was ten times that of slaves/tobacco and slaves/cotton." That to plant a sugar crop we have to dig a pit 3 feet square and a few inches deep into which one young plant is set. Then, of course, the thing has to grow. A mature sugar-cane plant is 3–9 feet tall. That's got to be cut at exactly the right point. Then we've got to crush it, boil it, refine it, from thick black syrup to fine white sugar, to make sure, as they say in Virginia, that we "got the niggah out." Now it's time to tend to our own gardens. Let's grow some sweet potatoes to "keep the niggah alive."

Sweet Potatoes

Like everything else, we have to start with something. Now we need a small 5
piece of potato with at least one of those scraggly roots hanging about for this native Central American tuber. This vegetable will stand more heat than almost

any other grown in the United States. It does not take to cool weather, and any kind of frost early or seasonal will kill the leaves, and if your soil gets cold the tubers themselves will not look very good. Get your soil ready at least two weeks before planting, weeding, turning, and generally disrupting the congealed and solid mass we refer to as dirt, so that your hands and the tubers may move easily through the soil, as will water and other nutrients.

6 *Once the soil is free of winter, two weeks after the last frost, plant the potato slips in 6–12 inch ridges, 3–4.5 feet apart. Separate the plants by 9–12 inches. If we space the plants more than that, our tubers may be grand, but way too big to make good use of in the kitchen. We should harvest our sweet potatoes when the tubers are not quite ripe, but of good size, or we can wait until the vines turn yellow. Don't handle our potatoes too roughly, which could lead to bruising and decay. If a frost comes upon us unexpectedly, take those potatoes out the ground right away. Our potatoes will show marked improvement during storage, which allows the starch in them to turn to sugar. Nevertheless let them lie out in the open for 2 to 3 hours to fully dry. Then move them to a moist and warm storage space. The growing time for our crop'll vary from 95 to 125 days.*

7 *The easiest thing to do with a sweet potato is to bake it. In its skin. I coat the thing with olive oil, or butter in a pinch. Wrap it in some aluminum foil, set it in the oven at 400 degrees. Wait till I hear sizzling, anywhere from 45 minutes to an hour after, in a very hot oven. I can eat it with my supper at that point or I can let it cool off for later. (One of the sexiest dates I ever went on was to the movies to see "El Mariachi." My date brought along chilled baked sweet potatoes and ginger beer. Much nicer than canola-sprayed "buttered" popcorn with too syrupy Coca-Cola, wouldn't you say?)*

Mustard Greens

8 *No, they are not the same as collards. We could say they, with their frilly edges and sinuous shapes, have more character, are more flirtatious, than collards. This green can be planted in the spring or the fall, so long as the soil is workable (not cold). It's not a hot weather plant, preferring short days and temperate climates. We can use the same techniques for mustard greens that we use for lettuce. Sowing the seeds in rows 12–18 inches apart, seedlings 4–8 inches apart. These plants should get lots of fertilizer to end up tender, lots of water, too. They should be harvested before they are fully mature. Now, you've got to be alert, because mustard greens grow fast, 25–40 days from the time you set them in the soil to harvest. When it comes time to reap what you've sown, gather the outer leaves when they are 3–4 inches long, tender enough; let the inner leaves then develop more or wait till it's hot and harvest the whole plant.*

9 *Now we cook the mustard greens just like the collards, or we don't have to cook it at all. This vegetable is fine in salads or on sandwiches and soups. If you shy away from pungent tastes, mix these greens with some collards, kale, or beet*

greens. That should take some of the kick out of them. I still like my peppers and vinegar, though. If we go back, pre-Columbus, the Caribs did, too. According to Spanish travelers, the Caribs, who fancied vegetables, added strong peppers called aji-aji to just about everything. We can still find aji-aji on some sauces from Spanish-speaking countries if we read the labels carefully. Like "La Morena." So appropriate.

Watermelon

The watermelon is an integral part of our actual life as much as it is a feature of our stereotypical lives in the movies, posters, racial jokes, toys, and early American portraits of the "happy darky." We could just as easily been eatin' watermelon in D. W. Griffith's "Birth of a Nation" as chicken legs. The implications are the same. Like the watermelon, we were a throwback of "African" pre-history, which isn't too off, since Lucy, the oldest Homo sapiens currently known is from Africa, too. 10

But I remember being instructed not to order watermelon in restaurants or to eat watermelon in any public places because it makes white people think poorly of us. They already did that, so I don't see what the watermelon was going to precipitate. Europeans brought watermelon with them from Africa anyway. In Massachusetts by 1629 it was recorded as "abounding." In my rebelliousness as a child, I got so angry about the status of the watermelon, I tried to grow some in the flower box on our front porch in Missouri. My harvest was minimal to say the least. 11

Here's how you can really grow you some watermelon. They like summer heat, particularly sultry, damp nights. If we can grow watermelons, we can grow ourselves almost any other kind of melon. The treatment is the same. Now, these need some space, if we're looking for a refrigerator-sized melon or one ranging from 25–30 pounds. Let them have a foot between plants in between rows 4–6 feet apart. They need a lot of fertilizer, especially if the soil is heavy and doesn't drain well. When the runners (vines) are a foot to a foot-and-a-half long, fertilize again about 8 inches from the plant itself. Put some more fertilizer when the first melons appear. Watermelons come in different varieties, but I'm telling you about the red kind. I have no primal response to a golden or blanched fleshed melon. Once your melons set on the vines and start to really take up some space, be sure not to forget to water the vines during the ripening process. 12

When is your watermelon ripe? You can't tell by thumping it nor by the curly tail at the point where the melon is still on the vine. The best way to know if your melon is ready is by looking at the bottom. The center turns from a light yellow to deep amber. Your melon'll have a powdery or mushy tasteless sorta taste if you let it ripen too long. 13

Surely you've seen enough pictures or been to enough picnics to know how to eat a watermelon, so I won't insult you with that information. However, there is a fractious continuing debate about whether to sprinkle sugar or salt on your watermelon slice. I am not going to take sides in this matter. 14

15 Some of us were carried to the New World specifically because we knew 'bout certain crops, know 'bout the groomin' and harvestin' of rice, for instance.

> Plantation owners were perfectly aware of the superiority . . . of African slaves from rice country. Littlefield (journalist) writes that "as early as 1700 ships from Carolina were reported in the Gambia River." . . . In a letter dated 1756, Henry Laurens, a Charleston merchant, wrote, "The slaves from the River Gambia are prefer'd to all others with us save the Gold Coast." The previous year he had written: "Gold Coast or Gambias are best; next to them the Windward Coast are prefer'd to Angolas."

16 These bits of information throw an entirely different, more dignified light on "colored" cuisine, for me. Particularly since I was raised on rice and my mother's people on both sides are indefatigable Carolinians, South, to be exact, South Carolinians. To some, our "phrenologically immature brains" didn't have consequence until our mastery of the cultivation of "cargo," "patna," "joponica," and finally Carolina rice, "small-grained, rather long and wiry, and remarkably white" was transferred to the books and records of our owners. Nevertheless, our penchant for rice was not dampened by its relationship to our bondage. Whether through force or will, we held on to our rice-eatin' heritage. I repeat, I was raised on rice. If I was Joe Williams, insteada singin' "Every day, every day, I sing the blues," I'd be sayin', "Oh, every day, almost any kinda way, I get my rice."

17 My poor mother, Eloise, Ellie, for short, made the mistake of marrying a man who was raised by a woman from Canada. So every day, he wanted a potato, some kinda potato, mashed, boiled, baked, scalloped, fried, just a potato. Yet my mother was raising a sixth generation of Carolinians, which meant we had to eat some kinda rice. Thus, Ellie was busy fixing potato for one and rice for all the rest every day, until I finally learnt how to do one or the other and gave her a break. I asked Ellie Williams how her mother, Viola, went about preparing the rice for her "chirren"—a Low-country linguistic lapse referring to off-spring like me. Anyway, this is what Mama said.

Mama's Rice

18 *"We'd buy some rice in a brown paper bag (this is in The Bronx). Soak it in a bit of water. Rinse it off and cook it the same way we do now." "How is that, Ma?" I asked. "Well, you boil a certain amount of water. Let it boil good. Add your rice and let it boil till tender. Stirring every so often because you want the water to evaporate. You lift your pot. You can tell if your rice is okay because there's no water there. Then you fluff it with a fork. You want every kind, extra, extra, what you call it. No ordinary olive oil will do.*

19 *"Heat this up. Just a little bit of it. You don't want no greasy rice, do you? Heat this until, oh, it is so hot that the smoke is coming quick. Throw*

in 3–4 cloves garlic, maybe 1 cup chopped onion too, I forgot. Let that sizzle and soften with $\frac{1}{2}$ cup each cilantro, pimiento, and everything. But don't let this get burned, no. So add your 4 cups water and 2 cups rice. Turn up the heat some more till there's a great boiling of rice, water, seasonings. The whole thing. Then leave it alone for a while with the cover on so all the rice cooks even. Now, when you check and see there's only a small bit of water left in the bottom of the pot, stir it all up. Turn the heat up again and wait. When there's no water left at all, at all. Just watch the steam coming up. Of course you should have a good pegau *by now, but the whole pot of your rice should be delicioso, ready even for my table. If you do as I say."*

For North Americans, a pot with burnt rice on the bottom is a scary concept. But all over the Caribbean, it's a different story entirely. In order to avoid making *asopao*—a rice moist and heavy with the sofrito or tomato-achiote mixture, almost like a thick soup where the rice becomes one mass instead of standing, each grain on its own—it is necessary to let the rice on the bottom of the pot get a crustlike bottom, assuring that all moisture has evaporated. My poor North American mother, Ellie, chastises me frequently for "ruining" good rice with all this spice. Then I remind her that outside North America we Africans were left to cook in ways that reminded us of our mother's cooking, not Jane Austen's characters. The rice tastes different, too. But sometimes I cheat and simply use Goya's Sazon—after all, I'm a modern woman. I shouldn't say that too loudly, though. Mathilde can hear all the way from her front porch any blasphemous notion I have about good cooking. No, it is her good cooking that I am to learn. I think it is more than appropriate that we know something about some of the crops that led to most of us African descendants of the Diaspora, being here, to eat anything at all. 20

But rather than end on a sour note, I am thinking of my classes with the great Brazilian dancer, choreographer and teacher Mercedes Baptista at the now legendary Clark Center. We learned a harvest dance, for there are many, but the movements of this celebratory ritual were lyrical and delicate, far from the tortured recounts of EuroAmericans to our "jigaboo" gatherings; no gyrations, repetitive shuffling that held no interest. Indeed, the simple movement of the arms, which we worked on for days until we got it, resembled a tropical port-à-bras worthy of any ballerina. Our hip movements, ever so subtle, with four switches to the left, then four to the right, all the while turning and covering space. The head leaning in the direction of the hips, the arms moving against it, till the next hip demanded counterpoint. 21

A healthy respect for the land, for what we produce for the blessing of a harvest begot dances of communal joy. On New Year's Eve in the late fifties, we danced the Madison; today it's a burning rendition of "The Electric Slide." Eighty-years-olds jammin' with toddlers after the weddin' toast. No, we haven't changed so much. 22

Content

1. What's the point of Shange's title? What *is* it "we really harvestin'"?
2. Shange gives directions on how to grow, prepare, and eat several foods—sweet potatoes, mustard greens, watermelon—and how to cook "Mama's Rice." Like many other directions written by experts, these seem easy to follow and the results seem assured. Why are most directions written so simply and positively?
3. "What Is It We Really Harvestin' Here?" was published in *Creative Nonfiction*, a publication usually read by creative writers, not in a home or cooking magazine. Why might this piece appeal to readers who are writers? Or to any readers who don't garden? Or cook? Or eat much "'colored' cusine"?

Strategies/Structures/Language

4. Shange's planting instructions are presented in a matrix of African-American political and social history (¶s 1–4), family history (¶s 16–17), and autobiography (¶s 20–22). How do these elements make the reading different from the usual instructions on how to perform a process, such as following a recipe or planting a garden?
5. Whom does Shange include in *we?* Is the *we* of the title and "We got a sayin'" (¶ 1, sentence 1), the same as the *we* of "*we* as a people" (¶ 1, sentence 2)? The same as the *we* of "And so we are performers in the fields" (¶ 3, sentence 2)? Why does it matter, to writer and readers, who *we* are?
6. How does Shange's style suit her subject? In this essay that is largely written in standard English, what are the effects of using dialect spelling (as in *chirren* [¶ 7]), or omitting the *-g* at the end of *ing* words, as in *puttin'* (¶ 1)? Why does Shange quote entire sentences in dialect: "Wen we hab a dance . . ." (¶ 3)? Why does Shange use dialect much more extensively in the first four paragraphs of the essay than later on?

For Writing

7. If you're a competent cook, write out a favorite recipe so others less experienced than you can prepare it. Identify unusual ingredients, the major steps to follow, and also any subprocesses that need to be done to prepare the dish. Have someone read (better yet, try out) your recipe. What questions do they ask? Incorporate the information from your answers into the recipe as you revise it.
8. Explain how to do or make something that's integral to your cultural background(s) (such as how to interpret or perform a particular religious ritual, celebrate a particular holiday, do a particular dance step, play a particular game, perform a specific athletic activity, engage in a flirtation or courtship). Embed your instructions, as Shange does, in a matrix of cultural, family, or personal history—use examples from real life to explain why certain things are done in a certain way, as well as how. If diagrams or photographs would clarify, add them as appropriate.
9. ***Journal Writing.*** Is preparing and eating food an important part of your social life? Explore the relationship between food and identity. Do you feel ambiguous about certain food traditions, as Shange describes African Americans of her

childhood being toward watermelon (¶ 11)? Or, are there foods, such as Shange describes in the being section "Mama's Rice" (¶s 18–20) that seem an inseparable part of who you are?

10. ***Dialogues.*** Compare the language and details Shange uses to emphasize the richness of " 'colored' cuisine" (¶ 16) with the language and details Michael Pollan uses in "The Meal" to critique the food industry. How does each writer use these descriptions of food to reinforce their point of view and conclusions?

11. ***Mixed Modes.*** Shange defines the Juba as a quintessentially "African" dance (¶ 2). What other activities and foods does she identify as particularly expressive of the culture of the "African descendants of the Diaspora" (¶ 20)? How much outside knowledge must you draw on—for example, from history and contemporary culture—to understand Shange's description of this culture?

NING YU

Ning Yu was born in 1955 in Beijing, People's Republic of China, and came to the United States in 1986 for graduate study. He earned a PhD in English from the University of Connecticut in 1993 and is now a professor of English and Chinese literature at Western Washington University, at work on a translation of 301 Chinese nature poems.

Ning Yu recounts some of the significant events of his youth in the following prize-winning essay. When he was in fourth grade, his school was closed down as a consequence of the "Great Proletarian Cultural Revolution," which overturned the existing social order. The intellectual class (the "blacks," in Yu's classification scheme) to which Yu's family belonged because his father was a professor of Chinese language and literature, were replaced on their jobs by members of the People's Liberation Army, "the reds," whose status—as we can see from Ning Yu's teachers—was determined by their political loyalty rather than their academic training. So Ning Yu learned one kind of English at school, the rote memorization of political slogans: "Down with the Soviet Neo-Czarists!" He explains that the Cultural Revolution stifled originality of language, as well as of thought. "Consequently," he says, "I used the clichés deliberately to create a realistic atmosphere for my story, and also ironically to attack the decade of clichés."

Ning Yu learned another kind of English, the rich, imaginative language of high-culture literature, from his father. On the verge of his fourth imprisonment as an intellectual (and therefore by definition subversive), Dr. Yu taught his teenage son the alphabet and some basic grammar. He gave his son a copy of Jane Austen's *Pride and Prejudice* and an old English-Chinese dictionary and told him to translate the novel—which Ning Yu "struggled through from cover to cover" during the nineteen months of his father's incarceration. Ning Yu's essay makes clear the relations among politics, social class, and education under the Maoist regime.

✧ Red and Black, or One English Major's Beginning

1 I have always told my friends that my first English teacher was my father. That is the truth, but not the whole truth. It was a freezing morning more than twenty years ago, we, some fifty-odd boys and girls, were shivering in a poorly heated classroom when the door was pushed open and in came a gust of wind and Comrade Chang Hong-gen, our young teacher. Wrapped in an elegant army overcoat, Comrade Chang strode in front of the blackboard and began to address us in outrageous gibberish. His gestures, his facial expressions, and his loud voice unmistakably communicated that he was lecturing us as a People's Liberation Army captain would address his soldiers before a battle—in revolutionary war movies, that is. Of course we didn't understand a word of the speech until he translated it into Chinese later:

> Comrades, red-guards, and revolutionary pupils:
>
> The Great Revolutionary Teacher Marx teaches us: "A foreign language is an important weapon in the struggle of human life." Our Great Leader, Great Teacher, Great Supreme-Commander, and Great Helmsman, Chairman Mao, has also taught us that it is not too difficult to learn a foreign language. "Nothing in the world is too difficult if you are willing to tackle it with the same spirit in which we conquered this mountain."
>
> Now, as you know, the Soviet Social Imperialists and the U.S. Imperialists have agreed on a venomous scheme to enslave China. For years the U.S. Imperialists have brought war and disaster to Vietnam; and you must have heard that the Soviet troops invaded our Jewel Island in Heilongjiang Province last month. Their evil purpose is obvious—to invade China, the Soviets from the north and the Americans from the south through Vietnam.
>
> We are not afraid of them, because we have the leadership of Chairman Mao, the invincible Mao Zedong Thought, and seven hundred million people. But we need to be prepared. As intellectual youth, you must not only prepare to sacrifice your lives for the Party and the Motherland, but also learn to stir up our people's patriotic zeal and to shatter the morale of the enemy troops. To encourage our own people, you must study Chairman Mao's works very hard and learn your lessons well with your teacher of Chinese; to crush the enemy, you must learn your English lessons well with me.

2 Then Comrade Chang paused, his face red and sweat beading on the tip of his nose. Though nonplussed, we could see that he was genuinely excited, but we were not sure whether his excitement was induced by "patriotic zeal" or the pleasure of hearing grandiose sounds issued from

his own lips. For my part, I suspected that verbal intoxication caused his excitement. Scanning the classroom, he seemed to bask in our admiration rather than to urge us to sacrifice our lives for the Party. He then translated the speech into Chinese and gave us another dose of eloquence:

> From now on, you are not pupils anymore, but soldiers—young, intellectual soldiers fighting at a special front. Neither is each English word you learn a mere word anymore. Each new word is a bullet shot at the enemy's chest, and each sentence a hand grenade.

Comrade Chang was from a "red" family. His name *hong* means red in Chinese, and *gen* means root, so literally, he was "Chang of Red Root." Students said that his father was a major in the People's Liberation Army, and his grandfather a general, and that both the father and the grandfather had "contributed a great deal to the Party, the Motherland, and the Chinese working people." When the "Great Proletarian Cultural Revolution" started, Mr. Chang had just graduated from the Beijing Foreign Languages Institute, a prestigious university in the capital where some thirty languages were taught to people "of red roots." Red youngsters were trained there to serve in the Foreign Ministry, mostly in Chinese embassies and consulates in foreign countries. We understood that Comrade Chang would work only for a token period in our ghetto middle school. At the time, the Foreign Ministry was too busy with the Cultural Revolution to hire new translators, but as soon as the "Movement" was over and everything back to normal, Comrade Chang, we knew, would leave us and begin his diplomatic career. 3

In the late 1960s the Revolution defined "intellectual" as "subversive." So my father, a university professor educated in a British missionary school in Tianjin, was regarded as a "black" element, an enemy of the people. In 1967, our family was driven out of our university faculty apartment, and I found myself in a ghetto middle school, an undeserving pupil of the red expert Comrade Chang. 4

In a shabby and ill-heated schoolroom I began my first English lesson, not "from the very beginning" by studying the alphabet, but with some powerful "hand grenades": 5

> Give up; no harm!
> Drop your guns!
> Down with the Soviet Neo-Czarists!
> Down with U.S. Imperialism!
> Long live Chairman Mao!
> We wish Chairman Mao a long, long life!
> Victory belongs to our people!

These sentences turned out to be almost more difficult and more dangerous to handle than real grenades, for soon the words became mixed up in our heads. So much so that not a few "revolutionary pupils" 6 reconstructed the slogans to the hearty satisfactions of themselves but to the horror of Comrade Chang:

> Long live the Soviet Neo-Czarists!
> Victory belongs to your guns!

Upon hearing this, Comrade Chang turned pale and shouted at us, "You idiots! Had you uttered anything like that in Chinese, young as you are, you could have been thrown into jail for years. Probably me too! Now you follow me closely: Long live Chairman Mao!"

7 "Long live Chairman Mao!" we shouted back.

8 "Long live Chairman Mao!"

9 "Long live Chairman Mao!"

10 "Down with the Soviet Neo-Czarists!"

11 "Down with the Soviet Neo-Czarists!"

12 Comrade Chang decided that those two sentences were enough for idiots to learn in one lesson, and he told us to forget the other sentences for the moment. Then he wrote the two sentences on the chalkboard and asked us to copy them in our English exercise books. Alas, how could anybody in our school know what that was!

13 I wrote the two sentences on my left palm and avoided putting my left hand in my pocket or mitten for the rest of the day. I also remembered what Comrade Chang said about being thrown into jail, for as the son of a "black, stinking bourgeois intellectual," I grasped the truth in his warning. The two English sentences were a long series of meaningless, unutterable sounds. Comrade Chang had the power to impose some Chinese meaning on my mind. So, before I forgot or confused the sounds, I invented a makeshift transliteration in Chinese for the phonetically difficult and politically dangerous parts of the sentences. I put the Chinese words *qui, mian,* and *mao* (cut, noodle, hair) under "Chairman Mao," and *niu za sui* (beef organ meat) under "Neo-Czarists." "Down with" were bad words applied to the enemies; "long live" were good words reserved for the great leader. These were easy to remember. So I went home with a sense of security, thinking the device helped me distinguish the Great Leader from the enemy.

14 The next morning, Comrade "Red Roots" asked us to try our weapons before the blackboard. Nobody volunteered. Then Comrade Chang began calling us by name. My friend "Calf" was the first to stand up. He did not remember anything. He didn't try to learn the words, and he told me to "forget it" when I was trying to memorize the weird sounds. In fact, none of my classmates remembered the sentences.

15 My fellow pupils were all "red" theoretically. But they were not Comrade Chang's type of red. Their parents were coolies, candy-peddlers, or bricklayers. Poor and illiterate. Before the 1949 revolution, these people led miserable lives. Even the revolution didn't improve their lives much, and parents preferred their children to do chores at home rather than

© Stephanie Maze/Corbis

What does it mean to become literate? Are there significant differences in this process among cultures, nationalities? Compare your own experience of learning to read and write English or another language with the processes of language learning that Ning Yu describes in this essay.

fool around with books, especially after the "Great Proletarian Cultural Revolution" started in 1966. Books were dangerous. Those who read books often ran into trouble for having ideas the Party didn't want them to have. "Look at the intellectuals," they said. "They suffer even more than us illiterates." They also knew that their children could not become "red experts" like Comrade Chang, because they themselves were working people who didn't contribute to the Party, the Motherland—or to the liberation of the working people themselves.

Thus my friends didn't waste time in remembering nonsense. 16 Still Comrade Chang's questions had to be answered. Since I was the only one in class not from a red family, my opinion was always the last asked, if asked at all. I stood up when Comrade Chang called my name. I had forgotten the English sounds too, for I took Calf's advice. But before I repeated the apology already repeated fifty times by my friends, I glanced at my left palm and inspiration lit up my mind. "Long live *qie mian mao!* Down with *niu za sui!*" My friends stared, and Comrade Chang glared at me. He couldn't believe his ears. "Say that again." I did. This time my classmates burst into a roar of laughter. "Cut noodle hair! Beef organ meat!" they shouted again and again.

"Shut up!" Comrade Chang yelled, trembling with anger and pointing at me with his right index finger. "What do you mean by 'cut noodle hair'? That insults our great leader Chairman Mao." Hearing that, the class 17 suddenly became silent. The sons and daughters of the "Chinese working people" knew how serious an accusation that could be. But Calf stood up and said: "Comrade Teacher, it is truly a bad thing that Ning Yu should associate Chairman Mao with such nonsense as 'cut noodle hair.' But he didn't mean any harm. He was trying to throw a hand grenade at the enemy. He also called the Soviets 'beef organ meat.' He said one bad thing (not enough respect for Chairman Mao) but then said a good thing (condemning the Soviets). One take away one is zero. So he didn't really do anything wrong, right?"

18 Again the room shook with laughter.

19 Now Comrade Chang flew into a rage and began to lecture us about how class enemies often say good things to cover up evil intentions. Calf, Chang said, was a red boy and should draw a line between himself and me, the black boy. He also threatened to report my "evil words" to the revolutionary committee of the middle school. He said that in the "urgent state of war" what I said could not be forgiven or overlooked. He told me to examine my mind and conduct severe self-criticism before being punished. "The great proletarian dictatorship," he said, "is all-powerful. All good will be rewarded and all evil punished when the right time comes." He left the classroom in anger without giving us any new hand grenades.

20 I felt ruined. Destroyed. Undone. I could feel icy steel handcuffs closing around my wrists. I could hear the revolutionary slogans that the mobs would shout at me when I was dragged off by the iron hand of the Proletarian Dictatorship. My legs almost failed me on my way home.

21 Calf knew better. "You have nothing to worry about, Third Ass."

22 I am the third child in my family, and it is a tradition of old Beijing to call a boy by number. So usually my family called me Thirdy. But in my ghetto, when the kids wanted to be really friendly, they added the word "ass" to your number or name. This address upset me when I first moved into the neighborhood. I was never comfortable with that affix during the years I lived there, but at that moment I appreciated Calf's kindness in using that affix. Words are empty shells. It's the feeling that people attach to a word that counts.

23 "I'll be crushed like a rotten egg by the iron fist of the Great Proletarian Dictatorship," I said.

24 "No way. Red Rooty is not going to tell on you. Don't you know he was more scared than you? He was responsible. How could you say such things if he had not taught you? You get it? You relax. *Qie mian mao!* You know, you really sounded like Rooty." Calf grinned.

25 Although Calf's wisdom helped me to "get it," relax I could not. My legs were as stiff as sticks and my heart beat against my chest so hard that I could hardly breathe. For many years I had tried to get rid of my "blackness" by hard work and good manners. But I could not succeed. No matter how hard I tried I could not change the fact that I was not "red." The Party denied the existence of intermediate colors. If you were not red, logically you could only be black. What Chang said proved what I guessed. But,

when cornered, even a rabbit may bite. Comrade Chang, I silently imagined, if I have to be crushed, you can forget about your diplomatic career. I created a drama in which Comrade Chang, the red root, and I, the black root, were crushed into such fine powder that one could hardly tell the red from the black. All one could see was a dark, devilish purple.

The next morning, I went to school with a faltering heart, expecting to be called out of the classroom and cuffed. Nothing happened. Comrade Chang seemed to have forgotten my transgression and gave us three handfuls of new "bullets." He slowed down too, placing more emphasis on pronunciation. He cast the "bullets" into hand grenades only after he was sure that we could shoot the "bullets" with certainty. 26

Nothing happened to me that day, or the next day, or the week after. Calf was right. As weeks passed, my dislike of Chang dwindled and I began to feel something akin to gratitude to him. Before learning his English tongue twisters, we only recited Chairman Mao's thirty-six poems. We did that for so long that I memorized the annotations together with the text. I also memorized how many copies were produced for the first, the second, and the third printing. I was bored, and Teacher Chang's tongue twisters brought me relief. Granted they were only old slogans in new sounds. But the mere sounds and the new way of recording the sounds challenged me. Still, as an old Chinese saying goes, good luck never lasts long. 27

Forty hand grenades were as many as the Party thought proper for us to hold. Before I mastered the fortieth tongue twister—"Revolutionary committees are fine"—our "fine" revolutionary committee ordered Comrade Chang to stop English lessons and to make us dig holes for air raid shelters. Comrade Chang approached this new task with just as much "patriotic zeal" as he taught English. In truth he seemed content to let our "bullets" and "hand grenades" rust in the bottom of the holes we dug. But I was not willing to let my only fun slip away easily. When digging the holes I repeated the forty slogans silently. I even said them at home in bed. One night I uttered a sentence as I climbed onto my top bunk. Reading in the bottom bunk, my father heard me and was surprised. He asked where I had learned the words. Then for the first time I told him about Comrade Chang's English lessons. 28

Now it may seem strange for a middle school boy not to turn to his family during a "political crisis." But at that time, it was not strange at all. By then my mother, my sister, and my brother had already been sent to the countryside in two different remote provinces. Getting help from them was almost impossible, for they had enough pressing problems themselves. Help from my father was even more impractical: he was already "an enemy of the people," and therefore whatever he said or did for me could only complicate my problems rather than resolve them. So I kept him in the dark. Since we had only each other in the huge city of eight million people, we shared many things, but not political problems. 29

30 Our home in the working class neighborhood was a single seventeen-square-meter room. Kitchen, bathroom, sitting room, study, bedroom, all in one. There was no ceiling, so we could see the black beams and rafters when we lay in bed. The floor was a damp and sticky dirt, which defied attempts at sweeping and mopping. The walls were yellow and were as damp as the dirt floor. To partition the room was out of the question. Actually my parents had sold their king-sized bed and our single beds, and bought two bunk beds in their stead. My mother and sister each occupied a top bunk, my father slept in one bottom bunk, and my brother and I shared the other. Red Guards had confiscated and burned almost all of my father's Chinese books, but miraculously they left his English books intact. The English books were stuffed under the beds on the dirt floor. We lived in this manner for more than a year till the family members were scattered all over China, first my siblings to a province in the northwest, and then my mother to southern China. They were a thousand miles from us and fifteen hundred miles from each other. After they left, I moved to the top bunk over my father, and we piled the books on the other bed. Thanks to the hard covers, only the bottom two layers of the books had begun to mold.

31 That evening, after hearing me murmuring in English, my father gestured for me to sit down on his bunk. He asked me whether I knew any sentences other than the one he had heard. I jumped at the opportunity to go through the inventory of my English arsenal. After listening to my forty slogans my father said: "You have a very good English teacher. He has an excellent pronunciation, standard Oxford pronunciation. But the sentences are not likely to be found in any books written by native English speakers. Did he teach you how to read?"

32 "I can read all those sentences if you write them out."

33 "If *I* write them? But can't *you* write them by yourself?"

34 "No."

35 "Did he teach you grammar?"

36 "No."

37 "Did he teach you the alphabet?"

38 "No."

39 My father looked amused. Slowly he shook his head, and then asked: "Can you recognize the words, the separate words, when they appear in different contexts?"

40 "I think so, but I'm not sure."

41 He re-opened the book that he was reading and turned to the first page and pointed with his index finger at the first word in the first sentence, signaling me to identify it.

42 I shook my head.

43 He moved the finger to the next word. I didn't know that either. Nor did I know the third word, the shortest word in the line, the word made up of a single letter. My father traced the whole sentence slowly, hoping

that I could identify some words. I recognized the bullet "in" and at once threw a hand grenade at him: "Beloved Chairman Mao, you are the red sun *in* our hearts." Encouraged, my father moved his finger back to the second word in the sentence. This time I looked at the word more closely but couldn't recognize it. "It's an 'is,'" he said. "You know 'are' but not 'is'! The third word in this sentence is an 'a'. It means 'one.'" It is the first letter in the alphabet and you don't know that either! What a teacher! A well-trained one too!" He then cleared his throat and read the whole sentence aloud: "It is a truth universally acknowledged, that a man in possession of a good fortune, must be in want of a wife."

The sounds he uttered reminded me of Chang's opening speech, but 44
they flowed out of my father's mouth smoothly. Without bothering about the meaning of the sentence, I asked my father to repeat it several times because I liked the rhythm. Pleased with my curiosity, my father began to explain the grammatical structure of the sentence. His task turned out to be much harder than he expected, for he had to explain terms such as "subject," "object," "nouns," "verbs" and "adjectives." To help me understand the structure of the English sentence, he had to teach me Chinese grammar first. He realized that the Great Proletarian Culture Revolution had made his youngest son literally illiterate, in Chinese as well as English.

That night, our English lessons started. He taught me the letters 45
A through F. By the end of the week, I had learned my alphabet. Afterward he taught the basics of grammar, sometimes using my hand grenades to illustrate the rules. He also taught me the international phonetic symbols and the way to use a dictionary. For reading materials, he excerpted simple passages from whatever books were available. Some were short paragraphs while others just sentences. We started our lessons at a manageable pace, but after a couple of months, for reasons he didn't tell me till the very last, he speeded up the pace considerably. The new words that I had to memorize increased from twenty words per day to fifty. To meet the challenge, I wrote the new words on small, thin slips of paper and hid them in the little red book of Chairman Mao, so that I could memorize them during the political study hours at school. In hole-digging afternoons I recited the sentences and sometimes even little paragraphs—aloud when I was sure that Chang was not around.

Before the sounds and shapes of English words became less elu- 46
sive, before I could confidently study by myself, my father told me that I would have to continue on my own. He was going to join the "Mao Zedong Thought Study Group" at his university. In those years, "Mao Zedong Thought Study Group" was a broad term that could refer to many things. Used in reference to my father and people like him, it had only one meaning: a euphemism for imprisonment. He had been imprisoned once when my mother and siblings were still in Bejing. Now it had come again. I asked, "Are you detained or arrested?" "I don't know," he said. "It's just a Study Group." "Oh," I said, feeling the weight of the words. Legally,

detention couldn't be any longer than fifteen days; arrest had to be followed by a conviction and a sentence, which also had a definite term. "Just a Study Group" could be a week or a lifetime. I was left on my own in a city of eight million people, my English lessons indefinitely postponed. What was worse, some people never returned alive from "Study Groups."

47 "When are you joining them?"

48 "Tomorrow."

49 I pretended to be "man" enough not to cry, but my father's eyes were wet when he made me promise to finish *Pride and Prejudice* by the time he came back.

50 After he left for the "Study Group," bedding roll on his shoulder, I took my first careful look at the book he had thrust into my hands. It was a small book with dark green cloth covers and gilt designs and letters on its spine. I lifted the front cover; the frontispiece had a flowery design and a woman figure on the upper right corner. Floating in the middle of the flowery design and as a mother, holding a baby, she held an armful of herbs, two apples or peaches, and a scroll. Her head tilted slightly toward her right, to an opened scroll intertwined with the flowers on the other side of the page. On the unrolled scroll, there were some words. I was thrilled to find that I could understand all the words in the top two lines with no difficulty except the last word: EVERYMAN, / I WILL GO WITH THEE. . . .

51 Two months after father entered the "Study Group," I stopped going to his university for my monthly allowance. The Party secretary of the bursar's office wore me out by telling me that my father and I didn't deserve to be fed by "working people." "Your father has never done any positive work," meaning the twenty years my father taught at the university undermined rather than contributed to socialist ideology. To avoid starvation, I picked up horse droppings in the streets and sold them to the farming communes in the suburb. Between the little cash savings my father left me and what I earned by selling dung, I managed an independent life. Meanwhile, I didn't forget my promise to my father. When I saw him again nineteen months later, I boasted of having thumbed his dictionary to shreds and struggled through Austen's novel from cover to cover. I hadn't understood the story, but I had learned many words.

52 My father was not surprised to find that I took pleasure in drudgery. He knew that looking up English words in a dictionary and wrestling with an almost incomprehensible text could be an exciting challenge. It provided an intellectual relief for a teenager living at a time when the entire country read nothing but Chairman Mao's works. "Don't worry whether you are red or black," my father said. "Just be yourself. Just be an ordinary everyman. Keep up with your good work, and when you learn English well enough, you'll be sure of a guide 'in your most need.' "

Content

1. An essay of dividing its subject often draws rigid boundaries between its categories so that they are mutually exclusive. Is that true in Ning Yu's essay? Are the "reds" in total opposition to the "blacks"? If there is any overlap or intermingling among these groups, where does it occur (see, for instance, ¶ 15)? Explain your answer.
2. What sorts of comparisons can Ning Yu count on his American readers to make between his childhood, schooling, living conditions, and their own? What sorts of information does he need to supply each time he introduces an unfamiliar concept? Has he done this successfully?
3. For what reasons—political, cultural, ethical—can Ning Yu expect Western readers to be sympathetic to the plight of himself and his father? Illustrate your answer with specific examples.

Strategies/Structures/Language

4. Much of the humor in this essay depends on the students' failure to understand the English slogans their equally uncomprehending teachers oblige them to memorize. Find some examples. What would these strike English-speaking readers as funny, but not the pupils?
5. Have you ever been given a "label"—based on your race, social class, gender, political or religious affiliation, place of residence (street or area, city or town, state)? If so, what was (or is) that label? How accurate are its connotations? Are they favorable, unfavorable, or a mixture? Does the label stereotype or limit the ways people are expected to react to it? Did (or do) you feel comfortable with that label?

For Writing

6. Have you or anyone you know well ever experienced persecution or harassment—intellectual, political, economic, racial, religious, or for other reasons? If so, write a paper explaining the causes, effects, and resolution (if any) of the problem. If it's extremely complex, select one or two aspects to concentrate on in your paper. Can you count on your audience to be sympathetic to your point of view? If not, what will you need to do to win them to your side?
7. ***Journal Writing.*** Have the values of your home ever clashed with those promoted in your school or in another environment (such as a club) away from home? Did you feel torn between loyalties? Alternatively, have you, like Yu's friend Calf, helped a friend through such a conflict? Explore how conflicts between family culture and society outside the home can be both difficult and foster personal growth.
8. ***Mixed Modes.*** Because Comrade Chang's students have not been taught the English alphabet or grammar, the "hand grenades" he has them memorize (¶ 5) do not "crush the enemy" (¶ 1), but, ironically, ricochet back and frighten him. Can you find other examples of irony in Yu's narrative?
9. ***Second Look.*** Does Yu's experience of learning English suggest that there are significant differences in the process of becoming literate among cultures and nationalities? Consider how the photograph in this essay conveys the process of learning to read and write and compare it with your own experience.
10. If you or someone you know has learned English (or another language) well enough to speak and read it fluently, write a brief "Literacy Autobiography" explaining the essence and the highlights of the process.

Additional Topics for Writing Process Analysis

(For strategies for writing process analysis, see 119.)

Multiple Strategies for Writing: Process Analysis

In writing on any of the process analysis topics below, you can choose among a variety of strategies to help explain a process and interpret its consequences:

- *definitions, explanations* of terms, equipment involved in the process
- a *narrative* of how the process proceeds, from start to finish
- *illustrations* and *examples*: to show what happens, and in what sequence
- *diagrams, drawings, flow charts, graphs* to clarify and explain
- *cause* and *effect*: to show why the process is justified or recommended, with what anticipated consequences
- *comparison* and *contrast*, between your recommendation and alternative ways of achieving the same or a similar result
- consideration of *short-term* and *long-term consequences* of a particular process

1. Write an essay in which you provide directions on how to perform a process—how to do or make something at which you are particularly skilled. In addition to the essential steps, you may wish to explain your own special technique or strategy that makes your method unique or better. Some possible subjects (which may be narrowed or adapted as you and your instructor wish) are these:

a. How to get a good job, permanent or summer
b. How to live meaningfully in a post 9/11 world (See Chapter 13, "World Peace.")
c. How to contribute to a "green" world, as an individual or member of a larger group (see photo insert)
d. How to scuba dive, hang-glide, rappel, jog, lift weights, train for a marathon or triathlon
e. How to do good for others, short term or long term
f. How to be happy
g. How to stay healthy, become stronger, gain or lose weight, stop smoking (see DiFranza, 124–33) or drinking (see Sanders, 192–203)
h. How to build a library of books, music, DVDs
i. How to shop at a garage sale or secondhand store
j. How to repair your own car, bicycle, computer, or other machine
k. How to live cheaply (but enjoyably)
l. How to study for a test—in general or in a specific subject
m. How to administer first aid for choking, drowning, burns, or some other medical emergency

n. How to get rich
o. Anything else you know that others might want to learn

2. Write an informative essay in which you explain how one of the following occurs or works. Although you should pick a subject you know something about, you may need to supplement your information by consulting outside sources.

a. How I made a major decision (to be—or not to be—a member of a particular profession, to practice a particular religion or lifestyle . . .)
b. How a computer (or amplifier, piano, microwave oven, or other machine) works
c. How to save energy through using a "green" product, such as a bicycle (specify kind), hybrid car, solar heating, and show how the device works
d. How a professional develops skill in his or her chosen field—that is, how one becomes a skilled electrical engineer, geologist, chef, tennis coach, surgeon . . . ; pick a field in which you're interested
e. How birds fly (or learn to fly), or some other process in the natural world
f. How a system of the body (circulatory, digestive, respiratory, skeletal, neurological) works
g. How the earth (or the solar system) was formed
h. How the scientific method (or a particular variation of it) functions in a particular field
i. How a well-run business (pick one of your choice—manufacturing, restaurant, clothing or hardware store, television repair service . . .) functions
j. How a specific area of our federal government (or your particular local or state government legislative, executive, judicial) came into existence, or has changed over time
k. How a system or process has gone wrong (may be satiric or humorous)
l. How a particular drug or other medicine was developed and/or how it works, including its benefits and hazards
m. How a great idea (on the nature of love, justice, truth, beauty . . .) found acceptance in a particular religion, culture, or smaller group
n. How a particular culture (ethnic, regional, tribal, religious) or subculture (preppies, yuppies, pacifists, punk rockers, motorcycle gangs . . .) developed, rose, and/or declined in a larger or smaller group

3. Write a humorous paper explaining a process of the kind identified below. You will need to provide a serious analysis of the method you propose, even though the subject itself is intended to be amusing. (See Verge's "The Habs" 107–11.)

a. How to make or do anything badly or inelegantly, without expertise or ability
b. How to be popular
c. How to survive in college

d. How to survive a broken love affair
e. How to be a model babysitter/son/daughter/student/employee/lover/spouse/parent
f. How to become a celebrity
g. Any of the topics in Writing Suggestions 1 or 2 above
h. How a process can go dreadfully wrong

Cause and Effect

Writers often explore the relationships between cause and effect. Sometimes they simply list the causes (or the consequences), and then either assume the consequences (or the causes) are obvious or let the readers draw their own conclusions. This is a common strategy of short poetry. Mary Oliver's "August" (183), for example, cites many natural causes that in combination create this perfect day of acceptance of nature and acceptance of self, epitomized in "this happy tongue."

Or they can probe more intensively, asking, "*Why* did something happen?" or "*What* are its consequences?" or both. Why did the United States develop as a democracy rather than as some other form of government? What have the effects of this form of government been on its population? Or you, as a writer, may choose to examine a chain reaction in which, like a Rube Goldberg cartoon device, Cause *A* produces Effect *B*, which in turn causes *C*, which produces Effect *D*: Peer pressure (Cause *A*) causes young men to drink to excess (Effect *B*), which causes them to drive unsafely (Cause *C*, a corollary of Effect *B*) and results in high accident rates in unmarried males under age twenty-five (Effect *D*).

Process analysis can also deal with events or phenomena in sequence, focusing on the *how* rather than the *why*. To analyze the process of drinking and driving would be to explain, as an accident report might, how Al C. O'Hall became intoxicated (he drank seventeen beers and a bourbon chaser in two hours at the Dun Inn) and how he then roared off at 120 miles an hour, lost control of his lightweight sports car on a curve, and plowed into an oncoming sedan.

Two conditions have to be met to prove a given cause:

B cannot occur without *A*.
Whenever *A* occurs, *B* must also occur.

Thus a biologist who observed, repeatedly, that photosynthesis *(B)* occurred in green plants whenever a light source *(A)* was present and that it only occurred under this condition could infer that light causes photosynthesis. This would be the immediate cause. The more *remote* or *ultimate cause* might be the source of the light if it were natural (the sun). Artificial light (electricity) would have a yet more remote cause, such as water or nuclear power.

But don't be misled by a coincidental time sequence. Just because *A* preceded *B* in time doesn't necessarily mean that *A* caused *B*. Although it may appear to rain every time you wash your car, the car wash doesn't cause the rain. To blame the car wash would be an example of the *post hoc, ergo propter hoc* fallacy (Latin for "after this, therefore because of this").

Indeed, in cause-and-effect papers ultimate causes may be of greater significance than immediate ones, especially when you're considering social, political, or psychological causes rather than exclusively physical phenomena. Looking for possible causes from multiple perspectives is a good way to develop ideas to write about. It's also a sure way to avoid oversimplification, attributing a single cause to an effect that results from several. Scott Russell Sanders's analysis of his father in "Under the Influence: Paying the Price of My Father's Booze" (192–203) presents an *argument*—as well as an *explanation*—and uses *comparison and contrast* to illustrate *cause and effect*. Sanders uses the single case of his father's alcoholism and its numerous, devastating effects on his family to serve as an analysis of alcoholism in general: the secret drinking, the unsafe driving, the weaving walk, his mother's accusations, his father's rage, the children cowering in fear, the fights, the sneakiness, and the unseemly behavior. Sanders's reaction to his father's drinking, as a child who blames himself as the cause of his father's horrifying behavior, may also be generalized to describe the impact of parental drinking on many children of alcoholics: "I lie there [in bed] hating him, loving him, fearing him, knowing I have failed him. I tell myself he drinks to ease the ache . . . I must have caused by disappointing him somehow, a murderous ache I should be able to relieve by doing all my chores, earning A's in school. . . . He would not . . . drink himself to death, if only I were perfect." Readers can be counted on to recognize that Sanders's childhood explanation is inaccurate and inadequate even as they acknowledge the devastating impact of the father's alcoholism on the entire family—his articulate son in particular.

The essays in this section treat cause and effect in a variety of ways. Because causes and effects are invariably intertwined, writers usually acknowledge the causes even when they're emphasizing the effects, and vice versa.

Two of the essays in this section—as well as others (see, for instance, Sanders, "The Inheritance of Tools" [143–50] and Yu, "Red and Black, or One English Major's Beginning" [166–74])—deal with the causes and effects of education, formal and informal, on the students involved, and with the consequences of that education—or lack of it—not only to the individual, but to society. Excerpts from Zitkala-Sa's *The School Days of an Indian Girl* (184–90) illustrate a host of constraints that are placed on Native American children uprooted from their homes and sent far away to boarding schools run by whites. These are reflected in the photograph of young girls from Omaha at a boarding school in Carlisle, Pennsylvania, in the 1880s (187). Whether the efforts to acclimate these children to white middle-class culture (symbolized by cutting off their braids, making them wear Anglo clothing, and obliging them to speak English rather than their tribal languages) were made from benign or more sinister motives, the effects were the same: alienation from and marginalization in both cultures. In re-creating the child's point of view, intended to represent all children in such schools, the author does not offer solutions, though she implies them.

Megan McGuire's "Wake Up Call" (230–36) addresses the subject of her informal education. How could she grow up to be levelheaded, self-reliant, and directed toward positive goals (a college education, a military career) when reared by parents so different—from both these goals and from each other? Her father was loving but on a disability pension, and her mother was underpaid, overworked, and—at best—inattentive. McGuire shows us a number of causes and their effects and then lets us figure out the interconnections ourselves.

Sanders's account of alcoholism is personal and biographical, not medical. Atul Gawande's "On Washing Hands" (206–12) brings a down-to-earth, personal, humane perspective to a medical subject so commonplace that it is often overlooked. Although Semmelweis had to argue 150 years ago that less-than-sterile hands caused infection, today it is no longer necessary to prove this obvious causal connection. Nevertheless, the fact that every year two million Americans become afflicted with hospital-induced infections and ninety thousand die is a shocking reminder of how cause and effect are neglected. How easy, how all-too-human it is for medical personnel, in hurrying from one sick person to another, to forget to wash their hands after greeting and treating patients, opening doors, and otherwise contaminating their hands (or gloves)—and more. Gawande also shows how it is possible for hospitals to keep the necessary sanitizing equipment close at hand in patients' rooms as well as in the sterile high-stakes territory of the operating room, the only place where thorough sanitation is maintained with consistent vigilance.

The cause-and-effect process Gawande explains seems simple in comparison with the complex issues involved in the causes and the consequences of global warming. In "The Physical Science behind Climate Change" (214–28), members of the 2007 Intergovernmental Panel on Climate Change—Collins, Colman, Haywood, Manning, and Mote—"place the probability that global warming has been caused by human activities at greater than 90 percent" (in contrast with a 66 percent probability reported in 2001). They contend that rapid increases in "the atmospheric concentrations of carbon dioxide, methane and nitrous oxide" in the past two hundred (but particularly the past twenty) years have been caused mostly by humans (aerosols, ozone, aircraft contrails), and explain why in considerable detail. They also discuss "The Consequences of Ongoing Warming" (224–25), which include rising temperatures and changes in precipitation as well as the consequences of these phenomena—"the state of the ocean and the cryosphere (sea ice, the great ice sheets in Greenland and Antarctica, glaciers, snow, frozen ground, and ice on lakes and rivers)" and numerous additional consequences worldwide, as indicated by the diagram and extensive captions. In "Our Moral Footprint" (227–28), Vaclav Havel, Czech president (1993–2003) and playwright, reinforces the scientists' evidence with a humanistic plea for moral responsibility: "Technological measures and regulations are important, but equally important is support for education, ecological training and ethics—a consciousness of the commonality of all living beings and an emphasis on shared responsibility." Failure to do this won't destroy the planet, he says, but it may destroy the human race.

A paper of cause-and-effect analysis requires you, as a thoughtful and careful writer, to know your subject well enough to avoid oversimplification and to shore up your analysis with specific, convincing details. You won't be expected to explain all the causes or effects of a particular phenomenon; that might be impossible for most humans, even the experts. But you can do a sufficiently thorough job with your chosen segment of the subject to satisfy yourself and help your readers to see it your way. Maybe they'll even come to agree with your interpretation. Why? Because. . . .

Strategies for Writing: Cause and Effect

1. What is the purpose of my cause-and-effect paper? Will I be focusing on the cause(s) of something, or its effect(s), short- or long-term? Will I be using cause and effect to explain a process? Analyze a situation? Present a prediction or an argument?
2. How much does my audience know about my subject? Will I have to explain some portions of the cause-and-effect relationship in more detail than others to compensate for their lack of knowledge? Or do they have sufficient background so I can focus primarily on new information or interpretations?
3. Is the cause-and-effect relationship I'm writing about valid? Or might there be other possible causes (or effects) that I'm overlooking? If I'm emphasizing causes, how far back do I want to go? If I'm focusing on effects, how many do I wish to discuss, and with how many examples?
4. Will I be using narration, description, definition, process analysis, argument, or other strategies in my explanation or analysis of cause(s) and effect(s)?
5. How technical or nontechnical will my language be? Will I need to qualify any of my claims or conclusions with "probably," or "in most cases," or other admissions that what I'm saying is not absolutely certain? What will my tone be—explanatory, persuasive, argumentative, humorous?

MARY OLIVER

Born in Cleveland, Ohio (1935), Mary Oliver attended both Ohio State University and Vassar College. In her first book of poems, *No Voyage, and Other Poems* (1963), the influence of moderns such as Edna St. Vincent Millay, William Carlos Williams, and James Wright was clearly evident, but her distinctive style and vision emerged in *Twelve Moons* (1979); *American Primitive* (1983), which won the Pulitzer Prize; *Dream Work* (1986); *House of Light* (1990); and *New and Selected Poems* (1992), which won a National Book Award. Oliver's main poetic interest is the natural world—its landscapes and especially its wealth of living things. Yet, as she explained to the *Bloomsbury Review*, she employs nature "in an emblematic way" to explore "the human condition." Oliver shares her advice to aspiring poets in *Rules for the Dance: A Handbook for Writing and Reading Metrical Verse* (1998). Recent volumes of poetry and essays include *The Leaf and the Cloud* (2000), *Owls and other Fantasies* (2003), *Three* (2005), *Thirst: Poems* (2006), and *Our World* (2007).

In "August," from *American Primitive*, late-summer ripeness draws the poet into the brambles, compelling the reader to follow. There is a sense of rapture and realization ("there is this happy tongue"), yet the reader is left with unresolved mysteries. If, amidst the blackberries, her body "accepts what it is," what is her body, then, and what relation does it bear to the undertone of dark and black images that haunts this poem?

August

When the blackberries hang
swollen in the woods, in the brambles
nobody owns, I spend

all day among the high
branches, reaching
my ripped arms, thinking

of nothing, cramming
the black honey of summer
into my mouth; all day my body

accepts what it is. In the dark
creeks that run by there is
this thick paw of my life darting among

the black bells, the leaves; there is
this happy tongue.

ZITKALA-SA

Zitkala-Sa (1878–1938) was the first Native American woman to write her autobiography by herself, without the help of an intermediary, such as an ethnographer, translator, editor, or oral historian. This unmediated authenticity gives her work unusual authority. She was a Yankton, born on the Pine Ridge Reservation in South Dakota, daughter of a full-blooded Sioux mother and a white father.

Zitkala-Sa wrote a number of autobiographical essays to call attention to the cultural dislocation and hardships caused when the whites in power sent Native American children to boarding schools hundreds of miles away from home and imposed western culture on them. In her own case, as she explains in "The Land of Red Apples," at the age of eight she left the reservation to attend a boarding school in Wabash, Indiana, run by Quaker missionaries. On her return, "neither a wild Indian nor a tame one," her distress and cultural displacement were acute, as "Four Strange Summers" makes clear. These were originally published in *Atlantic Monthly* (1900), as portions of *Impressions of an Indian Childhood* and *The School Days of an Indian Girl*.

Zitkala-Sa remained unhappily on the reservation for four years, then returned to the Quaker school, and at nineteen enrolled in the Quaker-run Earlham College in Indiana. Her marriage to Raymond Bonnin, a Sioux, enhanced her activism for Indian rights. She served as secretary of the Society of American Indians, and also edited *American Indian Magazine*. As a lobbyist and spokesperson for the National Council of American Indians, which she founded in 1926, she helped to secure passage of the Indian Citizenship Bill and other reforms. Yet she was an integrationist, not a separatist, and attempted to forge meaningful connections between cultures.

from *The School Days of an Indian Girl*

I The Land of Red Apples

1 There were eight in our party of bronzed children who were going East with the missionaries. Among us were three young braves, two tall girls, and we three little ones, Judéwin, Thowin, and I.

2 We had been very impatient to start on our journey to the Red Apple Country, which, we were told, lay a little beyond the great circular horizon of the Western prairie. Under a sky of rosy apples we dreamt of roaming as freely and happily as we had chased the cloud shadows on the Dakota plains. We had anticipated much pleasure from a ride on the iron horse, but the throngs of staring palefaces disturbed and troubled us.

On the train, fair women, with tottering babies on each arm, stopped 3
their haste and scrutinized the children of absent mothers. Large men, with heavy bundles in their hands, halted near by, and riveted their glassy blue eyes upon us.

I sank deep into the corner of my seat, for I resented being watched. 4
Directly in front of me, children who were no larger than I hung themselves upon the backs of their seats, with their bold white faces toward me. Sometimes they took their forefingers out of their mouths and pointed at my moccasined feet. Their mothers, instead of reproving such rude curiosity, looked closely at me, and attracted their children's further notice to my blanket. This embarrassed me, and kept me constantly on the verge of tears.

I sat perfectly still, with my eyes downcast, daring only now and 5
then to shoot long glances around me. Chancing to turn to the window at my side, I was quite breathless upon seeing one familiar object. It was the telegraph pole which strode by at short paces. Very near my mother's dwelling, along the edge of a road thickly bordered with wild sunflowers, some poles like these had been planted by white men. Often I had stopped, on my way down the road, to hold my ear against the pole, and, hearing its low moaning, I used to wonder what the paleface had done to hurt it. Now I sat watching for each pole that glided by to be the last one.

In this way I had forgotten my uncomfortable surroundings, when 6
I heard one of my comrades call out my name. I saw the missionary standing very near, tossing candies and gums into our midst. This amused us all, and we tried to see who could catch the most of the sweet-meats. The missionary's generous distribution of candies was impressed upon my memory by a disastrous result which followed. I had caught more than my share of candies and gums, and soon after our arrival at the school I had a chance to disgrace myself, which, I am ashamed to say, I did.

Though we rode several days inside of the iron horse, I do not recall 7
a single thing about our luncheons.

It was night when we reached the school grounds. The lights from 8
the windows of the large buildings fell upon some of the icicled trees that stood beneath them. We were led toward an open door, where the brightness of the lights within flooded out over the heads of the excited palefaces who blocked the way. My body trembled more from fear than from the snow I trod upon.

Entering the house, I stood close against the wall. The strong glaring 9
light in the large whitewashed room dazzled my eyes. The noisy hurrying of hard shoes upon a bare wooden floor increased the whirring in my ears. My only safety seemed to be in keeping next to the wall. As I was wondering in which direction to escape from all this confusion, two warm hands grasped me firmly, and in the same moment I was tossed high in midair. A rosy-checked paleface woman caught me in her arms. I was

both frightened and insulted by such trifling. I stared into her eyes, wishing her to let me stand on my own feet, but she jumped me up and down with increasing enthusiasm. My mother had never made a plaything of her wee daughter. Remembering this I began to cry aloud.

10 They misunderstood the cause of my tears, and placed me at a white table loaded with food. There our party were united again. As I did not hush my crying, one of the older ones whispered to me, "Wait until you are alone in the night."

11 It was very little I could swallow besides my sobs, that evening.

12 "Oh, I want my mother and my brother Dawée! I want to go to my aunt!" I pleaded; but the ears of the palefaces could not hear me.

13 From the table we were taken along an upward incline of wooden boxes, which I learned afterward to call a stairway. At the top was a quiet hall, dimly lighted. Many narrow beds were in one straight line down the entire length of the wall. In them lay sleeping brown faces, which peeped just out of the coverings. I was tucked into bed with one of the tall girls, because she talked to me in my mother tongue and seemed to soothe me.

14 I had arrived in the wonderful land of rosy skies, but I was not happy, as I had thought I should be. My long travel and the bewildering sights had exhausted me. I fell asleep, heaving deep, tired sobs. My tears were left to dry themselves in streaks, because neither my aunt nor my mother was near to wipe them away.

II The Cutting of My Long Hair

15 The first day in the land of the apples was a bitter-cold one; for the snow still covered the ground, and the trees were bare. A large bell rang for breakfast, its loud metallic voice crashing through the belfry overhead and into our sensitive ears. The annoying clatter of shoes on bare floors gave us no peace. The constant clash of harsh noises, with an undercurrent of many voices murmuring an unknown tongue, made a bedlam within which I was securely tied. And though my spirit tore itself in struggling for its lost freedom, all was useless.

16 A paleface woman, with white hair, came up after us. We were placed in a line of girls who were marching into the dining room. These were Indian girls, in stiff shoes and closely clinging dresses. The small girls wore sleeved aprons and shingled hair. As I walked noiselessly in my soft moccasins, I felt like sinking to the floor, for my blanket had been stripped from my shoulders. I looked hard at the Indian girls, who seemed not to care that they were even more immodestly dressed than I, in their tightly fitting clothes. While we marched in, the boys entered at an opposite door. I watched for the three young braves who came in our party. I spied them in the rear ranks, looking as uncomfortable as I felt.

© Corbis

When was this picture taken? How do you know these girls are Native Americans? Could they be of another ethnicity, country, or culture? What attributes of white middle-class culture are manifest in this photograph? Why has their native culture been suppressed, if not eradicated? How would the school personnel—then and now—interpret the girls' clothing, postures, and hair styles?

A small bell was tapped, and each of the pupils drew a chair from under the table. Supposing this act meant they were to be seated, I pulled out mine and at once slipped into it from one side. But when I turned my head, I saw that I was the only one seated, and all the rest at our table remained standing. Just as I began to rise, looking shyly around to see how chairs were to be used, a second bell was sounded. All were seated at last, and I had to crawl back into my chair again. I heard a man's voice at one end of the hall, and I looked around to see him. But all the others hung their heads over their plates. As I glanced at the long chain of tables, I caught the eyes of a paleface woman upon me. Immediately I dropped my eyes, wondering why I was so keenly watched by the strange woman. The man ceased his mutterings, and then a third bell was tapped. Every one picked up his knife and fork and began eating. I began crying instead, for by this time I was afraid to venture anything more. 17

But this eating by formula was not the hardest trial in that first day. Late in the morning, my friend Judéwin gave me a terrible warning. Judéwin knew a few words of English; and she had overheard the paleface woman talk about cutting our long, heavy hair. Our mothers had taught us that only unskilled warriors who were captured had their hair shingled by the enemy. Among our people, short hair was worn by mourners, and shingled hair by cowards! 18

19 We discussed our fate some moments, and when Judéwin said, "We have to submit, because they are strong," I rebelled.

20 "No, I will not submit! I will struggle first!" I answered.

21 I watched my chance, and when no one noticed I disappeared. I crept up the stairs quietly as I could in my squeaking shoes,—my moccasins had been exchanged for shoes. Along the hall I passed, without knowing whither I was going. Turning aside to an open door, I found a large room with three white beds in it. The windows were covered with dark green curtains, which made the room very dim. Thankful that no one was there, I directed my steps toward the corner farthest from the door. On my hands and knees I crawled under the bed, and cuddled myself in the dark corner.

22 From my hiding place I peered out, shuddering with fear whenever I heard footsteps near by. Though in the hall loud voices were calling my name, and I knew that even Judéwin was searching for me, I did not open my mouth to answer. Then the steps were quickened and the voices became excited. The sounds came nearer and nearer. Woman and girls entered the room. I held my breath, and watched them open closet doors and peep behind large trunks. Some one threw up the curtains, and the room was filled with sudden light. What caused them to stoop and look under the bed I do not know. I remember being dragged out, though I resisted by kicking and scratching wildly. In spite of myself, I was carried downstairs and tied fast in a chair.

23 I cried aloud, shaking my head all the while until I felt the cold blades of the scissors against my neck, and heard them gnaw off one of my thick braids. Then I lost my spirit. Since the day I was taken from my mother I had suffered extreme indignities. People had stared at me. I had been tossed about in the air like a wooden puppet. And now my long hair was shingled like a coward's! In my anguish I moaned for my mother, but no one came to comfort me. Not a soul reasoned quietly with me, as my own mother used to do: for now I was only one of many little animals driven by a herder. . . .

VI Four Strange Summers*

24 After my first three years of school, I roamed again in the Western country through four strange summers.

25 During this time I seemed to hang in the heart of chaos, beyond the touch or voice of human aid. My brother, being almost ten years my senior, did not quite understand my feelings. My mother had never gone inside of a schoolhouse, and so she was not capable of comforting her daughter who could read and write. Even nature seemed to have no place for me. I was neither a wee girl nor a tall one; neither a wild Indian nor

---

* Sections III, IV, and V are omitted.

a tame one. This deplorable situation was the effect of my brief course in the East, and the unsatisfactory "teenth" in a girl's years.

It was under these trying conditions that, one bright afternoon, as I sat restless and unhappy in my mother's cabin, I caught the sound of the spirited step of my brother's pony on the road which passed by our dwelling. Soon I heard the wheels of a light buckboard, and Dawée's familiar "Ho!" to his pony. He alighted upon the bare ground in front of our house. Tying his pony to one of the projecting corner logs of the low-roofed cottage, he stepped upon the wooden doorstep. 26

I met him there with a hurried greeting, and, as I passed by, he looked a quiet "What?" into my eyes. 27

When he began talking with my mother, I slipped the rope from the pony's bridle. Seizing the reins and bracing my feet against the dashboard, I wheeled around in an instant. The pony was ever ready to try his speed. Looking backward, I saw Dawée waving his hand to me. I turned with the curve in the road and disappeared. I followed the winding road which crawled upward between the bases of little hillocks. Deep water-worn ditches ran parallel on either side. A strong wind blew against my cheeks and fluttered my sleeves. The pony reached the top of the highest hill, and began an even race on level lands. There was nothing moving within that great circular horizon of the Dakota prairies save the tall grasses, over which the wind blew and rolled off in long, shadowy waves. 28

Within this vast wigwam of blue and green I rode reckless and insignificant. It satisfied my small consciousness to see the white foam fly from the pony's mouth. 29

Suddenly, out of the earth a coyote came forth at a swinging trot that was taking the cunning thief toward the hills and the village beyond. Upon the moment's impulse, I gave him a long chase and a wholesome fright. As I turned away to go back to the village, the wolf sank down upon his haunches for a rest, for it was a hot summer day; and as I drove slowly homeward, I saw his sharp nose still pointed at me, until I vanished below the margin of the hilltops. 30

In a little while I came in sight of my mother's house. Dawée stood in the yard, laughing at an old warrior who was pointing his forefinger, and again waving his whole hand, toward the hills. With his blanket drawn over one shoulder, he talked and motioned excitedly. Dawée turned the old man by the shoulder and pointed me out to him. 31

"Oh han!" (Oh yes) the warrior muttered, and went his way. He had climbed the top of his favorite barren hill to survey the surrounding prairies, when he spied my chase after the coyote. His keen eyes recognized the pony and driver. At once uneasy for my safety, he had come running to my mother's cabin to give her warning. I did not appreciate his kindly interest, for there was an unrest gnawing at my heart. 32

As soon as he went away, I asked Dawée about something else. 33

34 "No, my baby sister. I cannot take you with me to the party to-night," he replied. Though I was not far from fifteen, and I felt that before long I should enjoy all the privileges of my tall cousin, Dawée persisted in calling me his baby sister.

35 That moonlight night, I cried in my mother's presence when I heard the jolly young people pass by our cottage. There were no more young braves in blankets and eagle plumes, nor Indian maids with prettily painted cheeks. They had gone three years to school in the East, and had become civilized. The young men wore the white man's coat and trousers, with bright neckties. The girls wore tight muslin dresses, with ribbons at neck and waist. At these gatherings they talked English. I could speak English almost as well as my brother, but I was not properly dressed to be taken along. I had no hat, no ribbons, and no close-fitting gown. Since my return from school I had thrown away my shoes, and wore again the soft moccasins.

36 While Dawée was busily preparing to go I controlled my tears. But when I heard him bounding away on his pony, I buried my face in my arms and cried hot tears.

37 My mother was troubled by my unhappiness. Coming to my side, she offered me the only printed matter we had in our home. It was an Indian Bible, given her some years ago by a missionary. She tried to console me. "Here, my child, are the white man's papers. Read a little from them," she said most piously.

38 I took it from her hand, for her sake; but my enraged spirit felt more like burning the book, which afforded me no help, and was a perfect delusion to my mother. I did not read it, but laid it unopened on the floor, where I sat on my feet. The dim yellow light of the braided muslin burning in a small vessel of oil flickered and sizzled in the awful silent storm which followed my rejection of the Bible.

39 Now my wrath against the fates consumed my tears before they reached my eyes. I sat stony, with a bowed head. My mother threw a shawl over her head and shoulders, and stepped out into the night.

40 After an uncertain solitude, I was suddenly aroused by a loud cry piercing the night. It was my mother's voice wailing among the barren hills which held the bones of buried warriors. She called aloud for her brothers' spirits to support her in her helpless misery. My fingers grew icy cold, as I realized that my unrestrained tears had betrayed my suffering to her, and she was grieving for me.

41 Before she returned, though I knew she was on her way, for she had ceased her weeping, I extinguished the light, and leaned my head on the window sill.

42 Many schemes of running away from my surroundings hovered about in my mind. A few more moons of such a turmoil drove me away to the Eastern school. I rode on the white man's iron steed, thinking it would bring me back to my mother in a few winters, when I should be grown tall, and there would be congenial friends awaiting me. . . .

Content

1. To an extent, leaving the security of home and its familiar culture to go to school, with its inevitably somewhat different culture, presents problems for any child. To what extent are Zitkala-Sa's memories of being uprooted and sent away to school similar to those of any child in a similar circumstance, and to what extent are they exacerbated by the alien culture to which she is expected to adapt?
2. What was the rationale of those in power for sending Native American children away to boarding school? Why did parents allow their children to be sent away (see "The Land of Red Apples")? In what ways did this contribute to the adulteration and breakup of Native American culture (see all sections)?
3. Historically, the Quakers have a reputation for being respectful of civil rights and very sympathetic to the preservation of minority cultures. Quaker households, for instance, were often places of shelter for slaves escaping along the Underground Railway. Was the Quaker school to which Zitkala-Sa went an exception? What factors influenced her perception of the school when she was in residence and later when she wrote about it?

Strategies/Structures/Language

4. Zitkala-Sa is writing in standard English for an educated Anglo-American audience in 1900, many of whom might never have met a Native American, and who would have known very little about their schooling. What information does she need to supply to make the context of her narrative clear? Has she done this?
5. Zitkala-Sa's readers might be expected to share the viewpoint of the school personnel, in opposition to her own point of view, both as a character in her own story and as its narrator. By what means does she try to win readers to her point of view? Is she successful?
6. What are the effects of occasional passages in the language the Anglos attribute to Native Americans? See, for example, "palefaces" (¶ 2 and *passim*); "A few *more moons*. . . . I rode on the white man's *iron steed*, thinking it would bring me back to my mother in a *few winters*" (¶ 42).

For Writing

7. ***Journal Writing.*** As Zitkala-Sa does, tell the story of an experience of cultural displacement that you or someone you know well has experienced. Identify its causes and interpret its consequences, short- and long-term.
8. ***Dialogues.*** How might the experiences of ethnic minorities such as those that Zitkala-Sa describes have contributed to the development of what Eric Liu, in "Notes of a Native Speaker" (Chapter 12), calls an "ideology of race neutrality and self-reliance" (¶ 30)? How has forced cultural assimilation helped to create a culture that Richard Rodriguez describes in "Family Values" (Chapter 7) as beset by "social breakdown" even as it celebrates economic and social freedom (¶ 7)?
9. ***Mixed Modes.*** Zitkala-Sa describes the human and cultural cost of the policy of sending Native American children to white schools. Translate some of the specific ways in which she and her community suffer into a contemporary argument

about how cultural assimilation devalues individuality and collective identity. What kind of audience would be more persuaded by such an argument than by Zitkala-Sa's autobiographical narrative? Why, in your opinion, might she have written about cultural dislocation in this way? What would have been the impact had she listed the abuses of Native American culture at the hands of European Americans in the same way that Thomas Jefferson describes the wrongs of the British King in the Declaration of Independence (Chapter 10)?

10. ***Second Look.*** Consider the different ways the photograph in this essay might be interpreted—by a contemporary white, middle-class reader, a contemporary Native American, the girls themselves, their families, a historian, an anthropologist. How might each of these "readers" interpret the girls' clothing, postures, hair styles, and facial expressions? Discuss and compare your opinions with a partner or in a small group. Can you specify the reasons for your views?

SCOTT RUSSELL SANDERS

"Under the Influence," from *Secrets of the Universe* (1991), is full of examples that describe the effects of alcoholism—on the alcoholic father, on his wife, alternately distressed and defiant, and on his children, cowering with guilt and fear. Sanders uses especially the example of himself, the eldest son, who felt responsible for his father's drinking, guilty because he couldn't get him to stop, and obligated to atone for his father's sins through his own perfection and accomplishment. Although at the age of forty-four Sanders knows that his father was "consumed by disease rather than by disappointment," he writes to understand "the corrosive mixture of helplessness, responsibility, and shame that I learned to feel as the son of an alcoholic." Through the specific example of his family's behavior, Sanders illustrates the general problem of alcoholism that afflicts some "ten or fifteen million people." He expects his readers to generalize and to learn from his understanding.

Under the Influence: Paying the Price of My Father's Booze

1 My father drank. He drank as a gut-punched boxer gasps for breath, as a starving dog gobbles food—compulsively, secretly, in pain and trembling. I use the past tense not because he ever quit drinking but because he quit living. That is how the story ends for my father, age sixty-four, heart bursting, body cooling, slumped and forsaken on the linoleum of my brother's trailer. The story continues for my brother, my sister, my mother, and me, and will continue as long as memory holds.

In the perennial present of memory, I slip into the garage or barn to see my father tipping back the flat green bottles of wine, the brown cylinders of whiskey, the cans of beer disguised in paper bags. His Adam's apple bobs, the liquid gurgles, he wipes the sandy-haired back of a hand over his lips, and then, his bloodshot gaze bumping into me, he stashes the bottle or can inside his jacket, under the workbench, between two bales of hay, and we both pretend the moment has not occurred. 2

"What's up, buddy?" he says, thick-tongued and edgy. 3

"Sky's up," I answer, playing along. 4

"And don't forget prices," he grumbles. "Prices are always up. And taxes." 5

In memory, his white 1951 Pontiac with the stripes down the hood and the Indian head on the snout lurches to a stop in the driveway; or it is the 1956 Ford station wagon, or the 1963 Rambler shaped like a toad, or the sleek 1969 Bonneville that will do 120 miles per hour on straightaways; or it is the robin's-egg-blue pickup, new in 1980, battered in 1981, the year of his death. He climbs out, grinning dangerously, unsteady on his legs, and we children interrupt our game of catch, our building of snow forts, our picking of plums, to watch in silence as he weaves past us into the house, where he drops into his overstuffed chair and falls asleep. Shaking her head, our mother stubs out a cigarette he has left smoldering in the ashtray. All evening, until our bedtimes, we tiptoe past him, as past a snoring dragon. Then we curl fearfully in our sheets, listening. Eventually he wakes with a grunt, Mother slings accusations at him, he snarls back, she yells, he growls, their voices clashing. Before long, she retreats to their bedroom, sobbing—not from the blows of fists, for he never strikes her, but from the force of his words. 6

Left alone, our father prowls the house, thumping into furniture, rummaging in the kitchen, slamming doors, turning the pages of the newspaper with a savage crackle, muttering back at the late-night drivel from television. The roof might fly off, the walls might buckle from the pressure of his rage. Whatever my brother and sister and mother may be thinking on their own rumpled pillows, I lie there hating him, loving him, fearing him, knowing I have failed him. I tell myself he drinks to ease the ache that gnaws at his belly, an ache I must have caused by disappointing him somehow, a murderous ache I should be able to relieve by doing all my chores, earning A's in school, winning baseball games, fixing the broken washer and the burst pipes, bringing in the money to fill his empty wallet. He would not hide the green bottles in his toolbox, would not sneak off to the barn with a lump under his coat, would not fall asleep in the daylight, would not roar and fume, would not drink himself to death, if only I were perfect. 7

I am forty-four, and I know full well now that my father was an alcoholic, a man consumed by disease rather than by disappointment. What had seemed to me a private grief is in fact, of course, a public 8 scourge. In the United States alone, some ten or fifteen million people share his ailment, and behind the doors they slam in fury or disgrace, countless other children tremble. I comfort myself with such knowledge, holding it against the throb of memory like an ice pack against a bruise. Other people have keener sources of grief: poverty, racism, rape, war. I do not wish to compete to determine who has suffered most. I am only trying to understand the corrosive mixture of helplessness, responsibility, and shame that I learned to feel as the son of an alcoholic. I realize now that I did not cause my father's illness, nor could I have cured it. Yet for all this grownup knowledge, I am still ten years old, my own son's age, and as that boy I struggle in guilt and confusion to save my father from pain.

9 Consider a few of our synonyms for *drunk*: tipsy, tight, pickled, soused, and plowed; stoned and stewed, lubricated and inebriated, juiced and sluiced; three sheets to the wind, in your cups, out of your mind, under the table; lit up, tanked up, wiped out; besotted, blotto, bombed, and buzzed; plastered, polluted, putrefied; loaded or looped, boozy, woozy, fuddled, or smashed; crocked and shit-faced, corked and pissed, snockered and sloshed.

10 It is a mostly humorous lexicon, as the lore that deals with drunks—in jokes and cartoons, in plays, films and television skits—is largely comic. Aunt Matilda nips elderberry wine from the sideboard and burps politely during supper. Uncle Fred slouches to the table glassy-eyed, wearing a lampshade for a hat and murmuring, "Candy is dandy, but liquor is quicker." Inspired by cocktails, Mrs. Somebody recounts the events of her day in a fuzzy dialect, while Mr. Somebody nibbles her ear and croons a bawdy song. On the sofa with Boyfriend, Daughter Somebody giggles, licking gin from her lips, and loosens the bows in her hair. Junior knocks back some brews with his chums at the Leopard Lounge and stumbles home to the wrong house, wonders foggily why he cannot locate his pajamas, and crawls naked into bed with the ugliest girl in school. The family dog slurps from a neglected martini and wobbles to the nursery, where he vomits in Baby's shoe.

11 It is all great fun. But if in the audience you notice a few laughing faces turn grim when the drunk lurches onstage, don't be surprised, for these are the children of alcoholics. Over the grinning mask of Dionysus, the leering face of Bacchus, these children cannot help seeing the bloated features of their own parents. Instead of laughing, they wince, they mourn. Instead of celebrating the drunk as one freed from constraints, they pity him as one enslaved. They refuse to believe *in vino veritas*, having seen their befuddled parents skid away from truth toward folly and oblivion. And so these children bite their lips until the lush staggers into the wings.

12 My father, when drunk, was neither funny nor honest; he was pathetic, frightening, deceitful. There seemed to be a leak in him somewhere, and

he poured in booze to keep from draining dry. Like a torture victim who refuses to squeal, he would never admit that he had touched a drop, not even in his last year, when he seemed to be dissolving in alcohol before our very eyes. I never knew him to lie about anything, ever, except about this one ruinous fact. Drowsy, clumsy, unable to fix a bicycle tire, balance a grocery sack, or walk across a room, he was stripped of his true self by drink. In a matter of minutes, the contents of a bottle could transform a brave man into a coward, a buddy into a bully, a gifted athlete and skilled carpenter and shrewd businessman into a bumbler. No dictionary of synonyms for *drunk* would soften the anguish of watching our prince turn into a frog.

Father's drinking became the family secret. While growing up, we 13
children never breathed a word of it beyond the four walls of our house. To this day, my brother and sister rarely mention it, and then only when I press them. I did not confess the ugly, bewildering fact to my wife until his wavering and slurred speech forced me to. Recently, on the seventh anniversary of my father's death, I asked my mother if she ever spoke of his drinking to friends. "No, no, never," she replied hastily. "I couldn't bear for anyone to know."

The secret bores under the skin, gets in the blood, into the bone, and 14
stays there. Long after you have supposedly been cured of malaria, the fever can flare up, the tremors can shake you. So it is with the fevers of shame. You swallow the bitter quinine of knowledge, and you learn to feel pity and compassion toward the drinker. Yet the shame lingers and, because of it, anger.

For a long stretch of my childhood we lived on a military reservation 15
in Ohio, an arsenal where bombs were stored underground in bunkers and vintage airplanes burst into flames and unstable artillery shells boomed nightly at the dump. We had the feeling, as children, that we played within a minefield, where a heedless footfall could trigger an explosion. When Father was drinking, the house, too, became a minefield. The least bump could set off either parent.

The more he drank, the more obsessed Mother became with stop- 16
ping him. She hunted for bottles, counted the cash in his wallet, sniffed at his breath. Without meaning to snoop, we children blundered left and right into damning evidence. On afternoons when he came home from work sober, we flung ourselves at him for hugs and felt against our ribs the telltale lump in his coat. In the barn we tumbled on the hay and heard beneath our sneakers the crunch of broken glass. We tugged open a drawer in his workbench, looking for screwdrivers or crescent wrenches, and spied a gleaming six-pack among the tools. Playing tag, we darted around the house just in time to see him sway on the rear stoop and heave a finished bottle into the woods. In his good-night kiss we smelled the cloying sweetness of Clorets, the mints he chewed to camouflage his dragon's breath.

17 I can summon up that kiss right now by recalling Theodore Roethke's lines about his own father:

> The whiskey on your breath
> Could make a small boy dizzy;
> But I hung on like death:
> Such waltzing was not easy.

Such waltzing was hard, terribly hard, for with a boy's scrawny arms I was trying to hold my tipsy father upright.

18 For years, the chief source of those incriminating bottles and cans was a grimy store a mile from us, a cinderblock place called Sly's, with two gas pumps outside and a mangy dog asleep in the window. Inside, on rusty metal shelves or in wheezing coolers, you could find pop and Popsicles, cigarettes, potato chips, canned soup, raunchy postcards, fishing gear, Twinkies, wine, and beer. When Father drove anywhere on errands, Mother would send us along as guards, warning us not to let him out of our sight. And so with one or more of us on board, Father would cruise up to Sly's, pump a dollar's worth of gas or plump the tires with air, and then, telling us to wait in the car, he would head for the doorway.

19 Dutiful and panicky, we cried, "Let us go with you!"

20 "No," he answered. "I'll be back in two shakes."

21 "Please!"

22 "No!" he roared. "Don't you budge or I'll jerk a knot in your tails!"

23 So we stayed put, kicking the seats, while he ducked inside. Often, when he had parked the car at a careless angle, we gazed in through the window and saw Mr. Sly fetching down from the shelf behind the cash register two green pints of Gallo wine. Father swigged one of them right there at the counter, stuffed the other in his pocket, and then out he came, a bulge in his coat, a flustered look on his reddened face.

24 Because the mom and pop who ran the dump were neighbors of ours, living just down the tar-blistered road, I hated them all the more for poisoning my father. I wanted to sneak in their store and smash the bottles and set fire to the place. I also hated the Gallo brothers, Ernest and Julio, whose jovial faces beamed from the labels of their wine, labels I would find, torn and curled, when I burned the trash. I noted the Gallo brothers' address in California and studied the road atlas to see how far that was from Ohio, because I meant to go out there and tell Ernest and Julio what they were doing to my father, and then, if they showed no mercy, I would kill them.

25 While growing up on the back roads and in the country schools and cramped Methodist churches of Ohio and Tennessee, I never heard the word *alcoholic*, never happened across it in books or magazines. In the nearby towns, there were no addiction-treatment programs, no community mental-health centers, no Alcoholics Anonymous chapters, no

therapists. Left alone with our grievous secret, we had no way of understanding Father's drinking except as an act of will, a deliberate folly or cruelty, a moral weakness, a sin. He drank because he chose to, pure and simple. Why our father, so playful and competent and kind when sober, would choose to ruin himself and punish his family we could not fathom.

Our neighborhood was high on the Bible, and the Bible was hard on drunkards. "Woe to those who are heroes at drinking wine and valiant men in mixing strong drink," wrote Isaiah. "The priest and the prophet reel with strong drink, they are confused with wine, they err in vision, they stumble in giving judgment. For all tables are full of vomit, no place is without filthiness." We children had seen those fouled tables at the local truck stop where the notorious boozers hung out, our father occasionally among them. "Wine and new wine take away the understanding," declared the prophet Hosea. We had also seen evidence of that in our father, who could multiply seven-digit numbers in his head when sober but when drunk could not help us with fourth-grade math. Proverbs warned: "Do not look at wine when it is red, when it sparkles in the cup and goes down smoothly. At the last it bites like a serpent and stings like an adder. Your eyes will see strange things, and your mind utter perverse things." Woe, woe. 26

Dismayingly often, these biblical drunkards stirred up trouble for their own kids. Noah made fresh wine after the flood, drank too much of it, fell asleep without any clothes on, and was glimpsed in the buff by his son Ham, whom Noah promptly cursed. In one passage—it was so shocking we had to read it under our blankets with flashlights—the patriarch Lot fell down drunk and slept with his daughters. The sins of the fathers set their children's teeth on edge. 27

Our ministers were fond of quoting St. Paul's pronouncement that drunkards would not inherit the kingdom of God. These grave preachers assured us that the wine referred to in the Last Supper was in fact grape juice. Bible and sermons and hymns combined to give us the impression that Moses should have brought down from the mountain another stone tablet, bearing the Eleventh Commandment: Thou shalt not drink. 28

The scariest and most illuminating Bible story apropos of drunkards was the one about the lunatic and the swine. We knew it by heart: When Jesus climbed out of his boat one day, this lunatic came charging up from the graveyard, stark naked and filthy, frothing at the mouth, so violent that he broke the strongest chains. Nobody would go near him. Night and day for years, this madman had been wailing among the tombs and bruising himself with stones. Jesus took one look at him and said, "Come out of the man, you unclean spirits!" for he could see that the lunatic was possessed by demons. Meanwhile, some hogs were conveniently rooting nearby. "If we have to come out," begged the demons, 29 "at least let us go into those swine." Jesus agreed, the unclean spirits entered the hogs, and the hogs raced straight off a cliff and plunged into a lake. Hearing the story in Sunday school, my friends thought mainly of the pigs. (How big a splash did they make? Who paid for the lost pork?) But I thought of the redeemed lunatic, who bathed himself and put on clothes and calmly sat at the feet of Jesus, restored—so the Bible said—to "his right mind."

30 When drunk, our father was clearly in his wrong mind. He became a stranger, as fearful to us as any graveyard lunatic, not quite frothing at the mouth but fierce enough, quick-tempered, explosive; or else he grew maudlin and weepy, which frightened us nearly as much. In my boyhood despair, I reasoned that maybe he wasn't to blame for turning into an ogre: Maybe, like the lunatic, he was possessed by demons.

31 If my father was indeed possessed, who would exorcise him? If he was a sinner, who would save him? If he was ill, who would cure him? If he suffered, who would ease his pain? Not ministers or doctors, for we could not bring ourselves to confide in them; not the neighbors, for we pretended they had never seen him drunk; not Mother, who fussed and pleaded but could not budge him; not my brother and sister, who were only kids. That left me. It did not matter that I, too, was only a child, and a bewildered one at that. I could not excuse myself.

32 On first reading a description of delirium tremens—in a book on alcoholism I smuggled from a university library—I thought immediately of the frothing lunatic and the frenzied swine. When I read stories or watched films about grisly metamorphoses—Dr. Jekyll and Mr. Hyde, the mild husband changing into a werewolf, the kindly neighbor inhabited by a brutal alien—I could not help but see my own father's mutation from sober to drunk. Even today, knowing better, I am attracted by the demonic theory of drink, for when I recall my father's transformation, the emergence of his ugly second self, I find it easy to believe in being possessed by unclean spirits. We never knew which version of Father would come home from work, the true or the tainted, nor could we guess how far down the slope toward cruelty he would slide.

33 How far a man *could* slide we gauged by observing our backroad neighbors—the out-of-work miners who had dragged their families to our corner of Ohio from the desolate hollows of Appalachia, the tightfisted farmers, the surly mechanics, the balked and broken men. There was, for example, whiskey-soaked Mr. Jenkins, who beat his wife and kids so hard we could hear their screams from the road. There was Mr. Lavo the wino, who fell asleep smoking time and again, until one night his disgusted wife bundled up the children and went outside and left him in his easy chair to burn; he awoke on his own, staggered out coughing into the yard, and pounded her flat while the children looked on and the shack turned to ash. There was the truck driver, Mr. Sampson, who tripped over

AP Images

What are the conspicuous features of this photograph? Where does the light fall? Why is the young woman allowing the man to pour liquor into her open mouth instead of drinking it herself? What does the onlooker's smile indicate?

his son's tricycle one night while drunk and got mad, jumped into his semi, and drove away, shifting through the dozen gears, and never came back. We saw the bruised children of these fathers clump onto our school bus, we saw the abandoned children huddle in the pews at church, we saw the stunned and battered mothers begging for help at our doors.

Our own father never beat us, and I don't think he beat Mother, but 34
he threatened often. The Old Testament Yahweh was not more terrible in His rage. Eyes blazing, voice booming, Father would pull out his belt and swear to give us a whipping, but he never followed through, never needed to, because we could imagine it so vividly. He shoved us, pawed us with the back of his hand, not to injure, just to clear a space. I can see him grabbing Mother by the hair as she cowers on a chair during a nightly quarrel. He twists her neck back until she gapes up at him, and then he lifts over her skull a glass quart bottle of milk, and milk spilling down his forearm, and he yells at her, "Say just one more word, one goddamn word, and I'll shut you up!" I fear she will prick him with her sharp tongue, but she is terrified into silence, and so am I, and the leaking bottle quivers in the air, and milk seeps through the red hair of my father's uplifted arm, and the entire scene is there to this moment, the head jerked back, the club raised.

When the drink made him weepy, Father would pack, kiss each of 35
us children on the head, and announce from the front door that he was

moving out. "Where to?" we demanded, fearful each time that he would leave for good, as Mr. Sampson had roared away for good in his diesel truck. "Someplace where I won't get hounded every minute," Father would answer, his jaw quivering. He stabbed a look at Mother, who might say, "Don't run into the ditch before you get there," or "Good riddance," and then he would slink away. Mother watched him go with arms crossed over her chest, her face closed like the lid on a box of snakes. We children bawled. Where could he go? To the truck stop, that den of iniquity? To one of those dark, ratty flophouses in town? Would he wind up sleeping under a railroad bridge or on a park bench or in a cardboard box, mummied in rags like the bums we had seen on our trips to Cleveland and Chicago? We bawled and bawled, wondering if he would ever come back.

36 He always did come back, a day or a week later, but each time there was a sliver less of him.

37 In Kafka's *Metamorphosis*, which opens famously with Gregor Samsa waking up from uneasy dreams to find himself transformed into an insect, Gregor's family keep reassuring themselves that things will be just fine again "when he comes back to us." Each time alcohol transformed our father we held out the same hope, that he would really and truly come back to us, our authentic father, the tender and playful and competent man, and then all things would be fine. We had grounds for such hope. After his tearful departures and chapfallen returns, he would sometimes go weeks, even months, without drinking. Those were glad times. Every day without the furtive glint of bottles, every meal without a fight, every bedtime without sobs encouraged us to believe that such bliss might go on forever.

38 Mother was fooled by such a hope all during the forty-odd years she knew Greeley Ray Sanders. Soon after she met him in a Chicago delicatessen on the eve of World War II and fell for his butter-melting Mississippi drawl and his wavy red hair, she learned that he drank heavily. But then so did a lot of men. She would soon coax or scold him into breaking the nasty habit. She would point out to him how ugly and foolish it was, this bleary drinking, and then he would quit. He refused to quit during their engagement, however, still refused during the first years of marriage, refused until my older sister came along. The shock of fatherhood sobered him, and he remained sober through my birth at the end of the war and right on through until we moved in 1951 to the Ohio arsenal. The arsenal had more than its share of alcoholics, drug addicts, and other varieties of escape artists. There I turned six and started school and woke into a child's flickering awareness, just in time to see my father begin sneaking swigs in the garage.

39 He sobered up again for most of a year at the height of the Korean War, to celebrate the birth of my brother. But aside from that dry spell,

his only breaks from drinking before I graduated from high school were just long enough to raise and then dash our hopes. Then during the fall of my senior year—the time of the Cuban Missile Crisis, when it seemed that the nightly explosions at the munitions dump and the nightly rages in our household might spread to engulf the globe—Father collapsed. His liver, kidneys, and heart all conked out. The doctors saved him, but only by a hair. He stayed in the hospital for weeks, going through a withdrawal so terrible that Mother would not let us visit him. If he wanted to kill himself, the doctors solemnly warned him, all he had to do was hit the bottle again. One binge would finish him.

Father must have believed them, for he stayed dry the next 40
fifteen years. It was an answer to prayer, Mother said, it was a miracle. I believe it was a reflex of fear, which he sustained over the years through courage and pride. He knew a man could die from drink, for his brother Roscoe had. We children never laid eyes on doomed Uncle Roscoe, but in the stories Mother told us he became a fairy-tale figure, like a boy who took the wrong turn in the woods and was gobbled up by the wolf.

The fifteen-year dry spell came to an end with Father's retirement 41
in the spring of 1978. Like many men, he gave up his identity along with his job. One day he was a boss at the factory, with a brass plate on his door and a reputation to uphold; the next day he was a nobody at home. He and Mother were leaving Ontario, the last of the many places to which his job had carried them, and they were moving to a new house in Mississippi, his childhood stomping ground. As a boy in Mississippi, Father sold Coca-Cola during dances while the moonshiners peddled their brew in the parking lot; as a young blade, he fought in bars and in the ring, winning a state Golden Gloves championship; he gambled at poker, hunted pheasant, raced motorcycles and cars, played semiprofessional baseball, and, along with all his buddies—in the Black Cat Saloon, behind the cotton gin, in the woods—he drank hard. It was a perilous youth to dream of recovering.

After his final day of work, Mother drove on ahead with a car full of 42
begonias and violets, while Father stayed behind to oversee the packing. When the van was loaded, the sweaty movers broke open a six-pack and offered him a beer.

"Let's drink to retirement!" they crowed. "Let's drink to freedom! to 43
fishing! hunting! loafing! Let's drink to a guy who's going home!"

At least I imagine some such words, for that is all I can do, imag- 44
ine, and I see Father's hand trembling in midair as he thinks about the fifteen sober years and about the doctors' warning, and he tells himself, *Goddamnit, I am a free man*, and *Why can't a free man drink one beer after a lifetime of hard work*? and I see his arm reaching, his fingers closing, the can tilting to his lips. I even supply a label for the beer, a swaggering brand

that promises on television to deliver the essence of life. I watch the amber liquid pour down his throat, the alcohol steal into his blood, the key turn in his brain.

45 Soon after my parents moved back to Father's treacherous stomping ground, my wife and I visited them in Mississippi with our four-year-old daughter. Mother had been too distraught to warn me about the return of the demons. So when I climbed out of the car that bright July morning and saw my father napping in the hammock, I felt uneasy, and when he lurched upright and blinked his bloodshot eyes and greeted us in a syrupy voice, I was hurled back into childhood.

46 "What's the matter with Papaw?" our daughter asked.

47 "Nothing," I said. "Nothing!"

48 Like a child again, I pretended not to see him in his stupor, and behind my phony smile I grieved. On that visit and on the few that remained before his death, once again I found bottles in the workbench, bottles in the woods. Again his hands shook too much for him to run a saw, to make his precious miniature furniture, to drive straight down back roads. Again he wound up in the ditch, in the hospital, in jail, in the treatment center. Again he shouted and wept. Again he lied. "I never touched a drop," he swore. "Your mother's making it up."

49 I no longer fancied I could reason with the men whose names I found on the bottles—Jim Beam, Jack Daniel's—but I was able now to recall the cold statistics about alcoholism: ten million victims, fifteen million, twenty. And yet, in spite of my age, I reacted in the same blind way as I had in childhood, by vainly seeking to erase through my efforts whatever drove him to drink. I worked on their place twelve and sixteen hours a day, in the swelter of Mississippi summers, digging ditches, running electrical wires, planting trees, mowing grass, building sheds, as though what nagged at him was some list of chores, as though by taking his worries upon my shoulders I could redeem him. I was flung back into boyhood, acting as though my father would not drink himself to death if only I were perfect.

50 I failed of perfection; he succeeded in dying. To the end, he considered himself not sick but sinful. "Do you want to kill yourself?" I asked him. "Why not?" he answered. "Why the hell not? What's there to save?" To the end, he would not speak about his feelings, would not or could not give a name to the beast that was devouring him.

51 In silence, he went rushing off to the cliff. Unlike the biblical swine, however, he left behind a few of the demons to haunt his children. Life with him and the loss of him twisted us into shapes that will be familiar to other sons and daughters of alcoholics. My brother became a rebel, my sister retreated into shyness, I played the stalwart and dutiful son who would hold the family together. If my father was unstable, I would

be a rock. If he squandered money on drink, I would pinch every penny. If he wept when drunk—and only when drunk—I would not let myself weep at all. If he roared at the Little League umpire for calling my pitches balls, I would throw nothing but strikes. Watching him flounder and rage, I came to dread the loss of control. I would go through life without making anyone mad. I vowed never to put in my mouth or veins any chemical that would banish my everyday self. I would never make a scene, never lash out at the ones I loved, never hurt a soul. Through hard work, relentless work, I would achieve something dazzling—in the classroom, on the basketball court, in the science lab, in the pages of books—and my achievement would distract the world's eyes from his humiliation. I would become a worthy sacrifice, and the smoke of my burning would please God.

It is far easier to recognize these twists in my character than to undo 52
them. Work has become an addiction for me, as drink was an addiction for my father. Knowing this, my daughter gave me a placard for the wall: WORKAHOLIC. The labor is endless and futile, for I can no more redeem myself through work than I could redeem my father. I still panic in the face of other people's anger, because his drunken temper was so terrible. I shrink from causing sadness or disappointment even to strangers, as though I were still concealing the family shame. I still notice every twitch of emotion in those faces around me, having learned as a child to read the weather in faces, and I blame myself for their least pang of unhappiness or anger. In certain moods I blame myself for everything. Guilt burns like acid in my veins.

I am moved to write these pages now because my own son, at the age of 53
ten, is taking on himself the griefs of the world, and in particular the griefs of his father. He tells me that when I am gripped by sadness, he feels responsible; he feels there must be something he can do to spring me from depression, to fix my life and that crushing sense of responsibility is exactly what I felt at the age of ten in the face of my father's drinking. My son wonders if I, too, am possessed. I write, therefore, to drag into the light what eats at me—the fear, the guilt, the shame—so that my own children may be spared.

I still shy away from nightclubs, from bars, from parties where 54
the solvent is alcohol. My friends puzzle over this, but it is no more peculiar than for a man to shy away from the lions' den after seeing his father torn apart. I took my own first drink at the age of twenty-one, half a glass of burgundy. I knew the odds of my becoming an alcoholic were four times higher than for the children of nonalcoholic fathers. So I sipped warily.

I still do—once a week, perhaps, a glass of wine, a can of beer, noth- 55
ing stronger, nothing more. I listen for the turning of a key in my brain.

Content

1. This essay abounds in examples of alcoholism. Which examples are the most memorable? Are these also the most painful? The most powerful? Explain why.

2. Sanders says that in spite of all his "grown-up knowledge" of alcoholism, "I am still ten years old, my own son's age" (¶ 8) as he writes this essay. What does he mean by this? What kind of a character is Sanders in this essay? What kind of a character is his father? Is there any resemblance between father and son?

Strategies/Structures/Language

3. Is Sanders writing for alcoholic readers? Their families? People unfamiliar with the symptoms of alcoholism? Or is he writing mostly for himself, to try to come to terms with the effects of his father's alcoholism on him then and now?

4. Each section of this essay (¶s 1–8, 9–14, 15–24, 25–31, 32–36, 37–44, 45–52, 53–55) focuses on a different sort of example. What are they, and why are they arranged in this particular order?

5. Why does Sanders wait until late in the essay (¶ 39) to discuss his father's sobriety, and then devote only three paragraphs to a state that lasted fifteen years?

6. What is the tone of this essay? How does Sanders, one of the victims of alcoholism as both a child and an adult, avoid being full of self-pity? Is he angry at his father? How can you tell?

For Writing

7. ***Journal Writing.*** "Father's drinking became the family secret," says Sanders (¶ 13). Every family has significant secrets. Explain one of your family secrets, illustrating its effects on various family members, particularly on yourself. If you wish to keep the secret, don't show your essay to anyone; the point of writing this is to help yourself understand or come to terms with the matter.

8. Sanders depicts the impact of his father's alcoholism on the family as a personal perspective on a social problem. Define an economic, political, ecological, social, or personal problem (unemployment, waste disposal, AIDS, hunger, housing, racism, or another subject of your choice) so your readers can understand it from an unusual perspective—your own or that of your sources. Illustrate its causes, effects, or implications with several significant examples—perhaps those of a perpetrator or victim.

9. ***Dialogues.*** In "The Inheritance of Tools" (Chapter 4), Sanders describes how his father shows him how to use force constructively. Compare the images Sanders uses to convey the idea of construction with those he uses in "Under the Influence" to convey the idea of deterioration.

10. ***Mixed Modes.*** How does Sanders's use of biblical passages that refer to drunkenness (¶s 26–28) illustrate the family's understanding of alcoholism as "an act of will" (¶ 25)? How does the story about Jesus driving the demons from the lunatic (¶ 29) help the reader understand "the fear, the guilt, the shame" the narrator has endured for so long (¶ 53)?

11. ***Second Look.*** Interpret the photograph in this essay with respect to your own experience of drinking or that of your friends. Collaborate with someone whose experiences are different from yours. What generalizations or conclusions can you draw?

ATUL GAWANDE

Atul Gawande (born in 1965 in Brooklyn) earned an MA in politics, philosophy, and economics from Oxford in 1989. From Harvard Medical School he earned an MD in 1995 and a Master's in Public Health in 1999. He holds a joint appointment at both schools, in surgery and in health policy, and is a surgeon at Brigham and Women's Hospital in Boston and a staff writer for *The New Yorker*. His collection of essays, *Complications: A Surgeon's Notes on*

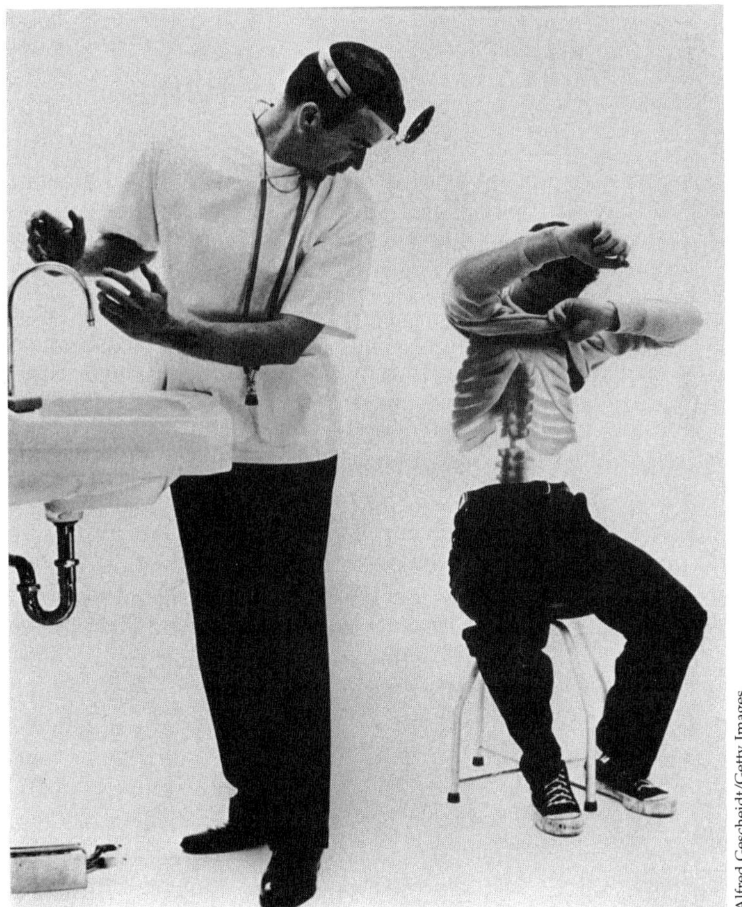

Alfred Gescheidt/Getty Images

What's going on in this photograph? What's missing?

an Imperfect Science (2002), performs "exploratory surgery on medicine itself, laying bare a science not in its idealized form but as it actually is—complicated, perplexing, profoundly human." Gawande takes readers into dramatic territory, the operating room, "where science is ambiguous, information is limited, the stakes are high, yet decisions must be made."

"On Washing Hands" first appeared in the *New England Journal of Medicine* in 2004 and is reprinted in Gawande's new book, *Better: A Surgeon's Notes on Performance* (2007). Gawande shows in this essay that hand-washing is far from a simple matter of policy; it is as complex to prescribe as it is critical to the lives of patients. Gawande shows how the work of preventing infection must overcome deeply ingrained habits and professional demands on health care workers, and he draws on the history of infectious disease to illustrate how cultural beliefs, personal antagonism, and professional competition play a crucial role in the advancement of medical knowledge.

On Washing Hands

1 One ordinary December day, I took a tour of my hospital with Deborah Yokoe, an infectious disease specialist, and Susan Marino, a microbiologist. They work in our hospital's infection-control unit. Their full-time job, and that of three others in the unit, is to stop the spread of infection in the hospital. This is not flashy work, and they are not flashy people. Yokoe is forty-five years old, gentle voiced, and dimpled. She wears sneakers at work. Marino is in her fifties and reserved by nature. But they have coped with influenza epidemics, Legionnaires' disease, fatal bacterial meningitis, and, just a few months before, a case that, according to the patient's brain-biopsy results, might have been Creutzfeld-Jakob disease—a nightmare, not only because it is incurable and fatal but also because the infectious agent that causes it, known as a prion, cannot be killed by usual heat-sterilization procedures. By the time the results came back, the neurosurgeon's brain-biopsy instruments might have transferred the disease to other patients, but infection-control team members tracked the instruments down in time and had them chemically sterilized. Yokoe and Marino have seen measles, the plague, and rabbit fever (which is caused by a bacterium that is extraordinarily contagious in hospital laboratories and feared as a bioterrorist weapon). They once instigated a nationwide recall of frozen strawberries, having traced a hepatitis A outbreak to a batch served at an ice cream social. Recently at large in the hospital, they told me, have been a rotavirus, a Norwalk virus, several strains of *Pseudomonas* bacteria, a superresistant *Klebsiella*, and the ubiquitous scourges of modern hospitals—resistant *Staphylococcus aureus* and *Enterococcus faecalis*, which are a frequent cause of pneumonias, wound infections, and bloodstream infections.

Each year, according to the U.S. Centers for Disease Control, two 2
million Americans acquire an infection while they are in the hospital. Ninety thousand die of that infection. The hardest part of the infection-control team's job, Yokoe says, is not coping with the variety of contagions they encounter or the panic that sometimes occurs among patients and staff. Instead, their greatest difficulty is getting clinicians like me to do the one thing that consistently halts the spread of infections: wash our hands.

There isn't much they haven't tried. Walking about the surgical 3
floors where I admit my patients, Yokoe and Marino showed me the admonishing signs they have posted, the sinks they have repositioned, the new ones they have installed. They have made some sinks automated. They have bought special five-thousand-dollar "precaution carts" that store everything for washing up, gloving, and gowning in one ergonomic, portable, and aesthetically pleasing package. They have given away free movie tickets to the hospital units with the best compliance. They have issued hygiene report cards. Yet still, we have not mended our ways. Our hospital's statistics show what studies everywhere else have shown—that we doctors and nurses wash our hands one-third to one-half as often as we are supposed to. Having shaken hands with a sniffling patient, pulled a sticky dressing off someone's wound, pressed a stethoscope against a sweating chest, most of us do little more than wipe our hands on our white coats and move on—to see the next patient, to scribble a note in the chart, to grab some lunch.

This is, embarassingly, nothing new. In 1847, at the age of 4
twenty-eight, the Viennese obstetrician Ignac Semmelweis famously deduced that, by not washing their hands consistently or well enough, doctors were themselves to blame for childbed fever. Childbed fever, also known as puerperal fever, was the leading cause of maternal death in childbirth in the era before antibiotics (and before the recognition that germs are the agents of infectious disease). It is a bacterial infection—most commonly caused by *Streptococcus*, the same bacteria that causes strep throat—that ascends through the vagina to the uterus after childbirth. Out of three thousand mothers who delivered babies at the hospital where Semmelweis worked, six hundred or more died of the disease each year—a horrifying 20 percent maternal death rate. Of mothers delivering at home, only 1 percent died. Semmelweis concluded that doctors themselves were carrying the disease between patients, and he mandated that every doctor and nurse on his ward scrub with a nail brush and chlorine between patients. The puerperal death rate immediately fell to 1 percent—incontrovertible proof, it would seem, that he was right. Yet elsewhere, doctors' practices did not change. Some colleagues were even offended by his claims; it was impossible to them that doctors could be killing their patients. Far from being hailed, Semmelweis was ultimately dismissed from his job.

5 Semmelweis's story has come down to us as Exhibit A in the case for the obstinacy and blindness of physicians. But the story was more complicated. The trouble was partly that nineteenth-century physicians faced multiple, seemingly equally powerful explanations for puerperal fever. There was, for example, a strong belief that miasmas of the air in hospitals were the cause. And Semmelweis strangely refused to either publish an explanation of the logic behind his theory or prove it with a convincing experiment in animals. Instead, he took the calls for proof as a personal insult and attacked his detractors viciously.

6 "You, Herr Professor, have been a partner in this massacre," he wrote to one University of Vienna obstetrician who questioned his theory. To a colleague in Wurzburg he wrote, "Should you, Herr Hofrath, without having disproved my doctrine, continue to teach your pupils [against it], I declare before God and the world that you are a murderer and the 'History of Childbed Fever' would not be unjust to you if it memorialized you as a medical Nero." His own staff turned against him. In Pest, where he relocated after losing his post in Vienna, he would stand next to the sink and berate anyone who forgot to scrub his or her hands. People began to purposely evade, sometimes even sabotage, his hand-washing regimen. Semmelweis was a genius, but he was also a lunatic, and that made him a failed genius. It was another twenty years before Joseph Lister offered his clearer, more persuasive, and more respectful plea for antisepsis in surgery in the British medical journal *Lancet*.

7 One hundred and forty years of doctors' plagues later, however, you have to wonder whether what's needed to stop them is precisely a lunatic. Consider what Yokoe and Marino are up against. No part of human skin is spared from bacteria. Bacterial counts on the hands range from five thousand to five million colony-forming units per square centimeter. The hair, underarms, and groin harbor greater concentrations. On the hands, deep skin crevices trap 10 to 20 percent of the flora, making removal difficult, even with scrubbing, and sterilization impossible. The worst place is under the fingernails. Hence the recent CDC guidelines requiring hospital personnel to keep their nails trimmed to less than a quarter of an inch and to remove artificial nails.

8 Plain soaps do, at best, a middling job of disinfecting. Their detergents remove loose dirt and grime, but fifteen seconds of washing reduces bacterial counts by only about an order of magnitude. Semmelweis recognized that ordinary soap was not enough and used a chlorine solution to achieve disinfection. Today's antibacterial soaps contain chemicals such as chlorhexidine to disrupt microbial membranes and proteins. Even with the right soap, however, proper hand washing requires a strict procedure. First, you must remove your watch, rings, and other jewelry (which are notorious for trapping bacteria). Next, you wet your hands in warm tap water. Dispense the soap and lather all

surfaces, including the lower one-third of the arms, for the full duration recommended by the manufacturer (usually fifteen to thirty seconds). Rinse off for thirty full seconds. Dry completely with a clean, disposable towel. Then use the towel to turn the tap off. Repeat after any new contact with a patient.

Almost no one adheres to this procedure. It seems impossible. On morning rounds, our residents check in on twenty patients in an hour. The nurses in our intensive care units typically have a similar number of contacts with patients requiring hand washing in between. Even if you get the whole cleansing process down to a minute per patient, that's still a third of staff time spent just washing hands. Such frequent hand washing can also irritate the skin, which can produce a dermatitis, which itself increases bacterial counts. 9

Less irritating than soap, alcohol rinses and gels have been in use in Europe for almost two decades but for some reason only recently caught on in the United States. They take far less time to use—only about fifteen seconds or so to rub a gel over the hands and fingers and let it air-dry. Dispensers can be put at the bedside more easily than a sink. And at alcohol concentrations of 50 to 95 percent, they are more effective at killing organisms, too. (Interestingly, pure alcohol is not as effective—at least some water is required to denature microbial proteins.) 10

Still, it took Yokoe over a year to get our staff to accept the 60 percent alcohol gel we have recently adopted. Its introduction was first blocked because of the staff's fears that it would produce noxious building air. (It didn't.) Next came worries that, despite evidence to the contrary, it would be more irritating to the skin. So a product with aloe was brought in. People complained about the smell. So the aloe was taken out. Then some of the nursing staff refused to use the gel after rumors spread that it would reduce fertility. The rumors died only after the infection-control unit circulated evidence that the alcohol is not systemically absorbed and a hospital fertility specialist endorsed the use of the gel. 11

With the gel finally in wide use, the compliance rates for proper hand hygiene improved substantially: from around 40 percent to 70 percent. But—and this is the troubling finding—hospital infection rates did not drop one iota. Our 70 percent compliance just wasn't good enough. If 30 percent of the time people didn't wash their hands, that still left plenty of opportunity to keep transmitting infections. Indeed, the rates of resistant *Staphylococcus* and *Enterococcus* infections continued to rise. Yokoe receives the daily tabulations. I checked with her one day not long ago, and sixty-three of our seven hundred hospital patients were colonized or infected with MRSA (the shorthand for methicillin-resistant *Staphylococcus aureus*) and another twenty-two had acquired VRE (vancomycin-resistant *Enterococcus*)—unfortunately, typical rates of infection for American hospitals. 12

13 Rising infection rates from superresistant bacteria have become the norm around the world. The first outbreak of VRE did not occur until 1988, when a renal dialysis unit in England became infested. By 1990, the bacteria had been carried abroad, and four in one thousand American ICU patients had become infected. By 1997, a stunning 23 percent of ICU patients were infected. When the virus for SARS—severe acute respiratory syndrome—appeared in China in 2003 and spread within weeks to almost ten thousand people in two dozen countries across the world (10 percent of whom were killed), the primary vector for transmission was the hands of health care workers. What will happen if (or rather, when) an even more dangerous organism appears—avian flu, say, or a new, more virulent bacteria? "It will be a disaster," Yokoe says.

14 Anything short of a Semmelweis-like obsession with hand washing has begun to seem inadequate. . . .

15 We always hope for the easy fix: the one simple change that will erase a problem in a stroke. But few things in life work this way. Instead, success requires making a hundred small steps go right—one after the other, no slipups, no goofs, everyone pitching in. We are used to thinking of doctoring as a solitary, intellectual task. But making medicine go right is less often like making a difficult diagnosis than like making sure everyone washes their hands.

16 It is striking to consider how different the history of the operating room after Lister has been from that of the hospital floor after Semmelweis. In the operating room, no one pretends that even 90 percent compliance with scrubbing is good enough. If a single doctor or nurse fails to wash up before coming to the operating table, we are horrified—and certainly not shocked if the patient develops an infection a few days later. Since Lister we have gone even further in our expectations. We now make sure to use sterile gloves and gowns, masks over our mouths, caps over our hair. We apply antiseptics to the patient's skin and lay down sterile drapes. We put our instruments through steam heat sterilizers or, if any are too delicate to tolerate the autoclave, through chemical sterilizers. We have reinvented almost every detail of the operating room for the sake of antisepsis. We have gone so far as to add an extra person to the team, known as the circulating nurse, whose central job is, essentially, to keep the team antiseptic. Every time an unanticipated instrument is needed for a patient, the team can't stand around waiting for one member to break scrub, pull the thing off a shelf, wash up, and return. So the circulator was invented. Circulators get the extra sponges and instruments, handle the telephone calls, do the paperwork, get help when it's needed. And every time they do, they're not just making the case go more smoothly. They are keeping the patient uninfected. By their very existence, they make sterility a priority in every case.

Stopping the epidemics spreading in our hospitals is not a problem of ignorance—of not having the know-how about what to do. It is a problem of compliance—a failure of an individual to apply that know-how correctly. But achieving compliance is hard. Why, after 140 years, the meticulousness of the operating room has not spread beyond its double doors is a mystery. But the people who are most careful in the surgical theater are frequently the very ones who are least careful on the hospital ward. I know because I have realized I am one of them. I generally try to be as scrupulous about washing my hands when I am outside the operating room as I am inside. And I do pretty well, if I say so myself. But then I blow it. It happens almost every day. I walk into a patient's hospital room, and I'm thinking about what I have to tell him concerning his operation, or about his family, who might be standing there looking worried, or about the funny little joke a resident just told me, and I completely forget about getting a squirt of that gel into my palms, no matter how many laminated reminder signs have been hung on the walls. Sometimes I do remember, but before I can find the dispenser, the patient puts his hand out in greeting and I think it too strange not to go ahead and take it. On occasion I even think, Screw it—I'm late, I have to get a move on, and what difference does it really make what I do this one time? 17

A few years ago, Paul O'Neill, the former secretary of the Treasury and CEO of the aluminum giant Alcoa, agreed to take over as head of a regional health care initiative in Pittsburgh, Pennsylvania. And he made solving the problem of hospital infections one of his top priorities. To show it could be solved, he arranged for a young industrial engineer named Peter Perreiah to be put on a single forty-bed surgical unit at a Pittsburgh veterans hospital. When he met with the unit's staff, a doctor who worked on the project told me, "Peter didn't ask, 'Why don't you wash your hands?' He asked, 'Why can't you?'" By far the most common answer was time. So, as an engineer, he went about fixing the things that burned up the staff's time. He came up with a just-in-time supply system that kept not only gowns and gloves at the bedside but also gauze and tape and other things the staff needed, so they didn't have to go back and forth out of the room to search for them. Rather than make everyone clean their stethoscopes, notorious carriers of infection, between patients, he arranged for each patient room to have a designated stethoscope on the wall. He helped make dozens of simplifying changes that reduced both the opportunities for spread of infection and the difficulties of staying clean. He made each hospital room work more like an operating room, in other words. He also arranged for a nasal culture to be taken from every patient upon admission, whether the patient seemed infected or not. That way the staff knew which 18 patients carried resistant bacteria and could preemptively use more stringent precautions for them—"search-and-destroy" the strategy is sometimes called. Infection rates for MRSA—the hospital contagion responsible for more deaths than any other—fell almost 90 percent, from four to six infections per month to about that many in an entire year. . . .

19 At one point during my tour with Yokoe and Marino, we walked through a regular hospital unit. And I finally began to see the ward the way they do. Flowing in and out of the patients' rooms were physical therapists, patient care assistants, nurses, nutritionists, residents, students. Some were good about washing. Some were not. Yokoe pointed out that three of the eight rooms had bright yellow precaution signs because of patients inside with MRSA or VRE. Only then did I realize we were on the floor of one of my own patients. One of those signs hung on his door.

20 He was sixty-two years old and had been in the hospital for almost three weeks. He had arrived in shock from another hospital, where an operation had gone awry. I performed an emergency splenectomy for him and then had to go back in again when the bleeding still didn't stop. He had an open abdominal wound and could not eat. He had to receive his nutrition intravenously. He was recovering, though. Three days after admission, he was out of the intensive care unit. Initial surveillance cultures were completely negative for resistant organisms. New cultures ten days after admission, however, came back positive for both MRSA and VRE. A few days after that, he developed fevers up to 102 degrees. His blood pressure began dropping. His heart rate climbed. He was septic. His central line—his lifeline for nutrition—had become infected, and we had to take it out.

21 Until that moment, when I stood there looking at the sign on his door, it had not occurred to me that I might have given him that infection. But the truth is I may have. One of us certainly did.

Content

1. Why, according to Gawande, do bacteria spread so easily (¶s 1, 7–8)?
2. Why do hospital workers resist efforts to improve hygiene? Why are operating room standards so much better and more strictly enforced than elsewhere in the hospital?
3. How does the story of Ignac Semmelweis's campaign to promote hand-washing (¶s 4–6) help explain the contemporary problem of ensuring that health-care workers thoroughly and regularly wash their hands?
4. What might be some of the difficulties in implementing the protocol for preventing the spread of infection developed by Peter Perreiah (¶ 18)? Would his system reduce the need for frequent hand-washing?

Strategies/Structures/Language

5. How does Gawande's description of a typical day in his life as a surgeon help the reader understand the problem of compliance with hygiene protocol (¶ 17)?

6. Why does Gawande begin and end his essay with the two members of his hospital's infection-control unit? Why does he end with the description of his own patient (¶s 20–22)?

For Writing

7. ***Journal Writing.*** Gawande describes some of the fears, prejudices, and habits that have hindered the regular use of alcohol gel among hospital staff. Why, in your opinion, are many individuals reluctant to follow expert advice? Have you or someone you know followed expert advice that turned out, in retrospect, to be right (or wrong)? What were the consequences of following or not following that advice?

8. ***Mixed Modes.*** Gawande observes that while thorough hand-washing or the use of alcohol gel is the single most important way to stop the spread of infection, campaigns to improve hygiene compliance often fail to check infections. Compare the steps followed in a hospital operating room to keep it antiseptic (¶ 16) with the system Perreiah developed (¶ 18) to reduce infections outside the operating room. How do they differ? Are the two protocols complementary?

9. ***Second Look.*** How might the image in this essay illustrate Gawande's surprise at discovering that one of the patients in the hospital with an infection was his own (¶s 20–22)? What potential sites of infection does this photograph include? What does the photograph suggest about the doctor-patient relationship?

10. Research the history of particular and significant medical advancements such as the development of vaccines or anesthesia; therapies to treat mental health problems such as addiction or war-related disorders; knowledge of preventive care such as nutrition; or the emergence of a professional specialty such as nursing. What role did particular scientists or other historical figures play in the diffusion and application of this knowledge? Did "the obstinacy and blindness" (¶ 5) of a group of individuals hinder the spread of this advance? Did the advance require people to change their behavior?

11. Gawande argues that although every year "two million Americans acquire an infection while they are in the hospital," the hardest task of a hospital infection-control team is "getting clinicians like me to do the one thing that consistently halts the spread of infections: wash our hands" (¶ 2). How can the public ensure that health care providers develop effective public health policies—and enforce them—such as reducing infections through hygiene protocol? Write an essay that addresses a public health concern and the role of health care providers or other institutions such as schools (see Joseph DiFranza's "Hooked from the First Cigarette," Chapter 4, or Marion Nestle's "Eating Made Simple," Chapter 6), and offer suggestions for how to resolve the problem. Write a letter either to your representative in the state legislature or Congress in which you analyze the problem and propose an action plan. Send a copy to the editor of your local newspaper.

CLIMATE CHANGE

WILLIAM COLLINS, ROBERT COLMAN, JAMES HAYWOOD, MARTIN R. MANNING, AND PHILIP MOTE

These authors were members of Working Group I of the Intergovernmental Panel on Climate Change (IPCC), which in 2007 presented the "fourth in a series of assessments of the state of knowledge" on climate change, "written and reviewed by hundreds of scientists worldwide." William Collins is a professor in the Department of Earth and Planetary Science at the University of California, Berkeley, and a senior scientist at Lawrence Berkeley National Laboratory and the National Center for Atmospheric Research in Boulder, Colorado. Robert Colman is a senior research scientist in the Climate Dynamics Group at the Australian Bureau of Meteorology Research Center in Melbourne. James Haywood is the manager of aerosol research in the Observational Based Research Group and the Chemistry, Climate, and Ecosystem Group at the Met Office in Exeter, England. Martin R. Manning is director of the IPCC WG I Support Unit at the National Oceanic and Atmospheric Administration Earth System Research Laboratory in Boulder, Colorado. Philip Mote is the climatologist of the state of Washington, and a research scientist in the Climate Impacts Group at the University of Washington.

These scientists coauthored both the longer report identified above and the analysis of "The Physical Science behind Climate Change," reprinted here from *Scientific American* (2007). They address critical issues relating to the fundamental question, "Are human activities primarily responsible for observed climate changes or might these be the result of some other cause?" and the implications of the fact that there is a 90% probability that humans are causing the problems.

*The Physical Science behind Climate Change**

1 For a scientist studying climate change, "eureka" moments are unusually rare. Instead progress is generally made by a painstaking piecing together of evidence from every new temperature measurement, satellite sounding or climate-model experiment. Data get checked and rechecked, ideas tested over and over again. Do the observations fit the predicted

* William Collins, Robert Colman, James Haywood, Martin R. Manning, and Philip Mote, "The Physical Science behind Climate Change," SCIENTIFIC AMERICAN, August 2007. Reprinted with permission. Copyright © 2007 by SCIENTIFIC AMERICAN, Inc. All rights reserved.

changes? Could there be some alternative explanation? Good climate scientists, like all good scientists, want to ensure that the highest standards of proof apply to everything they discover.

And the evidence of change *has* mounted as climate records have grown longer, as our understanding of the climate system has improved and as climate models have become ever more reliable. Over the past 20 years, evidence that humans are affecting the climate has accumulated inexorably, and with it has come ever greater certainty across the scientific community in the reality of recent climate change and the potential for much greater change in the future. This increased certainty is starkly reflected in the latest report of the Intergovernmental Panel on Climate Change (IPCC), the fourth in a series of assessments of the state of knowledge on the topic, written and reviewed by hundreds of scientists worldwide. 2

The panel released a condensed version of the first part of the report, on the physical science basis of climate change, in February. Called the "Summary for Policymakers," it delivered to policymakers and ordinary people alike an unambiguous message: scientists are more confident than ever that humans have interfered with the climate and that further 3

Jargon Buster

RADIATIVE FORCING . . . is the change in the energy balance of the earth from preindustrial times to the present.

LONG-LIVED GREENHOUSE GASES include carbon dioxide, methane, nitrous oxide and halocarbons. The observed increases in these gases are the result of human activity.

OZONE is a gas that occurs both in the earth's upper atmosphere and at ground level. At ground level ozone is an air pollutant. In the upper atmosphere, an ozone layer protects life on the earth from the sun's harmful ultraviolet rays.

SURFACE ALBEDO is the reflectivity of the earth's surface: a lighter surface, such as snow cover, reflects more solar radiation than a darker surface does.

AEROSOLS are airborne particles that come from both natural (dust storms, forest fires, volcanic eruptions) and man-made sources, such as the burning of fossil fuels.

CONTRAILS, or vapor trails, are condensation trails and artificial clouds made by the exhaust of aircraft engines.

TROPOSPHERE is the layer of the atmosphere close to the earth. It rises from sea level up to about 12 kilometers (7.5 miles).

STRATOSPHERE lies just above the troposphere and extends upward about 50 kilometers.

human-induced climate change is on the way. Although the report finds that some of these further changes are now inevitable, its analysis also confirms that the future, particularly in the longer term, remains largely in our hands—the magnitude of expected change depends on what humans choose to do about greenhouse gas emissions.

4 The physical science assessment focuses on four topics: drivers of climate change, changes observed in the climate system, understanding cause-and-effect relationships, and projection of future changes. Important advances in research into all these areas have occurred since the IPCC assessment in 2001. In the pages that follow, we lay out the key findings that document the extent of change and that point to the unavoidable conclusion that human activity is driving it.

Drivers of Climate Change

5 Atmospheric concentrations of many gases—primarily carbon dioxide, methane, nitrous oxide and halocarbons (gases once used widely as refrigerants and spray propellants)—have increased because of human activities. Such gases trap thermal energy (heat) within the atmosphere by means of the well-known greenhouse effect, leading to global warming. The atmospheric concentrations of carbon dioxide, methane and nitrous oxide remained roughly stable for nearly 10,000 years, before the abrupt and rapidly accelerating increases of the past 200 years [*see right illustrations in box on 217*]. Growth rates for concentrations of carbon dioxide have been faster in the past 10 years than over any 10-year period since continuous atmospheric monitoring began in the 1950s, with concentrations now roughly 35 percent above preindustrial levels (which can be determined from air bubbles trapped in ice cores). Methane levels are roughly two and a half times preindustrial levels, and nitrous oxide levels are around 20 percent higher.

6 How can we be sure that humans are responsible for these increases? Some greenhouse gases (most of the halocarbons, for example) have no natural source. For other gases, two important observations demonstrate human influence. First, the geographic differences in concentrations reveal that sources occur predominantly over land in the more heavily populated Northern Hemisphere. Second, analysis of isotopes, which can distinguish among sources of emissions, demonstrates that the majority of the increase in carbon dioxide comes from combustion of fossil fuels (coal, oil and natural gas). Methane and nitrous oxide increase derive from agricultural practices and the burning of fossil fuels.

7 Climate scientists use a concept called radiative forcing to quantify the effect of these increased concentrations on climate. Radiative forcing is the change that is caused in the global energy balance of the earth relative to preindustrial times. (Forcing is usually expressed as watts per

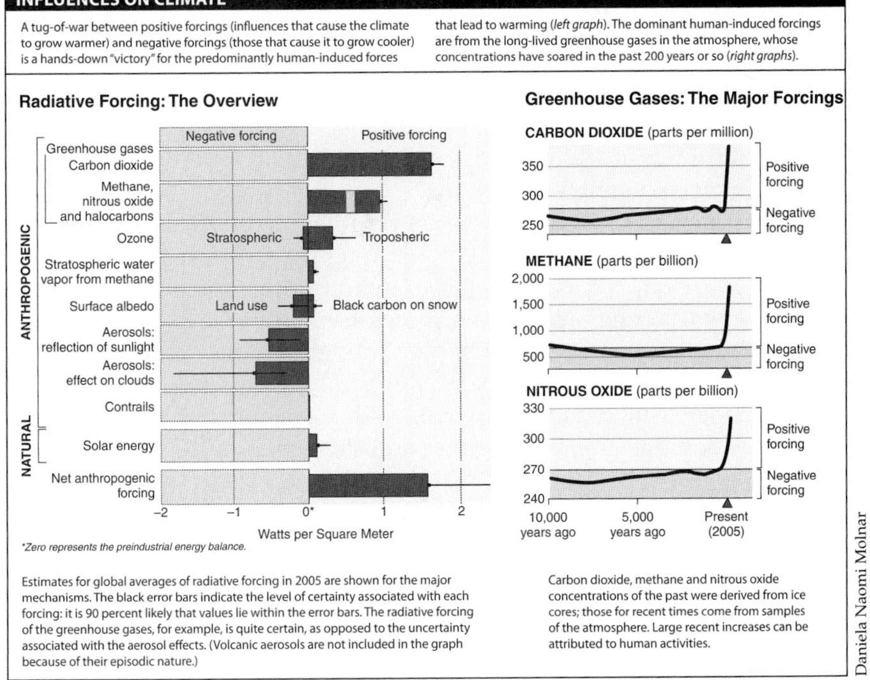

square meter.) A positive forcing induces warming; a negative forcing induces cooling. We can determine the radiative forcing associated with the long-lived greenhouse gases fairly precisely, because we know their atmospheric concentrations, their spatial distribution and the physics of their interaction with radiation.

Climate change is not driven just by increased greenhouse gas 8
concentrations; other mechanisms—both natural and human-induced—also play a part. Natural drivers include changes in solar activity and large volcanic eruptions. The report identifies several additional significant human-induced forcing mechanisms—microscopic particles called aerosols, stratospheric and tropospheric ozone, surface albedo (reflectivity) and aircraft contrails—although the influences of these mechanisms are much less certain than those of greenhouse gases [*see left illustration in box above*].

Investigators are least certain of the climatic influence of something 9
called the aerosol cloud albedo effect, in which aerosols from human origins interact with clouds in complex ways and make the clouds brighter, reflecting sunlight back to space. Another source of uncertainty comes from the direct effect of aerosols from human origins: How much do they reflect and absorb sunlight directly as particles? Overall these aerosol effects promote cooling that could offset the warming effect of long-lived greenhouse gases to some extent. But by how much? Could it overwhelm

the warming? Among the advances achieved since the 2001 IPCC report is that scientists have quantified the uncertainties associated with each individual forcing mechanism through a combination of many modeling and observational studies. Consequently, we can now confidently estimate the total human-induced component. Our best estimate is some 10 times larger than the best estimate of the natural radiative forcing caused by changes in solar activity.

10 This increased certainty of a net positive radiative forcing fits well with the observational evidence of warming discussed next. These forcings can be visualized as a tug-of-war, with positive forcings pulling the earth to a warmer climate and negative ones pulling it to a cooler state. The result is a no contest; we know the strength of the competitors better than ever before. The earth is being pulled to a warmer climate and will be pulled increasingly in this direction as the "anchorman" of greenhouse warming continues to grow stronger and stronger.

Observed Climate Changes

11 The many new or improved observational data sets that became available in time for the 2007 IPCC report allowed a more comprehensive assessment of changes than was possible in earlier reports. Observational records indicate that 11 of the past 12 years are the warmest since reliable records began around 1850. The odds of such warm years happening in sequence purely by chance are exceedingly small. Changes in three important quantities—global temperature, sea level and snow cover in the Northern Hemisphere [*see box on 220*]—all show evidence of warming, although the details vary. The previous IPCC assessment reported a warming trend of 0.6 ± 0.2 degree Celsius over the period 1901 to 2000. Because of the strong recent warming, the updated trend over 1906 to 2005 is now 0.74 ± 0.18 degree C. Note that the 1956 to 2005 trend alone is 0.65 ± 0.15 degree C, emphasizing that the majority of 20th-century warming occurred in the past 50 years. The climate, of course, continues to vary around the increased averages, and extremes have changed consistently with these averages—frost days and cold days and nights have become less common, while heat waves and warm days and nights have become more common.

12 The properties of the climate system include not just familiar concepts of averages of temperature, precipitation, and so on but also the state of the ocean and the cryosphere (sea ice, the great ice sheets in Greenland and Antarctica, glaciers, snow, frozen ground, and ice on lakes and rivers). Complex interactions among different parts of the climate system are a fundamental part of climate change—for example, reduction in sea ice increases the absorption of heat by the ocean and the heat flow between the ocean and the atmosphere, which can also affect cloudiness and precipitation.

13 A large number of additional observations are broadly consistent with the observed warming and reflect a flow of heat from the atmosphere

into other components of the climate system. Spring snow cover, which decreases in concert with rising spring temperatures in northern midlatitudes, dropped abruptly around 1988 and has remained low since. This drop is of concern because snow cover is important to soil moisture and water resources in many regions.

In the ocean, we clearly see warming trends, which decrease with 14
depth, as expected. These changes indicate that the ocean has absorbed more than 80 percent of the heat added to the climate system: this heating is a major contributor to sea-level rise. Sea level rises because water expands as it is warmed and because water from melting glaciers and ice sheets is added to the oceans. Since 1993 satellite observations have permitted more precise calculations of global sea-level rise, now estimated to be 3.1 ± 0.7 millimeters per year over the period 1993 to 2003. Some previous decades displayed similarly fast rates, and longer satellite records will be needed to determine unambiguously whether sea-level rise is accelerating. Substantial reductions in the extent of Arctic sea ice since 1978 (2.7 ± 0.6 percent per decade in the annual average, 7.4 ± 2.4 percent per decade for summer), increases in permafrost temperatures and reductions in glacial extent globally and in Greenland and Antarctic ice sheets have also been observed in recent decades. Unfortunately, many of these quantities were not well monitored until recent decades, so the starting points of their records vary.

Hydrological changes are broadly consistent with warming as 15
well. Water vapor is the strongest greenhouse gas; unlike other greenhouse gases, it is controlled principally by temperature. It has generally increased since at least the 1980s. Precipitation is very variable locally but has increased in several large regions of the world, including eastern North and South America, northern Europe, and northern and central Asia. Drying has been observed in the Sahel, the Mediterranean, southern Africa and parts of southern Asia. Ocean salinity can act as a massive rain gauge. Near-surface waters of the oceans have generally freshened in middle and high latitudes, while they have become saltier in lower latitudes, consistent with changes in large-scale patterns of precipitation.

Reconstructions of past climate—paleoclimate—from tree rings and 16
other proxies provide important additional insights into the workings of the climate system with and without human influence. They indicate that the warmth of the past half a century is unusual in at least the previous 1,300 years. The warmest period between A.D. 700 and 1950 was probably A.D. 950 to 1100, which was several tenths of a degree C cooler than the average temperature since 1980.

Attribution of Observed Changes

Although confidence is high both that human activities have caused 17
a positive radiative forcing and that the climate has actually changed, can we confidently link the two? This is the question of attribution: Are

human activities primarily responsible for observed climate changes, or is it possible they result from some other cause, such as some natural forcing or simply spontaneous variability within the climate system? The 2001 IPCC report concluded it was *likely* (more than 66 percent probable) that most of the warming since the mid-20th century was attributable to humans. The 2007 report goes significantly further, upping this to *very likely* (more than 90 percent probable).

18 The source of the extra confidence comes from a multitude of separate advances. For a start, observational records are now roughly five years longer, and the global temperature increase over this period has been largely consistent with IPCC projections of greenhouse gas–driven warming made in previous reports dating back to 1990. In addition, changes in more aspects of the climate have been considered, such as those in atmospheric circulation or in temperatures within the ocean. Such changes paint a consistent and now broadened picture of human intervention. Climate models, which

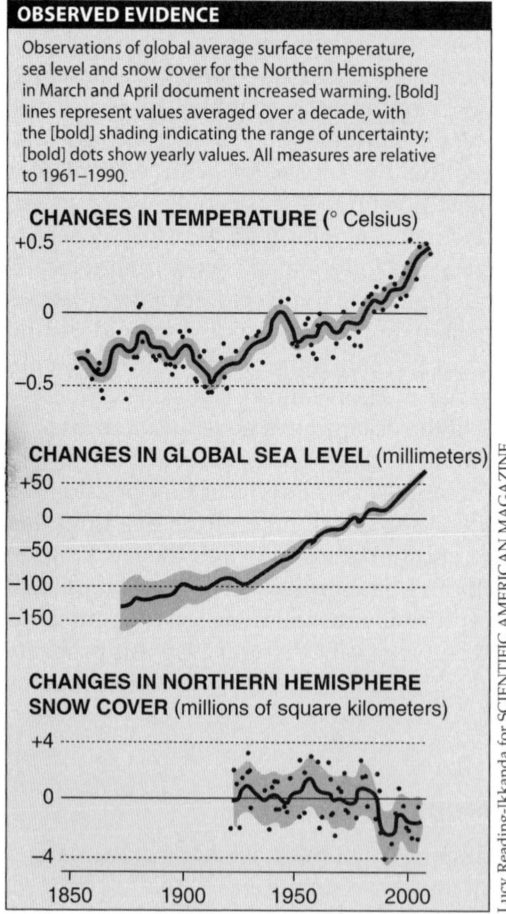

Lucy Reading-Ikkanda for SCIENTIFIC AMERICAN MAGAZINE.

are central to attribution studies, have also improved and are able to represent the current climate and that of the recent past with considerable fidelity. Finally, some important apparent inconsistencies noted in the observational record have been largely resolved since the last report.

The most important of these was an apparent mismatch between the instrumental surface temperature record (which showed significant warming over recent decades, consistent with a human impact) and the balloon and satellite atmospheric records (which showed little of the expected warming). Several new studies of the satellite and balloon data have now largely resolved this discrepancy—with consistent warming found at the surface and in the atmosphere. 19

An experiment with the real world that duplicated the climate of the 20th century with constant (rather than increasing) greenhouse gases would be the ideal way to test for the cause of climate change, but such an experiment is of course impossible. So scientists do the next best thing: they simulate the past with climate models. 20

Two important advances since the last IPCC assessment have increased confidence in the use of models for both attribution and projection of climate changes. The first is the development of a comprehensive, closely coordinated ensemble of simulations from 18 modeling groups around the world for the historical and future evolution of the earth's climate. Using many models helps to quantify the effects of uncertainties in various climate processes on the range of model simulations. Although some processes are well understood and well represented by physical equations (the flow of the atmosphere and ocean or the propagation of sunlight and heat, for example), some of the most critical components of the climate system are less well understood, such as clouds, ocean eddies and transpiration by vegetation. Modelers approximate these components using simplified representations called parameterizations. The principal reason to develop a multimodel ensemble for the IPCC assessments is to understand how this lack of certainty affects attribution and prediction of climate change. The ensemble for the latest assessment is unprecedented in the number of models and experiments performed. 21

The second advance is the incorporation of more realistic representations of climate processes in the models. These processes include the behavior of atmospheric aerosols, the dynamics (movement) of sea ice, and the exchange of water and energy between the land and the atmosphere. More models now include the major types of aerosols and the interactions between aerosols and clouds. 22

When scientists use climate models for attribution studies, they first run simulations with estimates of only "natural" climate influences over the past 100 years, such as changes in solar output and major volcanic eruptions. They then run models that include human-induced increases in greenhouse gases and aerosols. The results of such experiments are 23 striking. Models using only natural forcings are unable to explain the observed global warming since the mid-20th century, whereas they can do so when they include anthropogenic factors in addition to natural ones. Large-scale *patterns* of temperature change are also most consistent between models and observations when all forcings are included.

24 Two patterns provide a fingerprint of human influence. The first is greater warming over land than ocean and greater warming at the surface of the sea than in the deeper layers. This pattern is consistent with greenhouse gas–induced warming by the overlying atmosphere: the ocean warms more slowly because of its large thermal inertia. The warming also indicates that a large amount of heat is being taken up by the ocean, demonstrating that the planet's energy budget has been pushed out of balance. A second pattern of change is that while the troposphere (the lower region of the atmosphere) has warmed, the stratosphere, just above it, has cooled. If solar changes provided the dominant forcing, warming would be expected in both atmospheric layers. The observed contrast, however, is just that expected from the combination of greenhouse gas increases and stratospheric ozone decreases. This collective evidence, when subjected to careful statistical analyses, provides much of the basis for the increased confidence that human influences are behind the observed global warming. Suggestions that cosmic rays could affect clouds, and thereby climate, have been based on correlations using limited records; they have generally not stood up when tested with additional data, and their physical mechanisms remain speculative.

25 What about at smaller scales? As spatial and temporal scales decrease, attribution of climate change becomes more difficult. This problem arises because natural small-scale temperature variations are less "averaged out" and thus more readily mask the change signal. Nevertheless, continued warming means the signal is emerging on smaller scales. The report has found that human activity is likely to have influenced temperature significantly down to the continental scale for all continents except Antarctica.

26 Human influence is discernible also in some extreme events such as unusually hot and cold nights and the incidence of heat waves. This does not mean, of course, that individual extreme events (such as the 2003 European heat wave) can be said to be simply "caused" by human-induced climate change—usually such events are complex, with many causes. But it does mean that human activities have, more likely than not, affected the *chances* of such events occurring.

Projections of Future Changes

27 How will climate change over the 21st century? This critical question is addressed using simulations from climate models based on projections of future emissions of greenhouse gases and aerosols. The simulations suggest that, for greenhouse gas emissions at or above current rates, changes in climate will very likely be larger than the changes already observed

during the 20th century. Even if emissions were immediately reduced enough to stabilize greenhouse gas concentrations at current levels, climate change would continue for centuries. This inertia in the climate results from a combination of factors. They include the heat capacity of the world's oceans and the millennial timescales needed for the circulation to mix heat and carbon dioxide throughout the deep ocean and thereby come into equilibrium with the new conditions.

To be more specific, the models project that over the next 20 years, for 28
a range of plausible emissions, the global temperature will increase at an average rate of about 0.2 degree C per decade, close to the observed rate over the past 30 years. About half of this near-term warming represents a "commitment" to future climate change arising from the inertia of the climate system response to current atmospheric concentrations of greenhouse gases.

The long-term warming over the 21st century, however, is strongly 29
influenced by the future rate of emissions, and the projections cover a wide variety of scenarios, ranging from very rapid to more modest economic growth and from more to less dependence on fossil fuels. The best estimates of the increase in global temperatures range from 1.8 to 4.0 degrees C for the various emission scenarios, with higher emissions leading to higher temperatures. As for regional impacts, projections indicate with more confidence than ever before that these will mirror the *patterns* of change observed over the past 50 years (greater warming over land than ocean, for example) but that the *size* of the changes will be larger than they have been so far.

The simulations also suggest that the removal of excess carbon 30
dioxide from the atmosphere by natural processes on land and in the ocean will become less efficient as the planet warms. This change leads to a higher percentage of emitted carbon dioxide remaining in the atmosphere, which then further accelerates global warming. This is an important positive feedback on the carbon cycle (the exchange of carbon compounds throughout the climate system). Although models agree that carbon-cycle changes represent a positive feedback, the range of their responses remains very large, depending, among other things, on poorly understood changes in vegetation or soil uptake of carbon as the climate warms. Such processes are an important topic of ongoing research.

The models also predict that climate change will affect the physical 31
and chemical characteristics of the ocean. The estimates of the rise in sea level during the 21st century range from about 30 to 40 centimeters, again depending on emissions. More than 60 percent of this rise is caused by the thermal expansion of the ocean. Yet these model-based estimates do not include the possible acceleration of recently observed increases in ice loss from the Greenland and Antarctic ice sheets. Although scientific understanding of such effects is very limited, they could add an additional 10 to 20 centimeters to sea-level rises, and the possibility of significantly larger rises cannot be excluded. The chemistry of the ocean is also affected, as the increased concentrations of atmospheric carbon dioxide will cause the ocean to become more acidic.

FACING OUR FUTURE . . .

The Consequences of Ongoing Warming

Global warming is real and, as Working Group I of the IPCC stated in its January–February 2007 report, "very likely" to be largely the result of human activities for at least the past half a century. But is that warming significant enough to pose real problems? That determination fell to Working Group II, a similarly international assembly of scientists who focused on the vulnerability of natural and human environments to climate change.

In the April 2007 summary of its findings, Working Group II concluded that human-induced warming over the past three and a half decades has indeed had a discernible influence on many physical and biological systems. Observational evidence from all continents and most oceans shows that many natural systems are being affected by regional climate changes, particularly temperature increases. The ground in permafrost regions is becoming increasingly unstable, rock avalanches in mountainous areas are more frequent, trees are coming into leaf earlier, and some animals and plants are moving to higher latitudes or elevations.

Looking to the future, the group also projected that ongoing shifts in climate would affect the health and welfare of millions of people around the world. The severity of the effects would depend on precisely how much warming occurred. Among the most probable consequences:

- More frequent heat waves, droughts, fires, coastal flooding and storms will raise the toll of deaths, injuries and related diseases.
- Some infectious diseases, such as malaria, will spread to new regions.
- High concentrations of ground-level ozone will exacerbate heart and respiratory ailments.
- By the 2080s, rising sea levels will flood the homes and property of millions of people, especially in the large deltas of Asia and Africa and on small islands.

The harm from these changes will be most severe for impoverished communities. The poor are generally more dependent on climate-sensitive resources such as local water and food, and by definition their adaptive capacities are economically limited.

The effects of global warming would not be universally bad, particularly for the next few decades. For example, whereas higher temperatures would hurt the growth of important cereals in equatorial nations fairly quickly, they would for a time raise productivity on farms in mid- to high-latitude countries, such as the U.S. But once the temperature increase exceeded three degrees Celsius (5.4 degrees Fahrenheit), agricultural declines would set in even there, barring widespread adaptive changes.

Central and South America

- Gradual replacement of tropical forest by savanna in eastern Amazonia
- Replacement of semiarid vegetation by arid-land vegetation
- Species extinctions in many tropical areas
- Reduced water availability
- Loss of arable land in drier areas
- Decreased yields of some important crops
- Reduced livestock productivity

What Needs to be Done

The human race can respond to climate change in two ways: adaptation and mitigation. Adaptation means learning how to survive and prosper in a warmer world. Mitigation means limiting the extent of future warming by reducing the net release of greenhouse gases to the atmosphere. Given that rising temperatures are already encroaching on us and that an unstopped increase would be overwhelming, a strong combination of both adaptation and mitigation will be essential. Unfortunately, disagreements over the feasibility, costs and necessity of mitigation have notoriously bogged down global responses to date.

To project mitigation strategies for the looming problems—and their costs—Working Group III of the IPCC considered various estimates of economic expansion, population growth and fossil-fuel use for its 2007 report. The six resulting scenarios predict atmospheric concentrations of carbon dioxide equivalents (that is, greenhouse gases and aerosols equivalent to carbon dioxide) ranging from 445 parts per million to 1,130 ppm, with corresponding increases in temperatures from 2.0 to as much as 6.1 degrees C (approximately 3.6 to 11 degrees F) over preindustrial levels. To keep the temperature increase to the lowest of those projections, the group estimates that the world must stabilize atmospheric greenhouse gases at 445 ppm by 2015. (Current concentrations are approaching 400 ppm.) The scientists believe that any higher temperatures might trigger severe flooding in some places and severe drought in others, wipe out species and cause economic havoc.

The group's report looks in detail at the most promising technologies and policies for holding the gases at 445 ppm. It emphasizes the importance of improving energy efficiency in buildings and vehicles, shifting to renewable energy sources and saving forests as "carbon sinks." Policies include setting a target for global emissions, emissions trading schemes, caps, taxes and incentives.

But the IPCC scientists made their assessment before a study published online this past April in the *Proceedings of the National Academy of Sciences USA* reported that worldwide carbon dioxide emissions between 2000 and 2004 increased at three times the rate of the 1990s—from 1.1 to 3.2 percent a year. In other words, the actual global emissions since 2000 grew faster than those projected in the highest of the scenarios developed by the IPCC. That research indicates that the situation is more dire than even the bleak IPCC assessment forecasts.

The Regional Picture

The lists here indicate just some of the disturbing effects, beyond those enumerated in the discussion at the left, that Working Group II foresees in various parts of the world over the coming century. The group made most of these predictions with high or very high confidence. Find more details at www.ucar.edu/news/features/climatechange/regionalimpacts.jsp and at the IPCC Web site (www.ipcc.ch).

North America

- In the western mountains, decreased snowpack, more winter flooding and reduced summer flows
- An extended period of high fire risk and large increases in area burned
- Increased intensity, duration and number of heat waves in cities historically prone to them
- In coastal areas, increased stress on people and property as climate interacts with development and pollution

Europe

- Increased risk of inland flash floods
- In the south, more health-threatening heat waves and wildfires, reduced water availability and hydropower potential, endangered crop production and reduced summer tourism
- In the central and eastern areas, more health-threatening heat waves and peatland fires and reduced summer rainfall and forest productivity
- In the north, negative impacts eventually outweigh such initial benefits as reduced heating demand and increased crop yields and forest growth

Asia

- Increased flooding, rock avalanches and water resource disruptions as Himalayan glaciers melt
- Ongoing risk of hunger in several developing regions because of crop productivity declines combined with rapid population growth and urbanization

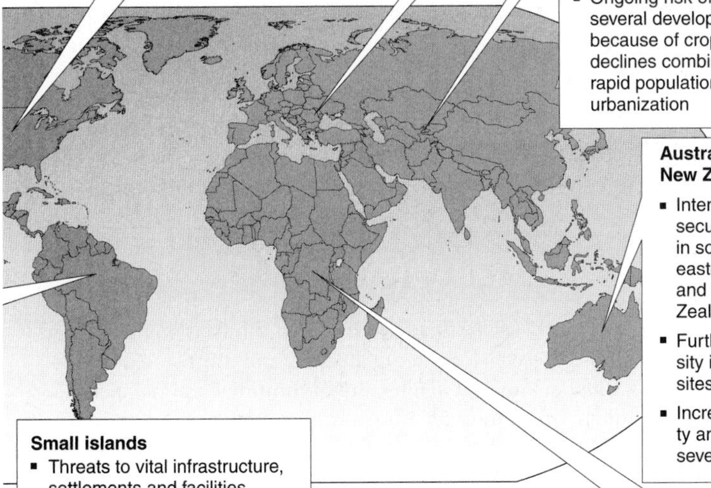

Australia and New Zealand

- Intensified water security problems in southern and eastern Australia and parts of New Zealand by 2030
- Further loss of biodiversity in ecologically rich sites by 2020
- Increased storm severity and frequency in several places

Small islands

- Threats to vital infrastructure, settlements and facilities because of sea-level rise
- Reduced water resources in many places by midcentury
- Beach erosion, coral bleaching and other deteriorating coastal conditions, leading to harmed fisheries and reduced value as tourist destinations
- Invasion by nonnative species, especially on mid- and high-latitude islands

Polar regions

- Thinning and shrinking of glaciers and ice sheets
- Changes in the extent of Arctic sea ice and permafrost
- Deeper seasonal thawing of permafrost

Africa

- Decreased water availability by 2020 for 75 million to 250 million people
- Loss of arable land, reduced growing seasons and reduced yields in some areas
- Decreased fish stocks in large lakes

Daniela Naomi Molnar

32 Some of the largest changes are predicted for polar regions. These include significant increases in high-latitude land temperatures and in the depth of thawing in permafrost regions and sharp reductions in the extent of summer sea ice in the Arctic basin. Lower latitudes will likely experience more heat waves, heavier precipitation, and stronger (but perhaps less frequent) hurricanes and typhoons. The extent to which hurricanes and typhoons may strengthen is uncertain and is a subject of much new research.

33 Some important uncertainties remain, of course. For example, the precise way in which clouds will respond as temperatures increase is a critical factor governing the overall size of the projected warming. The complexity of clouds, however, means that their response has been frustratingly difficult to pin down, and, again, much research remains to be done in this area.

34 We are now living in an era in which both humans and nature affect the future evolution of the earth and its inhabitants. Unfortunately, the crystal ball provided by our climate models becomes cloudier for predictions out beyond a century or so. Our limited knowledge of the response of both natural systems and human society to the growing impacts of climate change compounds our uncertainty. One result of global warming is certain, however. Plants, animals and humans will be living with the consequences of climate change for at least the next thousand years.

VACLAV HAVEL

Vaclav Havel (born in 1936 in Prague) is a writer, dramatist, politician, and human rights activist. He was repeatedly arrested and imprisoned in the 1970s and 1980s for speaking out against the Communist regime, including for his leading role in promoting the human rights manifesto Charter 77. Havel was elected President of Czechoslovakia in 1989 after the fall of the communist government in what has become known as the "Velvet Revolution." In 1993, he became the first President of the Czech Republic. He was reelected in 1998 and served until 2003. Havel has received multiple honorary doctorates, prizes, and awards, including the Gandhi Peace Prize in 2003 and the Presidential Medal of Freedom in 2008. In addition to plays and collections of poetry, he has written numerous books and articles on human rights, globalization, and Czech and European culture, history, and politics, including a political memoir, *To the Castle and Back*. In "Our Moral Footprint," first published in the *New York Times* in 2007, Havel appeals to readers to recognize the moral imperative of preserving the planet and argues that humanity should transcend its contemporary economic, cultural, and political conflicts and develop "a consciousness of the commonality of all living beings."

Our Moral Footprint

Over the past few years the questions have been asked ever more forcefully whether global climate changes occur in natural cycles or not, to what degree we humans contribute to them, what threats stem from them and what can be done to prevent them. Scientific studies demonstrate that any changes in temperature and energy cycles on a planetary scale could mean danger for all people on all continents. 1

It is also obvious from published research that human activity is a cause of change; we just don't know how big its contribution is. Is it necessary to know that to the last percentage point, though? By waiting for incontrovertible precision, aren't we simply wasting time when we could be taking measures that are relatively painless compared to those we would have to adopt after further delays? 2

Maybe we should start considering our sojourn on earth as a loan. There can be no doubt that for the past hundred years at least, Europe and the United States have been running up a debt, and now other parts of the world are following their example. Nature is issuing warnings that we must not only stop the debt from growing but start to pay it back. There is little point in asking whether we have borrowed too much or what would happen if we postponed the repayments. Anyone with a mortgage or a bank loan can easily imagine the answer. 3

The effects of possible climate changes are hard to estimate. Our planet has never been in a state of balance from which it could deviate through human or other influence and then, in time, return to its original state. The climate is not like a pendulum that will return to its original position after a certain period. It has evolved turbulently over billions of years into a gigantic complex of networks, and of networks within networks, where everything is interlinked in diverse ways. 4

Its structures will never return to precisely the same state they were in 50 or 5,000 years ago. They will only change into a new state, which, so long as the change is slight, need not mean any threat to life. 5

Larger changes, however, could have unforeseeable effects within the global ecosystem. In that case, we would have to ask ourselves whether human life would be possible. Because so much uncertainty still reigns, a great deal of humility and circumspection is called for. 6

We can't endlessly fool ourselves that nothing is wrong and that we can go on cheerfully pursuing our wasteful lifestyles, ignoring the climate threats and postponing a solution. Maybe there will be no major catastrophe in the coming years or decades. Who knows? But that doesn't relieve us of responsibility toward future generations. 7

I don't agree with those whose reaction is to warn against restricting civil freedoms. Were the forecasts of certain climatologists to come true, our freedoms would be tantamount to those of someone hanging from a 20th-story parapet. 8

9 Whenever I reflect on the problems of today's world, whether they concern the economy, society, culture, security, ecology or civilization in general, I always end up confronting the moral question: what action is responsible or acceptable? The moral order, our conscience and human rights—these are the most important issues at the beginning of the third millennium.

10 We must return again and again to the roots of human existence and consider our prospects in centuries to come. We must analyze everything open-mindedly, soberly, unideologically and unobsessively, and project our knowledge into practical policies. Maybe it is no longer a matter of simply promoting energy-saving technologies, but chiefly of introducing ecologically clean technologies, of diversifying resources and of not relying on just one invention as a panacea.

11 I'm skeptical that a problem as complex as climate change can be solved by any single branch of science. Technological measures and regulations are important, but equally important is support for education, ecological training and ethics—a consciousness of the commonality of all living beings and an emphasis on shared responsibility.

12 Either we will achieve an awareness of our place in the living and life-giving organism of our planet, or we will face the threat that our evolutionary journey may be set back thousands or even millions of years. That is why we must see this issue as a challenge to behave responsibly and not as a harbinger of the end of the world.

13 The end of the world has been anticipated many times and has never come, of course. And it won't come this time either. We need not fear for our planet. It was here before us and most likely will be here after us. But that doesn't mean that the human race is not at serious risk. As a result of our endeavors and our irresponsibility our climate might leave no place for us. If we drag our feet, the scope for decision-making—and hence for our individual freedom—could be considerably reduced.

Content

1. What evidence do the authors of "The Physical Science behind Climate Change" offer that human activities are responsible for the increase in greenhouse gases (¶s 5–6)? What natural mechanisms contribute to climate change (¶ 8)? What is a "net positive radiative forcing" and what factors contribute to it (¶s 9–10)?
2. What quantities and properties of our climate system do Collins et al. consider in their discussion of observational data (¶s 11–15)? How does this data indicate that our climate is changing?
3. Why did the IPCC 2007 report draw a stronger link between human activities and observed climate changes than its previous report ("The Physical Science Behind Climate Change," ¶s 17–26)? What did Working Group II of the IPCC add to those findings ("The Consequences of Ongoing Warming")?

4. How is our climate likely to change over the next century ("The Physical Science behind Climate Change," ¶s 27–32)? What are the consequences of those changes ("The Consequences of Ongoing Warming")? Why do scientists believe that future changes in climate will be larger than those the earth has seen in the past?
5. Why does Vaclav Havel ("Our Moral Footprint") believe that environmental policies should not depend on determining the extent to which human activity is driving global climate change? What kinds of policies does Havel suggest to accommodate this perspective?

Strategies/Structures/Language

6. Collins and his coauthors prepare the reader for a detailed discussion of scientific evidence for climate change by arguing that scientific progress "is generally made by a painstaking piecing together of evidence" (¶ 1). Find other examples of stylistic devices that prepare or guide the reader through their analysis. These devices might include asking a question that the text then answers, summarizing information already provided in order to build on that information, and using metaphors and examples.
7. Why does Havel compare the human relationship to the earth with a loan (¶ 3)? How does Havel's description of our planet (¶s 4–6) support his argument that we must "achieve an awareness of our place in the living and life-giving organism of our planet" (¶ 12)?

For Writing

8. ***Journal Writing.*** Havel says that since so much about our planet's climate is uncertain, "a great deal of humility and circumspection is called for" (¶ 6). Do you agree? How might our society learn to acquire "a consciousness of the commonality of all living beings" (¶ 11)?
9. ***Dialogues.*** Select one of the problems of managing the earth's natural resources (other than global warming) that Jared Diamond identifies in "The World as a Polder" (Chapter 10) and explain its connection and contribution to the problem of global warming and climate change. What kinds of adaptation and mitigation strategies does Diamond's analysis suggest would address the problem? Re-read both Diamond's discussion of the problem you have chosen and "Facing Our Future," including "The Regional Picture" (224–25), and discuss what the consequences of inaction in addressing this problem are likely to be and which regions of the world are likely to be hardest hit. What aspects of this problem suggest that international cooperation is necessary to adapt to a warmer future and mitigate its consequences? (See also photo insert.)
10. ***Mixed Modes.*** Choose one or more of the effects of global warming that Working Group II of the IPCC foresees in the coming century as described in "The Regional Picture" on 225. Research the issue(s) in a particular region and propose a combination of adaptation and mitigation strategies that are available in that region. Explain why your proposed solution is the best of the possible strategies.

MEGAN McGUIRE

Megan McGuire was born in 1983, grew up in Connecticut, and earned a BA in English and political science from the University of Connecticut in 2005. A member of the Army National Guard in college, she was commissioned as a Second Lieutenant soon after graduation. But this just scratches the surface.

Of her essay, she writes, "I generally do not reflect that often on my life growing up or how I got to where I am. I'm satisfied with what I've accomplished, who I am, and where I'm headed. I count myself lucky to have lived in two very different kinds of environments while growing up, one of which that was filled with love and support and fulfilled all the stereotypical ideas of childhood. I played outside until the streetlights came on and spent my summers at my grandparents' lake house. The other portion of my late childhood and adolescence was somewhat of a culture shock. Its forced independence created self-sufficiency and responsibility that, although acquired in a less than favorable way, have just as adequately contributed to my general successes in life as the more cushioned existence I experienced earlier. I never intended to record any portions of my life, but as a class assignment I began to do so and was surprised at the flooding of memories that I had almost forgotten. I was also surprised at how liberating it was to put parts of my life on paper. I felt as if I had inadvertently explained myself and who I am, answering some questions I didn't even know I had and revealing even more—a fulfilling experience that I plan to pursue further."

✧ *Wake Up Call*

1 *It was morning. My father just left my room. He had come in, as he came in every morning Monday through Friday, to inform me that it was no longer time for dreaming, the time had come to wake up and prepare for another monotonous day at school. Even at the age of ten the ability to wake up early eluded me. I gradually forced my eyes open, first briefly, then for a period of thirty seconds. Each time I opened my eyes I would stay awake a little longer. I did this every morning, partially denying that I had to leave the comfort of my warm bed, waiting for my second warning yell from down the hall that I was going to be late if I didn't wake up soon. I stared up at the canopy that covered my bed. I had begged for a canopy bed for years and one summer my father found one at a tag sale for a price we could afford. I loved that bed. It had a white frame and a royal blue canopy, with a miniature floral print. There were many times that I greatly desired something, and although I may have had to wait, I almost always got what I asked for if I wanted it long enough. Everyone has fleeting wants, but if the need was persistent, my father always came through.*

Along with the bed, I had always wanted a typewriter. As far back as I can remember I loved books. I don't remember learning to read, but I remember sitting on my father's lap while he read one of his big books, following along to the sound of his voice. We made constant trips to the local library; just being around books was exciting. I don't remember struggling to read but I remember the first book I ever read, an early learning book, a "Spot, the Dog" book, and I read it cover to cover. I became an insatiable reader and decided very young that I wanted to be a writer. For my birthday one year I was given an old typewriter, an antique. The keys were the traditional punch keys and I spent a good week figuring out how to insert the paper and not have my words type diagonally across the page. I soon learned that being a writer was not an easy task. First I actually needed to have something to write about and second, it was very time consuming. I decided, therefore, to enjoy my love of books and revisit the profession of writing at a later date, when I had something of significance to say. 2

School allowed an outlet for my desire to write by providing me topics to write about so I didn't have to think them up on my own. I enjoyed school but could never figure out why it required being up so early in the morning. It was a struggle, to be sure. This particular morning was no different. I eventually rolled out of bed. My clothes were still in a laundry basket by the door to my room. Dad was great, but he never seemed to get the hang of putting clothes away. I sifted through until I found something to wear. I chose a pair of jeans with a patch across the knee that my grandmother had sewn on for me and a black t-shirt decorated by yours truly using crafty puff paint, a trend at the time and very cool. I managed to find a pair of somewhat matching socks and donned them as well. I learned to do my own hair very early on. Dad never seemed to master anything beyond a lopsided ponytail and my older sister was far too busy being thirteen to help me, so I quickly braided my long blond hair and stepped off toward the kitchen, wishing I knew how to French-braid so I could have a nice hair-do like my girly classmates. Instead I looked as if I couldn't decide whether or not I wanted to be Barbie or Ken. 3

Breakfast consisted of a bowl of cereal which I inhaled quickly. My brother was still in bed. It might have been difficult waking me up for school, but it was impossible to wake up my brother. There was actually a time when he was dragged physically to school by my father and upon arriving he jumped out of the car, ran away, was chased down, caught and physically dragged into the building, kicking and screaming, by not only my father but the principal as well. It was disconcerting at the time and is now merely comical. I kissed Dad goodbye and hurried out of our apartment to the bus stop. My Dad was home when I left for school and I knew he would be home waiting for me at 3:20 when I stepped through the door. We were on state, I wasn't sure at the time what that meant, but I knew it meant Dad didn't have to work and at the grocery store we paid for food with colorful stamps that looked like my play money but apparently had more value. It also meant that during the holidays we went to the town hall and were given presents that were labeled "Girl 8–10" and "Boy 11–12" and we got to meet Santa. I knew we didn't have a lot of money, certainly not like my friend 4

Lauren who lived in a big old colonial house, had a playroom in addition to her own room, but I had a canopy bed, a typewriter, and I knew my Dad was always home if I needed him. There was never a day when I wasn't hugged or kissed or told I was loved. I was happy.

5 It is morning. My alarm clock is blaring in my ear from across the room for the second time. Snooze is a wonderful thing. I'm lucky this morning, my alarm clock actually works. It is possibly the oldest alarm clock, most certainly older then I am even at ten. The digital numbers sometimes fade on and off, but if I am lucky, it will burst to life at the appointed time in the morning and emit the most horrendous static sound, eventually forcing me awake. Rolling out of bed is easy, my bed consists of a mattress on the floor, the box spring adds some elevation to the mattress and acts as a substitute for a real frame. I sort through a large brown plastic garbage bag filled with clothes and find something suitable to wear. I put on a pair of stretchy elastic pants that were purchased at Ames as part of my back to school shopping and an oversized t-shirt that belonged to my mother. I can't seem to find a pair of socks. I vaguely remember leaving my laundry in the washing machine overnight. I walk into my older sister's room quietly and softly open her top drawer and steal a clean pair of socks. I stealthily exit the room and return to my own.

6 I share my room with my younger sister. I don't think our room was designed as a bedroom. The stairs lead directly to our room from the bottom floor and the two actual bedrooms and bathroom branch off our room that is something akin to a loft. My brother has one of the bedrooms and my older sister has the other. I hop into the bathroom, hairspray my hair into some wavelike fashion statement that epitomizes coolness and head downstairs. I spend a good twenty minutes leashing our four dogs up outside and as a result leave myself no time for breakfast. I head into the kitchen to see if there is anything quick I can grab and take with me. I try to be quiet, only a curtain separates my mother's room from the kitchen and I don't want to wake her up. She must have made it home late last night, I don't remember hearing her come in. I open the fridge, no milk. I grab a couple of pieces of bread and head out to the bus.

7 On the way down the dirt driveway I drag one of the large garbage barrels from the back of the house, Monday, trash day. It tips over when I snag it on a rock and all the contents spill out into the drive. Fabulous. I pick up what I can, trying not to get dirty. I stain my shirt. I don't have time to change and I don't think I have anything else clean to wear. My brother follows me outside, along with my younger sister. We wait outside the house for the bus. Our house is an old colonial that was moved from one side of town to its current location at some point in its history. It was placed on an unstable rocky foundation and as a result has settled nicely so that all the floors are bowed in one way or another. The paint

is a yellowish color and is excessively chipped, giving the surface a textured appearance. The house is blocked from sight on one side by large bushes and from the front by a large tree. I am ashamed of our house. It looks dilapidated and old, nothing like the nicely vinyl sided homes on the rest of our street. I am happy there are bushes and trees hiding it from sight.

I sit in the back corner of the class. In my other school it was cool to sit in the back, but apparently here the cool kids sit in front. Bad move. Everyone here wears jeans. If I had bought jeans I would have only been allowed to pick one outfit at Ames, so I bought stretch pants so I could have two outfits when school started. I still haven't determined how I am going to alternate what I wear. If I interchange tops with bottoms I still only have four outfits. There are five days in a school week, so I will have to repeat at least once. The other kids will remember what I wear. I want a pair of dark blue jeans like the pretty girl in the front row. She has dark hair in a French-braid, blue jeans and a pretty clean white shirt with ruffles on the collar. Her name is Kate. I know the answers to all the questions the teacher asks but I don't raise my hand. Smart kids are not cool. In my other school they called me Webster. I was like a dictionary. I get put in a remedial math level due to my less than enthusiastic effort but wish I had tried harder, all the cool kids were in advanced math. Tricky, tricky. 8

It is morning. I am freezing. I could swear the cold breeze outside comes right through the drafty closed window of my room. What time is it? My alarm clock didn't go off. I look across the room and the digital numbers are not there. No one is up. If I don't get up, no one gets up. My brother doesn't bother if I don't force him and my little sister relies on the same clock that we share in our room. My older sister doesn't need to get up. Her boyfriend and she sleep until he has to go to work at noon. She feels better now; the morning sickness isn't so bad anymore. I climb out of bed; the floor feels like a sheet of ice against my bare feet. I grab the oversized robe on the floor and put it over my already layered clothing. I flick the light switch and nothing happens. Was there a storm? How come there isn't any power? 9

The bathroom has a little more light; the window is on the one side of the house not smothered by vegetation. I glance in the mirror and notice that there is a black substance crusted under my nose and on my eyelashes. My little sister has it on her nose too. I wash my face off and head downstairs. The kerosene heater is covered in the black substance too; it must be some kind of soot. The TV won't turn on. I still have no idea what time it is. The thermostat is turned all the way down. We must be out of oil again. The living room houses the kerosene heater and is the warmest room in the house. Mom isn't home; she must have left for work already. On the dining room table is my permission slip that is due today. She forgot to sign it. I grab a pen and sign her name as authoritatively as 10

I can, and I realize it doesn't matter since I missed the bus anyway. I go to the bathroom downstairs, the ceramic on the toilet is ice cold so I try to hover over it in the same manner as I would a public bathroom. I try to flush, the water goes down but nothing replenishes the bowl, this seems somewhat odd. I crank the handle on the sink and the faucet responds with a funny noise and no water comes out.

11 I pick up the phone and dial Mom at work. At least something works. I'm on hold for about five minutes and she finally picks up. I get yelled at for not being in school. How could I have missed the bus? Does she have to be home to do everything? I'm ten years old, I should be able to wake up and get to school without her holding my hand. Where is Amber? Mom, we have no electricity and no water for some reason and the kerosene heater is broken and we need to go to the store when you get home, there isn't anything to eat. There's plenty to eat, make something, I'll be home around seven.

12 The fridge has milk and eggs and various condiments. It feels warm and the light doesn't turn on when I open the door. I go into the mudroom to look for something to make. The shelves are lined with jars filled with tomatoes, green beans and mixed vegetables. I remember the Saturday during the summer when Mom showed me how to jar the vegetables from the garden to preserve them. It was fun. I had never jarred vegetables before. Now they were the only things that looked back at me, the jars of vegetables and a box of brownie mix. At ten years old vegetables are still the less appetizing of the two, so I grab the box of brownie mix and head to the kitchen. I forget we have an electric stove. I take a couple of pieces of bread and head to the living room, still no TV.

13 I put on some clothes and take four dollars of change out of the change jar in my Mom's room. I walk the two miles to Cumberland Farms and buy some cookies and a couple of Airheads, my favorite kind of candy. I pass the library on the way back, situated in the old center of town, next to the police station and the old town hall. No TV, might as well get a book. I take out *The Witch of Blackbird Pond.* I love this book because it mentions the meadows near my house, the great expanse of fields that stretch from Rocky Hill to Wethersfield and through Glastonbury. I love going there when I want to feel alone and put my life into perspective. In the summer I lie in the field and watch the clouds float by.

14 When I get home everyone is up. I hear Amber yelling. She needs to get out of this place, this is bullshit, she can't wait to move out. She doesn't go to school right now, she'd be a freshman this year. I can't wait until high school. I spend my afternoon reading my book. Mom gets home at about 8:30. She's carrying a Styrofoam to-go container. She stopped at Angellino's for dinner on the way home with a girlfriend from work. The house is dark. I was able to find a candle and it was flickering on the dining room table. She smiles and takes three oil lamps out of a paper bag and sets them on the table. Late one month and they just shut you off. I have

a feeling we were late more than just one month but I don't say it. I learn that if you fill the toilet bowl with enough snow it will flush automatically. The pipes must have froze, when the hell is he going to come and fix that damn furnace, I pay way too much for this place. She says this, but I know I haven't seen the oil truck here in weeks. I use a towel and a bowl of water from a bottle to wash up by the light of the oil lamp. Amber and Mom are fighting. How can you go out for dinner? We have no food here, no electricity, no water. The argument continues until Mom slaps her. Amber leaves. I go downstairs and Mom shows me the jeans she bought. I think about the pair I've been industriously saving for every week by cleaning an old lady's house: four floors for $13.50. I wonder how much hers cost.

After a certain length of time if a family is without heat or running 15 water the town lets you stay in a hotel for free. The four of us share a room at the Suisse Chalet. I don't know where Amber is. I call it the Sleazy Chalet and everybody laughs. It's nice to watch TV. I haven't seen the Simpsons in four weeks. We stay at the Chalet for a week. Sometimes Mom would work really early and we wouldn't have a ride to school. It is a nice vacation. When we get home on Friday there is a pink notice on our back door. On Monday we are at the Howard Johnson's and our household goods are in storage. It is a much better motel. Bickford's is right at the bottom of the hill so I can walk and get pancakes if I'm hungry. Mike works there and now Amber does too, so I don't have to pay. I start at my new school next week. It's cool because it's the same town my Dad grew up in. He said some of his old teachers are still there. I'll be happy to get back to school. I've missed a lot.

It is afternoon. I just walked home from school. There's a pink note 16 on our door. Looks like I'm not graduating here, good thing I didn't order a class ring. I've seen four pink notes since eighth grade, this is nothing new. I'm an expert packer. It's just like Tetris, everything will fit if you do it right. I make sure I leave out everything that I'll need, clothes and schoolbooks. I also throw anything with sentimental value into a bag. So much gets lost.

Three weeks I have been living in New Britain. I can't stand it here. 17 I don't like this guy, Mom's friend or not. I'm sleeping on the floor living out of my duffel bag. Amber should be here any minute. She moved back to Connecticut from North Carolina just this week. What a relief. Should I leave a note for Mom? I wonder how long it will take her to notice I'm gone? I'm a coward. I have every reason to leave but I can't force myself to tell her I'm going. I need to get back to school or I won't graduate. What if she cries? What if she tries to make me feel guilty, like I'm abandoning her? She always "tries" so hard for us but it's not enough. I know I can do better on my own. No matter how hard I have to work, I will give myself stability.

I missed three weeks of school. Fortunately my new school doesn't 18 know this so I'm still on track to graduate. Mom hasn't called yet. I got a job. Maybe I'll have enough money to buy a car soon. Getting to work is difficult having no transportation other than my own two feet. Location severely limits my job options. My apartment is nice. My job has time and a half on Sunday so if I work every Sunday and at least five nights I'm hoping I'll be able to save a little. I wake up, go to school, go to work and study into the waning hours of the night. I'm always exhausted, only one more year until college. My grandmother always said that if I wanted to go to college I would have to work hard. Your mother won't help you and your father can't help you so you better study hard and get a scholarship. I study hard. I'm graduating in the top ten of my class but I haven't gotten any scholarships.

19 It's late. I just got home from work. My feet hurt. I'm 21 years old. I am a full-time student. I have two jobs and I am in the Army National Guard. I've lived on my own since I was 17. I'm always tired and always busy. My apartment is always warm, even if it means working more hours and there is food in my house. Sometimes I sit in my apartment and wonder what my life would be like if Dad hadn't gotten sick and I never moved in with my mother. We didn't have money, but I had a lot. I moved away and learned what it meant to work, what it meant to be hungry and cold, and what the world is really like. I saw what selfishness and bad habits could do. I learned about everything I didn't want to be. Maybe it was the combination of the two worlds. The beginning of my life was filled with love and support and I truly believed I could be anything I wanted to be as long as I worked hard. The latter portion of my adolescence taught me how to work hard. If I was never truly in want of anything would I be as motivated to be so much more than what I came from? I don't resent any part of my life. Everything that was has made me what I am. I'm lucky.

Content

1. McGuire presents examples of good and poor parenting. What are the components of each? Can you infer from her essay the factors that contribute to each parent's "style" of parenting? From the details McGuire presents, is it possible for readers to construct a more sympathetic interpretation of her mother than might initially meet the eye?
2. What kind of personality and character does McGuire have? Is this consistent throughout her childhood? How would you account for her strength of character and purpose?
3. Megan and her older sister appear to be turning out very differently during adolescence. To what extent can this be attributed to the parenting they have experienced? By the end of the narrative, McGuire is clearly headed for professional success and personal happiness. Has she overridden her upbringing, benefited from it, or both?

Strategies/Structures/Language

4. What is the tone of this piece? Is it consistent throughout? Self-pity and self-congratulation generally turn off readers; do you detect any shred of either in this piece? If so, where? If not, why not?

5. Throughout the essay, material objects assume symbolic value: how are readers expected to interpret the canopy bed (¶ 1), the "colorful stamps" (¶ 4), "presents labeled 'Girl 8–10'" (¶ 4), the various items of Megan's clothing (¶s 3, 4, 5, 8) and her mother's new jeans (¶ 8), the "dilapidated" old colonial house (¶ 7), the "pink notice" (¶s 15, 16)?

For Writing

6. ***Journal Writing.*** When and where did you feel safe as a child? Identify the external and psychological circumstances that contributed to that sense of security. Did you or do you associate that security with particular material objects or with specific activities?

7. ***Mixed Modes.*** This essay implies an ideal of parenting. With a partner, construct the definition of an ideal parent (or father or mother) whose good parenting would produce an ideal child. Identify and explain several characteristics of the ideal, both parent and child.

8. How can people emerge from disastrous upbringing as strong, capable, and powerful adults? Explain, analyzing the example of your own life or that of someone you know, or the life of a public figure including writers represented in *The Essay Connection* such as Frederick Douglass (Chapter 3) or Martin Luther King, Jr. (Chapter 10). You may wish to consult some of the writings on resilience, or positive psychology, by authors such as Martin Seligman and Mihaly Csikszentmihalyi (see, for example, *The American Psychologist*, January 2000 and March 2001 issues).

Additional Topics for Writing Cause and Effect

(For strategies for writing cause and effect, see 182.)

Multiple Strategies for Writing: Cause and Effect

In writing on any of the cause-and-effect topics below, you can employ assorted strategies to help explain either the causes or the effects, and to interpret their consequences:

- *definitions, explanations* of terms, equipment involved in the process
- *illustrations* and *examples*: to show what happens, and in what sequence
- *diagrams, drawings, flow charts, graphs* to clarify and explain
- *logical sequence of interrelated steps or ideas*
- consideration of *short-term* and *long-term consequences* of a particular effect—literal, material, psychological, emotional, economic, ethical, ecological, political or other
- examination of whether there is a *confusion* or *lack of clarity* between cause and effect; sometimes effects are mistaken for causes, and vice versa, or the wrong people or phenomena are credited with or blamed for a particular cause or effect

1. Write an essay, adapted to an audience of your choice, explaining either the causes or the effects of one of the following:

   a. Substance abuse by teenagers, young adults, or another group (see Sanders, "Under the Influence . . ." 192–203)
   b. America's 50 percent divorce rate (see Hall, "Killing Chickens" 120–23; McGuire, "Wake Up Call" 230–36)
   c. Genetic engineering (see McKibben, "Designer Genes" 572–82)
   d. Teenage pregnancy or smoking (see DiFranza "Hooked from the First Cigarette" 124–33)
   e. The popularity of a given television show, movie or rock star, film, book, or type of book (such as romance, Gothic, Western)
   f. Current taste in clothing, food, cars, architecture, interior decoration
   g. The Civil War; the Great Depression; World War II; the Vietnam War; the attack on the World Trade Center; or another historical event—such as the war in Iraq, Afghanistan, Darfur, Bosnia, or elsewhere
   h. The popularity of a particular spectator or active sport
   i. Your personality or temperament
   j. Success in college or in business
   k. Finding or losing one's religious faith
   l. Racial, sexual, or religious discrimination
   m. An increasingly higher proportion of working women (or mothers of young children)

n. Illiteracy
o. The American Dream that "if you work hard you're bound to succeed"
p. The actual or potential consequences of nuclear leaks, meltdowns, global warming, or natural disaster (see Collins et al., "The Physical Science behind Climate Change" 214–28)
q. Vanishing animal or plant species; or the depletion of natural resources (see Diamond, "The World as a Polder" 472–83)
r. The effects of outsourcing
s. Decrease in the number of people in training for skilled labor—electricians, plumbers, carpenters, tool and die makers, and others
t. A sudden change in personal status (from being a high school student to being a college freshman; from living at home to living away from home; from being dependent to being self-supporting; from being single to being married; from being childless to being a parent; from being married to widowed . . .)

2. Write a seemingly objective account of a social phenomenon or some other aspect of human behavior of which you actually disapprove, either because the form and context seem at variance, or because the phenomenon itself seems to you wrong, or to cause unanticipated problems, such as Anne Fadiman illustrates in "Under Water" (102–05), Deborah Tannen identifies in "Fast Forward: Technologically Enhanced Aggression" (308–15), and Bill McKibben analyzes in "Designer Genes" (572–82). You can justify your opinion (and convince your readers) through your choice of details and selection of a revealing incident or several vignettes. Ethical issues are suitable for a serious essay that examines the consequences of a process or set of beliefs, such as those Peter Singer addresses in "The Singer Solution to World Poverty" (535–41). Social and cultural phenomena are particularly suitable subjects for a comic essay—the causes or consequences of nerd or geek or yuppie or twenty-something behaviors—ways of spending money and leisure time and foolish, trivial, or wasteful things to spend it on.

PART III: CLARIFYING IDEAS

Description

When you describe a person, place, thing, experience, or phenomenon, you want your readers to understand it as you do and to experience its sounds, tastes, smells, or textures, both physical and emotional. You want to put your readers there—where you are, where your subject is—and enable them to see it through your eyes, interpret it through your understanding. Because you can't include everything, the details you select, the information you impart, will determine your emphasis, so pick the information that matters most to your point of view. You may decide to focus on only the big picture, the outline, the bare essentials, as do Kim Warp in "Rising Sea Levels—An Alternative Theory" (269) and Istvan Banyai in "Inflation" (285)—both convey considerable meaning in their cartoons by using minimal details. Or you may choose a closer perspective, concentrating on the small, revealing details as does Mark Twain in "Uncle John's Farm" (253–59), with its thickly sensuous descriptions of nature's bounty rendered through his childhood consciousness.

Your description can *exist for its own sake*, though in fact, few do. Most descriptions function in more than one way, for more than one purpose. A description, perhaps accompanied by a photograph or diagram, can exist *to show*—no surprise—*what something looks like or how it works*. Thus Linda Villarosa's "How Much of the Body Is Replaceable?" (250–51) simply presents the evidence to demonstrate that "from the top of the head to the tips of the toes, nearly every part of the body can be replaced. . . ." The accompanying diagram identifies the nature of the many replacement options—hair, brain, eyes, skin, heart, blood vessels, joints—with captions that explain the nature of the replacement and some of the research in progress. Issues of medical ethics, longevity, cost and allocation of medical time and resources, rationing, theology, and psychology—all of which would involve interpretation and might affect whether the replacements would actually be used—are off the table in this presentation.

Or *a description can serve as an argument*, with or without words. For instance, compare Villarosa's diagram with the two other graphic renderings of the human body in this chapter. Cartoonist Kim Warp's "Rising Sea Levels—An Alternative Theory" (269) makes its point about obesity by simply showing fat people happily eating while partially immersed in a rising body of water. In a comparable vein, Istvan Banyai's "Inflation" (285) needs no words to demonstrate—and implicitly argue against—astonishing inflation of both prices and the human body. His line drawings of the expanding figure on postage stamps from 1929–2050, with prices inflating from 3¢ to 1,000,000¢ during this time, say it all.

A description can also entertain. Another commentary on people's bodies, Suzanne Britt's "That Lean and Hungry Look" (281–83) concentrates on the temperaments, pastimes, and lifestyles of fat and thin people, rather than on the specifics of their bodies. Her generalizations—"Thin people believe in logic. Fat people see all sides. The sides fat people see are rounded blobs" (as depicted in the cartoons by both Warp and Banyai)—are intended to provide a humorous defense of the "convivial" fat, in comparison with the "oppressive" thin, whom readers will identify as general characters and personality types, rather than as specific individuals.

Such descriptions are inviting, welcoming. Mark Twain serves up nostalgia as he invites readers to visit "Uncle John's Farm" (253–59), with its appeal to the senses, for an abundance of sensory details are often the mainstay of description. Thus Twain evokes *sound* ("I know the crackling sound [a ripe watermelon] makes when the carving knife enters its end"); *smell* ("I can call back . . . [from] the deep woods, the earthy smells"); *touch* ("how snug and cozy one felt, under the blankets [on stormy nights]"); *taste* ("I know the taste of the watermelon which has been honestly come by, and I know the taste of the watermelon which has been acquired by art"); and *sight* ("I can see the white and black children grouped on the hearth, with the firelight playing on their faces and the shadows flickering upon the walls"). Twain calls on all our senses to take us to his beloved farm—and to love it as he does.

Indeed, most descriptions of places, like descriptions of people, phenomena, processes, and other subjects, are strongly influenced by the observer's aims, experiences, and values. Thus in much nontechnical writing the descriptions you provide are bound to be subjective, intended both to guide and influence your readers to see the topic your way rather than theirs. As a writer you can't afford to leave critical spaces blank; you must provide direction to influence your readers' interpretations. We have heard, to the point of cliché, that one picture is worth a thousand words, yet very often pictures need some words to expand and focus the interpretation to which the picture invites us. This is true not only of the cartoons on 269 and 285, for which we could come up with a variety of captions, but for all the pictures and diagrams throughout *The Essay Connection*, including Linda Villarosa's schematic diagram of replaceable parts of the body (250–51). Although the diagram shows us what parts are replaceable, we need written explanations to flesh out the figure.

Other *descriptions tell stories*, of people or places, re-creating the *emotional sense* of a person, place, or experience. Amanda Cagle's stunning creative nonfiction interpretation of her family's heritage and life "On the Banks of the Bogue Chitto" (245–49) views her Jena Choctaw family "through the dim and unreal morning shadows" in the Louisiana bayou where she was born and raised, where her free-spirited father taught her to shoot panthers with a bow and arrow. She describes her father in sensory language, "*listening* to the murmur of earthworms beneath his feet, *tasting* the first tomatoes, *watching* the swirls and ripples on the Bogue Chitto" [emphasis supplied]. Yet when her father "tried to conform to an employer's schedule, the rhythm of his own life always got in the way," and Cagle's description becomes an indictment of the white culture that has caused her teenage brother's unexplained suicide and her father's subsequent grief, breakdown, and entrapment in a dull, demeaning job as a mail carrier.

Michael Pollan's "The Meal" (261–68) describes in entertaining and explicit detail "the meal at the end of the industrial food chain . . . prepared by McDonald's and eaten in a moving car." To demonstrate that "well-designed fast food has a fragrance and flavor all its own," Pollan analyzes the "generic fast-food flavor" and composition of McNuggets, chicken pieces processed with thirteen corn-related products—which he lists and explains—and "several completely synthetic ingredients, quasiedible substances that . . . come from . . . a petroleum refinery or chemical plant." Along with "leavening agents" and antioxidants are "'anti-foaming agents' like dimethylpolysiloxene"—a probable carcinogen and an established cause of mutations, tumors, and reproductive problems; "it's also flammable." Pollan's lively description becomes an argument with every added nugget of information, an indictment of the destructive agricultural and manufacturing processes that transform potentially nutritious food into "a signifier of comfort food." "The more you concentrate on how it tastes, the less like anything it tastes."

In "Eating Made Simple" (270–79), Marion Nestle's nutrition research enables her to describe and interpret a mountain of conflicting diet advice on such topics as calories, meat, fish and heart disease, and sodas and obesity. Sound dietary principles remain constant, she says: "eat less; move more; eat fruits, vegetables and whole grains; and avoid too much junk food." Nestle explains nutritional issues involved in each and why the research—often on a single nutrient sponsored by industries that have an economic stake in the outcome—is confusing and contradictory. In a characteristic section, "Are Organics Healthier?" she identifies a typical fundamental conflict using a list (characteristic of description). The U.S. Department of Agriculture forbids producers of "Certified Organic Foods" from using "synthetic pesticides, herbicides, fertilizers, genetically modified seeds, irradiation or fertilizers derived from sewage sludge." Nevertheless, because the USDA's "principal mandate is to promote conventional agriculture"—which uses everything on this list—the USDA refuses to say that organic foods are either safer or more nutritious.

Though common sense would agree with these claims, supportive research is costly and scarce. In honesty, Nestle concludes that even if further research confirms that organic foods are more nutritious, "all fruits and vegetables contain certain useful nutrients, albeit in different combinations and concentrations," and that the main reason to buy organics is not for their presumed health benefits, but because "they are far less likely to damage the environment." Both Pollan and Nestle present a great deal of information in describing their subject and explaining the problems inherent in defining good nutrition; both analyze the information and imply—to the extent that their evidence allows them to do so—potential solutions to the problems they identify, but with the caution characteristic of good scientists and careful journalists. Although their presentations are balanced, in conclusion they tip the balance through selective details, flat-out assertion, tone, or a combination of these.

The point of Matt Nocton's careful description in "Harvest of Gold, Harvest of Shame" (286–90) is clear throughout because of his prevailing tone and choice of language. Tone, the prevailing mood of the essay, like a tone of voice conveys your attitude toward your subject and toward the evidence you present in support of your point. It is clear from the tone of all the essays in this chapter—indeed, all the essays in the entire *Essay Connection*—that the authors care deeply about their subjects. Nocton reports in a relatively objective tone on his personal experience with an aspect of farming—in this case, the harvesting of tobacco by a business that employs migrant and contract laborers, racial and ethnic minorities overseen by white bosses. Keeping himself out of the essay, he does not say in the essay that as a teenager, after two days on the job he was promoted to "bentkeeper" over the heads of minority employees with far more experience. Nevertheless, Nocton's concern for the workers and anger over their exploitation is apparent in the way he recounts the harvesting process, detail by detail, dirty, dusty, hot, and humiliating: each worker "must tie [a burlap sack] around his waist as a source of protection against the dirt and rocks that he will be dragging himself through for the next eight hours." Nocton's essay, like the creative nonfiction narratives by Amanda Cagle ("On the Banks of the Bogue Chitto" 245–49) and Meredith Hall ("Killing Chickens" 120–23) illustrate that these days, in nonfiction, anyway, unless it's satire, readers generally prefer understatement to overkill. There are always exceptions; the superabundance of good things at Twain's "Uncle John's Farm" (253–59) illustrates our—perhaps occasional—preference for overindulgence epitomized in Mae West's observation that "Too much of a good thing is—absolutely splendid." As the authors and illustrators in this chapter show us, there is a world of difference in descriptions, a compelling, complex world to explore. Whether we want the pictures wide-angled or narrow, distant or close up, sharply focused or fuzzy, is up to us—and our readers.

Strategies for Writing: Description

1. What is my main purpose in writing this descriptive essay? To present and interpret factual information about the subject? To re-create its essence as I have experienced it, or the person, as I have known him or her? To form the basis for a story, a cause-and-effect sequence, or an argument—overt or implied? What mixture of objective information and subjective impressions will best fit my purpose?
2. If my audience is completely unfamiliar with the subject, how much and what kinds of basic information will I have to provide so they can understand what I'm talking about? (Can I assume that they've seen lakes, but not necessarily Lake Tahoe, the subject of my paper? Or that they know other grandmothers, but not mine, about whom I'm writing?) If my readers are familiar with the subject, in what ways can I describe it so they'll discover new aspects of it?
3. What particular characteristics of my subject do I wish to emphasize? Will I use in this description details revealed by the senses—sight, sound, taste, smell, touch? Any other sort of information, such as a person's characteristic behavior, gestures, ways of speaking or moving or dressing, values, companions, possessions, occupation, residence, style of spending money, beliefs, hopes, vulnerabilities? Nonsensory details will be particularly necessary in describing an abstraction, such as somebody's temperament or state of mind.
4. How will I organize my description? From the most dominant to the least dominant details? From the most to the least familiar aspects (or vice versa)? According to what an observer is likely to notice first, second . . . last? Or according to some other pattern?
5. Will I use much general language, or will my description be highly specific throughout? Do I want to evoke a clear, distinct image of the subject? Or a mood—nostalgic, thoughtful, happy, sad, or otherwise?

AMANDA N. CAGLE

Amanda N. Cagle was born in Louisiana in 1979. She earned a BA in French (2000) and an MA in English (2001) at Mississippi State University, and a PhD in English at the University of Connecticut (2006) with a dissertation on American Indian women's poetry. Cagle's essays and poetry have appeared in *Ontario Review, Louisiana Review,* and *Revista Atenea.*

"On the Banks of the Bogue Chitto" won the Aetna Creative Nonfiction Award at the University of Connecticut and appeared in the Spring 2005 issue of the *Ontario Review*. The Bogue Chitto, which means "Big Creek" in Choctaw, winds through southern Louisiana and Mississippi.

✧ *On the Banks of the Bogue Chitto*

I was born on the banks of the Bogue Chitto. It was no accident. My mother wasn't caught miles from a hospital when she found herself in labor. She and my father purposefully walked from our plank-walled shotgun house into those woods and down to that bank. His arms supported her, and hers fitted over her taut belly like an insect's wings. It was early morning, and the light seemed false, my father used to say, like lamplight. Hung together in the gray were crows that fell lightly on the pines like a covering of ash. Even in January, the green kudzu vines curled tightly around the black bones of the cypress and the willow oak. My mother had already given birth to two children on the banks of the Bogue Chitto, and my father's mother, and her mothers, and many mothers before them had come to the same place. 1

This river is all the truth I've ever needed. It's where most of my family was born, where we were named, where we've found our food, where two of us have since chosen to die. It's where I've gone when the world's seemed too much. In this river, my grandmother proved herself to be the greatest catfish grabber in history by pulling an eighty-three-pound flathead to the banks. It's where my father was taught by his father to be a warrior. Where he taught me. I remember him standing on the bank beside me while I peered through the thickets and the dark roots of the forest floor to the slightest shift of shade and light. I stepped a few paces forward sure the very silence of the earth would follow me. I gently notched my arrow, pulled the bow taut, released the narrow shaft, and watched the panther's paw break into red blossoms. 2

When I think of my father, I like to remember times like these. I like to imagine that he is still the greatest of all the Jena Choctaw warriors. For many years, my brother Jason and I were convinced he was. When the Arrow Trucking Company would not let my father off work for Jason's seventh 3 birthday, he came ripping through our pasture at 5:00 in the morning with the big rig and its goods in tow. My father, Jason and I spent the morning picking Satsumas and the afternoon sitting on the banks of the Bogue Chitto chewing sugar cane which was heavy with the scent of hay and syrup.

4 That night, Jason and I slept in the cab of the 18-wheeler. We were not afraid that someone would steal up on us in the night to enter this mighty truck parked in our field. We knew our father would find a way to make things okay. Maybe the owner would come with a gun, and our father would tell a joke so funny that the man would laugh, pat him on the back and forget all about his truck. Maybe our father would hear the man coming and speed off into the night before he even arrived.

5 Of course, my father was fired from this job, as he would be from many others. He was not a very good employee. He wasn't good at making money or keeping it. He couldn't stand to be indoors, and as much as he tried to conform to an employer's schedule, the rhythm of his own life always got in the way. No job could hold him. When the needle-tooth garmade ripples in the river, my father forgot about work and headed out on the pirogue. When the cornfields stretched skyward and the watermelons grew too heavy for the vines, he could be found not at work but in the fields.

6 Somehow, I always expected him to be out there. When I was a child, I used to love to search for him through the dim and unreal morning shadows. He would be listening to the murmur of earthworms beneath his feet, tasting the first tomatoes, watching the swirls and ripples on the Bogue Chitto. These were his greatest moments. These were the times when he allowed himself to be free of the world. The water of the Bogue Chitto opened itself up to him, and he spent every day trapping and fishing along her banks.

7 I never thought nor hoped that there would come a time when the world owned him, when the water of the Bogue Chitto no longer flowed through him like a vein. But that time came when the state threatened to seize our land after my father had failed to come up with the money for the property taxes. He had lived on those thirty-three acres all of his life. The land had belonged to his father, his grandfather, and many fathers before them. He had tried to borrow money and to sell rebuilt car engines, but he couldn't get enough.

8 After the state assessed my father's land, they sent a social worker to assess his children. Jason, two cousins, and I ran into the woods when the social worker arrived. We watched the house from the tree line, unsure of what we were watching for. All I could picture was the man running after us with a giant net, scooping us up, and throwing us into his car.

9 Before long, we decided to head for the safety of our clubhouse, hidden deep in the tangled woods. Here we kept the bones we hunted and found like treasure. Most of them were from a neighbor's herd. The big bones came from sick cows that wandered off and starved or lay down between close trees and died. We had femurs, long and polished by the heat to a metallic whiteness. There were crescent ribs thin and pale as

David Muench/Stone/Getty Images

This mangrove swamp, with Spanish moss dripping from the branches, presents striking images of trees ethereal and eerie. Where is this located? Where is the shore? What's under the water? What time of day is it? What's the temperature? The humidity level? If people were in this picture, who would they be, and what would they be doing? Tell a story that interprets either the seen or the unseen (or both) in this photograph, and then see how closely your story corresponds to Amanda N. Cagle's "On the Banks of the Bogue Chitto."

the edges of the moon, a smooth hip bone with deep indentions as carefully hollowed out as the bowl of a pipe, and a skull nearly whole and full of black teeth with splintered roots. In these bones, we traced the lines of everything that had happened to us and everything that would.

One September Jason and I found a dog half eaten. His stomach was 10
ballooning out like a full sail, and we ran straight to the house. A panther, our father told us. In those woods, waiting for our father to send the social worker away, the wild moan of that panther stretched taut through the dim air like a scar.

We entered the house that night reluctantly. Our father was sitting on 11
the couch flipping through the phone book and writing down names and numbers. Early the next morning he went to town and did not return until nightfall. He continued to do this until he landed a job at the post office.

At first, he was just a temp, but he was scared and so he worked 12
hard to convince the post office to hire him full time. After a few years, he was given his own route. He arrived at dawn and returned home too late in the evening to work the fields or check the lines on the Bogue Chitto. But, for the first time in his life, he had a steady job, which meant the state would leave his land and his children alone.

13 My mother constantly praised his efforts. She was happy with the steady check and the health insurance. She had grown weary of his jumps between jobs and the anxious wait and hope for food upon his return from the woods. At first, he complained about the hours and the menial task of putting letters in a box, but my mother would simply rub his shoulders and tell him to suck it up. He did just that.

14 Over the next twelve years, he stopped telling stories about how to track deer, about when to plunge the arm deep into the mounded earth to feel for potatoes, and about how to interpret the cold and thin moan of the panther. Instead, he told us about who lived in what neighborhood and about the kind of mail they received. He especially liked to talk about the residents of the Indian Hills subdivision. There were no hills, he would say, and no Indians unless you counted Mr. Gupta.

15 If he had grown restless with the job, he didn't let us know it. He had settled into the expected routine. It was not the routine of a warrior, but I, more than my brother, understood what he had to lose. Nevertheless, I, like Jason, secretly hoped that he would turn in his uniforms. We longed for the days when we relied only on the Bogue Chitto to meet all of our needs. We missed the afternoons of sitting on her banks with our father and spitting muscadine seeds into the water. Sweet potato season passed us by; we harvested a few mustard greens but not enough to sell or freeze; there was squash, but no one stopped to watch it grow heavy with hips. The fall wind blew through the bald cypress, red maple, willow oak, and loblolly pine—the fragrance of death surrounded us, but none of us detected it.

16 In fact, it was a complete surprise. It still is and probably always will be. My father was the first to find out. Two officers arrived at the post office in an unmarked car, walked in and told him Jason was found on the bank of the Bogue Chitto. They were sure because there was a wallet beside the boy's body. There was a shotgun wound, self-inflicted. These things were a matter of fact. My father was so sure the officers were mistaken that he turned down a ride with them and drove himself to the morgue to confirm that the body was not that of his son. He later had to drive back to work to tell his supervisor that he would need a little time off from work; he was not sure how much.

17 He then told mother, the rest of the children, the grandparents and the cousins, and before long the entire Jena Choctaw tribe seemed to have descended on our house. I wondered for a moment if we would perform an old ceremony. The bone pickers of my grandfather's generation knew that in every bone there was an answer, but this was a different time. My father could do little more than pick out the nicest coffin he could afford. He purchased a plot of land that none of us had ever seen before. The man who sold it to him had a big round face and tight red fingers. He drew his boot heel across the plot and shook my father's hand.

18 My father spent the days following the funeral in the pastures cutting down what remained of the butterbeans, purple hulls and Satsuma. He paced along the banks of the Bogue Chitto and stared into its water. The

large animals living in the swamp water moved now like great shadows of a larger mystery. The river mud flaked in big cracks. My father sat on the bank like a smooth stone made by the waters of many a rain-lit night.

He returned to work too soon, and whatever he did there caused two more men in suits and an unmarked car to approach him. This time they came to our house, and they were not police but some type of high-ranking post office employees. They told him that he was in the midst of a nervous breakdown and that if he wanted to keep his job, he needed to check himself into the Woodland Hills Hospital for psychiatric treatment. When the men left, my cousins and I chased after them and threw small gravel rocks at their car. I didn't think for a moment that my father would go. I somehow expected him to follow behind us and to throw the furthest rock himself, but he did not. He sat inside on the couch while my mother pulled a suitcase from beneath their bed. 19

When I visited him at the hospital, his room was sterile and white. All of the blinds were down and the only sound was that of the hum of fluorescent lights. Sitting in the corner chair, under the falseness of the lamplight, he didn't look like anyone I had ever seen. 20

The family was invited to sit in on a few of the therapy sessions. Once the psychiatrist asked me to leave because she thought that I was interfering with my father's progress and disrupting the session. I had lashed out at him for taking the pills the psychiatrist had prescribed. I knew that neither the pills nor the stay at the white and sterile hospital would help him regain his balance. I wanted more than anything to be able to see him again as a warrior. I wanted him to leave the confines of the institution and return home to the ripening of the muscadines and the bedding of the catfish. 21

He did not stay long in that hospital. He returned to his job and to the routines of his life. The water of the Bogue Chitto must still run through him as it does through me, but he can no longer make the walls and ceilings that surround him vanish into fields of corn and horses, grain and cows, wandering ants and squirrels. There, where we used to sit, the marsh grass dances in the wind. Missing are the marks of our feet in the soft mud on the bank of the Bogue Chitto. Missing are the small prints that should hold the form of our bodies among the ancient creases and folds. 22

LINDA VILLAROSA

Linda Villarosa (born 1959) is a graduate of the University of Colorado and a former executive editor of *Essence Magazine*. She currently works as a freelance journalist based in New York City and has edited or coedited several books on parenting, adolescence, and health, including *Body & Soul: The Black Woman's Guide to Physical Health and Emotional Well-Being* (2003).

How Much of the Body Is Replaceable?*

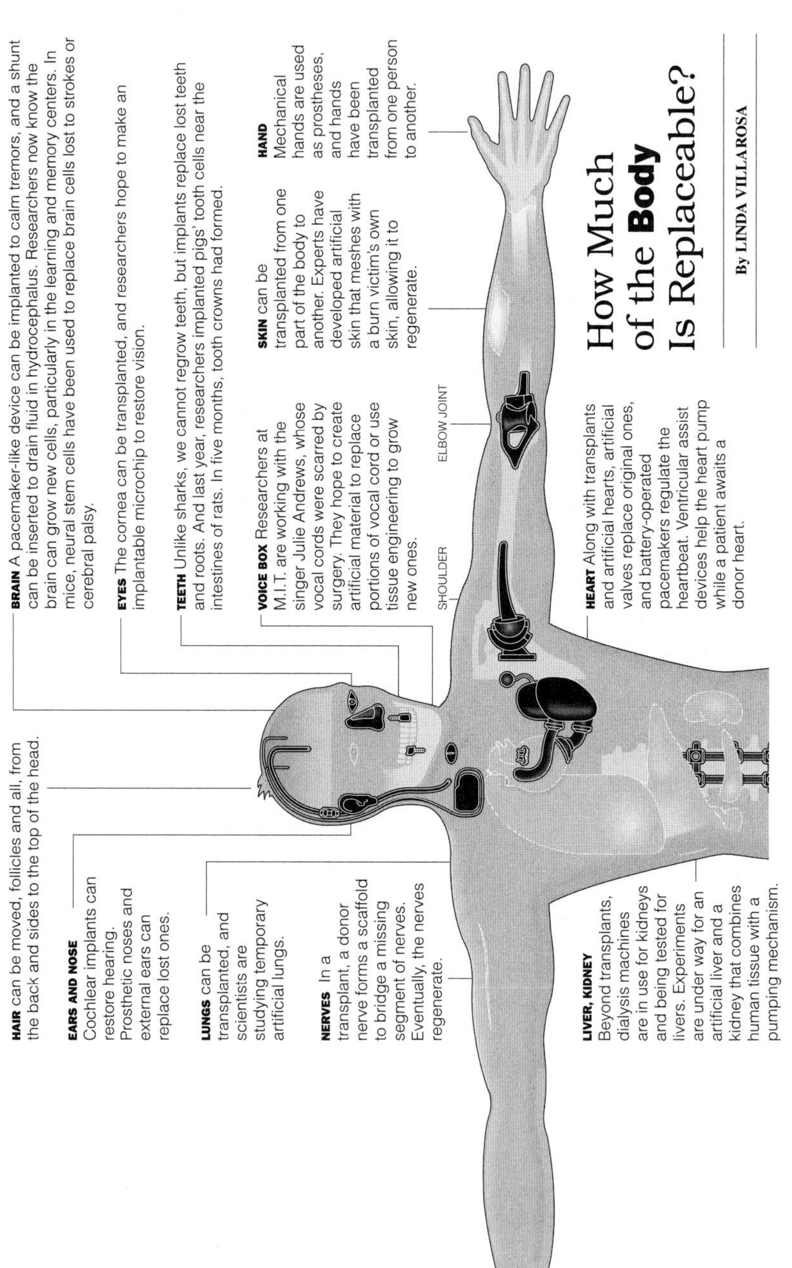

* From the NEW YORK TIMES, November 11, 2003. © 2003 NEW YORK TIMES. All rights reserved. Used by permission and protected by the Copyright Laws of the United States. The printing, copying, redistribution, or retransmission of the Material without express written permission is prohibited.

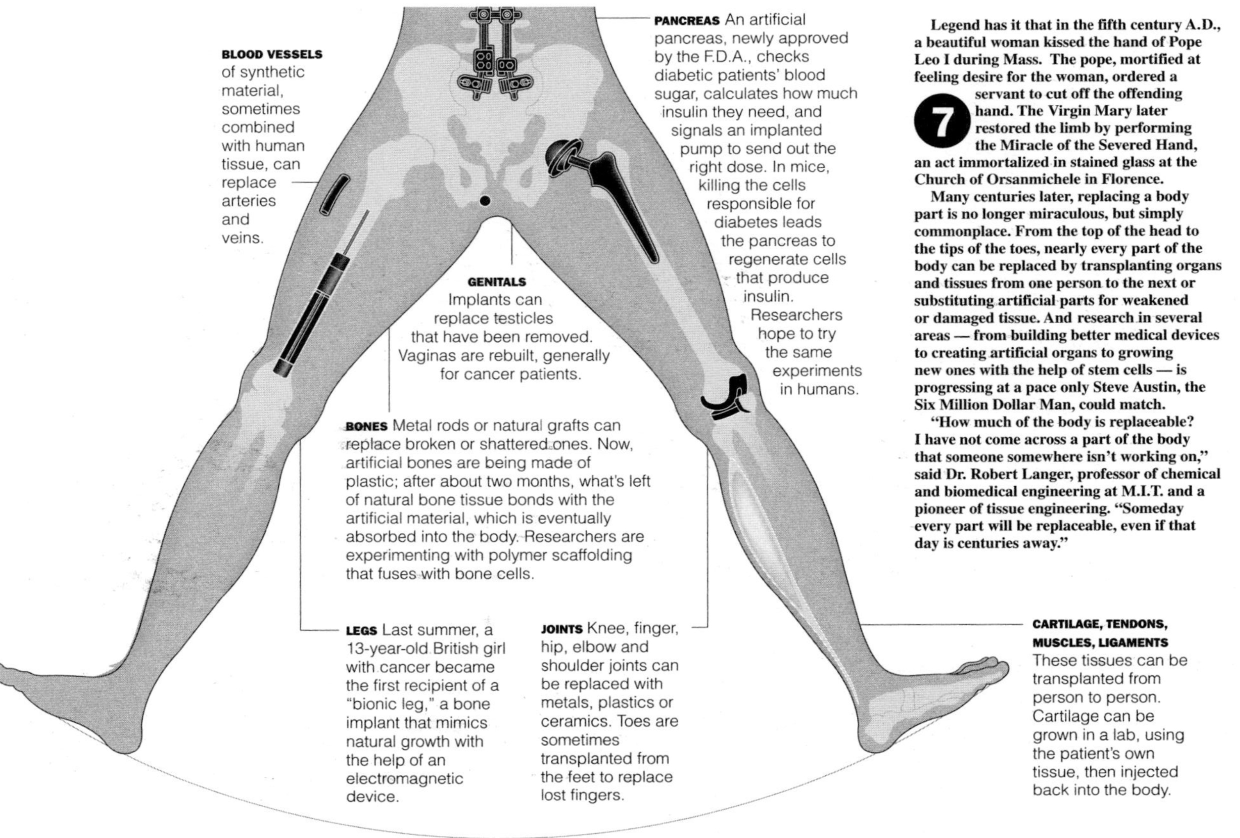

Legend has it that in the fifth century A.D., a beautiful woman kissed the hand of Pope Leo I during Mass. The pope, mortified at feeling desire for the woman, ordered a servant to cut off the offending hand. The Virgin Mary later restored the limb by performing the Miracle of the Severed Hand, an act immortalized in stained glass at the Church of Orsanmichele in Florence.

7

Many centuries later, replacing a body part is no longer miraculous, but simply commonplace. From the top of the head to the tips of the toes, nearly every part of the body can be replaced by transplanting organs and tissues from one person to the next or substituting artificial parts for weakened or damaged tissue. And research in several areas — from building better medical devices to creating artificial organs to growing new ones with the help of stem cells — is progressing at a pace only Steve Austin, the Six Million Dollar Man, could match.

"How much of the body is replaceable? I have not come across a part of the body that someone somewhere isn't working on," said Dr. Robert Langer, professor of chemical and biomedical engineering at M.I.T. and a pioneer of tissue engineering. "Someday every part will be replaceable, even if that day is centuries away."

Content

1. Villarosa refers to "the Six Million Dollar Man," from a television show about an action hero, who, after having been severely injured, was "put back together"—better than new—using artificial parts. *The Bionic Woman* took up a similar theme. What other shows or movies use this idea, and why is it a popular subject? If you have read Mary Shelley's *Frankenstein*, discuss to what extent it belongs to this tradition.

2. Many people currently alter their body voluntarily through plastic surgery. Do you suppose that at some time in the future people will elect to replace healthy body parts with stronger, more durable artificial ones? Explore the ethical implications of this possibility. For example, if professional athletes could buy themselves better knees, arms, or legs, what would the implications of this trend be for professional sports? What about students who might want to implant computing devices into their brain to enhance math ability? (See Bill McKibben, "Designer Genes" [Chapter 12], for an extension of this discussion.)

3. Villarosa's descriptions of replaceable body parts allude to ethically complex issues such as vivisection, prolonging life with mechanical devices, restoring body parts with donated organs, and human experimentation. Are such decisions ultimately personal? Should our society regulate such choices? For example, should the demand for donated organs be left to the free market? What are the pros and cons of establishing guidelines for medical research and experimentation?

For Writing

4. ***Journal Writing.*** Explore how the ethical issues Villarosa raises might influence the decision to replace your own or a loved one's body part(s). What criteria would you use to decide whether to take advantage of an experimental medical advance such as a transplant or artificial implant? Is medical intervention always, to some extent, experimentation? Discuss this with a writing partner and expand your discussion into an essay. Include relevant print or online sources.

5. ***Dialogues.*** How do Eisenberg's "Dialogue Boxes You Should Have Read More Carefully" (Chapter 10) and McKibben's "Designer Genes" (Chapter 12) suggest, like Villarosa's diagram, that technology has blurred the boundaries of human integrity? What issues does Marchetto's Op-Art "Why Haven't We Won the War on Cancer?" (Chapter 10) suggest about research on experimental medical procedures such as those Villarosa's diagram describes?

MARK TWAIN

Mark Twain (a riverman's term for "two fathoms deep," the pen name of Samuel Clemens [1835–1910]) celebrated in his writing a lifelong love affair with the Mississippi River and with the rural life along its banks. In *The Adventures of Tom Sawyer* (1876) and *The Adventures of Huckleberry Finn* (1885), he immortalized the riverfront town of Hannibal, Missouri, where he was born and whose folkways he absorbed. A prolific writer, Twain's works grew increasingly pessimistic as he experienced grief (the death of his beloved daughter) and economic reversals later in life. Nevertheless, in his *Autobiography* (published in 1924, fourteen years after his death), Twain depicted an idyllic but comically realistic picture of a country childhood, specific in time (pre–Civil War) and place (in the country, four miles from Florida, Missouri), yet timeless and ubiquitous. The autobiography shows us two central characters, the boy Sam Clemens, who enjoyed every aspect of his Uncle John Quarles's farm, and Mark Twain, the older, wiser, and sometimes more cynical author, who writes these reminiscences after alerting readers to bear in mind that he once could "remember anything, whether it had happened or not; but my faculties are decaying, now." What he remembers now is the spirit of the farm, the people who lived there, white and black, and how they lived in abiding harmony.

Twain reinforces that spirit with an abundance of sensory details—often the mainstay of description, as they are here. Thus he evokes a rich sensory intermingling in descriptions such as the following: "I can call back the solemn twilight [*sight*] and mystery of the deep woods, the earthy smells, the faint odors of the wild flowers [*smell*], the sheen of rain-washed foliage [*sight*], the rattling clatter of drops when the wind shook the trees, the far-off hammering of woodpeckers [*sound*]. . . . I can see the blue clusters of wild grapes . . . and I remember the taste of them and the smell" [*sight, taste, smell*] (¶ 13).

Uncle John's Farm*

For many years I believed that I remembered helping my grandfather drink his whiskey toddy when I was six weeks old, but I do not tell about that any more, now; I am grown old, and my memory is not as active as it used to be. When I was younger I could remember anything, whether it had happened or not; but my faculties are decaying, now, and soon I shall be so I cannot remember any but the things that [never] happened. It is sad to go to pieces like this, but we all have to do it. 1

My uncle, John A. Quarles, was a farmer, and his place was in the country four miles from Florida. He had eight children, and fifteen or twenty negroes, and was also fortunate in other ways. Particularly in his character. I have not come across a better man than he was. I was his guest for two or three months every year, from the fourth year after we removed to Hannibal till I was eleven or twelve years old. I have never consciously used him or his wife in a book, but his farm has come very handy to me in literature, once or twice. In *Huck Finn* and in *Tom Sawyer Detective* I moved it down to Arkansas. It was all of six hundred miles, but it was no trouble, it was not a very large farm; five hundred acres, perhaps, but I could have done it if it had been twice as large. And as for the morality of it, I cared nothing for that; I would move a State if the exigencies of literature required it. 2

* Title supplied

3 It was a heavenly place for a boy, that farm of my uncle John's. The house was a double log one, with a spacious floor (roofed in) connecting it with the kitchen. In the summer the table was set in the middle of that shady and breezy floor, and the sumptuous meals—well, it makes me cry to think of them. Fried chicken, roast pig, wild and tame turkeys, ducks and geese; venison just killed; squirrels, rabbits, pheasants, partridges, prairie-chickens; biscuits, hot batter cakes, hot buckwheat cakes, hot "wheat bread," hot rolls, hot corn pone; fresh corn boiled on the ear, succotash, butterbeans, string-beans, tomatoes, pease, Irish potatoes, sweet-potatoes; buttermilk, sweet milk, "clabber"; watermelons, muskmelons, cantaloupe—all fresh from the garden—apple pie, peach pie, pumpkin pie, apple dumplings, peach cobbler—I can't remember the rest. The way that the things were cooked was perhaps the main splendor—particularly a certain few of the dishes. For instance, the corn bread, the hot biscuits and wheat bread, and the fried chicken. These things have never been properly cooked in the North—in fact, no one there is able to learn the art, so far as my experience goes. The North thinks it knows how to make corn bread, but this is gross superstition. Perhaps no bread in the world is quite as good as Southern corn bread, and perhaps no bread in the world is quite so bad as the Northern imitation of it. The North seldom tries to fry chicken, and this is well; the art cannot be learned north of the line of Mason and Dixon, nor anywhere in Europe. . . .

4 It seems a pity that the world should throw away so many good things merely because they are unwholesome. I doubt if God has given us any refreshment which, taken in moderation, is unwholesome, except microbes. Yet there are people who strictly deprive themselves of each and every eatable, drinkable and smokable which has in any way acquired a shady reputation. They pay this price for health. And health is all they get for it. How strange it is; it is like paying out your whole fortune for a cow that has gone dry. . . .

5 The farmhouse stood in the middle of a very large yard, and the yard was fenced on three sides with rails and on the rear side with high palings; against these stood the smokehouse; beyond the palings was the orchard; beyond the orchard were the negro quarter and the tobacco-fields. The front yard was entered over a stile, made of sawed-off logs of graduated heights; I do not remember any gate. In a corner of the front yard were a dozen lofty hickory-trees and a dozen black-walnuts, and in the nutting season riches were to be gathered there.

6 Down a piece, abreast the house, stood a little log cabin against the rail fence; and there the woody hill fell sharply away, past the barns, the corn-crib, the stables and the tobacco-curing house, to a limpid brook which sang along over its gravelly bed and curved and frisked in and out and here and there and yonder in the deep shade of overhanging foliage and vines—a divine place for wading, and it had swimming-pools, too, which were forbidden to us and therefore much frequented by us. For

we were little Christian children, and had early been taught the value of forbidden fruit. . . .

I can see the farm yet, with perfect clearness. I can see all its belongings, all its details; the family room of the house, with a "trundle" bed in one corner and a spinning-wheel in another, a wheel whose rising and falling wail, heard from a distance, was the mournfulest of all sounds to me, and made me homesick and low-spirited, and filled my atmosphere with the wandering spirits of the dead; the vast fireplace, piled high, on winter nights, with flaming hickory logs from whose ends a sugary sap bubbled out but did not go to waste, for we scraped it off and ate it; the lazy cat spread out on the rough hearthstones, the drowsy dogs braced against the jambs and blinking; my aunt in one chimney-corner knitting, my uncle in the other smoking his corn-cob pipe; the slick and carpetless oak floor faintly mirroring the dancing flame-tongues and freckled with black indentations where fire-coals had popped out and died a leisurely death; half a dozen children romping in the background twilight; "split"-bottomed chairs here and there, some with rockers; a cradle—out of service, but waiting, with confidence; in the early cold mornings a snuggle of children, in shirts and chemises, occupying the hearthstone and procrastinating—they could not bear to leave that comfortable place and go out on the wind-swept floor-space between the house and kitchen where the general tin basin stood, and wash. 7

Along outside of the front fence ran the country road; dusty in the summertime, and a good place for snakes—they liked to lie in it and sun themselves; when they were rattlesnakes or puff adders, we killed them; when they were black snakes, or racers, or belonged to the fabled "hoop" breed, we fled, without shame; when they were "house snakes" or "garters" we carried them home and put them in Aunt Patsy's work-basket for a surprise; for she was prejudiced against snakes, and always when she took the basket in her lap and they began to climb out of it it disordered her mind. She never could seem to get used to them; her opportunities went for nothing. And she was always cold toward bats, too, and could not bear them; and yet I think a bat is as friendly a bird as there is. My mother was Aunt Patsy's sister, and had the same wild superstitions. A bat is beautifully soft and silky; I do not know any creature that is pleasanter to the touch, or is more grateful for caressings, if offered in the right spirit. I know all about these coleoptera, because our great cave, three miles below Hannibal, was multitudinously stocked with them, and often I brought them home to amuse my mother with. It was easy to manage if it was a school day, because then I had ostensibly been to school and hadn't any bats. She was not a suspicious person, but full of trust and confidence; and when I said "There's something in my coat pocket for you," she would put her hand in. But she always took it out again, herself; I didn't have to tell her. It was remarkable, the way she couldn't learn to like private bats. . . . 8

9 Beyond the road where the snakes sunned themselves was a dense young thicket, and through it a dim-lighted path led a quarter of a mile; then out of the dimness one emerged abruptly upon a level great prairie which was covered with wild strawberry-plants, vividly starred with prairie pinks, and walled in on all sides by forests. The strawberries were fragrant and fine, and in the season we were generally there in the crisp freshness of the early morning, while the dew-beads still sparkled upon the grass and the woods were ringing with the first songs of the birds.

10 Down the forest slopes to the left were the swings. They were made of bark stripped from hickory saplings. When they became dry they were dangerous. They usually broke when a child was forty feet in the air, and this was why so many bones had to be mended every year. I had no ill-luck myself, but none of my cousins escaped. There were eight of them, and at one time and another they broke fourteen arms among them. But it cost next to nothing, for the doctor worked by the year—$25 for the whole family. I remember two of the Florida doctors, Chowning and Meredith. They not only tended an entire family for $25 a year, but furnished the medicines themselves. Good measures, too. Only the largest persons could hold a whole dose. Castor-oil was the principal beverage. The dose was half a dipperful, with half a dipperful of New Orleans molasses added to help it down and make it taste good, which it never did. The next standby was calomel; the next, rhubarb; and the next, jalap. Then they bled the patient, and put mustard-plasters on him. It was a dreadful system, and yet the death-rate was not heavy. The calomel was nearly sure to salivate the patient and cost him some of his teeth. There were no dentists. When teeth became touched with decay or were otherwise ailing, the doctor knew of but one thing to do: he fetched his tongs and dragged them out. If the jaw remained, it was not his fault. Doctors were not called, in cases of ordinary illness; the family's grandmother attended to those. . . .

11 The country schoolhouse was three miles from my uncle's farm. It stood in a clearing in the woods, and would hold about twenty-five boys and girls. We attended the school with more or less regularity once or twice a week, in summer, walking to it in the cool of the morning by the forest paths, and back in the gloaming at the end of the day. All the pupils brought their dinners in baskets—corn-dodger, buttermilk and other good things—and sat in the shade of the trees at noon and ate them. It is the part of my education which I look back upon with the most satisfaction. My first visit to the school was when I was seven. A strapping girl of fifteen, in the customary sunbonnet and calico dress, asked me if I "used tobacco"—meaning did I chew it. I said, no. It roused her scorn. She reported me to all the crowd, and said—

12 "Here is a boy seven years old who can't chaw tobacco."

13 By the looks and comments which this produced, I realized that I was a degraded object; I was cruelly ashamed of myself. I determined

to reform. But I only made myself sick; I was not able to learn to chew tobacco. I learned to smoke fairly well, but that did not conciliate anybody, and I remained a poor thing, and characterless. I longed to be respected, but I never was able to rise. Children have but little charity for each other's defects.

As I have said, I spent some part of every year at the farm until 14
I was twelve or thirteen years old. The life which I led there with my cousins was full of charm, and so is the memory of it yet. I can call back the solemn twilight and mystery of the deep woods, the earthy smells, the faint odors of the wild flowers, the sheen of rain-washed foliage, the rattling clatter of drops when the wind shook the trees, the far-off hammering of woodpeckers and the muffled drumming of wood-pheasants in the remoteness of the forest, the snap-shot glimpses of disturbed wild creatures skurrying through the grass,—I can call it all back and make it as real as it ever was, and as blessed. I can call back the prairie, and its loneliness and peace, and a vast hawk hanging motionless in the sky, with his wings spread wide and the blue of the vault showing through the fringe of their end-feathers. I can see the woods in their autumn dress, the oaks purple, the hickories washed with gold, the maples and the sumacs luminous with crimson fires, and I can hear the rustle made by the fallen leaves as we ploughed through them. I can see the blue clusters of wild grapes hanging amongst the foliage of the saplings, and I remember the taste of them and the smell. I know how the wild blackberries looked, and how they tasted; and the same with the paw-paws, the hazelnuts and the persimmons; and I can feel the thumping rain, upon my head, of hickory-nuts and walnuts when we were out in the frosty dawn to scramble for them with the pigs, and the gusts of wind loosed them and sent them down. I know the stain of blackberries, and how pretty it is; and I know the stain of walnut hulls, and how little it minds soap and water; also what grudged experience it had of either of them. I know the taste of maple sap, and when to gather it, and how to arrange the troughs and the delivery tubes, and how to boil down the juice, and how to hook the sugar after it is made; also how much better hooked sugar tastes than any that is honestly come by, let bigots say what they will. I know how a prize watermelon looks when it is sunning its fat rotundity among pumpkin-vines and "simblins"; I know how to tell when it is ripe without "plugging" it; I know how inviting it looks when it is cooling itself in a tub of water under the bed, waiting; I know how it looks when it lies on the table in the sheltered great floor-space between house and kitchen, and the children gathered for the sacrifice and their mouths watering; I know the crackling sound it makes when the carving-knife enters its end, and I can see the split fly along in front of the blade as the knife cleaves its way to the other end; I can see its halves fall apart and display the rich red meat and the black seeds, and the heart standing up, a luxury fit for the elect; I know how a boy looks, behind a yard-long slice of that

melon, and I know how he feels; for I have been there. I know the taste of the watermelon which has been honestly come by, and I know the taste of the watermelon which has been acquired by art. Both taste good, but the experienced know which tastes best. I know the look of green apples and peaches and pears on the trees, and I know how entertaining they are when they are inside of a person. I know how ripe ones look when they are piled in pyramids under the trees, and how pretty they are and how vivid their colors. I know how a frozen apple looks, in a barrel down cellar in the winter-time, and how hard it is to bite, and how the frost makes the teeth ache, and yet how good it is, notwithstanding. I know the disposition of elderly people to select the specked apples for the children, and I once knew ways to beat the game. I know the look of an apple that is roasting and sizzling on a hearth on a winter's evening, and I know the comfort that comes of eating it hot, along with some sugar and a drench of cream. I know the delicate art and mystery of so cracking hickory-nuts and walnuts on a flatiron with a hammer that the kernels will be delivered whole, and I know how the nuts, taken in conjunction with winter apples, cider and doughnuts, make old people's tales and old jokes sound fresh and crisp and enchanting, and juggle an evening away before you know what went with the time. I know the look of Uncle Dan'l's kitchen as it was on privileged nights when I was a child, and I can see the white and black children grouped on the hearth, with the firelight playing on their faces and the shadows flickering upon the walls, clear back toward the cavernous gloom of the rear, and I can hear Uncle Dan'l telling the immortal tales which Uncle Remus Harris was to gather into his books and charm the world with, by and by; and I can feel again the creepy joy which quivered through me when the time for the ghost-story of the "Golden Arm" was reached—and the sense of regret, too, which came over me, for it was always the last story of the evening, and there was nothing between it and the unwelcome bed.

15 I can remember the bare wooden stairway in my uncle's house, and the turn to the left above the landing, and the rafters and the slanting roof over my bed, and the squares of moonlight on the floor, and the white cold world of snow outside, seen through the curtainless window. I can remember the howling of the wind and the quaking of the house on stormy nights, and how snug and cozy one felt, under the blankets, listening, and how the powdery snow used to sift in, around the sashes, and lie in little ridges on the floor, and make the place look chilly in the morning, and curb the wild desire to get up—in case there was any. I can remember how very dark that room was, in the dark of the moon, and how packed it was with ghostly stillness when one woke up by accident away in the night, and forgotten sins came flocking out of the secret chambers of the memory and wanted a hearing; and how ill chosen the time seemed for this kind of business; and how dismal was the hoo-hooing of the owl and the wailing of the wolf, sent mourning by on the night wind.

I remember the raging of the rain on that roof, summer nights, and how pleasant it was to lie and listen to it, and enjoy the white splendor of the lightning and the majestic booming and crashing of the thunder. It was a very satisfactory room; and there was a lightning-rod which was reachable from the window, an adorable and skittish thing to climb up and down, summer nights, when there were duties on hand of a sort to make privacy desirable. 16

I remember the 'coon and 'possum hunts, night, and the negroes, and the long marches through the black gloom of the woods, and the excitement which fired everybody when the distant bay of an experienced dog announced that the game was treed; then the wild scramblings and stumblings through briars and bushes and over roots to get to the spot; then the lighting of a fire and the felling of the tree, the joyful frenzy of the dogs and the negroes, and the weird picture it all made in the red glare—I remember it all well, and the delight that every one got out of it, except the 'coon. 17

I remember the pigeon seasons, when the birds would come in millions, and cover the trees, and by their weight break down the branches. They were clubbed to death with sticks; guns were not necessary, and were not used. I remember the squirrel hunts, and the prairie-chicken hunts, and the wild-turkey hunts, and all that; and how we turned out, mornings, while it was still dark, to go on these expeditions, and how chilly and dismal it was, and how often I regretted that I was well enough to go. A toot on a tin horn brought twice as many dogs as were needed, and in their happiness they raced and scampered about, and knocked small people down, and made no end of unnecessary noise. At the word, they vanished away toward the woods, and we drifted silently after them in the melancholy gloom. But presently the gray dawn stole over the world, the birds piped up, then the sun rose and poured light and comfort all around, everything was fresh and dewy and fragrant, and life was a boon again. After three hours of tramping we arrived back wholesomely tired, overladen with game, very hungry, and just in time for breakfast. 18

Content

1. Even though Twain's opening paragraph warns that he sometimes remembers something, "whether it had happened or not," what he says throughout this essay appears true and convincing. Why? Does anything seem too good to be true? What made the farm a "heavenly place for a boy"? Do his memories of children's broken bones (¶ 10) and his childhood shame at being unable to chew tobacco (¶s 11–13) diminish his pleasant recollections?

Strategies/Structures/Language

2. In places Twain's description involves long lists or catalogues—of foods (¶ 3), of the sights and sounds and activities of farm life (¶s 3–14), and of the seasons and seasonal activities (¶s 15–18). How does he vary the lists to keep them appealing?

3. Why does Twain pack so many details into such a long paragraph (¶ 14)? If he had broken it up, where could he have done so? With what effects?

4. In this largely descriptive account, Twain provides characterizations of the local doctors (¶ 10), many interpretations ("The life was. . . full of charm," [¶ 14]), and narration of incidents—for instance, of Aunt Patsy and the snakes (¶ 8). Explain how these techniques contribute to the overall picture of life on the farm.

5. Twain uses the language of an adult to recall events from his childhood. Find a typical passage in which he enables us to see the experience as a child would but to imply or offer an adult's interpretation.

For Writing

6. ***Journal Writing***. Identify a place that had considerable significance—pleasant, indifferent, unpleasant, or a mixture—for you as a child, and describe it. Use sensory details, where appropriate, to help your readers to re-create your experiences. The essays by Megan McGuire (230–36), Amanda N. Cagle (245–49), and Matt Nocton (286–90) provide good examples of how to do this.

7. Pick an aspect of your childhood relationship with a parent or other adult, or a critical experience in your precollege schooling, and describe it so the reader shares your experience. Compare, if you wish, with essays by Frederick Douglass (89–93), Anne Fadiman (102–06), Ning Yu (166–74), Scott Russell Sanders (143–50), or Megan McGuire (230–36).

8. "Our three basic needs, for food and security and love, are so mixed and mingled and entwined that we cannot straightly think of one without the others," says distinguished food writer M. F. K. Fisher. Write an essay focusing on the relationship between food and people: about how food has either shown you something about yourself; shaped your relationship with an individual, family, or group; or inspired adventures, culinary, philosophical, or otherwise. Your writing can range from how-to-do-it (gardening or recipes in context) to memories of events in which food (or its absence) played a major role—evoking succulence, hospitality, seduction, stress, an entire culture conveyed in a single dish or meal. Compare, if you wish, Megan McGuire's essay "Wake-Up Call" (Chapter 5) and Lynda Barry's graphic essay "Common Scents" (Chapter 8).

9. ***Dialogues.*** Compare Twain's descriptions of the sights, flavors, and textures of the life on the farm and surrounding countryside with Shange's (Chapter 4). What does each writer appear to have learned through the experiences he narrates? Compare, for example, Twain's references to "forbidden fruit" (¶ 6) and to the "fragrant and fine" "wild strawberry-plants" that grew "beyond the road where the snakes sunned themselves" (¶ 9). How do their descriptions suggest a process of internalizing the specific values of their respective cultures?

10. Twain celebrates the opulence of the South, including its cuisine (¶ 3), and disparages those who reject "good things merely because they are unwholesome" (¶ 4). What are some of the positive and negative ways that our society responds to abundance and wealth (see Charles C. Mann, "Forever Young" [Chapter 9],

and Robert Reich, "The Global Elite" [Chapter 10]? How do we glorify and also criticize extravagant lifestyles? What do these responses suggest about contemporary American culture?

MICHAEL POLLAN

Michael Pollan (born 1955) is the author of *Second Nature: A Gardener's Education* (2003); *The Botany of Desire: A Plant's Eye-View of the World* (2006); *The Omnivore's Dilemma: A Natural History of Four Meals* (2006); and *In Defense of Food: An Eater's Manifesto* (2008). He is a contributing writer to *The New York Times Magazine* and a Professor of Journalism at the University of California at Berkeley, where he directs the Knight Program in Science and Environmental Journalism. In "The Meal," excerpted from *The Omnivore's Dilemma*, Pollan examines how our relationship with the natural world has changed through the growth of industrial agriculture, the dominance of corn in the industrial food chain, and the consumption of processed food, of which corn constitutes a major part.

The Meal

The meal at the end of the industrial food chain that begins in an Iowa cornfield is prepared by McDonald's and eaten in a moving car. Or at least this was the version of the industrial meal I chose to eat; it could easily have been another. The myriad streams of commodity corn, after being variously processed and turned into meat, converge in all sorts of different meals I might have eaten, at KFC or Pizza Hut or Applebee's, or prepared myself from ingredients bought at the supermarket. Industrial meals are all around us, after all; they make up the food chain from which most of us eat most of the time. 1

My eleven-year-old son, Isaac, was more than happy to join me at McDonald's; he doesn't get there often, so it's a treat. (For most American children today, it is no longer such a treat: One in three of them eat fast food every single day.) Judith, my wife, was less enthusiastic. She's careful about what she eats, and having a fast-food lunch meant giving up a "real meal," which seemed a shame. Isaac pointed out that she could order one of McDonald's new "premium salads" with the Paul Newman dressing. I read in the business pages that these salads are a big hit, but even if they weren't, they'd probably stay on the menu strictly for their rhetorical usefulness. The marketers have a term for what a salad or veggie burger does for a fast-food chain: "denying the denier." These healthier menu items 2 hand the child who wants to eat fast food a sharp tool with which to chip away at his parents' objections. "But Mom, you can get the salad . . ."

3 Which is exactly what Judith did: order the Cobb salad with Caesar dressing. At $3.99, it was the most expensive item on the menu. I ordered a classic cheeseburger, large fries, and a large Coke. Large turns out to be a full 32 ounces (a quart of soda!) but, thanks to the magical economics of supersizing, it cost only 30 cents more than the 16-ounce "small." Isaac went with the new white-meat Chicken McNuggets, a double-thick vanilla shake, and a large order of fries, followed by a new dessert treat consisting of freeze-dried pellets of ice cream. That each of us ordered something different is a hallmark of the industrial food chain, which breaks the family down into its various demographics and markets separately to each one: Together we would be eating alone together, and therefore probably eating more. The total for the three of us came to fourteen dollars, and was packed up and ready to go in four minutes. Before I left the register I picked up a densely printed handout called "A Full Serving of Nutrition Facts: Choose the Best Meal for You."

4 We could have slipped into a booth, but it was such a nice day we decided to put the top down on the convertible and eat our lunch in the car, something the food and the car have both been engineered to accommodate. These days 19 percent of American meals are eaten in the car. The car has cup holders, front seat and rear, and, except for the salad, all the food (which we could have ordered, paid for, and picked up without opening the car door) can be readily eaten with one hand. Indeed, this is the genius of the chicken nugget: It liberated chicken from the fork and plate, making it as convenient, waste-free, and automobile-friendly as the precondimented hamburger. No doubt the food scientists at McDonald's corporate headquarters in Oak Brook, Illinois, are right now hard at work on the one-handed salad.

5 But though Judith's Cobb salad did present a challenge to front-seat dining, eating it at fifty-five miles per hour seemed like the thing to do, since corn was the theme of this meal: The car was eating corn too, being fueled in part by ethanol. Even though the additive promises to *diminish* air quality in California, new federal mandates pushed by the corn processors require refineries in the state to help eat the corn surplus by diluting their gasoline with 10 percent ethanol.

6 I ate a lot of McDonald's as a kid. This was in the pre-Wallerstein era, when you still had to order a second little burger or sack of fries if you wanted more, and the chicken nugget had not yet been invented. (One memorable childhood McDonald's meal ended when our station wagon got rear-ended at a light, propelling my milk shake across the car in creamy white lariats.) I loved everything about fast food: the individual portions all wrapped up like presents (not having to share with my three sisters was a big part of the appeal; fast food was private property at its best); the familiar meaty perfume of the French fries filling the car; and the pleasingly sequenced bite into a burger—the soft, sweet roll, the crunchy pickle, the savory moistness of the meat.

Well-designed fast food has a fragrance and flavor all its own, a 7
fragrance and flavor only nominally connected to hamburgers or French fries or for that matter to *any* particular food. Certainly the hamburgers and fries you make at home don't have it. And yet Chicken McNuggets do, even though they're ostensibly an entirely different food made from a different species. Whatever it is (surely the food scientists know), for countless millions of people living now, this generic fast-food flavor is one of the unerasable smells and tastes of childhood—which makes it a kind of comfort food. Like other comfort foods, it supplies (besides nostalgia) a jolt of carbohydrates and fat, which, some scientists now believe, relieve stress and bathe the brain in chemicals that make it feel good.

Isaac announced that his white-meat McNuggets were tasty, a defi- 8
nite improvement over the old recipe. McNuggets have come in for a lot of criticism recently, which might explain the reformulation. Ruling in 2003 in a lawsuit brought against McDonald's by a group of obese teenagers, a federal judge in New York had defamed the McNugget even as he dismissed the suit. "Rather than being merely chicken fried in a pan," he wrote in his decision, McNuggets "are a McFranksteinian creation of various elements not utilized by the home cook." After cataloging the thirty-eight ingredients in a McNugget, Judge Sweet suggested that McDonald's marketing bordered on deceptive, since the dish is not what it purports to be—that is, a piece of chicken simply fried—and, contrary to what a consumer might reasonably expect, actually contains more fat and total calories than a cheeseburger. Since the lawsuit, McDonald's has reformulated the nugget with white meat, and begun handing out "A Full Serving of Nutrition Facts."* According to the flyer, a serving of six nuggets now has precisely ten fewer calories than a cheeseburger. Chalk up another achievement for food science.

When I asked Isaac if the new nuggets tasted more like chicken 9
than he old ones, he seemed baffled by the question. "No, they taste like what they are, which is nuggets," and then dropped on his dad a withering two-syllable "duh." In this consumer's mind at least, the link between a nugget and the chicken in it was never more than notional, and probably irrelevant. By now the nugget constitutes its own genre of food for American children, many of whom eat nuggets every day. For Isaac, the nugget is a distinct taste of childhood, quite apart from chicken, and no doubt a future vehicle of nostalgia—a madeleine in the making.

Isaac passed one up to the front for Judith and me to sample. It looked 10
and smelled pretty good, with a nice crust and bright white interior reminiscent of chicken breast meat. In appearance and texture a nugget certainly alludes to fried chicken, yet all I could really taste was salt, that all-purpose fast-food flavor, and, okay, maybe a note of chicken bouillon

---

* In 2005 McDonald's announced it would begin printing nutrition information on its packaging.

informing the salt. Overall the nugget seemed more like an abstraction than a full-fledged food, an idea of chicken waiting to be fleshed out.

11 The ingredients listed in the flyer suggest a lot of thought goes into a nugget, that and a lot of corn. Of the thirty-eight ingredients it takes to make a McNugget, I counted thirteen that can be derived from corn: the corn-fed chicken itself; modified cornstarch (to bind the pulverized chicken meat); mono-, tri-, and diglycerides (emulsifiers, which keep the fats and water from separating); dextrose; lecithin (another emulsifier); chicken broth (to restore some of the flavor that processing leaches out); yellow corn flour and more modified cornstarch (for the batter); cornstarch (a filler); vegetable shortening; partially hydrogenated corn oil; and citric acid as a preservative. A couple of other plants take part in the nugget: There's some wheat in the batter, and on any given day the hydrogenated oil could come from soybeans, canola, or cotton rather than corn, depending on market price and availability.

12 According to the handout, McNuggets also contain several completely synthetic ingredients, quasiedible substances that ultimately come not from a corn or soybean field but from a petroleum refinery or chemical plant. These chemicals are what make modern processed foods possible, by keeping the organic materials in them from going bad or looking strange after months in the freezer or on the road. Listed first are the "leavening agents": sodium aluminum phosphate, monocalcium phosphate, sodium acid pyrophosphate, and calcium lactate. These are antioxidants added to keep the various animal and vegetable fats involved in a nugget from turning rancid. Then there are "antifoaming agents" like dimethylpolysiloxene, added to the cooking oil to keep the starches from binding to air molecules, so as to produce foam during the fry. The problem is evidently grave enough to warrant adding a toxic chemical to the food: According to the *Handbook of Food Additives*, dimethylpolysiloxene is a suspected carcinogen and an established mutagen, tumorigen, and reproductive effector; it's also flammable. But perhaps the most alarming ingredient in a Chicken McNugget is tertiary butylhydroquinone, or TBHQ, an antioxidant derived from petroleum that is either sprayed directly on the nugget or the inside of the box it comes in to "help preserve freshness." According to *A Consumer's Dictionary of Food Additives*, TBHQ is a form of butane (i.e., lighter fluid) the FDA allows processors to use sparingly in our food: It can comprise no more than 0.02 percent of the oil in a nugget. Which is probably just as well, considering that ingesting a single gram of TBHQ can cause "nausea, vomiting, ringing in the ears, delirium, a sense of suffocation, and collapse." Ingesting five grams of TBHQ can kill.

13 With so many exotic molecules organized into a food of such complexity, you would almost expect a chicken nugget to do something more spectacular than taste okay to a child and fill him up inexpensively. What it has done, of course, is to sell an awful lot of chicken for companies like Tyson, which invented the nugget—at McDonald's behest—in 1983. The nugget is the reason chicken has supplanted beef as the most popular meat in America.

14 Compared to Isaac's nuggets, my cheeseburger is a fairly simple construct. According to "A Full Serving of Nutrition Facts," the cheeseburger

contains a mere six ingredients, all but one of them familiar: a 100 percent beef patty, a bun, two American cheese slices, ketchup, mustard, pickles, onions, and "grill seasoning," whatever that is. It tasted pretty good, too, though on reflection what I mainly tasted were the condiments: Sampled by itself, the gray patty had hardly any flavor. And yet the whole package, especially on first bite, did manage to give off a fairly convincing burger-ish aura. I suspect, however, that owes more to the olfactory brilliance of the "grill seasoning" than to the 100 percent beef patty.

15 In truth, my cheeseburger's relationship to beef seemed nearly as metaphorical as the nugget's relationship to a chicken. Eating it, I had to remind myself that there was an actual cow involved in this meal—most likely a burned-out old dairy cow (the source of most fast-food beef) but possibly bits and pieces of a steer . . . as well. Part of the appeal of hamburgers and nuggets is that their boneless abstractions allow us to forget we're eating animals. I'd been on the feedlot in Garden City only a few months earlier, yet this experience of cattle was so far removed from that one as to be taking place in a different dimension. No, I could not taste the feed corn or the petroleum or the antibiotics or the hormones—or the feedlot manure. Yet while "A Full Serving of Nutrition Facts" did not enumerate these facts, they too have gone into the making of this hamburger, are part of its natural history. That perhaps is what the industrial food chain does best: obscure the histories of the foods it produces by processing them to such an extent that they appear as pure products of culture rather than nature—things made from plants and animals. Despite the blizzard of information contained in the helpful McDonald's flyer—the thousands of words and numbers specifying ingredients and portion sizes, calories and nutrients—all this food remains perfectly opaque. Where does it come from? It comes from McDonald's.

16 But that's not so. It comes from refrigerated trucks and from warehouses, from slaughterhouses, from factory farms in towns like Garden City, Kansas, from ranches in Sturgis, South Dakota, from food science laboratories in Oak Brook, Illinois, from flavor companies on the New Jersey Turnpike, from petroleum refineries, from processing plants owned by ADM and Cargill, from grain elevators in towns like Jefferson, and, at the end of that long and tortuous trail, from a field of corn and soybeans farmed by George Naylor in Churdan, Iowa.

17 It would not be impossible to calculate exactly how much corn Judith, Isaac, and I consumed in our McDonald's meal. I figure my 4-ounce burger, for instance, represents nearly 2 pounds of corn (based on a cow's feed conversion rate of 7 pounds of corn for every 1 pound of gain, half of which is edible meat). The nuggets are a little harder to translate into corn, since there's no telling how much actual chicken goes into a nugget; but if 6 nuggets contain a quarter pound of meat, that would have taken a chicken half a pound of feed corn to grow. A 32-ounce soda contains 86 grams of high-fructose corn syrup (as does a double-thick shake), which can be refined from a third of a pound of corn; so our 3 drinks used another 1 pound. Subtotal: six pounds of corn.

18 From here the calculations become trickier because, according to the ingredients list in the flyer, corn is everywhere in our meal, but in unspecified amounts. There's more corn sweetener in my cheeseburger, of all places: The bun and the ketchup both contain HFCS. It's in the salad dressing, too, and the sauces for the nuggets, not to mention Isaac's dessert. (Of the sixty menu items listed in the handout, forty-five contain HFCS.) Then there are all the other corn ingredients in the nugget: the binders and emulsifiers and fillers. In addition to corn sweeteners, Isaac's shake contains corn syrup solids, mono- and diglycerides, and milk from corn-fed animals. Judith's Cobb salad is also stuffed with corn, even though there's not a kernel in it: Paul Newman makes his dressing with HFCS, corn syrup, corn starch, dextrin, caramel color, and xanthan gum; the salad itself contains cheese and eggs from corn-fed animals. The salad's grilled chicken breast is injected with a "flavor solution" that contains maltodextrin, dextrose, and monosodium glutamate. Sure, there are a lot of leafy greens in Judith's salad too, but the overwhelming majority of the calories in it (and there are 500 of them, when you count the dressing) ultimately come from corn. And the French fries? You would think those are mostly potatoes. Yet since half of the 540 calories in a large order of fries come from the oil they're fried in, the ultimate source of these calories is not a potato farm but a field of corn or soybeans.

19 The calculation finally defeated me, but I took it far enough to estimate that, if you include the corn in the gas tank (a whole bushel right there, to make two and a half gallons of ethanol), the amount of corn that went into producing our movable fast-food feast would easily have overflowed the car's trunk, spilling a trail of golden kernels on the blacktop behind us.

20 Some time later I found another way to calculate just how much corn we had eaten that day. I asked Todd Dawson, a biologist at Berkeley, to run a McDonald's meal through his mass spectrometer and calculate how much of the carbon in it came originally from a corn plant. It is hard to believe that the identity of the atoms in a cheeseburger or a Coke is preserved from farm field to fast-food counter, but the atomic signature of those carbon isotopes is indestructible, and still legible to the mass spectrometer. Dawson and his colleague Stefania Mambelli prepared an analysis showing roughly how much of the carbon in the various McDonald's menu items came from corn, and plotted them on a graph. The sodas came out at the top, not surprising since they consist of little else than corn sweetener, but virtually everything else we ate revealed a high proportion of corn, too. In order of diminishing corniness, this is how the laboratory measured our meal: soda (100 percent corn), milk shake (78 percent), salad dressing (65 percent), chicken nuggets (56 percent), cheeseburger (52 percent), and French fries (23 percent). What in the eyes of the omnivore looks like a meal of impressive variety turns out, when viewed through the eyes of the mass spectrometer, to be the meal of a far

more specialized kind of eater. But then, this is what the industrial eater has become: corn's koala.

So what? Why should it matter that we have become a race of corn eaters such as the world has never seen? Is this necessarily a bad thing? The answer all depends on where you stand. 21

If where you stand is in agribusiness, processing cheap corn into forty-five different McDonald's items is an impressive accomplishment. It represents a solution to the agricultural contradictions of capitalism, the challenge of increasing food industry profits faster than America can increase its population. Supersized portions of cheap corn-fixed carbon solves the problem of the fixed stomach; we may not be expanding the number of eaters in America, but we've figured out how to expand each of their appetites, which is almost as good. Judith, Isaac, and I together consumed a total of 4,510 calories at our lunch—more than half as many as we each should probably consume in a day. We had certainly done our parts in chomping through the corn surplus. (We had also consumed a lot of petroleum, and not just because we were in a car. To grow and process those 4,510 food calories took at least ten times as many calories of fossil energy, the equivalent of 1.3 gallons of oil.) 22

If where you stand is on one of the lower rungs of America's economic ladder, our cornified food chain offers real advantages: not cheap food exactly (for the consumer ultimately pays the added cost of processing), but cheap calories in a variety of attractive forms. In the long run, however, the eater pays a high price for these cheap calories: obesity, type II diabetes, heart disease. 23

If where you stand is at the lower end of the *world*'s economic ladder, however, America's corn-fed food chain looks like an unalloyed disaster. I mentioned earlier that all life on earth can be viewed as a competition for the energy captured by plants and stored in carbohydrates, energy we measure in calories. There is a limit to how many of those calories the world's arable land can produce each year, and an industrial meal of meat and processed food consumes—and wastes—an unconscionable amount of that energy. To eat corn directly (as Mexicans and many Africans do) is to consume all the energy in that corn, but when you feed that corn to a steer or a chicken, 90 percent of its energy is lost—to bones or feathers or fur, to living and metabolizing as a steer or chicken. This is why vegetarians advocate eating "low on the food chain"; every step up the chain reduces the amount of food energy by a factor of ten, which is why in any ecosystem there are only a fraction as many predators as there are prey. But processing food also burns energy. What this means is that the amount of food energy lost in the making of something like a Chicken McNugget could feed a great many more children than just mine, and that behind the 4,510 calories the three of us 24 had for lunch stand tens of thousand of corn calories that could have fed a great many hungry people.

25 And how does this corn-fed food chain look if where you stand is in the middle of a field of corn? Well, it depends on whether you are the corn farmer or the plant. For the corn farmer, you might think the cornification of our food system would have redounded to his benefit, but it has not. Corn's triumph is the direct result of its overproduction, and that has been a disaster for the people who grow it. Growing corn and nothing but corn has also exacted a toll on the farmer's soil, the quality of the local water and the overall health of his community, the biodiversity of his landscape, and the health of all the creatures living on or downstream from it. And not *only* those creatures, for cheap corn has also changed, and much for the worse, the lives of several billion food animals, animals that would not be living on factory farms if not for the ocean of corn on which these animal cities float.

26 But return to that Iowa farm field for a moment and look at the matter—at us—from the standpoint of the corn plant itself. Corn, corn, corn as far as the eye can see, ten-foot stalks soldiering in perfect thirty-inch rows to the far horizon, an 80-million-acre corn lawn rolling across the continent. It's a good thing this plant can't form an impression of us, for how risible that impression would be: The farmers going broke cultivating it; the countless other species routed or emiserated by it; the humans eating and drinking it as fast as they can, some of them—like me and my family—in automobiles engineered to drink it, too. Of all the species that have figured out how to thrive in a world dominated by Homo sapiens, surely no other has succeeded more spectacularly—has colonized more acres and bodies—than *Zea mays*, the grass that domesticated its domesticator. You have to wonder why we Americans don't worship this plant as fervently as the Aztecs; like they once did, we make extraordinary sacrifices to it.

27 These, at least, were my somewhat fevered speculations, as we sped down the highway putting away our fast-food lunch. What is it about fast food? Not only is it served in a flash, but more often than not it's eaten that way too: We finished our meal in under ten minutes. Since we were in the convertible and the sun was shining, I can't blame the McDonald's ambiance. Perhaps the reason you eat this food quickly is because it doesn't bear savoring. The more you concentrate on how it tastes, the less like anything it tastes. I said before that McDonald's serves a kind of comfort food, but after a few bites I'm more inclined to think they're selling something more schematic than that—something more like a signifier of comfort food. So you eat more and eat more quickly, hoping somehow to catch up to the original idea of a cheeseburger or French fry as it retreats over the horizon. And so it goes, bite after bite, until you feel not satisfied exactly, but simply, regrettably, full.

(Study questions follow Nestle, 270–79.)

KIM WARP, *Rising Sea Levels— An Alternative Theory*

© The New Yorker Collection 2006 Kim Warp from cartoonbank.com. All rights reserved.

Write an alternative caption for this cartoon. If you wish, consult some of the 84 million Internet entries under "Fat Rights" for ideas. Is obesity an appropriate subject for humor? Why or why not?

MARION NESTLE

Marion Nestle (born 1938) is the Paulette Goddard Professor of Nutrition, Food Studies, and Public Health at New York University. She holds a PhD in molecular biology (1968) and an M.P.H. in public health nutrition (1986) from the University of California at Berkeley. Nestle has served on the FDA Food Advisory Committee and American Cancer Society committees that issue dietary guidelines for cancer prevention. She is the author of *Food Politics: How the Food Industry Influences Nutrition and Health* (2002) and *Safe Food Bacteria, Biotechnology, and Bioterrorism* (2003), as well as co-editor of *Taking Sides: Clashing Views on Controversial Issues in Food and Nutrition* (2004). Her most recent book, *What to Eat: An Aisle-by-Aisle Guide to Savvy Food Choices and Good Eating* (2006), won the James Beard Foundation Book Award. In "Eating Made Simple," first published in *Scientific American* in 2007, Nestle discusses the multiple factors that influence our diet, including the activities and marketing efforts of food companies, government guidelines and regulations, and nutrition research. She provides common sense guidelines to help consumers make well-informed food choices.

*Eating Made Simple**

1 As a nutrition professor, I am constantly asked why nutrition advice seems to change so much and why experts so often disagree. Whose information, people ask, can we trust? I'm tempted to say, "Mine, of course," but I understand the problem. Yes, nutrition advice seems endlessly mired in scientific argument, the self-interest of food companies and compromises by government regulators. Nevertheless, basic dietary principles are not in dispute: eat less; move more; eat fruits, vegetables and whole grains; and avoid too much junk food.

2 "Eat less" means consume fewer calories, which translates into eating smaller portions and steering clear of frequent between-meal snacks. "Move more" refers to the need to balance calorie intake with physical activity. Eating fruits, vegetables and whole grains provides nutrients unavailable from other foods. Avoiding junk food means to shun "foods of minimal nutritional value"—highly processed sweets and snacks laden with salt, sugars and artificial additives. Soft drinks are the prototypical junk food; they contain sweeteners but few or no nutrients.

3 If you follow these precepts, other aspects of the diet matter much less. Ironically, this advice has not changed in years. The noted cardiologist Ancel Keys (who died in 2004 at the age of 100) and his wife, Margaret, suggested similar principles for preventing coronary heart disease nearly 50 years ago.

4 But I can see why dietary advice seems like a moving target. Nutrition research is so difficult to conduct that it seldom produces unambiguous results. Ambiguity requires interpretation. And interpretation is influenced by the individual's point of view, which can become thoroughly entangled with the science.

Nutrition Science Challenges

5 This scientific uncertainty is not overly surprising given that humans eat so many different foods. For any individual, the health effects of diets are modulated by genetics but also by education and income levels, job satisfaction, physical fitness, and the use of cigarettes or alcohol. To simplify this situation, researchers typically examine the effects of single dietary components one by one.

6 Studies focusing on one nutrient in isolation have worked splendidly to explain symptoms caused by deficiencies of vitamins or minerals. But this approach is less useful for chronic conditions such as coronary heart disease and diabetes that are caused by the interaction of dietary,

---

* Marion Nestle, "Eating Made Simple," SCIENTIFIC AMERICAN, September 2007, pp. 60–69. Reprinted with permission. Copyright © 2007 by SCIENTIFIC AMERICAN, Inc. All rights reserved.

genetic, behavioral and social factors. If nutrition science seems puzzling, it is because researchers typically examine single nutrients detached from food itself, foods separate from diets, and risk factors apart from other behaviors. This kind of research is "reductive" in that it attributes health effects to the consumption of one nutrient or food when it is the overall dietary pattern that really counts most.

For chronic diseases, single nutrients usually alter risk by amounts 7
too small to measure except through large, costly population studies. As seen recently in the Women's Health Initiative, a clinical trial that examined the effects of low-fat diets on heart disease and cancer, participants were unable to stick with the restrictive dietary protocols. Because humans cannot be caged and fed measured formulas, the diets of experimental and control study groups tend to converge, making differences indistinguishable over the long run—even with fancy statistics.

It's the Calories

Food companies prefer studies of single nutrients because they can use 8
the results to sell products. Add vitamins to candies, and you can market them as health foods. Health claims on the labels of junk foods distract consumers from their caloric content. This practice matters because when it comes to obesity—which dominates nutrition problems even in some of the poorest countries of the world—it is the calories that count. Obesity arises when people consume significantly more calories than they expend in physical activity.

America's obesity rates began to rise sharply in the early 1980s. 9
Sociologists often attribute the "calories in" side of this trend to the demands of an overworked population for convenience foods—prepared, packaged products and restaurant meals that usually contain more calories than home-cooked meals.

But other social forces also promoted the calorie imbalance. The 10
arrival of the Reagan administration in 1980 increased the pace of industry deregulation, removing controls on agricultural production and encouraging farmers to grow more food. Calories available per capita in the national food supply (that produced by American farmers, plus imports, less exports) rose from 3,200 a day in 1980 to 3,900 a day two decades later.

The early 1980s also marked the advent of the "shareholder value 11
movement" on Wall Street. Stockholder demands for higher short-term returns on investments forced food companies to expand sales in a marketplace that already contained excessive calories. Food companies responded by seeking new sales and marketing opportunities. They encouraged formerly shunned practices that eventually changed social norms, such as frequent between-meal snacking, eating in book and clothing stores, and serving larger portions. The industry continued to sponsor organizations and journals that focus on nutrition-related subjects and

intensified its efforts to lobby government for favorable dietary advice. Then and now food lobbies have promoted positive interpretations of scientific studies, sponsored research that can be used as a basis for health claims, and attacked critics, myself among them, as proponents of "junk science." If anything, such activities only add to public confusion.

Supermarkets as "Ground Zero"

12 No matter whom I speak to, I hear pleas for help in dealing with supermarkets, considered by shoppers as "ground zero" for distinguishing health claims from scientific advice. So I spent a year visiting supermarkets to help people think more clearly about food choices. The result was my book *What to Eat*.

13 Supermarkets provide a vital public service but are not social services agencies. Their job is to sell as much food as possible. Every aspect of store design—from shelf position to background music—is based on marketing research. Because this research shows that the more products customers see, the more they buy, a store's objective is to expose shoppers to the maximum number of products they will tolerate viewing.

14 If consumers are confused about which foods to buy, it is surely because the choices require knowledge of issues that are not easily resolved by science and are strongly swayed by social and economic considerations. Such decisions play out every day in every store aisle.

Are Organics Healthier?

15 Organic foods are the fastest-growing segment of the industry, in part because people are willing to pay more for foods that they believe are healthier and more nutritious. The U.S. Department of Agriculture forbids producers of "Certified Organic" fruits and vegetables from using synthetic pesticides, herbicides, fertilizers, genetically modified seeds, irradiation or fertilizer derived from sewage sludge. It licenses inspectors to ensure that producers follow those rules. Although the USDA is responsible for organics, its principal mandate is to promote conventional agriculture, which explains why the department asserts that it "makes no claims that organically produced food is safer or more nutritious than conventionally produced food. Organic food differs from conventionally grown food in the way it is grown, handled and processed."

16 This statement implies that such differences are unimportant. Critics of organic foods would agree; they question the reliability of organic certification and the productivity, safety and health benefits of organic production methods. Meanwhile the organic food industry longs for research to address such criticisms, but studies are expensive and difficult to conduct. Nevertheless, existing research in this area has established

that organic farms are nearly as productive as conventional farms, use less energy and leave soils in better condition. People who eat foods grown without synthetic pesticides ought to have fewer such chemicals in their bodies, and they do. Because the organic rules require pretreatment of manure and other steps to reduce the amount of pathogens in soil treatments, organic foods should be just as safe—or safer—than conventional foods.

Similarly, organic foods ought to be at least as nutritious as conventional foods. And proving organics to be more nutritious could help justify their higher prices. For minerals, this task is not difficult. The mineral content of plants depends on the amounts present in the soil in which they are grown. Organic foods are cultivated in richer soils, so their mineral content is higher. 17

But differences are harder to demonstrate for vitamins or antioxidants (plant substances that reduce tissue damage induced by free radicals); higher levels of these nutrients relate more to a food plant's genetic strain or protection from unfavorable conditions after harvesting than to production methods. Still, preliminary studies show benefits: organic peaches and pears contain greater quantities of vitamins C and E, and organic berries and corn contain more antioxidants. 18

Further research will likely confirm that organic foods contain higher nutrient levels, but it is unclear whether these nutrients would make a measurable improvement in health. All fruits and vegetables contain useful nutrients, albeit in different combinations and concentrations. Eating a variety of food plants is surely more important to health than small differences in the nutrient content of any one food. Organics may be somewhat healthier to eat, but they are far less likely to damage the environment, and that is reason enough to choose them at the supermarket. 19

Dairy and Calcium

Scientists cannot easily resolve questions about the health effects of dairy foods. Milk has many components, and the health of people who consume milk or dairy foods is influenced by everything else they eat and do. But this area of research is especially controversial because it affects an industry that vigorously promotes dairy products as beneficial and opposes suggestions to the contrary. 20

Dairy foods contribute about 70 percent of the calcium in American diets. This necessary mineral is a principal constituent of bones, which constantly lose and regain calcium during normal metabolism. Diets must contain enough calcium to replace losses, or else bones become prone to fracture. Experts advise consumption of at least one gram of calcium a day to replace everyday losses. Only dairy foods provide this much calcium without supplementation. 21

22 But bones are not just made of calcium; they require the full complement of essential nutrients to maintain strength. Bones are stronger in people who are physically active and who do not smoke cigarettes or drink much alcohol. Studies examining the effects of single nutrients in dairy foods show that some nutritional factors—magnesium, potassium, vitamin D and lactose, for example—promote calcium retention in bones. Others, such as protein, phosphorus and sodium, foster calcium excretion. So bone strength depends more on overall patterns of diet and behavior than simply on calcium intake.

23 Populations that do not typically consume dairy products appear to exhibit lower rates of bone fracture despite consuming far less calcium than recommended. Why this is so is unclear. Perhaps their diets contain less protein from meat and dairy foods, less sodium from processed foods and less phosphorus from soft drinks, so they retain calcium more effectively. The fact that calcium balance depends on multiple factors could explain why rates of osteoporosis (bone density loss) are highest in countries where people eat the most dairy foods. Further research may clarify such counterintuitive observations.

24 In the meantime, dairy foods are fine to eat if you like them, but they are not a nutritional requirement. Think of cows: they do not drink milk after weaning, but their bones support bodies weighing 800 pounds or more. Cows feed on grass, and grass contains calcium in small amounts—but those amounts add up. If you eat plenty of fruits, vegetables and whole grains, you can have healthy bones without having to consume dairy foods.

A Meaty Debate

25 Critics point to meat as the culprit responsible for elevating blood cholesterol, along with raising risks for heart disease, cancer and other conditions. Supporters cite the lack of compelling science to justify such allegations; they emphasize the nutritional benefits of meat protein, vitamins and minerals. Indeed, studies in developing countries demonstrate health improvements when growing children are fed even small amounts of meat.

26 But because bacteria in a cow's rumen attach hydrogen atoms to unsaturated fatty acids, beef fat is highly saturated—the kind of fat that increases the risk of coronary heart disease. All fats and oils contain some saturated fatty acids, but animal fats, especially those from beef, have more saturated fatty acids than vegetable fats. Nutritionists recommend eating no more than a heaping tablespoon (20 grams) of saturated fatty acids a day. Beef eaters easily meet or exceed this limit. The smallest McDonald's cheeseburger contains 6 grams of saturated fatty acids, but a Hardee's Monster Thickburger has 45 grams.

27 Why meat might boost cancer risks, however, is a matter of speculation. Scientists began to link meat to cancer in the 1970s, but even after

decades of subsequent research they remain unsure if the relevant factor might be fat, saturated fat, protein, carcinogens or something else related to meat. By the late 1990s experts could conclude only that eating beef probably increases the risk of colon and rectal cancers and possibly enhances the odds of acquiring breast, prostate and perhaps other cancers. Faced with this uncertainty, the American Cancer Society suggests selecting leaner cuts, smaller portions and alternatives such as chicken, fish or beans—steps consistent with today's basic advice about what to eat.

Fish and Heart Disease

Fatty fish are the most important sources of long-chain omega-3 fatty 28
acids. In the early 1970s Danish investigators observed surprisingly low frequencies of heart disease among indigenous populations in Greenland that typically ate fatty fish, seals and whales. The researchers attributed the protective effect to the foods' content of omega-3 fatty acids. Some subsequent studies—but by no means all—confirm this idea.

Because large, fatty fish are likely to have accumulated methylmer- 29
cury and other toxins through predation, however, eating them raises questions about the balance between benefits and risks. Understandably, the fish industry is eager to prove that the health benefits of omega-3s outweigh any risks from eating fish.

Even independent studies on omega-3 fats can be interpreted differ- 30
ently. In 2004 the National Oceanic and Atmospheric Administration—for fish, the agency equivalent to the USDA—asked the Institute of Medicine (IOM) to review studies of the benefits and risks of consuming seafood. The ensuing review of the research on heart disease risk illustrates the challenge such work poses for interpretation.

The IOM's October 2006 report concluded that eating seafood 31
reduces the risk of heart disease but judged the studies too inconsistent to decide if omega-3 fats were responsible. In contrast, investigators from the Harvard School of Public Health published a much more positive report in the *Journal of the American Medical Association* that same month. Even modest consumption of fish omega-3s, they stated, would cut coronary deaths by 36 percent and total mortality by 17 percent, meaning that not eating fish would constitute a health risk.

Differences in interpretation explain how distinguished scientists 32
could arrive at such different conclusions after considering the same studies. The two groups, for example, had conflicting views of earlier work published in March 2006 in the *British Medical Journal*. That study found no overall effect of omega-3s on heart disease risk or mortality, although a subset of the original studies displayed a 14 percent reduction in total mortality that did not reach statistical significance. The IOM team interpreted the "nonsignificant" result as evidence for the need for caution, whereas the Harvard group saw the data as consistent with

studies reporting the benefits of omega-3s. When studies present inconsistent results, both interpretations are plausible. I favor caution in such situations, but not everyone agrees.

33 Because findings are inconsistent, so is dietary advice about eating fish. The American Heart Association recommends that adults eat fatty fish at least twice a week, but U.S. dietary guidelines say: "Limited evidence suggests an association between consumption of fatty acids in fish and reduced risks of mortality from cardiovascular disease for the general population . . . however, more research is needed." Whether or not fish uniquely protects against heart disease, seafood is a delicious source of many nutrients, and two small servings per week of the less predatory classes of fish are unlikely to cause harm.

Sodas and Obesity

34 Sugars and corn sweeteners account for a large fraction of the calories in many supermarket foods, and virtually all the calories in drinks—soft, sports and juice—come from added sugars.

35 In a trend that correlates closely with rising rates of obesity, daily per capita consumption of sweetened beverages has grown by about 200 calories since the early 1980s. Although common sense suggests that this increase might have something to do with weight gain, beverage makers argue that studies cannot prove that sugary drinks alone—independent of calories or other foods in the diet—boost the risk of obesity. The evidence, they say correctly, is circumstantial. But pediatricians often see obese children in their practices who consume more than 1,000 calories a day from sweetened drinks alone, and several studies indicate that children who habitually consume sugary beverages take in more calories and weigh more than those who do not.

36 Nevertheless, the effects of sweetened drinks on obesity continue to be subject to interpretation. In 2006, for example, a systematic review funded by independent sources found sweetened drinks to promote obesity in both children and adults. But a review that same year sponsored in part by a beverage trade association concluded that soft drinks have no special role in obesity. The industry-funded researchers criticized existing studies as being short-term and inconclusive, and pointed to studies finding that people lose weight when they substitute sweetened drinks for their usual meals.

37 These differences imply the need to scrutinize food industry sponsorship of research itself. Although many researchers are offended by suggestions that funding support might affect the way they design or interpret studies, systematic analyses say otherwise. In 2007 investigators classified studies of the effects of sweetened and other beverages on health

according to who had sponsored them. Industry-supported studies were more likely to yield results favorable to the sponsor than those funded by independent sources. Even though scientists may not be able to prove that sweetened drinks cause obesity, it makes sense for anyone interested in losing weight to consume less of them.

The examples I have discussed illustrate why nutrition science 38
seems so controversial. Without improved methods to ensure compliance with dietary regimens, research debates are likely to rage unabated. Opposing points of view and the focus of studies and food advertising on single nutrients rather than on dietary patterns continue to fuel these disputes. While we wait for investigators to find better ways to study nutrition and health, my approach—eat less, move more, eat a largely plant-based diet, and avoid eating too much junk food—makes sense and leaves you plenty of opportunity to enjoy your dinner.

© Lee Snider/The Image Works

Excess weight around the waist, the abdominal fat that contributes to the body's "apple shape," increases the risk of a host of serious medical problems: metabolic syndrome, type 2 diabetes, heart disease, high blood pressure, stroke, some types of cancer, sleep apnea, pulmonary hypertension, and cardiac arrhythmia. These risks are well known, yet estimates are that around 65% of Americans will become moderately to severely overweight during their lifetime. Why?

Tyler Hicks/The New York Times/Redux

People are scavenging for food in a garbage dump in Port-au-Prince, Haiti, the poorest country in the Western Hemisphere, with a per capita income of $400 per year, a life expectancy of 53 years, and 80% of the people living in poverty, half of whom cannot read. Contrast this situation with Americans' lifestyle and expectancy.

FLAWED FOOD PYRAMIDS

Fats, Oils and Sweets
USE SPARINGLY

Milk, Yogurt and Cheese Group
2–3 SERVINGS

Meat, Poultry, Fish, Dry Beans, Eggs and Nuts Group
2–3 SERVINGS

Vegetable Group
3–5 SERVINGS

Fruit Group
2–4 SERVINGS

Bread, Cereal, Rice and Pasta Group
6–11 SERVINGS

1992

2005

Whether you found the food pyramid created by the U.S. Department of Agriculture in 1992 beneficial or not, it was at least simple to use. The familiar triangular nutrition guide suggested how much of each food category—grains, dairy products, fruits and vegetables, meats and fats, oils and sweets—one should eat every day.

But in my opinion, the USDA's 2005 replacement, MyPyramid, is a disaster. The process the agriculture agency employed to replace the 1992 food pyramid (*left*) has been kept secret. It remains a mystery, for example, just how the department came up with a design for a new food guide that emphasizes physical activity but is devoid of food (*right*). According to the USDA staff, people should keep physically active, eat in moderation, make personalized food choices, eat a variety of foods in the recommended number of servings, and pursue gradual dietary improvement. The color and width of the vertical bands of MyPyramid are meant to denote food groups and servings, but the only way to know this in detail is to log on to a computer. Users must go to www.pyramid.gov and type in gender, age and activity level to obtain a "personalized" dietary plan at one of a dozen calorie levels.

People who seek advice from this site, and millions have, find diet plans notable for the large amounts of food they seem to recommend and for the virtual absence of appeals to "eat less" or to "avoid" certain foods. Critics, not surprisingly, discern the strong influence of food industry lobbyists here. I myself, for example, am expected to consume four cups of fruits and vegetables, six ounces of grains, five ounces of meat and, of course, three cups of milk a day, along with a couple of hundred "discretionary calories" that I can spend on junk foods. For all its flaws, the 1992 pyramid was easier to understand and use.

What MyPyramid really lacks is any notion of a hierarchical ranking of the items in a single food group in terms of nutritional desirability. The preliminary design of MyPyramid in 2004 looked much like the final version with one critical exception: it illustrated a hierarchy of desirable food choices. The grain band, for instance, placed whole-grain bread at the bottom (a positive ranking), pasta about halfway up (a middle rank) and cinnamon buns at the top ("eat less"). In the final version, the USDA eliminated all traces of hierarchy, presumably because food companies do not want federal agencies to advise eating less of their products, useful as such recommendations might be to an overweight public. ***—M.N.***

Illustration by Nick Rotondo

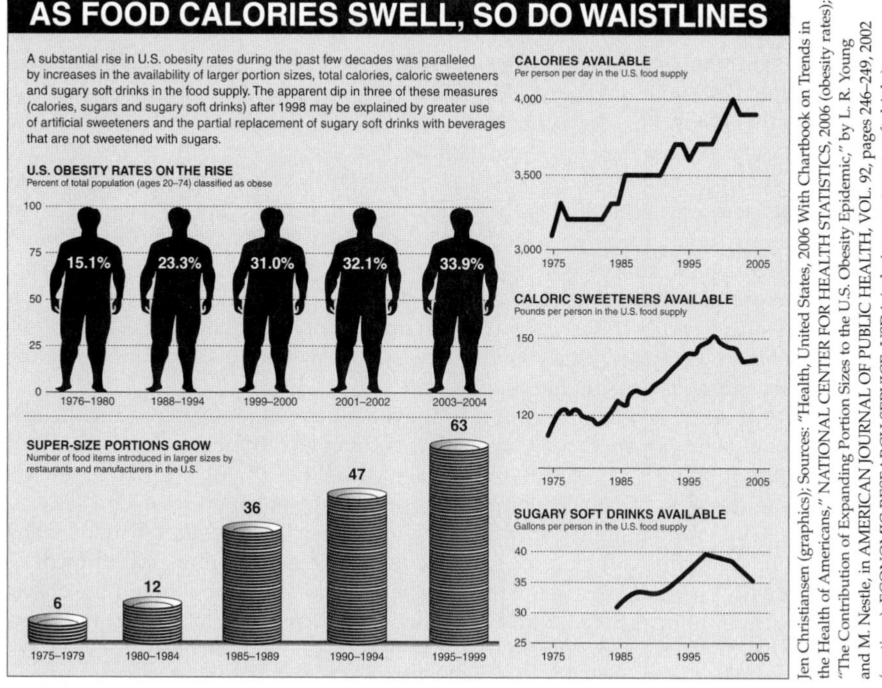

Jen Christiansen (graphics); Sources: "Health, United States, 2006 With Chartbook on Trends in the Health of Americans," NATIONAL CENTER FOR HEALTH STATISTICS, 2006 (obesity rates); "The Contribution of Expanding Portion Sizes to the U.S. Obesity Epidemic," by L. R. Young and M. Nestle, in AMERICAN JOURNAL OF PUBLIC HEALTH, VOL. 92, pages 246–249, 2002 (portions); ECONOMIC RESEARCH SERVICE, USDA (calories, sweeteners, soft drinks).

Content

1. What are some of the characteristics, according to Michael Pollan in "The Meal," of "the industrial food chain" (¶s 1–7)? How, in Pollan's view, has "industrial food" changed the way we eat (¶s 2–5)?

2. Pollan estimates the amount of corn he and his family consumed in one McDonald's meal (¶ 18) and concludes that this amount "would easily have overflowed the car's trunk" (¶ 19). What are some of the economic, health, environmental, and social effects of "this corn-fed food chain" (¶s 22–27)?

3. Why, according to Marion Nestle in "Eating Made Simple," do nutritional studies differ in their conclusions about healthy eating (¶s 5–7)? Why does Nestle argue that "it is the overall dietary pattern that really counts most" (¶ 6)?

4. What factors have contributed to recent increases in caloric intake (¶s 8–11)? How, according to Nestle, have food companies' marketing practices contributed to these changes in diet?

5. Explain why Nestle argues that food choices "are not easily resolved by science" (¶ 14). What are "Certified Organic" foods (¶ 15) and why might they be healthier to eat than conventionally grown crops (¶s 16–19)? Why does the consumption of dairy foods not necessarily ensure adequate consumption of calcium (¶s 21–24)? Explain why the health effects of meat consumption are in dispute (¶s 25–27) and the possible pros and cons of eating fish (¶s 28–32). Why did the Institute of Medicine and the Harvard School of Public Health differ in their conclusions about the role of omega-3 fats in the prevention of heart disease (¶s 30–32)?

Strategies/Structures/Language

6. Pollan quotes a federal judge's description of the Chicken McNugget as a "McFrankensteinian creation" (¶ 8). Find other examples of language in "The Meal" that emphasize the artificial and processed nature of industrial food. How does Pollan explain the appeal of fast food?

7. How does Pollan suggest that as industrial food becomes more removed from its source, it becomes less like "real" food and more like the language that describes it? He argues, for example, that the food McDonald's serves is "more like a signifier of comfort food" (¶ 27) than comfort food itself. Explain the connection he draws between what we eat and how we speak. Find examples in which Pollan suggests that industrial food is changing our experience of food, and our culture more generally, by changing the language we use to describe food. How do these examples explain his choice of title?

8. Nestle alludes to the different uses to which nutrition research is put, including as marketing by food companies (¶ 8) and the government's development of agricultural policies (¶s 15–16) and dietary guidelines (¶ 33). On what grounds does she question the quality of industry-supported nutrition research (¶s 8, 11, 20, 35–37)? Does she suggest that independent research is possible? Why does she "discern the strong influence of food industry lobbyists" in the development of USDA's MyPyramid ("Flawed Food Pyramids" diagram)? How might the charts in "As Food Calories Swell, So Do Waistlines" be interpreted to support the argument that the increase in "daily per capita consumption of sweetened beverages" (¶ 35) explains rising rates of obesity *and* the argument that "soft drinks have no special role in obesity" (¶ 36)?

9. In "Rising Sea Levels—An Alternative Theory" (269), Kim Warp combines two contemporary concerns, climate change and obesity, in a humorous application of fallacious reasoning. Why are the peripheral figures submerged? How do the two central figures explain the joke?

For Writing

10. ***Journal Writing.*** Pollan writes that hamburgers and chicken nuggets appeal to consumers in part because "their boneless abstractions allow us to forget we're eating animals" (¶ 15). Do you agree that consumers generally prefer to eat foods that are processed and packaged to distance them from their origins? Is this preference a question of habit? What is the impact of the widespread consumption of foods that "appear as pure products of culture rather than nature" (¶ 15)?

11. ***Dialogues.*** Both Pollan and Nestle allude to the environmental consequences of industrial food production: Pollan argues that the dominance of corn in the food chain damages soil and water quality as well as "the biodiversity of [the farmer's] landscape, and the health of all the creatures living on or downstream from it" (¶ 25), while Nestle argues that organic farms "use less energy and leave soils in better condition" than conventional agriculture (¶ 16). According to Jared Diamond in "The World as a Polder" (Chapter 10), how do modern farming techniques contribute to environmental degradation (¶s 8–9, 12, 13, 15)? How do Pollan and Nestle suggest that consumer and business behavior present obstacles to addressing these environmental concerns?

12. ***Second Look.*** In "The Meal," Pollan links obesity, among other conditions, to the consumption of "cheap calories" produced by the "cornified food chain" (¶ 23); in "Eating Made Simple," Nestle writes that "rising rates of obesity" represent a trend that correlates with the rise in the consumption of "sweetened beverages" (¶ 35). How does the photograph on 277 suggest that obesity is a public health issue? Explain how the anonymity, clothing, and arrangement of the two figures contribute to your reading of the photograph.

SUZANNE BRITT

Suzanne Britt was born in 1946 in Winston-Salem, North Carolina, and educated at Salem College and Washington University. Britt, who teaches English at Meredith College, describes herself as "stately, plump," and says, "I talk, eat, drink, walk around the block, read, have a stream of company, and sit on the grass outside. I try not to preach, do handicrafts, camp, bowl, argue, visit relatives, or serve on committees." "That Lean and Hungry Look," first published in *Newsweek*, is a contemporary example of a classical mode of literature—the "character"—a common form of description in which the stereotypical features of a character type ("the angry man") or role ("the schoolboy," "the housewife") are identified and often satirized.

Britt's humorous defense of fat people was first published in 1978, before obesity became a national epidemic. At that time, it would have been read as a lighthearted reinforcement of people's right to indulge in hot fudge sundaes and "two doughnuts and a big orange drink anytime they wanted it," augmented by double fudge brownies. But three decades later, obesity is considered a national epidemic. Sixty-seven percent of American adults—129.6 million—are estimated to be overweight, and 32 percent of those are categorized as "obese" (having more than 30 percent body fat). These figures do not include the 19 percent of overweight school-age children. By 2015 75% of adult Americans are predicted to be overweight, with obesity rising to 40% of the total (25% of children). Complications from obesity, including strokes, heart disease, high blood pressure, diabetes, some cancers, and kidney and gallbladder disorders, contribute to 300,000 deaths a year, lowering life expectancy and dramatically increasing health care costs—currently by over $100 billion a year. How do these sobering statistics affect the reading of "That Lean and Hungry Look" today?

That Lean and Hungry Look

Caesar was right. Thin people need watching. I've been watching them for most of my adult life, and I don't like what I see. When these narrow fellows spring at me, I quiver to my toes. Thin people come in all personalities, most of them menacing. You've got your "together" thin person, your mechanical thin person, your condescending thin 1 person, your tsk-tsk thin person, your efficiency expert thin person. All of them are dangerous.

2 In the first place, thin people aren't fun. They don't know how to goof off, at least in the best, fat sense of the word. They've always got to be a doing. Give them a coffee break, and they'll jog around the block. Supply them with a quiet evening at home, and they'll fix the screen door and lick S&H green stamps. They say things like "there aren't enough hours in the day." Fat people never say that. Fat people think the day is too damn long already.

3 Thin people make me tired. They've got speedy little metabolisms that cause them to bustle briskly. They're forever rubbing their bony hands together and eying new problems to "tackle." I like to surround myself with sluggish, inert, easygoing fat people, the kind who believe that if you clean it up today, it'll just get dirty again tomorrow.

4 Some people say the business about the jolly fat person is a myth, that all of us chubbies are neurotic, sick, sad people. I disagree. Fat people may not be chortling all day long, but they're a hell of a lot *nicer* than the wizened and shriveled. Thin people turn surly, mean and hard at a young age because they never learn the value of a hot-fudge sundae for easing tension. Thin people don't like gooey soft things because they themselves are neither gooey nor soft. They are crunchy and dull, like carrots. They go straight to the heart of the matter while fat people let things stay all blurry and hazy and vague, the way things actually are. Thin people want to face the truth. Fat people know there is no truth. One of my thin friends is always staring at complex, unsolvable problems and saying, "The key thing is . . ." Fat people never say that. They know there isn't any such thing as the key thing about anything.

5 Thin people believe in logic. Fat people see all sides. The sides fat people see are rounded blobs, usually gray, always nebulous and truly not worth worrying about. But the thin persons persists. "If you consume more calories than you burn," says one of my thin friends, "you will gain weight. It's that simple." Fat people always grin when they hear statements like that. They know better.

6 Fat people realize that life is illogical and unfair. They know very well that God is not in his heaven and all is not right with the world. If God was up there, fat people could have two doughnuts and a big orange drink anytime they wanted it.

7 Thin people have a long list of logical things they are always spouting off to me. They hold up one finger at a time as they reel off these things, so I won't lose track. They speak slowly as if to a young child. The list is long and full of holes. It contains tidbits like "get a

grip on yourself," "cigarettes kill," "cholesterol clogs," "fit as a fiddle," "ducks in a row," "organize" and "sound fiscal management." Phrases like that.

They think these 2,000-point plans lead to happiness. Fat people know happiness is elusive at best and even if they could get the kind thin people talk about, they wouldn't want it. Wisely, fat people see that such programs are too dull, too hard, too off the mark. They are never better than a whole cheesecake. 8

Fat people know all about the mystery of life. They are the ones acquainted with the night, with luck, with fate, with playing it by ear. One thin person I know once suggested that we arrange all the parts of a jigsaw puzzle into groups according to size, shape and color. He figured this would cut the time needed to complete the puzzle by at least 50 per cent. I said I wouldn't do it. One, I like to muddle through. Two, what good would it do to finish early? Three, the jigsaw puzzle isn't the important thing. The important thing is the fun of four people (one thin person included) sitting around a card table, working a jigsaw puzzle. My thin friend had no use for my list. Instead of joining us, he went outside and mulched the boxwoods. The three remaining fat people finished the puzzle and made chocolate, double-fudge brownies to celebrate. 9

The main problem with thin people is they oppress. Their good intentions, bony torsos, tight ships, neat corners, cerebral machinations and pat solutions loom like dark clouds over the loose, comfortable, spread-out, soft world of the fat. Long after fat people have removed their coats and shoes and put their feet up on the coffee table, thin people are still sitting on the edge of the sofa, looking neat as a pin, discussing rutabagas. Fat people are heavily into fits of laughter, slapping their thighs and whooping it up, while thin people are still politely waiting for the punch line. 10

Thin people are downers. They like math and morality and reasoned evaluating of the limitations of human beings. They have their skinny little acts together. They expound, prognose, probe and prick. 11

Fat people are convivial. They will like you even if you're irregular and have acne. They will come up with a good reason why you never wrote the great American novel. They will cry in your beer with you. They will put your name in the pot. They will let you off the hook. Fat people will gab, giggle, guffaw, gallumph, gyrate and gossip. They are generous, giving and gallant. They are gluttonous and goodly and great. What you want when you're down is soft and jiggly, not muscled and stable. Fat people know this. Fat people have plenty of room. Fat people will take you in. 12

Content

1. Britt is describing two categories of people, thin and fat. Does she stereotype them? If so, what does she gain from stereotyping? If not, how does she individualize each category? Is her depiction accurate? Why or why not?
2. Why has she chosen to overlook characteristics typical of either group—for instance, the effects on one's health of being either too fat or too thin? Does she treat thin people fairly? Does she intend to do so?
3. For the purpose of contrast, Britt has concentrated on the differences between fat and thin people. What similarities, if any, do they have? Are these related to their weight?

Strategies/Structures/Language

4. Throughout, Britt makes blanket generalizations about both thin and fat people. Does she support these? Is her evidence appropriate? Is it sufficiently comprehensive to make her case?
5. At what point in the essay do you realize that Britt is being humorous? Does her humor reinforce or undermine her point? Explain your answer.
6. Britt's language is conversational, sometimes slangy: "Thin people are downers. . . . They have their skinny little acts together" (¶ 11). In what ways does the language reinforce what Britt says about fat people?

For Writing

7. ***Journal Writing.*** Keep a food journal for a week and comment on your consumption patterns and moods in a serious and a satirical mode. Do your dietary patterns appear to affect your mood or vice versa? How does your relationship to food reflect your general outlook on life? Does observing your dietary habits inspire you to make any changes in your life?
8. ***Mixed Modes.*** Write a humorous essay in which you divide a larger category (such as students, parents, Southerners, Easterners, Californians) into subcategories as Britt does in the first paragraph, and then characterize each subcategory through comparing and contrasting its parts (working students, athletes, nerds, partiers). Writing collaboratively, each partner could describe one category or subcategory. If you like, borrow some of Britt's techniques, including her use of informal language ("too damn long already" ¶ 2); exaggeration ("always staring at complex, unsolvable problems" ¶ 4); alliteration ("bustle briskly" ¶ 3); and clichés ("God is not in his heaven" ¶ 6). Photographs, drawings, or cartoons can enhance the descriptions.
9. By yourself or with a partner, select one major cause of obesity in America today, research its causes, and provide a workable solution to the problem.
10. ***Second Look.*** Consider how the photograph of people scavenging for food in Haiti (278) challenges us to think about beautiful bodies, material well-being, and the environmental costs of our standard of living. In what ways does our society face conflicting messages about the health aspects and aesthetics of thinness? Why, for example, do we associate thinness with glamour? Does our obsession with dieting and exercise blind us to starvation in our own and neighboring countries?

ISTVAN BANYAI, *Inflation*

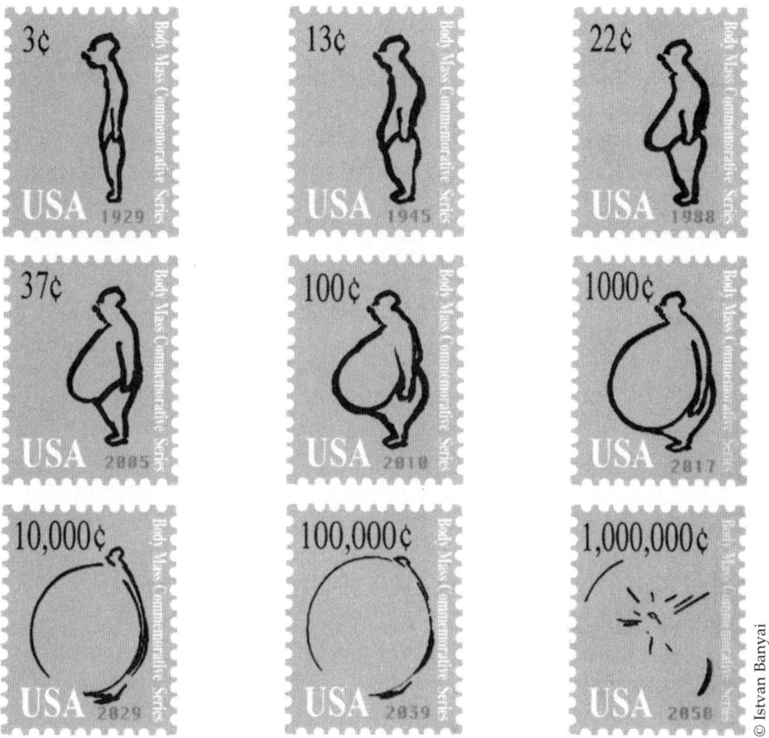

What's the story here? What changes—in the figure and in the cost of the postage stamp—occur in the successive panels? Do they need any captions? What's the point of using "Inflation" as a title? Can you think of any alternate titles that would work as well?

MATT NOCTON

Nocton (born 1975) has spent most of his life in the vicinity of his hometown, Simsbury, Connecticut, except for a year's sojourn in California—a cross-country trek that stimulated some of his best writing. He wrote the essay below as an English major at the University of Connecticut (BA 2002), and currently sells media advertising.

Nocton himself worked harvesting tobacco in Connecticut; the tobacco fields are adjacent to the state's largest airport, Bradley International Airport. "Harvest of Gold, Harvest of Shame" is the seventh revision Nocton submitted, every draft reinforcing the gulf between the bosses and the workers in the tobacco fields and sheds, every draft increasing his own awareness of the workers' exploited and powerless condition.

✧ Harvest of Gold, Harvest of Shame

1 Simsbury is a small affluent town located in the heart of the Connecticut River Valley. It is not a particularly exciting place and its high school students refer to it as "Simsboring." But in fact there is something unique about this quiet town. Simsbury is home to Culbro Tobacco Company's Farm No. 2. The Culbro Tobacco Company prides itself on growing the finest shade tobacco in the world. Its leaves are used to wrap expensive cigars.

2 Culbro employs three kinds of people: migrant workers, most of whom are from Jamaica and live on the farm headquarters, inner-city people, most of whom are Hispanic and are bussed from Hartford to Simsbury at 6:15 in the morning; and finally, a few local white residents. The latter are typically the men who oversee all of the other employees. Each supervisor is referred to as the "boss man" by the less fortunate workers. When a boss man speaks to one of his subordinates, the usual response comes either in the form of Spanglish, which most of the Hispanics speak, or Patoi, which is what the Jamaicans speak.

3 Working in tobacco fields is demanding and repetitious and the pay is minimum wage. In a typical day, a field worker is bussed to the field where he will be working with his group of roughly fifty to two hundred workers. When he gets off the bus he will find a pick-up truck parked nearby full of burlap and twine. He must tie this burlap around his waist as a source of protection against the dirt and rocks that he will be dragging himself through for the next eight hours. He will then find another pick-up truck containing wooden stakes with numbers on them. There he will find the stake with his number and stick it into the ground before the row of tobacco plants where he is about to work. A recorder or "bentkeeper" (so called because the distance between two tobacco posts is called a bent) stands under the blazing sun and monitors all the workers. He does this by looking at the numbers of each stake in each row. He flips through the pages on his clipboard until he finds the corresponding employee number. Then he checks the number of poles in the row and adds the number of "bents" in the row to a particular worker's sum total. He does this for fifty to two hundred laborers. At times when the rows are very short it is difficult to add all of the numbers fast enough to keep up with the pace of the pickers. The pickers who complete the most bents earn the most money. The bentkeeper is the only one authorized

to carry the clipboard and add the bent numbers. Every so often the unshaven field boss man with the coarse black mustache and cowboy hat calls the bentkeeper. "Hey, who was working in this row? Twelve six-four-five is still staked in here. Who was working next to twelve six-four-five?" The bentkeeper nervously hands over his clipboard and the boss man takes off his sunglasses and draws on his cigarette while he examines it.

4 "What the hell is this!?! This is an eight bent row! You've been adding nine! It changed from nine to eight way the hell back there! Look at the goddamn post! Goddamn are you blind or can't you read!?! Go fix it!" He shoves the clipboard into the bentkeeper's stomach and jumps in his truck. The truck kicks up dirt and a cloud of dust as it speeds down the rocky dirt road. It comes to an abrupt halt about one hundred yards down. As the bentkeeper tries to figure out where the bents changed from nine to eight and from which numbers he must deduct points, he hears the boss man in the distance. "Hey eleven two-nine-two! Were you working next to twelve six-four-five?! You're bruising the leaves! Look at this? See this? This is from your row! We can't use these! You're going too fast. Stop bruising the goddamn leaves or I'm going to dock ten bents from your total!"

5 The humiliated bentkeeper tries not to listen as he attempts to correct his blunder while keeping pace with the pickers at the same time. A tough looking Hispanic kid breaks his concentration. "Hey bentkeeper! How many I got?" He holds up his stake so the bentkeeper can see the number.

6 The bentkeeper flips through the pages, "Uhhmm . . . sixty-eight."

7 "What!? I got more than that!"

8 "No, you've got sixty-eight."

9 "Ahh man this is bullshit. How'd you get that job anyway?" The complaining worker walks over to the water truck to get a drink.

10 In the middle of two towering tobacco plants under the white netting eleven two-nine-two mumbles slowly in a deep raspy voice with smoke in his breath "Duh boss mon is crazy mon." He finishes his row and approaches the bentkeeper. "Hey mon, eleven two-nine-two, how many I got now?"

11 The bentkeeper replies "Yeah I know your number Stanley, you have one-hundred and fifteen."

12 Stanley's smile reveals a gold front tooth with a black clover on it, "Ohkay mon, yuh shades uh looking fat mon. All shades uh fat in my book mon."

13 After field "asparagus 1032," is finished, the nets are dropped and the boss man selects two unlucky souls to spray the field. They reluctantly don cumbersome yellow suits that resemble something NASA designed for the planned mission to Mars. The only obvious difference is that the sprayers wear back packs of insecticides rather than oxygen.

14 Beneath the foggy mask of his suit, David's pockmarked hairy face contorts into a nasty expression as he argues with his partner. Everyone hated David. He talked in the belligerent tongue of a junkyard dog. He was likened to a Neanderthal, though an allusion to something more ancient would probably suit him better. In the middle of the argument David blurts out, "I was in prison you know. . . . you know why I was there? . . . I killed a cop. . . . strangled him. . . . I'm on parole now." The significance of his comment seemed to bear no relation to the argument and his partner ignored it. He wasn't afraid of David.

15 All of the leaves from "asparagus 1032" are transported to the shed on a trailer pulled by a big blue Ford tractor. The shed operations are run by a short stocky Hispanic man who wears a blue Hawaiian tee shirt with buttons and flowers. Working in the shed is better than working in the field. Many women work in the shed. There, by means of a giant sewing machine, they monotonously sew tobacco leaves to a stick called a "lath." Every time a worker finishes fifty laths she gets credit for one bundle. That is recorded by the bundlekeeper who patrols the shed monitoring daily progress. When a sewer calls out "bundle!" the bundlekeeper acknowledges "bundle!" and he hurries over to the end of the shed and hoists the heavy bundle from the bundle stockpile onto his shoulder. He then carries it to the idle sewer and he drops the bundle of fifty laths on top of her sewing machine. He then withdraws his hole puncher and he punches a hole in her card. Every time he punches a sewer's card he punches the master card which he wears around his neck. The master card shows how many bundles the shed completes on a daily basis. The bundlekeeper is the only one authorized to carry the hole puncher and the master card. Every so often a "boss man" will summon the bundlekeeper over and yank the master card from the bundlekeeper's neck to examine it. Then the boss man marches up and down the shed to exercise his authority. Then he stops in a thick cloud of dust to bark his favorite motivational speech "you not gonna get paid if you don't speed up!" The sewers ignore him and try to keep up with their mindless sewing machines. Those who complete the most bundles make the most money.

16 Every time a lath is completed it is racked. Then a man who has precariously positioned himself on the bottom level of rafters in the shed reaches down to the rack and picks it up. He then passes it to his partner above him on the next level who passes it up to the man above him and so on until the lath reaches the highest level that is available for another row of lath. Each lath is suspended between two rafters in the barn. They are carefully packed about a foot and a half apart across the width of the shed on every level of rafters and along the length of the barn. It normally takes about three days or a million and a half tobacco leaves to fill a shed.

17 On the dry dusty floor of the shed, the sweaty bundlekeeper looks up and admires the beautiful ceiling as it is painted with enormous green

leaves with a splotch of a red shirt on one level and a yellow shirt above it and black arms with extended hands reaching to one another. For a moment he is gazing at the ceiling of the Sistine Chapel in Rome. He can imagine he is actually witnessing Michelangelo paint his masterpiece. For a moment the two men with extended hands remind the bundlekeeper of God in the heavens reaching to Adam. His imagination is suddenly snapped by a falling lath misplaced by an imperfect human being hanging from the rafters. The bundlekeeper ducks and after a loud 'thump!' he thanks God for his green hard hat.

As the clock rolls onto ten o'clock the boss man calls out "Coffee! 18
Last lath!" The sewers finish sewing their last fifty leaves and the squeaky machines fall silent. The silence is invaded by the chatter of relieved sewers who have temporarily escaped the heat and dust in the shed to drink their coffee outside under the shade of a nearby tree or the side of the barn. The men in the rafters descend to retrieve their coolers to snack on bread and beer for a leisurely ten minutes.

Work resumes promptly at ten after ten with the boss man's "back 19
to work!" The dissipating dust is replenished by a fresh cloud churned from the feet of a tired troop heading back to the barn. Next to the crack in the shed where a ray of sunlight illuminates floating dust particles, an old machine resumes its monotonous humming and clicking as a carefree Jamaican man whistles while feeding it leaves.

The boss man steps outside his dark shed for a breath of fresh air 20
and a chance to blow his nose and spit the gritty sand from his mouth. Then he sees the next load of green leaves preceding a light brown dust cloud in field "Ketchen 918" with the new hybrid seed. Those leaves cannot be mixed. He grows red in the face because the next shed has not yet been prepared for those leaves. He stomps over to his dust colored pickup truck to call base. After talking to the base coordinator he realizes that he will have to divide his crew into two sections with one half in one shed and another in the other shed. Now the bundlekeeper will have to run back and forth between the two sheds because of the field boss man's mistake. The stressed-out shed boss man invents another motivational speech "Hey, dees is not a carnival! dees is not the beach!" By lunch time the boss man has resumed his composure. He sneaks a peek at his watch and yells "last lath! break time! last lath!"

The shed workers rush to the water truck outside to wash their 21
hands before lunch. They sit in the weeds against the shady side of the shed and eat their lunches. The bundlekeeper and the shed boss eat in the pickup truck and listen to the Spanish radio. Out in the field the boss man calls "lunch time! Finish your rows!" The dirty and smelly pickers crawl out from underneath the nets and remove the tape from their fingers and try to wash the sticky tape, tobacco juices, and dirt from their fingertips. Then they head to the bus to find their coolers of beer and candy bars. They eat and drink for half an hour. Stanley puffs his harsh "Craven A"

cigarette between mouthfuls of ham and cheese and tries not to think about tobacco.

22 The bentkeeper and the field boss eat in the dusty pickup and the field boss lights his Marlboro and explains: "You know, when I yell at you it's nothing personal. I have to yell at you because it's my job. Man I know how it is, I was in your shoes once." The bentkeeper nods in agreement. His mind is on his lunch. It appears inedible. After growing tired of drinks and sandwiches that became warm and soggy in the hot sun for the past month, he has devised an unreliable system to solve that problem. Instead of just packing his lunch in ice, he actually freezes his entire lunch overnight. Unfortunately, when he opened his cooler on this hot day he discovered his peanut butter and jelly to be hard as a brick. Likewise his Boku juice boxes were still frozen solid.

23 As he sits there listening to his boss's rambling, he places his sandwich on the dash and he peels away the walls of his juice box and gnaws on it as if it were some kind of primitive popsicle. No matter how he prepares his lunch he can never seem to achieve a proper balance between hot and cold. When the sun is high and it's time to eat, he discovers either a frozen block of bread and jam or a soggy something suffering heat stroke.

24 At half past the hour Stanley strikes his stake into the dirt with a swift robotic motion. He sucks deeply on his cigarette and marches down to the end of the row. Large veins puff out of his forearm like the veins on the bottom green leaf that he snaps from the lower stalk of a thriving tobacco plant. Three more hours to go.

25 At the shed yet another blue tractor arrives with its precious load of fresh leaves. The shed boss man orders two rafter men down to disperse the containers of tobacco among the sewers. The bundlekeeper manages to help with the heavy containers between bundle runs. He is thoroughly exhausted and his eyes are bloodshot from the irritating smoke and dust in the shed. Although three hours remain every shed laborer is anticipating the boss man's "last lath! Get on the bus!"

26 At three-thirty in the hot afternoon three buses and two Chevy pickup trucks carry exhausted tobacco workers back to farm headquarters where the workers can rest before returning to work early tomorrow in the cool morning hours.

Content

1. Nocton identifies a variety of tasks the tobacco farm workers perform. What similarities are there among the jobs? What differences? Are readers to assume that all jobs are "demanding and repetitious and the pay is minimum wage" (¶ 3)? What's the difference between the tobacco harvesting process and the harvesting activities that Shange describes in "What Is It We Really Harvestin' Here?" (Chapter 4)?

2. Which workers are Hispanics and Jamaicans? Are any white Americans? Who performs which tasks?

3. Nocton evidently doesn't expect his readers to know much about the work of harvesting tobacco. What does he expect them to learn from reading his essay? What does he expect them to do as a consequence?

4. Is Nocton himself a worker in the scene he describes? If so, can you ascertain what his job is? What are your clues? In what ways, if any, does the effectiveness of his argument depend on the authority of his personal experience?

Strategies/Structures/Language

5. Nocton's language is slow and repetitive. How does the style fit the subject?

6. Where does Nocton use dialogue? With what effects?

7. In describing the process of harvesting and drying tobacco, Nocton also portrays the structure and members of a particular community, including its gender, social, and cultural divisions. What does his portrait of this community suggest about the relationship between the worker and the product of his or her labor? Is Nocton's comparison of the shed ceiling to the Sistine Chapel (¶ 17) ironic? What does this visionary moment suggest he has learned through his work experience?

8. ***Dialogues.*** Compare Nocton's description of working for The Culbro Tobacco Company with Michael Benedetto's experience of working the night shift in "Home Away from Home" (Chapter 9). How important are the locations for each writer? Why does Nocton focus on the terminology and process of harvesting tobacco while Benedetto focuses on his experience of a "vampire lifestyle" (¶ 3) and his own and his colleagues' reasons for working the night shift (¶ 7, 8, 11)? How would you characterize each writer's relationship to his work and employer?

For Writing

9. Have you or any family members or close friends ever held a minimum-wage job, or do you currently hold such a job? With a partner who has had comparable job experience, analyze your respective jobs and determine their common elements. Do they have aspects in common with the jobs Nocton describes? Are there any significant differences? Either together or individually, write a satiric paper about a typical day on the job, intended to serve as a critique and to imply a plan for better working conditions or employee benefits.

10. ***Mixed Modes.*** Have you ever thought about how any crop that provides common raw materials—wheat, sugar, potatoes, rice, coffee, cotton—is grown and harvested? Have you or your relatives ever worked in such harvests? Find out about the production of one of these crops and compare it with the tobacco harvest that Nocton describes. On the basis of your investigation, formulate some principles of how agricultural workers should be treated and what their compensation and protection should be.

Additional Topics for Writing Description

(For strategies for writing description, see 244.)

Multiple Strategies for Writing: Description

In writing on any of the description topics below, you can employ a number of options to enable your readers to interpret the subject according to the dimensions you present—those accessible by sight, sound, touch, taste, and smell or in psychological or emotional terms:

- *Illustrations* and *examples*, to show the whole, its components, and to interpret them
- *photographs, drawings, diagrams*, to clarify and explain
- *symbolic* use of literal details
- a *narrative*, or *logical sequence*, to provide coherence of interrelated parts
- *definitions, explanations, analyses* of the evidence
- *an implied or explicit argument* derived from the evidence and dependent on any of the above techniques

1. Places, for readers who haven't been there:
   a. Your dream house (or room)
   b. Your favorite spot on earth—or the place from hell
   c. A ghost town, or a dying or decaying neighborhood
   d. The site of a disaster or catastrophe, natural or man-made
   e. A foreign city or country you have visited
   f. A shopping mall or a particular store or restaurant, in use, under new management, or abandoned
   g. A factory, farm, store, or other place where you've worked
   h. The waiting room of an airport, hospital, physician's or dentist's office, or welfare office under a particular circumstance—routine or emergency
   i. A mountain, beach, lake, forest, desert, field, or other natural setting you know well
   j. Or compare and contrast two places you know well—two churches, houses, restaurants, vacation spots, schools, or any of the places identified in parts a–i, above; or a place before or after a renovation, a natural disaster, a long gap in time

See essays and poetry by O'Brien, 77–84; Shange, 158–63; Yu, 166–74; Oliver, 183; Zitkala-Sa, 184–90; Twain, 253–59; Nocton, 286–90; Cagle, 245–49; Asayesh, 330–32; and Khan, 333–36.

2. People you know for readers who don't know them:
   a. A close relative or friend
   b. A friend or relative with whom you were once very close but from whom you are presently separated, physically or psychologically
   c. An antagonist

d. Someone with an occupation or skill you want to know more about—you may want to interview the person to learn what skills, training, and personal qualities the job or activity requires
e. Someone who has participated, voluntarily or involuntarily, in a significant historical event
f. A bizarre or eccentric person, a "character"
g. A high achiever, mentor or role model, in business, education, sports, the arts or sciences, politics, religion
h. A person whose reputation, public or private, has changed dramatically, for better or worse

See essays and poetry by Alexie, 85–87; Sanders, 143–50; Pelizzon, 346–47; Cagle, 245–49; Britt, 281–83; McGuire, 230–36; Spinner, 300–01.

3. Situations or events, for readers who weren't there:

   a. A holiday, birthday, or community celebration; a high school or college party
   b. A crucial job interview
   c. A farmer's market, flea market, garage sale, swap meet, or auction
   d. An argument, brawl, or fight
   e. A performance of a play, concert, or athletic event
   f. A ceremony—a graduation, wedding, christening, bar or bat mitzvah, an initiation, the swearing-in of a public official
   g. A family or school reunion
   h. A confrontation—between team members and referees or the coach, employee and boss, strikers and scabs, protesters and police, political rivals (local, national, or international)

See essays, poetry, fiction, cartoon, and creative nonfiction by Fadiman, 102–05; Hall, 120–23; Sedaris, 318–20; Rodriguez, 321–28; Barry, 376–85; Tallent, 400–02; Chast, 409; King, Jr., 456–70.

4. Experiences or feelings, for readers with analogous experiences:

   a. Love—romantic, familial, patriotic, or religious (see Sanders, 143–50; Spinner, 300–01; Rodriguez, 321–28)
   b. Isolation or rejection (see Spiegelman, 96–97; Hogan, 99–101; Zitkala-Sa, 184–90)
   c. Fear (see Fadiman, 102–05)
   d. Aspiration (see Douglass, 89–93)
   e. Success (see McGuire, 230–36)
   f. Anger (see Douglass, 89–93)
   g. Peace, contentment, or happiness (see Hogan, 99–101; Doyle, 372–74)
   h. An encounter with birth or death (see O'Brien, 77–84)
   i. Coping with a handicap or disability—yours or that of someone close to you (see Hockenberry, 366–71; Sanders, 143–50)
   j. Knowledge and understanding—but after the fact (Fadiman, 102–05; Sanders, 143–50)
   k. Being a stranger in a strange land, as a traveler, immigrant, minority, or displaced person (Cagle, 245–49; Asayesh, 330–32; Khan, 333–36)

Division and Classification

To divide something is to separate it into its component parts, as the Roz Chast cartoon "Men Are from Belgium, Women Are from New Brunswick" (Chapter 9) indicates. As a writer you can divide a large, complex subject (people) into smaller segments, easier for you and your readers to deal with individually than to consider in a large, complicated whole (men and women). An even further refined analysis would interpret each component, as the dialogue in the cartoon does: "What men and women say" and "What they actually mean." As the section on process analysis indicates (see 115–19), writers usually employ division to explain the individual stages of a process—how the earth was formed, how a professional jockey (or potter or surgeon) performs his or her job, how a heat pump works. Process analysis also underlies explanations of how to make or do something, how to train your dog, or make biscotti, or use the newest version of the newest e-gadget.

You could also divide your subject in other ways—according to types of dogs, biscotti, or electronic equipment. And there would be still different ways to divide a discussion of dogs—by their size (miniature, small, medium, large); by the length of their hair (short or long); or according to their suitability as working dogs, guardians, pets, or show dogs.

As you start to divide your subject, you almost naturally begin to *classify* it as well, to sort it into categories of groups or families. You'll probably determine the subcategories according to some logical principle or according to characteristics common to members of particular subgroups. Don't stretch to create esoteric groupings (dogs by hair color, for example) if your common sense suggests a more natural way. Some categories simply make more sense than others. A discussion of dogs by breeds could be logically arranged in alphabetical order—Afghan, borzoi, bulldog, collie, Weimaraner. But a discussion that grouped dogs by type first and then breed would be easier to understand and more economical to write. For instance, you could consider all the common features of spaniels first, before dividing them into breeds of spaniels—cocker, springer, water—and discussing the differences.

How minutely you refine the subcategories of your classification system depends on the length of your writing, your focus, and your emphasis. You could use a *binary* (two-part) *classification*. This is a favorite technique of classifiers who wish to sort things into two categories, those with a particular characteristic and those without it (men and women, drinkers and nondrinkers, swimmers and nonswimmers). Thus, in an essay discussing the components of a large structure or organization—a farm, a corporation, a university—a binary classification might lead you to focus on management and labor or the university's academic and nonacademic functions. Twins are by definition a binary classification, unless they're treated as a single unit. In "Together in the Old Square Print, 1976," Jenny Spinner explores what it means to be an identical twin, whose meaning depends not only on its context but on who's doing the defining (see photo on 299). The biological classification is unvarying, but the social classification is shifting and complicated and as unique as each pair of twins or its individual members; for Jackie and Jenny do not think alike or behave alike even when they—hitherto inseparable—are entering first grade.

In "Make That a Double" (318–20), satirist David Sedaris makes the assumption that gender in French grammar is a straightforward binary classification scheme. In fact, as Sedaris correctly understands, a noun is indeed either masculine or feminine—and its gender "affects both its articles and its adjectives." The comic complication is one of logic—that if something is feminine or masculine in real life, its grammatical gender, or "sexual assignment," will logically correspond to that reality. Not so, as Sedaris discovers, "*Vagina* is masculine . . . while the word *masculinity* is feminine." His solution to the problem hinges on another classification system, singular and plural, for "the plural article does not reflect gender" and is consequently "the same for both the masculine and the feminine." That this requires him to buy two of everything, creating still other problems, seems a small price to pay for solving the grammatical dilemma.

Sometimes the divisions get more complicated because they are less clear-cut. The two essays on wearing the *hijab*, Gelareh Asayesh's "Shrouded in Contradiction" (330–32) and Sumbul Khan's "Mirror, Mirror on the Wall" (333–36), examine the combination of restrictions and freedom, comfort and discomfort, that wearing the veil allows women in (and out of) Islamic societies. This is an issue freighted with intense religious, social, and political implications, and so full of controversy that the personal stories here can only begin to touch on it. All of these complications are reinforced by a photograph taken in Pakistan in 2002 (331), in which veiled women, one carrying a child, pass in front of a phalanx of armed men in uniform.

In "Family Values" (321–28) Richard Rodriguez analyzes the subject from his perspective as a gay man about to come out to his parents. Each label of classification that he might use—*gay, queer, homosexual, joto, maricon*—has different connotations, as does each definition of *family* and, consequently, of *family values*. He then speculates on what it means for society to be arbitrarily divided into straight and gay, pointing out that each group performs overlapping roles and has varied sorts of investment in the family as they define it. Other definitions of family and family values are provided by still other categories of people: grandparents, parents, children (young and adult), politicians, immigrant groups from Asia and Mexico, Catholics and Protestants. Do so many labels, so many divisions and classifications, render them all insignificant? he implies. Are we not all one people? "My father opens the door to welcome me in."

In "Why Men Don't Last: Self-Destruction as a Way of Life" (302–05), Natalie Angier makes distinctions, based on biological and psychological research and statistical reports, between the self-destructive behavior of men and women—"women are about three times more likely than men to express suicidal thoughts or to attempt to kill themselves . . . but in the United States, four times more men than women die from the act each year." However, there are, she indicates, different ways to interpret these facts to show either that men are the greater risk takers ("given to showy displays of bravado, aggression and daring all for the sake of attracting a harem of mates") or that women are (because those who talk about suicide are more open to experience, including taking risks and seeking novelties). She makes other distinctions between men's and women's risk-taking behavior concerning homicide, alcohol and drug use, and gambling. For instance, although both men and women gamble, their "methods and preferences for throwing away big sums of money" are very different. Men try to "overcome the odds and beat the system" at table games "where they can feel powerful and omnipotent while everybody watches them," whereas women prefer "the solitary forms of gambling, the slot machines or video poker, where there isn't as much social scrutiny." Angier concludes by citing research that classifies boys by the extent to which they uphold traditional versus egalitarian views of masculinity; presumably the traditionalists would grow up to be more self-destructive than those who favored equal rights and responsibilities for women.

Deborah Tannen's works for general readers are characterized by numerous short divisions of the general topic, as both "Fast Forward: Technologically Enhanced Aggression" (308–15) and "Communication Styles" (403–07) indicate (both essays are graphically represented in the photograph of the tense angry man on 311). Each division makes her work easy to read and to understand. In particular, each division serves to classify the points in the arguments she makes, and each division is headed by a title that reinforces the point of that section. Although Tannen begins "Fast Forward" with positive examples of e-mail communication among coworkers and family members at short and long distance, the division titles reveal the way these divisions become an argument, that e-mail is really a form of "Technologically Enhanced Aggression" conducted through rapid and anonymous electronic communication. Thus the division titles claim, as they argue: "E-Mail Aggravates Aggression,"

"One-Way Communication Breeds Contempt," "Not So Fast!," "Stop That Law!" (what appears to legislators to be a "groundswell of popular protest is often the technologically enhanced protest of a few"—by fax, phone, letter, or e-mail), "Through the Magnifying Glass" (technology makes it much easier for critics of public figures to "ferret out inconsistencies" and make them look "unreliable" or "dishonest"), "'Who Is This? Why Are You Calling Here?'" (new technology makes it easier to act on the anger toward intrusive phone calls), and "Training Our Children to Kill" (by allowing them to play war video games).

Obviously, you can create as many categories and subcategories as are useful in enabling you and your readers to understand and interpret, the subject, as Marion Nestle does in "Eating Made Simple" (270–79). If you wanted to concentrate on the academic aspects of your own university, you might categorize them according to academic divisions—arts and sciences, business, education, music, public health. A smaller classification would examine the academic disciplines within a division—biology, English, history, mathematics. Or smaller yet, depending on your purpose—English literature, American literature, creative writing, linguistics—*ad infinitum,* as the anonymous jingle observes:

> Big fleas have little fleas, and these
> Have littler fleas to bite 'em,
> And these have fleas, and these have fleas,
> And so on ad infinitum.

In all six of the essays in this chapter, as well as Jenny Spinner's poem (300–01), the classification system provides the basis for the overall organization; but here as in most essays, the authors use many other techniques of writing in addition—narration, definition, description, analysis, illustration, and comparison and contrast.

In writing essays based on division, you might ask the following questions to help organize your materials: What are the parts of the total unit? How can these be subdivided to make the subject more understandable to my readers? In essays of classification, where you're sorting or grouping two or more things, you can ask: Into what categories can I sort these items? According to what principles—of logic, common characteristics, "fitness"? Do I want my classification to emphasize the similarities among groups or their differences? Once I've determined the groupings, am I organizing my discussion of each category in the same way, considering the same features in the same order? In many instances divisions and classifications are in the mind of the beholder. Is the glass half full or half empty? Your job as a writer is to help your readers recognize and accept the order of your universe.

Strategies for Writing: Division and Classification

1. Am I going to explain an existing system of classification, or am I going to invent a new one? Do I want to define a system by categorizing its components? Explain a process by dividing it into stages? Argue in favor of one category or another? Entertain through an amusing classification?
2. Do my readers know my subject but not my classification system? Know both subject and system? Or are they unacquainted with either? How will their knowledge (or lack of knowledge) of the subject or system influence how much I say about either? Will this influence the simplicity or complexity of my classification system?
3. According to what principle am I classifying or dividing my subject? Is it sensible? Significant? Does it emphasize the similarities or the differences among groups? Have I applied the principle consistently with respect to each category? How have I integrated my paper (to keep it from being just a long list), through providing interconnections among the parts and transitions between the divisions?
4. Have I organized my discussion of each category in the same way, considering the same features in the same order? Have I illustrated each category? Are the discussions of each category the same length? Should they be? Why or why not?
5. Have I used language similar in vocabulary level (equally technical, or equally informal) in each category? Have I defined any needed terms?

Photo courtesy Jenny Spinner.

Based on the depiction of the twin sisters in the following poem, which twin in the photograph would you identify as Jenny, the poem's author? And which is Jackie? On what do you base your reasoning?

JENNY SPINNER

Jenny Spinner (born 1970) grew up in the factory town of Decatur, Illinois, and was educated at Millikin University (BA 1992), Pennsylvania State University (MFA 1995), and the University of Connecticut (MA 1999, PhD 2004). She is an English professor at St. Joseph's University in Philadelphia. Spinner's dissertation focused on women essayists. Her essays, often about her sister and her family in Illinois, have appeared in the *Washington Post* and on National Public Radio. "Together in the Old Square Print, 1976" addresses her profound and intimate relationship with Jackie, her identical twin sister—and, until she became a mother, her only known blood relative, since the twins were adopted at birth.

Spinner explains the genesis of the poem: "In a creative writing class several semesters ago, I asked my students . . . to write a poem based on a photograph of themselves as children. I decided to give the assignment a whirl myself. The photograph upon which this poem is based was taken in 1976, the day my twin sister, Jackie, and I began first grade. I knew as soon as I touched it that this photo contained a poem. I remember vividly that traumatic day, the first day I was separated from my beloved sister and forced to make my way in the world as an individual. The poem attempts to describe what anyone looking at the picture can see—two look-alike little girls dressed in matching outfits, posed and poised. It also attempts to fill in what is beyond the physical edges of the photograph, the narrative of our first day of school. Finally, the poem brings in the seer, the adult poet who reflects on what she sees and emerges with some sort of truth. In this case, the truth is that I love(d) being a twin as much as I love(d) my sister. It made me feel unique, but that uniqueness, perhaps ironically, was bound to another. I was the first-born, scrambling out of the womb two minutes before my sister. Yet, I am the one who looked back, who was afraid to make her way in the world without her sister. Writing this poem taught me something I'd never before been able to articulate. It was a powerful, personal discovery."

✧ Together in the Old Square Print, 1976

Summer-brown, armed against
our inaugural day of first grade,
we are so alike in our *dernier cri*:
knee-high gingham dresses—
hers red, mine blue—
with coordinating tights
and brass-buckled Mary Janes.
Framed by the sleek pectinate line of our bangs,
our identical faces sprout, determined,
from our lace-ringed necks.
On the french doors behind us,
the camera flash forms a bright cross,
each of our heads hanging off an arm.
In just one hour, we will be led
into different classrooms,
our first separation since birth.
I will suffer through introductions
alone, hardly knowing
who I am without her,
and then I will cry.
And I won't stop until Mrs. Parnell
drags me across the hall
into the other first grade.
When my sister sees me
standing in the doorway, eyes aflame,
she looks up bewildered,

only then recognizing my absence.
For the rest of the day, I share
her small seat, drying my tears
in the heat of her body.
I don't feel shame, only
love bound back together.

But in the old print, all is yet to come.
At ease in our symmetry,
puffed sleeve against puffed sleeve,
we look out into the deceptive morning
that arrives with vague hints
of promises and premonitions:
Without her, I would be ordinary.
Afraid—and ordinary.

NATALIE ANGIER

Natalie Angier (born 1958) grew up in New York City and graduated from Barnard College in 1978. After working as a magazine staff writer at *Discover* and *Time* and as an editor at *Savvy*, she became a science reporter for the *New York Times* in 1990 and won a Pulitzer Prize in the following year. Her columns were published in 1995 as *The Beauty of the Beastly: New Views on the Nature of Life*. Topics include evolutionary biology ("Mating for Life?") DNA, scorpions, and central issues of life, death (by suicide or AIDS), and creativity. *Woman: An Intimate Geography* (1999) offers a spirited and controversial celebration of "the female body—its anatomy, its chemistry, its evolution, and its laughter," including both traditional (the womb, the egg) and nontraditional elements ("movement, strength, aggression, and fury"). Angier, who lists her hobby as "weightlifting," is also a mother; her work reflects the strengths of both. Her most recent book, *The Canon: A Whirligig Tour of the Beautiful Sciences* (2007), is an entertaining guide to science's controversies, mysteries, and beauties.

Angier's writing is characteristically clear, precise, and witty. She explains the unfamiliar in terms of the familiar, giving research a memorably human perspective. Thus, in "Why Men Don't Last," first published in the *New York Times* (Feb. 17, 1999), Angier examines significant differences between the biology of men and women, translating statistical and psychological research (on risk taking, compulsive gambling, suicidal behavior, masculinity) into language and concepts general readers can readily understand—without oversimplifying the subject or demeaning the audience.

Why Men Don't Last: Self-Destruction as a Way of Life

1 My father had great habits. Long before ficus trees met weight machines, he was a dogged exerciser. He did push-ups and isometrics. He climbed rocks. He went for long, vigorous walks. He ate sparingly and avoided sweets and grease. He took such good care of his teeth that they looked fake.

2 My father had terrible habits. He was chronically angry. He threw things around the house and broke them. He didn't drink often, but when he did, he turned more violent than usual. He didn't go to doctors, even when we begged him to. He let a big, ugly mole on his back grow bigger and bigger, and so he died of malignant melanoma, a curable cancer, at 51.

3 My father was a real man—so good and so bad. He was also Everyman.

4 Men by some measures take better care of themselves than women do and are in better health. They are less likely to be fat, for example; they exercise more, and suffer from fewer chronic diseases like diabetes, osteoporosis and arthritis.

5 By standard measures, men have less than half the rate of depression seen in women. When men do feel depressed, they tend to seek distraction in an activity, which, many psychologists say, can be a more effective technique for dispelling the mood than is a depressed woman's tendency to turn inward and ruminate. In the United States and many other industrialized nations, women are about three times more likely than men to express suicidal thoughts or to attempt to kill themselves.

6 And yet . . . men don't last. They die off in greater numbers than women do at every stage of life, and thus their average life span is seven years shorter. Women may attempt suicide relatively more often, but in the United States, four times more men than women die from the act each year.

7 Men are also far more likely than women to die behind the wheel or to kill others as a result of their driving. From 1977 to 1995, three and a half times more male drivers than female drivers were involved in fatal car crashes. Death by homicide also favors men; among those under 30, the male-to-female ratio is 8 to 1.

8 Yes, men can be impressive in their tendency to self-destruct, explosively or gradually. They are at least twice as likely as women to be alcoholics and three times more likely to be drug addicts. They have an eightfold greater chance than women do of ending up in prison. Boys are much more likely than girls to be thrown out of school for a conduct or antisocial personality disorder, or to drop out on their own surly initiative. Men gamble themselves into a devastating economic and emotional pit two to three times more often than women do.

"Between boys' suicide rates, dropout rates and homicide rates, and men's self-destructive behaviors generally, we have a real crisis in America," said William S. Pollack, a psychologist at Harvard Medical School and co-director of the Center for Men at McLean Hospital in Belmont, Mass. "Until recently, the crisis has gone unheralded." 9

It is one thing to herald a presumed crisis, though, and to cite a ream of gloomy statistics. It is quite another to understand the crisis, or to figure out where it comes from or what to do about it. As those who study the various forms of men's self-destructive behaviors realize, there is not a single, glib, overarching explanation for the sex-specific patterns they see. 10

A crude evolutionary hypothesis would have it that men are natural risk-takers, given to showy displays of bravado, aggression and daring all for the sake of attracting a harem of mates. By this premise, most of men's self-destructive, violent tendencies are a manifestation of their need to take big chances for the sake of passing their genes into the river of tomorrow. 11

Some of the data on men's bad habits fit the risk-taker model. For example, those who study compulsive gambling have observed that men and women tend to display very different methods and preferences for throwing away big sums of money. 12

"Men get enamored of the action in gambling," said Linda Chamberlain, a psychologist at Regis University in Denver who specializes in treating gambling disorders. "They describe an overwhelming rush of feelings and excitement associated with the process of gambling. They like the feeling of being a player, and taking on a struggle with the house to show that they can overcome the odds and beat the system. They tend to prefer the table games, where they can feel powerful and omnipotent while everybody watches them." 13

Dr. Chamberlain noted that many male gamblers engage in other risk-taking behaviors, like auto racing or hang gliding. By contrast, she said, "Women tend to use gambling more as a sedative, to numb themselves and escape from daily responsibilities, or feelings of depression or alienation. Women tend to prefer the solitary forms of gambling, the slot machines or video poker, where there isn't as much social scrutiny." 14

Yet the risk-taking theory does not account for why men outnumber women in the consumption of licit and illicit anodynes. Alcohol, heroin and marijuana can be at least as numbing and sedating as repetitively pulling the arm of a slot machine. And some studies have found that men use drugs and alcohol for the same reasons that women often overeat: as an attempt to self-medicate when they are feeling anxious or in despair. 15

"We can speculate all we want, but we really don't know why men drink more than women," said Enoch Gordis, the head of the National Institute on Alcohol Abuse and Alcoholism. Nor does men's comparatively 16 higher rate of suicide appear linked to the risk-taking profile. To the contrary, Paul Duberstein, an assistant professor of psychiatry and oncology at the University of Rochester School of Medicine, has found that people who complete a suicidal act are often low in a personality trait referred to as "openness to experience," tending to be rigid and inflexible in their behaviors. By comparison, those who express suicidal thoughts tend to score relatively high on the openness-to-experience scale.

17 Given that men commit suicide more often than women, and women talk about it more, his research suggests that, in a sense, women are the greater risk-takers and novelty seekers, while the men are likelier to feel trapped and helpless in the face of changing circumstances.

18 Silvia Cara Canetto, an associate professor of psychology at Colorado State University in Fort Collins, has extensively studied the role of gender in suicidal behaviors. Dr. Canetto has found that cultural narratives may determine why women attempt suicide more often while men kill themselves more often. She proposes that in Western countries, to talk about suicide or to survive a suicidal act is often considered "feminine," hysterical, irrational and weak. To actually die by one's own hand may be viewed as "masculine," decisive, strong. Even the language conveys the polarized, weak-strong imagery: a "failed" suicide attempt as opposed to a "successful" one.

19 "There is indirect evidence that there is negative stigma toward men who survive suicide," Dr. Canetto said. "Men don't want to 'fail,' even though failing in this case means surviving." If the "suicidal script" that identifies completing the acts as "rational, courageous and masculine" can be "undermined and torn to pieces," she said, we might have a new approach to prevention.

20 Dr. Pollack of the Center for Men also blames many of men's self-destructive ways on the persistent image of the dispassionate, resilient, action-oriented male—the Marlboro Man who never even gasps for breath. For all the talk of the sensitive "new man," he argues, men have yet to catch up with women in expanding their range of acceptable emotions and behaviors. Men in our culture, Dr. Pollack says, are pretty much limited to a menu of three strong feelings: rage, triumph, lust. "Anything else and you risk being seen as a sissy," he said.

21 In a number of books, most recently "Real Boys: Rescuing Our Sons From the Myths of Boyhood," he proposes that boys "lose their voice, a whole half of their emotional selves," beginning at age 4 or 5. "Their vulnerable, sad feelings and sense of need are suppressed or shamed out of them," he said—by their peers, parents, the great wide televised fist in their face.

22 He added: "If you keep hammering it into a kid that he has to look tough and stop being a crybaby and a mama's boy, the boy will start creating a mask of bravado."

That boys and young men continue to feel confused over the proper harmonics of modern masculinity was revealed in a study that Dr. Pollack conducted of 200 eighth-grade boys. Through questionnaires, he determined their scores on two scales, one measuring their "egalitarianism"—the degree to which they think men and women are equal, that men should change a baby's diapers, that mothers should work and the like—and the other gauging their "traditionalism" as determined by their responses to conventional notions, like the premise that men must "stand on their own two feet" and must "always be willing to have sex if someone asks." 23

On average, the boys scored high on both scales. "They are split on what it means to be a man," said Dr. Pollack. 24

The cult of masculinity can beckon like a siren song in baritone. Dr. Franklin L. Nelson, a clinical psychologist at the Fairbanks Community Mental Health Center in Alaska, sees many men who get into trouble by adhering to sentimental notions of manhood. "A lot of men come up here hoping to get away from a wimpy world and live like pioneers by old-fashioned masculine principles of individualism, strength and ruggedness," he said. They learn that nothing is simple; even Alaska is part of a wider, interdependent world and they really do need friends, warmth and electricity. 25

"Right now, it's 35 degrees below zero outside," he said during a January interview. "If you're not prepared, it doesn't take long at that temperature to freeze to death." 26

Content

1. Angier uses several categories of division in this piece: the "so good and so bad" habits of "Everyman" (¶ 3); the self-destructive habits and rates of men versus women (throughout); the division between the rugged individual versus the egalitarian helpmeet roles today's men are expected to play (¶s 23–25). Why do such divisions enable readers to clearly recognize similarities as well as differences?
2. Angier's explanations for these divisions are equally divided. What evidence does she offer to support the "crude evolutionary hypothesis" that "men are natural risk-takers, given to showy display of bravado, aggression and daring all for the sake of attracting a harem of mates" (¶ 11)? What evidence does she offer to contradict this hypothesis?
3. What might be some reasons why women talk about committing suicide more than men do, but that men actually have a higher rate of suicide than women do (¶s 16–19)?

Strategies/Structures/Language

4. What are the dangers and difficulties of categorizing behavior by gender? Why aren't the divisions and classifications Angier uses more clear-cut? Is this a phenomenon of the research she cites, of her writing, of the way things are in real life, or of some combination of the three?

5. Angier is writing as a reporter of other people's research. Do we know where she stands on the subject—which hypothesis for men's risk-taking behavior she believes? Is her essay slanted in favor of one opinion or another, either in terms of her examples or her language?

6. Should a reporter be neutral? Isn't the selection of evidence in itself a form of tipping the scale in favor of one side or another?

For Writing

7. ***Journal Writing.*** In what ways does American culture encourage men to develop a "mask of bravado" (¶ 22)? In your experience, are men punished when expressing their emotional needs? What aspects of the sex roles that you experienced as part of your childhood have you consciously changed or might want to change in raising your own children?

8. Have you ever done anything risky or dangerous to avoid looking like a wimp or to avoid falling into one or another stereotypical role for either men or women? Write a paper for an audience different from yourself; for instance, if you're a risk-taking man, write for a more prudent audience of women or men (if it makes a difference to your argument, specify which gender), and have such a reader critique your paper before you revise it.

9. ***Mixed Modes.*** Angier, like other science writers, has the difficult job of translating scientific research into language that newspaper readers can understand. From the following list of authors she cites on the role of gender in suicidal behaviors, choose one source and identify, with illustrations, the principles by which Angier works. Consider aspects such as document format, uses of evidence, presentation of data (via graphs, charts, statistics), technicality of language, definitions of scientific terms, citation of supporting research. Use illustrations, graphic as well as written, to clarify.

Canetto, Silvia Sara, and David Lester. "Gender, Culture, and Suicidal Behavior." *Transcultural Psychiatry* 35.2 (1998): 163–90.

Canetto, Silvia Sara, and Issac Sakinofsky. "The Gender Paradox in Suicide." *Suicide and Life-Threatening Behavior* 28.1 (Spring 1998): 1–23.

Chamberlain, Linda, Michael R. Ruetz, and William G. McCown. *Strange Attractors: Chaos, Complexity, and the Art of Family Therapy.* New York: Wiley, 1997.

Duberstein, Paul R., Yeates Conwell, and Christopher Cox. "Suicide in Widowed Persons." *American Journal of Geriatric Psychiatry* 6.4 (Fall 1998): 328–34.

Gordis, Enoch. "Alcohol Problems in Public Health Policy." *Journal of the American Medical Association* (Dec. 1997): 1781–87.

Pollack, William S. *Real Boys: Rescuing Our Sons from the Myths of Boyhood.* New York: Random, 1998.

Pollack, William S., and Ronald F. Levant, eds. *New Psychotherapy for Men.* New York: Wiley, 1998.

10. ***Dialogues.*** Angier argues that there is not one "overarching explanation for the sex-specific patterns" scientists who study self-destructive behaviors observe (¶ 10). Does Deborah Tannen's argument, in "Communication Styles" (Chapter 9), that boys learn to "use language to seize center stage" (¶ 3) and are

more comfortable demonstrating "verbal display" in the classroom (¶ 4) represent an overarching explanation for the sex-specific patterns she observes in the classroom? Does Tannen's argument represent an application of what Angier calls "the risk-taker model" (¶ 12)? Might what Angier calls the "cult of masculinity" (¶ 25) explain classroom behavior?

11. ***Second Look.*** What does the photo on 199 suggest about the reasons people engage in risky behaviors such as alcohol abuse? Are risky behaviors simply a part of growing up? Are such rites of passage different for men and women?

DEBORAH TANNEN

Deborah Tannen, born in Brooklyn in 1945, was partially deafened by a childhood illness. Her consequent interest in nonverbal communication and other aspects of conversation led ultimately to a doctorate in linguistics (University of California, Berkeley, 1979) and professorship at Georgetown University. Tannen's numerous studies of gender-related speech patterns draw on the combined perspectives of anthropology, sociology, psychology, and women's studies, as well as linguistics. Tannen brings a sensitive ear and keen analysis to communication related to gender, power, and status in the best-selling *That's Not What I Meant!: How Conversational Style Makes or Breaks Your Relations with Others* (1986), *You Just Don't Understand: Women and Men in Conversation* (1990), *Talking from 9 to 5* (1994), *I Only Say This Because I Love You* (2001), *Conversational Style: Analyzing Talk Among Friends* (2005), and *You're Wearing That?: Understanding Mothers and Daughters in Conversation* (2006).

"Fast Forward: Technologically Enhanced Aggression" comes from *The Argument Culture: Moving from Debate to Dialogue* (1998), a book devoted to analyzing the "pervasive warlike atmosphere that makes us approach public dialogue, and just about anything we need to accomplish, as if it were a fight." Our spirits, she says, are "corroded by living in an atmosphere of unrelenting contention—an argument culture" that "urges us to approach the world—and the people in it—in an adversarial frame of mind." Although argument can be useful, it often creates "more problems than it solves," as Tannen's analysis of various types of e-mail communication indicates. Each division of her analysis can be further categorized according to those who behave in the aggressive ways the section addresses and those who don't.

Fast Forward: Technologically Enhanced Aggression

1 I was the second person in my department to get a computer. The first was my colleague Ralph. The year was 1980. Ralph got a Radio Shack TRS 80; I got a used Apple 2-Plus. He helped me get started and before long helped me get on e-mail, the precursor of the Internet. Though his office was next to mine, we rarely had extended conversations except about department business. Shy and soft-spoken, Ralph mumbled so, I could barely tell he was speaking. But when we both were using e-mail, we started communicating daily in this (then) leisurely medium. We could send each other messages without fear of imposing, since the receiver determines when to log on and read and respond. Soon I was getting long, self-revealing messages from Ralph. We moved effortlessly among discussions of department business, our work, and our lives. Through e-mail Ralph and I became friends.

2 Ralph recently forwarded to me a message he had received from his niece, a college freshman. "How nice," I commented, "that you have such a close relationship with your niece. Do you think you'd be in touch with her if it weren't for e-mail?" "No," he replied. "I can't imagine we'd write each other letters regularly or call on the phone. No way." E-mail makes possible connections with relatives, acquaintances, or strangers that would not otherwise exist. And it enables more and different communication with people you are already close to. One woman discovered that e-mail brought her closer to her father. He would never talk much on the phone (as her mother would), but they have become close since they both got online.

3 Everywhere e-mail is enhancing or even transforming relationships. Parents keep in regular touch with children in college who would not be caught dead telephoning home every day. When I spent a year and a half in Greece in the late 1960s, I was out of touch with my family except for the mail—letters that took hours to compose and weeks to arrive. When my sister spent a year in Israel in the mid-1990s, we kept in touch nearly every day—and not only she and I. Prodded by her absence, within a month of her departure our third sister and my sisters' daughters all started using e-mail. Though she was so far away, my sister was in some ways in closer touch with the family than she would have been had she stayed home.

4 And another surprise: My other sister, who generally is not eager to talk about her feelings, opened up on e-mail. One time I called her and we spoke on the phone; after we hung up, I checked my e-mail and found she had revealed information there that she hadn't mentioned when we spoke. I asked her about it (on e-mail), and she explained, "The telephone

is so impersonal." At first this seemed absurd: How could the actual voice of a person right there be impersonal and the on-screen little letters detached from the writer be more personal? When I asked her about this, she explained: "The big advantage to e-mail is that you can do it at your time and pace; there is never the feeling that the phone is ringing and interrupting whatever it is you are doing." Writing e-mail is like writing in a journal; you're alone with your thoughts and your words, safe from the intrusive presence of another person.

E-Mail Aggravates Aggression

E-mail, and now the Internet and the World Wide Web, are creating 5
networks of human connection unthinkable even a few years ago. But at the same time that technologically enhanced communication enables previously impossible loving contact, it also enhances hostile and distressing communication. Along with the voices of family members and friends, telephone lines bring into our homes the annoying voices of solicitors who want to sell something—generally at dinnertime. (My father-in-law startles a telephone solicitor by saying, "We're eating dinner, but I'll call you back. What's your home phone number?" To the nonplussed caller, he explains, "Well, you're calling me at home; I thought I'd call you at home, too.") Even more unnerving, in the middle of the night may come frightening obscene calls and stalkers. From time to time the public is horrified to learn that even the most respected citizens can succumb to the temptation of anonymity that the telephone seems to offer—like the New York State Supreme Court chief justice who was harassing a former lover by mail and phone and the president of American University in Washington, D.C., who was found to be the source of obscene telephone calls to a woman he didn't even know.

But telephone lines can be traced (as President Richard Berendzen 6
learned) and voices can be recognized (as Judge Sol Wachtler discovered). The Internet ratchets up anonymity by homogenizing all messages into identical-appearing print and making it almost impossible to trace messages back to the computer that sent them. As the ease of using the Internet has resulted in more and more people logging on and sending messages to more and more others with whom they have a connection, it has also led to increased communication with strangers—and this has resulted in "flaming": vituperative messages that verbally attack. Flaming results from the anonymity not only of the sender but also of the receiver. It is easier to feel and express hostility against someone far removed whom you do not know personally, like the rage that some drivers feel toward an anonymous car that cuts them off. If the anonymous driver to whom you've flipped the finger turns out to be someone you know, the rush of shame you experience is evidence that anonymity was essential for your expression—and experience—of rage.

7 One of the most effective ways to defuse antagonism between two groups is to provide a forum for individuals from those groups to get to know each other personally. This is the logic behind programs that bring together, for example, African-American and Jewish youths or Israeli and Palestinian women. It was the means by which a troubled Vietnam veteran finally achieved healing: through a friendship with a man who had been the enemy he was trying to kill—a retired Vietnamese officer whose diary the American had found during the war and managed to return to its owner nearly twenty-five years later. When you get to know members of an "enemy" group personally, it is hard to demonize them, to see them as less than human.

8 What is happening in our lives is just the opposite: More and more of our communication is not face to face, and not with people we know. The proliferation and increasing portability of technology isolate people in a bubble. When I was a child, my family got the first television on our block, and the neighborhood children gathered in our dining room to watch Howdy Doody. Before long, every family had its own TV—but each had just one, so, in order to watch it, families came together. Now it is common for families to have more than one television, so the adults can watch what they like in one room and the children can watch their choice in another—or maybe each child has a private TV to watch alone. The spread of radio has followed the same pattern. Early radios were like a piece of furniture around which a family had to gather in order to listen. Now radio listeners may have a radio in every room, one in the car, and yet another, equipped with headphones, for walking or jogging. Radio and television began as sources of information that drew people together physically, even if their attention was not on each other. Now these technologies are exerting a centrifugal force, pulling people apart—and, as a result, increasing the likelihood that their encounters will be agonistic.

One-Way Communication Breeds Contempt

9 The head of a small business had a reputation among his employees as being a Jekyll-and-Hyde personality. In person he was always mild-mannered and polite. But when his employees saw a memo from him in their mail, their backs stiffened. The boss was famous for composing angry, even vicious memos that he often had to temper and apologize for later. It seemed that the presence of a living, breathing person in front of him was a brake on his hostility. But seated before a faceless typewriter or computer screen, his anger built and overflowed. A woman who had worked as a dean at a small liberal arts college commented that all the major problems she encountered with faculty or other administrators resulted from written memos, not face-to-face communication.

10 Answering machines are also a form of one-way communication. A piano teacher named Craig was president of a piano teachers'

© Larry Williams/Corbis

"Read" the picture as an illustration of Angier's "Why Men Don't Last" or Tannen's "Fast Forward: Technologically Enhanced Aggression," or both. How can you tell he's angry? Would you interpret the picture the same way if the figure were a woman rather than a man? Or if the figure looked more like a college student than a career person?

association that sponsored a yearly competition. Craig had nothing to do with the competition—someone else had organized and overseen it. So he felt helpless and caught off guard when he came home to a message that laid out in detail the caller's grievances about how the competition had been handled, and ended, "That's no way to run an organization!" Slam! When he heard the message, Craig thought, "Here I am, being the president as a service to keep things together, and I'm being attacked for something I had no control over. It made me wonder," he commented, "why I was doing it at all." Craig refused a second term in large part because of attacks like this—even though they were infrequent, while he frequently received lavish praise. Being attacked is perhaps unavoidable for those in authority, but in this case the technology played a role as well. It is highly unlikely the caller would have worked herself up into quite this frenzy, or concluded the conversation by hanging up on Craig, if she had gotten Craig himself and not his answering machine, let alone if she had talked to him in person.

In the heat of anger, it is easy to pick up a phone and make a call. 11
But when talking directly to someone, most people feel an impulse to tone down what they say. Even if they do not, the person they are attacking will respond after the first initial blast—by explaining, apologizing, or counterattacking. Whatever the response, it will redirect the

attacker's speech, perhaps aggravating the anger but also perhaps deflating it. If you write an angry letter, you might decide later not to send it or to tone it down. But if you make a call and reach voice mail or an answering machine, it's the worst of both worlds: You spout off in the heat of anger, there is no way to take back what you said or correct misinterpretations, and there is no response to act as a brake. In my research on workplace communication, I found that a large percentage of serious conflicts had been sparked by one-way communication such as memos, voice mail, and e-mail.

12 An experienced reporter at a newspaper heard that one of his colleagues, a feature writer, was working on a story about a topic he knew well. He had done extensive research on a related topic in the course of his own reporting. So he thought he'd be helpful: He sent her a long e-mail message warning her of potential pitfalls and pointing out aspects she should bear in mind. Rather than thanks, he received a testy reply informing him that she was quite capable of watching out for these pitfalls without his expert guidance, and that she too was a seasoned reporter, even though she had been at the paper a shorter time than he. Reading her angry reply, he gulped and sent an apology.

13 An advantage of e-mail is its efficiency: The reporter was able to send his ideas without taking the time to walk to another floor and talk face to face with his colleague. But had he done so, he would probably have presented his ideas differently, and she would have seen the spirit in which the advice was given. If not, it is unlikely he would have gotten so far in his advice giving before picking up that he was not coming across the way he intended, that she was taking offense. He then could have backtracked and changed the tone of his communication rather than laying it on thicker and thicker, continuing and expanding in a vein that was making her angrier by the second. What's more, if people meet regularly face to face, friendships begin to build that lay the foundation for future communication. It's harder for e-mail and memos to do that.

Not So Fast!

14 The potential for misunderstandings and mishaps with electronic communication expands in proportion to the potential for positive exchanges. For example, two workers exchanged e-mail about a report that had to be submitted. One of them wrote that a portion could better be handled by a third person—but added an unflattering remark about her. The recipient received the message at a busy time, noticed that it called for Person 3 to do something—and quickly and efficiently forwarded it to her, disparaging remark and all. E-mail makes it too easy to forward messages, too easy to reply before your temper cools, too easy to broadcast messages to large numbers of people without thinking about how every sentence

will strike every recipient. And there's plenty of opportunity for error: sending a message to the wrong person or having a message mysteriously appear on the screen of an unintended recipient.

Every improvement in technology makes possible new and 15
scarier kinds of errors. In one company, a manager set up an e-mail user-group list, so his messages would go to everyone in the department at once and their replies would also get distributed to everyone on the list. But several people sent him replies that they thought were private, not realizing everyone in the office would see them. Like a private conversation overheard, these "overread" messages to the manager came across to colleagues as kissing up, since people tend to use a more deferential tone in addressing a boss than a peer. It was embarrassing, but not as bad as the job applicant who mistakenly sent a message including his uncensored judgment about the person who interviewed him to that person. . . .

Who's to Judge?

One of the great contributions of the Internet is that it enables ordinary 16
people to put out information that previously would have been limited by such gatekeepers as newspaper editors and book publishers, or that would have required enormous amounts of time and money to publish and disseminate independently. In a few moments, anyone with the equipment and expertise can post information on the World Wide Web, and anyone else with the equipment and expertise can read it. This can be invaluable—for example, when individuals who have unusual medical conditions and their families exchange information and personal experience through specialized user groups. But there is a danger here as well. Editors, publishers, and other gatekeepers impose their judgment—for better or worse—on the accuracy of the material they publish. Those who download information from the Internet may be unable to judge the veracity and reliability of information.

A professor at a public university was assigned a student assistant 17
who had excellent computer skills. The assistant offered to help her make reading materials available to her class by placing them on a class Web site. He began by putting on the site readings and secondary sources that the professor had assigned or recommended. But he did not stop there. He went on to scour the Internet for anything related to the course topic and import it into the class Web site, too. When the professor discovered what he had done, she told him to remove these materials, since she did not have time to read everything he had imported to determine whether it was appropriate for the students to read. Some of it might have been irrelevant to the class and would distract them from the material she felt they should read. And some of it might be factually wrong. The idea that the professor thought she should read the material she was making

available to her students in order to judge its accuracy and suitability was foreign to the student assistant—and offensive. He argued that she was trying to infringe on the students' First Amendment right to have access to any kind of information at all.

18 This is a danger inherent in the Internet: At the same time that the ease of posting makes available enormous amounts of useful information, it also makes possible the dissemination of useless, false, or dangerous information—and makes it more difficult to distinguish between the two. To be sure, publishers and editors often make mistakes in publishing material they should not and rejecting material they should accept (as any author whose work has been rejected can tell you—and as evidenced by the many successful books that were rejected by dozens of editors before finally finding a home). Yet readers of reputable newspapers and magazines or books published by established presses know that what they are reading has been deemed reliable by professional editors. The Internet makes it more difficult for consumers to distinguish the veracity and reliability of information they come across.

19 The Internet can function as a giant and unstoppable rumor mill or as a conduit for such dangerous information as how to build a bomb. It can also facilitate aggressive behavior, as author Elaine Showalter discovered when she published a book, *Hystories*, in which she included chronic fatigue syndrome among a list of phenomena, such as alien abduction and satanic ritual abuse, that she identified as hysterical epidemics. Sufferers from chronic fatigue syndrome who were angered by the label "hysterical" used the Internet to share information about the author's public appearances, so they could turn out in force to harass and even threaten her. Law enforcement authorities have been unable to identify members of the Animal Liberation Front, who use violence and terrorism in their efforts to halt what they see as cruelty to animals, because their communication with one another takes place for the most part on the Internet rather than at face-to-face meetings. . . .

Like Peas Out of a Pod

20 Flaming is only one aspect of electronic communication. E-mail makes possible extended interaction among people who are physically distant from each other. But it also makes possible anonymity and in some cases—as with young people (mostly boys) who become computer "nerds"—begins to substitute for human interaction. Following a tragic incident in which a fifteen-year-old boy sexually assaulted and then murdered an eleven-year-old boy who happened to ring his doorbell selling candy and wrapping paper to raise money for his school, many people felt that the Internet shared a portion of the blame, because the murderer had himself been sexually abused by a pedophile he had met through the Internet. An aspect of this harrowing and bizarre event

which received less comment was that as the older boy had become obsessed with the Internet, he had gradually withdrawn from social interaction with his peers.

Advances in technology are part of a larger complex of forces moving people away from face-to-face interaction and away from actual experience—from hearing music performed, to hearing recordings of performances, to hearing digital re-creations of performances that some believe bear little resemblance to music as performed. From live dramatic performances in theaters, to silent movies shown in theaters with the accompaniment of live orchestras, to sound movies, to videos watched in the isolation of one's home. From local stores privately owned and owner-operated to chains owned by huge corporations based far away and staffed by minimum-wage employees who know little about the merchandise and have much less stake in whether customers leave the store happy or offended. 21

All of these trends have complex implications—many positive, but many troubling. Each new advance makes possible not only new levels of connection but also new levels of hostility and enhanced means of expressing it. People who would not dream of cutting in front of others waiting in a line think nothing of speeding along an empty traffic lane to cut ahead of others waiting in a line of cars. It is easy to forget that inside the car, or facing a computer screen, is a living, feeling person. 22

The rising level of public aggression in our society seems directly related to the increasing isolation in our lives, which is helped along by advances in technology. This isolation—and the technology that enhances it—is an ingredient in the argument culture. We seem to be better at developing technological means of communication than at finding ways to temper the hostility that sometimes accompanies them. We have to work harder at finding those ways. That is the challenge we now face. 23

Content

1. What connections does Tannen make between "advances in technology," "the increasing isolation in our lives," and "the rising level of public aggression in our society" (¶ 23)? Which types of evidence that she uses to make her case do you find the most convincing: personal anecdotes, contemporary news events, issues of public policy, or analyses of the way Americans in general live and behave? Why?
2. What are some of the advantages of technology as outlined by Tannen? Some of its disadvantages? Do the gains outweigh the losses in Tannen's analysis? In yours?
3. Tannen opens her essay with a discussion of the advantages of e-mail in building and maintaining close relationships (¶s 1–4). In paragraph 13, she

claims that "if people meet regularly face to face, friendships begin to build that lay the foundation for future communication. It's harder for e-mail and memos to do that." These positions are seemingly at odds with each other. Does she address or account for this apparent contradiction at any point in her essay?

4. What relationship does Tannen see between expressions of hostility such as "flaming" and "road rage" and the "anonymity not only of the sender but also of the receiver" (¶ 6)? Does your own experience corroborate her claim that "It is easier to feel and express hostility against someone far removed whom you do not know personally" (¶ 6) than it is to treat people with whom one has a personal connection in a hostile manner? Does Tannen offer any solutions to this problem? Can you or your fellow students resolve this issue, in discussion or in writing (see question 9).

Strategies/Structures/Language

5. Each division of Tannen's analysis can be further divided according to people who behave in the aggressive ways the section addresses and people who don't. Is anonymity, coupled with the ease and speed of sending insults by e-mail, the most compelling reason for such hostile behavior? What evidence does she offer that personal acquaintance with "members of an 'enemy' group" will humanize them (¶ 7) and thus have the potential for transforming a hostile relationship into a friendly one? Under what circumstances could personal acquaintance make relations worse rather than better?

6. Tannen's writing here and in "Communication Styles" (Chapter 9) is characterized by numerous subdivisions of her topic, identified by witty slogans ("One-Way Communication Breeds Contempt") and breezy headings ("Not So Fast!"). What is the effect on the total piece of these subdivisions and of the language in which they're written?

For Writing

7. Do you use different language in e-mails than you do in conversation? In hardcopy letters? What consistencies do you find in the language and other conventions of all three forms of communication? What differences? (For evidence you could look at some messages you've written and perhaps tape a conversation for analysis.) Tabulate your results in lists or a chart.

8. Use the data you and your classmates have collected in answering question 7 to write an essay that analyzes the use of technology by college students. You might, for example, set up a system of division and classification based on the categories suggested in question 7. Do you need to add other categories? You may wish to interview classmates to expand on their answers.

9. Tannen notes, "We seem to be better at developing technological means of communication than at finding ways to temper the hostility that sometimes accompanies them. We have to work harder at finding those ways. That is the challenge we now face" (¶ 23). If you use e-mail a lot (say, twenty or more messages a day), in collaboration with other e-mail users, draft a policy statement of appropriate e-mail etiquette for dealing with messages from people you don't

know personally, such as those in your school or workplace to whom you are accountable. Would you recommend treating people you know personally any different from strangers? Incorporate some of the evidence you've gleaned in your answer to question 7.

10. ***Journal Writing.*** Have you ever sent an e-mail or left a message on an answering machine that you later regretted? Retrace the process that led to your action. Would you have reacted in the same way had you communicated your feelings face-to-face to the other person? In situations where you are disappointed or angry, does the medium of communication—e-mail, phone, text-messaging—affect the way you communicate your feelings?

11. ***Second Look.*** How does the photo in this essay suggest that electronic communication and multitasking increase the opportunity for what Tannen calls ever "scarier kinds of errors" (¶ 15)? How does it illustrate her point that the speed and ease of electronic communications can foster hostility?

DAVID SEDARIS

David Sedaris was born in 1957 and graduated from the School of the Art Institute of Chicago in 1987. His national reputation as a humorist began in 1993 when he read excerpts from "The SantaLand Diaries" on National Public Radio, in a "nicely nerdy, quavering voice." These monologues, praised for their wit and deadpan delivery, anatomized various odd jobs he held after moving to New York—an elf in SantaLand at Macy's department store, an office worker, and an apartment cleaner. He explained to the *New York Times*, "I can only write when it's dark, so basically, my whole day is spent waiting for it to get dark. Cleaning apartments gives me something to do when I get up. Otherwise, I'd feel like a bum." His NPR appearances led to job offers—for both cleaning and writing—as well as contracts for *Barrel Fever* (1994) and *Naked* (1997).

In *Naked* and later books—*Me Talk Pretty One Day* (2000) and *Dress Your Family in Corduroy and Denim* (2004)—Sedaris has drawn his most memorable material from bittersweet renderings of his family: his father, "an eccentric IBM engineer who ruins miniature golf with dissertations on wind trajectory"; his mother, a secret alcoholic ("Drinking didn't count if you followed a glass of wine with a cup of coffee") who pushed her children outside on a snow day so she could drink in secret; and his siblings, alternately attractive and pathetic. Sedaris's presentations of his relationship with his partner, Hugh, are more mellow, as in "Make That a Double," which emphasizes the illogical and irrational (to English speakers) attributions of gender in French grammar: "Because it is a female and lays eggs, a chicken is masculine . . . while the word *masculinity* is feminine."

Make That a Double

1 There are, I have noticed, two basic types of French spoken by Americans vacationing in Paris: the Hard Kind and the Easy Kind. The Hard Kind involves the conjugation of wily verbs and the science of placing them alongside various other words in order to form such sentences as "I go him say good afternoon" and "No, not to him I no go it him say now."

2 The second, less complicated form of French amounts to screaming English at the top of your lungs, much the same way you'd shout at a deaf person or the dog you thought you could train to stay off the sofa. Doubt and hesitation are completely unnecessary, as Easy French is rooted in the premise that, if properly packed, the rest of the world could fit within the confines of Reno, Nevada. The speaker carries no pocket dictionary and never suffers the humiliation that inevitably comes with pointing to the menu and ordering the day of the week. With Easy French, eating out involves a simple "BRING ME A STEAK."

3 Having undertaken the study of Hard French, I'll overhear such requests and glare across the room, thinking, "That's *Mister* Steak to you, buddy." Of all the stumbling blocks inherent in learning this language, the greatest for me is the principle that each noun has a corresponding sex that affects both its articles and its adjectives. Because it is a female and lays eggs, a chicken is masculine. *Vagina* is masculine as well, while the word *masculinity* is feminine. Forced by the grammar to take a stand one way or the other, *hermaphrodite* is male and *indecisiveness* female.

4 I spent months searching for some secret code before I realized that common sense has nothing to do with it. *Hysteria, psychosis, torture, depression*: I was told that if something is unpleasant, it's probably feminine. This encouraged me, but the theory was blown by such masculine nouns as *murder, toothache*, and *Rollerblade*. I have no problem learning the words themselves, it's the sexes that trip me up and refuse to stick.

5 What's the trick to remembering that a sandwich is masculine? What qualities does it share with anyone in possession of a penis? I'll tell myself that a sandwich is masculine because if left alone for a week or two, it will eventually grow a beard. This works until it's time to order and I decide that because it sometimes loses its makeup, a sandwich is undoubtedly feminine.

6 I just can't manage to keep my stories straight. Hoping I might learn through repetition, I tried using gender in my everyday English. "Hi, guys," I'd say, opening a new box of paper clips, or "Hey, Hugh, have you seen my belt? I can't find her anywhere." I invented personalities for the objects on my dresser and set them up on blind dates. When things didn't work out with my wallet, my watch drove a wedge between my hairbrush and my lighter. The scenarios reminded me of my youth, when my sisters

and I would enact epic dramas with our food. Ketchup-wigged french fries would march across our plates, engaging in brief affairs or heated disputes over carrot coins while burly chicken legs guarded the perimeter, ready to jump in should things get out of hand. Sexes were assigned at our discretion and were subject to change from one night to the next—unlike here, where the corncob and the string bean remain locked in their rigid masculine roles. Say what you like about southern social structure, but at least in North Carolina a hot dog is free to swing both ways.

Nothing in France is free from sexual assignment. I was leafing through the dictionary, trying to complete a homework assignment, when I noticed the French had prescribed genders for the various land masses and natural wonders we Americans had always thought of as sexless, Niagara Falls is feminine and, against all reason, the Grand Canyon is masculine. Georgia and Florida are female, but Montana and Utah are male. New England is a she, while the vast area we call the Midwest is just one big guy. I wonder whose job it was to assign these sexes in the first place. Did he do his work right there in the sanitarium, or did they rent him a little office where he could get away from all the noise? 7

There are times when you can swallow the article and others when it must be clearly pronounced, as the word has two different meanings, one masculine and the other feminine. It should be fairly obvious that I cooked an omelette in a frying pan rather than in a wood stove, but it bothers me to make the same mistakes over and over again. I wind up exhausting the listener before I even get to the verb. 8

My confidence hit a new low when my friend Adeline told me that French children often make mistakes, but never with the sex of their nouns. "It's just something we grow up with," she said. "We hear the gender once, and then think of it as part of the word. There's nothing to it." 9

It's a pretty grim world when I can't even feel superior to a toddler. Tired of embarrassing myself in front of two-year-olds, I've started referring to everything in the plural, which can get expensive but has solved a lot of my problems. In saying a *melon,* you need to use the masculine article. In saying *the melons,* you use the plural article, which does not reflect gender and is the same for both the masculine and the feminine. Ask for two or ten or three hundred melons, and the number lets you off the hook by replacing the article altogether. A masculine kilo of feminine tomatoes presents a sexual problem easily solved by asking for two kilos of tomatoes. I've started using the plural while shopping, and Hugh has started using it in our cramped kitchen, where he stands huddled in the corner, shouting, "What do we need with four pounds of tomatoes?" 10

I answer that I'm sure we can use them for something. The only hard part is finding someplace to put them. They won't fit in the refrigerator, as I filled the last remaining shelf with the two chickens I bought from the butcher the night before, forgetting that we were still working our way through a pair of pork roasts the size of Duraflame logs. "We could 11 put them next to the radios," I say, "or grind them for sauce in one of the blenders. Don't get so mad. Having four pounds of tomatoes is better than having no tomatoes at all, isn't it?"

12 Hugh tells me that the market is off-limits until my French improves. He's pretty steamed, but I think he'll get over it when he sees the CD players I got him for his birthday.

Content

1. What is the underlying logic of Sedaris's premises, as a speaker of English, about the gender designations of a language? How does the French use of gender defy this logic? Grammar books don't treat this division humorously; why not? What's the difference between grammatical gender and sexual gender? Why does Sedaris find this contrast humorous?
2. Sedaris allegedly solves the problem by resorting to "referring to everything in the plural" (¶ 10), which, of course, since this is a comic piece, causes other problems. The solution is appropriate to comedy, but is it suitable for application to real-life situations? Explain.

Strategies/Structures/Language

3. Humorists often exaggerate, as Sedaris does in "Make That a Double." Find some instances of this. Why doesn't the obvious exaggeration trouble the humorist's readers or cause them to distrust the narrator?
4. What's the point of inventing "personalities for the objects" on the dresser and setting "them up on blind dates" (¶ 6) and other stratagems for learning grammatical gender? Do they work?
5. Having come to the logical conclusion of his humorous point, Sedaris stops. Is there more he could say? If so, what might that be? If not, what does this piece illustrate about why humorous writing is often short?

For Writing

6. As Sedaris does in "Make That a Double" and Britt does in "That Lean and Hungry Look" (Chapter 6), write a brief humorous essay that derives much of its humor from the system of division and classification of its subject. No topic is immune from outrageously irreverent humor; in "Possession" Sedaris, while visiting Anne Frank's secret annex, imagines how he would remodel it: "I'd get rid of the countertop and of course redo all the plumbing. . . and reclaim the fireplace. 'That's your focal point, there.'" Nevertheless, some topics are easier to work with than others; pick one you can handle comfortably, even though it might make your readers uncomfortable. Before turning it in, test it out on a classmate—on whose paper you will comment in turn.
7. ***Journal Writing.*** Identify some of the differences between your own culture and another one you know fairly well or have observed. If you speak the other language or dialect, explore the cultural differences the different languages suggest. Do you, like Sedaris, find some aspects of the other culture difficult to internalize?

8. ***Dialogues.*** Sedaris's humorous treatment of gender hints at a complex issue—the process through which we define gender socially (rather than biologically). What factors does Richard Rodriguez in "Family Values" (321–28) identify that underpin the meanings of masculinity and femininity in American culture? If, as Sedaris claims, "Nothing in France is free from sexual assignment" (¶ 7), are behaviors in American culture similarly assigned a gender?

RICHARD RODRIGUEZ

How Richard Rodriguez, born in San Francisco in 1944, the son of Mexican immigrants, should and can deal with his dual heritage is the subject of his autobiographical *Hunger of Memory: The Education of Richard Rodriguez* (1982). He spoke Spanish at home and didn't learn English until he began grammar school in Sacramento. Although for a time he refused to speak Spanish, he studied that language in high school as if it were a foreign language. Nevertheless, classified as Mexican-American, Rodriguez benefited from Affirmative Action programs, and on scholarships he earned a BA from Stanford (1967) and an MA from Columbia (1969). After that he studied Renaissance literature at the University of California, Berkeley. In 1992 he published *Days of Obligation: An Argument with my Mexican Father,* a collection of essays focusing on his complicated relations to the cultures of the Catholic Church, San Francisco's gay Castro District, and Mexico. His book, *Brown: The Last Discovery of America* followed in 2002.

For nearly three decades Rodriguez has been a nationally known commentator—in print and on radio and television—on issues of immigration, race, ethnicity, multiculturalism, and gender, but he did not come out as gay in his writings until around 1990. He opposes bilingual education and has consistently—and controversially—argued against the arbitrary and divisive classification of people into categories by race, religion, or ethnic origin for the purposes of Affirmative Action. In this essay Rodriguez turns his customarily critical gaze onto *family values;* he finds that American beliefs about family closeness and intimacy conflict with the centrifugal realities of American life.

Family Values

I am sitting alone in my car, in front of my parents' house—a middle-aged man with a boy's secret to tell. What words will I use to tell them? I hate the word *gay,* find its little affirming sparkle more pathetic than assertive. I am happier with the less polite *queer.* But to my parents I would say *homosexual,* avoid the Mexican slang *joto* (I had always heard it said in our 1

© Bob Daemmrich/The Image Works

This photograph was taken on October 11, 2003, National Coming Out Day, at a gay rights rally at the University of Texas, Austin. The middle student's T-shirt, the focal point of the picture, invites a reading. How do you "read" it? Does your interpretation of the message influence your interpretation of the student's sunglasses and his smile? Of his companions? Suppose the T-shirt were plain white. How would that affect your interpretation of the people in the photograph? Would you even remember it? By analogy, how could such a photograph, with and without messages on the T-shirt, illustrate Richard Rodriguez's "Family Values"? Now, look at David Sedaris's "Make That a Double" 318–20); is the author, who is openly gay, appearing in the equivalent of an unmarked shirt, or is he sending messages on the subject to his readers?

house with hints of condescension), though *joto* is less mocking than the sissy-boy *maricon.*

2 The buzz on everyone's lips now: Family values. The other night on TV, the vice president of the United States, his arm around his wife, smiled into the camera and described homosexuality as "mostly a choice." But how would he know? Homosexuality never felt like a choice to me.

3 A few minutes ago Rush Limbaugh, the radio guy with a voice that reminds me, for some reason, of a butcher's arms, was banging his console and booming a near-reasonable polemic about family values. Limbaugh was not very clear about which values exactly he considers to be family values. A divorced man who lives alone in New York?

4 My parents live on a gray, treeless street in San Francisco not far from the ocean. Probably more than half of the neighborhood is immigrant. India lives next door to Greece, who lives next door to Russia. I wonder what the Chinese lady next door to my parents makes of the politicians' phrase *family values.*

5 What immigrants know, what my parents certainly know, is that when you come to this country, you risk losing your children. The assurance of family—continuity, inevitably—is precisely what America encourages its children to overturn. *Become your own man.* We who are native to this country know this too, of course, though we are likely to deny it. Only a society so guilty about its betrayal of family would tolerate the pieties of politicians regarding family values.

6 On the same summer day that Republicans were swarming in Houston (buzzing about family values), a friend of mine who escaped family values awhile back and who now wears earrings resembling intrauterine devices, was complaining to me over coffee about the Chinese. The Chinese will never take over San Francisco, my friend said, because the Chinese do not want to take over San Francisco. The Chinese do not even see San Francisco! All they care about is their damn families. All they care about is double-parking smack in front of the restaurant on Clement Street and pulling granny out of the car—and damn anyone who happens to be in the car behind them or the next or the next.

7 Politicians would be horrified by such as American opinion, of course. But then what do politicians, Republicans or Democrats, really know of our family life? Or what are they willing to admit? Even in that area where they could reasonably be expected to have something to say—regarding the relationship of family life to our economic system—the politicians say nothing. Republicans celebrate American economic freedom, but Republicans don't seem to connect that economic freedom to the social breakdown they find appalling. Democrats, on the other hand, if more tolerant of the drift from familial tradition, are suspicious of the very capitalism that creates social freedom.

8 How you become free in America: Consider the immigrant. He gets a job. Soon he is earning more money than his father ever made (his father's authority is thereby subtly undermined). The immigrant begins living a life his father never knew. The immigrant moves from one job to another, changes houses. His economic choices determine his home address—not the other way around. The immigrant is on his way to becoming his own man.

9 When I was broke a few years ago and trying to finish a book, I lived with my parents. What a thing to do! A major theme of America is leaving home. We trust the child who forsakes family connections to make it on his own. We call that the making of a man.

10 Let's talk about this man stuff for a minute. America's ethos is anti-domestic. We may be intrigued by blood that runs through wealth—the Kennedys or the Rockefellers—but they seem European to us. Which is to say, they are movies. They are Corleones. Our real pledge of allegiance: We say in America that nothing about your family—your class, your race, your pedigree—should be as important as what you yourself achieve. We end up in 1992 introducing ourselves by first names.

11 What authority can Papa have in a country that formed its identity in an act of Oedipal rebellion against a mad British king? Papa is a joke in America, a stock sitcom figure—Archie Bunker or Homer Simpson. But my Mexican father went to work every morning, and he stood in a white smock, making false teeth, oblivious of the shelves of grinning false teeth mocking his devotion.

12 The nuns in grammar school—my wonderful Irish nuns—used to push Mark Twain on me. I distrusted Huck Finn, he seemed like a gringo kid I would steer clear of in the schoolyard. (He was too confident.) I realize now, of course, that Huck is the closest we have to a national hero. We trust the story of a boy who has no home and is restless for the river. (Huck's Pap is drunk.) Americans are more forgiving of Huck's wildness than of the sweetness of the Chinese boy who walks to school with his mama or grandma. (There is no worse thing in America than to be a mama's boy, nothing better than to be a real boy—all boy—like Huck, who eludes Aunt Sally, and is eager for the world of men.)

13 There's a bent old woman coming up the street. She glances nervously as she passes my car. What would you tell us, old lady, of family values in America?

14 America is an immigrant country, we say. Motherhood—parenthood—is less our point than adoption. If I had to assign gender to America, I would note the consensus of the rest of the world. When America is burned in effigy, a male is burned. Americans themselves speak of Uncle Sam.

15 Like the Goddess of Liberty, Uncle Sam has no children of his own. He steals children to make men of them, mocks all reticence, all modesty, all memory. Uncle Sam is a hectoring Yankee, a skinflint uncle, gaunt, uncouth, unloved. He is the American Savonarola—hater of moonshine, destroyer of stills, burner of cocaine. Sam has no patience with mama's boys.

16 You betray Uncle Sam by favoring private over public life, by seeking to exempt yourself, by cheating on your income taxes, by avoiding jury duty, by trying to keep your boy on the farm.

17 Mothers are traditionally the guardians of the family against America—though even Mom may side with America against queers and deserters, at least when the Old Man is around. Premature gray hair. Arthritis in her shoulders. Bowlegged with time, red hands. In their fiercely flowered housedresses, mothers are always smarter than fathers in America. But in reality they are betrayed by their children who leave. In a thousand ways. They end up alone.

18 We kind of like the daughter who was a tomboy. Remember her? It was always easier to be a tomboy in America than a sissy. Americans admired Annie Oakley more than they admired Liberace (who, nevertheless, always remembered his mother). But today we do not admire Annie Oakley when we see Mom becoming Annie Oakley.

The American household now needs two incomes, everyone says. Meaning: Mom is *forced* to leave home out of economic necessity. But lots of us know lots of moms who are sick and tired of being mom, or only mom. It's like the nuns getting fed up, teaching kids for all those years and having those kids grow up telling stories of how awful Catholic school was. Not every woman in America wants her life's work to be forgiveness. Today there are moms who don't want their husbands' names. And the most disturbing possibility: What happens when Mom doesn't want to be Mom at all? Refuses pregnancy? 19

Mom is only becoming an American like the rest of us. Certainly, people all over the world are going to describe the influence of feminism on women (all over the world) as their "Americanization." And rightly so. 20

Nothing of this, of course, will the politician's wife tell you. The politician's wife is careful to follow her husband's sentimental reassurances that nothing has changed about America except perhaps for the sinister influence of deviants. Like myself. 21

I contain within myself an anomaly at least as interesting as the Republican Party's version of family values. I am a homosexual Catholic, a communicant in a tradition that rejects even as it upholds me. 22

I do not count myself among those Christians who proclaim themselves protectors of family values. They regard me as no less an enemy of the family than the "radical feminists." But the joke about families that all homosexuals know is that we are the ones who stick around and make families possible. Call on us. I can think of 20 or 30 examples. A gay son or daughter is the only one who is "free" (married brothers and sisters are too busy). And, indeed, because we have admitted the inadmissible about ourselves (that we are queer)—we are adepts at imagination—we can even imagine those who refuse to imagine us. We can imagine Mom's loneliness, for example. If Mom needs to be taken to church or to the doctor or ferried between Christmas dinners, depend on the gay son or lesbian daughter. 23

I won't deny that the so-called gay liberation movement, along with feminism, undermined the heterosexual household, if that's what politicians mean when they say family values. Against churchly reminders that sex was for procreation, the gay bar as much as the birth-control pill taught Americans not to fear sexual pleasure. In the past two decades—and, not coincidentally, parallel to the feminist movement—the gay liberation movement moved a generation of Americans toward the idea of a childless adulthood. If the women's movement was ultimately more concerned about getting out of the house and into the workplace, the gay movement was in its way more subversive to puritan America because it stressed the importance of play. 24

Several months ago, the society editor of the morning paper in San Francisco suggested (on a list of "must haves") that every society dame must have at least one gay male friend. A ballet companion. A lunch date. 25

The remark was glib and incorrect enough to beg complaints from homosexual readers, but there was a truth about it as well. Homosexual men have provided women with an alternate model of masculinity. And the truth: The Old Man, God bless him, is a bore. Thus are we seen as preserving marriages? Even Republican marriages?

26 For myself, homosexuality is a deep brotherhood but does not involve domestic life. Which is why, my married sisters will tell you, I can afford the time to be a writer. And why are so many homosexuals such wonderful teachers and priests and favorite aunts, if not because we are freed from the house? On the other hand, I know lots of homosexual couples (male and female) who model their lives on the traditional heterosexual version of domesticity and marriage. Republican politicians mock the notion of a homosexual marriage, but ironically such marriages honor the heterosexual marriage by imitating it.

27 "The only loving couples I know," a friend of mine recently remarked, "are all gay couples."

28 This woman was not saying that she does not love her children or that she is planning a divorce. But she was saying something about the sadness of American domestic life: the fact that there is so little joy in family intimacy. Which is perhaps why gossip (public intrusion into the private) has become a national industry. All day long, in forlorn houses, the television lights up a freakish parade of husbands and mothers-in-law and children upon the stage of Sally or Oprah or Phil. They tell on each other. The audience ooohhhs. Then a psychiatrist-shaman appears at the end to dispense prescriptions—the importance of family members granting one another more "space."

29 The question I desperately need to ask you is whether we Americans have ever truly valued the family. We are famous, or our immigrant ancestors were famous, for the willingness to leave home. And it is ironic that a crusade under the banner of family values has been taken up by those who would otherwise pass themselves off as patriots. For they seem not to understand America, nor do I think they love the freedoms America grants. Do they understand why, in a country that prizes individuality and is suspicious of authority, children are disinclined to submit to their parents? You cannot celebrate American values in the public realm without expecting them to touch our private lives. As Barbara Bush remarked recently, family values are also neighborhood values. It may be harmless enough for Barbara Bush to recall a sweeter America—Midland, Texas, in the 1950s. But the question left begging is why we chose to leave Midland, Texas. Americans like to say that we can't go home again. The truth is that we don't want to go home again, don't want to be known, recognized. Don't want to respond in the same old ways. (And you know you will if you go back there.)

30 Little 10-year-old girls know that there are reasons for getting away from the family. They learn to keep their secrets—under lock and

key—addressed to Dear Diary. Growing up queer, you learn to keep secrets as well. In no place are those secrets more firmly held than within the family house. You learn to live in closets. I know a Chinese man who arrived in America about 10 years ago. He got a job and made some money. And during that time he came to confront his homosexuality. And then his family arrived. I do not yet know the end of this story.

The genius of America is that it permits children to leave home, it permits us to become different from our parents. But the sadness, the loneliness of America, is clear too. 31

Listen to the way Americans talk about immigrants. If, on the one hand, there is impatience when today's immigrants do not seem to give up their family, there is also a fascination with this reluctance. In Los Angeles, Hispanics are considered people of family. Hispanic women are hired to be at the center of the American family—to babysit and diaper, to cook and to clean and to ease the dying. Hispanic attachment to family is seen by many Americans, I think, as the reason why Hispanics don't get ahead. But if Asians privately annoy us for being so family oriented, they are also stereotypically celebrated as the new "whiz kids" in school. Don't Asians go to college, after all, to honor their parents? 32

More important still is the technological and economic ascendancy of Asia, particularly Japan, on the American imagination. Americans are starting to wonder whether perhaps the family values of Asia put the United States at a disadvantage. The old platitude had it that ours is a vibrant, robust society for being a society of individuals. Now we look to Asia and see team effort paying off. 33

In this time of national homesickness, of nostalgia, for how we imagine America used to be, there are obvious dangers. We are going to start blaming each other for the loss. Since we are inclined, as Americans, to think of ourselves individually, we are disinclined to think of ourselves as creating one another or influencing one another. 34

But it is not the politician or any political debate about family values that has brought me here on a gray morning to my parents' house. It is some payment I owe to my youth and to my parents' youth. I imagine us sitting in the living room, amid my mother's sentimental doilies and the family photographs, trying to take the measure of the people we have turned out to be in America. 35

A San Francisco poet, when he was in the hospital and dying, called a priest to his bedside. The old poet wanted to make his peace with Mother Church. He wanted baptism. The priest asked why. "Because the Catholic Church has to accept me," said the poet. "Because I am a sinner." 36

Isn't willy-nilly inclusiveness the point, the only possible point to be derived from the concept of family? Curiously, both President Bush and Vice President Quayle got in trouble with their constituents recently for expressing a real family value. Both men said that they would try to 37 dissuade a daughter or granddaughter from having an abortion. But, finally, they said they would support her decision, continue to love her, never abandon her.

38 There are families that do not accept. There are children who are forced to leave home because of abortions or homosexuality. There are family secrets that Papa never hears. Which is to say there are families that never learn the point of families.

39 But there she is at the window. My mother has seen me and she waves me in. Her face asks: Why am I sitting outside? (Have they, after all, known my secret for years and kept it, out of embarrassment, not knowing what to say?) Families accept, often by silence. My father opens the door to welcome me in.

Content

1. One of Rodriguez's main points in "Family Values" is that American beliefs about families clash with American realities. For example, politicians praise "family values," but "when you come to this country, you risk losing your children" (¶ 5) because they grow up to be different or move away. Identify several other beliefs about American families in this essay, and show how Rodriguez challenges these beliefs.

2. How does Rodriguez's status as a first-generation American affect his perception of American life? Give some examples of things he notices that less recent immigrants might not perceive. Similarly, consider his status as a gay man; does his sexual orientation allow him to perceive what others might miss?

3. This essay asserts that some American values cause results that are the opposite of what they intend to promote. For example, economic freedom and family traditions are both key values, but economic freedom means that "a major theme of America is leaving home" (¶ 9). What American traditions cause unintended results, according to Rodriguez?

Strategies/Structures/Language

4. "Family Values" begins and ends with a framing narrative—the episode in Rodriguez's life when he is just about to come out to his parents about his homosexuality. How effective is his use of a story to launch an argumentative essay?

5. Rodriguez uses generalizations that may provoke thought—or stretch the reader's credibility. For example, his friend states, "The only loving couples I know are all gay couples." What other generalizations play a role in the argument? To what extent do they help, or detract from, the essay's effectiveness?

6. Humor plays an important role in "Family Values." Consider passages such as "India lives next door to Greece, who lives next door to Russia" (¶ 4); or the moralizing of Rush Limbaugh, "a divorced man who lives alone in New York" (¶ 3); or "a friend of mine who escaped family values awhile back and who now wears earrings resembling intrauterine devices" (¶ 6). What other examples of humor do you notice? How is Rodriguez's use of humor effective in persuading the reader to accept his point of view?

For Writing

7. To what extent do you agree or disagree with Rodriguez's argument about American family values? With a friend, discuss what the most important values are in your respective families. On the basis of this discussion, explain whether Rodriguez does or doesn't succeed in convincing you that some American beliefs actually weaken the American family tradition or that family values are out of step with realities.

8. Research some of the issues that Rodriguez discusses to learn more about the trends that he sees. For example, you could find data or articles about adult children who move away from their place of birth or whose ability to outearn their parents greatly interferes with family cohesion. Or you could focus on the stability or instability of immigrant families (compare with Lynda Barry's "Common Scents" 376–85). Determine whether or not your findings confirm Rodriguez's conclusions, and discuss why this is so.

9. ***Journal Writing.*** Use a framing narrative, like Rodriguez's story about coming out to his parents, to discuss your own family experiences and the values you have come to accept or criticize.

10. ***Dialogues.*** Rodriguez writes that America encourages individualism: "leaving home" is "the making of a man" (¶ 9). In what ways might this individualism promote the self-destructive behavior Angier describes in "Why Men Don't Last" (302–05)? For example, does this emphasis on individualism encourage men to limit their feelings to "rage, triumph, [and] lust" (¶ 20)?

11. ***Mixed Modes.*** How does Rodriguez support his argument that "Only a society so guilty about its betrayal of family would tolerate the pieties of politicians regarding family values" (¶ 5)? Where does he suggest his own and others' feelings of guilt through expressions of envy, ridicule, or denial? For example, how do images of the "mama's boy" (¶ 12), Asian "whiz kids" (¶ 32), and family dynasties (¶ 10), or reactions to politicians' attitudes toward abortion (¶ 37) suggest Rodriguez's own and others' deep-seated and complex feelings about family?

12. ***Second Look.*** How does the photograph in this essay suggest that the family as an institution is changing? Discuss your interpretation of the photograph in relation to some specific change in your own understanding of what family means, perhaps with respect to divorce (see McGuire, "Wake Up Call," Chapter 5), a family member who has "come out," or one who has chosen a nontraditional career or life path.

GELAREH ASAYESH

"When a natural disaster hits, people talk for years about . . . the power of the earth tremor that remade the landscape of their lives. But the emotional disasters in our lives go largely unacknowledged, their repercussions unclaimed," says Gelareh Asayesh, in *Saffron Sky*, of her parents' decision in 1977 to move the family from Tehran, Iran (where she was born in 1961), to Chapel Hill, North Carolina. In Iran they lived in material comfort but in political opposition to the repressive Shah.

In Chapel Hill, as graduate students, they became outsiders, "wrenched from all that was loved and familiar" in Iran, "faced with an unspoken choice: to be alienated from the world around us or from our innermost selves." Although Asayesh was educated at the University of North Carolina-Chapel Hill and went on to become a journalist working for the *Boston Globe*, the *MiamI Herald*, and the *Baltimore Sun*, the appeals and tensions of these contradictory cultures have never been fully resolved.

In *Saffron Sky: A Life Between Iran and America* (1999), Asayesh explores the contrasts between these two ways of life, her ambivalent attitude toward her homeland intensified by her marriage to an American and her own parenthood. Returning to Iran in October 1990, just before the Persian Gulf war, Asayesh is newly aware of the world of "rigidity and restriction"—rules against wearing lipstick, or too sheer stockings, or letting the hair show—enforced by the intrusive gender police. Yet, as "Shrouded in Contradiction," published in the *New York Times Magazine* (November 2001), reveals, "To wear *hijab* is to invite contradiction. Sometimes I hate it. Sometimes I value it"—as a covering of both restriction and freedom.

Shrouded in Contradiction

1 I grew up wearing the miniskirt to school, the veil to the mosque. In the Tehran of my childhood, women in bright sundresses shared the sidewalk with women swathed in black. The tension between the two ways of life was palpable. As a schoolgirl, I often cringed when my bare legs got leering or contemptuous glances. Yet, at times, I long for the days when I could walk the streets of my country with the wind in my hair. When clothes were clothes. In today's Iran, whatever I wear sends a message. If it's a chador, it embarrasses my Westernized relatives. If it's a skimpy scarf, I risk being accused of stepping on the blood of the martyrs who died in the war with Iraq. Each time I return to Tehran, I wait until the last possible moment, when my plane lands on the tarmac, to don the scarf and long jacket that many Iranian women wear in lieu of a veil. To wear hijab—Islamic covering—is to invite contradiction. Sometimes I hate it. Sometimes I value it.

2 Most of the time, I don't even notice it. It's annoying, but so is wearing pantyhose to work. It ruins my hair, but so does the humidity in Florida, where I live. For many women, the veil is neither a symbol nor a statement. It's simply what they wear, as their mothers did before them. Something to dry your face with after your ablutions before prayer. A place for a toddler to hide when he's feeling shy. Even for a woman like me, who wears it with a hint of rebellion, *hijab* is just not that big a deal.

3 Except when it is.

4 "Sister, what kind of get-up is this?" a woman in black, one of a pair, asks me one summer day on the Caspian shore. I am standing in line to ride

© Reuters NewMedia/Corbis

In what ways is this photograph a graphic illustration of the elements of division and classification? Explain how it is a commentary on both Asayesh's "Shrouded in Contradiction" and Khan's "Mirror, Mirror on the Wall."

a gondola up a mountain, where I'll savor some ice cream along with vistas of sea and forest. Women in chadors stand wilting in the heat, faces gleaming with sweat. Women in makeup and clunky heels wear knee-length jackets with pants, their hair daringly exposed beneath sheer scarves.

None have been more daring than I. I've wound my scarf into a turban, leaving my neck bare to the breeze. The woman in black is a government employee paid to police public morals. "Fix your scarf at once!" she snaps. 5

"But I'm hot," I say. 6

"You're hot?" she exclaims. "Don't you think we all are?" 7

I start unwinding my makeshift turban. "The men aren't hot," I mutter. 8

Her companion looks at me in shocked reproach. "Sister, this isn't about men and women," she says, shaking her head. "This is about Islam." 9

I want to argue. I feel like a child. Defiant, but powerless. Burning with injustice, but also with a hint of shame. I do as I am told, feeling acutely conscious of the bare skin I am covering. In policing my sexuality, these women have made me more aware of it. 10

The veil masks erotic freedom, but its advocates believe *hijab* transcends the erotic—or expands it. In the West, we think of passion as a fever of the body, not the soul. In the East, Sufi poets used earthly passion 11 as a metaphor; the beloved they celebrated was God. Where I come from, people are more likely to find delirious passion in the mosque than in the bedroom.

12 There are times when I feel a hint of this passion. A few years after my encounter on the Caspian, I go to the wake of a family friend. Sitting in a mosque in Mashhad, I grip a slippery black veil with one hand and a prayer book with the other. In the center of the hall, there's a stack of Koranic texts decorated with green-and-black calligraphy, a vase of white gladioluses and a large photograph of the dearly departed. Along the walls, women wait quietly.

13 From the men's side of the mosque, the mullah's voice rises in lament. His voice is deep and plaintive, oddly compelling. I bow my head, sequestered in my veil while at my side a community of women pray and weep with increasing abandon. I remember from girlhood this sense of being exquisitely alone in the company of others. Sometimes I have cried as well, free to weep without having to offer an explanation. Perhaps they are right, those mystics who believe that physical love is an obstacle to spiritual love; those architects of mosques who abstained from images of earthly life, decorating their work with geometric shapes that they believed freed the soul to slip from its worldly moorings. I do not aspire to such lofty sentiments. All I know is that such moments of passionate abandon, within the circle of invisibility created by the veil, offer an emotional catharsis every bit as potent as any sexual release.

14 Outside, the rain pours from a sullen sky. I make my farewells and walk toward the car, where my driver waits. My veil is wicking muddy water from the sidewalk. I gather up the wet and grimy folds with distaste, longing to be home, where I can cast off this curtain of cloth that gives with one hand, takes away with the other.

[Suggestions for reading and writing about this essay are combined with those pertaining to Sumbul Khan's "Mirror, Mirror on the Wall" and appear on 336–38.]

SUMBUL KHAN

Sumbul Khan, born in Karachi, Pakistan, in 1978, attended the Indus Valley School of Art and Architecture for three years before transferring to the University of Connecticut and earning a BFA. "Mirror, Mirror on the Wall" was written in a freshman composition class during her first year at an American university. This was, Kahn says, "a tumultuous and yet very enriching time as it entailed adjusting to a completely different culture and finding my place in it as an international student." In writing the essay, she says, "I made a conscious effort to convey lucidly the logic behind the Muslim practice of wearing the veil and addressing the stereotypes that make it difficult sometimes to adhere to the practice, without alienating an audience that might have had varied perceptions of it."

Mirror, Mirror on the Wall, Who's the Fairest of Them All?

"One of those international students, can't help looking at them, can you?" 1

The snigger repeats itself in her mind as her fingers fasten the dark strands of hair in silver barrettes. She looks at the girl on the other side of the mirror and watches her face change as the white folds of cloth crop her countenance closely around its contours. The resemblance is evident and yet it is not her she sees today but the girl they see. 2

Rambling through her mind, seeking to find words that describe her to them, she sets herself on a plane outside of herself. It is as if she does not reside in her own body anymore but somewhere beyond its physical dimensions, from where she stares down at the effigy she calls, I. Is it the I that keeps coming in the way of adopting their ways? What is the I? What is it made of? 3

The I, for the moment, is only the piece of cloth that covers her hair, the *hejaab*. The garb of bondage, the symbol of primitive conformity, the virgin white *hejaab* that enshrouds her body that breathes every breath in self-abnegation. She wonders if that is what it really is? She peers into her eyes for an answer but the two pairs of eyes, both her own, stare transfixed at each other, neither knowing what to expect of which. 4

I was seventeen when it all began. Dunya had come home one day in tears: her husband had put a knife to her throat and threatened to kill her. They had been in the marriage for two years and not a day had gone by that he hadn't called her a whore and not meant it. *Was* Dunya a whore? Dunya was as untouched and pure as they come. Dunya was, however, a better doctor than him and, worse still, she belonged to a family that believed its daughters to be individual entities, not their husbands' doormats. The man was insecure. Having risen from adversity by dint of a little luck and a little help from kind relatives, his views were still as inflexible, as was typical of the men of his strata. Dunya, for him, was too self-sufficient for her culture and so Dunya was a whore. "It can't work, *Ammi*," she wept hysterically in their mother's arms. 5

6 That was the first failed marriage in the family and that too on the eve of the second daughter's wedding. Iman's wedding was fraught with uncertainty. It would have been postponed, for no one was up to celebrating, but putting off a wedding was said to bring bad luck. Hence it was decided that the wedding would be held the very day that it had been scheduled. It was the day after Dunya's divorce papers were filed.

7 The irony of it all did not go unnoticed and much was said in the neighborhood about *Miyan Saheb's* misfortune. Of course the punch line was, "When girls get sent to college they lose sight of their real station in life. How then, can marriages last?" After a year and a half of turning a deaf ear to such shows of sympathy and keeping their chins up with all the integrity parents with girls can have in South Asia, they hadn't the faintest idea what more was about to come their way.

8 It wasn't long before Iman came home too. Her divorce was not stomached as well as Dunya's, after all there was a third's marriage prospects to consider: who would marry her knowing both her elder sisters had failed to keep their husbands happy. They wouldn't see that the decision to opt out had been the girls' in both cases because there was something wrong with the men, but that didn't matter. No matter what the men were like, the girls had failed. The third will probably not make it either. It took six months of Iman being tossed back and forth between her father's and husband's house, before it was decided that it was unfair to make Iman live through hell for the sake of the youngest. If Allah willed the youngest to be happy, she would find her happiness regardless of whether her sisters were divorced or not. So that was that.

9 It was sometime in the middle of this frenzy that I, the youngest, struggled with the travails of adolescent girlhood in a male-dominated culture. Disillusioned by my sisters' experiences, I was probably the most cynical nineteen-year-old of my lot. So while my friends were looking for flippant high school sweethearts, I found myself thinking of independence—financial, social, physical and emotional—a career began to take form in my mind. Perhaps it was the need for stability, external and internal, that made me start reading up on Islam, the religion I was born in. And then I woke up one day and donned the *hejaab*. I was not going to be sized up by men, I would take control of my body and defy the objectification I felt as a woman. I would decide who was worthy enough to share my person with. It was a step towards liberation, as the readings on feminism later suggested, from the masculine gaze.

10 America. The land of opportunity. The land where Feminism was born. The land I thought would embrace me with open arms because I had broken the shackles of male dependence by deciding to live on my own. I celebrated my twenty-second birthday here. Life takes a perverse delight, though, in proving us wrong just when we think we're on top of things.

Her finger tips trace the circles around her eyes. Age. Is this what they say they feel at the big thirty? She counts her years up to thirty—eight more to go—no, it must be another feeling, she was too far behind to know quite what thirty felt like. It has been a while since she has thought back to a past so carefully locked away in the deep recesses of her mind. Perhaps this is one of those moments, when one feels so overcome by vulnerability that the strength of the everyday façade refuses to stay up, and all one's insecurities float before one's face laughing demonically, with vengeance. She looks back at them, the tiny specters that loom so large before her. 11

"Afghanistan wages war on women" had been the subject of the e-mail her friend had forwarded her. It had jabbed like a dagger in her gut. Even now she could feel the bile rising to her throat as she imagined women, covered like herself, being sentenced to death for being out with a male friend. 12

It's not their fault. How can they help but think of me as a victim? I can't even blame them for seeing me as an accomplice in the savagery of the Muslim world for wearing my *hejaab* so confidently. How can I explain my position against a backdrop of such ignorant transgression? What is wrong with the Afghan government? This is not what Islam propounds. Islam was the religion to give women the right to vote, the right to conduct trade, the right to marry who they pleased when the West was still grappling with corseted, powdered and puffed to perfection, chaperoned, puppets of the male will. What a mockery we make of our religion now! How in the face of this does one propose to anyone the feminist implications of *hejaab?* The fact that it sets a woman free from having to conform to the male standards of feminine beauty. Even in the most traditional of connotations, where it was a symbol of protection at a time against men who were at liberty to take any woman off the street, the *hejaab* was *for* the woman and now it is the very thing our men strangle us with! No, that isn't Islam, not to me, and not to a lot of Muslim men and women I know. There are those of us who still see the teachings in their true spirit. Yet, to a world that is fed only on the media, there appears to be no difference between those of us who understand their faith and those who warp it to suit their own interests. 13

Haven't there been transgressors in every religion, though? What of the ethnic cleansing in Bosnia? Christ, who died for the sins of mankind, would not have proposed killing every non-Christian left, right and center, yet the world doesn't generalize Christians as bigoted terrorists. Why is that objectivity extended to Christians—the level-headedness that says not all are alike and what is being done is wrong, wrong even to the spirit of the religion, in the name of which it is being done—and not to Muslims? 14

15 Her eyes wander from her face to the rest of her form, to her practically non-existent breasts. All through school if anyone had anything to say to her it was, "Honey, you need to let a man get to you." It was one of the gifts of repressed, single-sex, Convent schooling—girls deriding each other more openly than they would have were there boys around. Under the loose T-shirt however, they completely disappeared. Her thoughts drift to the pair of gray-green eyes that she had lately been seeking out in her drawing class. Eyes that barely ever rested on her longer than a second—how could they on a form so covered that it offered little incentive to look? Yet this is exactly what the point had been, to not allow a man to feast his eyes on her, but this one she was willing to give the prerogative to. The prerogative, however, only came with marriage and an American man was not about to forsake all the pleasures prettier girls may readily offer, just to have her.

16 It's something about the color of his eyes, I think, because in every other sense he's just an ordinary looking male. All that is keeping me from those eyes is my *hejaab*.

17 Is it worth it? This whole deal that I make of it? Can not having premarital sex guarantee that the man I ultimately choose to take would be right for me? He wasn't for Dunya or Iman. Yet would succumbing to this desire now guarantee that I would be able to secure a long-term relationship with this man-to-be?

18 No, if it failed, it would hurt all the more for then my husband's touch would never suffice. Perhaps then the *hejaab* in a way protects one from getting hurt, too; if there is nothing to compare against, at least the physical aspect of a conjugal bond would most likely be pleasurable with whomever the husband might be.

19 And yet, there is the present, the sordidly hurtful present that yearns, that longs, and that doesn't quite taste that particular mouth.

20 Her mouth curves into a sad wishful smile as her lower lip curls under the sharp bite of her teeth. For now, reverie has seized reign of her conscious self as a whiff of the fresh, sweet air that would waft across her room at home when the window was opened on to the garden. Her senses give in to its heady, tantalizing allure, unable to keep her from smiling. Far, oh-so-far, is the misery, the torment of being misunderstood, being unread. The anticipation of a new day, of the possibility of seeing him, propels her away from the self-analytical mirror to gather her things for the Tuesday morning studio.

Content

1. For what purpose or purposes is the *hijab* (or *hejaab*) worn? Why does Asayesh write, "In today's Iran, whatever I wear sends a message" (¶ 1)? What is the "message"? To whom is a message being sent? Is the message the same to every

viewer? Is this the same message that Khan sends when she wears the *hejaab* to class in America?

2. Both Asayesh and Khan have ambivalent feelings about wearing the *hijab*, the veil-like covering for women mandated in Islamic countries. What are these?

3. Both authors are bicultural: Asayesh is Iranian-American, and Khan, from Karachi, Pakistan, is studying in Connecticut. Are their conflicts related to the fact that they live in dual cultures? Or would these same conflicts exist if they lived in or held the values of a single culture?

Strategies/Structures/Language

4. Asayesh introduces her subject with a reference to wearing both miniskirts and veils. How does this reference help to convey the forms of division and classification she will pursue in her discussion? How does her conclusion help to tie her essay together?

5. The essays by Asayesh and Khan contain several contradictions. Identify them and explain how they contribute to the project of division and classification each undertakes in her essay.

6. Is Asayesh's definition of *hijab* adequate? Is Khan's? Do some research on *hijab* and explain why the definition each provides is either adequate or inadequate for the purposes of her essay.

7. In Asayesh's essay, who is "paid to police public morals" (¶ 5)? What does the policing of public morals entail? What is "the masculine gaze" to which Khan refers in paragraph 9? Is this also a form of control and "policing"? Compare and contrast, in discussion or in writing, the differences in the scrutiny of individual women's dress (and behavior) in the cultures depicted in these papers.

For Writing

8. Choose a particular article of clothing, describe it in detail (fabric, cost, quality, style), and trace the history of the changed messages it (as worn by a particular individual or group) has sent over time. You might consider the original purpose of the article (for example, a baseball cap, a fur coat, blue jeans, a military uniform) and then examine how and why the connotations of wearing this have changed—over time and when worn by different types of people. What message—cultural, economic, political, aesthetic, and/or other—is sent by each type of wearing?

9. Writing as an individual or with a partner, address the subject of what clothes your fellow students wear. Use the essays by Asayesh and Khan as points of reference. Analyze the clothing of a typical man and woman. In what respects are they similar? Different? Do any articles of clothing predominate? What "messages" do they send to particular audiences in particular contexts? What dictates this dress? Custom? Individual preference? Group behavior? Other factors?

10. Write an essay that proposes answers to Khan's questions in paragraph 13. How can those not familiar with the history of the *hejaab* "help but think of [Khan, Asayesh, or any woman who wears a *hejaab*] as a victim"? How can these and other women who choose to wear a *hejaab* for the reasons these authors identify avoid being seen as "an accomplice in the savagery of the Muslim world for wearing [their] *hejaab* so confidently" (¶ 13)?

11. ***Dialogues.*** Asayesh and Khan allude to different cultural conceptions of femininity. How does Judith Hall's juxtaposition of man and riddle in "Perilous Riddle" (Chapter 12) imply a particular conception of gender difference? How might this poem's central contradiction explain why Asayesh feels "like a child. Defiant, but powerless" (¶ 10) and illustrate Khan's experience of "the torment of being misunderstood, being unread" (¶ 20)? Or, examine the same topic with reference to Angier's "Why Men Don't Last" (302–05), Tannen's "Communication Styles" (Chapter 9), or Mann's "Forever Young" (Chapter 9).

12. ***Mixed Modes.*** Asayesh includes two narratives in her essay, one about her visit to the Caspian shore on a hot day, and the other about a wake in a mosque. Khan shifts point of view, between first and third person, to tell the stories of her life as an international student and of her sisters' divorces in Pakistan. How do these strategies illustrate each writer's themes?

13. ***Second Look.*** How might the photograph on 331 illustrate Asayesh's "sense of being exquisitely alone in the company of others" while wearing the *hijab* (¶ 13) or Khan's view of the *hejaab* that it "sets a woman free" (¶ 13)? How might the photograph explain each writer's ambivalence toward the veil?

Additional Topics for Writing Division and Classification

(For strategies for writing division and classification, see 298.)

Multiple Strategies for Writing: Division and Classification

In writing on any of the following division and classification topics, you can draw on various strategies to reinforce your organization into two or more parts or categories:

- *illustrations* and *examples,* to show the whole, its components, and to interpret them
- a systematic *analysis* of the component elements
- *photographs, drawings, diagrams,* to clarify and explain similarities and differences
- a *time sequence,* to show the formation or consequences of a particular division or classification
- *definitions, explanations, analyses* of the evidence
- an *argument, explicit* or *implicit,* to make the case for the superiority of one or more members of the classification over others—perhaps satiric or humorous

Note: So many of the readings in *The Essay Connection* lend themselves to division and classification that no specific works are identified here; the Table of Contents or Topical Table of Contents should suffice.

1. Write an essay in which you use division to analyze one of the following subjects. Explain or illustrate each of the component parts, showing how each part functions or relates to the functioning or structure of the who le. Remember to adapt your analysis to your reader's assumed knowledge of the subject. Is it extensive? meager? or somewhere in between? Are you, directly or indirectly, arguing for a particular interpretation?

    a. The organization of the college or university you attend
    b. An organization of which you are a member—team, band or orchestra, fraternity or sorority, social or political action group
    c. A typical (or atypical) weekday or weekend in your life
    d. Your budget, or the federal budget
    e. Your family
    f. Your hopes, fears
    g. A farm, factory, or other business
    h. Geologic periods or a zoological phylum
    i. Body types or temperament types
    j. A provocative poem, short story, novel, play, or television or film drama
    k. A hospital, city hall, bank, restaurant, supermarket, shopping mall

l. The organizational structure of a particular corporation or government office
m. Reasons for writing (or not writing)

2. Write an essay, adapted to your reader's assumed knowledge of the subject, in which you classify members of one of the following subjects. Make the basis of your classification apparent, consistent, and logical. You may want to identify each group or subgroup by a name or relevant term, actual or invented. The division or classification scheme could include a rationale for the superiority of one or more of its members.

a. Types of cars (or SUVs, minivans, or sports cars), boats, bicycles, or surfboards
b. People's temperaments or personality types
c. Vacations or holidays—including terrible trips
d. Styles of music, or types of a particular kind of music (classical, country and western, pop, folk, rock, hip hop)
e. People's styles of spending money
f. Types of restaurants, or subcategories (such as types of fast-food, upscale, or ethnic specialty restaurants)
g. Individual or family lifestyles
h. Types of post–high school educational institutions, or types of courses a given school offers
i. Religions or other systems of beliefs or values
j. Athletes or media celebrities or particular media treatment of these
k. Computers—types of hardware or software, or types of computer (or Internet or text messaging) users
l. Types of stores or shopping malls
m. Some phenomenon, activity, types of people or literature or entertainment that you like or dislike a great deal
n. Social or political groups

Definition

A definition can set limits or expand them. An objective definition may settle an argument; a subjective definition can provoke one. In either case, they answer the definer's fundamental question, What is X?

The composite photograph "Drivers Wanted" (363) offers a witty, visual definition of *square*—not cubed—for nearly everything depicted looks both flat and square except for the VW bug in the lower right-hand corner. Even objects usually conceived of as cubes—dishwasher, filing cabinet, cardboard box, house, eight-story building—look like two-dimensional squares in this rendering. Why are they shown in this way? Might their flat appearance be a pun on the meaning of *square*? Might the images be meant to convey the impression that although the VW is considered a square car, driven by square people, it is integral to life as we know it, and that life itself is composed of a superabundance of squares? If you don't "read" the ad this way, what alternatives can you offer?

The easiest way to define something is to identify it as a member of a class and then specify the characteristics that make it distinctive from all the other members of that class. You could define yourself as a "student," but that wouldn't be sufficient to discriminate between you as a college undergraduate and pupils in kindergarten, elementary, junior high, or high school, graduate students, or, for that matter, a person independently studying aardvarks, gourmet cooking, or the nature of the universe.

As you make any kind of writing more specific, you lower the level of abstraction, usually a good idea in definition. So you could identify—and thereby define—yourself by specifying "college student," or more specifically yet, your class status, "first-year college student," or "freshman," or "second year transfer." That might be sufficient for some contexts, such as filling out an application blank. But you might also need to indicate where you go to school "at Cuyahoga Community College" or "Michigan State University." (Initials won't always work—readers might think MSU means Memphis State, or Mississippi, or Montana.)

But if you're writing an entire essay devoted to defining exactly what kind of student you are, a phrase or sentence will be insufficient, even if expanded to include "a computer science major" or "a business major with an accounting specialty, and a varsity diver." Although the details of that definition would separate and thereby distinguish you from, certainly, most other members of your class, they wouldn't convey the essence of what you as a person are like in your student role.

You could consider that sentence your core definition, and expand each key word into a separate paragraph to create an essay-length definition that could include "college student," "accounting major," and "varsity diver."

But that still might not cover it. You could approach the subject through considering *cause-and-effect*. Why did you decide to go to college? Because you love to learn? Because you need to get specialized training for your chosen career? To get away from home? What have been the short-term effects of your decision to attend college? What are the long-term effects likely to be—on yourself, on your chosen field, perhaps on the world?

Or you might define yourself as a college student by *comparing and contrasting* your current life with that of a friend still in high school, or with someone who hasn't gone to college, or with a person you admire who has already graduated. If you work part- or full-time while attending college, you could write an *analysis* of its effect on your studying; or an *argument*, using yourself as an *extended example*, stating why it's desirable (or undesirable) for college students to work. Or, among many other possibilities, you could write a *narrative* of a typical week or semester at college. Each of these modes of writing could be an essay of definition. Each could be only partial, unless you wrote a book, for every definition is, by definition, selective. But each would serve your intended purpose. Each essay in this section represents a different common type of definition, but most use other types as well.

Definition According to Purpose. A definition according to purpose specifies the fundamental qualities an object, principle or policy, role, or literary or artistic work has—or should have—in order to fulfill its potential. Thus, such a definition might explicitly answer such questions as, What is the purpose of X? ("A parable is a simple story designed to teach a moral truth.") What is X for? ("Horror movies exist to scare the spectators.") What does X do? What is the role of X?

In her essay on the nature of skin, "A Supple Casing, Prone to Damage" (347–49), Natalie Angier answers all of these questions in thirteen compact, fact-filled paragraphs. She explains its purpose by identifying *what it does*: "Skin keeps the outside out and offers the first line of defense against the microbial multitudes. . . . If you didn't have your skin," she explains, "you would dehydrate and die." But skin is more than a protective cover; "With its rich array of sensory receptors, skin is the bridge between private and public, wary self and beckoning other. Through the touch of its mother, a baby learns it is loved." The rest of the essay incorporates *physical description* (how much skin do humans have? How thick is it? What is it made of? What does it look like?) with *process analysis* (how skin cells grow and change over time, including how they are affected by exposure to sunlight and by aging).

Descriptive Definition. A descriptive definition identifies the distinctive characteristics of an individual or group that set it apart from others. Thus a descriptive definition may begin by *naming* something, answering the question, What is X called? A possible answer might be Eudora Welty (unique among all other women); a walnut (as opposed to all other species of nuts); or *The Sound and the Fury* (and no other novel by William Faulkner).

A descriptive definition may also *specify the relationship among the parts of a unit or group*, responding to the questions, What is the structure of X? How is X organized? How is X put together or constituted—as in the periodic table or a diagram of the body, an engine, or any other mechanical device? Lynda Barry's "Common Scents" (376–85) also, through a series of cartoon panels, offers many combinations of smells, "mint, tangerines, and library books," "fried smelt, garlic, onions; 9,000 cigarettes; ½ a can of Adorne hair spray; Jade East aftershave" and more. . . . She uses these to evoke people's reactions both to the smells themselves and to the cultures and people who either denigrate or appreciate them, concluding, "Our house smelled like grease and fish and cigs, like Jade East and pork and dogs, like all the wild food my grandma boiled and fried. And if they could get *that* into a spray can, I'd buy it." The literal, descriptive definition might be, "You are what you smell like," but the connotative definition would depend not only on what the definers thought of the smells, but also on their opinions of the culture associated with that particular combination of odors.

Logical Definitions. Logical definitions answer two related questions: Into what general category does X fall? and How does it differ from all other members of that category? ("A porpoise is a marine mammal but differs from whales, seals, dolphins, and the others in its. . . .") Logical definitions are often used in scientific and philosophical writing, and indeed form the basis for the functional definition Howard Gardner presents in "Who Owns Intelligence?" (351–61).

There are five key principles for writing logical definitions:

1. For economy's sake, use the most specific category to which the item to be defined belongs, rather than broader categories. Thus Gardner confines his discussion to human beings, not animals nor even all primates.
2. Any division of a class must include all members of that class. *Negative definitions* explain what is excluded from a given classification and what is not.
3. Subdivisions must be smaller than the class divided. Intelligence, says Gardner, can be divided into various functional categories: "linguistic and logical-mathematical, musical, spatial, bodily-kinesthetic, naturalist, interpersonal, and intrapersonal."
4. Categories should be mutually exclusive; they should not overlap.
5. The basis for subdividing categories must be consistent throughout each stage of subdivision. Thus, claiming that Daniel Goleman, in his "otherwise admirable *Emotional Intelligence*," confuses emotional intelligence with "certain preferred patterns of behavior," Gardner prefers the term "emotional sensitivity" because this includes both "interpersonal and intrapersonal intelligences" and therefore applies to "people who are sensitive to emotions in themselves and in others."

Essential or Existential Definition. An essential definition might be considered a variation of a descriptive definition as it answers the question, "What is the essence, the fundamental nature of X?"—love, beauty, truth, justice, for instance. An existential definition presents the essence of its subject by answering the question, "What does it mean to be X?" or "What does it mean to live as an X" or "in a state of X?"—perhaps Chinese, supremely happy, married (or not), an AIDS victim. Thus, in "Clever and Poor," a poem of twenty-eight brief lines (346–47), Penelope Pelizzon captures the dramatic essence of the courtship of her parents, both clever, both poor, entering into marriage with a mixture of hope, ingenuity, and deception as definitions of these key concepts interlock, reinforce, sustain one another.

In the excerpt from his autobiography, *Moving Violations* (365–71), John Hockenberry offers a variety of definitions of his physical state that bleed into what—since he is paralyzed from his waist down—he is able to do, and not do, physically, emotionally, and socially (we already know that professionally he is a broadcast journalist). He offers contradictory labels—"I am a gimp, crip, physically challenged, differently abled, paralyzed"—in satiric, sardonic, in-your-face language. "Everything you think about me is right. Everything you think about me is wrong"—including assumptions about his "unlimited amounts of 'courage'" and his sexuality: "I have massive problems with my sexuality. Actually, there is no problem with sexuality. It's just not a problem." He questions the stereotypes that the able-bodied hold of people with disabilities: "What is 'normal' but another stereotype, no different than 'angry black man,' 'Asian math genius,' 'welfare mother,' or 'gay man with a lisp'?" As he writes to dispel the stereotypes, for "as each stereotype breaks down, it reveals a pattern of wrongs," his essay implictly urges readers to reinterpret, complicate, and thus redefine their understanding of "disability"—reinforced by the photograph of the person in the kayak, wheelchair strapped to the top (365).

Process Definitions. These are concerned with how things or phenomena get to be the way they are. How is X produced? What causes X? How does it work? What does it do, or not do? With what effects? How does change affect X itself? Such questions are often the basis for scientific definitions or explanations of social or scientific phenomena. In "Hegemony" (387–92), Christopher La Casse offers an ambiguous definition-in-slow-motion of the title term, defined by the *American Heritage Dictionary* as "the predominant influence, as of a state, region, or group, over another or others." This is, in Tim O'Brien's (76–84) terms, a true war story about a typical day in the life of any noncommissioned officer in the Iraq War, driving through anystreet, anywhere, being pelted by rocks and dirt thrown by anychildren at anyforeigninvader. Who is the predominant influence over whom? What's the point of this—or any—invasion? Of any war?

Ultimately, when you're writing an extended definition, you'll need to make it as clear, real, and understandable as possible. You could define a hummingbird as a very small, New World bird of the family *Trochilidae*, as dictionaries do—a somewhat abstract, comprehensive, technical definition. Or you could follow Brian Doyle's example in "Joyas Voladoras" (372–74). "Flying jewels" was the white explorers' name for hummingbirds. Doyle defines these feathered gems in terms of their heartbeats ("ten times a second"), how they fly ("whirring and zooming and nectaring," sometimes backward, visiting "a thousand flowers a day," diving "at sixty miles an hour," able to travel "more than five hundred miles without stopping"). He calls out their exotic names ("bearded helmetcrests and booted racket-tails, violet-tailed sylphs and . . . rainbow-bearded thornbills"), and identifies the "ferocious metabolism" made possible by "a thunderous wild heart the size of an infant's fingernail." In six eloquent paragraphs Doyle thus defines the meaning of hearts, moving from hummingbirds to whales and ultimately to humans, capturing the essence of how emotional hearts work: "You can brick up your heart as stout and tight and hard and cold and impregnable as you possibly can and down it comes in an instant, felled by a woman's second glance, a child's apple breath, the shatter of glass in the road. . . ." In delineating this delicate combination of strength and fragility, power and vulnerability, Doyle conveys the process of life itself. Like all good writers, Doyle's choices of specific details, illustrations, analogies, and anecdotes enable his readers to accept his definition, to see with his clear vision new ways to understand the subject, and to respect the boundaries he has set.

Strategies for Writing: Definition

1. What is the purpose of the definition (or definitions) I'm writing about? Do I want to explain the subject's particular characteristics? Identify its nature? Persuade readers of my interpretation of its meaning? Entertain readers with a novel, bizarre, or highly personal meaning? How long will my essay be? (A short essay will require a restricted subject that you can cover in the limited space.)
2. For whom am I providing the definition? Why are they reading it? Do they know enough about the background of the subject to enable me to deal with it in a fairly technical way? Or must I stick to the basics—or at least begin there? If I wish to persuade or entertain my readers, can I count on them to have a pre-existing definition in mind against which I can match my own?
3. Will my entire essay be a definition, or will I incorporate definition(s) as part of a different type of essay? What proportion of my essay will be devoted to definition? Where will I include definitions? As I introduce new terms or concepts? Where else, if at all?
4. What techniques of definition will I use: naming; providing examples, brief or extended; comparing and contrasting; considering cause and effect; analysis; argument; narrative; analogy; or a mixture? Will I employ primarily positive or negative means (i.e., X is, or X is not)?
5. How much denotative (objective) definition will I use in my essay? How much connotative (subjective) definition? Will my tone be serious? Authoritative? Entertaining? Sarcastic? Or otherwise?

V. PENELOPE PELIZZON

V. Penelope Pelizzon's (born 1968) first poetry collection, *Nostos* (Ohio University Press, 2000) won the Hollis Summers Prize and the Poetry Society of America's Norma Farber First Book Award. Her new poems, nonfiction essays, and critical writings on film have recently appeared in the *Hudson Review, Field*, the *Kenyon Review*, the *New England Review, 32Poems, Fourth Genre*, the *Yale Journal of Criticism, Post Script, American Studies*, and *Narrative*. Educated at the University of Massachusetts, Boston (BA, 1992), the University of California, Irvine (MFA, 1994), and the University of Missouri (PhD, 1998), in 2002 she joined the faculty at the University of Connecticut, where she directs the Creative Writing Program.

She says, "'Clever and Poor' is one of a tiny clutch of poems that survived from my MFA days and actually made it, years later, into my first book. I think of it as the first *real* poem I ever wrote. . . . It was the first poem I wrote where the form was inevitable given the subject matter—the subject created the shaping device of the two framing adjectives. This story, an account of my parents' first meeting, was one I had tried to write, in every possible genre, for several years. The problem was that it was such a fantastically interesting series of events, this postwar precursor to match.com, rife with physical privations, social barriers, and gender taboos. Obviously, it was very emotionally loaded for me, too. Hence the challenges: how to create a portrait that was *not merely descriptive* but dramatic, what point of view to adopt that was intimate but not editorializing. Perhaps most difficult was deciding what information to leave out. So for years I struggled with this as a long narrative poem, a short story, a dialogue. Nothing worked. Then one morning I woke up early and realized—insert cartoon lightbulb over head—that I could tell the whole story quite simply using those two words as a sort of balancing gesture, almost like a game. I wrote for less than an hour, and the result was 'Clever and Poor.' The poem taught me to trust that a story will tell you its true form (which is not to say that you won't have to wrestle near to death with it until it speaks)."

Clever and Poor

She has always been clever and poor,
especially here off the Yugoslav train
on a crowded platform of dust. Clever was
her breakfast of nutmeg ground in water

in place of rationed tea. Poor was the cracked
cup, the missing bread. Clever are the six

handkerchiefs stitched to the size of a scarf
and knotted at her throat. Poor is the thin coat

patched with cloth from the pockets
she then sewed shut. Clever is the lipstick,

Petunia Pink, she rubbed with a rag on her nails.
Poor nails, blue with the cold. Posed

in a cape to hide her waist, her photograph
was clever. Poor then was what she called

the last bills twisted in her wallet. Letter
after letter she was clever and more

clever, for months she wrote a newspaper man
who liked her in the picture. The poor

saved spoons of sugar, she traded them
for stamps. He wanted a clever wife. She was poor

so he sent a ticket: now she could come to her wedding
by train. Poor, the baby left with the nuns.

Because she is clever, on the platform to meet him
she thinks *Be generous with your eyes*. What is poor

is what she sees. Cracks stop the station clock,
girls with candle grease to sell. Clever, poor,

clever and poor, her husband, more nervous
than his picture, his shined shoes tied with twine.

NATALIE ANGIER

For biographical information, see 301.

In "A Supple Casing, Prone to Damage," originally published in 2007 in the *New York Times*, Natalie Angier offers an informative primer on the composition and history of our skin while also conveying its beauty and its frailty—which makes it especially vulnerable to sun damage.

A Supple Casing, Prone to Damage*

Grimly determined this past summer to enjoy myself and humor 1
my family, I foolishly ventured outdoors during daylight hours on multiple occasions, including three pointless trips to the beach. Although I always wore sunscreen, sunglasses, a hat and as much clothing as I could get away with and not look like a homeless person, I nevertheless ended

---

* From the NEW YORK TIMES, September 4, 2007, © 2007 NEW YORK TIMES. All rights reserved. Used by permission and protected by the Copyright Laws of the United States. The printing, copying, redistribution, or retransmission of the Material without express written permission is prohibited.

up with a few unwanted solar souvenirs. There's a kind of a praline speckling to my forearms now, reverse sandal stripes on my feet, and a bright white wristwatch outline should I ever need help accessorizing in a cave.

2 As I survey the sharp tan lines and flaking faces that surround me, I see that I am hardly alone. When it comes to how we treat our birthday suits, it seems, we are like 2-year-olds: more concerned with the wrapping and ribbons than with the present itself. We spend billions of dollars a year on makeup and skin-care products, yet we're slipshod about the one measure that dermatologists emphasize is essential for the long-term health, strength and bounce of our skin: guarding it against ultraviolet radiation.

3 That means applying full-spectrum sunscreen every day of the year, and by the gob, not the gossamer, and reapplying it later even if you're in a bad mood and don't feel like it. It also means skipping the tanning salons, forever decoupling the words "fit" and "tanned," and retreating from the fiercest light of midday, back to a shady oasis, where you can contemplate the complexity, multidexterity and deep beauty of the organ called skin.

4 That skin merits designation as an organ is not an effort to lend scientific seriousness to a body part often considered superficial compared with meaty organ kingpins like the heart, liver and brain. For one thing, as burn victims demonstrate all too tragically, you can no more survive without your skin than you can without your lungs. For another, according to Nina G. Jablonski, a professor of anthropology at Penn State University and author of "Skin: A Natural History," the definition of an organ is a set of tissues working together toward a common end and outfitted with an independent supply of blood and nerves. "Skin is like that," she said. "It has its own blood supply, its own nerve supply and its own set of commitments, which are many and wondrous."

5 Skin keeps the outside out and offers the first line of defense against the microbial multitudes that might otherwise make of us bed, breakfast and birthing room. Skin keeps the inside in, keeps our fluids from leaking out and allows us to carry our own piece of sea. If you didn't have your skin, according to Elaine Fuchs, who studies the biology of skin and hair at Rockefeller University, you would dehydrate and die.

6 With its rich array of sensory receptors, skin is the bridge between private and public, wary self and beckoning other. Through the touch of its mother, a baby learns it is loved.

7 By many measures, skin is the largest organ of the human body, averaging 20 square feet in surface area—roughly enough to cover the top of a twin mattress—and weighing about nine pounds. It consists of some 20 types of cells divided into two basic domains, the thin part we see and the thick understory we pinch. The top layer, or epidermis, is about the thickness of cellophane, although that thickness varies considerably

across the body, from a thin point a mere five cells across on the scalp, to serious thickness of hundreds of cells on the palms of the hands and the balls of the feet. The epidermis is constantly sloughing off from above and being rebuilt from a pool of dividing stem cells at the innermost epidermal layer. Over a period of about four weeks, a newborn skin cell will detach from the starter pool and begin heading upward, gradually shedding such unnecessary cellular baggage as its nucleus, and cross-linking its primary content, the tough, stretchy protein keratin, into ever tighter bundles, and secreting a drizzle of greasy lipids that help lend skin its Saran-wrap seal.

By the time a fully matured epidermal cell reaches the light, 8
Dr. Fuchs said, it's essentially a dead sack full of highly cross-linked keratin filaments. Much of the dust in your house consists of just such shed keratin sacks.

Also embedded in the epidermis are the melanocytes, cells that 9
make the melanin pigments that color our skin varying shades of brown, ocher and glue. Melanin serves as the skin's primary defense against excess ultraviolet radiation, and tanning is the result of stepped-up melanin production, the body's frantic effort to protect the DNA molecules of underlying skin cells from gluttonous doses of sun.

In most animals, including our close kin the chimpanzee, mel- 10
anocyte production centers on the hair follicles, coloring the fur while leaving the underlying skin pale. But as early humans shed their pelts, Dr. Jablonski said, the better to sweat away heat in their increasingly active hunting and gathering lives, the demand for protective melanic output moved into the skin.

Skin needs ultraviolet radiation to begin the synthesis of vitamin D, 11
but dermatologists say you can probably get the necessary electromagnetic input from a mere 20 minutes of sun exposure a week, as you go about your daily affairs, sunblocked and sans beach.

Beneath the epidermis is the thicker dermis, the part of an animal's hide 12
that is chemically tanned to give us leather. The dermis is a clotted forest of blood vessels, nerves, sweat glands, hair follicles, piloerector muscles to make the product of those follicles stand on end, immune cells to battle infection, and fibroblasts, the all-important cells that synthesize collagen. More than three-quarters of skin's dry weight consists of collagen, proteins that look and act like ropes and help anchor the dermis to the restless epidermal roofline above. Interwoven with collagen are pliant twists of the protein elastin, the source of our skin's power to spring back into shape after stretching.

Our skin bends over backward and puts itself out and saves face 13
and rejuvenates and exfoliates for us, year after year, but time takes its toll. With age it gets thinner, losing collagen and elastin and the fingerlike anchors that help keep our epidermis in place. The connective fibers that remain become stiffer and weaker and more chaotically cross-linked. Chronic sun exposure can hasten the breakdown by 10 years or more, which is why come next summer, I plan to go spelunking.

Content

1. Why does skin merit "designation as an organ" (¶s 4–5)? What are the differences between the epidermis and the dermis (¶s 7, 12)?
2. Why does the skin tan (¶s 9–10)? What evolutionary function do scientists believe tanning served (¶ 10)?
3. What is the function of collagen? Of elastin (¶ 12)? How does sun exposure damage skin (¶ 13)?

Strategies/Structures/Language

4. Identify some of the metaphors Angier uses to describe our skin. For example, the epidermis is constantly "being rebuilt from a pool of dividing stem cells" (¶ 7) and the dermis "is a clotted forest" (¶ 12). How do these metaphors help the reader understand the skin's characteristics and functions? How do these metaphors help persuade the reader of the "complexity, multidexterity and deep beauty" (¶ 3) of skin?
5. Is Angier's sole purpose to persuade readers to avoid damaging their skin? How does Angier suggest our attitude toward our skin reflects other social and cultural behaviors? Why, for example, does she characterize skin as "the bridge between private and public" (¶ 6) and the color of skin pigments as "brown, ocher and glue" (¶ 9)?

For Writing

6. ***Journal Writing.*** Does a tan body seem to imply a fit one? Explore your own perceptions of suntanned skin. Do you find tanned skin attractive despite knowing that tanned skin is also damaged skin? What factors influence you in your perception of tanning and of various shades of skin color generally?
7. ***Dialogues.*** How does Gawande's "On Washing Hands" (206–12) offer an alternative view of skin compared to Angier's? How might these two texts complement each other?

HOWARD GARDNER

Howard Gardner (born 1943) studied cognitive and social psychology at Harvard (BA, 1965, PhD, 1971) and became codirector of Project Zero at the Harvard Graduate School of Education, studying the ways children and adults learn. He is currently the Hobbs Professor in Cognition and Education at Harvard and an adjunct research professor of neurology at Boston University School of Medicine. Gardner has written over twenty books and hundreds of articles, most of them focusing on creativity and intelligence. Among his most recent works are *Changing Minds: The Art and Science of Changing Our Own and Other People's Minds* (2004) and *Multiple Intelligences: New Horizons, the Development and Education of the Mind* (2006).

In his best-known book, *Frames of Mind: The Theory of Multiple Intelligences* (1983), he postulates that there are seven distinct cognitive realms in the human brain and that each governs a particular kind of intelligence. Those intelligences most commonly considered—and tested—by the American educational establishment are *linguistic*, the ability to communicate through language, and *logical-mathematical*, the ability to come up with and use abstract concepts. To these Gardner adds five other intelligences: *spatial*, the ability to perceive and reimage the physical world; *bodily-kinesthetic*, the ability to use the body in skilled or creative ways; *musical*, the ability to distinguish, remember, and manipulate tone, melody, and rhythm; *interpersonal*, the ability to understand other people; and *intrapersonal*, the ability to understand one's self and have a conscious awareness of one's emotions. A decade later Gardner added an eighth intelligence: *naturalist*, the ability to have an intuitive understanding about plants and animals. Despite criticism from people who say Gardner's multiple intelligences are really talents (something we can get along without, as opposed to traditionally defined intelligence, which is indispensable) and that they can't be easily measured, to many educators he evokes "the reverence teenagers lavish on a rock star." "Who Owns Intelligence?" first published in the *Atlantic Monthly* in February 1999, addresses these issues in attempting, once again, to pin down intelligence and who owns it—a particularly significant issue as the twenty-first century grapples with expanding concepts of intellectual property, ranging from book manuscripts, musical compositions, and mechanical inventions to websites, applications of gene therapy, and esoteric chemical and technical processes.

Who Owns Intelligence?

Almost a century ago Alfred Binet, a gifted psychologist, was asked by the French Ministry of Education to help determine who would experience difficulty in school. Given the influx of provincials to the capital, along with immigrants of uncertain stock, Parisian officials believed they needed to know who might not advance smoothly through the system. Proceeding in an empirical manner, Binet posed many questions to youngsters of different ages. He ascertained which questions when answered correctly predicted success in school, and which questions when answered incorrectly foretold school difficulties. The items that discriminated most clearly between the two groups became, in effect, the first test of intelligence. 1

Binet is a hero to many psychologists. He was a keen observer, a careful scholar, an inventive technologist. Perhaps even more important for his followers, he devised the instrument that is often considered psychology's greatest success story. Millions of people who have never heard Binet's name have had aspects of their fate influenced by 2 instrumentation that the French psychologist inspired. And thousands of psychometricians—specialists in the measurement of psychological variables—earn their living courtesy of Binet's invention.

3 Although it has prevailed over the long run, the psychologists' version of intelligence is now facing its biggest threat. Many scholars and observers—and even some iconoclastic psychologists—feel that intelligence is too important to be left to the psychometricians. Experts are extending the breadth of the concept—proposing many intelligences, including emotional intelligence and moral intelligence. They are experimenting with new methods of ascertaining intelligence, including some that avoid tests altogether in favor of direct measures of brain activity. They are forcing citizens everywhere to confront a number of questions: What is intelligence? How ought it to be assessed? And how do our notions of intelligence fit with what we value about human beings? In short, experts are competing for the "ownership" of intelligence in the next century.

4 The outline of the psychometricians' success story is well known. Binet's colleagues in England and Germany contributed to the conceptualization and instrumentation of intelligence testing—which soon became known as IQ tests. (An IQ, or intelligence quotient, designates the ratio between mental age and chronological age. Clearly we'd prefer that a child in our care have an IQ of 120, being smarter than average for his or her years, than an IQ of 80, being older than average for his or her intelligence). Like other Parisian fashions of the period, the intelligence test migrated easily to the United States. First used to determine who was "feeble-minded," it was soon used to assess "normal" children, to identify the "gifted," and to determine who was fit to serve in the Army. By the 1920s the intelligence test had become a fixture in educational practice in the United States and much of Western Europe.

5 Early intelligence tests were not without their critics. Many enduring concerns were first raised by the influential journalist Walter Lippmann, in a series of published debates with Lewis Terman, of Stanford University, the father of IQ testing in America. Lippmann pointed out the superficiality of the questions, their possible cultural biases, and the risks of trying to determine a person's intellectual potential with a brief oral or paper-and-pencil measure.

6 Perhaps surprisingly, the conceptualization of intelligence did not advance much in the decades following Binet's and Terman's pioneering contributions. Intelligence tests came to be seen, rightly or wrongly, as primarily a tool for selecting people to fill academic or vocational niches. In one of the most famous—if irritating—remarks about intelligence testing, the influential Harvard psychologist E. G. Boring declared, "Intelligence is what the tests test." So long as these tests did what they were supposed to do (that is, give some indication of school success), it did not seem necessary or prudent to probe too deeply into their meaning or to explore alternative views of the human intellect.

Psychologists who study intelligence have argued chiefly about three questions. The first: Is intelligence singular, or does it consist of various more or less independent intellectual faculties? The purists—ranging from the turn of-the-century English psychologist Charles Spearman to his latter-day disciples Richard J. Herrnstein and Charles Murray (of *The Bell Curve* fame)—defend the notion of a single overarching "g," or general intelligence. The pluralists—ranging from L. L. Thurstone, of the University of Chicago, who posited seven vectors of the mind, to J. P. Guilford, of the University of Southern California, who discerned 150 factors of the intellect—construe intelligence as composed of some or even many dissociable components. In his much cited *The Mismeasure of Man* (1981) the paleontologist Stephen Jay Gould argued that the conflicting conclusions reached on this issue reflect alternative assumptions about statistical procedures rather than the way the mind is. Still, psychologists continue the debate, with a majority sympathetic to the general-intelligence perspective. 7

The public is more interested in the second question: Is intelligence (or are intelligences) largely inherited? This is by and large a Western question. In the Confucian societies of East Asia individual differences in endowment are assumed to be modest, and differences in achievement are thought to be due largely to effort. In the West, however, many students of the subject sympathize with the view—defended within psychology by Lewis Terman, among others—that intelligence is inborn and one can do little to alter one's intellectual birthright. 8

Studies of identical twins reared apart provide surprisingly strong support for the "heritability" of psychometric intelligence. That is, if one wants to predict someone's score on an intelligence test, the scores of the biological parents (even if the child has not had appreciable contact with them) are more likely to prove relevant than the scores of the adoptive parents. By the same token, the IQs of identical twins are more similar than the IQs of fraternal twins. And, contrary to common sense (and political correctness), the IQs of biologically related people grow closer in the later years of life. Still, because of the intricacies of behavioral genetics and the difficulties of conducting valid experiments with human child-rearing, a few defend the proposition that intelligence is largely environmental rather than heritable, and some believe that we cannot answer the question at all. 9

Most scholars agree that even if psychometric intelligence is largely inherited, it is not possible to pinpoint the sources of differences in average IQ between groups, such as the fifteen-point difference typically observed between African-American and white populations. That is because in our society the contemporary—let alone the historical—experiences of these two groups cannot be equated. One could ferret out the differences (if any) between black and white populations only in a society that was truly color-blind. 10

11 One other question has intrigued laypeople and psychologists: Are intelligence tests biased? Cultural assumptions are evident in early intelligence tests. Some class biases are obvious—who except the wealthy could readily answer a question about polo? Others are more subtle. Suppose the question is what one should do with money found on the street. Although ordinarily one might turn it over to the police, what if one had a hungry child? Or what if the police force were known to be hostile to members of one's ethnic group? Only the canonical response to such a question would be scored as correct.

12 Psychometricians have striven to remove the obviously biased items from such measures. But biases that are built into the test situation itself are far more difficult to deal with. For example, a person's background affects his or her reaction to being placed in an unfamiliar locale, being instructed by someone dressed in a certain way, and having a printed test booklet thrust into his or her hands. And as the psychologist Claude M. Steele has argued in these pages (see "Race and the Schooling of Black Americans," April, 1992), the biases prove even more acute when people know that their academic potential is being measured and that their racial or ethnic group is widely considered to be less intelligent than the dominant social group. . . .

13 Paradoxically, one of the clearest signs of the success of intelligence tests is that they are no longer widely administered. In the wake of legal cases about the propriety of making consequential decisions about education on the basis of IQ scores, many public school officials have become test-shy. By and large, the testing of IQ in the schools is restricted to cases involving a recognized problem (such as a learning disability) or a selection procedure (determining eligibility for a program that serves gifted children).

14 Despite this apparent setback, intelligence testing and the line of thinking that underlies it have actually triumphed. Many widely used scholastic measures, chief among them the SAT (renamed the Scholastic Assessment Test a few years ago), are thinly disguised intelligence tests that correlate highly with scores on standard psychometric instruments. Virtually no one raised in the developed world today has gone untouched by Binet's seemingly simple invention of a century ago.

Multiple Intelligences

15 The concept of intelligence has in recent years undergone its most robust challenge since the days of Walter Lippmann. Some who are informed by psychology but not bound by the assumptions of the psychometricians have invaded this formerly sacrosanct territory. They have put forth their own ideas of what intelligence is, how (and whether) it should be measured, and which values should be invoked in considerations of the human intellect. For the first time in many years the intelligence establishment is

clearly on the defensive—and the new century seems likely to usher in quite different ways of thinking about intelligence.

One evident factor in the rethinking of intelligence is the perspective introduced by scholars who are not psychologists. Anthropologists have commented on the parochialism of the Western view of intelligence. Some cultures do not even have a concept called intelligence, and others define intelligence in terms of traits that we in the West might consider odd—obedience, good listening skills, or moral fiber, for example. Neuroscientists are skeptical that the highly differentiated and modular structure of the brain is consistent with a unitary form of intelligence. Computer scientists have devised programs deemed intelligent; these programs often go about problem-solving in ways quite different from those embraced by human beings or other animals. 16

Even within the field of psychology the natives have been getting restless. Probably the most restless is the Yale psychologist Robert J. Sternberg. A prodigious scholar, Sternberg, who is forty-nine, has written dozens of books and hundreds of articles, the majority of them focusing in one or another way on intelligence. Sternberg began with the strategic goal of understanding the actual mental processes mobilized by standard test items, such as the solving of analogies. But he soon went beyond standard intelligence testing by insisting on two hitherto neglected forms of intelligence: the "practical" ability to adapt to varying contexts (as we all must in these days of divorcing and downsizing), and the capacity to automate familiar activities so that we can deal effectively with novelty and display "creative" intelligence. 17

Sternberg has gone to greater pains than many other critics of standard intelligence testing to measure these forms of intelligence with the paper-and-pencil laboratory methods favored by the profession. And he has found that a person's ability to adapt to diverse contexts or to deal with novel information can be differentiated from success at standard IQ-test problems. . . . 18

The psychologist and journalist Daniel Goleman has achieved worldwide success with his book *Emotional Intelligence* (1995). Contending that this new concept (sometimes nicknamed EQ) may matter as much as or more than IQ, Goleman draws attention to such pivotal human abilities as controlling one's emotional reactions and "reading" the signals of others. In the view of the noted psychiatrist Robert Coles, author of *The Moral Intelligence of Children* (1997), among many other books, we should prize character over intellect. He decries the amorality of our families, hence our children; he shows how we might cultivate human beings with a strong sense of right and wrong, who are willing to act on that sense even when it runs counter to self-interest. Other, frankly popular accounts deal with leadership intelligence (LQ), executive intelligence (EQ or ExQ), and even financial intelligence. 19

20 Like Coles's and Goleman's efforts, my work on "multiple intelligences" eschews the psychologists' credo of operationalization and test-making. I began by asking two questions: How did the human mind and brain evolve over millions of years? and How can we account for the diversity of skills and capacities that are or have been valued in different communities around the world?

21 Armed with these questions and a set of eight criteria, I have concluded that all human beings possess at least eight intelligences: linguistic and logical-mathematical (the two most prized in school and the ones central to success on standard intelligence tests), musical, spatial, bodily-kinesthetic, naturalist, interpersonal, and intrapersonal.

22 I make two complementary claims about intelligence. The first is universal. We all possess these eight intelligences—and possibly more. Indeed, rather than seeing us as "rational animals," I offer a new definition of what it means to be a human being, cognitively speaking: *Homo sapiens sapiens* is the animal that possesses these eight forms of mental representation.

23 My second claim concerns individual differences. Owing to the accidents of heredity, environment, and their interactions, no two of us exhibit the same intelligences in precisely the same proportions. Our "profiles of intelligence" differ from one another. This fact poses intriguing challenges and opportunities for our education system. We can ignore these differences and pretend that we are all the same; historically, that is what most education systems have done. Or we can fashion an education system that tries to exploit these differences, individualizing instruction and assessment as much as possible.

Intelligence and Morality

24 As the century of Binet and his successors draws to a close, we'd be wise to take stock of, and to anticipate, the course of thinking about intelligence. Although my crystal ball is no clearer than anyone else's (the species may lack "future intelligence"), it seems safe to predict that interest in intelligence will not go away.

25 To begin with, the psychometric community has scarcely laid down its arms. New versions of the standard tests continue to be created, and occasionally new tests surface as well. Researchers in the psychometric tradition churn out fresh evidence of the predictive power of their instruments and the correlations between measured intelligence and one's life chances. And some in the psychometric tradition are searching for the biological basis of intelligence: the gene or complex of genes that may affect intelligence, and neural structures that are crucial for intelligence, or telltale brain-wave patterns that distinguish the bright from the less bright.

26 Beyond various psychometric twists, interest in intelligence is likely to grow in other ways. It will be fed by the creation of machines that display

intelligence and by the specific intelligence or intelligences. Moreover, observers as diverse as Richard Herrnstein and Robert B. Reich, President Clinton's first Secretary of Labor, have agreed that in coming years a large proportion of society's rewards will go to those people who are skilled symbol analysts—who can sit at a computer screen (or its technological successor), manipulate numbers and other kinds of symbols, and use the results of their operations to contrive plans, tactics, and strategies for enterprises ranging from business to science to war games. These people may well color how intelligence is conceived in decades to come—just as the need to provide good middle-level bureaucrats to run an empire served as a primary molder of intelligence tests in the early years of the century.

Surveying the landscape of intelligence, I discern three struggles between opposing forces. The extent to which, and the manner in which, these various struggles are resolved will influence the lives of millions of people. I believe that the three struggles are interrelated; that the first struggle provides the key to the other two; and that the ensemble of struggles can be resolved in an optimal way. 27

The first struggle concerns the breadth of our definition of intelligence. One camp consists of the purists, who believe in a single form of intelligence—one that basically predicts success in school and in school-like activities. Arrayed against the purists are the progressive pluralists, who believe that many forms of intelligence exist. Some of these pluralists would like to broaden the definition of intelligence considerably, to include the abilities to create, to lead, and to stand out in terms of emotional sensitivity or moral excellence. 28

The second struggle concerns the assessment of intelligence. Again, one readily encounters a traditional position. Once chiefly concerned with paper-and-pencil tests, the traditionally oriented practitioner is now likely to use computers to provide the same information more quickly and more accurately. But other positions abound. Purists disdain psychological tasks of any complexity, preferring to look instead at reaction time, brain waves, and other physiological measures of intellect. In contrast, simulators favor measures closely resembling the actual abilities that are prized. And skeptics warn against the continued expansion of testing. They emphasize the damage often done to individual life chances and self-esteem by a regimen of psychological testing, and call for less technocratic, more humane methods—ranging from self-assessment to the examination of portfolios of student work to selection in the service of social equity. 29

The final struggle concerns the relationship between intelligence and the qualities we value in human beings. Although no one would baldly equate intellect and human worth, nuanced positions have emerged on this issue. Some (in the *Bell Curve* mold) see intelligence as closely related to a person's ethics and values; they believe that brighter people are more likely to appreciate moral complexity and to behave judiciously. Some call for a sharp distinction between the realm of intellect on the one hand, and 30 character, morality, or ethics on the other. Society's ambivalence on this issue can be discerned in the figures that become the culture's heroes. For every Albert Einstein or Bobby Fischer who is celebrated for his intellect, there is a Forrest Gump or a Chauncey Gardiner who is celebrated for human—and humane—traits that would never be captured on any kind of intelligence test. . . .

The Borders of Intelligence

31 Writing as a scholar rather than as a layperson, I see two problems with the notion of emotional intelligence. First, unlike language or space, the emotions are not contents to be processed; rather, cognition has evolved so that we can make sense of human beings (self and others) that possess and experience emotions. Emotions are part and parcel of all cognition, though they may well prove more salient at certain times or under certain circumstances: they accompany our interactions with others, our listening to great music, our feelings when we solve—or fail to solve—a difficult mathematical problem. If one calls some intelligences emotional, one suggests that other intelligences are not—and that implication flies in the face of experience and empirical data.

32 The second problem is the conflation of emotional intelligence and a certain preferred pattern of behavior. This is the trap that Daniel Goleman sometimes falls into in his otherwise admirable *Emotional Intelligence.* Goleman singles out as emotionally intelligent those people who use their understanding of emotions to make others feel better, to solve conflicts, or to cooperate in home or work situations. No one would dispute that such people are wanted. However, people who understand emotion may not necessarily use their skills for the benefit of society.

33 For this reason I prefer the term "emotional sensitivity"—a term (encompassing my interpersonal and intrapersonal intelligences) that could apply to people who are sensitive to emotions in themselves and in others. Presumably, clinicians and salespeople excel in sensitivity to others, poets and mystics in sensitivity to themselves. And some autistic or psychopathological people seem completely insensitive to the emotional realm. I would insist, however, on a strict distinction between emotional sensitivity and being a "good" or "moral" person. A person may be sensitive to the emotions of others but use that sensitivity to manipulate or to deceive them, or to create hatred.

34 I call, then, for a delineation of intelligence that includes the full range of contents to which human beings are sensitive, but at the same time designates as off limits such valued but separate human traits as creativity, morality, and emotional appropriateness. I believe that such a delineation makes scientific and epistemological sense. It reinvigorates the elastic band without stretching it to the breaking point. It helps to resolve the two remaining struggles: how to assess, and what kinds of human beings to admire.

Once we decide to restrict intelligence to human information-processing and product-making capacities, we can make use of the established technology of assessment. That is, we can continue to use paper-and-pencil or computer-adapted testing techniques while looking at a broader range of capacities, such as musical sensitivity and empathy with others. And we can avoid ticklish and possibly unresolvable questions about the assessment of values and morality that may well be restricted to a particular culture and that may well change over time. 35

Still, even with a limited perspective on intelligence, important questions remain about which assessment path to follow—that of the purist, the simulator, or the skeptic. Here I have strong views. I question the wisdom of searching for a "pure" intelligence—be it general intelligence, musical intelligence, or interpersonal intelligence. I do not believe that such alchemical intellectual essences actually exist; they are a product of our penchant for creating terminology rather than determinable and measurable entities. Moreover, the correlations that have thus far been found between supposedly pure measures and the skills that we actually value in the world are too modest to be useful. 36

What does exist is the use of intelligences, individually and in concert, to carry out tasks that are valued by a society. Accordingly, we should be assessing the extent to which human beings succeed in carrying out tasks of consequence that presumably involve certain intelligences. To be concrete, we should not test musical intelligence by looking at the ability to discriminate between two tones or timbres; rather, we should be teaching people to sing songs or play instruments or transform melodies and seeing how readily they master such feats. At the same time, we should abjure a search for pure emotional sensitivity—for example, a test that matches facial expressions to galvanic skin response. Rather, we should place (or observe) people in situations that call for them to be sensitive to the aspirations and motives of others. For example, we could see how they handle a situation in which they and colleagues have to break up a fight between two teenagers, or persuade a boss to change a policy of which they do not approve. 37

Here powerful new simulations can be invoked. We are now in a position to draw on technologies that can deliver realistic situations or problems and also record the success of subjects in dealing with them. A student can be presented with an unfamiliar tune on a computer and asked to learn that tune, transpose it, orchestrate it, and the like. Such exercises would reveal much about the student's intelligence in musical matters. 38

Turning to the social (or human, if you prefer) realm, subjects can be presented with simulated interactions and asked to judge the shifting motivations of each actor. Or they can be asked to work in an interactive hypermedia production with unfamiliar people who are trying to accomplish some sort of goal, and to respond to their various moves and 39 countermoves. The program can alter responses in light of the moves of the subject. Like a high-stakes poker game, such a measure should reveal much about the interpersonal or emotional sensitivity of a subject.

40 A significant increase in the breadth—the elasticity—of our concept of intelligence, then, should open the possibility for innovative forms of assessment far more realistic than the classic short-answer examinations. Why settle for an IQ or an SAT test, in which the items are at best remote proxies for the ability to design experiments, write essays, critique musical performances, and so forth? Why not instead ask people actually (or virtually) to carry out such tasks? And yet by not opening up the Pandora's box of values and subjectivity, one can continue to make judicious use of the insights and technologies achieved by those who have devoted decades to perfecting mental measurement.

41 To be sure, one can create a psychometric instrument for any conceivable human virtue, including morality, creativity, and emotional intelligence in its several senses. Indeed, since the publication of Daniel Goleman's book dozens of efforts have been made to create tests for emotional intelligence. The resulting instruments are not, however, necessarily useful. Such instruments are far more likely to satisfy the test maker's desire for reliability (a subject gets roughly the same score on two separate administrations of the test) than the need for validity (the test measures the trait that it purports to measure).

42 Such instruments-on-demand prove dubious for two reasons. First, beyond some platitudes, few can agree on what it means to be moral, ethical, a good person: consider the differing values of Jesse Helms and Jesse Jackson, Margaret Thatcher and Margaret Mead. Second, scores on such tests are much more likely to reveal test-taking savvy (skills in language and logic) than fundamental character.

43 In speaking about character, I turn to a final concern: the relationship between intelligence and what I will call virtue—those qualities that we admire and wish to hold up as examples for our children. No doubt the desire to expand intelligence to encompass ethics and character represents a direct response to the general feeling that our society is lacking in these dimensions; the expansionist view of intelligence reflects the hope that if we transmit the technology of intelligence to these virtues, we might in the end secure a more virtuous population.

44 I have already indicated my strong reservations about trying to make the word "intelligence" all things to all people—the psychometric equivalent of the true, the beautiful, and the good. Yet the problem remains: how, in a post-Aristotelian, post-Confucian era in which psychometrics looms large, do we think about the virtuous human being?

45 My analysis suggests one promising approach. We should recognize that intelligences, creativity, and morality—to mention just three desiderata—are separate. Each may require its own form of measurement or assessment, and some will prove far easier to assess objectively than

others. Indeed, with respect to creativity and morality, we are more likely to rely on overall judgments by experts than on any putative test battery. At the same time, nothing prevents us from looking for people who combine several of these attributes—who have musical and interpersonal intelligence, who are psychometrically intelligent and creative in the arts, who combine emotional sensitivity and a high standard of moral conduct.

Let me introduce another analogy at this point. In college admissions much attention is paid to scholastic performance, as measured by College Board examinations and grades. However, other features are also weighed, and sometimes a person with lower test scores is admitted if he or she proves exemplary in terms of citizenship or athletics or motivation. Admissions officers do not confound these virtues (indeed, they may use different scales and issue different grades), but they recognize the attractiveness of candidates who exemplify two or more desirable traits. 46

We have left the Eden of classical times, in which various intellectual and ethical values necessarily commingled, and we are unlikely ever to re-create it. We should recognize that these virtues can be separate and will often prove to be remote from one another. When we attempt to aggregate them, through phrases like "emotional intelligence," "creative intelligence," and "moral intelligence," we should realize that we are expressing a wish rather than denoting a necessary or even a likely coupling. 47

We have an aid in converting this wish to reality: the existence of powerful examples—people who succeed in exemplifying two or more cardinal human virtues. To name names is risky—particularly when one generation's heroes can become the subject of the next generation's pathographies. Even so, I can without apology mention Niels Bohr, George C. Marshall, Rachel Carson, Arthur Ashe, Louis Armstrong, Pablo Casals, Ella Fitzgerald. 48

In studying the lives of such people, we discover human possibilities. Young human beings learn primarily from the examples of powerful adults around them—those who are admirable and also those who are simply glamorous. Sustained attention to admirable examples may well increase the future incidence of people who actually do yoke capacities that are scientifically and epistemologically separate. 49

In one of the most evocative phrases of the century the British novelist E. M. Forster counseled us, "Only connect." I believe that some expansionists in the territory of intelligence, though well motivated, have prematurely asserted connections that do not exist. But I also believe that as human beings, we can help to forge connections that may be important for our physical and psychic survival. 50

Just how the precise borders of intelligence are drawn is a question we can leave to scholars. But the imperative to broaden our definition of intelligence in a responsible way goes well beyond the academy. Who "owns" intelligence promises to be an issue even more critical in the next century than it has been in this era of the IQ test. 51

Content

1. What is intelligence? Compare and contrast some of the types Gardner refers to, which may be divided into two groups, the sort that "predicts success in school and in school-like activities" (¶s 4–10, 28) and all other kinds, including "the abilities to create, to lead, and to stand out in terms of emotional sensitivity or moral excellence" (¶ 28).
2. How can intelligence of a particular sort best be measured?
3. Who owns intelligence? The people who possess it? The society or social subgroup that determines what sorts of intelligence are valuable, necessary, appreciated—and those that aren't? The testers? How does Gardner's essay address this issue?

Strategies/Structures/Language

4. Find examples in Gardner's essay of the following common techniques of definition, and comment on their effectiveness in conveying one or more meanings of intelligence:

   a. Illustration
   b. Comparison and contrast
   c. Negation (saying what something is not)
   d. Analysis
   e. Explanation of a process (how something is measured or works)
   f. Identification of causes or effects
   g. Simile, metaphor, or analogy
   h. Reference to authority or the writer's own expertise
   i. Reference to the writer's or others' personal experience or observation

5. ***Mixed Modes.*** Gardner's essay is full of arguments: for his definition of intelligence, against competing definitions; for various practical ways of measuring intelligence, against particular sorts of testing. Identify some of the assertions and evidence he uses to support his claims. Are they credible?
6. Does Gardner believe it's possible to expand the definition of *intelligence* to include virtue (¶ 43), to make it encompass qualities he'd like it to have?
7. Can people change definitions of words to make them mean what they want them to mean? Or does every term have borders around it (¶ 51)? If so, who creates and enforces the boundaries?

For Writing

8. Write your own definition either of *intelligence* in general or of a specific type of intelligence such as one that Gardner discusses in his essay. You may need to define some of these yourself or consult other sources for the intelligences Gardner only touches on: a. psychometric intelligence (¶s 4–10); b. the "'practical'" ability to adapt to varying contexts (¶ 17); the "ability to deal with novel information" (¶ 18); emotional intelligence (¶s 19, 31–33); moral intelligence (¶s 19, 41–45); or creativity (¶s 41–45). Or define a form of intelligence on Gardner's personal list that includes "linguistic, logical-mathematical, musical, spatial, bodily-kinesthetic, naturalist, interpersonal, and intrapersonal." (See Gardner's book *Frames of Mind* [1983] or any

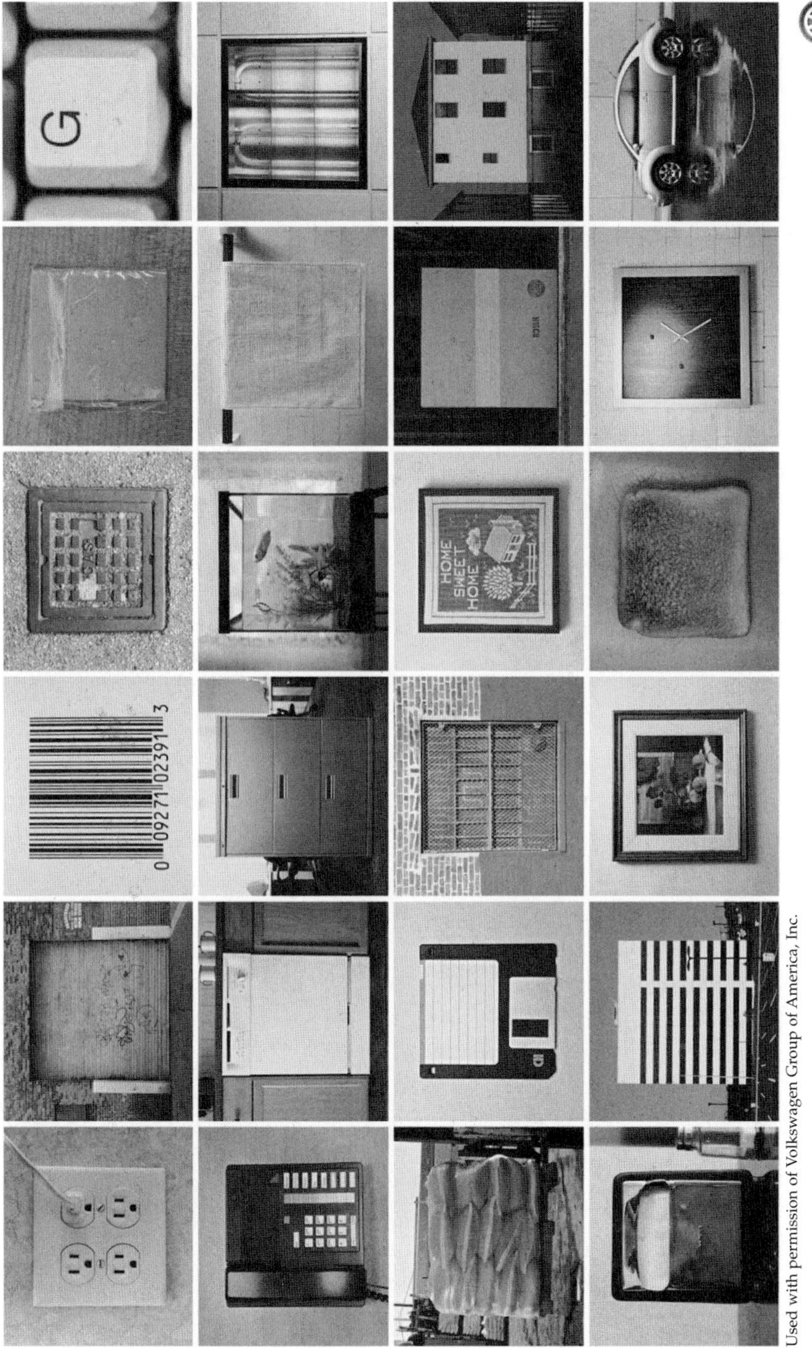

Used with permission of Volkswagen Group of America, Inc.

Possible ways to "read" this photograph are discussed on the first page of this chapter.

other of Gardner's numerous writings on the subject.) Use one or more techniques of definition identified in question 4, and, assuming that you yourself fulfill your own definition of *intelligent*, supplement your more general definition with a specific firsthand example, and abundant illustrations, verbal and graphic.

9. Write a definition of an abstract concept for readers who may not have thought much about it—such as *love, truth, beauty, justice, greed, pride,* or *the good life*—but who have probably used it often in everyday life, something intangible that can be identified in terms of its effects, causes, manifestations, or other nonphysical properties. Use one or more techniques of definition identified above and illustrate your definition with one or two specific examples with which you are familiar. Then use the examples as a basis for making generalizations that apply to other aspects of the concept.

10. ***Journal Writing.*** Explore the definition of intelligence that you developed for question 8. How would you or have you used your understanding of intelligence in teaching somebody a particular skill? How might you apply your knowledge of the kinds of intelligence you excel in to your own learning processes?

11. ***Second Look.*** How might Malcolm Venville's linked photographs on the previous page illustrate Gardner's argument that human beings possess different kinds of intelligences and that "Owing to the accidents of heredity, environment, and their interactions, no two of us exhibit the same intelligences in precisely the same proportions" (¶ 23)? Explore how differences in the functionality, aesthetics, texture, spatial organization, size, and temporality of the objects pictured suggest the breadth and variety of human intelligence. What qualities of the square do these photographs suggest are universal or particular to a specific object? What do such qualities suggest about the human brain?

JOHN HOCKENBERRY

John Hockenberry (born in 1956 in Dayton, Ohio) is an award-winning journalist who has written for many publications, including *The New York Times, The New Yorker, Wired,* and the *Washington Post.* Formerly a correspondent for NBC (1996–2005), he has worked as a Middle East correspondent for National Public Radio, where he anchored "The DNA Files" (1998–2003). He has published a novel, *A River Out of Eden* (2001), and written a one-man show, *Spoke Man* (1996), that appeared off-Broadway. His memoir, *Moving Violations: War Zones, Wheelchairs and Declarations of Independence* (1995), from which this excerpt is taken, recounts the 1976 car accident that left him a paraplegic. In this excerpt Hockenberry describes the stereotypes attached to the physically disabled individual. Using confrontational and conversational language, as well as biting humor, Hockenberry critiques the ways in which contemporary American culture, particularly through the medium of television, thrives on the perpetuation of stereotypes, including those focused on race and the disabled.

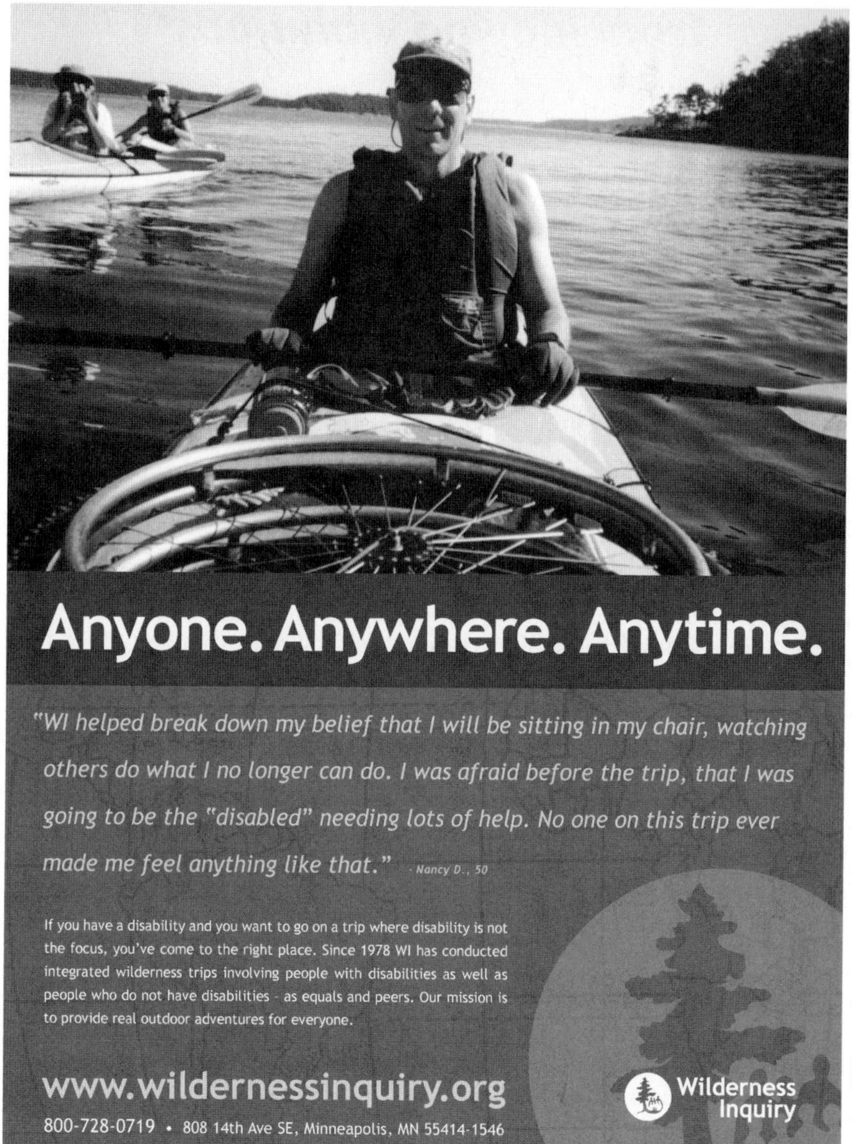

Anyone. Anywhere. Anytime.

"WI helped break down my belief that I will be sitting in my chair, watching others do what I no longer can do. I was afraid before the trip, that I was going to be the "disabled" needing lots of help. No one on this trip ever made me feel anything like that." - Nancy D., 50

If you have a disability and you want to go on a trip where disability is not the focus, you've come to the right place. Since 1978 WI has conducted integrated wilderness trips involving people with disabilities as well as people who do not have disabilities - as equals and peers. Our mission is to provide real outdoor adventures for everyone.

www.wildernessinquiry.org

800-728-0719 • 808 14th Ave SE, Minneapolis, MN 55414-1546

Wilderness Inquiry

Wilderness Inquiry sponsors a variety of national and international trips that involve camping, hiking, kayaking, canoeing, and other outdoor experiences on land, sea, and rivers—in wilderness, national parks, and game preserves. Their trips accommodate people of all ages and abilities. Given the language of the ad, how would you expect this kayaker, his wheelchair strapped to the top of his kayak, to be treated on this trip?

from *Moving Violations**

1 People often ask me what I would prefer to be called. Do they think I have an answer?

2 I'm a crip for life. I cannot walk. I have "lost the use of my legs." I am paralyzed from the waist down. I use a wheelchair. I am wheelchair-bound. I am confined to a wheelchair. I am a paraplegic. I require "special assistance for boarding." I am a gimp, crip, physically challenged, differently abled, paralyzed. I am a T-5 para. I am sick. I am well. I have a T4–6 incomplete dural lesion, a spinal cord injury, a broken back, "broken legs" to Indian cabbies in New York who always ask, "What happened to your legs, Mister?"

3 I have a spastic bladder, pneumatic tires, air in all four of my tires. Solid wheelchair tires are for hospitals and weenies. No self-respecting crip would be caught dead in one. I use a catheter to take a whiz. I require no leg bag. That's for the really disabled. I have no van with a wheelchair lift anymore. Those are for the really disabled, and thank God I'm not one of them. I need no motor on my wheelchair. Those are for the really disabled, and I am definitely not one of those. From mid-chest down I have no sensation. I am numb all the way to my toes.

4 I know what they're all thinking. My dick doesn't work. The truth? My dick works sometimes. My dick works without fail. I have two dicks. I have totally accepted my sexuality. I have massive problems with my sexuality. Actually, there is no problem with sexuality. It's just not a problem. I think we can just drop this subject of sexuality because it's not an issue. Not at all. The truth? I had a little problem there in the beginning, then I learned how to compensate. Now everything is fine. It's actually better than fine. To be perfectly honest, I am the sexual version of crack. There are whole clinics set up for people who became addicted to sleeping with me. All right, the truth? Not so fast.

5 You do not have to feel guilty for causing my situation even though your great-great-grandparents may have been slave owners. You do have to feel guilty and fawning and contrite if I ever catch you using a wheelchair stall in an airport men's room or parking in a disabled space. I feel as though I caused my situation and deserve to be cast from society, on which I am a burden. I am a poster boy demanding a handout. I am the 800 number you didn't call to donate money. I am the drum major in Sally Struther's parade of wretches. I watch the muscular dystrophy telethon every year without fail. I would like to have Jerry Lewis sliced thinly and packed away in Jeffrey Dahmer's freezer. I am not responsible for my situation and roll around with a chip on my shoulder ready to lash out at and assault any person making my life difficult, preferably with a deadly weapon.

---

* From MOVING VIOLATIONS by John Hockenberry. Copyright © 1995 John Hockenberry. Reprinted by permission of Hyperion. All rights reserved.

I have unlimited amounts of "courage," which is evident to everyone but myself and other crips. I get around in a wheelchair. I am a wheelchair "racer." I am just rolling to work. I am in denial. I have accepted my disability and have discovered within myself a sublime reservoir of truth. I can't accept my disability, and the only truth I am aware of is that my life is shit and that everyone is making it worse. I am a former food stamp recipient. I am in the 35 percent tax bracket. I am part of the disability rights movement. I am a sell-out wannabe TV star media scumbag who has turned his broken back on other crips. 6

I am grateful for the Americans with Disabilities Act, which has heralded a new era of civil rights in this country. I think the Americans with Disabilities Act is the most useless, empty, unenforceable law of the last quarter-century. It ranks up there as one of the most pansy-assed excuses for a White House news conference in U.S. history. I think that the disabled community is a tough, uncompromising coalition of activists. I think the disabled community is a back-biting assembly of noisy, mutually suspicious clowns who would eagerly sell out any revolution just to appear on a telethon, or in the White House Rose Garden, or in a Levis' commercial. 7

I cannot reach the cornflakes in my cupboard. I cannot do a handstand. I cannot use most revolving doors. I cannot rollerblade. Bowling is more of a waste of time than it used to be. (One of the chief advantages of being in a wheelchair is always having an excuse not to go bowling, even though I do miss the shoes.) I'm telling you these things because I want us to share, and for you to understand my experiences and then, together, bridge the gulf between us. I want you all to leave me alone. 8

I'm a guy in a chair, crip for life. Everything you think about me is right. Everything you think is wrong. 9

What is "normal" but another stereotype, no different than "angry black man," "Asian math genius," "welfare mother," or "gay man with a lisp"? Each stereotype thrives in direct proportion to the distance from each class of persons it claims to describe. Get close to the real people and these pretend images begin to break up, but they don't go easily. As each stereotype breaks down, it reveals a pattern of wrongs. Losing a stereotype is about being wrong retroactively. For a person to confront such assumptions they must admit an open-ended wrong for as long as those assumptions have lived inside them. There is the temptation to hold on to why you believed in stereotypes. "I was told gays were like that as a child." "I never knew many blacks, and that's what my parents believed about them." "I was once frightened and disgusted by a person in a wheelchair." To relinquish a stereotype is to lose face by giving up a mask. 10

We trade in masks in America. Especially in politics. Politicians love to talk about the "American people" and what they allegedly want or don't want. But who are they, really? The America evoked most often today by politicians and pundits is a closet full of masks denoting race, nationality, and a host of other characteristics. America's 11 definitive social unit of measurement is no longer the family, nor is it the extended family. On the other end of the scale, it is not the village or hamlet, neighborhood or block, city, state, or region. I grew up in America at a time when its logo was the racially balanced commercial image of four or five children, one black, white, Asian, female, and disabled (optional) romping in an idyllic, utopian, and quite nonexistent playground.

12 You can still occasionally see this image in the children's fashion supplement to *The New York Times Magazine*. These are happy measuring sticks of a demographic formula, perfect faces of social equilibrium to distract from the fact that each child is usually clad in the designer fabric hard currency equivalent of the GNP of Guyana or Cameroon. In the eighties the fashion chain Benetton crossed the old American emblem with the UN General Assembly and produced its own utopian logo of a meticulously integrated, multiracial youth army, no disabled (not optional).

13 We once portrayed these idealized young people as seeds of a racially harmonious society we dreamed would come. Now those children shout down the long narrow lenses of music video cameras, or gun each other down on the streets. Our communities have become multiracial, just as the dream foretold. But they are not utopias. Integration is no guarantee of harmony. It is what most of the world has known since the end of World War Two. It is this nation's last, cruel lesson of the twentieth century.

14 Today, if one measures America at all, it is in audience units. America is the union of all the multiracial groups of ostensibly "normal" people, ranging from submissive and polite to angry and aggressive, who can be seated in a television studio in front of a talk-show host. There they stare at, and react to, the famous hosts, the famous guests, or anyone else on stage. Mad people, older people, teenagers, victims, predators, all of the species in America's great political aviary pass in front of the audience. America turns its thumbs up or down, then goes to a commercial break. There is no verdict. There is just the din of many verdicts. As the camera scans the audience, the people who can be anticipated to have a distinct opinion, or more likely, an outrage, are handed the microphone. "Why don't you just leave him if he beats you?" "It's people like you skinheads who spread hate in this country." America punctuates each of these outraged questions and challenges with applause, jeers, and shouts.

15 I caught the delivery of verdicts from one such clump of Americana between commercial breaks on the "Oprah Winfrey" show some time after my accident. I had always thought of myself as a face in the audience. On this show I saw myself on the stage with a group of four married couples, each with a disabled partner. Three of the couples contained a partner in a wheelchair; the other was a blind woman and her sighted

husband. The theme of the show that day was something like "One of them is fine and the other one is defective. How do they manage?" The audience applauded with an enthusiasm they reserved for First Ladies, and Oprah herself had that deep, breathy voice that television talk-show hosts reserve for the inspirational subjects—the serious themes that justify all of those celebrity interviews and fluff. Here, "Crips and Their Spouses" was gripping television.

The couples represented an odd composite of the crip population. 16 This was Oprah's idea of the crips next door, and that next door, in this case, was not necessarily the state institution. Just your average run-of-the-mill crip and spouse combo package. There were no Vietnam vets on this panel, no wheelchair jocks, no quadriplegics, no gunshot ghetto homies with their stripped-down Quickie ultra-lights, and, of course, they had neglected to call me.

Three of the couples might as well have had lamp shades on their 17 heads. They were nonthreatening, overweight, jolly, well-adjusted types with a hint of acne, all wearing loud, baggy shirts. These are the people the audience was used to giving a wide berth on the bus and then ignoring. One of the women was in a dented, ill-fitting wheelchair with gray hospital wheels. They said things like, "Hey, Oprah, it just takes more planning. It's no big deal." They laughed a lot. The audience imagined working near one of these people; it did not have to imagine being one.

One of the couples was different; a thin guy in a wheelchair and 18 his pretty, young, unparalyzed wife. They had dated in college before his "accident." They were nearly dressed and clearly held the most fascination for the audience members. "How difficult was it for you after his accident?" Oprah addressed herself to the young woman when she wanted to know some detail. No, she had never thought of breaking up with him after the accident. "It's no different than anything else that might make a relationship difficult." The audience began to applaud while Oprah nodded. On their faces was a kind of sentimental approval. The audience wanted her to know that she could have left him . . . she would have had the perfect excuse . . . no jury would have convicted, certainly not in that audience. She seemed slightly sensitive about this point because she insisted again that she had not thought of breaking up the relationship, and that it really was just another thing, like a joint checking account, for a couple to deal with.

The joint checking account line really got them. "I just want to say 19 that I think you are such an inspiration to us all," an audience member addressed the panel. It didn't really matter what the panelists said, especially the young couple. It only mattered what the audience thought about the young man's plight and his courageous girlfriend. It was far more important to assume that he was broken, that she was tied to him now selflessly, and that they would make the best of things. "Yes, Oprah; we manage just fine," she said in her small voice with her husband's nodding assent. Oprah addressed the young man once. "You must be so happy to have someone like Amy," or whatever her name was.

20 I was rooting for these folks to hold their own. Though I was just a little older, I could tell that I had logged lots more wheelchair time than the young guy on TV. I could feel what was coming, I saw the audience greedily looking them up and down. I saw what we were supposed to think about them. He: strong, brave, and struck down in his youth. She: stronger and braver for spending her youth with him. On their faces you could see that the conditions of this public execution were just beginning to dawn on them.

21 But it was just Oprah. It was all in good fun. I was making too much of a television talk show. They weren't forced to go out onto that stage. A voice inside said, "If you weren't so angry and dysfunctional, John, maybe you would be invited to go on 'Oprah' too."

22 It didn't take long for Oprah to deliver. "So there's one thing I want to know." She looks directly at the young girl as the hungry crowd buzzes with anticipation. Oh, my god, she's going to ask. Like a car accident in the movies, the world slows down at this point. I can see the smile freeze on the face of the young woman. The crowd goes wild. The camera cuts away to Oprah.

23 "What I want to know is . . ."

24 She pauses for sincerity. The crowd is totally with her. The woman must know what's about to happen. She must have been asked a million times. I wondered if the guy knew. The guy probably had no idea. Or maybe it was a condition for going on the show. I'm screaming at the TV now: "Tell her it's none of her damn business. We're counting on you out here. Tell Oprah to stuff it!"

25 Oprah delivers.

26 "Amy, can he do it?"

27 Loud gasp from the crowd. I imagine that it must have sounded this way when Sydney Carton's head was lopped off in *A Tale of Two Cities*. The camera immediately cuts to the woman's face, which has blushed a deep red. She tries something of a laugh, glances at her husband, who is out of the shot. Eventually, when the noise dies down, she says, "Yes, he can, Oprah." She giggles.

28 The camera pulls wide, and the two onstage seem very small. He takes her hand for comfort. The crowd bursts into applause. Even the other crips on stage are applauding. He withdraws his hand, as though it had been placed in hot oil. The camera cuts back to Oprah, who is nodding to the crowd half-heartedly, trying to get them to stop clapping. She looks somewhere between a very satisfied Perry Mason and a champion mud wrestler. Now we know what the show was really about. It wasn't just Oprah; the whole crowd seemed to care only about this. The oddest thing was that after the question and the embarrassed answer the audience seemed to think they now knew how "it" was done. What did they

know? They knew that they had the guts to ask this question; they didn't really care about the answer.

Oprah, here's something I have always wanted to know. Do black guys really have giant dicks? The angry voice yelled at the television and then turned it off. Is that what people think when they stare? What constitutes "doing it"? There was no answer for them. There was no answer for me. Questions like these were the weapon. They need no real answer and apparently are always loaded in the chambers of people's curiosity. Stereotypes bring forth righteous anger and deep humiliation. At the same time, they are completely understandable, like an old piece of furniture you have walked by every day of your life. . . . 29

Content

1. What criteria does Hockenberry suggest determines who is "really disabled" (¶ 3)? Why does he insist that he's "not one of those" (¶ 3)?
2. According to Hockenberry, what presumptions do the nondisabled make about the disabled (¶s 4–5)? Why does he represent these presumptions as extreme and opposing? Why does Hockenberry tell the reader, "Everything you think about me is right. Everything you think is wrong" (¶ 9)?
3. Hockenberry writes that "Each stereotype thrives in direct proportion to the distance from each class of persons it claims to describe" (¶ 10). Why are stereotypes difficult to give up? What are the benefits of "giving up a mask" (¶ 10)?
4. Hockenberry writes, "Our communities have become multiracial, just as the dream foretold. But they are not utopias." Why, according to him, hasn't America become "a racially harmonious society" (¶ 13)?
5. As Hockenberry describes his reaction to the *Oprah* episode, he slows his pace, carefully describing the different characters and the angles of the camera, and recounting his own speech as well as that of the people on camera (¶s 15–28). What is the effect of this careful pacing? How does this strategy build on Hockenberry's earlier discussion of stereotypes? Why does he compare Oprah's intrusive question with an equally intrusive and obnoxious question about black men in the final paragraph (¶ 29)?

Strategies/Structures/Language

6. How does Hockenberry's language suggest that television has increasingly come to dominate and define American culture? Find examples such as "your average run-of-the-mill crip and spouse combo package" (¶ 16) and explain how such phrases support Hockenberry's cultural critique.
7. Why does Hockenberry compare this *Oprah Winfrey* show with an execution (¶s 20, 27) and a trial by jury (¶ 17)? How does he prepare the reader for this narrative (¶ 14)?
8. How does Hockenberry use clichés such as "I am in denial" (¶ 6) and "a new era of civil rights in this country" (¶ 7)? What do these clichés suggest about his view of stereotypes and his characterization of American culture as "a closet full of masks" (¶ 11)?

For Writing

9. What is the impact of television shows in which participants reveal their personal lives? Under what circumstances might you be persuaded to participate in such a show? Is Hockenberry being ironic when he writes, "A voice inside said, 'If you weren't so angry and dysfunctional, John, maybe you would be invited to go on "Oprah" too'" (¶ 21)? Write an essay that examines our culture's attitudes toward television shows that encourage self-exposure.

10. ***Second Look.*** The photograph for adventure vacations on 365 features a wheelchair-bound man kayaking. Does this advertisement speak to the disabled or the nondisabled? What does Hockenberry's analysis suggest about his views of representing the disabled in nontraditional ways? Might he disparage the implication that a wheelchair-bound kayaker has "unlimited amounts of 'courage'" (¶ 6)?

BRIAN DOYLE

Brian Doyle is an award-winning essayist and editor of the University of Portland's *Portland Magazine*. He has published work in the *Atlantic Monthly, Orion, Harper's,* and the *Best American Essays* anthologies (1998, 1999, 2003, and 2005). His collections of creative nonfiction include *Saints Passionate and Peculiar* (2002), *Leaping: Revelations and Epiphanies* (2003), and *The Grail: A Year of Ambling and Shambling Through an Oregon Vineyard in Pursuit of the Best Pinot Noir Wine in the Whole Wild World* (2006). His first collection of poems, *Epiphanies & Elegies: Very Short Stories* was published in 2007. "Joyas Voladoras," which first appeared in *The American Scholar* (2004), evokes through its descriptive definitions of the hearts of various creatures the frailty of life, the mystery of the web that connects all living things, and the essential solitary nature of our sojourn on the earth.

Joyas Voladoras

1 Consider the hummingbird for a long moment. A hummingbird's heart beats ten times a second. A hummingbird's heart is the size of a pencil eraser. A hummingbird's heart is a lot of the hummingbird. *Joyas voladoras,* flying jewels, the first white explorers in the Americas called them, and the white men had never seen such creatures, for hummingbirds came into the world only in the Americas, nowhere else in the universe, more than three hundred species of them whirring and zooming and nectaring in hummer time zones nine times removed from ours, their hearts hammering faster than we could clearly hear if we pressed our elephantine ears to their infinitesimal chests.

Each one visits a thousand flowers a day. They can dive at sixty miles an hour. They can fly backward. They can fly more than five hundred miles without pausing to rest. But when they rest they come close to death: on frigid nights, or when they are starving, they retreat into torpor, their metabolic rate slowing to a fifteenth of their normal sleep rate, their hearts sludging nearly to a halt, barely beating, and if they are not soon warmed, if they do not soon find that which is sweet, their hearts grow cold, and they cease to be. Consider for a moment those hummingbirds who did not open their eyes again today, this very day, in the Americas: bearded helmetcrests and booted racket-tails, violet-tailed sylphs and violet-capped woodnymphs, crimson topazes and purple-crowned fairies, red-tailed comets and amethyst woodstars, rainbow-bearded thornbills and glittering-bellied emeralds, velvet-purple coronets and golden-bellied star-frontlets, fiery-tailed awlbills and Andean hillstars, spatuletails and pufflegs, each the most amazing thing you have never seen, each thunderous wild heart the size of an infant's fingernail, each mad heart silent, a brilliant music stilled. 2

Hummingbirds, like all flying birds but more so, have incredible enormous immense ferocious metabolisms. To drive those metabolisms they have racecar hearts that eat oxygen at an eye-popping rate. Their hearts are built of thinner, leaner fibers than ours. Their hearts are built of thinner, leaner fibers than ours. Their arteries are stiffer and more taut. They have more mitochondria in their heart muscles—anything to gulp more oxygen. Their hearts are stripped to the skin for the war against gravity and inertia, the mad search for food, the insane idea of flight. The price of their ambition is a life closer to death; they suffer more heart attacks and aneurysms and ruptures than any other living creature. It's expensive to fly. You burn out. You fry the machine. You melt the engine. Every creature on earth has approximately two billion heartbeats to spend in a lifetime. You can spend them slowly, like a tortoise, and live to be two hundred years old, or you can spend them fast, like a hummingbird, and live to be two years old. 3

The biggest heart in the world is inside the blue whale. It weighs more than seven tons. It's as big as a room. It *is* a room, with four chambers. A child could walk around in it, head high, bending only to step through the valves. The valves are as big as the swinging doors in a saloon. This house of a heart drives a creature a hundred feet long. When this creature is born it is twenty feet long and weighs four tons. It is waaaaay bigger than your car. It drinks a hundred gallons of milk from its mama every day and gains two hundred pounds a day, and when it is seven or eight years old it endures an unimaginable puberty and then it essentially disappears from human ken, for next to nothing is known of the mating habits, travel patterns, diet, social life, language, social structure, diseases, spirituality, wars, stories, despairs, and arts of the blue whale. There are perhaps ten thousand blue whales in the world, 4 living in every ocean on earth, and of the largest mammal who ever lived we know nearly nothing. But we know this: the animals with the largest hearts in the world generally travel in pairs, and their penetrating moaning cries, their piercing yearning tongue, can be heard underwater for miles and miles.

5 Mammals and birds have hearts with four chambers. Reptiles and turtles have hearts with three chambers. Fish have hearts with two chambers. Insects and mollusks have hearts with one chamber. Worms have hearts with one chamber, although they may have as many as eleven single-chambered hearts. Unicellular bacteria have no hearts at all; but even they have fluid eternally in motion, washing from one side of the cell to the other, swirling and whirling. No living being is without interior liquid motion. We all churn inside.

6 So much held in a heart in a lifetime. So much held in a heart in a day, an hour, a moment. We are utterly open with no one, in the end—not mother and father, not wife or husband, not lover, not child, not friend. We open windows to each but we live alone in the house of the heart. Perhaps we must. Perhaps we could not bear to be so naked, for fear of a constantly harrowed heart. When young we think there will come one person who will savor and sustain us always; when we are older we know this is the dream of a child, that all hearts finally are bruised and scarred, scored and torn, repaired by time and will, patched by force of character, yet fragile and rickety forevermore, no matter how ferocious the defense and how many bricks you bring to the wall. You can brick up your heart as stout and tight and hard and cold and impregnable as you possibly can and down it comes in an instant, felled by a woman's second glance, a child's apple breath, the shatter of glass in the road, the words "I have something to tell you," a cat with a broken spine dragging itself into the forest to die, the brush of your mother's papery ancient hand in the thicket of your hair, the memory of your father's voice early in the morning echoing from the kitchen where he is making pancakes for his children.

Content

1. Doyle characterizes the hummingbird as a tiny creature with "thunderous wild heart" and "ferocious" metabolism. What additional information does his list of the types of hummingbirds convey to the reader (¶ 2)? Why does he spend nearly an entire paragraph describing the hummingbird's heart and then end it with a reference to the tortoise (¶ 3)? What aspects of the heart does this description emphasize?

2. Doyle links the first three paragraphs of his essay to the last three paragraphs with the sentence, "Every creature on earth has approximately two billion heartbeats to spend in a lifetime" (¶ 3). How are the hearts he describes similar and yet different?

3. Doyle chooses the enormous blue whale, a creature of which "we know nearly nothing" (¶ 4), to contrast with the tiny hummingbird. Why does the size of the blue whale's heart suffice for his purposes?

Strategies/Structures/Language

4. Doyle uses a variety of stylistic devices, including *onomatopoeia* ("whirring and zooming," ¶ 1); *scesis onomaton*, or repetitive synonymous phrases ("You burn out. You fry the machine. You melt the engine." ¶ 3); *metaphors* ("as big as the swinging doors in a saloon," ¶ 4); *alliteration* ("harrowed heart," ¶ 6); *anaphora*, or beginning successive sentences with the same words ("Perhaps we must. Perhaps we could not bear to be so naked," ¶ 6); and *parallelism* ("our elephantine ears to their infinitesimal chests," ¶ 1). Find other examples of these devices and explain what kind of effects they create. How, for example, do such devices create contrasting sounds and images, emphasize specific themes, or evoke emotion?
5. Doyle makes references to children (¶s 2, 4) and the newborn blue whale (¶ 4). How do these references anticipate and resonate in the final paragraph?
6. Why does the writer introduce the final paragraph with the short statement "We all churn inside" (¶ 5)?

For Writing

7. ***Journal Writing.*** Is the belief that there will be "one person who will savor and sustain us always" a childish dream (¶ 6)? Can we ever share ourselves completely? Would we want to? Why do we seem to desire such closeness when we are young only to discover that we are ultimately alone? What does vulnerability and intimacy mean to you? Explore these issues in an essay; share it only if you wish.
8. ***Dialogues.*** Compare the pattern, or structure, of Doyle's essay with Linda Hogan's spiritual essay "Waking" (99–101). What shape does each essay suggest? How does each shape create a different idea of our spiritual selves?
9. ***Second Look.*** Doyle writes that "all hearts finally are bruised and scarred, scored and torn, repaired by time and will . . ." (¶ 6). Reread Natalie Angier's "A Supple Casing, Prone to Damage" (347–49) and write an essay about how skin, like the heart, also tells the story of our lives. Refer in your discussion to the photograph of the African American woman with a mop on 451 and/or the photograph of people in Haiti scavenging for food on 278.

LYNDA BARRY

Lynda Barry (born 1956), daughter of a Filipino mother and an American father, grew up in an interracial neighborhood in Seattle. When she began Evergreen State College Barry "wanted to be a fine artist." "Cartoons to me were really base." Then she realized that her drawings could make her friends laugh, and shortly after she graduated, in 1978, she created

"Ernie Pook's Comeek," a wry, witty, and feminist strip now syndicated in over sixty newspapers in the United States, Canada, Russia, and Hungary. Barry's eighth comic collection is *It's So Magic* (1994); her second novel is *Cruddy* (1998). *One! Hundred! Demons!*, her autobiography in graphic novel format, was published in 2003 and followed by *What It Is* in 2008.

"Common Scents" (from *One! Hundred! Demons!*) illustrates what Barry told an interviewer, "There was always a lot of commotion in the house, mostly in the kitchen. We didn't have a set dinner or lunch or breakfast time; when we wanted to eat there was always food on the stove . . . At the time it was a little frustrating for me, because I looked to all the world like a regular little white American kid, but at home we were eating real different food and there was sometimes octopus in the refrigerator and stuff that was scary looking to my friends... We ate with our hands, and when you say that, people think that you're also squatting on the floor . . . but it wasn't like that. There's a whole etiquette to the way that you eat with your hands, just like you hold a fork. And it was lively and unusual, an atmosphere where I . . . could pretty much do whatever I wanted to do."

Common Scents

1

Lynda Barry, *Common Scents*, copyright © 2002 by Lynda Barry, from "One! Hundred! Demons!" Reprinted courtesy of Darhansoff, Verrill, Feldman Literary Agents. All Rights Reserved.

2

3

I HAVE ALWAYS NOTICED THE SMELL OF OTHER PEOPLE'S HOUSES, BUT WHEN I WAS A KID I WAS FASCINATED BY IT. NO TWO HOUSES EVER SMELLED ALIKE, EVEN IF THE PEOPLE USED THE SAME AIR FRESHENER.
WHAT'S THAT KIND AGAIN?
FRESH EVERGREEN GLEN.
YEAH. AT THE BIDMAN'S THEY GOT THE SAME KIND BUT HERE IT SMELLS LIKE A FRESH, UM, BUS BATHROOM.
SOME OF THE SMELLS WERE UNCOMPLICATED, LIKE THE CAT PEE SMELL OF THE HOUSE NEXT DOOR. THE LADY HAD 14 CATS. IT WAS HARD TO STAY AND VISIT. SHE SOMETIMES BURNED INCENSE WHICH ALSO SMELLED LIKE CAT PEE.
(BREATHING THROUGH MY MOUTH)
HAVE SOME PEANUT BRITTLE, DEAR. JUST PICK THE FUR OFF IF YOU'RE FUSSY, BUT IT WON'T HURT YOU NONE.

4

BUT THERE WERE BAD MYS-
TERIES TOO, LIKE THE MYSTERY
OF THE BLEACH PEOPLE WHOSE
HOUSE GAVE OFF FUMES YOU
COULD SMELL FROM THE STREET.
WE KEPT WAITING FOR THAT
HOUSE TO EXPLODE. THE BUGS
DIDN'T EVEN GO IN THEIR YARD.

ALSO GIVING OFF BLEACH FUMES

HEYA, JANINA.

HEYA.

'N I ASK YOU A PERSONAL THING?

POSSIBLY.

HOW COME YOUR HOUSE SMELLS LIKE THAT?

SMELLS LIKE WHAT?

5

SOME SMELLS WERE MYS-
TERIOUSLY WONDERFUL LIKE
AT THE PALINKI'S WHERE IT WAS
A COMBINATION OF MINT, TAN-
GERINES, AND LIBRARY BOOKS.
BUT HOW? I NEVER SAW ANY
OF THOSE THINGS THERE.

WHAT'S YOUR KIND OF AIR FRESHENER, BECAUSE THAT'S THE KIND I WANT MY MOM TO GET.

I DON'T USE AIR FRESHENER, DEAR.

WELL, THAT'S WEIRD BECAUSE YOUR HOUSE SMELLS PERFECT.

6
OF COURSE THE BIGGEST MYSTERY OF ALL WAS MY OWN HOUSE. I COULDN'T SMELL IT AT ALL. I DIDN'T THINK IT HAD A SMELL, WHICH WAS STRANGE CONSIDERING ALL THAT WENT ON THERE.
JADE EAST AFTER SHAVE
9,000 CIGARETTES
½ A CAN OF ADORNE HAIR SPRAY
N'AKO! MA BUNGO!
ANG SARAP-SARAP! EAT! EAT!
JUNGLE GARDENIA PERFUME
FRIED SMELT, GARLIC, ONIONS.
DOG THAT ROLLS ON THINGS.
7
I PROBABLY HAD THE STRONGEST SMELLING HOUSE IN THE NEIGHBORHOOD EXCEPT FOR THE BLEACH PEOPLE, BUT I HAD NO IDEA WHAT IT SMELLED LIKE TO OTHERS UNTIL I HEARD A COMMENT ABOUT IT.
MY MOM SAYS YOUR PEOPLE FRY WEIRD FOOD AND SAVE THE GREASE AND ALSO THAT YOU BOIL PIG'S BLOOD WHICH IS THE REASON FOR THE SMELL.
WHAT SMELL?

8

THE TRUTH WAS WE DID SAVE OUR GREASE IN A HILLS BROTHERS COFFEE CAN AND YES, MY GRANDMA DID COOK THINGS LIKE PIG'S BLOOD STEW. BOILING AND FRYING WENT ON IN THE HOUSE EVERY DAY.

THAT'S WHY I'M NOT SPOSTA COME OVER, 'CAUSE THE SMELL GETS ON MY CLOTHES, MAKES MY MOM SICK.

9

THE GIRL WHO SHOCKED ME WITH THE NEWS ABOUT THE SMELL OF MY HOUSE WAS THE ONE WHOSE HOUSE SMELLED LIKE THE FRESH BUS BATHROOM. HER MOTHER WAS THE MOST DISINFECTING, AIR FRESHENER SPRAYING PERSON THAT EVER LIVED.

10

SHE HAD THOSE CAR FRESHENER CHRISTMAS TREE THINGS HANGING EVERYWHERE. EVEN THE MARSHMALLOW TREATS SHE MADE HAD A FRESH PINE-SPRAY FLAVOR. SHE WAS FREE WITH HER OBSERVATIONS ABOUT THE SMELL OF OTHERS.

YOUR ORIENTALS HAVE AN ARRAY, WITH YOUR CHINESE SMELLING STRONGER THAN YOUR JAPANESE AND YOUR KOREANS FALLING SOMEWHERES IN THE MIDDLE AND DON'T GET ME STARTED ON YOUR FILIPINOS.

11

SHE DETAILED THE SMELLS OF BLACKS, MEXICANS, ITAL-IANS, SOME PEOPLE I NEVER HEARD OF CALLED "BO-HUNKS" AND THE DIFFERENCE IT MADE IF THEY WERE WET OR DRY, FAT OR SKINNY. NATURALLY I BROUGHT THIS INFORMATION HOME.

AIE N'AKO! WHITE LADIES SMELL BAD TOO, NAMAN! SHE NEVER WASH HER POOKIE! HER KILI-KILI ALWAYS SWEAT-SWEATING! THE OLD ONES SMELL LIKE E-HEE! THAT LADY IS TUNG-AH!

12

MY GRANDMA WAS A PHILO-
SOPHICAL SORT OF PERSON
WHO ALWAYS HAD AN INTER-
ESTING TAKE ON THINGS.
YOU KNOW, MY DARLING, GOD HAS MADE EVERY PEOPLE! AND EVERY PEOPLE MAKES TA-EE! AND EVERY TA-EE SMELLS BAD! ASK THIS LADY DOES PERFUME COME OUT OF HER PUEET? N'AKO, I DON'T THINK SO, DARLING! IT IS NOT GOD'S WAY. YOU TELL HER!

13

THE AIR FRESHENER LADY
MOVED BEFORE I COULD COM-
MUNICATE MY GRANDMOTHER'S
WISDOM TO HER. IT TOOK THE
NEW PEOPLE A YEAR TO
CHASE HER SMELL OUT.
LORD, I HAVE SCRUBBED EVERY FLOOR, WALL AND CEILING AND IT STILL COMES AT ME.
I DON'T SMELL IT.
ACTUALLY IT SMELLS WAY BETTER. ACTUALLY IT SMELLS LIKE BURNT POPCORN AND GREEN KOOL-AID WHICH IS EXCELLENT.

14

I FORGOT ABOUT HER UNTIL I WAS IN BED THE OTHER NIGHT, READING SOME TRUE CRIME STORIES.

WOW. HONEY, LISTEN TO THIS ONE. THIS LADY KILLS HER HUSBAND AND HIDES HIS BODY IN THE ATTIC BUT HE STARTS TO SMELL, RIGHT?

DEAR GOD, NOT AGAIN.

UH HUH.

SO SHE STARTS BUYING THOSE AIR FRESHENERS YOU CAN STICK ON THINGS, YOU KNOW? LIKE, SHE BUYS TONS OF THEM

UH-HUH.

15

I STARTED THINKING ABOUT MY OLD NEIGHBOR. I DON'T THINK SHE HAD A BODY IN HER ATTIC BUT THERE WAS SOMETHING SHE WAS TRYING TO SPRAY AWAY. SHE SAW SMELLY DEVILS EVERYWHERE.

I MEAN, SHE WAS OBSESSED, YOU KNOW?

YES, PEOPLE WHO GIVE THEMSELVES TO THE AIR FRESHENER GODS HAVE DARK SECRETS INDEED. THEY ARE AMONG THE DAMNED.

ZZZZZZZZ

WILL HAVE NO MEMORY OF SAYING THIS IN THE MORNING.

16

17

I'VE NEVER HEARD A SINGLE PERSON EVER SAY THEY LOVED THE SMELL OF AIR FRESHENER AND YET THERE ARE SO MANY PEOPLE WHO FILL THEIR HOMES WITH IT.
PLUG-INS
DANGLERS
POP UPS
STICK ONS
LIGHT BULB SCENT RINGS
POTPOURRI MIXES
SPRAYS
AIR WICKS
SCENTED CANDLE NIGHTMARE
CAT PEE INCENSE
WHEN COMBINED WITH NATURAL BUT POWER-FILLED SMELLS, THE RESULTS CAN BE TRAUMATIC.
CHERRY POP-UP FRIED LIVER
VANILLA-SPICE DIAPER PAIL
STRAWBERRY-DREAMSCAPE PLUG-IN FRIED FLOUNDER
TROPICAL PASSION AROMA THERAPY CAT BOX
PINEY WOODS PIG'S BLOOD STEW BREAKDOWN

18

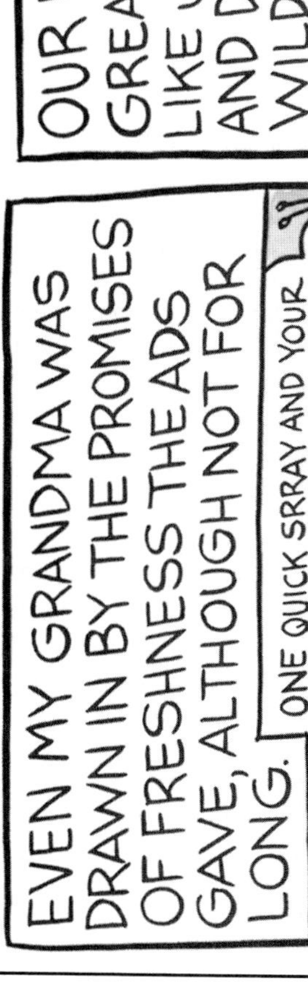
EVEN MY GRANDMA WAS DRAWN IN BY THE PROMISES OF FRESHNESS THE ADS GAVE, ALTHOUGH NOT FOR LONG.

ONE QUICK SRRAY AND YOUR HOUSE IS SPRINGTIME FRESH!
AIE NAKO, LADY. I TRIED IT. IT SMELLS WORSE THAN THE PUEET OF A VAMPIRE!
YOU'LL NEVER WORRY ABOUT FRYING FISH AGAIN!
IF I HAVE FISH, I AM NOT WORRIED! I AM THANKING GOD!

19

OUR HOUSE SMELLED LIKE GREASE AND FISH AND CIGS, LIKE JADE EAST AND PORK AND DOGS, LIKE ALL THE WILD FOOD MY GRANDMA BOILED AND FRIED. AND IF THEY COULD GET THAT INTO A SPRAY CAN, I'D BUY IT.
N'AKO, LYNDA! THIS DURAN FRUITS SMELLS SO BADLY BUT TASTE SO GOODLY! YOU TRY IT! GOD MADE IT! MY GOLLY! EAT! EAT!

Content

1. Good works of visual art, like good essays or stories, stand up to careful rereading; they can't be entirely taken in or understood at a single glance. Skim "Common Scents" and then go back and review it carefully. What topics and meanings come into sharp focus on the second reading?

2. Explain the meaning of the caption of panel 7: "I probably had the strongest-smelling house in the neighborhood except for the bleach people, but I had no idea what it smelled like to others until I heard a comment about it." Can you identify some of the more exotic smells, such as "pigs blood stew" (panel 8) and duran (panel 19)?

Strategies/Structures/Language

3. None of Barry's characters look very attractive—in fact, by some criteria they'd be considered ugly. In what respects are they sympathetic or unsympathetic—just as characters are in a totally verbal story? In what ways does their appearance reinforce Barry's point?

4. What latitude does Barry have in using drawings with dialogue that she wouldn't have if the story were told entirely in writing?

For Writing/Drawing

5. If you're artistically inclined, tell a story that presents a social commentary through a series of six to eight pictures (or more, if you get carried away) with captions that reinforce the pictures and perhaps explain them. If your artistic abilities are limited, either work with a partner who can draw or use someone else's cartoons or drawings and substitute your own captions. In either case, write an analysis of what you've done, and why, to show how the illustrations and the text reinforce one another.

6. "Common Scents" obliges readers to think about smells—of people (and ethnic stereotypes of their smells), of food, of environments: "[The air freshener lady] detailed the smells of blacks, Mexicans, Italians . . . 'bo-hunks' and the difference it made if they were wet or dry, fat or skinny" (panel 11)—and to examine their prejudices concerning these smells. In fact, American culture in general may be prejudiced against most odors, given the fact that in the United States many people try to remove all odors except those of some flowers and some foods. Explain why this is so. In what ways have Barry's drawings raised your critical awareness of this practice? Would a national culture with a greater range and variety of acceptable smells be preferable?

7. ***Journal Writing.*** When you were growing up, how was your family different from your friends' families? Explore the ways in which you found your friends' homes and families attractive, strange, or uncomfortable. As in question 5, use your own or someone else's drawings to illustrate your memories and perceptions.

8. ***Dialogues.*** Write a paper in which you analyze and compare Barry's "Common Scents" or another cartoon sequence with a social point, such as Art Spiegelman's "Mein Kampf" (96–97), another sequence by Spiegelman, or one of Garry Trudeau's *Doonesbury* comic strips (533).

CHRISTOPHER LaCASSE

Christopher LaCasse earned from the University of Connecticut BAs in English and Education, and a MA in Education. For six years he was a member of the Connecticut Army National Guard, and as a Staff Sergeant in the Engineer Corps he was removed from college in mid-semester and sent to Iraq for a year's tour of duty 2003–04. While in Ar Ramadi, in the milieu of war, he began work on the memoir from which "Hegemony" eventually evolved, written over time to gain distance and perspective on both the war and his writing style. Back in school after his return from Iraq, LaCasse also completed his last two years in the National Guard, listening to his fellow soldiers telling and retelling stories; trying to make sense of what had come to pass; and learning to write narrative in the first person, with many voices, perspectives, memories in play as the narrative develops. He is currently working on a MA in English at the University of Delaware. As a soldier and an engineer, LaCasse writes with great ambivalence about working with the Iraqi people, juxtaposed against a devastated landscape.

✧ *Hegemony*

"Don'll be the SAW [Squad Automatic Weapon—a light machine gun] gunner because Brian's feet are too swollen from those bites—the sand fleas got him good. He can't even put on his boots," James tells us this as he settles into the front seat. He clips the radio handmic to the chin strap of his helmet and pushes the engine start button. The truck shivers to a start; it clears its throat, coughing exhaust from its stack, and settles. Jeff nods from the ring-mount where he swivels around—the sun reflects off his shades. Don and I take up positions on each side of the truck behind a wall of sandbags and plate steel. "When we get there," James turns around in the seat—he peers through the back of the cab window, "Sanders will take care of the mail." He refers to Staff Sergeant Sanders, the convoy NCOIC [non-commissioned officer in charge], who was given a name and a building number—his task is to seek out this specific point of contact in order to sort out the mail situation. Since our unit was moved to Al Asad Airbase, our mail has been shipped elsewhere—Balad, and soldiers grow restless waiting to read the first letters sent from home—voices of families and loved ones amidst epistolary scribbling. 1

Winds whistle over the edges of the truck as we move along. As I listen to the rushing winds, I wonder if Sanders will stumble upon a bag of mail waiting to be shipped to Balad. I imagine a few letters sent by friends and family—at least one sent by her. I wonder if the words will be of the same girl who wore khaki shorts that nipped her butt, who led me, barefoot, between cliff and shattered waves, to a nook on Watch Hill. I remember 2 the waves, crashing on the edges of the rock face, and how the breakers sounded like an explosion while the brewing storm stirred the winds to a fierce howl. The girl, who confided all—her voice growing gentle, just above a whisper, as she sat on the cooling sands with granules running between her toes. She spoke secrets to the salt night. I carried her through tall dune grass, piggyback along a path with her warm breath behind my ear, confessing fears of snakes and the future. The waves washed up and white dissolving suds recoiled back, fleeing to the sea behind us.

3 We drive and drive; racing the sun; four gun-trucks bury needles, engines whining to their highest pitch—we careen against the setting sun, and James, like a mad man howling over the engine, jerks the wheel hard right: an explosion, a sharp pop, a local truck whizzing by in the opposite direction; in a blur, horns blaring and trailing away; "What the—" another cuss lost on the wind behind us, and Don, who ducked and turned his face away from the shattering glass, now fixes his barrel and follows the truck until his weapon points to the rear; the local truck vanishes in the distance. The mirror, in shards along the road, twinkles as we pull away.

4 "He was in the middle of the road," James shouts behind his seat through the small window of the cab. His eyes, blue and hysterical, glare for a moment before whipping back around. Jeff swivels on the ring-mount looking angry. I imagine he was jostled pretty hard up there. Don, digging into the sandbag wall, shakes his head. We hurtle toward Baghdad International Air Port, a race against nightfall.

5 We meet the HETs [Heavy Equipment Transport—a tractor trailer truck designed to carry M1 Abrams tanks] in a remote holding area. Sanders's humvee speeds off. When he returns to us an hour later, he has no bag of letters to offer. "Somewhere" is where we stand now—the out-of-the-way side of the airport, this open plain where overgrowth has concealed old tarmac—airstrips that are hidden in tall grass like forgotten ghost towns, and stretching far and wide above, the vast skyline allows the setting sun to fall for what seems forever—we watch the slow bulb descend with nothing else around. We watch colors of the sun. They bleed oranges across the horizon—along the tops of palms and distant buildings. These colors join the graying sky, holding for minutes, before darkening to night.

6 The HET drivers appear to have settled after a long day's drive. Some of the drivers, bootless and stripped down to brown tees, are sprawled around a make-shift camp site. Several find sleep already. They stretch out across various areas of their trucks: cots appear on truck rooftops, along tractor trailer beds, or some soldiers settle in the cab itself to avoid the sand fleas. Around a little campfire of burning garbage, they chat in melodious southern tongues—shouting jests in accents almost indecipherable. Those who remain by the fire draw attention to one buddy who strolls out into the field with a roll of toilet paper and an E-tool [entrenching tool].

Night deepens, and we toss on our cots to the moans of a woman 7 somewhere in the city. She bellows in Arabic. Our thoughts mingle with the solemnity of her utterances, entering the sacrosanct nature of her pain. Her sobs are met on the night air by nothing—nothing muffles her cries that carry for miles; her wailing pierces our sleep.

We wake early to our hands splashing cold water on our faces, 8 automatic, routine. We shave, leaning against a humvee hood, taking turns using the vehicle's mirror. A tin shaving cup vibrates on the hood. The cup is left on the hood, and someone's black stubble lines the edges as the used shaving water appears creamy like milk. We snack on MREs and check our gear while engines of tractor trailer trucks begin to emerge in unison. As the HETs lumber out behind Sanders's lead humvee, we wait our turn, counting these oversized trucks before slipping into the middle of the convoy. The trucks weave between the last bastion-barriers exiting the post's north entrance, turning slowly across both lanes while Sanders's humvee blocks traffic: the entire convoy enters the congested urban area of Baghdad known as the flea market where hundreds of Iraqis swarm the streets, on foot or in car, walking or weaving, skirting between traffic. We creep through the city as locals blast their horns—their cars leap broken curbs, flying down the sidewalk, across dirt front lawns—cars hustle past the traffic jam with determined anarchy. Children buzz around a front porch like a swarm of hornets. The men squat, wearing the long white or gray dishdasha—they watch their children, staring at us—expressionless. Through sunglasses, we return their deadpan gaze.

I think back to the professor who stood in front of the class firing 9 out theory. A single word comes to mind as I look out over the impossible numbers of people—people who tramp through the streets to the strident rhythms of any city, and as they sit on their stoops without job or income, I think of this one word: hegemony.

Across the street, children skim rocks and tiptoe at the edges of a 10 pond. The urban pond, stretching along roadside in an empty lot, is fed by a broken water main. I imagine this ruptured pipeline was created by HE [high explosive] impacts while only the ruins of a building lie nearby. Little ones continue to slosh knee deep in the dark puddles, and some are pulled away kicking—kicking and squirming as we pull away, nearing the most active section of the flea market. Our trucks slow to a stop, and men, crossing the street, slide between our bumpers, strolling before our iron sights, seemingly oblivious to our muzzles. These men walk to greet locals who sell goods from thatch shelves, chanting—canticles of salesmen rising up above thatched huts to a panoramic backdrop of buildings: some left in debris—some, where roofs slope inward, suggest structural damage, as if earthquakes shook loose the foundations. Other lots are completely cleared but for leftover mortar brick and rebar that litters the ground.

11 "I don't like this," Don mutters. "Why aren't we moving? LaCasse, why aren't we moving? This is ridiculous," his voice, rising to a yell, is met by the incessant honking of horns. "We're sitting ducks here. Sergeant James, what's going on up there?" With the length of the thirty-two HETs, we are spread across what seems a mile of urban jungle. The streets are festering with suspicious eyes. Our eyes scan roofs, windows, alleyways, crowds. Cars scramble off the road to our right and coast by tossing clouds of dirt from their passing tires. Like the initial drops of a rain, we hear something tapping the steel-plated sides of our truck. A storm of pebbles begins dinging the truck: crowds of little children charge, pitch stones, and return to the corner of the house to regroup, reload, and charge again. Above my head, Jeff cusses, dodging a stone. He cusses down at the children from his ring-mount. A baseball-size rock clangs against the steel below Don in a rich baritone song.

12 "Did you see that?" Jeff yells. "Did you see who threw that, LaCasse—keep an eye on those trucks and cars approaching from the rear." I watch throngs of children rush toward the road. They launch their rocks. As one child throws and bends down for another, two or three more pass by his sides; they step closer and sling handfuls of dirt up at me. My eyes meet the eyes of a child; he lingers by the porch, steps closer to his father. All happens at once—the simultaneity of time: James fidgets in the front seat. He presses the handmic under his Kevlar—yells from the front seat, but we don't hear him, though his gestures appear frantic. Don turns and looks to me, puts a finger to his ear and shrugs. I motion that I don't understand what James is yelling. I shrug. Jeff dips his head into the cab from the ring-mount. The world seems to slow and speed at once—primordial perhaps (something not right) something uncanny sneaks into our minds. A look, a gesture, a fulgurating flicker in James's eyes. Before Jeff can pop back up from the cab and relay the message, James shouts louder. He turns in the seat, the radio cord, hung from the helmet, wraps around his chest.

13 "Shots fired—Shots fired." The child, stone in hand, cocked back and ready to fire; his knuckles white with a tight grip. Our eyes, caught for a moment, the stone, slackening in his hand. Other children—swimming around him, their chants a maddening blur: a dream sequence—a mob scene. Jeff, spinning, turning: the big gun tilted toward the crowd. Don, cussing—his face red with cussing. The sun, spilling from above, catching passing windshields of cars zipping by our blindside. Faces everywhere. Faces in the crowd and eyes from above on rooftops and in windows. Alleyways of eyes and expressionless faces—buildings with blacked out windows—vacant stares: watching everything; watching us. "Shots fired."—James, screaming to us before turning his attention out the window.

14 "What are we doing here? Why aren't we moving?"

"Watch those men behind that car. Watch those by the building 15
corner."

"Where are you scanning?" 16

"Everywhere." 17

"Watch the rear—cars approaching on our rear." 18

"Watch out for those rocks. Watch out for those little—"cussing. 19

I watch the children, hurried by a man, scurrying away. James turns 20
twisting his body in the seat to yell out the back window. "Shots fired on the right—the right side"—*my side.* "It was on *your* side—up ahead at one of the HETs," James shouts. "But watch both sides." My left hand leaves the hand guard and gropes for the AT4 [anti-tank, single shot weapon]. The two anti-tank weapons are bound loosely with bungee cords against the back of the cab. I prop my foot on the ammunition can. Within the can there are four fragmentation grenades and a few flares of different colors. I can almost feel the tightly packed explosives jostle in the tin can below my boot. I glance up at Jeff, lonely in the ring-mount, hands clenching the MK19 automatic grenade launcher, which fires sixty 40mm rounds per minute. I consider the amount of fire power we possess and the continuous surge of bodies through the streets. Jeff spins; his big gun like a carnival ride, searches the masses; sun spills over his glasses, and James turns again.

"Two gunmen in the alley . . . behind a blue and white pickup truck 21
with mattresses in the back . . ." *Bizarre*: gunmen behind mattresses. The handmic is pressed to James's ear. "They're aiming at the MK19," he tells us, spitting out expletives between words. For a moment in the sun—the glittering across Jeff's sunglasses—a beautiful light. The fat swinging barrel of his cannon. A crowd, a countless crowd—swarming and passing between our bumpers. Don, hunkering down, quieter now, his machine-gun trained on the crowd. Shouting. A car horn in one long shill. "LaCasse, right side, watch it." Cars tumbling past our blindside. "Watching it?" Shouts. Arabic and babble, everywhere. *Yella Yella*—let's go. Another car; dusting my sector. My foot, stepping over a sandbag, an uncapped water bottle chugging out its contents upon the truck bed—like suds, spilled on a beach, sliding up the shores and thinning out—it dissolves.

"LaCasse?" 22

"I know—got it." I realize nakedness—pure vulnerability: exposure 23
to a great wide open—to a thousand eyes burning holes in my back. An understanding descends. I examine the crowds, rooftops, alleyways, and cars speeding up from behind. A calm acceptance: the entire back half of the truck is open with no sandbags—no steel. I understand rooftop-vantage points—we're all easy targets. Even the steel and sandbags wouldn't do much against an RPG [rocket propelled grenade] or a decent sniper. Standing just below Jeff, I wonder when the gunmen will finally pull the trigger. Time stills herself. I wonder if James is thinking of his two sons—his wife. I can sense Don behind me, his face reddened by the

sun—by his high blood pressure, searching for the two gunmen concealed in the crowd. They'll surely slip away in the mass of bodies.

24 "This is over-the-top." The term strikes me. "Over-the-top" was an infantryman's most feared command echoed down the trenches. Officers would call out "over-the-top," and grunts would pull themselves up, over the parapets, over the barbed wire—charging across the kill zone with eyes trained forward—running until flanks fell lifeless to the entrenched and battle-hardened Germans dug in to machinegun pits; the "rat-tat-tat" and crackling of rifles across the plain of "no man's land" would often answer this call.

25 "It's about time," says Don as the city rolls behind us. "Why did we go this way?" he asks Jeff. Jeff's dark tint glasses are unreadable. He seems to shake his head, twice, ever so slightly. I have no idea how long our wait in traffic lasted; I forgot to check my watch. Onto the highway, and with the open desert at our sides, we move in silence. The faces of Don and Jeff seem emotionless—they stare off on the horizon without a word. The city has passed behind us, allowing villages to spring up when the desert is met by the river. We reach one village and this village passes, letting the great empty desert rejoin the roadsides. We pass the town of Hit and notice tons of steel rusting away. D7 and D8 high-track dozers cluster in the sandy lots. Their color is rust as tracks are twisted in great heaps. Some machines are left without ROPs [Rollover Protection]. These beasts continue stiffening with time, marking yet another signpost of the economic lull. Jeff spins around for a moment. He gazes at what passes behind us.

26 "Did I earn my combat patch?" He laughs to himself for a minute. Women, alone in the fields, without men beside them, are garbed from head to toe in black; they kneel in the green fields. I think I see a child stand up from the tall grass near the field's edge. The child appears to have sprouted up like a wild flower or perhaps a weed. Jeff, with his back to the road ahead, continues watching the scenes that fall behind our passing wheels. He pushes sunglasses up the bridge of his nose and then swings forward. We are left with only the sound of the wind rushing over the truck.

Content

1. What are the four soldiers' initial objectives (¶s 1–5)? Which objectives does LaCasse explicitly state and which are implied? Why does LaCasse leave the girl he remembers unnamed (¶ 2)?
2. Based on LaCasse's descriptions of the camp's sleeping and hygiene arrangements, the night air and landscape, and the soldiers' daily routine, how would you characterize his perception of the American involvement in Iraq (¶s 6–8)?
3. How does LaCasse characterize the residents of Baghdad (¶ 8–10)? Why does "the flea market" (¶ 8) remind him of the word "hegemony" (¶ 9)?

4. In what sense are the children a threat to the convoy (¶s 11–13)? What do LaCasse's descriptions of the children, crowds, and buildings suggest about the nature and difficulty of the Americans soldiers' mission? How do the well-armed Americans soldiers become so vulnerable (¶s 20–23)?

Strategies/Structures/Language

5. LaCasse uses several common—almost clichéd—expressions, including "sitting ducks" (¶ 11), "shots fired" (¶ 13), "easy targets" (¶ 23), and "rat-tat-tat" (¶ 24). How do these phrases help orient the reader in an unfamiliar environment? What kind of response do they elicit from the reader? How do they set up a contrast with the Arabic phrase "Yella Yella" (¶ 21)?

6. How do LaCasse's references to wind, sea, waves, beach, and sand provide a thread that runs through the text? How do they suggest both familiarity and strangeness, present and past, safety and danger?

7. Why doesn't LaCasse tells us more about his fellow soldiers' appearances and backgrounds? Why doesn't he describe the child whose eyes lock with his own (¶ 13) or the child he spots in the field (¶ 26)? How do his spare descriptions help define his experience?

For Writing

8. ***Journal Writing.*** Does your reading of LaCasse's narrative or of other soldiers' stories have an impact on your political beliefs or your perceptions of American foreign policy? If you have family or friends who have served in Iraq or Afghanistan, or in another conflict, describe how their experiences have helped to shape your understanding of that conflict. Can civilians ever understand the soldier's experience? Can soldiers ever allow themselves the luxury of a political stance?

9. ***Dialogues.*** Tim O'Brien writes in "How to Tell a True War Story" (77–84), "Send guys to war, they come home talking dirty" (¶ 9). How does LaCasse convey what O'Brien calls the "obscenity" of war (¶ 9)? Does LaCasse's view of the concept of "hegemony" apply to O'Brien's description of the American involvement in Vietnam?

10. ***Mixed Modes.*** LaCasse's descriptions of the heavily armed American soldiers highlight their vulnerability rather than their invincibility. Write an essay in which you describe the complexities of a particular and specific power struggle. What are the inherent weaknesses and vulnerabilities of the apparently more powerful party? How does the weaker party gain strength from his or her position? Use, if you like, Frederick Douglass's "Resurrection" (89–93), Ning Yu's "Red and Black" (166–74), or Natalie Angier's "Why Men Don't Last" (302–05) for inspiration or ideas. Describe each party's position with concrete details and the step-by-step process through the dynamics of the relationship shift.

Additional Topics for Writing Definition

(For strategies for writing definition, see 345.)

Multiple Strategies for Writing: Definition

Definition is an essential component of many kinds of writing; it is often necessary to define terms, components, or concepts as the basis for explaining something or conducting an argument. Conversely, you may employ a variety of other strategies in writing definitions:

- *illustrations* and *examples*, to show the meaning of the entire term or its components, and to interpret them
- *photographs, drawings, diagrams, maps* as alternatives to "a thousand words"
- a *time sequence*, to show the formation or consequences of a particular term
- *explanations* and *analyses* of the term
- *comparison* and *contrast; division* and *classification*, to illustrate the parts of the whole
- a *narrative*, on occasion, to allow the meaning of the term to emerge gradually as the tale unfolds
- *negation*—what a term isn't

1. Write or draw (as Barry does, 376–85) an extended definition of one or more of the following trends, concepts, abstractions, phenomena, or institutions. Be sure to identify your audience, limit your subject, and illustrate your essay with specific examples.

   a. Peace (see "World Peace," Chapter 13)
   b. War (see O'Brien, 76–84; LaCasse, 387–92)
   c. Intelligence (see Gardner, 351–61)
   d. Ethics, or an ethical issue (Reich, 490–98; Singer, 535–41)
   e. Personality or character
   f. Physical fitness (see Nestle, 270–79; Hockenberry, 365–71)
   g. Optimism or depression (economic or psychological)
   h. The nature of friendship or love (see Doyle, 372–74)
   i. Marriage (either, the ideal marriage, or the ideal versus the reality)
   j. Parenthood (see Sanders, 192–203; Rodriguez, 321–28)
   k. Education—formal or informal (see Fadiman, 102–05; Zitkala-Sa, 184–59; Turkle, 411–17; Sedaris, 318–20)
   l. Public service
   m. A good job or profession; work; or a very bad job (see Nocton, 286–90; Benedetto, 436–38)
   n. An ecological issue (see Diamond, 472–83; Gore, 618–20; photo insert)

o. A scientific or technical phenomenon of your choice (an eclipse, the "big bang" theory of creation, genetic engineering, DNA, the MX missile) (see McKibben, 572–82)
p. A sport, game, hobby, or recreational activity (see Verge, 107–11)

2. Explain a particular value system or belief system, such as the following:

a. Democracy, communism, socialism, or some other political theory or form of government
b. Protestantism (or a particular sect), Catholicism, Judaism (or a particular branch—Orthodox, Conservative, Reform), Buddhism (or a particular sort), Islam, or some other religion
c. A theoretical system and some of its major ramifications (feminism, Marxism, postcolonialism, Freudianism, postmodernism)

3. Prepare a dictionary of fifteen jargon or slang words used in your academic major, in your hobby, or in some other activity you enjoy, such as playing a particular sport or game, listening to a specific type of music, or working on a computer system.

Comparison and Contrast

Writers compare people, places, things, or qualities to identify their similarities, and contrast them to identify the differences. What you say about one subject usually helps to illuminate or explain the other, as we understand very well when trying to decide which college to attend, whom to hang out with (or avoid), whether (or not) to buy a car, and if so, what kind. Such explanations have the added advantage of answering questions that hinge on the similarities and differences under consideration. Your commentary can also provide the basis for judging the relative merits and demerits of the subject at hand.

For instance, comparison and contrast can help you determine whether to choose a liberal arts or technical education, and what your future will be like with whichever you select. It can help you explain the resemblances between the works of Faulkner and Hemingway, and the differences—and to justify your preference for one author over the other. Comparison and contrast can help you decide whom to vote for, what movie to see (or avoid), where to live, whether (and whom) to marry. A thoroughgoing, detailed comparison and contrast of the reasons for the quality of life with and without handguns, public transportation, or conservation of natural resources can provide a convincing argument for your choice.

But not everything will work. The subjects you select should have some obvious qualities in common to make the comparison and contrast fruitful. If you try to compare very dissimilar things, as the Mad Hatter does in *Alice in Wonderland* ("Why is a raven like a writing desk?"), you'll have to stretch for an answer ("Because they both begin with an *r* sound.") that may be either silly or irrelevant. But other comparisons by their very nature can command appropriate contrasts. Roz Chast's perceptive cartoon, "An Excerpt from Men Are from Belgium, Women Are from New Brunswick" (409), details major gender-related differences between the communication styles of men and women. Deborah Tannen's "Communication Styles" (403–07) is based on an extended exploration of differences in the way men and women students behave in the classroom. For instance, Tannen has found that men speak in class more often than women do. They're more at ease in the "public" classroom setting and enjoy the "debate-like form that discussion may take," while women students are "more comfortable speaking in private to a small group of people they know well" in nonconfrontational dialogue. Compare this essay with Elizabeth Tallent's short story

"No One's a Mystery" (400–02), which consists of a dialogue between an older man and a younger woman; as might be expected to make the story compelling, the man has very different views of the relationship delineated than the woman does. This intriguing contrast permits comparisons between the speakers, in addition to possible generalizations about the nature of such relationships, questions that could also be asked of the examples in Tannen's analysis and Chast's cartoon. "Whose side are we on in each?" is a question that provokes still more comparisons and contrasts.

In writing an essay of comparison and contrast you'll need to justify your choice of subject, unless the grounds for comparison are obvious. You'll also have to limit your comparison, for no single essay—or even an entire book—can fully address the possibilities of most subjects. Michael Benedetto's "Home Away from Home" (436–38) makes a number of razor-sharp comparisons between his life—working the night shift at "one of those colossal warehouses that doubled as a hardware store," which required him to be alert and functioning from 10 p.m. to 6 a.m—and the lives of everyone else whose schedules were the reverse, as different as night and day. Some comparisons depend on what occurs at a given time in the lives of day and night workers; the more complex and less easy to tease out are the motives of the night workers—those who are in it for the long haul, and those of Michael himself, who knew that "Once summer was over I could quit."

The basis for the fundamental comparison and contrast in Charles C. Mann's "Forever Young" (422–33) is readily apparent. Because U.S. life expectancy in the past century has increased from forty-seven to seventy-seven, the "orderly succession of generations," from youth to old age, is being and will continue to be overturned as people live longer and longer. This fact enables many comparisons: between the formerly old (47 is no longer old!) and the currently old (but what does that mean—65? 75? 120?). Between the genuinely young (whatever age that means) and the old (whatever age that means). Between affluent elders and impecunious youngsters. Between the wealthy who can afford whatever it costs to stay alive to be old and the less affluent who will die younger and more naturally. Between the more-healthy elderly who can hang onto high-paying jobs and the youth indefinitely suspended in "quasi-adulthood" as "parasitic singles" whose opportunities to lead mature, independent lives are on hold until the old get out of the workforce. And many more issues, susceptible to interpretations that are biological, philosophical, medical, and ethical as well as economic. Or, as Carolita Johnson's cartoon of two babes in bikinis (435) puts it, "I never thought turning eighty would be so much fun!"

There are several common ways to organize an essay of comparison and contrast. Sherry Turkle's "How Computers Change the Way We Think" (411–17) is based on *before-and-after* considerations of how the omnipresence of computers has changed our ways of seeing and knowing the world and "our place in it." Among the changes are today's dramatically different conceptions of privacy, authentic selves, "powerful ideas" versus PowerPoint (which "encourages presentation, not conversation"), and the deleterious effects of rapid word processing on thinking.

Other common patterns become apparent when you examine the ways you might organize your thoughts about buying a new car. Let's say you're making lists that will be the basis of an essay to help you make decisions on type (minivan, pickup, sports car, sedan), make and model, age (new or used), cost, special features (four-wheel drive, built-in CD player), and financing (buy or lease). If you've just begun to think about the subject, you could deal with each issue topic by topic, most usefully in the order listed here: type, make and model, and so on. Or you could deal with each subject as a whole before moving on to the next. If you've already decided on the particular type and price of the car—say, a small used vehicle costing between $8,000 and $10,000— then you might find it more useful to devote one section, say, to the Honda Civic, another to the GEO Prizm, and a third to the Smart Car, considering all features of each car in the same order: size, handling, reliability, fuel economy, safety, sportiness, and final cost. Why the same order for each car? Because you'll confuse yourself and your readers if you follow a different organizational pattern for each car; everyone needs to know where to look in each discussion to find comparable information. Another way to organize the information would be to group all the similarities about the cars in one section and all the differences in another, arranged in order from the most important (to you) to the least. Eventually, you'll summarize your conclusion: "While I like the first car better because it's sportier and more fun to drive, and the second is great on hills and curves, I guess I'm stuck with the third because I know I can get a good deal from my great uncle, who kept it in his garage all winter and never drove it over fifty."

The pattern of comparison and contrast that emerges may depend on how long the paper is; the longer the discussion, the less easy it is for readers to remember what they need to. Try out a sample section on members of your class or writing group and see whether they can understand the points of comparison you're trying to make; if they can't, then try another method of arrangement.

Whatever pattern of comparison and contrast you use, a topic outline can help you to organize such papers, and to make sure you've covered equivalent points for each item in the comparison. However you organize the paper, you don't have to give such equal emphasis to the similarities and to the differences; some may simply be more important than others. But you do have to make your chosen points of comparison relevant. Comparison and contrast is particularly useful as a technique in explanations. You can compare something that readers don't know much about (foreign sports cars) with something that's familiar (family sedans).

As we've seen, essays of comparison and contrast may include other types of writing, particularly description, narration, and analysis. Classification and division often determine the points to be covered in such essays: my actual life versus my ideal life, country living versus city living, life on the East (or West) Coast versus life in the Midwest, middle-class life versus upper-class life. . . . And essays of comparison and contrast themselves become, at times, illustrations or arguments, direct or indirect, overt or more subtle. Long live the differences and the zest they provide.

Strategies for Writing: Comparison and Contrast

1. Will my essay focus on the similarities between two or more things (comparison) or the differences (contrast), or will I be discussing both similarities and differences? Why do I want to make the comparison or contrast? To find, explore, or deny overt or less apparent resemblances among the items? To decide which one of a pair or group is better or preferable? Or to use the comparison or contrast to argue for my preference?
2. Are my readers familiar with one or more of the objects of my comparison? If they are familiar with them all, then can I concentrate on the unique features of my analysis? (If they are familiar with only one item, start with the known before discussing the unknown. If they are unacquainted with everything, for purposes of explanation you might wish to begin with a comparison that focuses on the common elements among the items under discussion.)
3. How global or minute will my comparison be (i.e., do I want to make only a few points of comparison or contrast, or many)? Will my essay make more sense to my readers if I present each subject as a complete unit before discussing the next? Or will the comparison or contrast be more meaningful if I proceed point by point?
4. Have I ruled out trivial and irrelevant comparisons? Does each point have a counterpart that I have treated in an equivalent manner, through comparable analysis or illustration, length, and language?
5. Suppose I like or favor one item of the comparison or contrast over the others. Am I obliged to treat every item equally in language and tone, or can my tone vary to reinforce my interpretation?

ELIZABETH TALLENT

Elizabeth Tallent (born in Washington, D.C., in 1954) grew up in the Midwest and majored in anthropology at Illinois State University (BA, 1975). Her first volume of stories, *In Constant Flight* (1983), centered on characters alienated from each other and detached from their own lives, while her novels *Museum Pieces* (1985), *Time with Children* (1987), and *Honey* (1993) unflinchingly examined couples, marriage, children, and houses. Tallent's fiction appears regularly in periodicals such as *Granta* and the *New Yorker*, and anthologies such as *Best American Short Stories*. She has also published a critical study, *Married Men and Magic Tricks: John Updike's Erotic Heroes* (1982). Her academic career includes teaching positions at the University of California at Irvine, the Iowa Writers Workshop, and the University of California, Davis. Currently, she is a professor at Stanford University, where she also served as Director of Creative Writing from 1994 to 1996. "No One's a Mystery," from *Time with Children*, describes a close encounter between an adulterous couple and the husband's wife. With a bit of dialogue and a few images, smells, and sounds, the characters, situation, past, present, and future spring into view. Like any good short story, "No One's a Mystery" rewards rereading. What do you notice upon your second or third reading that previously escaped your attention?

No One's a Mystery

1 For my eighteenth birthday Jack gave me a five-year diary with a latch and a little key, light as a dime. I was sitting beside him scratching at the lock, which didn't seem to want to work, when he thought he saw his wife's Cadillac in the distance, coming toward us. He pushed me down onto the dirty floor of the pickup and kept one hand on my head while I inhaled the musk of his cigarettes in the dashboard ashtray and sang along with Rosanne Cash on the tape deck. We'd been drinking tequila and the bottle was between his legs, resting up against his crotch, where the seam of his Levi's was bleached linen-white, though the Levi's were nearly new. I don't know why his Levi's always bleached like that, along the seams and at the knees. In a curve of cloth his zipper glinted, gold.

2 "It's her," he said. "She keeps the lights on in the daytime. I can't think of a single habit in a woman that irritates me more than that." When he saw that I was going to stay still he took his hand from my head and ran it through his own dark hair.

3 "Why does she?" I said.

4 "She thinks it's safer. Why does she need to be safer? She's driving exactly fifty-five miles an hour. She believes in those signs: 'Speed Monitored by Aircraft.' It doesn't matter that you can look up and see that the sky is empty."

5 "She'll see your lips move, Jack. She'll know you're talking to someone."

6 "She'll think I'm singing along with the radio."

7 He didn't lift his hand, just raised the fingers in salute while the pressure of his palm steadied the wheel, and I heard the Cadillac honk twice, musically; he was driving easily eighty miles an hour. I studied his boots. The elk heads stitched into the leather were bearded with frayed thread, the toes were scuffed, and there was a compact wedge of muddy manure between the heel and the sole—the same boots he'd been wearing for the two years I'd known him. On the tape deck Rosanne Cash sang, "Nobody's into me, no one's a mystery."

8 "Do you think she's getting famous because of who her daddy is or for herself?" Jack said.

9 "There are about a hundred pop tops on the floor, did you know that? Some little kid could cut a bare foot on one of these, Jack."

10 "No little kids get into this truck except for you."

11 "How come you let it get so dirty?"

12 "'How come,'" he mocked. "You even sound like a kid. You can get back into the seat now, if you want. She's not going to look over her shoulder and see you."

13 "How do you know?"

14 "I just know," he said. "Like I know I'm going to get meat loaf for supper. It's in the air. Like I know what you'll be writing in that diary."

15 "What will I be writing?" I knelt on my side of the seat and craned around to look at the butterfly of dust printed on my jeans. Outside the window Wyoming was dazzling in the heat. The wheat was fawn and yellow and parted smoothly by the thin dirt road. I could smell the water in the irrigation ditches hidden in the wheat.

16 "Tonight you'll write, 'I love Jack. This is my birthday present from him. I can't imagine anybody loving anybody more than I love Jack.'"

17 "I can't."

18 "In a year you'll write, 'I wonder what I ever really saw in Jack. I wonder why I spent so many days just riding around in his pickup. It's true he taught me something about sex. It's true there wasn't ever much else to do in Cheyenne.'"

19 "I won't write that."

20 "In two years you'll write, 'I wonder what that old guy's name was, the one with the curly hair and the filthy dirty pickup truck and time on his hands.'"

21 "I won't write that."

22 "No?"

23 "Tonight I'll write, 'I love Jack. This is my birthday present from him. I can't imagine anybody loving anybody more than I love Jack.'"

24 "No, you can't," he said. "You can't imagine it."

25 "In a year I'll write, 'Jack should be home any minute now. The table's set—my grandmother's linen and her old silver and the yellow candles left over from the wedding—but I don't know if I can wait until after the trout à la Navarra to make love to him.'"

26 "It must have been a fast divorce."

27 "In two years I'll write, 'Jack should be home by now. Little Jack is hungry for his supper. He said his first word today besides "Mama" and "Papa." He said "kaka."' "

28 Jack laughed. "He was probably trying to finger-paint with kaka on the bathroom wall when you heard him say it."

29 "In three years I'll write, 'My nipples are a little sore from nursing Eliza Rosamund.' "

30 "Rosamund. Every little girl should have a middle name she hates."

31 " 'Her breath smells like vanilla and her eyes are just Jack's color of blue.' "

32 "That's nice," Jack said.

33 "So, which one do you like?"

34 "I like yours," he said. "But I believe mine."

35 "It doesn't matter. I believe mine."

36 "Not in your heart of hearts, you don't."

37 "You're wrong."

38 "I'm not wrong," he said. "And her breath would smell like your milk, and it's kind of a bittersweet smell, if you want to know the truth."

Content

1. How many things can you infer from the slice of life Tallent offers you? Use your knowledge of people, relationships, and the information Tallent provides to sum up everything she conveys about the characters and situation *without having to tell you directly.*
2. Is this story mainly about differences or similarities? Certainly the age difference between the two characters is a major issue, yet there may be other contrasts operating as well. Can you draw out any differences in personality, temperament, or values? Is gender a factor? From another point of view, what do Jack and the narrator have in common? Do they share any attitudes toward life?
3. Whose view of the future are you likely to believe? What evidence in the story corroborates your prediction?

DEBORAH TANNEN

For biographical information, see 307.

Much of Deborah Tannen's research, like her writing, is based on comparative analyses of the contrasting behavior of men and women in a variety of situations. "Communication Styles" was originally published as "Teachers' Classroom Strategies Should Recognize that Men and Women Use Language Differently" in the *Chronicle of Higher Education* (June 19, 1991). Here Tannen explores differences in the ways that men and women students interact, and how the size, informality, and composition of the group influences who speaks up and who remains silent.

Communication Styles

When I researched and wrote my book, *You Just Don't Understand: Women and Men in Conversation*, the furthest thing from my mind was reevaluating my teaching strategies. But that has been one of the direct benefits of having written the book. 1

The primary focus of my linguistic research always has been the language of everyday conversation. One facet of this is conversational style: how different regional, ethnic, and class backgrounds, as well as age and gender, result in different ways of using language to communicate. *You Just Don't Understand* is about the conversational styles of women and men. As I gained more insight into typically male and female ways of using language, I began to suspect some of the causes of the troubling facts that women who go to single-sex schools do better in later life, and that when young women sit next to young men in classrooms, the males talk more. This is not to say that all men talk in class, nor that no women do. It is simply that a greater percentage of discussion time is taken by men's voices. 2

The research of sociologists and anthropologists such as Janet Lever, Marjorie Harness Goodwin, and Donna Eder has shown that girls and boys learn to use language differently in their sex-separate peer groups. Typically, a girl has a best friend with whom she sits and talks, frequently telling secrets. It's the telling of secrets, the fact and the way that they talk to each other, that makes them best friends. For boys, activities are central: Their best friends are the ones they do things with. Boys also tend to play in larger groups that are hierarchical. High-status boys give orders and push low-status boys around. So boys are expected to use language to seize center stage: by exhibiting their skills, displaying their knowledge, and challenging and resisting challenges. 3

These patterns have stunning implications for classroom interaction. Most faculty members assume that participating in class discussion is a necessary part of successful performance. Yet speaking in a classroom is more congenial to boys' language experience than to girls', since it entails putting oneself forward in front of a large group of people, many of whom are strangers and at least one of whom is sure to judge speakers' knowledge and intelligence by their verbal display. 4

Another aspect of many classrooms that makes them more hospitable to most men than to most women is the use of debate-like formats as a learning tool. Our educational system, as Walter Ong argues persuasively in his book *Fighting for Life* (Cornell University Press, 1981), is fundamentally male in that the pursuit of knowledge is believed to be achieved by ritual opposition: public display followed by argument and challenge. Father Ong demonstrates that ritual opposition—what he calls "adversativeness" or "agonism"—is fundamental to the way most males 5 approach almost any activity. (Consider, for example, the little boy who shows he likes a little girl by pulling her braids and shoving her.) But ritual opposition is antithetical to the way most females learn and like to interact. It is not that females don't fight, but that they don't fight for fun. They don't *ritualize* opposition.

6 Anthropologists working in widely disparate parts of the world have found contrasting verbal rituals for women and men. Women in completely unrelated cultures (for example, Greece and Bali) engage in ritual laments: spontaneously produced rhyming couplets that express their pain, for example, over the loss of loved ones. Men do not take part in laments. They have their own, very different verbal ritual: a contest, a war of words in which they vie with each other to devise clever insults.

7 When discussing these phenomena with a colleague, I commented that I see these two styles in American conversation: Many women bond by talking about troubles, and many men bond by exchanging playful insults and put-downs, and other sorts of verbal sparring. He exclaimed: "I never thought of this, but that's the way I teach: I have students read an article, and then I invite them to tear it apart. After we've torn it to shreds, we talk about how to build a better model."

8 This contrasts sharply with the way I teach: I open the discussion of readings by asking, "What did you find useful in this? What can we use in our own theory building and our own methods?" I note what I see as weaknesses in the author's approach, but I also point out that the writer's discipline and purposes might be different from ours. Finally, I offer personal anecdotes illustrating the phenomena under discussion and praise students' anecdotes as well as their critical acumen.

9 These different teaching styles must make our classrooms wildly different places and hospitable to different students. Male students are more likely to be comfortable attacking the readings and might find the inclusion of personal anecdotes irrelevant and "soft." Women are more likely to resist discussion they perceive as hostile, and, indeed, it is women in my classes who are most likely to offer personal anecdotes.

10 A colleague who read my book commented that he had always taken for granted that the best way to deal with students' comments is to challenge them; this, he felt it was self-evident, sharpens their minds and helps them develop debating skills. But he had noticed that women were relatively silent in his classes, so he decided to try beginning discussion with relatively open-ended questions and letting comments go unchallenged. He found, to his amazement and satisfaction, that more women began to speak up.

11 Though some women in his class clearly liked this better, perhaps some of the men liked it less. One young man in my class wrote in a questionnaire about a history professor who gave students questions to think about and called on people to answer them: "He would then play

devil's advocate . . . *i.e.*, he debated us. . . . That class *really* sharpened me intellectually. . . . We as students do need to know how to defend ourselves." This young man valued the experience of being attacked and challenged publicly. Many, if not most, women would shrink from such "challenge," experiencing it as public humiliation.

A professor at Hamilton College told me of a young man who 12
was upset because he felt his class presentation had been a failure. The professor was puzzled because he had observed that class members had listened attentively and agreed with the student's observations. It turned out that it was this very agreement that the student interpreted as failure: Since no one had engaged his ideas by arguing with him, he felt they had found them unworthy of attention.

So one reason men speak in class more than women is that many 13
of them find the "public" classroom setting more conducive to speaking, whereas most women are more comfortable speaking in private to a small group of people they know well. A second reason is that men are more likely to be comfortable with the debate-like form that discussion may take. Yet another reason is the different attitudes toward speaking in class that typify women and men.

Students who speak frequently in class, many of whom are men, 14
assume that it is their job to think of contributions and try to get the floor to express them. But many women monitor their participation not only to get the floor but to avoid getting it. Women students in my class tell me that if they have spoken up once or twice, they hold back for the rest of the class because they don't want to dominate. If they have spoken a lot one week, they will remain silent the next. These different ethics of participation are, of course, unstated, so those who speak freely assume that those who remain silent have nothing to say, and those who are reining themselves in assume that the big talkers are selfish and hoggish.

When I looked around my classes, I could see these differing ethics 15
and habits at work. For example, my graduate class in analyzing conversation had 20 students, 11 women and 9 men. Of the men, four were foreign students: two Japanese, one Chinese, and one Syrian. With the exception of the three Asian men, all the men spoke in class at least occasionally. The biggest talker in the class was a woman, but there were also five women who never spoke at all, only one of whom was Japanese. I decided to try something different.

I broke the class into small groups to discuss the issues raised in the 16
readings and to analyze their own conversational transcripts. I devised three ways of dividing the students into groups: one by the degree program they were in, one by gender, and one by conversational style, as closely as I could guess it. This meant that when the class was grouped according to conversational style, I put Asian students together, fast talkers together, and quiet students together. The class split into groups six times during the semester, so they met in each grouping twice. I told students to regard the

groups as examples of interactional data and to note the different ways they participated in different groups. Toward the end of the term, I gave them a questionnaire asking about their class and group participation.

17 I could see plainly from my observation of the groups at work that women who never opened their mouths in class were talking away in the small groups. In fact, the Japanese woman commented that she found it particularly hard to contribute to the all-woman group she was in because "I was overwhelmed by how talkative the female students were in the female-only group." This is particularly revealing because it highlights that the same person who can be "oppressed" into silence in one context can become the talkative "oppressor" in another. No one's conversational style is absolute; everyone's style changes in response to the context and others' styles.

18 Some of the students (seven) said that they preferred the same-gender groups; others preferred the same-style groups. In answer to the question "Would you have liked to speak in class more than you did?" six of the seven who said Yes were women; the one man was Japanese. Most startlingly, this response did not come only from quiet women; it came from women who had indicated they had spoken in class never, rarely, sometimes, and often. Of the 11 students who said the amount they had spoken was fine, 7 were men. Of the four women who checked "fine," two added qualifications indicating it wasn't completely fine: One wrote in "maybe more," and one wrote, "I have an urge to participate but often feel I should have something more interesting/relevant/wonderful/intelligent to say!!"

19 I counted my experiment a success. Everyone in the class found the small groups interesting, and no one indicated he or she would have preferred that the class not break into groups. Perhaps most instructive, however, was the fact that the experience of breaking into groups, and of talking about participation in class, raised everyone's awareness about classroom participation. After we had talked about it, some of the quietest women in the class made a few voluntary contributions, though sometimes I had to insure their participation by interrupting the students who were exuberantly speaking out.

20 Americans are often proud that they discount the significance of cultural differences: "We are all individuals," many people boast. Ignoring such issues as gender and ethnicity becomes a source of pride: "I treat everyone the same." But treating people the same is not equal treatment if they are not the same.

21 The classroom is a different environment for those who feel comfortable putting themselves forward in a group than it is for those who find the prospect of doing so chastening, or even terrifying. When a professor asks, "Are there any questions?," students who can formulate statements the fastest have the greatest opportunity to respond. Those who need significant time to do so have not really been given a chance at all, since by the time they are ready to speak, someone else has the floor.

In a class where some students speak out without raising hands, those who feel they must raise their hands and wait to be recognized do not have equal opportunity to speak. Telling them to feel free to jump in will not make them feel free; one's sense of timing, of one's rights and obligations in a classroom, are automatic, learned over years of interaction. They may be changed over time, with motivation and effort, but they cannot be changed on the spot. And everyone assumes his or her own way is best. When I asked my students how the class could be changed to make it easier for them to speak more, the most talkative woman said she would prefer it if no one had to raise hands, and a foreign student said he wished people would raise their hands and wait to be recognized. 22

My experience in this class has convinced me that small-group interaction should be part of any class that is not a small seminar. I also am convinced that having the students become observers of their own interaction is a crucial part of their education. Talking about ways of talking in class makes students aware that their ways of talking affect other students, that the motivations they impute to others may not truly reflect others' motives, and that the behaviors they assume to be self-evidently right are not universal norms. 23

The goal of complete equal opportunity in class may not be attainable, but realizing that one monolithic classroom-participation structure is not equal opportunity is itself a powerful motivation to find more-diverse methods to serve diverse students—and every classroom is diverse. 24

Content

1. In your experience, are boys (more often than girls) "expected to use language to seize center stage: by exhibiting their skills, displaying their knowledge, and challenging and resisting challenges" (¶ 3)? How does this translate into classroom performance (¶s 4, 7)? In your experience, is Ong's claim true that "ritual opposition . . . is fundamental to the way most males approach almost any activity" (¶ 5)?
2. "Treating people the same is not equal treatment if they are not the same" (¶ 20). Explain how this idea applies in a classroom.
3. Does Tannen argue that the differences between men's and women's communication styles are biologically or culturally determined? Does she equate student talkativeness in class with an inquiring mind? With intelligent preparation? Or does she base her equation exclusively on gender? Explain your answers.

Strategies/Structures/Language

4. Tannen's article follows the format of physical and social science research: statement of the problem, review of the literature, identification of research methodology, explanation of the research procedure, interpretation of the research findings, and generalizations to other situations or recommendations for either further research or practical applications or both. Show where each stage occurs in this article.

5. "No one's conversational style is absolute; everyone's style changes in response to the context and others' styles" (¶ 17). Explain, with reference to your own experience and other students' behavior in your classes—and out.

For Writing

6. ***Journal Writing.*** Do some primary investigation to replicate Tannen's observation that "when young women sit next to [presumably she means *share the same classroom*, not necessarily *sit in immediate proximity to*] young men in classrooms, the males talk more" (¶ 2). Is this true in any or all of your classes? Typically, do men speak more than women in classes taught by men? Do women speak more or less than men in classes taught by women? Do the ages and life experiences of men and women influence the extent of their class participation? Generalize from your findings and interpret them with regard to Tannen's findings. Do you think the men and women students at your school are typical of students at all American colleges or only at colleges of the type that yours represents (private or public community college, four-year undergraduate school, research university)?

7. Do you agree with Tannen's conclusion that "small-group interaction should be part of any class that is not a small seminar" (¶ 23)? If so, why? If not, why not? What demands does this format place on the students? What does this format imply about the way we learn?

8. Write an essay about any of the Content questions. Base your essay on your own experience, and reinforce it with three interviews—one with a student of a different gender from yours, another with a student of a different racial background, another with a student from a different socio-economic class. (To control for teaching style and content, all the students should be enrolled in the same course at the same time.) To what extent are your conclusions influenced by your informants' class and ethnicity, in comparison with their gender?

9. ***Dialogues.*** Do men and women use electronic communication differently? While Tannen argues in "Communication Styles" that "women . . . resist [classroom] discussion they perceive as hostile" (¶ 9), she does not distinguish between men's and women's use of "technologically enhanced communication" in "Fast Forward" (308–15). In that essay Tannen discusses the use of e-mail to send "hostile and distressing communication" (¶ 5); is this practice gender specific? Does electronic communication diminish differences in the ways men and women communicate? How does electronic communication change behaviors traditionally associated with gender? Write an essay that extends Tannen's analysis of gender differences in communicating to the world of electronic communication.

ROZ CHAST

Roz Chast (born in 1954 in Brooklyn) has published nine collections of her work, most recently *Theories of Everything* (2006), in which "An Excerpt from Men Are from Belgium, Women Are from New Brunswick" was published. She received a BFA in 1977 from Rhode Island School of Design. Chast began publishing in the *New Yorker* in 1979 and has continued to do so ever since. She has also provided cartoons and editorial illustrations for many other magazines, among them *Vogue, National Lampoon, Scientific American, Time,* and *Mother Jones*. She has illustrated children's books, including *The Alphabet from A to Y with Bonus Letter Z!* (2007), and contributed to various *New Yorker* collections of cartoons. "Men Are from Belgium, Women Are from New Brunswick" decodes gender-specific ways of communicating in everyday life and illustrates the multitude of conflicting emotions that can simmer beneath the surface of apparently straightforward and banal language. (Note that the title below applies to the entire cartoon; it is not an excerpt.)

An Excerpt from Men Are from Belgium, Women Are from New Brunswick

© The New Yorker Collection 1997 Roz Chast from cartoonbank.com. All Rights Reserved.

Content

1. Does Chast's depiction of communication between the sexes correspond to your experience? Does Chast's graphic illustration of the process of communication challenge gender stereotypes? Why or why not? How would the verbal and nonverbal responses change if the "guy" rather than the "gal" in the cartoon had cooked the meatloaf? What clues, if any, indicate that this cartoon narrative was created by a "gal"? Would a "guy's" work have been the same? If not, in what significant ways would it have been different?

2. How do the columned format and the images in this cartoon work together to convey both a humorous and serious side of this subject? Is there a resolution to the conflict between the two characters? What does the image of the licensed professional (therapist? marriage counselor?) contribute to the reader's understanding of this mini-narrative?

Strategies/Structures/Language

3. How does Chast extract humor from the situation by small shifts in language and emphasis?

4. What can you deduce about the character's personalities from their language and from the artist's use of punctuation, underlining, and capitalization? What is the effect of hand-written, as opposed to typed, text?

For Writing

5. ***Journal Writing.*** In what types of situations do people avoid stating what they mean? How do intonation, word choice, gestures, and facial expressions contribute to the complexities of such communications? Are mixed signals an inherent part of communication? Include in your response a specific situation in which you felt that you could not say what you felt. Were you able to convey your views nevertheless? Why or why not?

6. ***Dialogues.*** Compare Chast's depiction of what women and men "actually mean" with Art Spiegelman's understated treatment of the Holocaust in "Mein Kampf" (96–97). For example, what do the artist's references to the Holocaust suggest about his feelings toward his family's history? What does his reassurance to his son that "King Kong" is "only a story" imply about his attitude toward the Holocaust? In comparison, what unstated messages do Chast's characters' statements and thoughts suggest about their relationship with one another?

7. Deborah Tannen argues in "Communication Styles" in this chapter that many men and women have different styles of learning that are based on their preferred ways of communicating. Using Chast's comic as a starting point, present an argument that explains some of the differences in communication styles between men and women (or two other groups such as parents/children; children of particular ages/stages in life; teachers/students; doctors/patients . . .). What are the social and psychological factors that explain these differences? Support your argument with specific, convincing details.

SHERRY TURKLE

Sherry Turkle is a clinical psychologist and sociology professor at Massachusetts Institute of Technology. She was born in 1948 in New York City, and was educated at Harvard (BA, 1970; PhD, 1976). Her research and writing focus on the cultural and psychological implications of computer technology. She looks at "computers as carriers of culture, as objects that give rise to new metaphors, to new relationships between people and machines, between different people, and most significantly between people and their ways of thinking about themselves." Her books include *The Second Self: Computers and the Human Spirit* (1984) and *Life on the Screen: Identity in the Age of the Internet* (1995) In addition to identities as "Turkle the social scientist," the author, and the professor, she adds others: "the cyberspace explorer, the woman who might log on as a man, or as another woman, or as, simply, ST" (from "Why Am We?"). "How Computers Change the Way We Think" was originally published in the *Chronicle of Higher Education* on January 30, 2004.

How Computers Change the Way We Think

The tools we use to think change the ways in which we think. The invention of written language brought about a radical shift in how we process, organize, store, and transmit representations of the world. Although writing remains our primary information technology, today when we think about the impact of technology on our habits of mind, we think primarily of the computer. 1

My first encounters with how computers change the way we think came soon after I joined the faculty at the Massachusetts Institute of Technology in the late 1970s, at the end of the era of the slide rule and the beginning of the era of the personal computer. At a lunch for new faculty members, several senior professors in engineering complained that the transition from slide rules to calculators had affected their students' ability to deal with issues of scale. When students used slide rules, they had to insert decimal points themselves. The professors insisted that that required students to maintain a mental sense of scale, whereas those who relied on calculators made frequent errors in orders of magnitude. Additionally, the students with calculators had lost their ability to do "back of the envelope" calculations, and with that, an intuitive feel for the material. 2

That same semester, I taught a course in the history of psychology. There, I experienced the impact of computational objects on students' ideas about their emotional lives. My class had read Freud's essay on 3 slips of the tongue, with its famous first example: The chairman of a parliamentary session opens a meeting by declaring it closed. The students discussed how Freud interpreted such errors as revealing a person's mixed emotions. A computer-science major disagreed with Freud's approach. The mind, she argued, is a computer. And in a computational dictionary—like we have in the human mind—"closed" and "open" are designated by the same symbol, separated by a sign for opposition. "Closed" equals "minus open." To substitute "closed" for "open" does not require the notion of ambivalence or conflict.

4 "When the chairman made that substitution," she declared, "a bit was dropped; a minus sign was lost. There was a power surge. No problem."

5 The young woman turned a Freudian slip into an information-processing error. An explanation in terms of meaning had become an explanation in terms of mechanism.

6 Such encounters turned me to the study of both the instrumental and the subjective sides of the nascent computer culture. As an ethnographer and psychologist, I began to study not only what the computer was doing *for* us, but what it was doing *to* us, including how it was changing the way we see ourselves, our sense of human identity.

7 In the 1980s, I surveyed the psychological effects of computational objects in everyday life—largely the unintended side effects of people's tendency to project thoughts and feelings onto their machines. In the 20 years since, computational objects have become more explicitly designed to have emotional and cognitive effects. And those "effects by design" will become even stronger in the decade to come. Machines are being designed to serve explicitly as companions, pets, and tutors. And they are introduced in school settings for the youngest children.

8 Today, starting in elementary school, students use e-mail, word processing, computer simulations, virtual communities, and PowerPoint software. In the process, they are absorbing more than the content of what appears on their screens. They are learning new ways to think about what it means to know and understand.

9 What follows is a short and certainly not comprehensive list of areas where I see information technology encouraging changes in thinking. There can be no simple way of cataloging whether any particular change is good or bad. That is contested terrain. At every step we have to ask, as educators and citizens, whether current technology is leading us in directions that serve our human purposes. Such questions are not technical; they are social, moral, and political. For me, addressing that subjective side of computation is one of the more significant challenges for the next decade of information technology in higher education. Technology does not determine change, but it encourages us to take certain directions. If we make those directions clear, we can more easily exert human choice.

Thinking about privacy

Today's college students are habituated to a world of online blogging, instant messaging, and Web browsing that leaves electronic traces. Yet they have had little experience with the right to privacy. Unlike past generations of Americans, who grew up with the notion that the privacy of their mail was sacrosanct, our children are accustomed to electronic surveillance as part of their daily lives. 10

I have colleagues who feel that the increased incursions on privacy have put the topic more in the news, and that this is a positive change. But middle-school and high-school students tend to be willing to provide personal information online with no safeguards, and college students seem uninterested in violations of privacy and in increased governmental and commercial surveillance. Professors find that students do not understand that in a democracy, privacy is a right, not merely a privilege. In 10 years, ideas about the relationship of privacy and government will require even more active pedagogy. (One might also hope that increased education about the kinds of silent surveillance that technology makes possible may inspire more active political engagement with the issue.) 11

Avatars or a self?

Chat rooms, role-playing games, and other technological venues offer us many different contexts for presenting ourselves online. Those possibilities are particularly important for adolescents because they offer what Erik Erikson described as a moratorium, a time out or safe space for the personal experimentation that is so crucial for adolescent development. Our dangerous world—with crime, terrorism, drugs, and AIDS—offers little in the way of safe spaces. Online worlds can provide valuable spaces for identity play. 12

But some people who gain fluency in expressing multiple aspects for self may find it harder to develop authentic selves. Some children who write narratives for their screen avatars may grow up with too little experience of how to share their real feelings with other people. For those who are lonely yet afraid of intimacy, information technology has made it possible to have the illusion of companionship without the demands of friendship. 13

From powerful ideas to PowerPoint

In the 1970s and early 1980s, some educators wanted to make programming part of the regular curriculum for K–12 education. They argued that because information technology carries ideas, it might as well carry the most powerful ideas that computer science has to offer. It is ironic that in most elementary schools today, the ideas being carried by information technology are not ideas from computer science like procedural thinking, but more likely to be those embedded in productivity tools like PowerPoint presentation software. 14

15 PowerPoint does more than provide a way of transmitting content. It carries its own way of thinking, its own aesthetic—which not surprisingly shows up in the aesthetic of college freshmen. In that aesthetic, presentation becomes its own powerful idea.

16 To be sure, the software cannot be blamed for lower intellectual standards. Misuse of the former is as much a symptom as a cause of the latter. Indeed, the culture in which our children are raised is increasingly a culture of presentation, a corporate culture in which appearance is often more important than reality. In contemporary political discourse, the bar has also been lowered. Use of rhetorical devices at the expense of cogent argument regularly goes without notice. But it is precisely because standards of intellectual rigor outside the educational sphere have fallen that educators must attend to how we use, and when we introduce, software that has been designed to simplify the organization and processing of information.

17 In "The Cognitive Style of PowerPoint" (Graphics Press, 2003), Edward R. Tufte suggests that PowerPoint equates bulleting with clear thinking. It does not teach students to begin a discussion or construct a narrative. It encourages presentation, not conversation. Of course, in the hands of a master teacher, a PowerPoint presentation with few words and powerful images can serve as the jumping-off point for a brilliant lecture. But in the hands of elementary-school students, often introduced to PowerPoint in the third grade, and often infatuated with its swooshing sounds, animated icons, and flashing text, a slide show is more likely to close down debate than open it up.

18 Developed to serve the needs of the corporate boardroom, the software is designed to convey absolute authority. Teachers used to tell students that clear exposition depended on clear outlining, but presentation software has fetishized the outline at the expense of the content.

19 Narrative, the exposition of content, takes time. PowerPoint, like so much in the computer culture, speeds up the pace.

Word processing vs. thinking

20 The catalog for the Vermont Country Store advertises a manual typewriter, which the advertising copy says "moves at a pace that allows time to compose your thoughts." As many of us know, it is possible to manipulate text on a computer screen and see how it looks faster than we can think about what the words mean.

21 Word processing has its own complex psychology. From a pedagogical point of view, it can make dedicated students into better writers because it allows them to revise text, rearrange paragraphs, and experiment with the tone and shape of an essay. Few professional writers would part with their computers; some claim that they simply cannot think without their hands on the keyboard. Yet the ability to quickly fill the page, to see it before you can think it, can make bad writers even worse.

A seventh grader once told me that the typewriter she found in her mother's attic is "cool because you have to type each letter by itself. You have to know what you are doing in advance or it comes out a mess." The idea of thinking ahead has become exotic. 22

Taking things at interface value

We expect software to be easy to use, and we assume that we don't have to know how a computer works. In the early 1980s, most computer users who spoke of transparency meant that, as with any other machine, you could "open the hood" and poke around. But only a few years later, Macintosh users began to use the term when they talked about seeing their documents and programs represented by attractive and easy-to-interpret icons. They were referring to an ability to make things work without needing to go below the screen surface. Paradoxically, it was the screen's opacity that permitted that kind of transparency. Today, when people say that something is transparent, they mean that they can see how to make it work, not that they know how it works. In other words, transparency means epistemic opacity. 23

The people who built or bought the first generation of personal computers understood them down to the bits and bytes. The next generation of operation systems were more complex, but they still invited that old-time reductive understanding. Contemporary information technology encourages different habits of mind. Today's college students are already used to taking things at (inter) face value; their successors in 2014 will be even less accustomed to probing below the surface. 24

Simulation and its discontents

Some thinkers argue that the new opacity is empowering, enabling anyone to use the most sophisticated technological tools and to experiment with simulation in complex and creative ways. But it is also true that our tools carry the message that they are beyond our understanding. It is possible that in daily life, epistemic opacity can lead to passivity. 25

I first became aware of that possibility in the early 1990s, when the first generation of complex simulation games were introduced and immediately became popular for home as well as school use. SimLife teaches the principles of evolution by getting children involved in the development of complex ecosystems; in that sense it is an extraordinary learning tool. During one session in which I played SimLife with Tim, a 13-year-old, the screen before us flashed a message: "Your orgot is being eaten up." "What's an orgot?" I asked. Tim didn't know. "I just ignore that," he said confidently. "You don't need to know that kind of stuff to play." 26

For me, that story serves as a cautionary tale. Computer simulations enable their users to think about complex phenomena as dynamic, evolving 27 systems. But they also accustom us to manipulating systems whose core assumptions we may not understand and that may not be true.

28 We live in a culture of simulation. Our games, our economic and political systems, and the ways architects design buildings, chemists envisage molecules, and surgeons perform operations all use simulation technology. In 10 years the degree to which simulations are embedded in every area of life will have increased exponentially. We need to develop a new form of media literacy: readership skills for the culture of simulation.

29 We come to written text with habits of readership based on centuries of civilization. At the very least, we have learned to begin with the journalist's traditional questions: who, what, when, where, why, and how. Who wrote these words, what is their message, why were they written, and how are they situated in time and place, politically and socially? A central project for higher education during the next 10 years should be creating programs in information-technology literacy, with the goal of teaching students to interrogate simulations in much the same spirit, challenging their built-in assumptions.

30 Despite the ever-increasing complexity of software, most computer environments put users in worlds based on constrained choices. In other words, immersion in programmed worlds puts us in reassuring environments where the rules are clear. For example, when you play a video game, you often go through a series of frightening situations that you escape by mastering the rules—you experience life as a reassuring dichotomy of scary and safe. Children grow up in a culture of video games, action films, fantasy epics, and computer programs that all rely on that familiar scenario of almost losing but then regaining total mastery: There is danger. It is mastered. A still-more-powerful monster appears. It is subdued. Scary. Safe.

31 Yet in the real world, we have never had a greater need to work our way out of binary assumptions. In the decade ahead, we need to rebuild the culture around information technology. In that new socio-technical culture, assumptions about the nature of mastery would be less absolute. The new culture would make it easier, not more difficult, to consider life in shades of gray, to see moral dilemmas in terms other than a battle between Good and Evil. For never has our world been more complex, hybridized, and global. Never have we so needed to have many contradictory thoughts and feelings at the same time. Our tools must help us accomplish that, not fight against us.

32 Information technology is identity technology. Embedding it in a culture that supports democracy, freedom of expression, tolerance, diversity, and complexity of opinion is one of the next decade's greatest challenges. We cannot afford to fail.

33 When I first began studying the computer culture, a small breed of highly trained technologists thought of themselves as "computer people." That is no longer the case. If we take the computer as a carrier of a way of

knowing, a way of seeing the world and our place in it, we are all computer people now.

Content

1. What new technologies does Turkle claim are changing the way people think? Have you experienced the changes in thought patterns that she describes, such as the tendency of PowerPoint presentations to "close down debate" (¶ 17) or of word processing to "make bad writers even worse" (¶ 21)?
2. Is there any technology or program that Turkle should add to her list, based on your experience? What mind-altering computing experiences have you had that she doesn't mention?
3. At the end of the article, Turkle asserts that current computing habits and software may undermine "democracy, freedom of expression, tolerance, diversity, and complexity of opinion" (¶ 32). Look over the article again to determine the precise reasons she gives to support these conclusions. Which arguments do you find to be the most convincing? Why?
4. Do you ever intentionally try to get away from technology, or have you ever had to be away from the Internet or the computer for an extended period of time? Did you notice any changes in your thinking process or attitudes as a result? Explain what happened and whether the experience was positive or negative.

Strategies/Structures/Language

5. One of the main strategies Turkle uses is the past/present contrast, such as the idea that the typewriter allowed people to put more thought into their writing (¶ 22). What other examples can you find of Turkle comparing current technology to past technology? To what extent are these comparisons effective at persuading the reader to accept her conclusions?

For Writing

6. With a group of classmates, determine how much experience each person has with the technologies that Turkle mentions. For example, how many of your colleagues have experience with PowerPoint? How many participate in chat rooms, role-playing games, simulation games, or use a screen avatar? Discuss with the group whether any of these technologies may be changing or shaping your basic thought processes, and write a collaborative paper reporting on and analyzing your findings.
7. Can you think of some solutions to the issues that Turkle raises in her article? To what extent can we lessen computer technology's negative impact on our thinking? Is the solution technological, or would it help to educate the public about the dangers Turkle outlines? Write a paper explaining how some, or all, of the issues Turkle discusses could be resolved.
8. Can you think of any computing technology that might help humans to *improve* their thought processes? Invent a program or online service that could help enhance mental functioning or perhaps enhance the democratic process,

freedom of expression, or tolerance. Write a proposal persuading readers to support your effort to make your invention available to the public, stressing the way it will improve the way we think.

9. ***Dialogues.*** Turkle raises privacy issues (¶s 10–11) that James Fallows, in "Tinfoil Underwear" (151–57), and Michael J. Bugeja, in "Facing the Facebook" (601–04), also discuss. Do you agree that today's students are, as Turkle argues, "uninterested in violations of privacy" (¶ 11)? Which aspects of Fallows's and Bugeja's discussions seem most relevant to students today? Which of these aspects might "inspire more active political engagement," as Turkle hopes (¶ 11)?

BEN STEIN

Ben Stein (born 1944) is an American Renaissance man. He grew up outside Washington, DC, the son of Herb Stein, an economic advisor to Presidents Nixon and Ford. Educated at Columbia University and Yale Law School, Stein has been a poverty lawyer, a trial lawyer for the U.S. Trade Commission, and a law professor at Pepperdine University. Stein is also an actor known for his deadpan comic monotone, most memorably featured in *Ferris Bueller's Day Off* (1986). He has also appeared in many film and TV roles (including appearances in *Seinfeld* and *Married . . . With Children*) and as a recognizable voice-over and personality in commercials and ad spoofs. The game show he co-hosted, "Win Ben Stein's Money," was awarded seven Emmys during its 1997–2003 run.

Stein began his literary career as a speechwriter for Presidents Nixon and Ford. He has written numerous books, including *How to Ruin Your Love Life* (2003), *How to Ruin Your Financial Life* (2004), *How to Ruin the United States of America* (2008), and various investment guides. He is an economics columnist for *Yahoo! Finance* online and for the Sunday *New York Times*, in which "Connected, Yes, but Hermetically Sealed" was first published in 2008. Although considered a political and economic conservative, his views cannot be easily pigeonholed (for example, he has criticized the U.S. tax code as favoring the wealthy). Stein's writing often takes a strong ethical stance; this essay critiques current technological devices such as the cell phone and the PDA, which, in Stein's view, have "basically replaced thought."

Connected, Yes, but Hermetically Sealed

1 "Man is born free, and everywhere he is in chains," said Jean-Jacques Rousseau.

2 What would Rousseau have made of the modern-day balls and chains with which we shackle ourselves? They are not made of steel or iron, but of silicon and plastic and digits and electrons and waves zooming through the air. These are the chains of all kinds of devices, like

the BlackBerry, the iPhone and the Voyager. These are the chains with which we have bound ourselves, losing much of our solitude and our ability to see the world around and inside us.

Consider an airplane flight. We are soaring across the country. We listen to music. We read books and newspapers. We sleep and dream. If you are like me, you look at the cloud formations and listen to Mozart's Clarinet Concerto in A major. Maybe you talk to your neighbors. 3

You are free to think and to reflect on existence and on your own small role in it. You are free to have long thoughts and memories of high school and college and the first time you met your future spouse. 4

Then, the airplane lands. Cellphones and P.D.A.s snap into action. Long rows of lights light up on tiny little screens. These are people we absolutely have to talk to. Voice messages pour in, telling of children who got speeding tickets, of margin calls, of jobs offered and lost. The bonds of obligation, like handcuffs, are clapped back onto our wrists, and we shuffle off to the servitude of our jobs and our mundane tasks. A circuit is completed: the passengers who were human beings a few moments earlier become part of an immense, all-engulfing machine of communication and control. Human flesh and spirit become plastic and electronic machinery. 5

What if we didn't have cellphones or P.D.A.s? We would still have duties and families and bosses, but they would not be at our heels, yipping at us constantly, barking at us to do this or that or worry about this or that. We would have some moat of time and space around ourselves. Not now. 6

Consider another example: Walk down the Avenue of the Americas in Manhattan, between Central Park South and 45th Street. Almost every man and woman is on the phone or scanning the screen of a BlackBerry. No one looks at anyone else (except me; I stare openly and voraciously). It is as if each person were in a cocoon of electrons and self-obsession and obligation. Each of these people might as well be wearing a yoke around his neck. 7

There is no community here—or on the streets of any other city. Beverly Hills, my home, is far worse. There, people are hermetically sealed off from one another, not taking in the air or the stupendous buildings or the sky or just the miracle of confronting the earth as it is. 8

Or consider our beloved young people. I see them in Beverly Hills, in Malibu, among magnificent homes, next to the mighty Pacific, walking along avenues of mansions and towering palm trees. They walk in rows of three, each on a cellphone, not even talking to the people next to her. 9

I keep thinking of my happiest moments of youth, walking along Sligo Creek Parkway in Silver Spring, Md., coming home from Parkside Elementary School (long ago closed) or along Dale Drive, coming home from Montgomery Blair High School. I could smell the leaves burning in the late fall, think the long thoughts that young people are supposed to have, and dream of my adult life, when I would have the love of a great woman and a Corvette. Those were moments of power. 10

11 Now, there is no thought or reverie. There is nothing but gossip and making plans to shop or watch television. The cellphone and the P.D.A. have basically replaced thought. When I was a young White House speech writer, we communed with one another and otherwise read and wrote quietly in our offices. We had mental space. No more.

12 I spent much of the summer in my beloved Sandpoint, Idaho, far north in the Panhandle, overlooking Lake Pend Oreille. People there still have some freedom of thought. They walk along the streets without phones. They ride in their boats and water-ski or fish without any talking over the airwaves. They talk to one another. They look up at the sky. Children line up to swing on a rope over Sand Creek and then drop into the creek. Businesspeople walk to their appointments, greeting the people they see, not talking to a small plastic box. In other words, they are connected to the glorious Bonner County sky and water and land, and, most of all, connected to their own ruminations.

13 What would we do if cellphones and P.D.A.s disappeared? We would be forced to think again. We would have to confront reality. My own life is spent mostly with men and women of business. I have been at this for a long time now, and what I have seen of the loss if solitude and dignity is terrifying among those who travel and work, or even who stay still and work. They are slaves to connectedness. Their work has become their indentured servitude. Their children and families are bound to the same devices, too.

14 But try a day without that invasion of your privacy. Or a week. You will be shocked at what you discover. It's called life. It's called nature. It's called getting to know yourself. I have a close friend who is in prison. He used to be imprisoned by this P.D.A. He has many stories, but the most haunting one is about how, without his phone, without his P.D.A., he has come to know, for the first time, who he is.

15 Will the rest of us ever get the chance? Will we ever throw away the chains that go "ping" in our pocket? Or have we irrevocably become machines ourselves?

Content

1. Stein uses Rousseau's observation, "Man is born free, and everywhere he is in chains," to characterize the "modern-day balls and chains with which we shackle ourselves" (¶ 1). Are you attached to any device made of "silicon and plastic and digits and electrons and waves zooming through the air"? If so, to which one(s)? Is Stein's observation accurate? Do the benefits of these outweigh their disadvantages?
2. Which is your favorite device? Why? What does it enable you to do that you couldn't do without it?
3. Is Stein right; have "the cellphone and the P.D.A. basically replaced thought" with "gossip and making plans to shop or watch television" (¶ 11)? Affirm or refute this on the basis of your own observations.

Strategies/Structures/Language

4. Stein uses negative metaphors, "balls and chains" and "shackles," to characterize the effect of portable electronic devices on their users. Is this appropriate? Substitute a positive metaphor for the negative comparison; how does this change the argument?

5. What does Stein mean by "reality" (¶ 13)? What about "life," "nature,"and "getting to know yourself" (¶ 14)? Pick one of these terms and define it in relation to the concepts in this essay.

For Writing

6. ***Journal Writing.*** Keep track for one 24-hour period of your use of the sorts of devices that Stein is talking about—iPods, iPhones, BlackBerrys, P.D.A.s, or comparable equipment. How much time do you spend using each device? Does this represent a typical day's use? How would you spend the equivalent time if you didn't have these?

7. As Stein recommends, "Try a day without that invasion of your privacy. Or a week" (¶ 14). What do you discover as a consequence? How will your discoveries influence your subsequent behavior?

8. ***Dialogues.*** Draw a cartoon with captions in the manner of Chast's "An Excerpt from Men Are from Belgium, Women Are from New Brunswick" (409) in which you illustrate gender differences—if any—between the way men and women talk on cellphones or other comparable device.

9. Or, draw a cartoon with captions to illustrate differences—if any—between the ways teenagers or college students use an insulating electronic device and the ways older adults use them.

10. ***Mixed Modes.*** Draw a cartoon satirizing the use of any device made of "silicon and plastic and digits and electrons and waves zooming through the air," in the manner of Chast or Lynda Barry (376–85).

11. Write "A Modest Proposal" for the regulation of abolition of cellphones, PDAs, or other electronic device in the manner of Jonathan Swift's "A Modest Proposal" (524–30).

12. ***Second Look.*** Write an essay in which you either agree with or debate Stein's conclusion, that if "cellphones and P.D.A.s disappeared . . . we would be forced to think again" (¶ 13). Did people think more deeply before the arrival of these devices? Is thinking the inevitable or necessary alternative to being "wired" most of the time? How else might they spend the time? For better or for worse?

CHARLES C. MANN

Charles C. Mann's journalistic writing and books focus on the fascinating and complex interconnections among science, technology, and commerce. He is an award-winning correspondent for *Science, Wired*, and *The Atlantic Monthly*; his work has been published in many newspapers and magazines, nationally and internationally, including the *Boston Globe, Fortune, Geo* (Germany), the *New York Times, Paris-Match* (France), *Quark* (Japan), *Smithsonian, Der Stern* (Germany), *Technology Review* (MIT), *Vanity Fair*, and the *Washington Post*. His most recent book, *1491: New Revelations of the Americas Before Columbus* (2005), won the U.S. National Academy of Sciences' Keck award for best book of the year. "Forever Young," which first appeared in *The Atlantic Monthly* in 2005 titled "The Coming Death Shortage," explores "the social conflicts that will ensue as the interests of increasingly long-lived older generations diverge from those of their heirs." Mann argues that the "intergenerational warfare" that increased longevity will instigate unprecedented change since "almost every aspect of society is based on the orderly succession of generations."

Forever Young*

1 ANNA NICOLE SMITH'S role as a harbinger of the future is not widely acknowledged. Born Vickie Lynn Hogan, Smith first came to the attention of the American public in 1993, when she earned the title Playmate of the Year. In 1994 she married J. Howard Marshall, a Houston oil magnate said to be worth more than half a billion dollars. He was eighty-nine and wheelchair-bound; she was twenty-six and quiveringly mobile. Fourteen months later Marshall died. At his funeral the widow appeared in a white dress with a vertical neckline. She also claimed that Marshall had promised half his fortune to her. The inevitable litigation sprawled from Texas to California and occupied batteries of lawyers, consultants, and public relations specialists for more than seven years.

2 Even before Smith appeared, Marshall had disinherited his older son. And he had infuriated his younger son by lavishing millions on a mistress, an exotic dancer, who then died in a bizarre face-lift accident. To block Marshall senior from squandering on Smith money that Marshall junior regarded as rightfully his, the son seized control of his father's assets by means that the trial judge later said were so "egregious," "malicious," and "fraudulent" that he regretted being unable to fine the younger Marshall more than $44 million in punitive damages.[1]

---

* Copyright © 2005 The Atlantic Monthly Group, as first published in THE ATLANTIC MONTHLY. Distributed by Tribune Media Services.

[1] After this article was submitted, a federal appellate court ruled that the Anna Nicole Smith case properly should have been decided not by the federal court in California that awarded her $88 million but by the Texas probate court that had previously ruled wholly against her. Smith appealed to the U.S. Supreme Court, joined by the Bush administration, which wished to preserve federal jurisdiction over state probate proceedings. The court ruled 9–0 for Smith in May 2006, sending the case back to appellate court. No matter who finally wins this *Bleak House* legal battle, though, the case remains emblematic of the social conflicts that will ensue as the interests of increasingly long-lived older generations diverge from those of their heirs. [*Atlantic* editors' footnote.] Smith herself died in 2007, age thirty-nine, legal issues unresolved.

In its epic tawdriness the Marshall affair was natural fodder for the tabloid media. Yet one aspect of it may soon seem less a freak show than a cliche. If an increasingly influential group of researchers is correct, the lurid spectacle of intergenerational warfare will become a typical social malady. 3

The scientists' argument is circuitous but not complex. In the past century U.S. life expectancy has climbed from forty-seven to seventy-seven, increasing by nearly two thirds. Similar rises happened in almost every country. And this process shows no sign of stopping: according to the United Nations, by 2050 global life expectancy will have increased by another ten years. Note, however, that this tremendous increase has been in *average* life expectancy—that is, the number of years that most people live. There has been next to no increase in the *maximum* lifespan, the number of years that one can possibly walk the earth—now thought to be about 120. In the scientists' projections, the ongoing increase in average lifespan is about to be joined by something never before seen in human history: a rise in the maximum possible age at death. 4

Stem-cell banks, telomerase amplifiers, somatic gene therapy—the list of potential longevity treatments incubating in laboratories is startling. Three years ago a multi-institutional scientific team led by Aubrey de Grey, a theoretical geneticist at Cambridge University, argued in a widely noted paper that the first steps toward "engineered negligible senescence"—a rough-and-ready version of immortality—would have "a good chance of success in mice within ten years." The same techniques, De Grey says, should be ready for human beings a decade or so later. "In ten years we'll have a pill that will give you twenty years," says Leonard Guarente, a professor of biology at Massachusetts Institute of Technology. "And then there'll be another pill after that. The first hundred-and-fifty-year-old may have already been born." 5

Critics regard such claims as wildly premature. In March ten respected researchers predicted in the *New England Journal of Medicine* that "the steady rise in life expectancy during the past two centuries may soon come to an end," because rising levels of obesity are making people sicker. The research team leader, S. Jay Olshansky, of the University of Illinois School of Public Health, also worries about the "potential impact of infectious disease." Believing that medicine can and will overcome these problems, his "cautious and I think defensibly optimistic estimate" is that the average lifespan will reach eighty-five or ninety—in 2100. Even this relatively slow rate of increase, he says, will radically alter the underpinnings of human existence. "Pushing the outer limits of lifespan" will force the world to confront a situation no society has ever faced before: an acute shortage of dead people. 6

The twentieth-century jump in life expectancy transformed society. Fifty years ago senior citizens were not a force in electoral politics. Now the 7

AARP is widely said to be the most powerful organization in Washington. Medicare, Social Security, retirement, Alzheimer's, snowbird economies, the population boom, the golfing boom, the cosmetic-surgery boom, the nostalgia boom, the recreational-vehicle boom, Viagra—increasing longevity is entangled in every one. Momentous as these changes have been, though, they will pale before what is coming next.

8 From religion to real estate, from pensions to parent-child dynamics, almost every aspect of society is based on the orderly succession of generations. Every quarter century or so, children take over from their parents—a transition as fundamental to human existence as the rotation of the planet about its axis. In tomorrow's world, if the optimists are correct, grandparents will have living grandparents; children born decades from now will ignore advice from people who watched the Beatles on *The Ed Sullivan Show*. Intergenerational warfare—the Anna Nicole Smith syndrome—will be but one consequence. Trying to envision such a world, sober social scientists find themselves discussing pregnant seventy-year-olds, offshore organ farms, protracted adolescence, and lifestyles policed by insurance companies. Indeed, if the biologists are right, the coming army of centenarians will be marching into a future so unutterably different that they may well feel nostalgia for the long-ago days of three score and ten.

9 The oldest in vitro fertilization clinic in China is located on the sixth floor of a no-star hotel in Changsha, a gritty flyover city in the south-central portion of the country. It is here that the clinic's founder and director, Lu Guangxiu, pursues her research into embryonic stem cells.

10 Most cells *don't* divide, in spite of what elementary school students learn—they just get old and die. The body subcontracts out the job of replacing them to a special class of cells called stem cells. Embryonic stem cells—those in an early-stage embryo—can grow into any kind of cell: spleen, nerve, bone, whatever. Rather than having to wait for a heart transplant, medical researchers believe, a patient could use stem cells to grow a new heart: organ transplant without an organ donor.

11 The process of extracting stem cells destroys an early-stage embryo, which has led the Bush administration to place so many strictures on stem-cell research that scientists complain it has been effectively banned in this country. A visit to Lu's clinic not long ago suggested that ultimately Bush's rules won't stop anything. Capitalism won't let them.

12 During a conversation Lu accidentally brushed some papers to the floor. They were faxes from venture capitalists in San Francisco, Hong Kong, and Stuttgart. "I get those all the time," she said. Her operation was short of money—a chronic problem for scientists in poor countries. But it had something of value: thousands of frozen embryos, an inevitable byproduct of in vitro fertilizations. After obtaining permission from patients, Lu uses the embryos in her work. It is possible that she has access to more embryonic stem cells than all U.S. researchers combined.

Sooner or later, in one nation or another, someone like Lu will cut a deal: frozen embryos for financial backing. Few are the stemcell researchers who believe that their work will not lead to tissue-and-organ farms and that these will not have a dramatic impact on the human lifespan. If Organs 'Я' Us is banned in the United States, Americans will seek out longevity centers elsewhere. As Stephen S. Hall wrote in *Merchants of Immortality*, biotechnology increasingly resembles the software industry. Dependence on venture capital, loathing of regulation, pathological secretiveness, penchant for hype, willingness to work overseas—they're all there. Already the U.S. Patent Office has issued four hundred patents concerning human stem cells. 13

Longevity treatments will almost certainly drive up medical costs, says Dana Goldman, the director of health economics at the RAND Corporation, and some might drive them up significantly. Implanted defibrillators, for example, could constantly monitor people's hearts for signs of trouble, electrically regulating the organs when they miss a beat. Researchers believe that the devices would reduce heart-disease deaths significantly. At the same time, Goldman says, they would by themselves drive up the nation's health-care costs by "many billions of dollars" (Goldman and his colleagues are working on nailing down how much), and they would be only one of many new medical interventions. In developed nations antiretroviral drugs for AIDS typically cost about $15,000 a year. According to James Lubitz, the acting chief of the aging and chronic-disease statistics branch of the Centers for Disease Control's National Center for Health Statistics, there is no a priori reason to suppose that lifespan extension will be cheaper, that the treatments will have to be administered less frequently, or that their inventors will agree to be less well compensated. To be sure, as Ramez Naam points out in *More Than Human*, which surveys the prospects for "biological enhancement," drugs inevitably fall in price as their patents expire. But the same does not necessarily hold true for medical procedures: heart bypass operations are still costly, decades after their invention. And in any case there will invariably be newer, more effective, and more costly drugs. Simple arithmetic shows that if 80 million U.S. senior citizens were to receive $15,000 worth of treatment every year, the annual cost to the nation would be $1.2 trillion—"the kind of number," Lubitz says, "that gets people's attention." 14

The potential costs are enormous, but the United States is a rich nation. As a share of gross domestic product, the cost of U.S. health care roughly doubled from 1980 to the present, explains David M. Cutler, a health-care economists at Harvard. yet unlike many cost increases, this one signifies that people are better off. "Would you rather have a heart attack with 1980 medicine at the 1980 price?" Clutler asks. "We get more and better treatments now, and we pay more for the additional services. I don't look at that and see an obvious disaster." 15

16 The critical issue, in Goldman's view, will be not the costs per se but determining who will pay them. "We're going to have a very public debate about whether this will be covered by insurance," he says. "My sense is that it won't. It'll be like cosmetic surgery—you pay out of pocket." Necessarily, a pay-as-you-go policy would limit access to longevity treatments. If high-level antiaging therapy were expensive enough, it could become a perk for movie stars, politicians, and CEOs. One can envision Michael Moore fifty years from now, still denouncing the rich in political tracts delivered through the next generation's version of the Internet—neural implants, perhaps. Donald Trump, a 108-year-old multibillionaire in 2054, will be firing the children of the apprentices he fired in 2004. Meanwhile, the maids, chauffeurs, and gofers of the rich will stare mortality in the face.

17 Short of overtly confiscating rich people's assets, it would be hard to avoid this divide. Yet as Goldman says, there will be "furious" political pressure to avert the worst inequities. For instance, government might mandate that insurance cover longevity treatments. In fact, it is hard to imagine any democratic government foolhardy enough *not* to guarantee access to those treatments, especially when the old are increasing in number and political clout. But forcing insurers to cover longevity treatments would only change the shape of the social problem. "Most everyone will want to take [the treatment]," Goldman says. "So that jacks up the price of insurance, which leads to more people uninsured. Either way, we may be bifurcating society."

18 Ultimately, Goldman suggests, the government would probably end up paying outright for longevity treatments—an enormous new entitlement program. How could it be otherwise? Older voters would want it because it is in their interest; younger ones would want it because they, too, will age. "At the same time," he says, "nobody likes paying taxes, so there would be constant pressure to contain costs."

19 To control spending, the program might give priority to people with healthy habits; no point in retooling the genomes of smokers, risk takers, and addicts of all kinds. A kind of reverse eugenics might occur, in which governments would freely allow the birth of people with "bad" genes but would let nature take its course on them as they aged. Having shed the baggage of depression, addiction, mental retardation, and chemical-sensitivity syndrome, tomorrow's legions of perduring old would be healthier than the young. In this scenario moralists and reformers would have a field day.

20 Meanwhile, the gerontocratic elite will have a supreme weapon against the young: compound interest. According to a 2004 study by three researchers at the London Business School, historically the average rate of real return on stock markets worldwide has been about 5 percent. Thus a twenty-year-old who puts $10,000 in the market in 2010 should expect by 2030 to have about $27,000 in real terms—a tidy

increase. But that happy forty-year-old will be in the same world as septuagenarians and octogenarians who began investing their money during the Carter administration. If someone who turned seventy in 2010 had invested $10,000 when he was twenty, he would have about $115,000. In the same twenty-year period during which the young person's account would grew from $10,000 to $27,000, the old person's account would grow from $115,000 to $305,000. Inexorably, the gap between them will widen.

The result would be a tripartite society: the very old and very rich on top, beta-testing each new treatment on themselves; a mass of the ordinary old, forced by insurance into supremely healthy habits, kept alive by medical entitlement; and the diminishingly influential young. In his novel *Holy Fire* (1996) the science fiction writer and futurist Bruce Sterling conjured up a version of this dictator-ship-by-actuary: a society in which the cautions, careful centenarian rules, supremely fit and disproportionately affluent, if a little frail, look down with ennui and mild contempt on their juniors. Marxist class warfare, upgraded to the biotech era! 21

In the past, twenty-and thirty-year-olds had the chance of sudden windfalls in the form of inheritances. Some economists believe that bequests from previous generations have provided as much as a quarter of the start-up capital for each new one—money for college tuitions, new houses, new businesses. But the image of an ingenue's getting a leg up through a sudden bequest from Aunt Tilly will soon be a relic of late-millennium romances. 22

Instead of helping their juniors begin careers and families, tomorrow's rich oldsters will be expending their disposable income to enhance their memories, senses, and immune systems. Refashioning their flesh to ever higher levels of performance, they will adjust their metabolisms on computers, install artificial organs that synthesize smart drugs, and swallow genetically tailored bacteria and viruses that clean out arteries, fine-tune neurons, and repair broken genes. Should one be reminded of H. G. Wells's *The Time Machine*, in which humankind is divided into two species, the ethereal Eloi and the brutish, underground-dwelling Morlocks? "As I recall," Goldman told me recently, "in that book it didn't work out very well for the Eloi." 23

When lifespans extend indefinitely, the effects are felt throughout the life cycle, but the biggest social impact may be on the young. According to Joshua Goldstein, a demographer at Princeton, adolescence will in the future evolve into a period of experimentation and education that will last from the teenage years into the midthirties. In a kind of *wanderjahr* prolonged for decades, young people will try out jobs on a temporary basis, float in and out of their parents' homes, hit the Europass-and-hostel circuit, pick up extra courses and degrees, and live with different people in different places. 24

In the past the transition from youth to adulthood usually followed an orderly sequence: education, entry into the labor force, marriage, and parenthood. For tomorrow's thirtysomethings, suspended in what Goldstein calls "quasi-adulthood," these steps may occur in any order.

25 From our short-life-expectancy point of view, quasi-adulthood may seem like a period of socially mandated fecklessness—what Leon Kass, the chair of the President's Council on Bioethics, has decried as the coming culture of "protracted youthfulness, hedonism, and sexual license." In Japan, ever in the demographic forefront, as many as one out of three young adults is either unemployed or working part-time, and many are living rent-free with their parents. Masahiro Yamada, a sociologist at Tokyo Gakugei University, has sarcastically dubbed them *parasaito shinguru*, or "parasite singles." Adult offspring who live with their parents are common in aging Europe, too. In 2003 a report from the British Prudential finacial-services group awarded the 6.8 million British in this category the mocking name of "kippers"—"kids in parents' pockets eroding retirement savings."

26 To Kass, the main cause of this stasis is "the successful pursuit of longer life and better health." Kass's fulminations easily lend themselves to ridicule. Nonetheless, he is in many ways correct. According to Yuji Genda, an economist at Tokyo University, the drifty lives of parasite singles are indeed a byproduct of increased longevity, mainly because longer-lived seniors are holding on to their jobs. Japan, with the world's oldest population, has the hightest percentage of working senior citizens of any developed nation: one out of three men over sixty-five is still on the job. Everyone in the nation, Genda says, is "tacitly aware" that the old are "blocking the door."

27 In a world of two-hundred-year-olds "the rate of rise in income and status perhaps for the first hundred years of life will be almost negligible," the crusty maverick economist Kenneth Boulding argued in a prescient article from 1965. "It is the propensity of the old, rich, and powerful to die that gives the young, poor, and powerless hope." (Boulding died in 1993, opening up a position for another crusty maverick economist.)

28 Kass believes that "human beings, once they have attained the burdensome knowledge of good and bad, should not have access to the tree of life." Accordingly, he has proposed a straightforward way to prevent the problems of youth in a society dominated by the old: "Resist the siren song of the conquest of aging and death." Senior citizens, in other words, should let nature take its course once humankind's biblical seventy-year lifespan is up. Unfortunately, this solution is self-canceling, since everyone who agrees with it is eventually eliminated. Opponents, meanwhile, live on and on. Kass, who is sixty-six, has another four years to make his case.

29 Increased longevity may add to marital strains. The historian Lawrence Stone was among the first to note that divorce was rare in

previous centuries partly because people died so young that bad unions were often dissolved by early funerals. As people lived longer, Stone argued, divorce became "a functional substitute for death." Indeed, marriages dissolved at about the same rate in 1860 as in 1960, except that in the nineteenth century the dissolution was more often due to the death of a partner, and in the twentieth century to divorce. The corollary that children were as likely to live in households without both biological parents in 1860 as in 1960 is also true. Longer lifespans are far from the only reason for today's higher divorce rates, but the evidence seems clear that they play a role. The prospect of spending another twenty years sitting across the breakfast table from a spouse whose charm has faded must have already driven millions to divorce lawyers. Adding an extra decade or two can only exacerbate the strain.

Worse, child-rearing, a primary marital activity, will be even more 30
difficult than it is now. For the past three decades, according to Ben J. Wattenberg, a senior fellow at the American Enterprise Institute, birth rates around the world have fallen sharply as women have taken advantage of increased opportunities for education and work outside the home. "More education, more work, lower fertility," he says. The title of Wattenberg's latest book, published in October 2004, sums up his view of tomorrow's demographic prospects: *Fewer*. In his analysis, women's continuing movement outside the home will lead to a devastating population crash—the mirror image of the population boom that shaped so much of the past century. Increased longevity will only add to the downward pressure on birth rates, by making childbearing even more difficult. During their twenties, as Goldstein's quasi-adults, men and women will be unmarried and relatively poor. In their thirties and forties they will finally grow old enough to begin meaningful careers—the worst time to have children. Waiting still longer will mean entering the maelstrom of reproductive technology, which seems likely to remain expensive, alienating, and prone to complications. Thus the parental paradox: increased longevity means *less* time for pregnancy and child-rearing, not more.

Even when women manage to fit pregnancy into their careers, 31
they will spend a smaller fraction of their lives raising children than ever before. In the mid-nineteenth century, white women in the United States had a life expectancy of about forty years and typically bore five or six children. (I specify Caucasians because records were not kept for African Americans.) These women literally spent more than half their lives caring for offspring. Today U.S. white women have a life expectancy of nearly eighty and bear an average of 1.9 children—below replacement level. If a woman spaces two births close together, she may spend only a quarter of her days in the company of offspring under the age of eighteen. Children will become ever briefer parentheses in long, crowded adult existences. It seems inevitable that the bonds between generations will fray.

32 Purely from a financial standpoint, parenthood has always been a terrible deal. Mom and Dad fed, clothed, housed, and educated the kids but received little in the way of tangible return. Ever since humankind began acquiring property, wealth has flowed from older generations to younger ones. Even in those societies where children herded cattle and tilled the land for their aged progenitors, the older generation consumed so little and died off so quickly that the net movement of assets and services was always downward. "Of all the misconceptions that should be banished from discussions of aging," F. Landis MacKellar, an economist at the International Institute for Applied Systems Analysis, in Austria, wrote in the journal *Population and Development Review* in 2001, "the most persistent and egregious is that in some simpler and more virtuous age children supported their parents."

33 This ancient pattern changed at the beginning of the twentieth century, when government pension and social security schemes spread across Europe and into the Americas. Within the family parents still gave much more than they received, according to MacKellar, but under the new state plans the children in effect banded together outside the family and collectively reimbursed the parents. In the United States workers pay less to Social Security than they eventually receive; retirees are subsidized by the contributions of younger workers. But on the broadest level financial support from the young is still offset by the movement of assets within families—a point rarely noted by critics of "greedy geezers."

34 Increased longevity will break up this relatively equitable arrangement. Here concerns focus less on the super-rich than on middle-class senior citizens, those who aren't surfing the crest of compound interest. These people will face a Hobson's choice. On the one hand, they will be unable to retire at sixty-five, because the young would end up bankrupting themselves to support them—a reason why many would-be reformers propose raising the retirement age. On the other hand, it will not be feasible for most of tomorrow's nonagenarians and centenarians to stay at their desks, no matter how fit and healthy they are.

35 The case against early retirement is well known. In economic jargon the ratio of retirees to workers is known as the "dependency ratio," because through pension and Social Security payments people who are now in the work force funnel money to people who have left it. A widely cited analysis by three economists at the Organization for Economic Cooperation and Development estimated that in 2000 the overall dependency ratio in the United States was 21.7 retirees for every 100 workers, meaning (roughly speaking) that everyone older than sixty-five had five younger workers contributing to his pension. By 2050 the dependency ratio will have almost doubled, to 38 per 100; that is, each retiree will be

supported by slightly more than two current workers. If old-age benefits stay the same, in other words, the burden on younger workers, usually in the form of taxes, will more than double.

This may be an underestimate. The OECD analysis did not assume 36
any dramatic increase in longevity or the creation of any entitlement program to pay for longevity care. If both occur, as gerontological optimists predict, the number of old will skyrocket, as will the cost of maintaining them. To adjust to these "very bad fiscal effects," says the OECD economist Pablo Antolin, one of the report's coauthors, societies have only two choices: "raising the retirement age or cutting the benefits." He continues, "This is arithmetic—it can't be avoided." The recent passage of a huge new prescription-drug program by an administration and Congress dominated by the "party of small government" suggests that benefits will not be cut. Raising the age of retirement might be more feasible politically, but it would lead to a host of new problems—see today's Japan.

In the classic job pattern, salaries rise steadily with seniority. 37
Companies underpay younger workers and overpay older workers as a means of rewarding employees who stay at their jobs. But as people have become more likely to shift firms and careers, the pay increases have become powerful disincentives for companies to retain employees in their fifties and sixties. Employers already worried about the affordability of older workers are not likely to welcome calls to raise the retirement age; the last thing they need is to keep middle managers around for another twenty or thirty years. "There will presumably be an elite group of super-rich who would be immune to all these pressures," Ronald Lee, an economic demographer at the University of California at Berkeley, says. "Nobody will kick Bill Gates out of Microsoft as long as he owns it. But there will be a lot of pressure on the average old person to get out."

In Lee's view, the financial downsizing need not be inhumane. One 38
model is the university, which shifted older professors to emeritus status, reducing their workload in exchange for reduced pay. Or, rather, the university *could* be a model: age-discrimination litigation and professors' unwillingness to give up their perks, Lee says, have largely torpedoed the system. "It's hard to reduce someone's salary when they are older," he says. "For the person, it's viewed as a kind of disgrace. As a culture we need to get rid of that idea."

The Pentagon has released few statistics about the hundreds or thousands 39
of insurgents captured in Afghanistan and Iraq, but one can be almost certain that they are disproportionately young. Young people have ever been in the forefront of political movements of all stripes. University students protested Vietnam, took over the U.S. embassy in Tehran, filled Tiananmen Square, served as the political vanguard for the Taliban. "When we are forty," the young writer Filippo Marinetti promised in the 1909

Futurist Manifesto, "other younger and stronger men will probably throw us in the wastebasket like useless manuscripts—we want it to happen!"

40 The same holds true in business and science. Steve Jobs and Stephen Wozniak founded Apple in their twenties; Albert Einstein dreamed up special relativity at about the same age. For better and worse, young people in developed nations will have less chance to shake things up in tomorrow's world. Poorer countries, where the old have less access to longevity treatments, will provide more opportunity, political and financial. As a result, according to Fred C. Iklé, an analyst with the Center for Strategic and International Studies, "it is not fanciful to imagine a new cleavage opening up in the world order." On one side would be the " 'bioengineered' nations," societies dominated by the "becalmed temperament" of old people. On the other side would be the legions of youth—"the protagonists," as the political theorist Samuel Huntington has described them, "of protest, instability, reform, and revolution."

41 Because poorer countries would be less likely to be dominated by a gerontocracy, tomorrow's divide between old and young would mirror the contemporary division between rich northern nations and their poorer southern neighbors. But the consequences might be different—unpredictably so. One assumes, for instance, that the dictators who hold sway in Africa and the Middle East would not hesitate to avail themselves of longevity treatments, even if few others in their societies could afford them. Autocratic figures like Arafat, Franco, Perón, and Stalin often leave the scene only when they die. If the human lifespan lengthens greatly, the dictator in Gabriel García Márquez's *The Autumn of the Patriarch*, who is "an indefinite age somewhere between 107 and 232 years," may no longer be regarded as a product of magical realism.

42 Bioengineered nations, top-heavy with the old, will need to replenish their labor forces. Here immigration is the economist's traditional solution. In abstract terms, the idea of importing young workers from poor regions of the world seems like a win-win solution: the young get jobs, the old get cheap service. In practice, though, host nations have found that the foreigners in their midst are stubbornly . . . foreign. European nations are wondering whether they really should have let in so many Muslims. In the United States, traditionally hospitable to migrants, bilingual education is under attack and the southern border is increasingly locked down. Japan, preoccupied by *Nihonjinron* (theories of "Japaneseness"), has always viewed immigrants with suspicion if not hostility. Facing potential demographic calamity, the Japanese government has spent millions trying to develop a novel substitute for immigrants: robots smart and deft enough to take care of the aged.

43 According to Ronald Lee, the Berkeley demographer, rises in life expectancy have in the past stimulated economic growth. Because they arose mainly from reductions in infant and child mortality, these rises produced more healthy young workers, which in turn led to more-productive

societies. Believing they would live a long time, those young workers saved more for retirement than their forebears, increasing society's stock of capital—another engine of growth. But these positive effects are offset when increases in longevity come from old people's neglecting to die. Older workers are usually less productive than younger ones, earning less and consuming more. Worse, the soaring expenses of entitlement programs for the old are likely, Lee believes, "to squeeze out government expenditures on the next generation," such as education and childhood public-health programs. "I think there's evidence that something like this is already happening among the industrial countries," he says. The combination will force a slowdown in economic growth: the economic pie won't grow as fast. But there's a bright side, at least potentially. If the fall in birth rates is sufficiently vertiginous, the number of people sharing that relatively smaller pie may shrink fast enough to let everyone have a bigger piece. One effect of the longevity-induced "birth dearth" that Wattenburg fears, in other words, may be higher per capita incomes.

For the past thirty years the United States has financed its budget 44
deficits by persuading foreigners to buy U.S. Treasury bonds. In the nature of things, most of these foreigners have lived in other wealthy nations, especially Japan and China. Unfortunately for the United States, those other countries are marching toward longevity crises of their own. They, too, will have fewer young, productive workers. They, too, will be paying for longevity treatments for the old. They, too, will be facing a grinding economic slowdown. For all these reasons they may be less willing to finance our government. If so, Uncle Sam will have to raise interest rates to attract investors, which will further depress growth—a vicious circle.

Longevity-induced slowdowns could make young nations more 45
attractive as investment targets, especially for the cash-strapped pension-and-insurance plans in aging countries. The youthful and ambitious may well follow the money to where the action is. If Mexicans and Guatemalans have fewer rich old people blocking their paths, the river of migration may begin to flow in the other direction. In a reverse brain drain, the Chinese coast guard might discover half-starved American postgraduates stuffed into the holds of smugglers' ships. Highways out of Tijuana or Nogales might bear road signs telling drivers to watch out for *norteamericano* families running across the blacktop, the children's Hello Kitty backpacks silhouetted against a yellow warning background.

Given that today nobody knows precisely how to engineer major 46
increases in the human lifespan, contemplating these issues may seem premature. Yet so many scientists believe that some of the new research will pay off, and that lifespans will stretch like taffy, that it would be shortsighted not to consider the consequences. And the potential changes are so enormous and hard to grasp that they can't be understood and planned for at the last minute. "By definition," says Aubrey de Grey, the Cambridge geneticist, "you live with longevity for a very long time."

Content

1. Why does Mann begin his essay with the court case over J. Howard Marshall's estate? What's at the heart of "intergenerational warfare" (¶ 3)?

2. Mann reports that average life expectancy is predicted to reach the late 80s or early 90s by the end of this century (¶s 4, 6). According to Mann, what are some of the issues associated with increases in average life expectancy (¶s 7–8)? Which of these issues are primarily socioeconomic (Social Security), personal or behavioral (Viagra), or ethical ("pregnant seventy year-olds")? Which seem the most serious? Which seem to call for public policy decisions? Discuss Carolita Johnson's cartoon ("I never thought turning eighty would be so much fun," 435) in respect to the ethical and social policy issues it raises.

3. Why are embryonic stem cells in demand? According to Mann, why are attempts to restrict stem-cell research futile (¶s 10–13)?

4. Why are medical procedures that expand longevity likely to drive up health care costs (¶ 14)? What issues does Mann raise in his discussion of who will pay for these longevity treatments (¶s 16–19)? Why does Mann argue that "it would be hard to avoid this divide" between those who can access these treatments and those who can't (¶ 17)? What forces might increase general access to longevity treatments and what pressures might restrict such access (¶s 17–18)?

5. Why, according to Mann, does the prospect of a longer average life expectancy suggest the development of "a tripartite society" (¶ 21)? What assumptions does he make about voting behavior (¶ 18), public policy (¶s 18–19), savings rates (¶ 20), and spending habits (¶ 23) in predicting this outcome?

6. How does Mann believe longer life spans will affect the young (¶s 24–27)? Marriage and the family (¶s 29–31)? The intergenerational flow of wealth (¶s 32–34)? The structure of the labor market (¶s 35–37)? The divide between the developed and undeveloped countries (¶s 40–42)? Economic growth (¶s 43–45)?

Strategies/Structures/Language

7. Mann argues that longevity treatments might lead to a "kind of reverse eugenics" (¶ 19). Explain the steps in his line of reasoning. What assumptions does he make? Do you detect any flaws in his argument? Find other examples of claims Mann makes that depend on debatable assumptions. For example, examine his claim that "tomorrow's rich oldsters will be expending their disposable income to enhance their memories, senses, and immune systems" (¶ 23) and that "increased longevity means *less* time for pregnancy and child-rearing, not more" (¶ 30). Can you make a counterargument to these claims based on the evidence and logic Mann provides?

For Writing

8. ***Journal Writing.*** Many films and books explore the human desire to prolong life indefinitely through science, black magic, or a vampire's bite. Explore the fascination with such narratives, perhaps by analyzing in detail a film or novel that you particularly like. How does the narrative resolve the quest for immortality? How does it characterize death?

9. ***Dialogues.*** Mann argues that capitalism will invariably lead to the development of "longevity centers" (¶s 11–13) whose treatments will be in near-universal demand (¶ 17). Bill McKibben, in "Designer Genes" (572–82), similarly argues that market forces dictate that in our consumerist culture germline genetic engineering, once introduced, "will accelerate endlessly and unstoppably into the future" (¶ 38). How does each author depict social forces opposing such developments? Write an essay based on the evidence and arguments in "Forever Young" and "Designer Genes" in which you argue that social and community structures will work to restrict market forces in the allocation of medical advances such as longevity treatments and genetic engineering. Do you expect your current position to change as you yourself grow older? As you deal with—and make decisions for and about—aging parents or grandparents?

10. ***Mixed Modes.*** Mann includes several terms in his description of the social conflicts that might arise with increasing life expectancy, including "*maximum* lifespan" (¶ 4), "engineered negligible senescence" (¶ 5), "embryonic stem cells" (¶ 10), "kippers" (¶ 25), "the dependency ratio" (¶ 35), "gerontocracy" (¶ 41), and "*Nihonjinron*" (¶ 42). How are the definitions of these terms—and others—critical to his argument? How does he introduce each definition? Where in the paragraph does the definition appear? What is the pattern of these definitions? Why is it effective?

"I never thought turning eighty would be so much fun!"

© The New Yorker Collection 2006 Carolita Johnson from cartoonbank.com. All rights reserved.

MICHAEL BENEDETTO

Michael Benedetto (born 1985) explains the genesis of his prize-winning "Home Away from Home": "Every summer break during college I would return to my hometown of Bristol, a small city in Connecticut, and try to find a summer job for a few months before slipping back into the college lifestyle." Every job was different; some predictable, like lifeguarding and landscaping, others more unusual, "like being a wildlife specialist at a summer camp despite the fact I was an English major, but the most interesting one by far is described at length in my essay."

Benedetto, who graduated from the University of Connecticut with a BA in 2007, is pursuing a career in publishing. He says, "Hopefully [I] will not have to return to the third shift any time soon. I still follow my professor's advice to this day: 'If you want to be a writer you simply have to write. Write every day and read everything you can. That's the only way you'll improve.'"

✧ *Home Away from Home*

1 I would wake up around four in the afternoon, maybe six or seven o'clock on a bad day, and eat dinner with my family. "So, how was everyone's day?" my mother would ask, and I'd hear stories about school and work, whatever went on while I was asleep. At nine I'd make my lunch; peanut-butter and jelly, or maybe just a T.V. dinner to nuke later then head out to my car. Things always felt strange, especially those first few weeks, driving past traffic jams, heading away from home rather than towards it. Like a salmon swimming up stream, I returned to the place I had been the night before, and most other nights before that.

2 As I pulled into the oversized, near-empty parking lot, I'd see the day people walking out to their cars with their empty coolers. I went in through the double automatic doors and locked them behind me. No one would be getting in or out until the sun came up, I hoped I would make it through the night. My boss would zoom up to the front of the store on a motorized pallet-jack and bark orders at me, always wearing the same work boots, the same dirty flannel jacket. The first few hours were the worst; I'd work slowly in anticipation of the long night ahead.

3 Working the night shift was a challenge, everyone there could tell you that. It wasn't a terrible job; it had its benefits and the pay was good. It wasn't even the work that was so hard, but the time you weren't at work. Times when you'd get home and hate the sun for keeping you awake, or leaving a friend's house at nine thirty on a Friday night because you had to go to work for eight hours. You have to make the transition to this vampire lifestyle, sleeping with the shades drawn all day, being removed

from the rest of regular society. You spend most of your time with the rest of the night crew, a handful of guys who live just like you, and they all had their reasons for living the way they did, otherwise they'd be at home in bed like everyone else.

The place where I worked was one of those colossal warehouses that doubled as a hardware store. During the day young couples and contractors would walk the aisles with oversized carriages and fill them with paint and tools, laminate tile flooring, light fixtures, potted plants, and Jacuzzi hot tubs. Anything a person would need to build a house, you could probably find it there. But at night the place was empty, and every sound echoed off the cavernous ceiling. 4

I started work in June and was honored with the title of the "new guy," which meant I got to do all the jobs no one else wanted. Nights when it rained I'd grab a yellow poncho and work outside in the gardening area. Moving big potted plants or hauling around thirty pound bags of dehydrated manure and wood chips. One time someone drove a fork lift into a pyramid style display of Driveway Cleanup. Driveway Cleanup is like tar in a bucket, it's used to fill in cracks and generally make your driveway look nice and neat. So when thirty containers of it were cut in half by fork lift spikes, and the black ooze spilled all over the floor, it was my job to help shovel it up before it dried. It's not easy to wash that stuff off your skin either, I must have smelled it on me for the rest of the week. 5

It wasn't always so difficult, however. Sometimes I'd get an easy job because I was the only one who couldn't drive a forklift. Nights when we'd get big shipments in, there would be pallets stacked in long lines outside the store. The doors would have to be left open so machines could easily move in and out. It was my job to sit in a lawn chair and make sure no one walked in and stole any toilet bowls or sliding glass doors at four in the morning. I guess this was a real problem they've had before. 6

And of course there were always breaks. We took three breaks a night: two for fifteen minutes, and a half hour "lunch" break at two a.m. This was fun because I got to find out why all the guys thought working from ten at night to six in the morning was such a good idea. Like I said, everybody had their reasons. Some guys worked nights because they couldn't handle the day shift. My boss was one of those guys, he couldn't handle dealing with customers, but he was good at his job, so he was in charge of the night crew and was forced to take anger management classes every Tuesday and Thursday. Others worked at night because they'd been laid off and they needed to find a job fast, to pay bills and child support. Luckily for them, not many people wanted the job. Some of my fellow employees slept during break, so they could be ready and alert for their second job that started at seven. 7

Then they'd ask me why I worked there, and I honestly couldn't say. I was one of the younger guys on the night crew, so I didn't have to 8 worry about getting enough overtime to pay my mortgage. "Don't you have better things to do than stay here all night?" they'd ask me. I probably could've found something better to do, but for some reason I always returned.

9 Around five thirty the day crew started coming back in. This was the awkward transition period. People, freshly showered with nice work clothes and huge mugs of coffee would start getting ready for the daylight hours. I'd be wearing tattered jeans and a filthy shirt, covered in sweat, waiting to go home and shower, then pass out in my bed. Promptly at six I'd punch out and head to my car, waving good morning to the day crew as I left. I'd drive home in the opposite direction of everyone else, just as the sun was coming up.

10 I usually got home at six thirty and fought with my siblings for the shower as they awoke. Then I'd eat breakfast with everyone while they rushed around getting their things in order. "So," my mom would ask "how was your night," and I'd tell her all the exciting goings on that took place the night before. Then everyone evacuated the house and I was left alone. I'd go to my room and draw the blinds, get into bed so I'd be well rested to wake up that night for work.

11 Some mornings while in bed, as the day light got brighter through the windows, I thought about that question: why did I decide to live this way? Why did I decide to join the ranks of the living-dead? Stumbling around all night, bleary-eyed and miserable, hiding from the sun. Maybe it was the money. Maybe I was like my boss and couldn't stand people constantly pestering me. Or maybe it was something more unnatural; the darkness and quiet drawing me in, forcing me to return to that place every night despite the way it made me feel. The way it broke me down and made me miserable. Whatever the reason, I didn't like what it was doing to me. Before drifting off to sleep I thanked God I wasn't trapped there like the others. Since I couldn't find my reason for living that way, that meant I didn't have to. Once summer was over I could quit; go back to living during the day, and sleeping at night.

Content

1. What differences between day jobs and night jobs at a big box store are apparent from Benedetto's "Home Away from Home"? What factors would impel a worker to choose one over the other?
2. How do day or night jobs reflect the personalities and interests of the workers depicted in Benedetto's essay? Other workers you know personally? The life Benedetto expects to resume once he goes back to school?
3. What are some significant differences between "hard" and "easy" work, either as Benedetto explains it or the sort of work that "The Global Elite" do (see Robert Reich, 490–98)?

Strategies/Structures/Language

4. Which is more appropriate language to characterize Benedetto's night job, the title, "Home Away from Home" or "this vampire lifestyle" (¶ 3)? Why? Or are both equally appropriate but for different reasons?

5. What is Benedetto's attitude toward his job? How does the tone of the essay reveal this? What details does he use to reinforce this?

For Writing

6. ***Journal Writing.*** Have you ever had a job you didn't like? For how long did you hold it? Or do you still have the job? If so, can you do anything to make it better? If not, why don't you quit? Are the reasons Benedetto gives in ¶ 11 for holding on to his job good ones?

7. If you've ever held a night job, compare your experiences with Benedetto's.

8. ***Dialogues.*** Judging from Benedetto's description, the night workers on his job are primarily if not exclusively men. Why? What sorts of work might women do in this environment? Compare the options with Roz Chast's "An Excerpt from Men Are from Belgium, Women Are from New Brunswick" (409) or Sherry Turkle's "Communication Styles" (411–17).

9. Imagine a store after hours, as Benedetto depicts it. If workers remain attached to cellphones, P.D.A.s, or other electronic devices that Ben Stein discusses in "Connected, Yes, but Hermetically Sealed" (418–20), how would their use affect on-the-job performance? Interaction among the workers?

10. ***Second Look.*** What are the main differences between a "summer job" for a college student and a permanent job that you might expect to have after graduation? Compare with Robert Reich, "The Global Elite" (490–98).

Additional Topics for Writing Comparison and Contrast

(For strategies for writing comparison and contrast, see 399.)

Multiple Strategies for Writing: Comparison and Contrast

In writing on any of the comparison and contrast topics below, you can employ assorted strategies to make the comparisons more meaningful and the contrasts sharp and distinctive, and to interpret their significance.

- *definitions* of essential terms, component parts
- *verbal illustrations* and *examples*, to show the meaning or significance of the comparison and contrast
- *photographs, drawings, diagrams, maps*, to reinforce the verbal illustrations
- *explanations* and *analyses* of the similarities and differences
- *division* and *classification*, to illustrate the parts of the whole
- a *narrative*, on occasion, to allow the meaning of the term to emerge gradually as the tale unfolds
- *negation*, to show why one part is unlike the other

1. Write an essay, full of examples, that compares and contrasts any of the following pairs:

   a. Two people with a number of relevant characteristics in common (two of your teachers, roommates, friends, lovers, employers, clergy, relatives playing the same role—that is, two of your siblings, two of your grandparents, a father or mother and a stepparent)
   b. Two cities or regions of the country you know well, or two neighborhoods you have lived in
   c. Two comparable historical figures with similar positions, such as two presidents, two senators, two generals, two explorers, two immigrants from the same home country
   d. Two religions or two sects or churches within the same religion
   e. Two utopian communities (real or imaginary)
   f. Two explanations or interpretations of the same scientific, economic, religious, psychological, or political phenomenon (for instance, creationism versus Darwinism; Freudian versus Skinnerian theory of behavior)
   g. The cuisine of two different countries or two or more parts of a country (Greek versus French cooking; Szechuan, Cantonese, and Peking Chinese food)

2. Write a balanced essay involving a comparison and contrast of one of the subjects below that justifies your preference for one over the other. Write for a reader who is likely to debate your choice.

   a. An American-made versus foreign-made product (specify the country, the manufacturers, and the make/model or other distinguishing characteristics)
   b. The styles of two performers—musicians, actors or actresses, dancers, athletes participating in the same sport, comedians
   c. The work of two writers, painters, theater or film directors; or two (or three) works by the same writer or painter
   d. Two political parties, candidates for the same office, campaigns, or machines, past or present
   e. Two colleges or universities (or programs or sports teams within them) that you know well
   f. Two styles of friendship, courtship, marriage, or family (both may be contemporary, or you may compare and contrast past and present styles)
   g. Two academic majors, professions, or careers
   h. Life in the mainstream or on the margin (specify of which group, community, or society)

3. Write an essay, by yourself or with a partner, for an audience of fellow students, comparing the reality with the ideal of one of the following:

   a. Dating or courtship styles
   b. Your current job and the most satisfying job you could have
   c. Your current accomplishment in a particular area (sports, a performing art, a skill, or a level of knowledge) with what you hope to attain
   d. Friendship
   e. Parenthood
   f. Your present dwelling and your dream house
   g. The way you currently spend your leisure time, or money, the way you'd like to spend it, and the way you think you *ought* to spend it
   h. The present state of affairs versus the future prospects of some issue of social significance, such as world population, ecology, the control of nuclear arms, the activities and treatment of international terrorists, an appropriate climate for world peace. These are huge topics; you will need to refine them further to discuss in a single paper.

PART IV: *ARGUING DIRECTLY AND INDIRECTLY*

Appealing to Reason: Deductive and Inductive Arguments

When you write persuasively you're trying to move your readers to either belief or action or both, as the Declaration of Independence (450–54) reveals. You can do this through appealing to their reasons, their emotions, or their sense of ethics, as you know if you've ever tried to prove a point on an exam or change an attitude in a letter to the editor. Photographer Gordon Parks's "American Gothic" 1942 (451) that accompanies The Declaration is an homage to Grant Wood's famous "American Gothic" 1929 painting, in which two motionless, iconic figures in front of a plain white wooden farmhouse stare impassively at the viewer, the balding farmer, in overalls and a black suit jacket, holding erect a three-pronged pitchfork as if to protect himself and his aproned wife. By posing the African American cleaning woman, flanked by an erect broom and mop whose volume nearly equals hers, in front of an American flag, Parks combines title and image to comment on the inequalities of opportunity, ownership, and citizenship in the land of the free, and to argue for change. Other pictures, cartoons, and visual images can also make their points with eloquent succinctness. Evan Eisenberg's satiric commentary, "Dialogue Boxes You Should Have Read More Carefully" (486) critiques Microsoft's near-monopoly, while Marisa Acocella Marchetto's "Why Haven't We Won the War on Cancer?" (488) is a visual op-ed plea for greater federal funding for cancer research. In Chapter 11 we discuss appeals to emotion and ethics; here we'll concentrate on argumentation.

An argument, as we're using the term here, does not mean a knockdown confrontation over an issue: "Philadelphia is the most wonderful place in the world to live!" "No, it's not. Social snobbery has ruined the City of Brotherly Love." Nor is an argument hard-sell brainwashing that admits of no alternatives: "America—love it or leave it!" When you write an argument, however, as a reasonable writer you'll present a reasonable proposition that states what you believe. ("In the twenty-first century, the United States will continue to remain the best country in the world for freedom, democracy, and the opportunity to succeed.") You'll need to offer logic, evidence, and perhaps emotional appeals, to try to convince your readers of the merits of what you say. Sometimes, but not always, you'll also argue that they should adopt a particular course of action. ("Consequently, the United States should establish an 'open door' immigration policy to enable the less fortunate to enjoy these benefits, too." Or "Consequently, the United States should severely restrict immigration, to prevent overcrowding and enable every citizen to enjoy these hard-won benefits.")

Unless you're writing an indirect argument that makes its point through satire, irony, an imagined character whose actions or life story illustrate a point (see Jonathan Swift, "A Modest Proposal," [524–30]), or some other oblique means, you'll probably want to identify the issue at hand and justify its significance early in the essay: "Mandatory drug testing is essential for public officials with access to classified information." If it's a touchy subject, you may wish at this point to demonstrate good will toward readers likely to disagree with you by showing the basis for your common concern: "Most people would agree that it's important to protect children and adolescents from harmful influences." You could follow this by acknowledging the merits of their valid points: "And it's also true that drug abuse is currently a national crisis, and deserves immediate remedy." You'll need to follow this with an explanation of why, nevertheless, your position is better than theirs: "But mandatory drug testing for everyone would be a violation of their civil liberties, incredibly costly, and subject to abuse through misuse of the data."

There are a number of suitable ways to organize the body of your argument. If your audience is inclined to agree with much of what you say, you might want to put your strongest point first and provide the most evidence for that, before proceeding to the lesser points, arranged in order of descending importance:

1. Mandatory drug testing for everyone is unconstitutional.
   (three paragraphs)
2. Mandatory drug testing would be extremely costly, an expense grossly disproportionate to the results.
   (two paragraphs)
3. The results of mandatory drug testing would be easy to abuse—to falsify, to misreport, to misinterpret.
   (one paragraph)
4. Consequently, mandatory drug testing for everyone would cause more problems than it would solve.
   (conclusion—one paragraph)

For an antagonistic audience you could do the reverse, beginning with the points easiest to accept or agree with and concluding with the most difficult. Or you could work from the most familiar to the least familiar parts.

No matter what organizational pattern you choose, you'll need to provide supporting evidence—through specific examples, facts and figures, the opinions of experts, case histories, narratives, analogies, considerations of cause and effect. Any or all of these techniques can be employed in either *inductive* or *deductive* reasoning. Chances are that most of your arguments will proceed by induction. You might use an individual example intended as representative of the whole, as Scott Russell Sanders does in "Under the Influence: Paying the Price of My Father's Booze" (192–203), anatomizing his father's alcoholism to illustrate the alcoholic's characteristic behavior.

Or you might use a larger number of examples and apply inductive reasoning to prove a general proposition. Research scientists and detectives work this way, as do some social commentators and political theorists. Robert Reich identifies the characteristics of "The Global Elite" (490–98) and uses them both to counteract the myths that the United States is a benevolent, egalitarian society and to argue against the separatism—moral and economic secession—that upper-income Americans currently practice to dissociate themselves from responsibilities toward the rest of society.

An essay of deductive reasoning proceeds from a general proposition to a specific conclusion. The model for a deductive argument is the syllogism, a three-part sequence that begins with a major premise, is followed by a minor premise, and leads to a conclusion. Aristotle's classic example of this basic logical pattern is

> Major premise: All men are mortal.
> Minor premise: Socrates is a man.
> Conclusion: Therefore, Socrates is mortal.

Sometimes an essay will identify all parts of the syllogism; sometimes one or more parts will be implied. In "The Declaration of Independence" (450–54), Thomas Jefferson and his coauthors explore the consequences of the explicitly stated propositions that "all men are created equal" and that, as a consequence, their "unalienable Rights" cannot be denied.

In his classic essay, "Letter from Birmingham Jail" (456–70), Martin Luther King, Jr.—shown in a 1966 photograph on 457 escorting black children to a newly integrated school—argues for the proposition that "one has a moral responsibility to disobey unjust laws" and uses a vast range of resources to demonstrate his point. He uses biblical and historical examples to explain the situation in Birmingham; illustrations from his own life and from the lives of his own children and other victims of racial segregation; and more generalized incidents of brutal treatment of "unarmed, nonviolent Negroes."

He identifies the process of nonviolent resistance: "collection of the facts to determine whether injustices exist; negotiation; self-purification; and direct action" (¶ 6). In the course of making his main argument, Dr. King addresses a host of lesser arguments: "Why direct action? . . . Isn't negotiation a better path?" (¶ 10); Why not give local politicians time to act? (¶ 12); Wait! What's the rush? (¶s 13, 23–25); "How can you advocate breaking some laws and obeying others?" (¶ 15), with a related consideration, What is the difference between a just and an unjust law? (¶s 16 ff); "I would agree with St. Augustine that 'an unjust law is no law at all'" (¶ 15). Isn't your nonviolent approach "extremist" (¶s 31 ff)? Why not let the white church handle this (¶s 32–35)? All of Dr. King's illustrations and answers lead to one conclusion: "We will reach the goal of freedom in Birmingham and all over the nation, because the goal of America is freedom. Abused and scorned though we may be, our destiny is tied up with America's destiny" (¶ 44).

No matter what your argumentative strategy, you will want to avoid *logical fallacies,* errors of reasoning that can lead you to the wrong conclusion. The most common logical fallacies to be aware of are the following:

- *Arguing from analogy*: Comparing only similarities between things, concepts, or situations while overlooking significant differences that might weaken the argument. "Having a standing army is just like having a loaded gun in the house. If it's around, people will want to use it."
- *Argumentation ad hominem* (from Latin, "argument to the man"): Attacking a person's ideas or opinions by discrediting him or her as a person. "Napoleon was too short to be a distinguished general." "She was seen at the Kit Kat Lounge three nights last week; she can't possibly be a good mother."
- *Argument from doubtful or unidentified authority*: Treating an unqualified, unreliable, or unidentified source as an expert on the subject at hand. "They say you can't get pregnant the first time." "'History is bunk!' said Henry Ford."
- *Begging the question*: Regarding as true from the start what you set out to prove; asserting that what is true is true. "Rapists and murderers awaiting trial shouldn't be let out on bail" assumes that the suspects have already been proven guilty, which is the point of the impending trial.
- *Arguing in a circle*: Demonstrating a premise by a conclusion and a conclusion by a premise. "People should give 10 percent of their income to charity because that is the right thing to do. Giving 10 percent of one's income to charity is the right thing to do because it is expected."
- *Either/or reasoning*: Restricting the complex aspects of a difficult problem or issue to only one of two possible solutions. "You're not getting any younger. Marry me or you'll end up single forever."
- *Hasty generalization*: Erroneously applying information or knowledge of one or a limited number of representative instances to an

entire, much larger category. "Poor people on welfare cheat. Why, just yesterday I saw an SUV parked in front of the tenement at 9th and Main."

- *Non sequitur* (from the Latin, "it does not follow"): Asserting as a conclusion something that doesn't follow from the first premise or premises. "The Senator must be in cahoots with that shyster developer, Landphill. After all, they were college fraternity brothers."
- *Oversimplification*: Providing simplistic answers to complex problems. "Ban handguns and stop murderous assaults in public schools."
- *Post hoc ergo propter hoc* (from Latin, "after this, therefore because of this"): Confusing a cause with an effect and vice versa. "Bicyclists are terribly unsafe riders. They're always getting into accidents with cars." Or confusing causality with proximity: just because two events occur in sequence doesn't necessarily mean that the first caused the second. Does war cause famine, or is famine sometimes the cause of war?

After you've written a logical argument, have someone who disagrees with you read it critically to look for loopholes. Your critic's guidelines could be the same questions you might ask yourself while writing the paper, as indicated in the process strategies below. If you can satisfy yourself and a critic, you can take on the world. Or is that a logical fallacy?

Strategies for Writing: Appealing to Reason: Deductive and Inductive Arguments

1. Do I want to convince my audience of the truth of a particular matter? Do I want essentially to raise their consciousness of an issue? Do I want to promote a belief or refute a theory? Or do I want to move my readers to action? If action, what kind? To change their minds, attitudes, or behavior? To right a wrong, or alter a situation?
2. At the outset, do I expect my audience to agree with my ideas? To be neutral about the issues at hand? Or to be opposed to my views? Can I build into my essay responses to my readers' anticipated reactions, such as rebuttals to their possible objections? Do I know enough about my subject to be able to do this?
3. What is my strongest (and presumably most controversial) point, and where should I put it? At the beginning, if my audience agrees with my views? At the end, after a gradual buildup, for an antagonistic audience? How much development (and consequent emphasis) should each point have? Will a deductive or inductive format best express my thesis?

4. What will be my best sources of evidence? My own experience? The experiences of people I know? Common sense or common knowledge? Opinion from experts in a relevant field? Scientific evidence? Historic records? Economic, anthropological, or statistical data?
5. What tone will best reinforce my evidence? Will my audience also find this tone appealing? Convincing? Would an appropriate tone be sincere? Straightforward? Objective? Reassuring? Confident? Placating? What language can I use to most appropriately convey this tone?

© Library of Congress/Snark Archives © Photo12/The Image Works

Marilyn Nelson chose this 1922 photograph, "Parade of the KKK," to accompany the publication of her poem, "Friends in the Klan." Why did the Ku Klux Klan wear white robes and hoods while employing terrorism, violence, and lynching to promote white supremacy? How would their costumes have been seen by Klan members? By potential victims—not only African American, but Catholic or Jewish? How could "The Professor," George Washington Carver, possibly have a "friend in the Klan"? And pray for him?

MARILYN NELSON

Marilyn Nelson, daughter of an Air Force pilot and a teacher, was born in Cleveland in 1946. Brought up on different military bases, Nelson started writing while still in elementary school. Her college degrees are from the University of California, Davis (BA, 1968), the University of Pennsylvania (MA, 1970), and the University of Minnesota (PhD, 1979). She is a widely published poet (as Marilyn Waniek before 1995) whose academic career has been primarily at the University of Connecticut. Recipient of numerous honors and fellowships (including a Guggenheim), in 2002 she was chosen as Connecticut Poet Laureate. *The Homeplace* (1990) honors her family, from Rufus Atwood (slave name "Pomp"), c. 1845–1915, to her father and his dashing, heroic group of black World War II aviators, the Tuskegee Airmen.

> Suddenly when I hear airplanes overhead—
> big, silver ones
> whose muscles fill the sky—
> I listen: That sounds like

someone I know.
And the sky looks much closer.

Nelson's numerous award-winning books include *The Fields of Praise,* which was a National Book Award finalist and recipient of the 1999 Poets' Prize, and *Carver: A Life in Poems,* which was both a Newbery Honor Book and a Coretta Scott King Honor book. Her work ranges widely, from a rendition of Euripides' play *Hecuba* to several books for children, including *Fortune's Bones: The Manumission Requiem* and *A Wreath for Emmett Till,* both published in 2005. In 2004 she opened her home, Soul Mountain, as a writers' retreat. "When I have time and energy, I make quilts," she says.

Carver: A Life in Poems (2001), from which "Friends in the Klan" is reprinted, consists of fifty-nine vignettes that tell the story of George Washington Carver, pioneering African-American educator and scientist. In "Friends in the Klan" Nelson employs natural, straightforward language with a subtle manipulation of poetic form to create a portrait of grace and disgrace at a historical juncture where the personal and the political collide.

Friends in the Klan (1923)

Black veterans of WWI experienced
such discrimination in veterans' hospitals
that the Veterans' Administration, to save face,
opened in Tuskegee a brand-new hospital,
for Negroes only. Under white control.
(White nurses, who were legally excused
from touching blacks, stood holding their elbows
and ordering colored maids around, white shoes
tapping impatiently.)
The Professor joined
the protest. When the first black doctor arrived
to jubilation, the KKK uncoiled
its length and hissed. *If you want to stay alive*
be away Tuesday. Unsigned. But a familiar hand.
The Professor stayed. And he prayed for his friend in the Klan.

THOMAS JEFFERSON

Politician, philosopher, architect, inventor, and writer, Thomas Jefferson (1743–1826) was born near Charlottesville, Virginia, and was educated at the College of William and Mary. He served as a delegate to the Continental Congress in 1775, as governor of the Commonwealth of Virginia, and as third president of the United States. With help from Benjamin Franklin and John Adams, he wrote *The Declaration of Independence* in mid-June 1776, and after further revision by the Continental Congress in Philadelphia, it was signed on July 4. Frequently called "an expression of the American mind," Jefferson's Declaration is based on his acceptance of democracy as the ideal form of government, a belief also evidenced in his refusal to sign the Constitution until the Bill of Rights was added. Jefferson died at Monticello, his home in Charlottesville, on July 4, 1826, the fiftieth anniversary of the signing of the Declaration.

The Declaration is based on a deductive argument, with the fundamental premises stated in the first sentence of the second paragraph, "We hold these truths to be self-evident. . . ." The rest of the argument follows logically—patriots among the Colonists who read this might say inevitably—from the premises of this emphatic, plainspoken document. What evidence is there in the Declaration that the British might react to it as a hot-headed manifesto, perhaps even a declaration of war? Can a cluster of colonies simply secede by fiat?

The Declaration of Independence

1 When in the course of human events, it becomes necessary for one people to dissolve the political bands which have connected them with another, and to assume among the Powers of the earth, the separate and equal station to which the Laws of Nature and of Nature's God entitle them, a decent respect to the opinions of mankind requires that they should declare the causes which impel them to the separation.

2 We hold these truths to be self-evident, that all men are created equal, that they are endowed by their Creator with certain unalienable Rights, that among these are Life, Liberty and the pursuit of Happiness. That to secure these rights, Governments are instituted among Men deriving their just powers from the consent of the governed. That whenever any Form of Government becomes destructive of these ends, it is the Right of People to alter or to abolish it, and to institute new Government, laying its foundation on such principles and organizing its powers in such form, as to them shall seem most likely to effect their Safety and Happiness. Prudence, indeed, will dictate that Governments long established should not be changed for light and transient causes; and accordingly all experience hath shown, that mankind are more disposed to suffer, while

© Gordon Parks/Corbis

In 1942, as a photographer for the Farm Security Administration, a Depression Era government agency, Gordon Parks took this after-hours picture of Ella Watson, a cleaning woman who worked in his office building. As a fellow African American, he had experienced virulent bigotry and discrimination in the nation's capital, and understood that Ms. Watson's own "disastrous life" could be used to symbolize this version of "American Gothic," the title of the picture. How do you interpret this combination of a slight figure with a very large broom and mop in front of a huge American flag? In what ways does this picture comment on "The Declaration of Independence" (450–54), Martin Luther King, Jr.'s "Letter from Birmingham Jail" (456–70), and Sojourner Truth's "Ain't I a Woman?" (521)?

evils are sufferable, than to right themselves by abolishing the forms to which they are accustomed. But when a long train of abuses and usurpations pursuing invariably the same Object evinces a design to reduce them under absolute Despotism, it is their right, it is their duty, to throw off such government, and to provide new Guards for their future security. Such has been the patient sufferance of these Colonies; and such is now the necessity which constrains them to alter their former Systems of Government. The history of the present King of Great Britain is a history of repeated injuries and usurpations, all having in direct object the establishment of an absolute Tyranny over these States. To prove this, let Facts be submitted to a candid world.

He has refused his Assent to Laws, the most wholesome and neces- 3
sary for the public good.

4 He had forbidden his Governors to pass Laws of immediate and pressing importance, unless suspended in their operation till his Assent should be obtained; and when so suspended, he has utterly neglected to attend them.

5 He has refused to pass other Laws for the accommodation of large districts of people, unless those people would relinquish the right of Representation in the Legislature, a right inestimable to them and formidable to tyrants only.

6 He has called together legislative bodies at places unusual, uncomfortable, and distant from the depository of their Public Records, for the sole purpose of fatiguing them into compliance with his measures.

7 He has dissolved Representative Houses repeatedly, for opposing with manly firmness his invasions on the rights of the people.

8 He has refused for a long time, after such dissolutions, to cause others to be elected; whereby the Legislative Powers, incapable of Annihilation, have returned to the People at large for their exercise; the State remaining in the mean time exposed to all the dangers of invasion from without, and convulsions within.

9 He has endeavoured to prevent the population of these States; for that purpose obstructing the Laws of Naturalization of Foreigners; refusing to pass others to encourage their migration hither, and raising the conditions of new Appropriations of Lands.

10 He has obstructed the Administration of Justice, by refusing his Assent to Laws for establishing Judiciary Powers.

11 He has made Judges dependent on his Will alone, for the tenure of their offices, and the amount and payment of their salaries.

12 He has erected a multitude of New Offices, and sent hither swarms of Officers to harass our People, and eat out their substance.

13 He has kept among us, in time of peace, Standing Armies without the Consent of our Legislature.

14 He has affected to render the Military independent of and superior to the Civil Power.

15 He has combined with others to subject us to jurisdictions foreign to our constitution, and unacknowledged by our laws; giving his Assent to their acts of pretended Legislation:

16 For quartering large bodies of armed troops among us:

17 For protecting them, by a mock Trial, from Punishment for any Murders which they should commit on the Inhabitants of these States:

18 For cutting off our Trade with all parts of the world:

19 For imposing Taxes on us without our Consent:

20 For depriving us in many cases, of the benefits of Trial by Jury:

21 For transporting us beyond Seas to be tried for pretended offenses:

22 For abolishing the free System of English Laws in a Neighbouring Province, establishing therein an Arbitrary government, and enlarging its boundaries so as to render it at once an example and fit instrument for introducing the same absolute rule into these Colonies:

For taking away our Charters, abolishing our most valuable Laws, 23
and altering fundamentally the Forms of our Governments:

For suspending our own Legislatures, and declaring themselves 24
invested with Power to legislate for us in all cases whatsoever.

He has abdicated Government here, by declaring us out of his Pro- 25
tection and waging War against us.

He has plundered our seas, ravaged our Coasts, burnt our towns 26
and destroyed the Lives of our people.

He is at this time transporting large Armies of foreign Mercenaries 27
to compleat works of death, desolation and tyranny, already begun with circumstances of Cruelty & perfidy scarcely paralleled in the most barbarous ages, and totally unworthy the Head of a civilized nation.

He has constrained our fellow Citizens taken Captive on the high 28
Seas to bear Arms against their Country, to become the executioners of their friends and Brethren, or to fall themselves by their Hands.

He has excited domestic insurrections amongst us, and has endea- 29
voured to bring on the inhabitants of our frontiers, the merciless Indian Savages, whose known rule of warfare, is an undistinguished destruction of all ages, sexes and conditions.

In every stage of these Oppressions We Have Petitioned for Redress 30
in the most humble terms: Our repeated petitions have been answered only by repeated injury. A Prince, whose character is thus marked by every act which may define a Tyrant, is unfit to be the ruler of a free People.

Not have We been wanting in attention to our British brethren. We 31
have warned them from time to time of attempts by their legislature to extend an unwarrantable jurisdiction over us. We have reminded them of the circumstances of our emigration and settlement here. We have appealed to their native justice and magnanimity and we have conjured them by the ties of our common kindred to disavow these usurpations, which would inevitably interrupt our connections and correspondence. They too have been deaf to the voice of justice and of consanguinity. We must, therefore acquiesce in the necessity, which denounces our Separation, and hold them, as we hold the rest of mankind, Enemies in War, in Peace Friends.

We, therefore, the Representatives of the United States of America, 32
in General Congress, Assembled, appealing to the Supreme Judge of the world for the rectitude of our intentions, do, in the Name, and by Authority of the good People of these Colonies, solemnly publish and declare, That these United Colonies are, and of Right ought to be Free and Independent States; that they are Absolved from all Allegiance to the British Crown and that all political connection between them and the State of Great Britain, is and ought to be totally dissolved; and that as Free and Independent States, they have full power to levy War, conclude Peace, contract Alliances, establish Commerce, and to do all other Acts and Things which Independent States may of right do. And for the support of this Declaration, with a firm reliance on the protection of Divine

Providence, we mutually pledge to each other our lives, our Fortunes and our sacred Honor.

Content

1. What are "the Laws of Nature and of Nature's God" to which Jefferson refers in paragraph 1? Why doesn't he specify what they are? Is a brief allusion to them in the first paragraph sufficient support for the fundamental premise of the second paragraph?
2. What is Jefferson's fundamental premise (¶ 2)? Does he ever prove it? Does he need to?
3. In paragraphs 3–31 the Declaration states a series of the American colonists' grievances against the British King, George III. What are some of these grievances? Can they be grouped into categories related to the "unalienable rights" Jefferson has specified at the outset, the rights to "Life, Liberty and the pursuit of Happiness"?
4. From the nature of the grievances Jefferson identifies, what ideal of government does he have in mind? Can such a government exist among colonial peoples, or only in an independent nation?

Strategies/Structures/Language

5. Could the American colonists have expected the British simply to agree that separation had become necessary? Or is *The Declaration of Independence* in effect a declaration of war? How does the conclusion (¶ 32) appear to be the inevitable consequence of the reasoning that precedes it? Are there any feasible alternatives? How do Jefferson's choice of words (semantics) and sentence structure (syntax) imply that separation is the inevitable effect of the king's actions?
6. Why has Jefferson listed the grievances in the order in which they appear?
7. Is *The Declaration of Independence* written primarily for an audience of the British King and his advisors? Who else would be likely to be vitally involved?
8. What is the tone of this document? How would Jefferson have expected this tone to have affected King George III and associates? How might the same tone have affected the American patriots of 1776?

For Writing

9. ***Journal Writing.*** Are the ideals celebrated in the *Declaration of Independence* relevant today? Or, does the wording of the *Declaration* seem specific to the historical context in which it was written? What passages do you find particularly relevant or obsolete with respect to contemporary society? Which of Jefferson's grievances can be translated into and applied to contemporary issues?
10. Use your journal (question 9) to write an essay in which you discuss the extent to which the federal government of the United States exhibits one or more of the ideals of government that Jefferson promoted in *The Declaration of Independence*.

11. Write your own "declaration of independence," in which you justify setting yourself (or yourself as a member of a particular social, occupational, economic, ethnic, or cultural group) free from an oppressor or oppressive group.

12. ***Dialogues.*** While Jefferson structures the *Declaration* around the legitimacy of the colonies' political separation from the British Crown, Martin Luther King, Jr., (below) stresses the fundamental unity of all Americans, including those who try to hinder racial justice: "We are caught in an inescapable network of mutuality, tied in a single garment of destiny" (¶ 4). How does King convince his reader that racial justice necessitates an end to segregation, rather than promoting autonomy, as the *Declaration* argues of political justice? Where does King's logic depart from Jefferson's in crucial ways?

13. ***Second Look.*** Equality and the enjoyment of "certain unalienable Rights" (¶ 2) were, in 1776, concepts restricted to men of European descent. How does Gordon Parks's photograph of the African American woman (451) juxtapose class, gender, and race with the ideals of "Life, Liberty, and the pursuit of Happiness" (¶ 2)? How does the photograph's focus and the arrangement of the flag (off-center, blurred), the sharp quality of the woman's dotted dress and broom, and the tilt of her head and shadowed features all work together to elicit a particular interpretation?

MARTIN LUTHER KING, JR.

"Letter from Birmingham Jail," a literary and humanitarian masterpiece, reveals why Martin Luther King, Jr. was the most influential leader of the American civil rights movement in the 1950s and 1960s, and, why, with Mahatma Gandhi, he was one of this century's most influential advocates for human rights. King was born in Atlanta in 1929, the son of a well-known Baptist clergyman, educated at Morehouse College, and ordained in his father's denomination.

A forceful and charismatic leader, Dr. King became at twenty-six a national spokesperson for the civil rights movement when in 1955 he led a successful boycott of the segregated bus system of Montgomery, Alabama. Dr. King became president of the Southern Christian Leadership Conference and led the sit-ins and demonstrations—including the 1964 march on Washington, D.C., which climaxed with his famous "I Have a Dream" speech—that helped to ensure passage of the 1964 Civil Rights Act and the Voting Rights Act of 1965. He received the Nobel Peace Prize in 1964, its youngest winner. Toward the end of his life, cut short by assassination in 1968, Dr. King was increasingly concerned with improving the rights and the lives of the nation's poor, irrespective of race, and with ending the war in Vietnam. His birthday became a national holiday in 1986.

In 1963 King wrote the letter reprinted below while imprisoned for "parading without a permit." Though ostensibly replying to eight clergymen—Protestant, Catholic, and Jewish—who feared violence in the Birmingham desegregation demonstrations, King actually intended his letter for the worldwide audience his civil rights activities commanded. Warning that America had more to fear from passive moderates ("the appalling silence of good people") than from extremists, King defended his policy of "nonviolent direct action" and explained why he was compelled to disobey "unjust laws"—supporting his argument with references to Protestant, Catholic, and Jewish examples ("Was not Jesus an extremist for love. . . ."), as well as to the painful examples of segregation in his own life.

Letter from Birmingham Jail*

April 16, 1963

1 *My Dear Fellow Clergymen:*
While confined here in the Birmingham city jail, I came across your recent statement calling my present activities "unwise and untimely." Seldom do I pause to answer criticism of my work and ideas. If I sought to answer all the criticisms that cross my desk, my secretaries would have little time for anything other than such correspondence in the course of the day, and I would have no time for constructive work. But since I feel that you are men of genuine good will and that your criticisms are sincerely set forth, I want to try to answer your statement in what I hope will be patient and reasonable terms.

2 I think I should indicate why I am here in Birmingham, since you have been influenced by the view which argues against "outsiders coming in." I have the honor of serving as president of the Southern Christian Leadership Conference, an organization operating in every southern state, with headquarters in Atlanta, Georgia. We have some eighty-five affiliated organizations across the South, and one of them is the Alabama Christian Movement for Human Rights. Frequently we share staff, educational and financial resources with our affiliates. Several months ago the affiliate here in Birmingham asked us to be on call to engage in a nonviolent direct-action program if such were deemed

* AUTHOR'S NOTE: This response to a published statement by eight fellow clergymen from Alabama (Bishop C. C. J. Carpenter, Bishop Joseph A. Durick, Rabbi Hilton L. Grafman, Bishop Paul Hardin, Bishop Holan B. Harmon, the Reverend George M. Murray, the Reverend Edward V. Ramage and the Reverend Earl Stallings) was composed under somewhat constricting circumstances. Begun on the margins of the newspaper in which the statement appeared while I was in jail, the letter was continued on scraps of writing paper supplied by a friendly Negro trusty, and concluded on a pad my attorneys were eventually permitted to leave me. Although the text remains in substance unaltered, I have indulged in the author's prerogative of polishing it for publication.

© Bettmann/Corbis

Dr. Martin Luther King, Jr., and other notable figures in the 60s Civil Rights movement—Andy Young (left), Joan Baez, and Hosea Williams (next to Baez)—are escorting black children into a newly integrated school in Grenada, Mississippi, on September 20, 1966. What arguments are embedded in this picture? What is the point of having such a high profile delegation of escorts? Where would this picture have first been published? Reprinted? Who would be expected to view it? With what reaction(s)? What has happened since this picture was taken to make this a telling scene in American history rather than a typical first-day-of-school picture today? Compare this with the first-day-of-school photograph of the six-year-old Spinner twins (299).

necessary. We readily consented, and when the hour came we lived up to our promise. So I, along with several members of my staff, am here because I was invited here. I am here because I have organizational ties here.

But more basically, I am in Birmingham because injustice is here. Just as the prophets of the eighth century B.C. left their villages and carried their "thus saith the Lord" far beyond the boundaries of their home towns, and, just as the Apostle Paul left his village of Tarsus and carried the gospel of Jesus Christ to the far corners of the Greco-Roman world, so am I compelled to carry the gospel of freedom beyond my own home town. Like Paul, I must constantly respond to the Macedonian call for aid. 3

Moreover, I am cognizant of the interrelatedness of all communities and states. I cannot sit idly by in Atlanta and not be concerned about 4 what happens in Birmingham. Injustice anywhere is a threat to justice everywhere. We are caught in an inescapable network of mutuality, tied in a single garment of destiny. Whatever affects one directly, affects all indirectly. Never again can we afford to live with the narrow, provincial "outside agitator" idea. Anyone who lives inside the United States can never be considered an outsider anywhere within its bounds.

5 You deplore the demonstrations taking place in Birmingham. But your statement, I am sorry to say, fails to express a similar concern for the conditions that brought about the demonstrations. I am sure that none of you would want to rest content with the superficial kind of social analysis that deals merely with effects and does not grapple with underlying causes. It is unfortunate that demonstrations are taking place in Birmingham, but it is even more unfortunate that the city's white power structure left the Negro community with no alternative.

6 In any nonviolent campaign there are four basic steps: collection of the facts to determine whether injustices exist; negotiation; self-purification; and direct action. We have gone through all these steps in Birmingham. There can be no gainsaying the fact that racial injustice engulfs this community. Birmingham is probably the most thoroughly segregated city in the United States. An ugly record of brutality is widely known. Negroes have experienced grossly unjust treatment in the courts. There have been more unsolved bombings of Negro homes and churches in Birmingham than in any other city in the nation. These are the hard brutal facts of the case. On the basis of these conditions, Negro leaders sought to negotiate with the city fathers. But the latter consistently refused to engage in good-faith negotiation.

7 Then, last September, came the opportunity to talk with leaders of Birmingham's economic community. In the course of the negotiations, certain promises were made by the merchants—for example, to remove the stores' humiliating racial signs. On the basis of these promises, the Reverend Fred Shuttlesworth and the leaders of the Alabama Christian Movement for Human Rights agreed to a moratorium on all demonstrations. As the weeks and months went by, we realized that we were the victims of a broken promise. A few signs, briefly removed, returned; the others remained.

8 As in so many past experiences, our hopes had been blasted, and the shadow of deep disappointment settled upon us. We had no alternative except to prepare for direct action, whereby we would present our very bodies as a means of laying our case before the conscience of the local and the national community. Mindful of the difficulties involved, we decided to undertake a process of self-purification. We began a series of workshops on nonviolence, and we repeatedly asked ourselves: "Are you able to accept blows without retaliating?" "Are you able to endure the ordeal of jail?" We decided to schedule our direct-action program for the Easter season, realizing that except for Christmas, this is the main shopping period

of the year. Knowing that a strong economic-withdrawal program would be the by-product of direct action, we felt that this would be the best time to bring pressure to bear on the merchants for the needed change.

Then it occurred to us that Birmingham's mayoralty election was 9
coming up in March, and we speedily decided to postpone action until after election day. When we discovered that the Commissioner of Public Safety, Eugene "Bull" Connor, had piled up enough votes to be in the run-off, we decided again to postpone action until the day after the run-off so that the demonstrations could not be used to cloud the issues. Like many others, we waited to see Mr. Connor defeated, and to this end we endured postponement after postponement. Having aided in this community need, we felt that our direct-action program could be delayed no longer.

You may well ask: "Why direct action? Why sit-ins, marches and so 10
forth? Isn't negotiation a better path?" You are quite right in calling for negotiation. Indeed this is the very purpose of direct action. Nonviolent direct action seeks to create such a crisis and foster such a tension that a community which has constantly refused to negotiate is forced to confront the issue. It seeks so to dramatize the issue that it can no longer be ignored. My citing the creation of tension as part of the work of the nonviolent-resister may sound rather shocking. But I must confess that I am not afraid of the word "tension." I have earnestly opposed violent tension, but there is a type of nonviolent tension which is necessary for growth. Just as Socrates felt that it was necessary to create a tension in the mind so that individuals could rise from the bondage of myths and half-truths to the unfettered realm of creative analysis and objective appraisal, so must we see the need for nonviolent gadflies to create the kind of tension in society that will help men rise from the dark depths of prejudice and racism to the majestic heights of understanding and brotherhood.

The purpose of our direct-action program is to create a situation so 11
crisis-packed that it will inevitably open the door to negotiation. I therefore concur with you in your call for negotiation. Too long has our beloved Southland been bogged down in a tragic effort to live in monologue rather than dialogue.

One of the basic points in your statement is that the action that 12
I and my associates have taken in Birmingham is untimely. Some have asked: "Why didn't you give the new city administration time to act?" The only answer that I can give to this query is that the new Birmingham administration must be prodded about as much as the outgoing one, before it will act. We are sadly mistaken if we feel that the election of Albert Boutwell as mayor will bring the millennium to Birmingham. While Mr. Boutwell is a much more gentle person than Mr. Connor, they are both segregationists, dedicated to maintenance of the status quo. I have hope that Mr. Boutwell will be reasonable enough to see the futility of massive resistance to desegregation. But he will not see

this without pressure from devotees of civil rights. My friends, I must say to you that we have not made a single gain in civil rights without determined legal and nonviolent pressure. Lamentably, it is an historical fact that privileged groups seldom give up their privileges voluntarily. Individuals may see the moral light and voluntarily give up their unjust posture; but, as Reinhold Niebuhr has reminded us, groups tend to be more immoral than individuals.

13 We know through painful experience that freedom is never voluntarily given by the oppressor; it must be demanded by the oppressed. Frankly, I have yet to engage in a direct-action campaign that was "well-timed" in the view of those who have not suffered unduly from the disease of segregation. For years now I have heard the word "Wait!" It rings in the ear of every Negro with piercing familiarity. This "Wait" has almost always meant "Never." We must come to see, with one of our distinguished jurists, that "justice too long delayed is justice denied."

14 We have waited for more than 340 years for our constitutional and Godgiven rights. The nations of Asia and Africa are moving with jetlike speed toward gaining political independence, but we still creep at horse-and-buggy pace toward gaining a cup of coffee at a lunch counter. Perhaps it is easy for those who have never felt the stinging darts of segregation to say, "Wait." But when you have seen vicious mobs lynch your mothers and fathers at will and drown your sisters and brothers at whim; when you have seen hate-filled policemen curse, kick and even kill your black brothers and sisters; when you see the vast majority of your twenty million Negro brothers smothering in an airtight cage of poverty in the midst of an affluent society; when you suddenly find your tongue twisted and your speech stammering as you seek to explain to your six-year-old daughter why she can't go to the public amusement park that has just been advertised on television, and see tears welling up in her eyes when she is told that Funtown is closed to colored children, and see ominous clouds of inferiority beginning to form in her little mental sky, and see her beginning to distort her personality by developing an unconscious bitterness toward white people; when you have to concoct an answer for a five-year-old son who is asking: "Daddy, why do white people treat colored people so mean?"; when you take a cross-country drive and find it necessary to sleep night after night in the uncomfortable corners of your automobile because no motel will accept you; when you are humiliated day in and day out by nagging signs reading "white" and "colored"; when your first name becomes "nigger," your middle name becomes "boy" (however old you are) and your last name becomes "John," and your wife and mother are never given the respected title "Mrs."; when you are harried by day and haunted by night by the fact that you are a Negro, living constantly at tiptoe stance, never quite knowing what to expect next, and are plagued with inner fears and outer resentments; when you are forever fighting a degenerating sense of "nobodiness"—then you will understand why we

find it difficult to wait. There comes a time when the cup of endurance runs over, and men are no longer willing to be plunged into the abyss of despair. I hope, sirs, you can understand our legitimate and unavoidable impatience.

You express a great deal of anxiety over our willingness to break 15
laws. This is certainly a legitimate concern. Since we so diligently urge people to obey the Supreme Court's decision of 1954 outlawing segregation in the public schools, at first glance it may seem rather paradoxical for us consciously to break laws. One may well ask: "How can you advocate breaking some laws and obeying others?" The answer lies in the fact that there are two types of laws: just and unjust. I would be the first to advocate obeying just laws. One has not only a legal but a moral responsibility to obey just laws. Conversely, one has a moral responsibility to disobey unjust laws. I would agree with St. Augustine that "an unjust law is no law at all."

Now, what is the difference between the two? How does one deter- 16
mine whether a law is just or unjust? A just law is a man-made code that squares with the moral law or the law of God. An unjust law is a code that is out of harmony with the moral law. To put it in the terms of St. Thomas Aquinas: An unjust law is a human law that is not rooted in eternal law and natural law. Any law that uplifts human personality is just. Any law that degrades human personality is unjust. All segregation statutes are unjust because segregation distorts the soul and damages the personality. It gives the segregator a false sense of superiority and the segregated a false sense of inferiority. Segregation, to use the terminology of the Jewish philosopher Martin Buber, substitutes an "I-it" relationship for an "I-thou" relationship and ends up relegating persons to the status of things. Hence segregation is not only politically, economically and sociologically unsound, it is morally wrong and sinful. Paul Tillich has said that sin is separation. Is not segregation an existential expression of man's tragic separation, his awful estrangement, his terrible sinfulness? Thus it is that I can urge men to obey the 1954 decision of the Supreme Court, for it is morally right; and I can urge them to disobey segregation ordinances, for they are morally wrong.

Let us consider a more concrete example of just and unjust laws. An 17
unjust law is a code that a numerical or power majority group compels a minority group to obey but does not make binding on itself. This is *difference* made legal. By the same token, a just law is a code that a majority compels a minority to follow and that it is willing to follow itself. This is *sameness* made legal.

Let me give another explanation. A law is unjust if it is inflicted on a 18
minority that, as a result of being denied the right to vote, had no part in enacting or devising the law. Who can say that the legislature of Alabama which set up that state's segregation laws was democratically elected? Throughout Alabama all sorts of devious methods are used to prevent

Negroes from becoming registered voters, and there are some counties in which even though Negroes constitute a majority of the population, not a single Negro is registered. Can any law enacted under such circumstances be considered democratically structured?

19 Sometimes a law is just on its face and unjust in its application. For instance, I have been arrested on a charge of parading without a permit. Now, there is nothing wrong in having an ordinance which requires a permit for a parade. But such an ordinance becomes unjust when it is used to maintain segregation and to deny citizens the First-Amendment privilege of peaceful assembly and protest.

20 I hope you are able to see the distinction I am trying to point out. In no sense do I advocate evading or defying the law, as would the rabid segregationist. That would lead to anarchy. One who breaks an unjust law must do so openly, lovingly, and with a willingness to accept the penalty. I submit that an individual who breaks a law that conscience tells him is unjust, and who willingly accepts the penalty of imprisonment in order to arouse the conscience of the community over its injustice, is in reality expressing the highest respect for the law.

21 Of course, there is nothing new about this kind of civil disobedience. It was evidenced sublimely in the refusal of Shadrach, Meshach and Abednego to obey the laws of Nebuchadnezzar, on the ground that a higher moral law was at stake. It was practiced superbly by the early Christians, who were willing to face hungry lions and the excruciating pain of chopping blocks rather than submit to certain unjust laws of the Roman Empire. To a degree, academic freedom is a reality today because Socrates practiced civil disobedience. In our own nation, the Boston Tea Party represented a massive act of civil disobedience.

22 We should never forget that everything Adolf Hitler did in Germany was "legal" and everything the Hungarian freedom fighters did in Hungary was "illegal." It was "illegal" to aid and comfort a Jew in Hitler's Germany. Even so, I am sure that, had I lived in Germany at the time, I would have aided and comforted my Jewish brothers. If today I lived in a Communist country where certain principles dear to the Christian faith are suppressed, I would openly advocate disobeying that country's anti-religious laws.

23 I must make two honest confessions to you, my Christian and Jewish brothers. First, I must confess that over the past few years I have been gravely disappointed with the white moderate. I have almost reached the regrettable conclusion that the Negro's great stumbling block in his stride toward freedom is not the White Citizen's Counciler or the Ku Klux Klanner, but the white moderate, who is more devoted to "order" than to justice; who prefers a negative peace which is the absence of tension to a positive peace which is the presence of justice; who constantly says: "I agree with you in the goal you seek, but I cannot agree with your methods of direct action"; who paternalistically

believes he can set the timetable for another man's freedom; who lives by a mythical concept of time and who constantly advises the Negro to wait for a "more convenient season." Shallow understanding from people of good will is more frustrating than absolute misunderstanding from people of ill will. Lukewarm acceptance is much more bewildering than outright rejection.

I had hoped that the white moderate would understand that law 24
and order exist for the purpose of establishing justice and that when they fail in this purpose they become the dangerously structured dams that block the flow of social progress. I had hoped that the white moderate would understand that the present tension in the South is a necessary phase of the transition from an obnoxious negative peace, in which the Negro passively accepted his unjust plight, to a substantive and positive peace, in which all men will respect the dignity and worth of human personality. Actually, we who engage in non-violent direct action are not the creators of tension. We merely bring to the surface the hidden tension that is already alive. We bring it out in the open, where it can be seen and dealt with. Like a boil that can never be cured so long as it is covered up but must be opened with all its ugliness to the natural medicines of air and light, injustice must be exposed, with all the tension its exposure creates, to the light of human conscience and the air of national opinion before it can be cured.

In your statement you assert that our actions, even though peace- 25
ful, must be condemned because they precipitate violence. But is this a logical assertion? Isn't this like condemning a robbed man because his possession of money precipitated the evil act of robbery? Isn't this like condemning Socrates because his unswerving commitment to truth and his philosophical inquiries precipitated the act by the misguided populace in which they made him drink hemlock? Isn't this like condemning Jesus because his unique God-consciousness and never-ceasing devotion to God's will precipitated the evil act of crucifixion? We must come to see that, as the federal courts have consistently affirmed, it is wrong to urge an individual to cease his efforts to gain his basic constitutional rights because the quest may precipitate violence. Society must protect the robbed and punish the robber.

I had also hoped that the white moderate would reject the myth 26
concerning time in relation to the struggle for freedom. I have just received a letter from a white brother in Texas. He writes: "All Christians know that the colored people will receive equal rights eventually, but it is possible that you are in too great a religious hurry. It has taken Christianity almost two thousand years to accomplish what it has. The teachings of Christ take time to come to earth." Such an attitude stems from a tragic misconception of time, from the strangely irrational notion that there is something in the very flow of time that will inevitably cure all ills. Actually, time itself is neutral; it can be used either

destructively or constructively. More and more I feel that the people of ill will have used time much more effectively than have the people of good will. We will have to repent in this generation not merely for the hateful words and actions of the bad people but for the appalling silence of the good people. Human progress never rolls in on wheels of inevitability; it comes through the tireless efforts of men willing to be coworkers with God, and without this hard work, time itself becomes an ally of the forces of social stagnation. We must use time creatively, in the knowledge that the time is always ripe to do right. Now is the time to make real the promise of democracy and transform our pending national elegy into a creative psalm of brotherhood. Now is the time to lift our national policy from the quicksand of racial injustice to the solid rock of human dignity.

27 You speak of our activity in Birmingham as extreme. At first I was rather disappointed that fellow clergymen would see my nonviolent efforts as those of an extremist. I began thinking about the fact that I stand in the middle of two opposing forces in the Negro community. One is a force of complacency, made up in part of Negroes who, as a result of long years of oppression, are so drained of self-respect and a sense of "somebodiness" that they have adjusted to segregation; and in part of a few middle-class Negroes who, because of a degree of academic and economic security and because in some ways they profit by segregation, have become insensitive to the problems of the masses. The other force is one of bitterness and hatred, and it comes perilously close to advocating violence. It is expressed in the various black nationalist groups that are springing up across the nation, the largest and best-known being Elijah Muhammad's Muslim movement. Nourished by the Negro's frustration over the continued existence of racial discrimination, this movement is made up of people who have lost faith in America, who have absolutely repudiated Christianity, and who have concluded that the white man is an incorrigible "devil."

28 I have tried to stand between these two forces, saying that we need emulate neither the "do-nothingism" of the complacent nor the hatred and despair of the black nationalist. For there is the more excellent way of love and nonviolent protest. I am grateful to God that, through the influence of the Negro church, the way of nonviolence became an integral part of our struggle.

29 If this philosophy had not emerged, by now many streets of the South would, I am convinced, be flowing with blood. And I am further convinced that if our white brothers dismiss as "rabble-rousers" and "outside agitators" those of us who employ nonviolent direct action, and if they refuse to support our non-violent efforts, millions of Negroes will, out of frustration and despair, seek solace and security in black-nationalist ideologies—a development that would inevitably lead to a frightening racial nightmare.

Oppressed people cannot remain oppressed forever. The yearning 30
for freedom eventually manifests itself, and that is what has happened to the American Negro. Something within has reminded him of his birthright of freedom, and something without has reminded him that it can be gained. Consciously or unconsciously, he has been caught up by the *Zeitgeist*, and with his black brothers of Africa and his brown and yellow brothers of Asia, South America and the Caribbean, the United States Negro is moving with a sense of great urgency toward the promised land of racial justice. If one recognizes this vital urge that has engulfed the Negro community, one should readily understand why public demonstrations are taking place. The Negro has many pent-up resentments and latent frustrations, and he must release them. So let him march; let him make prayer pilgrimages to the city hall; let him go on freedom rides—and try to understand why he must do so. If his repressed emotions are not released in nonviolent ways, they will seek expression through violence; this is not a threat but a fact of history. So I have not said to my people: "Get rid of your discontent." Rather, I have tried to say that this normal and healthy discontent can be channeled into the creative outlet of nonviolent direct action. And now this approach is being termed extremist.

But though I was initially disappointed at being categorized as an 31
extremist, as I continued to think about the matter I gradually gained a measure of satisfaction from the label. Was not Jesus an extremist for love: "Love your enemies, bless them that curse you, do good to them that hate you, and pray for them which despitefully use you, and persecute you." Was not Amos an extremist for justice: "Let justice roll down like waters and righteousness like an ever-flowing stream." Was not Paul an extremist for the Christian gospel: "I bear in my body the marks of the Lord Jesus." Was not Martin Luther an extremist: "Here I stand; I cannot do otherwise, so help me God." And John Bunyan: "I will stay in jail to the end of my days before I make a butchery of my conscience." And Abraham Lincoln: "This nation cannot survive half slave and half free." And Thomas Jefferson: "We hold these truths to be self-evident, that all men are created equal. . . ." So the question is not whether we will be extremists, but what kind of extremists we will be. Will we be extremists for hate or for love? Will we be extremists for the preservation of injustice or for the extension of justice? In that dramatic scene on Calvary's hill three men were crucified. We must never forget that all three were crucified for the same crime—the crime of extremism. Two were extremists for immorality, and thus fell below their environment. The other, Jesus Christ, was an extremist for love, truth and goodness, and thereby rose above his environment. Perhaps the South, the nation and the world are in dire need of creative extremists.

I had hoped that the white moderate would see this need. Perhaps 32
I was too optimistic; perhaps I expected too much. I suppose I should

have realized that few members of the oppressor race can understand the deep groans and passionate yearnings of the oppressed race, and still fewer have the vision to see that injustice must be rooted out by strong, persistent and determined action. I am thankful, however, that some of our white brothers in the South have grasped the meaning of this social revolution and committed themselves to it. They are still all too few in quantity, but they are big in quality. Some—such as Ralph McGill, Lillian Smith, Harry Golden, James McBride Dabbs, Ann Braden and Sarah Patton Boyle—have written about our struggle in eloquent and prophetic terms. Others have marched with us down nameless streets of the South. They have languished in filthy, roach-infested jails, suffering the abuse and brutality of policemen who view them as "dirty nigger-lovers." Unlike so many of their moderate brothers and sisters, they have recognized the urgency of the moment and sensed the need for powerful "action" antidotes to combat the disease of segregation.

33 Let me take note of my other major disappointment. I have been so greatly disappointed with the white church and its leadership. Of course, there are some notable exceptions. I am not unmindful of the fact that each of you has taken some significant stands on this issue. I commend you, Reverend Stallings, for your Christian stand on this past Sunday, in welcoming Negroes to your worship service on a nonsegregated basis. I commend the Catholic leaders of this state for integrating Spring Hill College several years ago.

34 But despite these notable exceptions, I must honestly reiterate that I have been disappointed with the church. I do not say this as one of those negative critics who can always find something wrong with the church. I say this as a minister of the gospel, who loves the church; who was nurtured in its bosom; who has been sustained by its spiritual blessings and who will remain true to it as long as the cord of life shall lengthen.

35 When I was suddenly catapulted into the leadership of the bus protest in Montgomery, Alabama, a few years ago, I felt we would be supported by the white church. I felt that the white ministers, priests and rabbis of the South would be among our strongest allies. Instead, some have been outright opponents, refusing to understand the freedom movement and misrepresenting its leaders; all too many others have been more cautious than courageous and have remained silent behind the anesthetizing security of stained-glass windows.

36 In spite of my shattered dreams, I came to Birmingham with the hope that the white religious leadership of this community would see the justice of our cause and, with deep moral concern, would serve as the channel through which our just grievances could reach the power structure. I had hoped that each of you would understand. But again I have been disappointed.

37 I have heard numerous southern religious leaders admonish their worshipers to comply with a desegregation decision because it is the

law, but I have longed to hear white ministers declare: "Follow this decree because integration is morally right and because the Negro is your brother." In the midst of blatant injustices inflicted upon the Negro, I have watched white churchmen stand on the sideline and mouth pious irrelevancies and sanctimonious trivialities. In the midst of a mighty struggle to rid our nation of racial and economic injustice, I have heard many ministers say: "Those are social issues, with which the gospel has no real concern." And I have watched many churches commit themselves to completely other-worldly religion which makes a strange, un-Biblical distinction between body and soul, between the sacred and the secular.

I have traveled the length and breadth of Alabama, Mississippi 38
and all the other southern states. On sweltering summer days and crisp autumn mornings I have looked at the South's beautiful churches with their lofty spires pointing heavenward. I have beheld the impressive outlines of her massive religious-education buildings. Over and over I have found myself asking: "What kind of people worship here? Who is their God? Where were their voices when the lips of Governor Barnett dripped with words of interposition and nullification? Where were they when Governor Wallace gave a clarion call for defiance and hatred? Where were their voices of support when bruised and weary Negro men and women decided to rise from the dark dungeons of complacency to the bright hills of creative protest?"

Yes, these questions are still in my mind. In deep disappointment 39
I have wept over the laxity of the church. But be assured that my tears have been tears of love. There can be no deep disappointment where there is not deep love. Yes, I love the church. How could I do otherwise? I am in the rather unique position of being the son, the grandson and the great-grandson of preachers. Yes, I see the church as the body of Christ. But, oh! How we have blemished and scarred that body through social neglect and through fear of being nonconformists.

There was a time when the church was very powerful—in the time 40
when the early Christians rejoiced at being deemed worthy to suffer for what they believed. In those days the church was not merely a thermometer that recorded the ideas and principles of popular opinion; it was a thermostat that transformed the mores of society. Whenever the early Christians entered a town, the people in power became disturbed and immediately sought to convict the Christians for being "disturbers of the peace" and "outside agitators." But the Christians pressed on, in the conviction that they were "a colony of heaven," called to obey God rather than man. Small in number, they were big in commitment. They were too God-intoxicated to be "astronomically intimidated." By their effort and example they brought an end to such ancient evils as infanticide and gladiatorial contests.

Things are different now. So often the contemporary church is a weak, 41
ineffectual voice with an uncertain sound. So often it is an archdefender

of the status quo. Far from being disturbed by the presence of the church, the power structure of the average community is consoled by the church's silent—and often even vocal—sanction of things as they are.

42 But the judgment of God is upon the church as never before. If today's church does not recapture the sacrificial spirit of the early church, it will lose its authenticity, forfeit the loyalty of millions, and be dismissed as an irrelevant social club with no meaning for the twentieth century. Every day I meet young people whose disappointment with the church has turned into outright disgust.

43 Perhaps I have once again been too optimistic. Is organized religion too inextricably bound to the status quo to save our nation and the world? Perhaps I must turn my faith to the inner spiritual church, the church within the church, as the true *ekklesia* and the hope of the world. But again I am thankful to God that some noble souls from the ranks of organized religion have broken loose from the paralyzing chains of conformity and joined us as active partners in the struggle for freedom. They have left their secure congregations and walked the streets of Albany, Georgia, with us. They have gone down the highways of the South on tortuous rides for freedom. Yes, they have gone to jail with us. Some have been dismissed from their churches, have lost the support of their bishops and fellow ministers. But they have acted in the faith that right defeated is stronger than evil triumphant. Their witness has been the spiritual salt that has preserved the true meaning of the gospel in these troubled times. They have carved a tunnel of hope through the dark mountain of disappointment.

44 I hope the church as a whole will meet the challenge of this decisive hour. But even if the church does not come to the aid of justice, I have no despair about the future. I have no fear about the outcome of our struggle in Birmingham, even if our motives are at present misunderstood. We will reach the goal of freedom in Birmingham and all over the nation, because the goal of America is freedom. Abused and scorned though we may be, our destiny is tied up with America's destiny. Before the pilgrims landed at Plymouth, we were here. Before the pen of Jefferson etched the majestic words of the Declaration of Independence across the pages of history, we were here. For more than two centuries our forebears labored in this country without wages; they made cotton king; they built the homes of their masters while suffering gross injustice and shameful humiliation—and yet out of a bottomless vitality they continued to thrive and develop. If the inexpressible cruelties of slavery could not stop us, the opposition we now face will surely fail. We will win our freedom because the sacred heritage of our nation and the eternal will of God are embodied in our echoing demands.

45 Before closing I feel impelled to mention one other point in your statement that has troubled me profoundly. You warmly commended the Birmingham police force for keeping "order" and "preventing violence."

I doubt that you would have so warmly commended the police force if you had seen its dogs sinking their teeth into unarmed, nonviolent Negroes. I doubt that you would so quickly commend the policemen if you were to observe their ugly and inhumane treatment of Negroes here in the city jail; if you were to watch them push and curse old Negro women and young Negro girls; if you were to see them slap and kick old Negro men and young boys; if you were to observe them as they did on two occasions, refuse to give us food because we wanted to sing our grace together. I cannot join you in your praise of the Birmingham police department.

It is true that the police have exercised a degree of discipline in han- 46
dling the demonstrators. In this sense they have conducted themselves rather "nonviolently" in public. But for what purpose? To preserve the evil system of segregation. Over the past few years I have consistently preached that nonviolence demands that the means we use must be as pure as the ends we seek. I have tried to make clear that it is wrong to use immoral means to attain moral ends. But now I must affirm that it is just as wrong, or perhaps even more so, to use moral means to preserve immoral ends. Perhaps Mr. Connor and his policemen have been rather nonviolent in public, as was Chief Pritchett in Albany, Georgia, but they have used the moral means of nonviolence to maintain the immoral end of racial injustice. As T. S. Eliot has said: "The last temptation is the greatest treason: To do the right deed for the wrong reason."

I wish you had commended the Negro sit-inners and demonstrators 47
of Birmingham for their sublime courage, their willingness to suffer and their amazing discipline in the midst of great provocation. One day the South will recognize its real heroes. They will be the James Merediths, with the noble sense of purpose that enables them to face jeering and hostile mobs, and with the agonizing loneliness that characterizes the life of the pioneer. They will be old, oppressed, battered Negro women, symbolized in a seventy-two-year-old woman in Montgomery, Alabama, who rose up with a sense of dignity and with her people decided not to ride segregated buses, and who responded with ungrammatical profundity to one who inquired about her weariness: "My feet is tired, but my soul is at rest." They will be the young high school and college students, the young ministers of the gospel and a host of their elders, courageously and nonviolently sitting in at lunch counters and willingly going to jail for conscience' sake. One day the South will know that when these disinherited children of God sat down at lunch counters, they were in reality standing up for what is best in the American dream and for the most sacred values in our Judaeo-Christian heritage, thereby bringing our nation back to those great wells of democracy which were dug deep by the founding fathers in their formulation of the Constitution and the Declaration of Independence.

Never before have I written so long a letter. I'm afraid it is much too 48
long to take your precious time. I can assure you that it would have been

much shorter if I had been writing from a comfortable desk, but what else can one do when he is alone in a narrow jail cell, other than write long letters, think long thoughts and pray long prayers?

49 If I have said anything in this letter that overstates the truth and indicates an unreasonable impatience, I beg you to forgive me. If I have said anything that understates the truth and indicates my having a patience that allows me to settle for anything less than brotherhood, I beg God to forgive me.

50 I hope this letter finds you strong in faith. I also hope that circumstances will soon make it possible for me to meet each of you, not as an integrationist or a civil-rights leader but as a fellow clergyman and a Christian brother. Let us all hope that the dark clouds of racial prejudice will soon pass away and the deep fog of misunderstanding will be lifted from our fear-drenched communities, and in some not too distant tomorrow the radiant stars of love and brotherhood will shine over our great nation with all their scintillating beauty.

Yours for the cause of Peace and Brotherhood,
Martin Luther King, Jr.

Content

1. In paragraph 4 King makes several assertions on which he bases the rest of his argument. What are they? Does he ever prove them, or does he assume that readers will take them for granted?
2. In paragraph 5 King asserts that Birmingham's "white power structure left the Negro community with no alternative" but to commit civil disobedience. Does he ever prove this? Does he need to? Is it a debatable statement?
3. What, according to King, are the "four basic steps" in "any nonviolent campaign" (¶ 6)? What is the goal of "nonviolent direct action" (¶ 10)? What is the constructive, "nonviolent tension" (¶ 10) King favors?
4. Why has King been disappointed by white moderates (¶s 23–32)? By the white church (¶s 33–44)? What does he want white moderates to do? What does he claim that the church should do?
5. How does King deal with the argument that civil rights activists are too impatient, that they should go slow because "it has taken Christianity almost two thousand years to accomplish what it has" (¶ 26)? How does he refute the argument that he is an extremist (¶ 27)?

Strategies/Structures/Language

6. How does King establish, in the salutation and first paragraph, his reasons for writing? The setting in which he writes? His intended audience? In what ways does he demonstrate a sensitive, reasonable tone?
7. King's letter ostensibly replies to that of the eight clergymen. Find passages in which he addresses them, and analyze the voice he uses. In what relation to the clergymen does King see himself? He also has a secondary audience; who are its

members? Locate passages that seem especially directed to this second audience. In what relation to this audience does King see himself?

8. Why does King cite the theologians Aquinas (a Catholic), Buber (a Jew), and Tillich (a Protestant) in paragraph 16? What similarities link the three?

9. After defending his actions against the criticisms of the clergymen, King takes the offensive in paragraphs 23–44. How does he signal this change?

10. Which parts of King's letter appeal chiefly to reason? To emotion? How are the two types of appeals interrelated?

11. King uses large numbers of rhetorical questions throughout this essay (see ¶s 18, 25, 31, 38, 39). Why? With what effects?

12. How does King define a "just law" (¶s 16, 17)? An "unjust law" (¶s 16, 17)? Why are these definitions crucial to the argument that follows?

For Writing

13. With a partner, write a position paper identifying the circumstances, if any, under which breaking the law is justifiable. If you use Dr. King's definition of just and unjust law (¶s 15–20) or make any distinction, say, between moral law and civil law, be sure to explain what you mean. You may, if you wish, use examples with which you are personally familiar. Or you may elaborate on some of the examples King uses (¶ 22) or on examples from King's own civil rights activities, such as the boycotts in the early 1950s of the legally segregated Montgomery bus system (¶ 35).

14. If you are a member of a church, or attend a church regularly, address members of the congregation on what, if any, commitment you think your church should make to better the lives of other groups who do not attend that church. Does this commitment extend to civil disobedience?

15. Would you ever be willing to go to jail for a cause? What cause or types of causes? Under what circumstances? If you knew that a prison record might bar you from some privileges in some states (such as practicing law or medicine), would you still be willing to take such a risk?

16. ***Journal Writing.*** Write a narrative about a historical event that occurred during your lifetime, perhaps the election of Barack Obama as the fourty-fourth President of the United States. To what extent were you aware that you were living through a moment of history-in-the-making? Did you fully realize how the event would change the world or your life? Did you go back to the event and re-tell it to yourself to make sense of it?

17. ***Dialogues.*** Given King's characterization of the church as "the body of Christ" (¶ 39), how might he interpret the fight Frederick Douglass recounts in "Resurrection" (89–93)? When and under what circumstances might he consider violence justifiable? How might he interpret Douglass's fight as a metaphorical struggle for what calls "somebodiness" (¶ 27)?

18. ***Second Look.*** How does the photograph in this essay of Dr. King and other civil rights figures escorting children to school illustrate King's belief in the efficacy of nonviolent direct action? Why are the mothers of the children absent from the photograph? How does the arrangement of the people photographed affect your interpretation of this historical moment? For example, the only woman pictured, Joan Baez, who is white and a celebrity, stands in the center of the group, while each child is sheltered by the male adults. What kinds of assumptions about race and gender does this photograph challenge?

JARED DIAMOND

Jared Diamond (born in Boston, 1937) says of his life's work: "I've set myself the modest task of trying to explain the broad pattern of human history, on all the continents, for the last 13,000 years. Why did history take such different evolutionary courses for peoples of different continents? This problem has fascinated me for a long time, but it's now ripe for a new synthesis because of recent advances in many fields seemingly remote from history, including molecular biology, plant and animal genetics, and biogeography, archaeology, and linguistics."

The triple orientation of his work has prepared him well to accomplish this aim. After earning a BA from Harvard (1958) and PhD from Cambridge University (1961) in physiology and membrane biophysics he taught physiology at UCLA Medical School. For over twenty years, he concurrently did research on the ecology of New Guinea and the evolution of birds there, leading over seventeen research expeditions. His more recent work, incorporating a broad knowledge of evolutionary biology, physiology, anthropology, and biogeography, has led to a professorship in geography at UCLA. Recipient of innumerable awards, including a Guggenheim Fellowship, Japan's Cosmos Prize, and a National Science Medal, he won the Pulitzer Prize for *Guns, Germs, and Steel* (1998) and the *Los Angeles Times* Book Award for *The Third Chimpanzee* (1992). In *Collapse: How Societies Choose to Fail or Succeed* (2005), from which the following piece is excerpted, Diamond argues that human mismanagement of natural resources is responsible for the downfall of several major civilizations and colonies, including the Mayan and Easter Island cultures and the Nordic settlements in Greenland, and that contemporary society faces equally serious threats from our inefficient and extravagant exploitation of our environment. Here Diamond lists the major environmental challenges we currently face, describes the urgency of these interrelated problems, and calls on all nations to respond in a coordinated effort to prevent the chaos that will ensue from a depleted earth.

The World as a Polder

1 Let's begin with the natural resources that we are destroying or losing: natural habitats, wild food sources, biological diversity, and soil.

2 1. At an accelerating rate, we are destroying natural habitats or else converting them to human-made habitats, such as cities and villages, farmlands and pastures, roads, and golf courses. The natural habitats whose losses have provoked the most discussion are forests, wetlands, coral reefs, and the ocean bottom. . . . More than half of the world's original area of forest has already been converted to other uses, and

at present conversion rates one-quarter of the forests that remain will become converted within the next half-century. Those losses of forests represent losses for us humans, especially because forests provide us with timber and other raw materials, and because they provide us with so-called ecosystem services such as protecting our watersheds, protecting soil against erosion, constituting essential steps in the water cycle that generates much of our rainfall, and providing habitat for most terrestrial plant and animal species. Deforestation was a or *the* major factor in all the collapses of past societies described . . . In addition, . . . issues of concern to us are not only forest destruction and conversion, but also changes in the structure of wooded habitats that do remain. Among other things, that changed structure results in changed fire regimes that put forests, chaparral woodlands, and savannahs at greater risk of infrequent but catastrophic fires.

Other valuable natural habitats besides forests are also being 3
destroyed. An even larger fraction of the world's original wetlands than of its forests has already been destroyed, damaged, or converted. Consequences for us arise from wetlands' importance in maintaining the quality of our water supplies and the existence of commercially important freshwater fisheries, while even ocean fisheries depend on mangrove wetlands to provide habitat for the juvenile phase of many fish species. About one-third of the world's coral reefs—the oceanic equivalent of tropical rainforests, because they are home to a disproportionate fraction of the ocean's species—have already been severely damaged. If current trends continue, about half of the remaining reefs would be lost by the year 2030. That damage and destruction result from the growing use of dynamite as a fishing method, reef over-growth by algae ("seaweeds") when the large herbivorous fish that normally graze on the algae become fished out, effects of sediment runoff and pollutants from adjacent lands cleared or converted to agriculture, and coral bleaching due to rising ocean water temperatures. It has recently become appreciated that fishing by trawling is destroying much or most of the shallow ocean bottom and the species dependent on it.

2. Wild foods, especially fish and to a lesser extent shellfish, contribute 4
a large fraction of the protein consumed by humans. In effect, this is protein that we obtain for free (other than the cost of catching and transporting the fish), and that reduces our needs for animal protein that we have to grow ourselves in the form of domestic livestock. About two billion people, most of them poor, depend on the oceans for protein. If wild fish stocks were managed appropriately, the stock levels could be maintained, and they could be harvested perpetually. Unfortunately, the problem known as the tragedy of the commons has regularly undone efforts to manage fisheries sustainably, and the great majority of valuable fisheries already either have collapsed or are in steep decline. Past societies that overfished included Easter Island, Mangareva, and Henderson.

5 Increasingly, fish and shrimp are being grown by aquaculture, which in principle has a promising future as the cheapest way to produce animal protein. In several respects, though, aquaculture as commonly practiced today is making the problem of declining wild fisheries worse rather than better. Fish grown by aquaculture are mostly fed wild-caught fish and thereby usually consume more wild fish meat (up to 20 times more) than they yield in meat of their own They contain higher toxin levels than do wild-caught fish. Cultured fish regularly escape, interbreed with wild fish, and thereby harm wild fish stocks genetically, because cultured fish strains have been selected for rapid growth at the expense of poor survival in the wild (50 times worse survival for cultured salmon than for wild salmon). Aquaculture runoff causes pollution and eutrophication. The lower costs of aquaculture than of fishing, by driving down fish prices, initially drive fishermen to exploit wild fish stocks even more heavily in order to maintain their incomes constant when they are receiving less money per pound of fish.

6 3. A significant fraction of wild species, populations, and genetic diversity has already been lost, and at present rates a large fraction of what remains will be lost within the next half-century. Some species, such as big edible animals, or plants with edible fruits or good timber, are of obvious value to us. . . .

7 But biodiversity losses of small inedible species often provoke the response, "Who cares? Do you really care less for humans than for some lousy useless little fish or weed, like the snail darter or Furbish lousewort?" This response misses the point that the entire natural world is made up of wild species providing us for free with services that can be very expensive, and in many cases impossible, for us to supply ourselves. Elimination of lots of lousy little species regularly causes big harmful consequences for humans, just as does randomly knocking out many of the lousy little rivets holding together an airplane. The literally innumerable examples include: the role of earthworms in regenerating soil and maintaining its texture (one of the reasons that oxygen levels dropped inside the Biosphere 2 enclosure, harming its human inhabitants and crippling a colleague of mine, was a lack of appropriate earthworms, contributing to altered soil/atmosphere gas exchange); soil bacteria that fix the essential crop nutrient nitrogen, which otherwise we have to spend money to supply in fertilizers; bees and other insect pollinators (they pollinate our crops for free, whereas it's expensive for us to pollinate every crop flower by hand); birds and mammals that disperse wild fruits (foresters still haven't figured out how to grow from seed the most important commercial tree species of the Solomon Islands, whose seeds are naturally dispersed by fruit bats, which are becoming hunted out); elimination of whales, sharks, bears, wolves, and other top predators in the seas and on the land, changing the whole food chain beneath

them; and wild plants and animals that decompose wastes and recycle nutrients, ultimately providing us with clean water and air.

4. Soils of farmlands used for growing crops are being carried away by water and wind erosion at rates between 10 and 40 times the rates of soil formation, and between 500 and 10,000 times soil erosion rates on forested land. Because those soil erosion rates are so much higher than soil formation rates, that means a net loss of soil. For instance, about half of the topsoil of Iowa, the state whose agriculture productivity is among the highest in the U.S., has been eroded in the last 150 years. On my most recent visit to Iowa, my hosts showed me a churchyard offering a dramatically visible example of those soil losses. A church was built there in the middle of farmland during the 19th century and has been maintained continuously as a church ever since, while the land around it was being farmed. As a result of soil being eroded much more rapidly from fields than from the churchyard, the yard now stands like a little island raised 10 feet above the surrounding sea of farmland. 8

Other types of soil damage caused by human agricultural practices include salinization; . . . losses of soil fertility, because farming removes nutrients much more rapidly than they are restored by weathering of the underlying rock; and soil acidification in some areas, or its converse, alkalinization, in other areas. All of these types of harmful impacts have resulted in a fraction of the world's farmland variously estimated at between 20% and 80% having become severely damaged, during an era in which increasing human population has caused us to need more farmland rather than less farmland. Like deforestation, soil problems contributed to the collapses of all past societies discussed . . . 9

The next three problems involve ceilings—on energy, freshwater, and photosynthetic capacity. In each case the ceiling is not hard and fixed but soft: we can obtain more of the needed resource, but at increasing costs. 10

5. The world's major energy sources, especially for industrial societies, are fossil fuels: oil, natural gas, and coal. While there has been much discussion about how many big oil and gas fields remain to be discovered, and while coal reserves are believed to be large, the prevalent view is that known and likely reserves of readily accessible oil and natural gas will last for a few more decades. This view should not be misinterpreted to mean that all of the oil and natural gas within the Earth will have been used up by then. Instead, further reserves will be deeper underground, dirtier, increasingly expensive to extract or process, or will involve higher environmental costs. Of course, fossil fuels are not our sole energy sources, and I shall consider problems raised by the alternatives below. 11

6. Most of the world's freshwater in rivers and lakes is already being utilized for irrigation, domestic and industrial water, and in situ uses 12

such as boat transportation corridors, fisheries, and recreation. Rivers and lakes that are not already utilized are mostly far from major population centers and likely users, such as in Northwestern Australia, Siberia, and Iceland. Throughout the world, freshwater underground aquifers are being depleted at rates faster than they are being naturally replenished, so that they will eventually dwindle. Of course, freshwater can be made by desalinization of seawater, but that costs money and energy, as does pumping the resulting desalinized water inland for use. Hence desalinization, while it is useful locally, is too expensive to solve most of the world's water shortages. The Anasazi and Maya were among the past societies to be undone by water problems, while today over a billion people lack access to reliable safe drinking water.

13 7. It might at first seem that the supply of sunlight is infinite, so one might reason that the Earth's capacity to grow crops and wild plants is also infinite. Within the last 20 years, it has been appreciated that that is not the case, and that's not only because plants grow poorly in the world's Arctic regions and deserts unless one goes to the expense of supplying heat or water. More generally, the amount of solar energy fixed per acre by plant photosynthesis, hence plant growth per acre, depends on temperature and rainfall. At any given temperature and rainfall the plant growth that can be supported by the sunlight falling on an acre is limited by the geometry and biochemistry of plants, even if they take up the sunlight so efficiently that not a single photon of light passes through the plants unabsorbed to reach the ground. The first calculation of this photosynthetic ceiling, carried out in 1986, estimated that humans then already used (e.g., for crops, tree plantations, and golf courses) or diverted or wasted (e.g., light falling on concrete roads and buildings) about half of the Earth's photosynthetic capacity. Given the rate of increase of human population, and especially of population impact (see point 12 below), since 1986, we are projected to be utilizing most of the world's terrestrial photosynthetic capacity by the middle of this century. That is, most energy fixed from sunlight will be used for human purposes, and little will be left over to support the growth of natural plant communities, such as natural forests.

14 The next three problems involve harmful things that we generate or move around: toxic chemicals, alien species, and atmospheric gases.

15 8. The chemical industry and many other industries manufacture or release into the air, soil, oceans, lakes, and rivers many toxic chemicals, some of them "unnatural" and synthesized only by humans, others present naturally in tiny concentrations (e.g., mercury) or else synthesized by living things but synthesized and released by humans in quantities much larger than natural ones (e.g., hormones). The first of these toxic chemicals to achieve wide notice were insecticides, pesticides, and herbicides,

whose effects on birds, fish, and other animals were publicized by Rachel Carson's 1962 book *Silent Spring*. Since then, it has been appreciated that the toxic effects of even greater significance for us humans are those on ourselves. The culprits include not only insecticides, pesticides, and herbicides, but also mercury and other metals, fire-retardant chemicals, refrigerator coolants, detergents, and components of plastics. We swallow them in our food and water, breathe them in our air, and absorb them through our skin. Often in very low concentrations, they variously cause birth defects, mental retardation, and temporary or permanent damage to our immune and reproductive systems. Some of them act as endocrine disruptors, i.e., they interfere with our reproductive systems by mimicking or blocking effects of our own sex hormones. They probably make the major contribution to the steep decline in sperm count in many human populations over the last several decades, and to the apparently increasing frequency with which couples are unable to conceive, even when one takes into account the increasing average age of marriage in many societies. In addition, deaths in the U.S. from air pollution alone (without considering soil and water pollution) are conservatively estimated at over 130,000 per year.

Many of these toxic chemicals are broken down in the environment 16 only slowly (e.g., DDT and PCBs) or not at all (mercury), and they persist in the environment for long times before being washed out. Thus, cleanup costs of many polluted sites in the U.S. are measured in the billions of dollars (e.g., Love Canal, the Hudson River, Chesapeake Bay, the *Exxon Valdez* oil spill, and Montana copper mines). But pollution at those worst sites in the U.S. is mild compared to that in the former Soviet Union, China, and many Third World mines, whose cleanup costs no one even dares to think about.

9. The term "alien species" refers to species that we transfer, inten- 17 tionally or inadvertently, from a place where they are native to another place where they are not native. Some alien species are obviously valuable to us as crops, domestic animals, and landscaping. But others devastate populations of native species with which they come in contact, either by preying on, parasitizing, infecting, or outcompeting them. The aliens cause these big effects because the native species with which they come in contact had no previous evolutionary experience of them and are unable to resist them (like human populations newly exposed to smallpox or AIDS). There are by now literally hundreds of cases in which alien species have caused one-time or annually recurring damages of hundreds of millions of dollars or even billions of dollars. Modern examples include Australia's rabbits and foxes, agricultural weeds like Spotted Knapweed and Leafy Spurge pests and pathogens of trees and crops and livestock (like the blights that wiped out American chestnut trees and devasted American elms), the water hyacinth that chokes waterways, the zebra mussels that choke power plants, and the lampreys that devastated the

former commercial fisheries of the North American Great Lakes. Ancient examples include the introduced rats that contributed to the extinction of Easter Island's palm tree by gnawing its nuts, and that ate the eggs and chicks of nesting birds on Easter, Henderson, and all other Pacific islands previously without rats.

18 10. Human activities produce gases that escape into the atmosphere, where they either damage the protective ozone layer (as do formerly widespread refrigerator coolants) or else act as greenhouse gases that absorb sunlight and thereby lead to global warming. The gases contributing to global warming include carbon dioxide from combustion and respiration, and methane from fermentation in the intestines of ruminant animals. Of course, there have always been natural fires and animal respiration producing carbon dioxide, and wild ruminant animals producing methane, but our burning of firewood and of fossil fuels has greatly increased the former, and our herds of cattle and of sheep have greatly increased the latter.

19 For many years, scientists debated the reality, cause, and extent of global warming: are world temperatures really historically high now, and, if so, by how much, and are humans the leading cause? Most knowledgeable scientists now agree that, despite year-to-year ups and downs of temperature that necessitate complicated analyses to extract warming trends, the atmosphere really has been undergoing an unusually rapid rise in temperature recently, and that human activities are the or a major cause. The remaining uncertainties mainly concern the future expected magnitude of the effect: e.g., whether average global temperatures will increase by "just" 1.5 degrees Centigrade or by 5 degrees Centigrade over the next century. Those numbers may not sound like a big deal, until one reflects that average global temperatures were "only" 5 degrees cooler at the height of the last Ice Age.

20 While one might at first think that we should welcome global warming on the grounds that warmer temperatures mean faster plant growth, it turns out that global warming will produce both winners and losers. Crop yields in cool areas with temperatures marginal for agriculture may indeed increase, while crop yields in already warm or dry areas may decrease. In Montana, California, and many other dry climates, the disappearance of mountain snowpacks will decrease the water available for domestic uses, and for irrigation that actually limits crop yields in those areas. The rise in global sea levels as a result of snow and ice melting poses dangers of flooding and coastal erosion for densely populated low-lying coastal plains and river deltas already barely above or even below sea level. The areas thereby threatened include much of the Netherlands, Bangladesh, and the seaboard of the eastern U.S., many low-lying Pacific islands, the deltas of the Nile and Mekong Rivers, and coastal and riverbank cities of the United Kingdom (e.g., London), India, Japan, and the Philippines. Global warming will also produce big

secondary effects that are difficult to predict exactly in advance and that are likely to cause huge problems, such as further climate changes resulting from changes in ocean circulation resulting in turn from melting of the Arctic ice cap.

The remaining two problems involve the increase in human population: 21

11. The world's human population is growing. More people require more food, space, water, energy, and other resources. Rates and even the direction of human population change vary greatly around the world, with the highest rates of population growth (4% per year or higher) in some Third World countries, low rates of growth (1% per year or less) in some First World countries such as Italy and Japan, and negative rates of growth (i.e., decreasing populations) in countries facing major public health crises, such as Russia and AIDS-affected African countries. Everybody agrees that the world population is increasing, but that its annual percentage rate of increase is not as high as it was a decade or two ago. However, there is still disagreement about whether the world's population will stabilize at some value above its present level (double the present population?), and (if so) how many years (30 years? 50 years?) it will take for population to reach that level, or whether population will continue to grow. 22

There is long built-in momentum to human population growth because of what is termed the "demographic bulge" or "population momentum," i.e., a disproportionate number of children and young reproductive-age people in today's population, as a result of recent population growth. That is, suppose that every couple in the world decided tonight to limit themselves to two children, approximately the correct number of children to yield an unchanging population in the long run by exactly replacing their two parents who will eventually die (actually, around 2.1 children when one considers mortality, childless couples, and children who won't marry). The world's population would nevertheless continue to increase for about 70 years, because more people today are of reproductive age or entering reproductive age than are old and post-reproductive. The problem of human population growth has received much attention in recent decades and has given rise to movements such as Zero Population Growth, which aim to slow or halt the increase in the world's population. 23

12. What really counts is not the number of people alone, but their impact on the environment. If most of the world's 6 billion people today were in cryogenic storage and neither eating, breathing, nor metabolizing, that large population would cause no environmental problems. Instead, our numbers pose problems insofar as we consume resources and generate wastes. That per-capita impact—the resources consumed, and the wastes put out, by each person—varies greatly around the world, being 24

highest in the First World and lowest in the Third World. On the average, each citizen of the U.S., western Europe, and Japan consumes 32 times more resources such as fossil fuels, and puts out 32 times more wastes, than do inhabitants of the Third World.

25 But low-impact people are becoming high-impact people for two reasons: rises in living standards in Third World countries whose inhabitants see and covet First World lifestyles; and immigration, both legal and illegal, of individual Third World inhabitants into the First World, driven by political, economic, and social problems at home. Immigration from low-impact countries is now the main contributor to the increasing populations of the U.S. and Europe. By the same token, the overwhelmingly most important human population problem for the world as a whole is not the high rate of population increase in Kenya, Rwanda, and some other poor Third World countries, although that certainly does pose a problem for Kenya and Rwanda themselves, and although that is the population problem most discussed. Instead, the biggest problem is the increase in total human impact, as the result of rising Third World living standards, and of Third World individuals moving to the First World and adopting First World living standards.

26 There are many "optimists" who argue that the world could support double its human population, and who consider only the increase in human numbers and not the average increase in per-capita impact. But I have not met anyone who seriously argues that the world could support 12 times its current impact, although an increase of that factor would result from all Third World inhabitants adopting First World living standards. (That factor of 12 is less than the factor of 32 that I mentioned in the preceding paragraph, because there are already First World inhabitants with high-impact lifestyles, although they are greatly outnumbered by Third World inhabitants.) Even if the people of China alone achieved a First World living standard while everyone else's living standard remained constant, that would double our human impact on the world.

27 People in the Third World aspire to First World living standards. They develop that aspiration through watching television, seeing advertisements for First World consumer products sold in their countries, and observing First World visitors to their countries. Even in the most remote villages and refugee camps today, people know about the outside world. Third World citizens are encouraged in that aspiration by First World and United Nations development agencies, which hold out to them the prospect of achieving their dream if they will only adopt the right policies, like balancing their national budgets, investing in education and infrastructure, and so on.

28 But no one in First World governments is willing to acknowledge the dream's impossibility: the unsustainability of a world in which the Third World's large population were to reach and maintain current First World living standards. It is impossible for the First World to resolve

that dilemma by blocking the Third World's efforts to catch up: South Korea, Malaysia, Singapore, Hong Kong, Taiwan, and Mauritius have already succeeded or are close to success; China and India are progressing rapidly by their own efforts; and the 15 rich Western European countries making up the European Union have just extended Union membership to 10 poorer countries of Eastern Europe, in effect thereby pledging to help those 10 countries catch up. Even if the human populations of the Third World did not exist, it would be impossible for the First World alone to maintain its present course, because it is not in a steady state but is depleting its own resources as well as those imported from the Third World. At present, it is untenable politically for First World leaders to propose to their own citizens that they lower their living standards, as measured by lower resource consumption and waste production rates. What will happen when it finally dawns on all those people in the Third World that current First World standards are unreachable for them, and that the First World refuses to abandon those standards for itself? Life is full of agonizing choices based on trade-offs, but that's the cruelest trade-off that we shall have to resolve: encouraging and helping all people to achieve a higher standard of living, without thereby undermining that standard through overstressing global resources.

I have described these 12 sets of problems as separate from each other. 29
In fact, they are linked: one problem exacerbates another or makes its solution more difficult. For example, human population growth affects all 11 other problems: more people means more deforestation, more toxic chemicals, more demand for wild fish, etc. The energy problem is linked to other problems because use of fossil fuels for energy contributes heavily to greenhouse gases, the combating of soil fertility losses by using synthetic fertilizers requires energy to make the fertilizers, fossil fuel scarcity increases our interest in nuclear energy which poses potentially the biggest "toxic" problem of all in case of an accident, and fossil fuel scarcity also makes it more expensive to solve our freshwater problems by using energy to desalinize ocean water. Depletion of fisheries and other wild food sources puts more pressure on livestock, crops, and aquaculture to replace them, thereby leading to more topsoil losses and more eutrophication from agriculture and aquaculture. Problems of deforestation, water shortage, and soil degradation in the Third World foster wars there and drive legal asylum seekers and illegal emigrants to the First World from the Third World.

Our world society is presently on a non-sustainable course, and any 30
of our 12 problems of non-sustainability that we have just summarized would suffice to limit our lifestyle within the next several decades. They are like time bombs with fuses of less than 50 years. For example, destruction of accessible lowland tropical rainforest outside national parks is

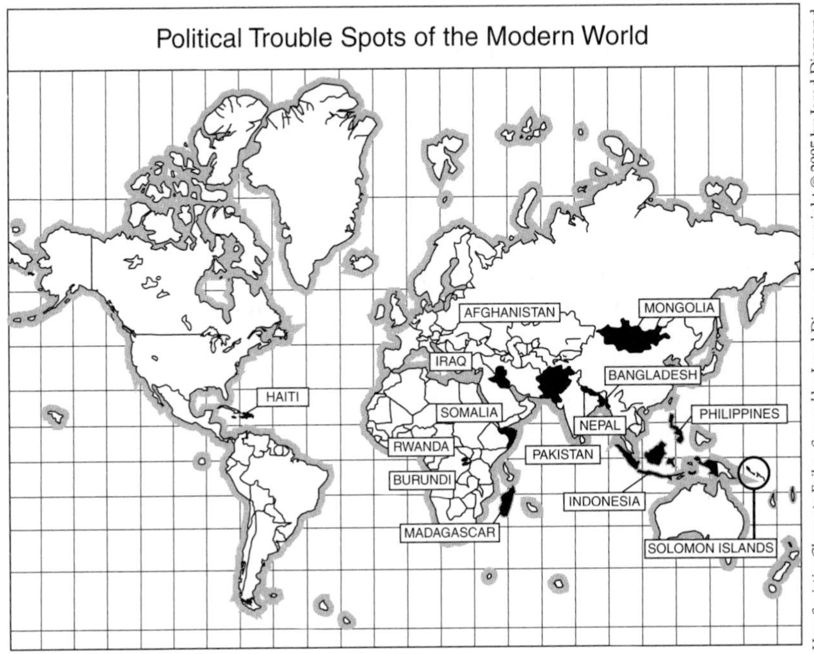

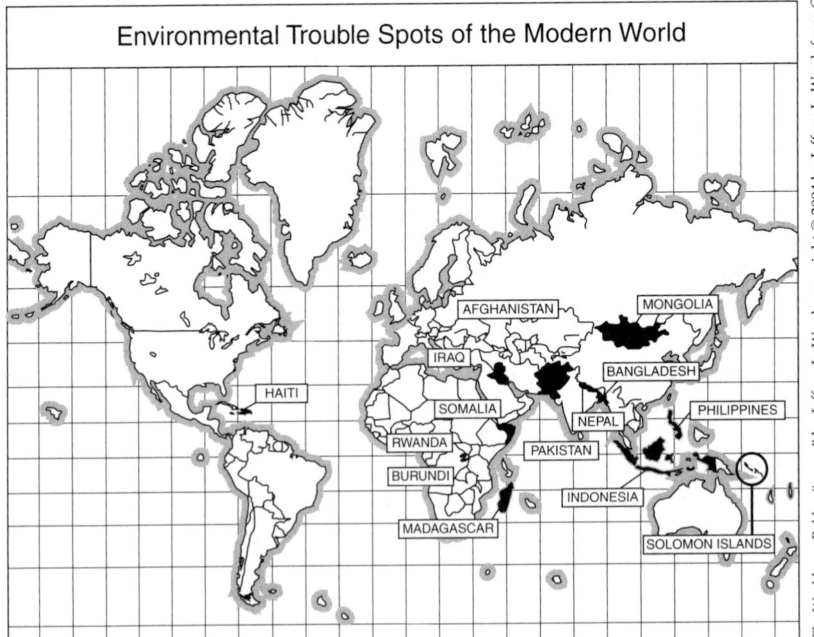

The World as a Polder, "maps" by Jeffrey L. Ward, copyright © 2004 by Jeffrey L. Ward, from *Collapse: How Societies Choose to Fail or Succeed* by Jared Diamond, copyright © 2005 by Jared Diamond. Used by permission of Viking Penguin, a division of Penguin Group (USA) Inc.

The black areas in each map indicate "trouble spots," political in the top map, environmental in the lower map. To what extent are these trouble spots the same? Identify some reasons why these are congruent.

already virtually complete in Peninsular Malaysia, will be complete at current rates within less than a decade in the Solomon Islands, the Philippines, on Sumatra, and on Sulawesi, and will be complete around the world except perhaps for parts of the Amazon Basin and Congo Basin within 25 years. At current rates, we shall have depleted or destroyed most of the world's remaining marine fisheries, depleted clean or cheap or readily accessible reserves of oil and natural gas, and approached the photosynthetic ceiling within a few decades. Global warming is projected to have reached a degree Centigrade or more, and a substantial fraction of the world's wild animal and plant species are projected to be endangered or past the point of no return, within half a century. People often ask, "What is the single most important environmental/population problem facing the world today?" A flip answer would be, "The single most important problem is our misguided focus on identifying the single most important problem!" That flip answer is essentially correct, because any of the dozen problems if unsolved would do us grave harm, and because they all interact with each other. If we solved 11 of the problems, but not the 12th, we would still be in trouble, whichever was the problem that remained unsolved. We have to solve them all.

Thus, because we are rapidly advancing along this non-sustainable course, the world's environmental problems *will* get resolved, in one way or another, within the lifetimes of the children and young adults alive today. The only question is whether they will become resolved in pleasant ways of our own choice, or in unpleasant ways not of our choice, such as warfare, genocide, starvation, disease epidemics, and collapses of societies. While all of those grim phenomena have been endemic to humanity throughout our history, their frequency increases with environmental degradation, population pressure, and the resulting poverty and political instability. 31

Examples of those unpleasant solutions to environmental and population problems abound in both the modern world and the ancient world. The examples include the recent genocides in Rwanda, Burundi, and the former Yugoslavia; war, civil war, or guerrilla war in the modern Sudan, Philippines, and Nepal, and in the ancient Maya homeland; cannibalism on prehistoric Easter Island and Mangareva and among the ancient Anasazi; starvation in many modern African countries and on prehistoric Easter Island; the AIDS epidemic already in Africa, and incipiently elsewhere; and the collapse of state government in modern Somalia, the Solomon Islands, and Haiti, and among the ancient Maya. An outcome less drastic than a worldwide collapse might "merely" be the spread of Rwanda-like or Haiti-like conditions to many more developing countries, while we First World inhabitants retain many of our First World amenities but face a future with which we are unhappy, beset by more chronic terrorism, wars, and disease outbreaks. But it is doubtful that the First World could retain its separate lifestyle in the face of desperate waves of immigrants fleeing from collapsing Third World countries, in numbers much larger than the current unstoppable influx. . . . 32

Content

1. According to Diamond, what problems do the destruction of natural habitats (¶s 2–3), the decline of wild species (including those we eat) (¶s 4–7), and the erosion of farm soil (¶s 8–9) create for humankind? How are these problems interrelated?

2. What is the earth's "photosynthetic capacity" and how does Diamond define the "ceiling" on this capacity (¶ 13)? How do extraction and environmental costs imply a similar ceiling on the energy derived from fossil fuels (¶ 11)? What are the various costs of utilizing alternatives to freshwater aquifers (¶ 12)?

3. What impact do toxic chemicals have on our health and environment (¶s 15–16)? How does the introduction of alien species disrupt a local ecosystem (¶ 17)? How do atmospheric gases contribute to climate change (¶s 18–19)? How might climate change affect farming and coastal communities (¶ 20)?

4. Why are rates of population growth only a part of the problem of environmental degradation (¶s 22–24)? Why is the per capita impact of the human population likely to rise with further increases in rates of population growth (¶s 25–27)? What factors does Diamond refer to that affect the size, growth, and impact of human populations (¶s 22–26)?

5. Why, in Diamond's view, are First World standards of living unsustainable (¶ 28)? Why is it unlikely that the Third World will one day enjoy First World living standards (¶s 27–30)? How might the destruction of natural resources lead to the collapse of a community, or even of an entire society (¶s 29–32)?

Strategies/Structures/Language

6. Diamond emphasizes the costs of environmental damage and the economic value of natural resources: biodiversity, for example, provides "services that can be very expensive, and in many cases, impossible, for us to supply ourselves" (¶ 7). Find other examples of Diamond's application of cost/benefit analysis to the management of natural resources. What consequences of environmental damage does he not mention? Who is Diamond's audience? How does he want his readers to respond to the problems of managing increasingly precious natural resources?

7. Diamond argues that global "society is presently on a non-sustainable course" (¶ 30). What specific evidence does Diamond offer that supports the idea that economic development overstresses the world's natural resources? How does his characterization of resource depletion in terms of rates of consumption—for example of forests (¶ 2) and coral reefs (¶ 3)—illustrate the nature of the problem as well as ways of developing appropriate responses?

8. How does Diamond characterize the First and Third Worlds? What roles, according to Diamond, do developing and developed nations play in depleting or managing the world's natural resources? Why doesn't Diamond suggest ways that countries might cooperate to manage global resources better? What assumptions about political structures such as the United Nations and the European Union does he appear to make in arguing that "warfare, genocide, starvation, disease epidemics, and collapses of societies" (¶ 31) will be the consequences of environmental degradation?

9. Why, in the maps on 482, does Diamond emphasize the link between political instability and stress on the environment? Which aspects of his overall argument do these maps illustrate? How might you re-label each

country or region on the map to illustrate its ability to sustain its current rates of consumption?

For Writing

10. Diamond writes that each citizen of First World countries "consumes 32 times more resources such as fossil fuels" than inhabitants of Third World countries (¶ 24). Do some research on the environmental impact of your own consumption of, for example, fossil fuels; processed foods; water; and plastics, paper, and other wastes. What is your environmental or ecological "footprint"? What facilities or incentives does your town, city, or state offer to encourage a greener lifestyle? How might you reduce your impact on the environment?

11. ***Dialogues.*** Matthew Allen argues in "The Rhetorical Situation of the Scientific Paper and the 'Appearance' of Objectivity" (500–10) that the scientist-writer "persuades his or her audience largely through the *appearance* of objectivity" (¶ 3). Does Diamond's goal of persuading the reader of the urgency of the problem of environmental degradation compromise the integrity of his analysis? Could you interpret his data differently? Select two or three pieces of evidence from the essay and describe how Diamond's use of what Allen calls "rhetoric and exigence" (¶ 10) creates a specific interpretation of that evidence.

12. ***Second Look.*** What does the photograph of people in Haiti scavenging for food (278) suggest about scarcity and waste? How does it suggest that the value of resources depends on scarcity, the technology of extracting value from waste, and rates of consumption? Does the process the photograph describes suggest that Haitian society is on the verge of collapse? Would your interpretation of the photograph change if you had relatives in Haiti? Does the closeness of the country—culturally, geographically, ethnically, economically—affect your response to the image?

CARTOON ARGUMENTS

EVAN EISENBERG

Evan Eisenberg (born 1955) studied philosophy and classics at Harvard and Princeton and biology at the University of Massachusetts, Amherst, preparatory to becoming a journalist specializing in nature, culture, music, and technology. In addition to two books, *The Recording Angel: Explorations in Phonography* (1987, 2005) and *The Ecology of Eden* (1988), offering a model of how to prevent environmental disaster, Eisenberg's serious works have appeared in *The Atlantic, The New Republic, The New York Times, Natural History*, and other periodicals. His humorous pieces have been featured in *The New Yorker* (where "Dialogue Boxes" first appeared, in 2005), *Esquire, Slate, Salon*, and elsewhere. This piece provides a strong critique of Microsoft in a concise form, readily accessible to any computer user. As you read, note not only the text in the dialogue boxes, but the icons and the—very limited—options for response.

Dialogue Boxes You Should Have Read More Carefully

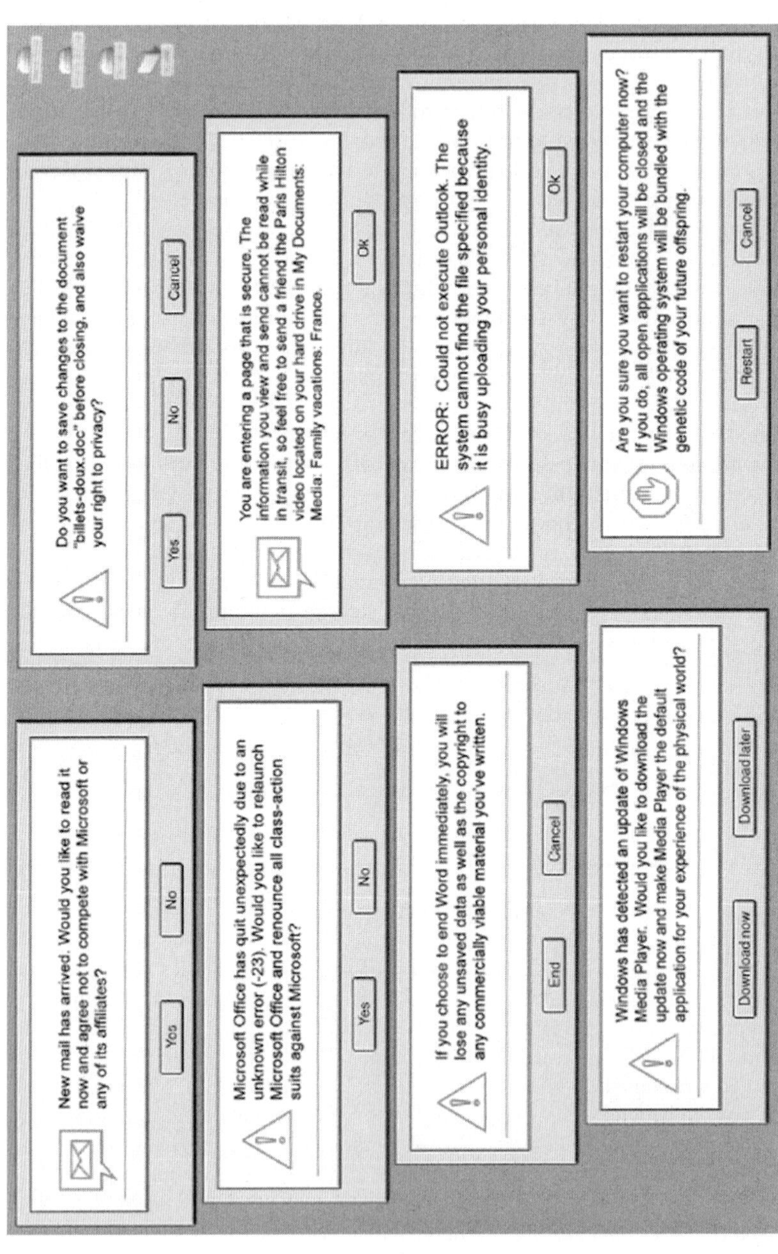

Evan Eisenberg, "Dialogue Boxes You Should Have Read More Carefully." Copyright © 2004 by Evan Eisenberg. Reprinted by permission of the author. This selection first appeared in *The New York Times*.

MARISA ACOCELLA MARCHETTO

As a child, Marisa Acocella Marchetto fell in love with cartooning when her family, on vacation, stayed in a house formerly occupied by humorist and cartoonist James Thurber, whose quirky line drawings covered the walls. She is the creator of "The Strip," the first regular cartoon feature in *The New York Times*, where this Op-Art comic also appeared in 2007. Her first graphic novel, *Just Who the Hell is SHE, Anyway?* (1995), was based on a character, SHE, created for *Mirabella* magazine; other cartoons have appeared in *The New Yorker* and *Glamour*. Her most recent book, *Cancer Vixen: A True Story* (2006), is a memoir of Marchetto's refusal to be victimized by the sudden onset of breast cancer, discovered shortly before her wedding to a New York restauranteur. For this work Marchetto was awarded The Humanitarian Award by The Breast Cancer Research Foundation in 2006.

In this op-art comic, Marchetto illustrates the stark reality that cancer research depends on generous funding—always precarious, always threatened, always subject to competing interests—and is unlikely to succeed without it. By introducing readers to one of the "generals in the war on cancer" and his colleagues, she humanizes the world of scientific research and its competitive pressures.

Cartoonist Marisa Acocella Marchetto is the author of the graphic memoir CANCER VIXEN (Knopf).

Content

1. Each of Eisenberg's dialogue boxes embeds an argument about Microsoft. Identify the argument of each and the specific charge against Microsoft's relation to those who use its operating system.
2. Now consider all the arguments together. What's their point?
3. By what benchmarks does Marchetto argue that cancer research is underfunded? Why are clinical trials necessary?
4. Why does Marchetto present the state of cancer research as a conversation between herself and Dr. Norton?

Strategies/Structures/Language

5. In Eisenberg's dialogue boxes, what's missing from some of the limited choices in the actions the computer user can take? Identify these, and explain what will happen if the user chooses one or another of the permissible alternatives.
6. Eisenberg conducts his argument by letting readers do most of the work and come to all of the conclusions. How can he be sure they'll read the boxes the way he wants them to and arrive at the same conclusions that he does?
7. How closely has Eisenberg imitated Microsoft's language?
8. How does Marchetto characterize Dr. Norton? How does she characterize cancer researchers and the research process? Do Marchetto's descriptions challenge any stereotyped ideas about scientists and scientific research?
9. Why does Marchetto (through Dr. Norton) compare cancer research budgets with the tobacco industry's spending on advertising and with national soft drink consumption? What do these comparisons suggest about public health priorities and health education? How does she expect readers to respond to this information?

For Writing

10. Find cartoons that make arguments, and analyze several to show how they do it—either through only visual means or through a combination of words

and images. Editorial or political cartoons are a good source. If you work with a partner, you can check your interpretations against each other's.

11. Present an argument of your own in cartoon format, using either a single or multiple panel. If you can't draw, you can provide your own captions for existing cartoons. See, for instance, *The New Yorker's* website, www.cartoonbank.com.

12. ***Dialogues.*** Compare Marchetto's op-art comic and Lynda Barry's graphic narrative "Common Scents" (376–85). In what ways is each a traditional story with a beginning, middle, and end, and a climax and resolution? How does each narrative challenge an unstated assumption or belief and so act as an "anti-story," or one that undermines an existing story? Who, or what, is the protagonist in each narrative? What stake does each narrator have in the outcome of the story she tells? Would you characterize the narrators as observers, supporting actors, stand-ins for the reader, victims, or heroes? How does the relationship between the narrator and reader differ in each narrative? How does each artist challenge your ideas about what stories—and comics—are supposed to do? If you wish, expand your analysis to address the same issues in Art Spiegelman's "Mein Kampf (My Struggle)" (96–97).

ROBERT REICH

Robert Reich (born 1946), earned a BA at Dartmouth College (1968) and a JD degree from Yale Law School (1973), was a Rhodes scholar at Oxford, and taught at Harvard's John F. Kennedy School of Government, and at Brandeis University before moving in 2005 to a professorship at the University of California, Berkeley's Goldman School of Public Policy. In 2003 he received the Václav Havel Prize for his "contributions to social thought." Active in politics since his student days, Reich interned for Senator Robert Kennedy; coordinated Eugene McCarthy's 1968 presidential campaign; and was secretary of labor during Clinton's first term as president (1993–1996). *Locked in the Cabinet* (1997) discusses his experiences.

Many of Reich's books on economics are intended for a general audience, including *Tales of a New America: The Anxious Liberal's Guide to the Future* (1988); and *Reason: Why Liberals will Win the Battle for America* (2004). *The Next American Frontier* (1983) provided a rationale for the Democratic party's economic policy, explaining that "government intervention sets the boundaries, decides what's going to be marketed, sets the rules of the game through procurement policies, tax credits, depreciation allowances, loans and loan guarantees." *Tales of a New America* defines four economic myths: "Mob at the Gate" labels foreigners as adversaries to American citizens; "The Triumphant Individual" reinforces the myth of the American Dream; "The Benevolent Community" claims that Americans act out of social responsibility to one another; and "The Rot at the Top" accuses the elite class of corruption and abuse of their power. "The Global Elite," first published in the *New York Times Magazine* (1991) provides factual information to counteract the myths of a benevolent, egalitarian society and implicitly argues for a more equitable—and democratic—distribution of our country's wealth.

The Global Elite

1 The idea of "community" has always held a special attraction for Americans. In a 1984 speech, President Ronald Reagan celebrated America's "bedrock"—"its communities where neighbors help one another, where families bring up kids together, where American values are born." Governor Mario M. Cuomo of New York, with a very different political leaning, has been almost as lyrical. "Community . . . is the reality on which our national life has been founded," he said in 1987.

2 There is only one problem with this picture. Most Americans no longer live in traditional communities. They live in suburban subdivisions bordered by highways and sprinkled with shopping malls, or in tony condominiums and residential clusters, or in ramshackle apartment buildings and housing projects. Most of them commute to work and socialize on some basis other than geographic proximity. And most people pick up and move to a different neighborhood every five years or so.

3 But Americans generally have one thing in common with their neighbors: They have similar incomes. And that simple fact lies at the heart of the new community. This means that their educational backgrounds are likely to be similar, that they pay roughly the same in taxes, and that they indulge in the same consumer impulses. "Tell me someone's ZIP code," the founder of a direct-mail company once bragged, "and I can predict what they eat, drink, drive—even think."

4 Americans who own their homes usually share one political cause with their neighbors: a near obsessive concern with maintaining or upgrading property values. And this common interest is responsible for much of what has brought neighbors together in recent years. Complete strangers, although they may live on the same street or in the same condominium complex, suddenly feel intense solidarity when it is rumored that low-income housing will be constructed in their midst or that a poorer school district will be consolidated with their own.

5 The renewed emphasis on "community" in American life has justified and legitimized these economic enclaves. If generosity and solidarity end at the border of similarly valued properties, then the most fortunate can be virtuous citizens at little cost. Since most people in one neighborhood or town are equally well off, there is no cause for a guilty conscience.

If inhabitants of another area are poorer, let them look to one another. Why should *we* pay for *their* schools?

So the argument goes, without acknowledging that the critical assumption has already been made: "We" and "they" belong to fundamentally different communities. Through such reasoning, it has become possible to maintain a self-image of generosity toward, and solidarity with, one's "community" without bearing any responsibility to "them"—the other "community." 6

America's high earners—the fortunate top fifth—thus feel increasingly justified in paying only what is necessary to insure that everyone in their community is sufficiently well educated and has access to the public services they need to succeed. 7

Last year, the top fifth of working Americans took home more money than the other four-fifths put together—the highest portion in postwar history. These high earners will relinquish somewhat more of their income to the Federal Government this year than in 1990 as a result of last fall's tax changes, although considerably less than in the late 1970s, when the tax code was more progressive. But the continuing debate over whether the wealthy are paying their fair share of taxes obscures a larger issue, with more profound implications for America: The fortunate fifth is quietly seceding from the rest of the nation. 8

This is occurring gradually, without much awareness by members of the top group—or, for that matter, by anyone else. And the Government is speeding this process as Washington shifts responsibility for many public services to state and local governments. 9

The secession is taking several forms. In many cities and towns, the wealthy have in effect withdrawn their dollars from the support of public spaces and institutions shared by all and dedicated the savings to their own private services. As public parks and playgrounds deteriorate, there is a proliferation of private health clubs, golf clubs, tennis clubs, skating clubs, and every other type of recreational association in which costs are shared among members. Condominiums and the omnipresent residential communities dun their members to undertake work that financially strapped local governments can no longer afford to do well—maintaining roads, mending sidewalks, pruning trees, repairing street lights, cleaning swimming pools, paying for lifeguards, and, notably, hiring security guards to protect life and property. (The number of private security guards in the United States now exceeds the number of public police officers.) 10

Of course, wealthier Americans have been withdrawing into their own neighborhoods and clubs for generations. But the new secession is more dramatic because the highest earners now inhabit a different economy from other Americans. The new elite is linked by jet, modem, fax, satellite, and fiber-optic cable to the great commercial and recreational centers of the world, but it is not particularly connected to the rest of the nation. 11

12 That is because the work this group does is becoming less tied to the activities of other Americans. Most of their jobs consist of analyzing and manipulating symbols—words, numbers, or visual images. Among the most prominent of these "symbolic analysts" are management consultants, lawyers, software and design engineers, research scientists, corporate executives, financial advisors, strategic planners, advertising executives, television and movie producers, and other workers whose job titles include terms like "strategy," "planning," "consultant," "policy," "resources," or "engineer."

13 These workers typically spend long hours in meetings or on the telephone and even longer hours in planes or hotels—advising, making presentations, giving briefings, and making deals. Periodically, they issue reports, plans, designs, drafts, briefs, blueprints, analyses, memorandums, layouts, renderings, scripts, or projections. In contrast with people whose jobs tend to be tedious and repetitive, symbolic analysts find their work varied and intellectually challenging. In fact, the work is often enjoyable.

14 These symbolic analysts are in ever greater demand in a world market that places an increasing value on identifying and solving problems. Requests for their software designs, financial advice, or engineering blueprints come from all parts of the globe. This largely explains why most (but by no means all) symbolic analysts have become wealthier, even as the ever-growing worldwide supply of unskilled labor continues to depress the wages of other Americans.

15 Successful Americans have not completely disengaged themselves from the lives of their less fortunate compatriots. Some devote substantial resources and energies to helping the rest of society, not through their tax payments, but through voluntary efforts. "Generosity is a reflection of what one does with his or her resources—and not what he or she advocates the government do with everyone's money," Ronald Reagan said in 1984.

16 The argument is fair enough. Government is not the only device for redistributing wealth. In his speech accepting the Presidential nomination at the Republican National Convention in 1988, George Bush said that the real magnanimity of America was to be found in a "brilliant diversity" of private charities, "spread like stars, like a thousand points of light in a broad and peaceful sky."

17 No nation congratulates itself more enthusiastically on its charitable acts than America; none engages in a greater number of charity balls, bake sales, benefit auctions, and border-to-border hand holdings for good causes. Much of this is sincerely motivated and admirable.

18 But close examination reveals that many of these acts of benevolence do not help the needy. Particularly suspect is the private givings of those in the top income-tax bracket. Studies have revealed that their

largess does not flow mainly to social services for the poor—to better schools, health clinics, or recreational centers. Instead, most voluntary contributions of wealthy Americans go to the places and institutions that entertain, inspire, cure, or educate wealthy Americans—art museums, opera houses, theaters, orchestras, ballet companies, private hospitals, and elite universities.

And even these charitable contributions are relatively skimpy. Last 19 year, American households with incomes of less than $10,000 gave an average of 5.5 percent of their earnings to charity or to a religious organization; those making more than $100,000 a year gave only 2.9 percent. After the 1986 tax-code overhaul reduced the benefits of charitable giving, the very rich became even stingier. According to Internal Revenue Service data, taxpayers earning $500,000 or more slashed their average donations to $16,062 in 1988 from $47,432 in 1980.

Corporate philanthropy is following the same general pattern. In 20 recent years, the largest American corporations have been sounding the alarm about the nation's fast deteriorating primary and secondary schools. Few are more eloquent and impassioned about the need for better schools than American executives. "How well we educate all of our children will determine our competitiveness globally, and our economic health domestically, and our communities' character and vitality," said a report of The Business Roundtable, a New York–based association of top executives.

Accordingly, there are numerous "partnerships" between corpo- 21 rations and public schools: scholarships for poor children qualified to attend college, and programs in which businesses adopt individual schools by making conspicuous donations of computers, books, and, on occasion, even money. That such activities are loudly touted by public relations staffs should not detract from the good they do.

Despite the hoopla, business donations to education and charitable 22 causes actually tapered off markedly in the 1980s, even as the economy boomed. In the 1970s, corporate giving to education jumped an average of 15 percent a year. In 1990, however, giving was only 5 percent over that in 1989; and in 1989 it was 3 percent over 1988. Moreover, most of this money goes to colleges and universities—in particular, to the alma maters of symbolic analysts, who expect their children and grandchildren to follow in their footsteps. Only 1.5 percent of corporate giving in the late 1980s was to public primary and secondary schools.

Notably, these contributions have been smaller than the amounts 23 corporations are receiving from states and communities in the form of subsidies or tax breaks. Companies are quietly procuring such deals by threatening to move their operations—and jobs—to places around the world with a more congenial tax climate. The paradoxical result has been even less corporate revenue to spend on schools and other community services than before. The executives of General Motors, for example, who have been among the loudest to proclaim the need for better schools, have also been among the most relentless in pursuing local tax abatements and in challenging their tax assessments. G.M.'s successful efforts to reduce its taxes in North Tarrytown, N.Y., where the company has had a factory since 1914, cut local revenues by $1 million in 1990, part of a larger shortfall that forced the town to lay off scores of teachers.

24 The secession of the fortunate fifth has been apparent in how and where they have chosen to work and live. In effect, most of America's large urban centers have splintered into two separate cities. One is composed of those whose symbolic and analytic services are linked to the world economy. The other consists of local service workers—custodians, security guards, taxi drivers, clerical aides, parking attendants, salespeople, restaurant employees—whose jobs are dependent on the symbolic analysts. Few blue-collar manufacturing workers remain in American cities. Between 1953 and 1984, for example, New York City lost 600,000 factory jobs; in the same interval, it added about 700,000 jobs for symbolic analysts and service workers.

25 The separation of symbolic analysts from local service workers within cities has been reinforced in several ways. Most large cities now possess two school systems—a private one for the children of the top-earning group and a public one for the children of service workers, the remaining blue-collar workers, and the unemployed. Symbolic analysts spend considerable time and energy insuring that their children gain entrance to good private schools, and then small fortunes keeping them there—dollars that under a more progressive tax code might finance better public education.

26 People with high incomes live, shop, and work within areas of cities that, if not beautiful, are at least esthetically tolerable and reasonably safe; precincts not meeting these minimum standards of charm and security have been left to the less fortunate.

27 Here again, symbolic analysts have pooled their resources to the exclusive benefit of themselves. Public funds have been spent in earnest on downtown "revitalization" projects, entailing the construction of clusters of post-modern office buildings (complete with fiber-optic cables, private branch exchanges, satellite dishes, and other communications equipment linking them to the rest of the world), multilevel parking garages, hotels with glass enclosed atriums, upscale shopping plazas and galleries, theaters, convention centers, and luxury condominiums.

28 Ideally, these complexes are entirely self-contained, with air-conditioned walkways linking residences, businesses, and recreational space. The lucky resident is able to shop, work, and attend the theater without risking direct contact with the outside world—that is, the other city.

29 When not living in urban enclaves, symbolic analysts are increasingly congregating in suburbs and exurbs where corporate headquarters have been relocated, research parks have been created, and where bucolic

universities have spawned entrepreneurial ventures. Among the most desirable of such locations are Princeton, N.J.; northern Westchester and Putnam Counties in New York; Palo Alto, Calif.; Austin, Tex.; Bethesda, Md.; and Raleigh-Durham, N.C.

Engineers and strategists of American auto companies, for example, do not live in Flint or Saginaw, Mich., where the blue-collar workers reside; they cluster in their own towns of Troy, Warren, and Auburn Hills. Likewise, the vast majority of financial specialists, lawyers, and executives working for the insurance companies of Hartford would never consider living there; after all, Hartford is the nation's fourth-poorest city. Instead, they flock to Windsor, Middlebury, West Hartford, and other towns that are among the wealthiest in the country. 30

This trend, too, has been growing for decades. But technology has accelerated it. Today's symbolic analysts linked directly to the rest of the globe can choose to live and work in the most pastoral of settings. 31

The secession has been encouraged by the Federal Government. For the last decade, Washington has in effect shifted responsibility for many public services to local governments. At their peak, Federal grants made up 25 percent of state and local spending in the late 1970s. Today, the Federal share has dwindled to 17 percent. Direct aid to local governments, in the form of programs introduced in the Johnson and Nixon Administrations, has been the hardest hit by budget cuts. In the 1980s, Federal dollars for clean water, job training and transfers, low-income housing, sewage treatment, and garbage disposal shrank by some $50 billion a year, and Washington's share of spending on local transit declined by 50 percent. (The Bush Administration has proposed that states and localities take on even more of the costs of building and maintaining roads, and wants to cut Federal aid for mass transit.) In 1990, New York City received only 9.6 percent of all its revenue from the Federal Government, compared with 16 percent in 1981. 32

States have quickly transferred many of these new expenses to fiscally strapped cities and towns, with a result that by the start of the 1990s, localities were bearing more than half the costs of water and sewage, roads, parks, welfare, and public schools. In New York State, the local communities' share has risen to about 75 percent of these costs. 33

Cities and towns with affluent inhabitants can bear these burdens relatively easily. Poorer ones, faced with the twin problem of lower incomes and greater demand for social services, have had far more difficulty. And as the gap between the richest and poorest communities has widened, the shift in responsibility for public services to cities and towns has functioned as another means of relieving wealthier Americans of the cost of aiding less fortunate citizens. 34

The result has been a growing inequality in basic social and community services. While the city tax rate in Philadelphia, for example, is about triple that of communities around it, the suburbs enjoy far better schools, hospitals, recreation, and police protection. Eighty-five percent 35 of the richest families in the greater Philadelphia area live outside the city limits, and 80 percent of the region's poorest live inside. The quality of a city's infrastructure—roads, bridges, sewage, water treatment—is likewise related to the average income of its inhabitants.

36 The growing inequality in government services has been most apparent in the public schools. The Federal Government's share of the costs of primary and secondary education has dwindled to about 6 percent. The bulk of the cost is divided about equally between the states and local school districts. States with a higher concentration of wealthy residents can afford to spend more on their schools than other states. In 1989, the average public-school teacher in Arkansas, for example, received $21,700; in Connecticut, $37,300.

37 Even among adjoining suburban towns in the same state the differences can be quite large. Consider three Boston-area communities located within minutes of one another. All are predominantly white, and most residents within each town earn about the same as their neighbors. But the disparity of incomes between towns is substantial.

38 Belmont, northwest of Boston, is inhabited mainly by symbolic analysts and their families. In 1988, the average teacher in its public schools earned $36,100. Only 3 percent of Belmont's eighteen-year-olds dropped out of high school, and more than 80 percent of graduating seniors chose to go on to a four-year college.

39 Just east of Belmont is Somerville, most of whose residents are low-wage service workers. In 1988, the average Somerville teacher earned $29,400. A third of the town's eighteen-year-olds did not finish high school, and fewer than a third planned to attend college.

40 Chelsea, across the Mystic River from Somerville, is the poorest of the three towns. Most of its inhabitants are unskilled, and many are unemployed or only employed part time. The average teacher in Chelsea, facing tougher educational challenges than his or her counterparts in Belmont, earned $26,200 in 1988, almost a third less than the average teacher in the more affluent town just a few miles away. More than half of Chelsea's eighteen-year-olds did not graduate from high school, and only 10 percent planned to attend college.

41 Similar disparities can be found all over the nation. Students at Highland Park High School in a wealthy suburb of Dallas, for example, enjoy a campus with a planetarium, indoor swimming pool, closed-circuit television studio and state-of-the-art science laboratory. Highland Park spends about $6,000 a year to educate each student. This is almost twice that spent per pupil by the towns of Wilmer and Hutchins in southern Dallas County. According to Texas education officials, the richest school district in the state spends $19,300 a year per pupil; its poorest, $2,100 a year.

42 The courts have become involved in trying to repair such imbalances, but the issues are not open to easy judicial remedy.

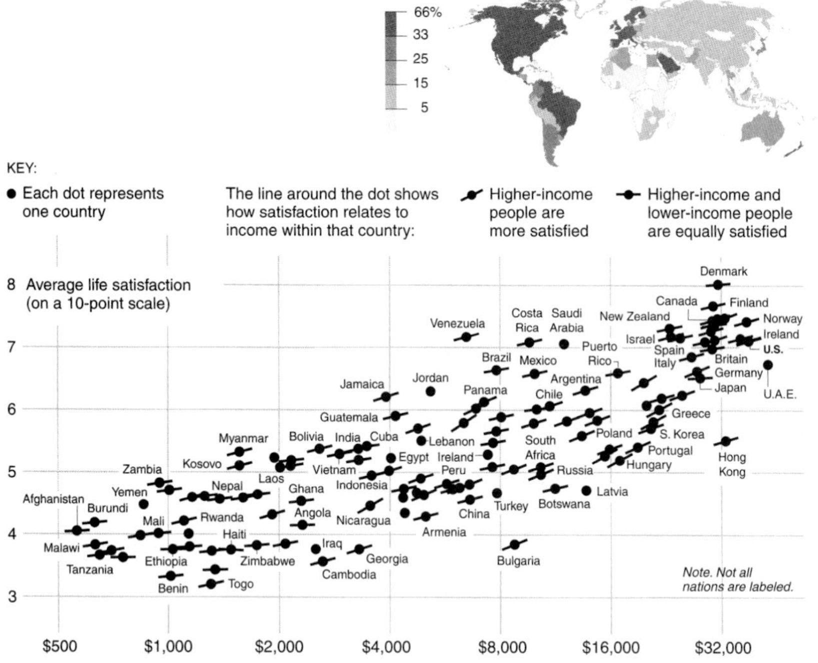

G.D.P. per capita, converted to dollars at prices that equalize purchasing power. [Note the relationship between income and amount of individual satisfaction. Compare this diagram with the two maps on 482. To what degree do the "Political Trouble Spots of the Modern World" and the "Environmental Trouble Spots of the Modern World" indicated on these maps correspond to the diagram of individual satisfaction above? Explain this correspondence. For additional commentary see 499, question 12.]

Betsey Stevenson and Justin Wolters, Wharton School at the University of Pennsylvania. *The New York Times*, April 16, 2008. © 2008, *The New York Times*. Reprinted by permission.

The four-fifths of Americans left in the wake of the secession of the fortunate fifth include many poor blacks, but racial exclusion is neither the primary motive for the separation nor a necessary consequence. Lower-income whites are similarly excluded, and high-income black symbolic analysts are often welcomed. The segregation is economic rather than racial, although economically motivated separation often results in *de facto* racial segregation. Where courts have found a pattern of racially motivated segregation, it usually has involved lower-income white communities bordering on lower-income black neighborhoods. 43

In states where courts have ordered equalized state spending in school districts, the vast differences in a town's property values—and thus local tax revenues—continue to result in substantial inequities. Where courts or state governments have tried to impose limits on what affluent communities can pay their teachers, not a few parents in upscale towns have simply removed their children from the public schools and applied the money they might otherwise have willingly paid in higher 44 taxes to private school tuitions instead. And, of course, even if statewide expenditures were better equalized, poorer states would continue to be at a substantial disadvantage.

45 In all these ways, the gap between America's symbolic analysts and everyone else is widening into a chasm. Their secession from the rest of the population raises fundamental questions about the future of American society. In the new global economy—in which money, technologies, and corporations cross borders effortlessly—a citizen's standard of living depends more and more on skills and insights, and on the infrastructure needed to link these abilities to the rest of the world. But the most skilled and insightful Americans, who are already positioned to thrive in the world market, are now able to slip the bonds of national allegiance, and by so doing disengage themselves from their less-favored fellows. The stark political challenge in the decades ahead will be to reaffirm that, even though America is no longer a separate and distinct economy, it is still a society whose members have abiding obligations to one another.

Content

1. Does Reich prove convincingly that "the fortunate fifth [those Americans with the highest income] is quietly seceding from the rest of the nation" (¶ 8)? To what extent does your receptivity to his argument depend on whether or not you consider yourself or your family a member of the "fortunate fifth"?
2. Who are "symbolic analysts" (¶s 12–14, 25–31)? Does Reich demonstrate that these persons comprise a significant portion of the "fortunate fifth"? Why does he identify their job titles (¶ 12), activities (¶ 13), lifestyles (¶s 25–28), and places of work and residence (¶s 28–30) in long lists? In what ways does he expect his readers to interpret these lists?
3. Reich illustrates many of the points of his argument with reference to the public schools in rich and poor districts (¶s 36–44, for example). Why does he focus on schools?
4. If Reich has convinced you of his premise (see question 1 above), has he also convinced you of his conclusion that "the most skilled and insightful Americans . . . are now able to slip the bonds of national allegiance, and by so doing disengage themselves from their less-favored fellows. The stark political challenge . . . will be to reaffirm that . . . [America] is still a society whose members have abiding obligations to one another" (¶ 45)? If he has convinced you, what does he want you to do as a consequence? If he hasn't convinced you, why hasn't he?

Strategies/Structures/Language

5. The specific statistical information and other figures in Reich's 1991 article change annually, if not more often. Is their alteration within the next decade likely to affect either Reich's argument or your receptivity to it? Since numbers are always in flux, why use them in an argument?

6. Reich's sentences are fairly long, but his paragraphs are short, usually from one to three sentences. (The longest paragraph, ¶ 32, has eight sentences.) This is because the article was originally published in a newspaper, the *New York Times Magazine*; newspapers provide paragraph breaks not to indicate where the material logically breaks or changes course but to rest readers' eyes as they roam the page. What is the effect, if any, of such a large number of short paragraphs in a serious article?

7. Which side does Reich favor? At what point in the argument does he expect his readers to realize this?

8. Does Reich's division of workers into "symbolic and analytic services" and "local service workers" cover most people in cities? Where do "blue-collar manufacturing workers" live (see ¶ 24)? Are such labels necessary or helpful in constructing the argument Reich makes?

For Writing

9. Argue, by yourself or with a team, as Reich does but using your own examples (and some of his factual information, among other sources) that, as Reich concludes, "even though America is no longer a separate and distinct economy, it is still a society whose members have abiding obligations to one another" (¶ 45). One way to address the subject is to consider the implications of a particular public policy issue (such as school busing, property taxation, equalization of school funding across rich and poor districts, gated residential communities with private security guards, privatization of Social Security). See, for example, Martin Luther King, Jr.'s, "Letter from Birmingham Jail" (456–70), and the essays by Matt Nocton (286–90) and Peter Singer (535–41).

10. ***Journal Writing.*** What factors, other than income, bring people together in a geographical community, whether a suburban or urban neighborhood, a small town within a metropolitan area, or a rural town? In your experience, does ethnicity, religion, or a particular interest, perhaps recreational activities, play a major role in defining a community? To what extent do these factors correlate with income levels? Is income level the defining factor in your community's character?

11. ***Dialogues.*** Is it socially desirable for the upper fifth in income to "secede" from "the rest of the nation," as Reich asserts in paragraph 8 and challenges thereafter? How might American attitudes toward wealth that Reich describes foster the emergence of a separate, elite workforce? Do Americans consider poverty a form of failure or disgrace, as Singer's "The Singer Solution to World Poverty" (535–41) implies? Expand your answer by incorporating part of Martin Luther King, Jr.'s, analysis of systemic discrimination against African Americans. Does such a social structure encourage or discourage excellence?

12. What does the chart on 497 suggest about the relationship between economic growth and the well-being of a nation's citizens? Speculate why the citizens of countries at lower levels of GDP per capita tend to report equal levels of satisfaction regardless of income differences. Why might the lower-income citizens of some countries with high levels of GDP per capita report less satisfaction with their lives relative to higher-income citizens? Which countries represent the outliers (the data points on the margins of the dominant statistical relationship)? What factors might be responsible for their position relative to other countries?

13. ***Second Look.*** Consider Reich's argument with respect to the photograph of Native American schoolgirls (187) or the cleaning woman in front of the American flag (451). How do these images suggest that exclusion defines what is American? Does the "new elite" as Reich defines it (¶ 11) grow out of a history rooted in the disenfranchisement or forced assimilation of specific ethnic groups? Is the idea of a unified American culture a pretense that conceals social inequity? In what ways do Lange's photograph of the "Migrant Mother" (536) and Adams's photograph of the Tsurutani family at the Manzanar Relocation Center (592) expand or complicate your answers?

MATTHEW ALLEN

Matthew Allen (born 1980) earned a BA at Brigham Young University (2005) and is currently pursuing graduate studies in English Language and Linguistics at Purdue University. After brief stints in law and government, Allen taught high school English and ESL in Massachusetts. Allen spent a few years in Europe and daydreams about returning.

In several ways, Allen says, "'The Rhetorical Situation of the Scientific Paper' is the culmination of my undergraduate studies. First, I drew on the different disciplines I had studied, including biology, psychology, and English language and linguistics, as I researched and wrote this paper. Second, the countless revisions I went through for this paper showed me how much I had matured as a writer. For years, I dreaded criticism so much that I refused to proofread or redraft my work. After becoming an editor and writing tutor [at BYU's Writing Center], I finally realized the value of feedback and revision." Allen says his paper went through more than six major revisions before it was published in *Young Scholars in Writing: Undergraduate Research in Writing and Rhetoric* (2004). In it, Allen argues that the "experimental report, like all written accounts, is an interpretation, subject to creativity, convention, form, and style" (¶ 26).

✧ The Rhetorical Situation of the Scientific Paper and the "Appearance" of Objectivity

1 Mention the words *rhetoric* and *science* together, and many people see an intrinsic contradiction. After all, two hallmarks of modern science are objectivity and empirical method, whereas rhetoric bears the marks of a long and sometimes sordid history of sophistic oratory and biased argumentation. Gerald Holton describes this distinction: Rhetoric

is often perceived as the art of persuasion, while science is generally seen as the art of demonstration (173). This idea implies, to use a figure of speech, that rhetoric and science should not be seen together in public. The distinction between the two, however, is probably more fabricated than genuine. Scholars, especially during the last several decades, have argued that scientific practice and discourse do have rhetorical and persuasive elements.

Published scientific papers bridge the gap between a scientist's work and the public's knowledge of that work. Research that goes unpublished, to use an image from Robert Day, is like a tree falling in a forest when no one is around—there is no "sound" without an audience (1). In order for this knowledge to be received and accepted by the intended audience, generally the scientific community, the research or experimental report must follow certain conventions, not the least of which are methodological validity and pertinence to the existing body of scientific knowledge. The authors of scientific papers must demonstrate the validity and objectivity of their findings and make them seem interesting and relevant to already-established conclusions. In effect, this is a rhetorical situation: a speaker (the author) communicates knowledge about a particular subject to an audience via the scientific paper, intending, on some level, to persuade that audience. 2

What is most interesting about the rhetorical situation of the scientific paper is that the writer persuades his or her audience largely through the *appearance of* objectivity. Many people, as Charles Bazerman points out, think that writing based on scientific premises is not really writing at all (14), that it is an unbiased vessel for transmitting truth. But in this essay, I analyze Renske Wassenberg, Jeffrey E. Max, Scott D. Lindgren, and Amy Schatz's article, "Sustained Attention in Children and Adolescents after Traumatic Brain Injury: Relation to Severity of Injury, Adaptive Functioning, ADHD and Social Background" (herein referred to as "Sustained Attention in Children and Adolescents"), recently published in *Brain Injury,* to illustrate that the writer of an experimental report in effect creates an exigence and then addresses it through rhetorical strategies that contribute to the appearance of objectivity. 3

Scientific Inquiry and Objectivity

It would seem that the objective nature of modern science precludes any possibility of rhetoric's entering into scientific writing. The assumption is that writing is interpretive and science is not. This notion results from an apparently sound connection: scientific writing is scientific; science is objective; therefore, scientific writing is objective. Objectivity certainly is one of the key goals and primary assumptions of scientific practice and writing. Nevertheless, it is inaccurate to think that the subjective human element can be completely eliminated through even the most objective 4 scientific method. As Peter Medawar suggests, "There is no such thing as unprejudiced observation. Every act of observation we make is biased. What we see or otherwise sense is a function of what we have seen or sensed in the past" (230).

5 While the historic public face of science may exude objectivity, there is a pervasive, if less openly discussed, subjective side. Even if scientists were able to collect data in a purely objective way, Brent Slife and Richard Williams contend that "we cannot ignore the necessity of *interpreting* the data yielded by scientific method" (5, emphasis in original). Although computer programs may seem to be doing unbiased interpreting in some cases, human beings must ultimately give meaning to data, however raw they may or may not be. For example, an experiment that measured the brain waves of laboratory rats under certain conditions might yield a group of numbers, a data set. That data set would be virtually meaningless (i.e., it would not tell the researchers what they had found) until it was organized in some coherent way. But what kind of organization would be most coherent? A graph, a table, perhaps a qualitative description? Each organizational approach might produce different findings, but many approaches will be equally valid. The choice of methods and organization of data will ultimately depend on the point of view of the person doing the interpreting and the scientific needs of the project. A computer might flawlessly organize data a particular way, but that computer was programmed by someone. The point is that ideas outside of the actual data set must be projected onto the data set before it means anything. As Slife and Williams explain, "in this sense, data can never be facts until they have been given an interpretation that is dependent on ideas that do not appear in the data themselves" (6).

6 This type of evidence leads to Bazerman's assertion that the "popular belief of this past century that scientific language is simply a transparent transmitter of natural facts is . . . of course wrong" (14). Medawar goes even further, declaring that the scientific paper gives "a totally misleading narrative of the processes of thought that go into the making of scientific discoveries" (233). One of his points is that there is a creative side to science, a side often sacrificed to an assumed objectivity. Creativity is more subjective than objective, and so alternative interpretations exist.

Experimental Papers and Persuasive Argument

7 Despite attempts to influence the reader, the type of rhetoric involved in scientific writing does not, as Kristine Hansen emphasizes, involve "bombast, flowery phrases, or appeals to emotion, all aimed at deceiving" (xvi). Rather, contend John Schuster and Richard Yeo, "scientific argumentation is essentially persuasive argument and therefore is rightly termed *rhetorical* in the sense defined by students of 'the new rhetoric,' where 'rhetoric' denotes the entire field of discursive

structures and strategies used to render arguments persuasive in given situations" (xii). As scientists write reports of original research, all the while conforming to certain accepted structures and styles, such as logic, clarity, and empiricism, they still give a rhetorical shape to their writing. Gerald Holton describes this process as a "proactive rhetoric of assertion"—when a scientist becomes convinced of something, he or she hopes to persuade others about that same idea or phenomenon when the work is published (176).

There are practical motivations beyond contributing to scientific knowledge for using scientific rhetoric to emphasize the importance of publishable research. Scientists, according to Day, are primarily measured by and known for their publications (ix). In the competitive world of academics and research, scientists need to publish to gain prestige and promotions. Poorly written, nonstandard, or unconvincing papers are naturally less likely to be chosen for publication. 8

The Rhetorical Situation and Its Exigence

According to Lloyd Bitzer, rhetoric is always situational; it is a pragmatic response "to a situation of a certain kind," functioning "ultimately to produce action or change in the world" (3). The rhetorical situation, according to Bitzer, has several key features, but my primary concern is with exigence, which is central to understanding scientific rhetoric. An exigence, as defined by Bitzer, is "an imperfection marked by urgency; it is a defect, an obstacle, something waiting to be done, a thing which is other than it should be" (6). An exigence such as winter or death that cannot be altered through rhetoric or through any other means is not a rhetorical exigence (6). This understanding of exigence is further elucidated by Bitzer's definition of rhetoric: 9

> In short, rhetoric is a mode of altering reality, not by direct application of energy to objects, but by the creation of discourse which changes reality through the mediation of thought and action. The rhetor alters reality by bringing into existence a discourse of such a character that the audience, in thought and action, is so engaged that it becomes mediator of change. In this sense rhetoric is always persuasive. (3)

This concept of rhetoric and exigence is exemplified in many of the speeches and writings of Martin Luther King, Jr. King believed that the racially inequitable social conditions around him could be altered through speech and subsequent action. King helped to change the reality of racial inequality through rhetoric, including his famous "I Have a Dream" speech. His discourse engaged, and continued to engage, his audience, often prompting people to action. King did not himself rewrite legislation or policies, but his rhetoric contributed to the actions of those who did. 10

11 In a scientific paper, the reality being altered is the accumulating knowledge of the scientific community. The rhetorical exigence is, in Lawrence Prelli's words, the "gap in the collective body of knowledge" (23). Simply put, a scientist performs an experiment to better understand a law, principle, or phenomenon and then creates and publishes a scientific paper to communicate the results to the scientific community. In a sense, the scientist is "fixing" a problem—he or she has come to a better understanding of something than anyone else and is therefore able to fill in that "gap" in knowledge. As Prelli suggests, "[a] scientific orientation inclines one to define rhetorical situations in terms of the presence or absence of objectively verifiable information and the consonance of new evidence with already-accepted knowledge" (23).

12 Prelli seems to imply, justifiably, that scientific rhetoric is secondary to scientific knowledge and practice. If the new knowledge cannot be scientifically verified and reconciled with traditional knowledge, the rhetorical aspects of the paper alone, the strategies used to make the new knowledge seem like an answer, are useless. The scientist must first have identified a problem in order to propose the answer he or she has found. Experimental reports, Bazerman says, are special in this way because they describe "an event created so that it might be told" (59). Scientists formulated problems, according to their methodologies, in order to solve them—in essence, they create more than discover the rhetorical situation because they construct an exigence.

13 In "Sustained Attention in Children and Adolescents," the authors express their exigence when they state the study's primary objective: "To examine the relationship of child and family psychological variables and traumatic brain injury (TBI) severity as it relates to sustained attention" (751). The driving question is clear: What, if any, is the relationship between psychosocial variables and TBI? This question certainly is compelling and worthwhile, but was it discovered or created? The authors imply a creative process of arriving at their exigence:

> Attention problems are commonly reported after TBI in children. There is little known about the effects of TBI on specific attentional components: orienting to sensory stimuli, executive functions and maintaining the alert state. The focus of this study is on sustained attention (i.e. the capacity to maintain arousal and alertness over time). According to Dennis et al., sustained attention is a regulator of cognitive activities needed for academic tasks, adaptive functioning and social interactions. A deficiency in sustained attention may, therefore, have a significant impact on the child's development in the acute and chronic stages of TBI. (752)

14 As this paragraph from the introduction illustrates, the authors created an exigence by building upon previous research and their own insights and by constructing a logical hypothesis (eventually an entire

study) to address that exigence. In essence, they arrived at their research question through inference. The exigence, however valid, was essentially created through a careful, thoughtful, and creative process. The authors' review of the literature did not inevitably lead to their hypothesis. They creatively took two factors (pre-TBI psychological variables and post-TBI sustained attention) and postulated a relationship between them. Yet, the connection is scientifically valid: many of their ideas have been discussed or established in previous research, and they can test their new ideas empirically.

Rhetorical Strategies Used to Shape the Persuasive Paper

In effect, the authors of experimental papers address the exigence of the rhetorical situation through a carefully crafted rhetoric. The writing, as Bazerman says, "appears to hide itself" (14). This subtle approach is a specific rhetorical strategy: there seems to be no style—hence, no rhetoric—when in fact there is one. The writing style in most experimental reports intentionally deemphasizes creativity and human voice. The general choice is to use rhetoric that is persuasive through emphasizing logic and objectivity over creativity. Such rhetorical aspects of scientific writing tend to be subsumed or hidden by the larger goal of conveying meaning clearly and impartially. 15

For example, the passive voice, whereby the writer can easily omit the agent (the "doer" in the clause), is more prevalent in scientific writing than in most other genres. The editors of *Merriam Webster's Dictionary of English Usage* point out that while the active voice is generally preferable, "a few [usage] commentators find the passive useful in scientific writing (one even believes it to be necessary) because of the tone of detachment and impersonality that it helps establish" (721). 16

The authors of "Sustained Attention in Children and Adolescents" definitely agree with this remark about the importance of the passive voice. An analysis of the first 118 or so lines of the article (the introduction and part of the method section) attests to the author's careful choice of language: over one-third of the verb constructions are passives (about 26 of 70). For most non-scientific published writing, passive constructions tend to be around 10 to 15 percent, a ratio that the article noticeably surpasses (*Merriam Webster's* 720) The significance of this frequent use of passives is that actions and findings (i.e., non-human elements) are emphasized over human elements. The agent is noticeably missing in the following passive sentences from the article: 17

- The Paediatric Assessment of Cognitive Efficiency (PACE) was used in this study to test two types of deficits, inattention and impulsiveness. (752)

- Inattention and impulsiveness were not further elucidated because the two error measures, omission and commission errors, were not independently analyzed. (752)
- It was hypothesized that children with severe TBI will produce significantly more errors on the PACE than children with mild/moderate TBI. (753)
- No differences were found between the Mild/Moderate and Severe TBI group in regards to demographic characteristics. (754)

18 For each of these actions, there must have been an agent, someone using the assessment, choosing not to further elucidate certain factors, hypothesizing, and failing to find differences. The authors' use of the passive voice to emphasize the action and deemphasize the agent (the authors omit the agent in nearly every passive construction in the first 118 lines) certainly does create a "tone of detachment and impersonality," even one of objectivity.[1]

19 The standard organization of scientific papers is another way to emphasize the factual and objective over the interpretive and subjective. The organization helps portray the paper's information logically and persuasively. The modern research paper, as Day explains, has the basic universal form of IMRAD—Introduction, Methods, Results, and Discussion—because this form is "so eminently logical" (11). Holton dubs this rationale the "well-tested machinery of logic and analysis, the direct evidence of the phenomena" (174). Plainly stated, the scientific paper is structured according to a scientific ideal: the method is set forth, and the results are reported, analyzed, and discussed. The organization by sequential sections is logical; the analysis is scientific because the discussion (the possibly non-scientific human element) is kept separate from the results. This type of organization, Medawar argues, implies an inductive process of unbiased observation leading to generalization (229). While the accuracy of this method may be questioned, it is logically convincing because, as Louis Pasteur purportedly told his students, it makes the results seem inevitable (Holton 174).

20 "Sustained Attention in Children and Adolescents" strictly adheres to the IMRAD method of organization. The report contains an introduction; a methods section, which is further broken down into six subsections; a results section; and a discussion. The authors could have chosen another method of organization, but doing so would probably have reduced the likelihood of their getting the article published, and had it been published in a novel format, frequent readers of research reports would likely have been put off to some degree. As it stands, readers of "Sustained Attention in Children and Adolescents" waste no time getting to the crux of the study—it's right there in the introduction and discussion—but all the technical evidence is still available. One interesting aspect of this particular study is that it is essentially part of a "soft" or social science. The

variables in the study are all centered on human beings, studied according to various psychological tests. The patently scientific organization of the paper, however, seems to leave no question that this study was done according to "hard" science principles.

The same type of logical persuasion exemplified in the IMRAD organization is common in the introductions of many papers, a part of the report designed to emphasize the relevance and necessity of the particular findings to preexisting scientific evidence. John Swales found that scientists tend to use a very specific rhetorical strategy, what he termed the Create a Research Space (CARS) communication move schema (Golebiowski 1). After analyzing dozens of research paper introductions from various fields (e.g., physics, biology and medicine, and social sciences), Swales and subsequent researchers found that nearly every one of them contained three to six rhetorical organization "moves" aimed at making the paper seem important and relevant. 21

Swales' CARS model consists of three principle communicative moves: Move 1—establish centrality within the research; Move 2—establish a niche within the research; and Move 3—occupy the niche with the present research (Golebiowski 1–2). These moves help the author clearly state the exigence (the lack of knowledge) and the proposed solution (the present research). Scientists can use the introduction of the scientific paper to relate their research to others and to show how important the present findings are to the corpus of scientific knowledge. Findings that are relevant and timely should indeed be welcomed and accepted by the larger community, and so carefully introducing one's topic makes all the more sense. 22

These principal CARS communicative moves are central to the introduction of "Sustained Attention in Children and Adolescents." The authors establish centrality within their research area, Move 1, by briefly discussing traumatic brain injury (TBI) in children and adolescents and by stating that "childhood TBI [is] a significant public health problem" because it "is the leading cause of child deaths in the US and one of the most frequent causes of interruption to normal child development" (751). The authors also discuss previous research, eventually building up to their own research, and thereby establish their study's relevance through the implication that they share the same central assumptions and information base. 23

The authors establish a niche within the research, Move 2, primarily by indicating a gap in the research and by claiming that they will build upon the research of a previous study. After reviewing the general topic of TBI, the authors claim, "There is little known about the effects of TBI on specific attentional components: orienting to sensory stimuli, executive functions and maintaining the alert state" (752). They immediately move to occupy this niche, Move 3, by stating. "The focus of this study is on sustained attention (i.e. the capacity to maintain arousal and alertness over time)" (752). After identifying sustained attention as their primary 24 area of interest, the authors continue moving from general to specific and from Move 2 to Move 3. They review the literature dealing with sustained attention and then, in the last paragraph of the introduction, identify one study in particular from which they will proceed: "The present study aims to extend the findings of Taylor et al. in several ways" (753). The authors' intention seems clear: find something new without radically departing from what other researchers have already established.

Conclusion

25 Indubitably, scientific reports further our understanding of the world and the phenomena around us. James Watson and Francis Crick's famous paper that established the double helix structure of DNA, for example, radically altered biological studies (and in many ways, society at large). In "Sustained Attention in Children and Adolescents," the researchers found that people treating children with traumatic brain injury need to "consider pre-injury child and family psychosocial characteristics in addition to severity of injury" (751). While not as revolutionary as Watson and Crick's paper, the authors point out that their study helps fill a dearth of medical knowledge. Their findings are probably very important to those affected by TBI and those treating them.

26 It is important, however, to recognize that just as all scientific data are interpreted, this experimental report, like all written accounts, is an interpretation, subject to creativity, convention, form, and style. For example, the very tests used in the research and the results of those tests may not really show what the authors understood them to show. The authors inferred a connection between the tests and the test results and their eventual interpretations. The tests themselves are fundamentally based on theories, as are all scientific methods, but are essentially treated by the authors as being objective (at least if they are administered under ideal circumstances). A "soft" science experiment, this study is reported in "hard" science fashion.

27 Writing experimental reports is an especially provocative practice because through these studies today's hypotheses and theories become tomorrow's scientific facts and laws. In Sundar Sarukkai's words, "The writing of science is not only a representation of the ideas of science; it is also integral to the creation of new meaning and truth claims" (1). In one sense, the "creation of new meaning and truth claims" implies a rhetorical situation, where the writing is meant to persuade. Certainly, scientists and researchers should be aware of embedded rhetorical strategies. But given the profound and pervasive influence of science in Western culture, we should all—scientist or not—be attentive to how our knowledge is shaped.

28 I would like to thank Beth Hedengren and Kristine Hansen for generously sharing their time and knowledge to help me develop this article.

Notes

1. By way of comparison, James Watson and Francis Crick's famous article in *Nature* proposing the structure of DNA contains about 24 percent passive constructions, markedly fewer than "Sustained Attention in Children and Adolescents'" approximately 37 percent. Subtract the passive constructions in Watson and Crick's article that include the agent and the number drops to around 17 percent. The comparison between the two articles is useful because it shows that using the passive voice is a choice—a strategy to create a certain ethos, in this case, one of objectivity.

Works Cited

Bazerman, Charles. *Shaping Written Knowledge: The Genre and Activity of the Experimental Article in Science.* Madison: U of Wisconsin P, 1988.

Bitzer, Lloyd F. "The Rhetorical Situation." *Philosophy and Rhetoric* 1 (1968): 1–14.

Day, Robert A. *How to Write and Publish a Scientific Paper.* 4th ed. Phoenix: Oryx, 1994.

Golebiowski, Zosia. "Application of Swales' Model in the Analysis of Research Papers by Polish Authors." *International Review of Applied Linguistics in Language Teaching* 37.3 (1999). Online. *Academic Search Elite.* 14 Mar. 2003.

Hansen, Kristine. *A Rhetoric for the Social Sciences: A Guide to Academic and Professional Communications.* Upper Saddle River, NJ: Prentice Hall, 1998.

Holton, Gerald. "Quanta, Relativity, and Rhetoric." *Persuading Science: The Art of Scientific Rhetoric.* Ed. Marcello Pera and William R. Shea. Canton, MA: Science History, 1991. 173–203.

Medawar, Peter. "Is the Scientific Paper a Fraud?" *BBC Third Programme, Listener.* BBC. London, UK. 1963. Rpt. in *The Threat and the Glory: Reflections on Sciences and Scientists.* Ed. David Pyke. New York: HarperCollins, 1990. 228–33.

Merriam-Webster's Dictionary of English Usage. Springfield: Merriam-Webster, 1994.

Prelli, Lawrence J. *A Rhetoric of Science: Inventing Scientific Discourse.* Columbia: U of South Carolina P, 1989.

Sarukkai, Sundar. *Translating the World: Science and Language.* Lanham: Washington, D.C., 2002.

Schuster, John A., and Richard R. Yeo. Introduction. *The Politics and Rhetoric of Scientific Method: Historical Studies.* Boston: D. Reidel, 1986. ix–xxxvii.

Slife, Brent D., and Richard N. Williams. *What's Behind the Research: Discovering Hidden Assumptions in the Behavioral Sciences.* Thousand Oaks: Sage, 1995.

Wassenberg, Renske, Jeffrey E. Max, Scott D. Lindgren, and Amy Schatz. "Sustained Attention in Children and Adolescents after Traumatic Brain Injury: Relation to Severity of Injury, Adaptive Functioning, ADHD and Social Background." *Brain Injury* 18 (2004): 751–64.

Watson, J. D., and F. H. C. Crick, "Molecular Structure of Nucleic Acids: A Structure for Deoxyribose Nucleic Acid." *Nature* 4356 (1953): 737–38.

Content

1. What evidence does Allen provide to corroborate Peter Medawar's observation that "there is no such thing as unprejudiced observation. Every act of observation we make is biased" (¶ 4)? If this is so, why does scientific writing have the reputation for being objective and unbiased?
2. Is data meaningless without interpretation (¶ 4)? Is objective interpretation—of anything—impossible? What rhetorical strategies do scientists use to present their evidence convincingly?
3. Explain Allen's conclusion that "scientists formulate problems, according to their methodologies, in order to solve them—in essence, they create more than discover the rhetorical situation because they construct an exigence" (¶ 12). What does he mean by "rhetorical situation"? By "exigence"?
4. In what ways has Allen demonstrated his conclusion, that "this experimental report ["Sustained Attention"], like all written accounts, is an interpretation, subject to creativity, convention, form, and style" (¶ 26)?

Strategies/Structures/Language

5. Allen has undertaken the difficult task of trying to summarize a thirteen-page scientific paper and analyze its rhetorical strategies in ten paragraphs (¶s 15–24). Although he has done an exemplary job, this section of the paper is nevertheless difficult to understand. Why?
6. Might some of the difficulties in understanding this paper be due to the specialized vocabularies of (a) rhetorical analysis or (b) the language of "Sustained Attention?" Does Allen define new rhetorical concepts the first time he uses a new word or term?

For Writing

7. Either independently or with a partner, analyze a published scientific or social scientific paper in your field, or one of the scientific or social science essays in *The Essay Connection* (such as those by Gawande, "On Washing Hands" 206–12; Angier, "Why Men Don't Last" 302–05; Tannen, "Fast Forward: Technologically Enhanced Aggression" 308–15; Mann, "Forever Young" 422–33; Diamond, "The World as a Polder" 472–83; or another) to show why, where, and how they are interpretive (and therefore not objective). *Note*: This does *not* mean these essays are unreliable; indeed, they are all of high quality, though not without controversy.

Additional Topics for Writing Appealing to Reason: Deductive and Inductive Arguments

(For strategies for appealing to reason, see 446–47.)

Multiple Strategies for Writing: Arguments

Arguments commonly employ assorted strategies to make their points as compelling as possible and to interpret their significance. Among these are the following:

- *definitions* of essential terms, component parts. These may be objective or favorable to the writer's point of view.
- *illustrations* and *examples,* to show the meaning or significance of the key issues
- *explanations* and *analyses* of the salient points
- *comparison* and *contrast* of the pro and con positions
- *division* and *classification* of the relevant subtopics and side issues
- a *narrative,* on occasion, either at the beginning to humanize the abstract or theoretical issue under consideration or at the end to allow the full import of the argument to make a final impact
- *cause* and *effect,* to show the beneficial consequences of the arguer's point of view and the detrimental consequences of the opposition's stance

1. By yourself or with a partner, write a logical, clearly reasoned, well-supported argument appropriate to the subject in organization, language, and tone and appealing to your designated audience. Be sure you have in mind a particular reader or group of readers who you know (or suspect) are likely to be receptive or hostile to your position, or uncommitted people whose opinion you're trying to influence.

   a. Tackling a particular ecological issue—you pick the controversy—is (or is not) worth the effort and expense.
   b. Smoking, drinking, or using "recreational" drugs is (is not) worth the risks.
   c. Economic prosperity is (is not) more important to our country than conservation and preservation of our country's resources.
   d. The Social Security system should (should not) be preserved in its present form for current and future generations.
   e. Everyone should (should not) be entitled to comprehensive medical care (supply one: from the cradle to the grave; in early childhood; while a student; in old age; if they're unable to pay for it).
   f. Drunk drivers should (should not) be jailed, even for a first offense.
   g. Cell phone use should (should not) be prohibited for drivers of motor vehicles when in use or in other venues (public transportation; elevators; restaurants; locker rooms)

h. Companies manufacturing products that may affect consumers' health or safety (such as food, drugs, liquor, automobiles, pesticides) should (should not) have consumer representatives on their boards of directors.
i. The civil rights, women's liberation, gay liberation, or some comparable movement has (has not) accomplished major and long-lasting benefits for the group it represents.
j. Intercollegiate athletic teams that are big business should (should not) hire their players; intercollegiate athletes should (should not) have professional status.
k. Strong labor unions should (should not) be preserved.
l. The costs of America's space program are worth (far exceed) the benefits.
m. The federal government should (should not) take over the nation's health care system.
n. The Patriot Act should (should not) be repealed.
o. The possibility of identity theft is (is not) a reasonable tradeoff for ease of Internet usage.

2. Write a letter to your campus, city, or area newspaper in which you take a stand on an issue, defending or attacking it. You could write on one of the topics in Additional Topics 1 above or differ with a recent column or editorial. Hot button issues are fine if you have appropriate support for your argument. Send in your letter (keep a copy for yourself), and see if it is published. If so, what kind of response did it attract?

3. Write to your state or federal legislator, urging the passage or defeat of a particular piece of legislation currently being considered. (You will probably find at least one side of the issue being reported in the newspapers or a newsmagazine.) An extra: If you receive a reply, analyze it to see whether it addresses the specific points you raise. In what fashion? Does it sound like an individual response or a form letter?

Appealing to Emotion and Ethics

The essence of an emotional appeal is passion. You write from passion, and you expect your readers to respond with equal fervor. "I have a dream." "The only thing we have to fear is fear itself." "We have nothing to offer but blood, toil, tears, and sweat." "The West wasn't won with a loaded gun!" You'll be making your case, combining appeals to reason, emotion, and ethics in specific, concrete, memorable ways that you expect to have an unusually powerful impact on your readers. So your writing will probably be more colorful than it might be in less emotional circumstances, with a high proportion of vivid examples, narratives, anecdotes, character sketches, analogies ("Will Iraq or North Korea or *X* be another Vietnam?"), and figures of speech, including metaphors ("a knee-jerk liberal"), and similes ("The Southern Senator had a face like an old Virginia ham and a personality to match.").

You can't incite your readers, either to agree with you or to take action on behalf of the cause you favor, by simply bleeding all over the page. The process of writing and rewriting and revising again (see Donald Murray, "The Maker's Eye: Revising Your Own Manuscripts" [58–62]) will act to cool your red-hot emotion and will enable you to modulate in subsequent drafts what you might have written the first time just to get it out of your system: "Hell, no! We won't go!" As the essays in this section and elsewhere reveal, writers who appeal most effectively to their readers' emotions themselves exercise considerable control over the organization and examples they use to make their points.

They also keep particularly tight rein over their own emotions, as revealed in the tone and connotations of their language, crucial in an emotional appeal. Tone, the prevailing mood of the work, like a tone of voice conveys your attitude toward your subject and toward the evidence you present in support of your point.

Seamus Heaney's poem, "Horace and the Thunder" (517), written in the wake of the attacks on the World Trade Center and the Pentagon on September 11, 2001, presents cataclysm in matter-of-fact terms: "Anything can happen, the tallest things/be overturned. . . . " This is illustrated by the photograph (518) of a firefighter seeking a drink while the remains of the World Trade Center disintegrate amidst the ash and debris of that fateful attack that, as Heaney says, "Shook the earth." As with every other earthshaking event ("Ground gives," observes Heaney), we looked at our world one way before and another way—or many other ways—afterward. Did the world change? Or did we? And in what ways—significant, casual, or even trivial? How, we might have asked then and we can still ponder, will terrorist attacks and the infinite possibilities of future terrorism, specific or vague, affect the ways we live our lives; plan our futures; and look at our neighbors, our friends, and enemies—revealed as a consequence of that attack and American retaliation.

In "About Suffering" (542–47), Sheryl R. Kennedy describes a visit to a soldier, Luke, at Walter Reed Army Medical Center. Luke lost his leg in the Iraq war, and his world has changed, changed utterly. Kennedy's sympathetic but unsentimental examination of his condition, and of human suffering generally, leads to her implicit question, "How much of this suffering—if any—was warranted?" Her answer is implied in the soldier's bitterness, her own fear of visiting "traumatically brain injured patients," of seeing "the vacant eyes and 'persistent vegetative states,'" her grief at "thinking of Luke's once beautiful leg" cremated, "history repeating itself by another young man just doing his job."

To establish a climate that encourages readers to sympathize emotionally, you as a writer can present telling facts and allow the readers to interpret them, rather than continually nudging the audience with verbal reminders to see the subject your way.

If you are appealing to your readers' emotions through irony, the tone of your words, their music, is likely to be at variance with their overt message—and to intentionally undermine it. Thus the narrator of Swift's "A Modest Proposal" (524–30) can, with an impassive face, advocate that year-old children of the poor Irish peasants be sold for "a most delicious, nourishing, and wholesome food, whether stewed, roasted, baked, or broiled"; and, in an additional inhumane observation, "I make no doubt that it will equally serve in a fricassee or a ragout."

The connotations, overtones of the language, are equally significant in emotional appeals, as they subtly (or not so subtly) reinforce the overt, literal meanings of the words. Lincoln, arriving at Gettysburg in 1863 to deliver the speech that would rank among the most memorable in American history, deliberately uses biblical language ("Fourscore" instead of "eighty"), biblical phrasing, biblical cadences to reinforce the solemnity of the occasion—dedication of the graveyard at Gettysburg. This language also underscores the seriousness of the Civil War, then in progress, and its profound consequences. In contrast to the majesty of Lincoln's language, Swift's narrator depersonalizes human beings, always calling the children *it*, with an impersonal connotation, and never employing the humanizing terms of *he, she*, or *baby*. The *it* emphasizes the animalistic connotations of the narrator's references to a newborn as "a child just dropped from its dam," further dehumanizing both mother and child.

Language, tone, and message often combine to present an *ethical appeal*—a way of impressing your readers that you as the author (and perhaps as a character in your own essay) are a knowledgeable person of good moral character, good will, and good sense. Consequently, you are a person of integrity, and to be believed as a credible, reasonable advocate of the position you take in your essay.

Thus Peter Singer, in "The Singer Solution to World Poverty" (535–41), employs straightforward language, logic, and clear-cut examples to open his readers' eyes to ethical issues that many people who consider themselves ethical either ignore or disregard. In a matter-of-fact way, Singer, an ethicist who is considered controversial because of the logical extent (some would say extremes) his principles lead to, identifies a simple principle for supporting the world's poor: "Whatever money you're spending on luxuries, not necessities, should be given away."

The brief appeal of Sojourner Truth's charismatic oratory, "Ain't I a Woman?" (521), makes the feminist argument for gender (and racial) equality to the 1851 Ohio Women's Rights Convention; alas, this is still alive and valid over a century and a half after she delivered it. As with Singer's solution to world poverty, Truth's statements are brief and require the audience to do much of the work, filling in the evidence and the logic behind the refrain "Ain't I a woman?"

Although ethical appeals usually tap our most profound moral values, they can be made in humorous ways, often by satire, as implied even in the title of Sherman Alexie's "What Sacagawea Means to Me" (85–87). Alexie uses language common in academic writing (one type of "establishment") to criticize the establishment's treatment of minorities (Native Americans). When Open design studio published the satiric op-art column "Introducing **new** GoValue!™ service" (532) in May, 2006—with the slogan "Your money is important to us"—there were many problems with airline travel that were easy to satirize: issues of space, luggage delays, bad (or nonexistent) food. Since then, the difficulties of air travel have multiplied—making it easy for frustrated readers (and passengers) to add many more "forbidden" boxes to this cartoon.

Social satire—as we can see from these writings as well as from Swift's "A Modest Proposal"—always implies the need for reform. Self-satire, however, as Jason Verge presents his Montreal Canadien fanhood in "The Habs" (107–11) may just be poking fun at one's human fallibilities.

Because they usually make their point indirectly, fables, parables, and other stories with subtle moral points are often used to appeal to readers' emotions and ethical sense. The photographs of winsome (never repulsive, never ugly!) waifs often grace fundraising advertisements for famine relief, amplified by biographies of their pitiful lives; only our contributions can save them. One of the dangers in using such poster-child appeals is the possibility that you'll include too many emotional signals or ultraheavy emotional language and thereby write a paper that repels your readers by either excessive sentimentality or overkill.

Works by student writers in this book, such as Amanda Cagle's "On the Banks of the Bogue Chitto" (245–49) and Megan McGuire's "Wake Up

Call" (230–36), deal directly with the impact of very difficult issues (poverty, instability, divorce, disability, suicide) on their families, particularly as they affected the authors as children growing up—resilient, resourceful, creative. Their language and examples, precise but unsentimental, are more appealing to readers—and ultimately more moving—than any "alas, poor me" approach would be. All embed powerful ethical issues.

Indeed, appeals to emotion and ethics are often intertwined. Such appeals are everywhere—for example, in the connotations of descriptions and definitions. Furthermore, if your readers like and trust you, they're more likely to believe what you say and to be moved to agree with your point of view. The evidence in a scientific report, however strong in itself, is buttressed by the credibility of the researcher. The sense of realism, the truth of a narrative, is enhanced by the credibility of the narrator. We believe Lincoln and Sheryl Kennedy and we trust the spirit of satirist Swift, even if we believe he is exaggerating, if not downright inventing, the substance of his narrative. Hearts, common sense, sensibility, and sympathy compel agreement where minds hesitate. Don't hesitate to make ethical use of this understanding.

Strategies for Writing: Appealing to Emotion and Ethics

1. Do I want to appeal primarily to my readers' emotions (and which emotions) or to their ethical sense of how people ought to behave? (Remember that in either case the appeals are intertwined with reason—see Chapter 10, "Appealing to Reason: Deductive and Inductive Arguments.")
2. To what kinds of readers am I making these appeals? What ethical or other personal qualities should I as an author exhibit? How can I lead my readers to believe that I am a person of sound character and good judgment?
3. What evidence can I choose to reinforce my appeals and my authorial image? Examples from my own life? The experiences of others? References to literature or scientific research? What order of arrangement would be most convincing? From the least emotionally moving or involving to the most? Or vice versa?
4. How can I interpret my evidence to move my readers to accept it? Should I explain very elaborately, or should I let the examples speak for themselves? If you decide on the latter, try out your essay on someone unfamiliar with the examples to see if they are in fact self-evident.
5. Do I want my audience to react with sympathy? Pity? Anger? Fear? Horror? To accomplish this, should I use much emotional language? Should my appeal be overt, direct? Or would indirection, understatement, be more effective? Would irony—saying the opposite of what I really mean (as Swift does)—be more appropriate than a direct approach? Could I make my point more effectively with a fable, parable, comic tale, or invented persona than with a straightforward analysis and overt commentary?

SEAMUS HEANEY

Seamus Heaney, Ireland's best-known contemporary poet, was born in 1939 on a farm in County Derry, Northern Ireland. He considers the fact that his heritage includes "both the Ireland of the cattle-herding Gaelic past and the Ulster of the Industrial Revolution" to be significant in his work. For the past thirty years he has lived alternately in Dublin and the United States. Since 1981 he has taught at Harvard for portions of every academic year, currently as Ralph Waldo Emerson Poet in Residence. Like his predecessor and countryman, W.B. Yeats, Heaney's poetry deals in passionate yet clear language with love and loss, peace and war as interpreted through Irish history and lore. And, like Yeats, Heaney received the Nobel Prize in Literature (1985) for his poetry, the year he published *Station Island*. Other books include *The Haw Lantern* (1987), *Seeing Things* (1991), *The Spirit Level* (1996), and translations of Beowulf (1999) and *Antigone* (2004). Heaney's work has won a rare combination of critical esteem—as signaled by numerous awards and prestigious academic appointments (including five years as professor of poetry at Oxford)—and great popular acclaim, as attested by the large sales of his books and the hundreds of fans ("Heaneyboppers" included) who attend his readings. His most recent collection of poetry, *District and Circle* (2006), was awarded the T. S. Eliot Prize.

Horace and the Thunder

After Horace, Odes, 1, 34.

Anything can happen. You know how Jupiter
Will mostly wait for clouds to gather head
Before he hurls the lightning? Well, just now,
He galloped his thunder-cart and his horses

Across a clear blue sky. It shook the earth
And the clogged underearth, the River Styx,
The winding streams, the Atlantic shore itself.
Anything can happen, the tallest things

Be overturned, those in high places daunted,
Those overlooked regarded. Stropped-beak Fortune
Swoops, making the air gasp, tearing off the crest of one,
Setting it down bleeding on the next.

Ground gives. The heaven's weight
Lifts up off Atlas like a kettle lid,
Capstones shift, nothing resettles right.
Smoke-furl and boiling ashes darken day.

© Yoni Brook/Corbis

This photograph by Yoni Brook was captioned "Firefighter Michael Sauer drinks and washes his face at a fire hydrant hours after the collapse of the World Trade Center on September 11," 2001. What is the connection between the now-iconic collapsing tower walls and the fire hydrant in the foreground? Does the hydrant ring over the firefighter's head resemble a halo?

This photograph won first place in "September 11-News" category for the 59th Annual Picture of the Year Awards and is identified as an "Essay." What makes it an essay? *What stories does it tell? What meanings do the viewers supply? Could this photograph also be considered a* poem, *equivalent to Seamus Heaney's poetic statement in "Horace and the Thunder"?*

ABRAHAM LINCOLN

Abraham Lincoln (1809–1865) was a self-made, self-taught son of Kentucky pioneers. He served four terms in the Illinois state legislature before being elected to Congress in 1847. As sixteenth president of the United States (1861–1865), Lincoln's supreme efforts were devoted to trying to secure the passage of the Thirteenth Amendment to outlaw slavery and to preserve the still young United States of America from the forces expressed through and beyond the bloody Civil War that threatened to destroy its young men, its economy, and the very government itself.

The Gettysburg Address

Four score and seven years ago our fathers brought forth on this continent, a new nation, conceived in liberty, and dedicated to the proposition that all men are created equal. 1

Now we are engaged in a great civil war, testing whether that nation, or any nation so conceived and so dedicated, can long endure. We are met on a great battlefield of that war. We have come to dedicate a portion of that field, as a final resting place for those who here gave their lives that the nation might live. It is altogether fitting and proper that we should do this. 2

But, in a larger sense, we cannot dedicate—we cannot consecrate—we cannot hallow—this ground. The brave men, living and dead, who struggled here, have consecrated it, far above our poor power to add or detract. The world will little note, nor long remember what we say here, but it can never forget what they did here. It is for us the living, rather, to be dedicated here to the unfinished work which they who fought here have thus far so nobly advanced. It is rather for us to be here dedicated to the great task remaining before us—that from these honored dead we take increased devotion—that we here highly resolve that these dead shall not have died in vain—that this nation, under God, shall have a new birth of freedom—and that government of the people, by the people, for the people, shall not perish from the earth. 3

Content

1. What principles of the founding of the United States does Lincoln emphasize in the first sentence? Why are these so important to the occasion of his address? To the theme of this address?
2. What does Lincoln imply and assert is the relation of life and death? Birth and rebirth?

Strategies/Structures/Language

3. Why would Lincoln, knowing that his audience expected longer orations, deliberately have decided to make his speech so short? Lincoln's speech commemorated a solemn occasion: the dedication of a major battlefield of the ongoing Civil War. Wouldn't such a short speech have undermined the significance of the event?
4. Identify the language and metaphors of birth that Lincoln uses throughout this address. For what purpose? With what effect?
5. Why did Lincoln use biblical language and phrasing conspicuously at the beginning and end of the address, such as "four score and seven years ago" instead of the more common "eighty-seven"?
6. Lincoln uses many *antitheses*—oppositions, contrasts. Identify some and show how they reinforce the meaning.

7. Another important rhetorical device is the *tricolon,* "the division of an idea into three harmonious parts, usually of increasing power,"—for example, "government of the people, by the people, for the people. . . ." Find others and show why they are so memorable.

For Writing

8. Write a short, dignified speech for a solemn occasion, real or imaginary. Let the majesty of your language and the conspicuous rhetorical patterns of your sentences and paragraphs (through such devices as antithesis and parallelism) reinforce your point.

9. Rewrite the "Gettysburg Address" as it might have been spoken by a more recent president or other politician, using language, paragraphing, and sentence structures characteristic of the speaker and the times. One such speech, a parody, is William Safire's "Carter's Gettysburg Address," which begins: "Exactly two hundred and one years, five months and one day ago, our forefathers—and our foremothers, too, as my wife, the First Lady, reminds me—our highly competent Founding Persons brought forth on this land mass a new nation, or entity, dreamed up in liberty and dedicated to the comprehensive program of insuring that all of us are created with the same basic human rights."

SOJOURNER TRUTH

Sojourner Truth (1797–1883) was born Isabella Baumfree to a family of slaves on an estate in Ulster County, New York. She was sold several times, enduring the hardships of slavery with the help of her religious faith. She fled her owners in 1827, was taken in by the Van Wagener family, whose name she assumed for a time, and became an inspirational evangelical preacher. In 1843, a spiritual calling led her to change her name to Sojourner Truth and set out as a traveling preacher, living on the kindness of strangers, and eventually joining an abolitionist cooperative community in Massachusetts. After the breakup of the community, she dictated her memoirs to one of its members, Olive Gilbert, which William Lloyd Garrison published as *The Narrative of Sojourner Truth* (1850). Her book provided her with an income and gave her more opportunities to speak out against slavery and in support of women's rights. During the Civil War, she worked with freed slaves at a government refugee camp in Virginia and was employed by the National Freedman's Relief Association in Washington, DC. She met President Abraham Lincoln in 1864. Truth delivered her most famous speech at the 1851 Ohio Women's Rights Convention. While some historians have suggested that the speech was embellished afterward and prior to publication—perhaps by adding repetitions of the phrase "ain't I a woman?"—it nevertheless stands as a model of persuasive and inspirational oratory.

Ain't I a Woman?

Well, children, where there is so much racket there must be something out of kilter. I think that 'twixt the negroes of the South and the women at the North, all talking about rights, the white men will be in a fix pretty soon. But what's all this here talking about? 1

That man over there says women need to be helped into carriages, and lifted over ditches, and to have the best place everywhere. Nobody ever helps me into carriages, or over mud-puddles, or gives me any best place! And ain't I a woman? Look at me! Look at my arm! I have ploughed and planted, and gathered into barns, and no man could head me! And ain't I a woman? I could work as much and eat as much as a man—when I could get it—and bear the lash as well! And ain't I a woman? I have borne thirteen children, and seen them most all sold off to slavery, and when I cried out with my mother's grief, none but Jesus heard me! And ain't I a woman? 2

Then they talk about this thing in the head; what's this they call it? [Intellect, someone whispers.] That's it, honey. What's that got to do with women's rights or negro's rights? If my cup won't hold but a pint, and yours holds a quart, wouldn't you be mean not to let me have my little half-measure full? 3

Then that little man in black there, he says women can't have as much rights as men, 'cause Christ wasn't a woman! Where did your Christ come from? Where did your Christ come from? From God and a woman! Man had nothing to do with Him. 4

If the first woman God ever made was strong enough to turn the world upside down all alone, these women together ought to be able to turn it back, and get it right side up again! And now they is asking to do it, the men better let them. 5

Obliged to you for hearing me, and now old Sojourner ain't got nothing more to say. 6

Content

1. Identify the arguments Truth makes in support of gender equality. Does she suggest that female equality will diminish or enhance the position of white men? Why does she comment that "the white men will be in a fix pretty soon" (¶ 1)?
2. What evidence does Truth offer her audience to back up her arguments? Why is she a credible witness?
3. Some historians have presented evidence that Truth's audience at the 1851 Ohio Women's Rights Convention received her warmly and favorably rather than, as this version of the speech implies, in the face of some hostility. Why might she or other women's rights activists have changed the speech prior to publication? Does this ambiguity about the authenticity of a historical event change your interpretation of her speech? If so, how?

Strategies/Structures/Language

4. How does the phrase "ain't I a woman?" underscore Truth's argument? Why do repetitions of this key phrase move the reader?
5. Truth was a dedicated political activist (see 520). Why does she claim to be unfamiliar with the word "intellect" (¶ 3)?
6. Why does Truth begin by referring to her audience as "children" (¶ 1)? How does her question "But what's all this here talking about" build on this foundation (¶ 1)?
7. What does the metaphor "my cup" refer to (¶ 3)? How does this metaphor introduce Sojourner's argument that Christ was born of "God and a woman" (¶ 4)?

For Writing

8. ***Journal Writing.*** Explore the memory of an inspirational experience, whether spiritual (e.g., during prayer or a sermon), intellectual (e.g., in the classroom), or aesthetic (e.g., through experiencing or creating a work of art). How important was language to this experience? Did the experience transcend language? How might you recreate such an experience or communicate it to others?
9. ***Dialogues.*** Compare Truth's relationship to her own body with Zara Rix's in "Corporality" (606–12). Consider Rix's experience of her body as "a strange, alien thing" (¶ 33) and as the repository of "others' stories" (¶ 1). How does Truth's voice marginalize and yet draw attention to her body? What does her use of her body as evidence suggest about her relationship to her personal history and that of her fellow African Americans?
10. ***Second Look.*** Dorothea Lange's photograph of Florence Owens Thompson and her children (536) has become known as "Migrant Mother." How might you read this photograph as a portrait of feminine weakness and/or strength? How does it suggest, as Sojourner Truth argues, that "women together ought to be able to turn [the world] . . . right side up again" (¶ 5)? How does the arrangement of the three children influence your interpretation of the photograph? Does learning that Florence Owens Thompson was Native American and a labor activist influence your interpretation of her portrait?

JONATHAN SWIFT

Jonathan Swift, author of *Gulliver's Travels* (1726) and other satiric essays, poems, and tracts, was well acquainted with irony. Born in Dublin in 1667, the son of impoverished English Anglicans, he obtained a degree from Trinity College, Dublin, in 1685 only by "special grace." When James II arrived in Ireland in 1688, he initiated pro-Catholic, anti-Protestant policies

© Tischler Fotografen/Peter Arnold, Inc.

A well-dressed Chinese schoolgirl in uniform stands and waits amidst rubble in an urban slum neighborhood in Shengen, beyond which gleam the modern high-rise buildings that signal renewal and hope of a way up and out. This photograph, like the "We shall overcome" photograph of Dr. Martin Luther King, Jr., Joan Baez, and others escorting African-American schoolchildren to a newly integrated school in 1966 (457), makes direct and indirect arguments about children, human rights, and society. What are some of these arguments? What evidence does each photograph provide for your interpretation? What do you have to supply from your knowledge of history or culture?

that remained in force until the ascendancy of William III. Swift, along with many Anglo-Irish, was forced to flee to England, was eventually ordained as an Anglican priest, and rose prominently in London literary and political circles until 1713. Although he had hoped for a church appointment in England, his desertion of the Whig Party for the Tories was ironically rewarded with an appointment as dean of St. Patrick's (Anglican) Cathedral in Dublin, which he regarded as virtual exile. Nevertheless, despite his religious differences with the Irish people, Swift became a beloved leader in the Irish resistance to English oppression, motivated less by partisan emotions than by his own "savage indignation" against injustice. He died in 1745.

Swift wrote "A Modest Proposal" in the summer of 1729, after three years of drought and crop failure had forced over 35,000 peasants to leave their homes and wander the countryside looking for work, food, and shelter for their starving families, ignored by the insensitive absentee landowners. The "Proposal" carries the English landowners' treatment of the Irish to its logical—but repugnant—extreme: if they are going to devour any hope the Irish have of living decently, why don't they literally eat the Irish children? The persona Swift creates is logical, consistent, seemingly rational—and utterly inhumane, an advocate of infanticide and cannibalism. Yet nowhere in the "Proposal" does the satirist condemn the speaker; he relies on the readers' sense of morality for that. This tactic can be dangerous, for a reader who misses the irony may take the "Proposal" at face value. But Swift's intended readers, English (landlords included) as well as Irish who could act to alleviate the people's suffering, understood very well what he meant. The victims themselves, largely illiterate, would probably have been unaware of this forceful plea on their behalf.

A Modest Proposal

1 It is a melancholy object to those who walk through this great town or travel in the country, when they see the streets, the roads, and cabin doors, crowded with beggars of the female sex, followed by three, four, or six children, all in rags and importuning every passenger for an alms. These mothers, instead of being able to work for their honest livelihood, are forced to employ all their time in strolling to beg sustenance for their helpless infants: who as they grow up either turn thieves for want of work, or leave their dear native country to fight for the pretender in Spain, or sell themselves to the Barbadoes.

2 I think it is agreed by all parties that this prodigious number of children in the arms, or on the backs, or at the heels of their mothers, and frequently of their fathers, is in the present deplorable state of the kingdom a very great additional grievance; and, therefore, whoever could find out a fair, cheap, and easy method of making these children sound, useful members of the commonwealth, would deserve so well of the public as to have his statue set up for a preserver of the nation.

3 But my intention is very far from being confined to provide only for the children of professed beggars; it is of a much greater extent, and shall take in the whole number of infants at a certain age who are born of parents in effect as little able to support them as those who demand our charity in the streets.

4 As to my own part, having turned my thoughts for many years upon this important subject, and maturely weighed the several schemes of our projectors, I have always found them grossly mistaken in their computation. It is true, a child just dropped from its dam may be supported by her milk for a solar year, with little other nourishment; at most not above the value of two shillings, which the mother may certainly get, or the value in scraps, by her lawful occupation of begging; and it is exactly at one year old that I propose to provide for them in such

a manner as instead of being a charge upon their parents or the parish, or wanting food and raiment for the rest of their lives, they shall on the contrary contribute to the feeding, and partly to the clothing, of many thousands.

There is likewise another great advantage in my scheme, that it will 5
prevent those voluntary abortions, and that horrid practice of women murdering their bastard children, alas! too frequent among us! sacrificing the poor innocent babes I doubt more to avoid the expense than the shame, which would move tears and pity in the most savage and inhuman breast.

The number of souls in this kingdom being usually reckoned one 6
million and half, of these I calculate there may be about two hundred thousand couple whose wives are breeders; from which number I subtract thirty thousand couple who are able to maintain their own children (although I apprehend there cannot be so many, under the present distress of the kingdom); but this being granted, there will remain an hundred and seventy thousand breeders. I again subtract fifty thousand for those women who miscarry, or whose children die by accident or disease within the year. There only remain an hundred and twenty thousand children of poor parents annually born. The question therefore is, how this number shall be reared and provided for? which, as I have already said, under the present situation of affairs, is utterly impossible by all the methods hitherto proposed. For we can neither employ them in handicraft or agriculture; we neither build houses (I mean in the country) nor cultivate land; they can very seldom pick up a livelihood by stealing, till they arrive at six years old, except where they are of towardly parts; although I confess they learn the rudiments much earlier; during which time they can, however, be properly looked upon only as probationers; as I have been informed by a principal gentleman in the country of Cavan, who protested to me that he never knew above one or two instances under the age of six, even in a part of the kingdom so renowned for the quickest proficiency in that art.

I am assured by our merchants, that a boy or a girl before twelve 7
years old is no saleable commodity; and even when they come to this age they will not yield above three pounds, or three pounds and a half a crown at most on the Exchange; which cannot turn to account either to the parents or kingdom, the charge of nutriment and rags having been at least four times that value.

I shall now therefore humbly propose my own thoughts, which 8
I hope will not be liable to the least objection.

I have been assured by a very knowing American of my acquaintance 9
in London, that a young healthy child well nursed is at a year old the most delicious, nourishing, and wholesome food, whether stewed, roasted, baked, or broiled; and I make no doubt that it will equally serve in a fricassee or a ragout.

10 I do therefore humbly offer it to public consideration that of the hundred and twenty thousand children already computed, twenty thousand may be reserved for breed, whereof only one fourth part to be males; which is more than we allow to sheep, black cattle, or swine; and my reason is, that these children are seldom the fruits of marriage, a circumstance not much regarded by our savages; therefore, one male will be sufficient to serve four females. That the remaining hundred thousand may, at a year old, be offered in sale to the persons of quality and fortune through the kingdom; always advising the mother to let them suck plentifully in the last month, so as to render them plump and fat for a good table. A child will make two dishes at an entertainment for friends; and when the family dines alone, the fore or hind quarter will make a reasonable dish, and seasoned with a little pepper or salt will be very good boiled on the fourth day, especially in winter.

11 I have reckoned upon a medium that a child just born will weigh twelve pounds, and in a solar year, if tolerably nursed, will increase to twenty-eight pounds.

12 I grant this food will be somewhat dear, and therefore very proper for landlords, who, as they have already devoured most of the parents, seem to have the best title to the children.

13 Infant's flesh will be in season throughout the year, but more plentiful in March, and a little before and after: for we are told by a grave author, an eminent French physician, that fish being a prolific diet, there are more children born in Roman Catholic countries about nine months after Lent than at any other season; therefore, reckoning a year after Lent, the markets will be more glutted than usual, because the number of popish infants is at least three to one in this kingdom: and therefore it will have one other collateral advantage, by lessening the number of papists among us.

14 I have already computed the charge of nursing a beggar's child (in which list I reckon all cottagers, laborers, and four-fifths of the farmers) to be about two shillings per annum, rags included; and I believe no gentleman would repine to give ten shillings for the carcass of a good fat child, which, as I have said, will make four dishes of excellent nutritive meat, when he has only some particular friend or his own family to dine with him. Thus the squire will learn to be a good landlord, and grow popular among the tenants; the mother will have eight shillings net profit, and be fit for work till she produces another child.

15 Those who are more thrifty (as I must confess the times require) may flay the carcass; the skin of which artificially dressed will make admirable gloves for ladies, and summer boots for fine gentlemen.

16 As to our city of Dublin, shambles may be appointed for this purpose in the most convenient parts of it, and butchers we may be assured will

not be wanting: although I rather recommend buying the children alive, and dressing them hot from the knife as we do roasting pigs.

A very worthy person, a true lover of his country, and whose virtues 17
I highly esteem, was lately pleased in discoursing on this matter to offer a refinement upon my scheme. He said that many gentlemen of this kingdom, having of late destroyed their deer, he conceived that the want of venison might be well supplied by the bodies of young lads and maidens, not exceeding fourteen years of age nor under twelve; so great a number of both sexes in every country being now ready to starve for want of work and service; and these to be disposed of by their parents, if alive, or otherwise by their nearest relations. But with due deference to so excellent a friend and so deserving a patriot, I cannot be altogether in his sentiments; for as to the males, my American acquaintance assured me from frequent experience that their flesh was generally tough and lean, like that of our schoolboys by continual exercise, and their taste disagreeable; and to fatten them would not answer the charge. Then as to the females, it would, I think, with humble submission be a loss to the public, because they soon would become breeders themselves: and besides, it is not improbable that some scrupulous people might be apt to censure such a practice (although indeed very unjustly), as a little bordering upon cruelty; which, I confess, has always been with me the strongest objection against any project, how well soever intended.

But in order to justify my friend, he confessed that this expedient 18
was put into his head by the famous Psalmanazar, a native of the island Formosa, who came from thence to London about twenty years ago: and in conversation told my friend, that in his country when any young person happened to be put to death, the executioner sold the carcass to persons of quality as a prime dainty; and that in his time the body of a plump girl of fifteen, who was crucified for an attempt to poison the emperor, was sold to his imperial majesty's prime minister of state, and other great mandarins of the court, in joints from the gibbet, at four hundred crowns. Neither indeed can I deny, that if the same use were made of several plump young girls in this town, who without one single groat to their fortunes cannot stir abroad without a chair, and appear at the playhouse and assemblies in foreign fineries which they never will pay for, the kingdom would not be the worse.

Some persons of a desponding spirit are in great concern about that 19
vast number of poor people, who are aged, diseased, or maimed, and I have been desired to employ my thoughts what course may be taken to ease the nation of so grievous an encumbrance. But I am not in the least pain upon that matter, because it is very well known that they are every day dying and rotting by cold and famine, and filth and vermin, as fast as can be reasonably expected. And as to the young laborers, they are now in

as hopeful a condition: they cannot get work, and consequently pine away for want of nourishment, to a degree that if at any time they are accidentally hired to common labor, they have not strength to perform it; and thus the country and themselves are happily delivered from the evils to come.

20 I have too long digressed, and therefore shall return to my subject. I think the advantages by the proposal which I have made are obvious and many, as well as of the highest importance.

21 For first, as I have already observed, it would greatly lessen the number of papists, with whom we are yearly overrun, being the principal breeders of the nation as well as our most dangerous enemies; and who stay at home on purpose to deliver the kingdom to the Pretender, hoping to take their advantage by the absence of so many good Protestants, who have chosen rather to leave their country than stay at home and pay tithes against their conscience to an Episcopal curate.

22 Secondly, The poor tenants will have something valuable of their own, which by law may be made liable to distress and help to pay their landlord's rent, their corn and cattle being already seized, and money a thing unknown.

23 Thirdly, Whereas the maintenance of a hundred thousand children from two years old and upward, cannot be computed at less than ten shillings a piece per annum, the nation's stock will be thereby increased fifty thousand pounds per annum, beside the profit of a new dish introduced to the tables of all gentlemen of fortune in the kingdom who have any refinement in taste. And the money will circulate among ourselves, the goods being entirely of our own growth and manufacture.

24 Fourthly, The constant breeders beside the gain of eight shillings sterling per annum by the sale of their children, will be rid of the charge of maintaining them after the first year.

25 Fifthly, This food would likewise bring great custom to taverns, where the vintners will certainly be so prudent as to procure the best receipts for dressing it to perfection, and consequently have their houses frequented by all the fine gentlemen, who justly value themselves upon their knowledge in good eating; and a skillful cook who understands how to oblige his guests, will contrive to make it as expensive as they please.

26 Sixthly, This would be a great inducement to marriage, which all wise nations have either encouraged by rewards or enforced by laws and penalties. It would increase the care and tenderness of mothers toward their children, when they were sure of a settlement for life to the poor babes, provided in some sort by the public, to their annual profit instead of expense. We should see an honest emulation among the married women, which of them would bring the fattest child to the market. Men would become as fond of their wives during the time of their pregnancy as they are now of their mares in foal, their cows in calf, their sows when they are ready to farrow; nor offer to beat or kick them (as is too frequent a practice) for fear of a miscarriage.

Many other advantages might be enumerated. For instance, the addition of some thousand carcasses in our exportation of barreled beef, the propagation of swine's flesh, and improvement in the art of making good bacon, so much wanted among us by the great destruction of pigs, too frequent at our table; which are no way comparable in taste or magnificence to a well-grown, fat, yearling child, which roasted whole will make a considerable figure at a lord mayor's feast or any other public entertainment. But this and many others I omit, being studious of brevity. 27

Supposing that one thousand families in this city would be constant customers for infants' flesh, besides others who might have it at merry-meetings, particularly at weddings and christenings, I compute that Dublin would take off annually about twenty thousand carcasses; and the rest of the kingdom (where probably they will be sold somewhat cheaper) the remaining eighty thousand. 28

I can think of no one objection that will possibly be raised against this proposal, unless it should be urged that the number of people will be thereby much lessened in the kingdom. This I freely own, and it was indeed one principal design in offering it to the world. I desire the reader will observe, that I calculate my remedy for this one individual kingdom of Ireland and for no other that ever was, is, or I think ever can be upon earth. Therefore let no man talk to me of other expedients; of taxing our absentees at five shillings a pound: of using neither clothes nor household furniture except what is of our own growth and manufacture: of utterly rejecting the materials and instruments that promote foreign luxury: of curing the expensiveness of pride, vanity, idleness, and gaming in our women: of introducing a vein of parsimony, prudence, and temperance: of learning to love our country, in the want of which we differ even from Laplanders and the inhabitants of Topinamboo: of quitting our animosities and factions, nor acting any longer like the Jews, who were murdering one another at the very moment their city was taken: of being a little cautious not to sell our country and conscience for nothing: of teaching landlords to have at least one degree of mercy toward their tenants; lastly, of putting a spirit of honesty, industry, and skill into our shopkeepers; who, if a resolution could now be taken to buy only our native goods, would immediately unite to cheat and exact upon us in the price, the measure, and the goodness, nor could ever yet be brought to make one fair proposal of just dealing, though often and earnestly invited to it. 29

Therefore I repeat, let no man talk to me of these and the like expedients, till he has at least some glimpse of hope that there will be ever some hearty and sincere attempts to put them in practice. 30

But as to myself, having been wearied out for many years with offering vain, idle, visionary thoughts, and at length utterly despairing of success, I fortunately fell upon this proposal; which, as it is wholly new, so it 31 has something solid and real, of no expense and little trouble, full in our own power, and whereby we can incur no danger in disobliging England. For this kind of commodity will not bear exportation, the flesh being of too tender a consistence to admit a long continuance in salt, although perhaps I could name a country which would be glad to eat up our whole nation without it.

32 After all, I am not so violently bent upon my own opinion as to reject any offer proposed by wise men, which shall be found equally innocent, cheap, easy, and effectual. But before something of that kind shall be advanced in contradiction to my scheme, and offering a better, I desire the author or authors will be pleased maturely to consider two points. First, as things now stand, how they will be able to find food and raiment for a hundred thousand useless mouths and backs. And secondly, there being a round million of creatures in human figure throughout this kingdom, whose subsistence put into a common stock would leave them in debt two millions of pounds sterling, adding those who are beggars by profession to the bulk of farmers, cottagers, and laborers, with the wives and children who are beggars in effect; I desire those politicians who dislike my overture, and may perhaps be so bold as to attempt an answer, that they will first ask the parents of these mortals, whether they would not at this day think it a great happiness to have been sold for food at a year old in the manner I prescribe, and thereby have avoided such a perpetual scene of misfortunes as they have since gone through by the oppression of landlords, the impossibility of paying rent without money or trade, the want of common sustenance, with neither house nor clothes to cover them from the inclemencies of the weather, and the most inevitable prospect of entailing the like or greater miseries upon their breed for ever.

33 I profess, in the sincerity of my heart, that I have not the least personal interest in endeavoring to promote this necessary work, having no other motive than the public good of my country, by advancing our trade, providing for infants, relieving the poor, and giving some pleasure to the rich. I have no children by which I can propose to get a single penny; the youngest being nine years old, and my wife past child-bearing.

Content

1. What is the overt thesis of Swift's essay? What is its implied (and real) thesis? In what ways do these theses differ?
2. What are the primary aims and values of the narrator of the essay? Identify the economic advantages of his proposal that he offers in paragraphs 9–16. How do the narrator's alleged aims and values differ from the aims and values of Swift as the essay's author?

3. What do the advantages that the narrator offers for his proposal (¶s 21–26) reveal about the social and economic conditions of Ireland when Swift was writing?

4. Why is it a "very knowing *American*" (emphasis added) who has assured the narrator of the suitability of year-old infants for food (¶ 9)?

5. Swift as the author of the essay expects his readers to respond to the narrator's cold economic arguments on a humane, moral level. What might such an appropriate response be?

Strategies/Structures/Language

6. What persona (a created character) does the speaker of Swift's essay have? How are readers to know that this character is not Swift himself?

7. Why does the narrator use so many mathematical computations throughout? How do they reinforce his economic argument? How do they enhance the image of his cold-bloodedness?

8. Why did Swift choose to present his argument indirectly rather than overtly? What advantages does this indirect, consistently ironic technique provide? What disadvantages does it have (for instance, do you think Swift's readers are likely to believe he really advocated eating babies)?

9. What is the prevailing tone of the essay? How does it undermine what the narrator says? How does the tone reinforce Swift's implied meaning?

10. Why does Swift say "a child just dropped from its dam" (¶ 4) instead of "just born from his mother"? What other language reinforces the animalistic associations (see, for instance, "breeders" in ¶ 17)?

For Writing

11. ***Journal Writing.*** Why do satire and parody often score more political points than straightforward reportage and editorial writing? Explore a memorable television show or Internet site that uses satire and parody to make a political statement. When does the humor work and when does it miss the mark? Does the humor ever cut too close to the bone? What's the purpose of political satire in our culture?

12. ***Dialogues.*** Either individually or as part of a team, write a Modest Proposal of your own. Pick some problem that you think needs to be solved, and propose, for a critical audience, a radical solution—a dramatic way to preserve endangered species, use genetic engineering, or eliminate identity theft or addiction, for example. You may draw on Diamond's "The World as a Polder" (472–83); McKibben's "Designer Genes" (572–82); Fallows's "Tinfoil Underwear" (151–57); or DiFranza's "Hooked from the First Cigarette" (124–33).

13. Write an essay in which a created character, a narrative persona, speaks ironically (as Swift's narrator does) about your subject. The character's values should be at variance with the values you and your audience share. For instance, if you want to propose stiff penalties for drunk driving, your narrator could be a firm advocate of drinking, and of driving without restraint, and could be shown driving unsafely while under the influence of alcohol, indifferent to the dangers.

ETHICAL ARGUMENTS: VISUAL VERSIONS

OPEN

Open is an edgy design studio in New York City. The name suggests "Come on in, we're OPEN."

Introducing new GoValue!™ service

1 It was reported recently that Airbus was considering standing-room-only "seats" for its planes. Passengers would be strapped to padded backboards, allowing airlines to squeeze in more people. Sounds like a great idea. But why stop there?

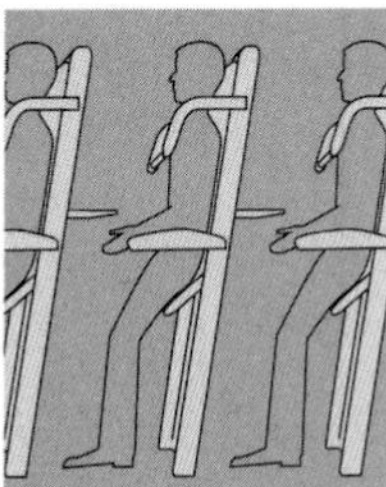

StandingRoom™
Everybody knows airline seats are uncomfortable. Now we're doing something about it!

BeHassleFree™
Do flight attendants bug you during a flight? Well, we got rid of them. Now you can have some peace and quiet!

FlexTravelTime™
Go with the flow! Your flight might get there up to 48 hours after its scheduled arrival time. Relax! What's the rush?

TravelExtraLite™
We've eliminated all cargo compartments and overhead storage bins. No more lugging all those heavy bags!

HealthYesNow™
Everybody knows snacks and soft drinks are bad for you. So we don't serve them! Or any other food.

PrivacyPlusXT™
Since we've removed the lavatories from our planes, you can use the restroom in the comfort of your own home.

EcoFastUltra™
Our new windowless planes are more aero-dynamic, increasing fuel efficiency by .001%. Happy Earth Day!

Your money is important to us. ValueFunAir

Courtesy OPEN

GARRY TRUDEAU

Garry Trudeau (born in New York City in 1948) launched his comic strip, *Doonesbury*, in 1970 just as he graduated from Yale. The strip was an instant hit; for forty years the characters of Zonker, Boopsie, Lacey, Duke, and Joanie Caucus have remained American icons, participating in consistent satire of contemporary events, politics, personalities, and lifestyles—whether privileged or counterculture. Indeed, many of the 1,400 newspapers nationally and internationally in which the strip appears print it on their editorial pages rather than with the rest of the comics. In 1975 Trudeau won a Pulitzer Prize for editorial cartooning; he was a Pulitzer Prize finalist in 1989, 2004, and 2005. His work has been collected in over 60 editions and has appeared in film and on Broadway. "Satire is an ungentlemanly art," says Trudeau. "It's lacking in balance. It's unfair"—and thus keeps the complacent on razor's edge. No one is immune, even the greatest fans—such as college students satirized in the following strip.

Doonesbury

DOONESBURY © 2008 G.B. Trudeau. Reprinted with permission of UNIVERSAL PRESS SYNDICATE. All rights reserved.

Content

1. The strategy of Open's satire, like that of many satires, is to take an idea that was initially presented as a straightforward proposal and then derive a number of ridiculous analogies to reveal the weaknesses and flaws of the original. So, what's wrong with Airbus's idea of having "standing-room-only" seats on its planes, in which passengers would be strapped to padded backboards, allowing up to 200 more passengers per planeload?

2. The standing-room information, originally published in *The New York Times*, April 25, 2006, was incorrect; the satire was published in the *Times* on May 1, 2006. A retraction published May 3, 2006, in *Plane News* and elsewhere says that although Airbus had "researched that idea in 2003, it has since abandoned" the plan; moreover, because the Airbus A380 superjumbo jet could "accommodate 853 passengers in regular seats, standing-room positions would not be needed." Does knowledge of the truth diminish the point of the satire?

3. If your college culture decreed that partying started on Thursday night, rather than Wednesday as depicted in the Doonesbury strip, would that fact change the point of the strip? Your reaction to it?

Strategies/Structures/Language

4. The purpose of satire is often to right a wrong (see Swift's "A Modest Proposal" 524–30) or to reform ill-conceived plans. Since standing-room seats never took off, what's the point of paying attention to this satire now?
5. Satire often works through exaggeration of actual facts. What's exaggerated in the "**new** GoValue!™ Service"? In the *Doonesbury* strip? What's not?
6. Show how both satires, through clever graphics combined with ironic language, cause readers—including those in the target populations—to laugh. At whom or what are readers laughing?

For Writing

7. In the few years since the "**new** GoValue!™ Service" was published, airlines have continued to cut costs and to expect more money and/or more sacrifices from passengers. Have any of the proposals in this op-art editorial come to pass? Does the existence of these—or their equivalents—lend credibility to the satire? With a partner, (if you wish), preferably a frequent flyer, write your own "Modest Proposal" concerning current airline travel, or a Passengers' Bill of Rights, straightforward or satiric.
8. Present the ideas you generated in question 7 in the form of icons, avatars, or cartoons.

PETER SINGER

Designated in 2005 by *Time* magazine as one of the "world's most influential people," philosopher Peter Singer is known for challenging conventional notions of ethical correctness. Born in Melbourne, Australia, in 1946 to a family decimated by the Nazi holocaust, Singer was educated at the University of Melbourne (BA, 1967; MA, 1969) and Oxford University (B Phil, 1971). After teaching at Oxford and New York University, he served as Chair of the Philosophy Department at Monash University in Australia and led the Centre for Human Bioethics there (1983–1998). Currently, he is a professor of Bioethics at Princeton University. Singer first gained attention as a protector of animal rights with *Animal Liberation* (1975), in which he criticized "speciesism"—the valuing of human rights above those of other species. He continued to explore the ethics of human–animal relations with *In Defense of Animals* (1985), *Animal Factories* (1990), and *The Great Ape Project* (1994). In *Making Babies* (1985), *Should the Baby Live?* (1985), and *Rethinking Life and Death* (1995), he addressed problems of science, technology, conception, and human life. Singer's views on end-of-life issues are consistent with his utilitarian approach to wealth advocated in "The Singer Solution to World Poverty"—that what is the greatest good for the greatest number should prevail. Their application, to animals, infants, and the elderly has aroused considerable controversy. More recent books include *One World: The Ethics of Globalization* (2002), *The President of Good and Evil: The Ethics of George W. Bush* (2004), *How Ethical is Australia*? (2005), and *The Way We Eat: Why Our Food Choices Matter* (2006).

"The Singer Solution to World Poverty" is a wake-up call for ethical responsibility—a reminder that serious questions of right and wrong behavior lie just beyond the horizon of middle-class awareness. Singer starkly presents the death and degradation that come with child poverty, creates the "Bugatti senario" to test the reader's ethical commitments (to saving an expensive car or a child's life), and even provides an 800 number for immediate action.

The Singer Solution to World Poverty

In the Brazilian film *Central Station*, Dora is a retired schoolteacher who makes ends meet by sitting at the station writing letters for illiterate people. Suddenly she has an opportunity to pocket a thousand dollars. All she has to do is persuade a homeless nine-year-old-boy to follow her to an address she has been given. (She is told he will be adopted by wealthy foreigners.) She delivers the boy, gets the money, spends some of it on a television set, and settles down to enjoy her new acquisition. Her neighbor spoils the fun, however, by telling her that the boy was too old to be adopted—he will be killed and his organs sold for transplantation. Perhaps Dora knew this all along, but after her neighbor's plain speaking, she spends a troubled night. In the morning Dora resolves to take the boy back. 1

Suppose Dora had told her neighbor that it is a tough world, other people have nice new TVs too, and if selling the kid is the only way she can get one, well, he was only a street kid. She would then have become, in the eyes of the audience, a monster. She redeems herself only by being prepared to bear considerable risks to save the boy. 2

At the end of the movie, in cinemas in the affluent nations of the world, people who would have been quick to condemn Dora if she had not rescued the boy go home to places far more comfortable than her apartment. In fact, the average family in the United States spends almost one third of its income on things that are no more necessary to them than Dora's new TV was to her. Going out to nice restaurants, buying new clothes because the old ones are no longer stylish, vacationing at beach resorts—so much of our income is spent on things not essential to the preservation of our lives and health. Donated to one of a number of charitable agencies, that money could mean the difference between life and death for children in need. 3

All of which raises a question: in the end, what is the ethical distinction between a Brazilian who sells a homeless child to organ peddlers and an American who already has a TV and upgrades to a better one, knowing that the money could be donated to an organization that would use it to save the lives of kids in need? 4

Library of Congress Prints and Photographs Division Washington DC, LC-USF34-T01-009058-C

This photo, titled "Migrant Mother," is Dorothea Lange's best-known picture. What stories does it tell? How do these stories relate to Sojourner Truth's "Ain't I a Woman?" (521), Jonathan Swift's "Modest Proposal" (524–30), and Peter Singer's "Solution to World Poverty"? When poverty and maternity are the common denominator, does it matter that the woman, in real life Florence Owens Thompson, an Oklahoma Cherokee, is neither African American nor Irish? Does it matter that the photograph enabled Lange to attain professional reputation and reward, while the subject remained impoverished and unknown?

5 Of course, there are several differences between the two situations that could support different moral judgments about them. For one thing, to be able to consign a child to death when he is standing right in front of you takes a chilling kind of heartlessness; it is much easier to ignore an appeal for money to help children you will never meet. Yet for a utilitarian philosopher like myself—that is, one who judges whether acts are right or wrong by their consequences—if the upshot of the American's failure to donate the money is that one more kid dies on the streets of a Brazilian city, then it is in some sense just as bad as selling the kid to the organ peddlers. But one doesn't need to embrace my utilitarian ethic to

see that at the very least, there is a troubling incongruity in being so quick to condemn Dora for taking the child to the organ peddlers while at the same time not regarding the American consumer's behavior as raising a serious moral issue.

In his 1996 book, *Living High and Letting Die*, the New York University philosopher Peter Unger presented an ingenious series of imaginary examples designed to probe our intuitions about whether it is wrong to live well without giving substantial amounts of money to help people who are hungry, malnourished, or dying from easily treatable illnesses like diarrhea. Here's my paraphrase of one of these examples: 6

Bob is close to retirement. He has invested most of his savings in a very rare and valuable old car, a Bugatti, which he has not been able to insure. The Bugatti is his pride and joy. In addition to the pleasure he gets from driving and caring for his car, Bob knows that its rising market value means that he will always be able to sell it and live comfortably after retirement. One day when Bob is out for a drive, he parks the Bugatti near the end of a railway siding and goes for a walk up the track. As he does so, he sees that a runaway train, with no one aboard, is running down the railway track. Looking farther down the track, he sees the small figure of a child very likely to be killed by the runaway train. He can't stop the train and the child is too far away to warn of the danger, but he can throw a switch that will divert the train down the siding where his Bugatti is parked. Then nobody will be killed—but the train will destroy his Bugatti. Thinking of his joy in owning the car and the financial security it represents, Bob decides not to throw the switch. The child is killed. For many years to come, Bob enjoys owning his Bugatti and the financial security it represents. 7

Bob's conduct, most of us will immediately respond, was gravely wrong. Unger agrees. But then he reminds us that we too have opportunities to save the lives of children. We can give to organizations like UNICEF or Oxfam America. How much would we have to give one of these organizations to have a high probability of saving the life of a child threatened by easily preventable diseases? (I do not believe that children are more worth saving than adults, but since no one can argue that children have brought their poverty on themselves, focusing on them simplifies the issues.) Unger called up some experts and used the information they provided to offer some plausible estimates that include the cost of raising money, administrative expenses, and the cost of delivering aid where it is most needed. By his calculation, $200 in donations would help a sickly two-year-old transform into a healthy six-year-old—offering safe passage through childhood's most dangerous years. To show how practical philosophical argument can be, Unger even tells his readers that they can easily donate funds by using their credit card and calling one of these toll-free numbers: (800) 367-5437 for UNICEF; (800) 693-2687 for Oxfam America. 8

9 Now you too have the information you need to save a child's life. How should you judge yourself if you don't do it? Think again about Bob and his Bugatti. Unlike Dora, Bob did not have to look into the eyes of the child he was sacrificing for his own material comfort. The child was a complete stranger to him and too far away to relate to in an intimate, personal way. Unlike Dora too, he did not mislead the child or initiate the chain of events imperiling him. In all these respects, Bob's situation resembles that of people able but unwilling to donate to overseas aid and differs from Dora's situation.

10 If you still think that it was very wrong of Bob not to throw the switch that would have diverted the train and saved the child's life, then it is hard to see how you could deny that it is also very wrong not to send money to one of the organizations listed above. Unless, that is, there is some morally important difference between the two situations that I have overlooked.

11 Is it the practical uncertainties about whether aid will really reach the people who need it? Nobody who knows the world of overseas aid can doubt that such uncertainties exist. But Unger's figure of $200 to save a child's life was reached after he had made conservative assumptions about the proportion of the money donated that will actually reach its target.

12 One genuine difference between Bob and those who can afford to donate to overseas aid organizations but don't is that only Bob can save the child on the tracks, whereas there are hundreds of millions of people who can give $200 to overseas aid organizations. The problem is that most of them aren't doing it. Does this mean that it is all right for you not to do it?

13 Suppose that there were more owners of priceless vintage cars—Carol, Dave, Emma, Fred, and so on, down to Ziggy—all in exactly the same situation as Bob, with their own siding and their own switch, all sacrificing the child in order to preserve their own cherished car. Would that make it all right for Bob to do the same? To answer this question affirmatively is to endorse follow-the-crowd ethics—the kind of ethics that led many Germans to look away when the Nazi atrocities were being committed. We do not excuse them because others were behaving no better.

14 We seem to lack a sound basis for drawing a clear moral line between Bob's situation and that of any reader of this article with $200 to spare who does not donate it to an overseas aid agency. These readers seem to be acting at least as badly as Bob was acting when he chose to let the runaway train hurtle toward the unsuspecting child. In the light of this conclusion, I trust that many readers will reach for the phone and donate that $200. Perhaps you should do it before reading further.

15 Now that you have distinguished yourself morally from people who put their vintage cars ahead of a child's life, how about treating yourself and

your partner to dinner at your favorite restaurant? But wait. The money you will spend at the restaurant could also help save the lives of children overseas! True, you weren't planning to blow $200 tonight, but if you were to give up dining out just for one month, you would easily save that amount. And what is one month's dining out compared to a child's life? There's the rub. Since there are a lot of desperately needy children in the world, there will always be another child whose life you could save for another $200. Are you therefore obliged to keep giving until you have nothing left? At what point can you stop?

Hypothetical examples can easily become farcical. Consider Bob. 16
How far past losing the Bugatti should he go? Imagine that Bob had got his foot stuck in the track of the siding, and if he diverted the train, then before it rammed the car it would also amputate his big toe. Should he still throw the switch? What if it would amputate his foot? His entire leg?

As absurd as the Bugatti scenario gets when pushed to extremes, 17
the point it raises is a serious one: only when the sacrifices become very significant indeed would most people be prepared to say that Bob does nothing wrong when he decides not to throw the switch. Of course, most people could be wrong; we can't decide moral issues by taking opinion polls. But consider for yourself the level of sacrifice that you would demand of Bob, and then think about how much money you would have to give away in order to make a sacrifice that is roughly equal to that. It's almost certainly much, much more than $200. For most middle-class Americans, it could easily be more like $200,000.

Isn't it counterproductive to ask people to do so much? Don't we run the 18
risk that many will shrug their shoulders and say that morality, so conceived, is fine for saints but not for them? I accept that we are unlikely to see, in the near or even medium-term future, a world in which it is normal for wealthy Americans to give the bulk of their wealth to strangers. When it comes to praising or blaming people for what they do, we tend to use a standard that is relative to some conception of normal behavior. Comfortably off Americans who give, say, 10 percent of their income to overseas aid organizations are so far ahead of most of their equally comfortable fellow citizens that I wouldn't go out of my way to chastise them for not doing more. Nevertheless, they should be doing much more, and they are in no position to criticize Bob for failing to make the much greater sacrifice of his Bugatti.

At this point various objections may crop up. Someone may say, "If 19
every citizen living in the affluent nations contributed his or her share, I wouldn't have to make such a drastic sacrifice, because long before such levels were reached the resources would have been there to save the lives of all those children dying from lack of food or medical care. So why should I give more than my fair share?" Another, related objection is that

the government ought to increase its overseas aid allocations, since that would spread the burden more equitably across all taxpayers.

20 Yet the question of how much we ought to give is a matter to be decided in the real world—and that, sadly, is a world in which we know that most people do not, and in the immediate future will not, give substantial amounts to overseas aid agencies. We know too that at least in the next year, the United States government is not going to meet even the very modest United Nations–recommended target of 0.7 percent of gross national product; at the moment it lags far below that, at 0.09 percent, not even half of Japan's 0.22 percent or a tenth of Denmark's 0.97 percent. Thus, we know that the money we can give beyond that theoretical "fair share" is still going to save lives that would otherwise be lost. While the idea that no one need do more than his or her fair share is a powerful one, should it prevail if we know that others are not doing their fair share and that children will die preventable deaths unless we do more than our fair share? That would be taking fairness too far.

21 Thus, this ground for limiting how much we ought to give also fails. In the world as it is now, I can see no escape from the conclusion that each one of us with wealth surplus to his or her essential needs should be giving most of it to help people suffering from poverty so dire as to be life-threatening. That's right: I'm saying that you shouldn't buy that new car, take that cruise, redecorate the house, or get that pricy new suit. After all, a thousand-dollar suit could save five children's lives.

22 So how does my philosophy break down in dollars and cents? An American household with an income of $50,000 spends around $30,000 annually on necessities, according to the Conference Board, a nonprofit economic research organization. Therefore, for a household bringing in $50,000 a year, donations to help the world's poor should be as close as possible to $20,000. The $30,000 required for necessities holds for higher incomes as well. So a household making $100,000 could cut a yearly check for $70,000. Again, the formula is simple: whatever money you're spending on luxuries, not necessities, should be given away.

23 Now, evolutionary psychologists tell us that human nature just isn't sufficiently altruistic to make it plausible that many people will sacrifice so much for strangers. On the facts of human nature, they might be right, but they would be wrong to draw a moral conclusion from those facts. If it is the case that we ought to do things that, predictably, most of us won't do, then let's face that fact head-on. Then, if we value the life of a child more than going to fancy restaurants, the next time we dine out we will know that we could have done something better with our money. If that makes living a morally decent life extremely arduous, well, then that is the way things are. If we don't do it, then we should at least know that we are failing to live a morally decent life—not because it is good to wallow in guilt but because knowing where we should be going is the first step toward heading in that direction.

When Bob first grasped the dilemma that faced him as he stood by that railway switch, he must have thought how extraordinarily unlucky he was to be placed in a situation in which he must choose between the life of an innocent child and the sacrifice of most of his savings. But he was not unlucky at all. We are all in that situation. 24

Content

1. What was your reaction to the "Bugatti scenario," which Singer describes as a "hypothetical example" designed to test the reader's ethics? Do you agree that Bob's conduct was "gravely wrong" (¶ 8)? What about the incremental version of the scenario—how much is the child's life worth? A toe, a foot, a leg? (¶ 16).
2. Singer describes his philosophical stance as utilitarian; he "judges whether acts are right or wrong by their consequences" (¶ 5). How does the utilitarian point of view inform "The Singer Solution"? What actions and what consequences is the article concerned with? Where does Singer stress consequences as a criterion for decision making?

Strategies/Structures/Language

3. Emotion can lead to motion: Authors can move readers to action by arousing intense feelings and then providing an outlet for them. Singer appeals to emotion with the *Central Station* example and the idea of children starving to death. However, he expects the reader to rationally test their ethics in the "Bugatti scenario" and the call for overseas aid donations. Did your emotional reactions to the portrayals of poverty help you make up your mind, or did they get in the way of your ethical deliberations?
4. Consider to what extent Singer uses visual images in his argument. What are some scenes or pictures that remained in your mind after you read the article? Why does Singer rely on imagery? Do you think his use of imagery is effective?

For Writing

5. Do you think that Singer presents a highly effective solution to world poverty? Should his ideas perhaps replace current methods of poverty relief? Write an argument explaining why you agree with Singer's program, or explain how you disapprove of the "Singer Solution" and why.
6. ***Journal Writing.*** Is there an ethical situation to which you feel that a utilitarian point of view does *not* apply? When are considerations of efficiency and expediency relevant to ethical situations? Does a utilitarian approach require a moral or ethical framework?
7. ***Dialogues.*** Do you agree with Singer's utilitarian argument that "only when the sacrifices become very significant indeed would most people be prepared to say that Bob does nothing wrong when he decides not to throw the switch" (¶ 17)? (See question 1.) Compare Singer's assumptions with those Swift's narrator makes in advancing a utilitarian solution to mass starvation in "A Modest Proposal" (524–30). Why does Singer's utilitarian stance lead to a dramatically different conclusion than Swift's?

8. With a classmate, develop an ethical test to help readers confront an issue that you feel is important. Using Singer's methods, construct a hypothetical example that offers the readers choices and helps them come to a decision about a difficult moral problem. Test it out on several classmates, and write a paper reporting and interpreting your findings. What values do these allocations represent? Do you share these? Why or why not?

SHERYL KENNEDY

Sheryl Kennedy (born 1951) writes, "In January of 1969, I left college after one semester, ready to experience first-hand the tumult of the sixties: I hopped on a Greyhound bus and hit the streets of Boston ready to join the revolution. I thought I didn't need the classroom experience to get an education—I was wrong." Thirty-eight years later she returned to the University of Connecticut, experiencing, in Lawrence Ferlinghetti's words, "a new rebirth of wonder," for which she thanks professors Gerry and Charles Van Doren.

Her essay, "About Suffering," which won second prize in the university-wide creative nonfiction contest, was written in a freshman writing class in response to an assigned poem, W. H. Auden's "Musee des Beaux Arts." Kennedy explains, "My friend Staff Sergeant Luke Murphy had just gotten his leg blown off in Iraq. I was devastated for him and confused by the apathy concerning those wounded in the war. The middle section, *The Ploughman Speaks*, was written first. I really did feel his voice come through me!" Kennedy updated her commentary in June, 2008: Today, two years later, "the number of wounded is officially over 30,000, not counting the many thousands suffering mental and emotional trauma (PTSD). Toe and finger losses are not counted as amputations (I'm not sure about eyes), and a patient sustaining multiple amputations is only counted as one injured person, so the figures can be deceiving. I continue to comb many related sites, including the Department of Defense, for information about the wounded, traumatized and the 'non-combat related' deaths, of which many are suicides. However, since there is no way to put an exact number on the amputations, I wonder if we should say 'phantoms of countless limbs,' instead of an estimated number."

✧ *About Suffering*

1 Sometime after Luke's tragedy, I began listening to W. H. Auden reading his poetry on tape. Driving the back roads of Connecticut, with the sound of his nasal voice and Oxford accent becoming increasingly familiar as he read, I was deeply moved by one poem, *Musee des Beaux Arts*, Auden's poetic reaction to an exhibit of Brueghel paintings

in the Brussels museum. I listened to the poem over and over again. For days, it played in a continuous loop and became the soundtrack that marked the beginning of my understanding of what had happened. Every word was important to me because of Luke.

It begins: About suffering they were never wrong, 2
The old Masters . . .

The old masters knew that people's suffering always takes place 3
while we are busy doing other things, Auden writes—"eating, or opening a window, or just walking dully along." The poem goes on to describe *The Fall of Icarus*, painted in the 17th century by Pieter Brueghel the Elder, which shows an industrious scenario: a farmer busily plowing his field near a shepherd and his flock, all overlooking a sunlit bay where a portly friar casts a fishing line and glorious ships are setting sail for the open sea. But there is more in the picture: Icarus is falling out of the sky into the water—and as Auden tells us, "the sun shone As it had to on the white legs disappearing into the green . . ." Why has no one noticed? Why does the ploughman turn his back? Doesn't he hear the splash or the boy's cry? Why is the ship, laden with its riches, just sailing calmly on its way?

I traveled with Auden's voice a companion on my daily rounds. 4
His poem, a powerful testament to indifference written in the early days of World War II, played again and again on my aging tape deck until one day the sound quality began to disintegrate, Auden's voice fading in and out with a crackling sound like static on a radio. I thought the tape had finally worn out, and reached over to remove it when I became alarmed by a bizarre disturbance in the air. I was scarcely able to drive as an other-worldly echo, dim at first then louder and louder, a new voice, sharp and insistent, heavily accented, finally overtook Auden's . . .

Part One: The Ploughman Speaks

Forgive me Mr. Auden, but I am a poor farmer who has waited three 5
hundred and eighty years to tell my story. Your poem is an interesting one, but I feel I must enlighten you concerning the part that I played in the painting you describe. I remember the morning that Pieter Brueghel the Elder came to the edge of my miserable plot of rocky soil to watch me struggle through the mud with my rude plow. As I regarded him out of the corner of my eye, he cleaned and sorted his expensive brushes and leisurely set up his easel in the morning sunlight, took out his paints and began to dabble about. He never greeted me nor asked about my family. He loves to paint us, the "peasantry" (we are so colorful and quaint!), but his interest is not in us as people, but rather in his own high-minded ideas. For all these years I have carried the burden of representing those who turn away from the suffering of others when it was Brueghel who turned away!

6 Mr. Auden, let me tell you what suffering I left at home that morning. After burying our youngest child only two days before, I had stayed up all the previous night helping my wife nurse our daughter through the very same fever that had taken our son. Marta is numb with grief and still she must wash the clothes, tend the garden, milk the cow, scrub the floors on her hands and knees, prepare food for me and our children. I closed the door that morning upon the cries of my children so that I might go to my fields to coax some good hay and a few carrots, leeks and turnips out of the sand and rocks. Did Brueghel care to know any of this? Did he, with his keen artistic eye, notice my hollow red-rimmed eyes, my gnarled hands, the sad stoop of my weary back?

7 Does Brueghel, the great master, truly understand suffering? Can he see what is right in front of his eyes? Mr. Brueghel sees only what he wants to see: a lone man plowing in a picturesque field overlooking the sea, a ship in full sail, Brother Halleck trying for a fish, my own young brother tending his flock. A pretty picture on the surface I will grant you, except for the white legs slipping into the water. A picture that many must have seen and exclaimed, "Look at that farmer, how he turns away! What kind of man is he?"

8 From what am I turning away? A foolish young criminal who seeks to escape his fate by flying like a bird? A boy who wastes his time in dreaming and expects hard working people to be torn away from their enterprise to come to his rescue? I did not turn away, but rather continued in the direction of my plow, completely unaware of the boy and his white legs. We did not see him, Mr. Auden! We did not see nor hear him in his plight, or we certainly would have left our work and clambered down the rocks to his rescue. I was too far away, and Brother Halleck is as blind as a bat. My own young brother Iain was counting his sheep . . . and of course the shipmates navigating their glorious craft laden with riches—all of their eyes were cast toward the open sea. You are an intelligent man, you know who saw the boy—it was Brueghel, of course. But he was too busy painting the interesting tragedy to cry out!

9 So there it is, the truth at last. I am blameless! I will sleep tonight, even in my own suffering and grief, knowing that I have told my story, which is the story of an innocent man.

Part Two: An Important Failure

10 On April 24 [2006] the phone rang just after breakfast while I was opening the kitchen window to the fresh spring air. It was Sally Murphy, who has been my friend since we were in our twenties, calling from Florida. "It's Luke," she choked, "he's had an accident." She went on to explain the circumstances of the tragedy. Her son's Humvee in Iraq had come under fire, and Luke was struck violently by flying shrapnel from an improvised explosive device and was now clinging to life in an army field hospital near Baghdad. She told me

that his left leg had been blown off, that doctors were struggling to save his right leg, severely mangled, large chunks of muscle gone, tendons and nerves ripped and burned. She explained how Luke, with these grievous injuries, had dragged himself from the burning vehicle, taken a head count of his men, calmed them down, radioed for help. What remained of his left leg had been amputated by medics in the back of a truck on the way to the field hospital in an attempt to save him from bleeding to death.

Sally told me that her first reaction to the early morning phone call from the Army was dismissive. "No, I'm sorry, you must have the wrong number, it is not my son you are talking about . . ." Her blonde Luke, second of three sons, an extraordinarily handsome man of twenty-four years with piercing blue eyes and an impish smile. A friendly kid who loved a good laugh and a good argument and had been dubbed "Luke the Lawyer" in junior high. 11

I was stunned into silence; I didn't know what to say to my friend. How does one receive this gruesome news on a bright spring day, standing in a sunny kitchen, drying the last blue flowered dish, the smell of coffee and toast still strong in the air? What sense could I make of this day, what could I do or say now that would be of any importance? I felt guilty and ashamed that I had not done enough to prevent Luke from going to war. We had failed Luke, I had failed Luke. I felt nausea, revulsion at my comfort, my health, my life. And I felt anger; murderous rage at the powers that had sent Luke ten thousand miles away but did not protect him. 12

In August I made my first trip to Ward 57 of Walter Reed Army Medical Center to visit Luke. I was told by those who had been there before me that visiting the huge army hospital would be a powerful experience, but difficult to see, difficult to know what to say or do. It would be uncomfortable. I thought I was ready, but nothing could have prepared me for what I witnessed as I walked onto the enormous ward, brilliantly lit, room after room full of men just like Luke, missing arms, legs, hands, eyes. The empty beds made up immaculately with white sheets, starched and bleached, purposefully left empty in readiness for those who would be coming in tonight, tomorrow, next week. To walk down the hallway of the ward might invite a near collision with a patient rounding a corner on two prosthetic legs, one arm missing, or a grief-stricken family just arriving to see their wounded child for the first time. 13

I found Luke in good spirits and feeling strong, and later noticed his arm muscles rippling as he wheeled down the long halls, showing me around and joking with the nurses. He casually pointed out his old rooms, rooms where he had lain during the first months in agonizing pain from multiple surgeries, experiencing recurring unexplained high fevers, drugged and sick, his one leg immobilized with countless titanium pins attached to a heavy external fixator. 14

© Robert Galbraith/Corbis

On Memorial Day 2005, Veterans for Peace constructed this "Arlington West" memorial on the beach at Santa Monica, California, to commemorate their comrades killed in the Iraq War. Compare and contrast the story the images in the foreground tell—the kneeling soldier amidst the crosses on the sand, however temporary—with the beachgoers at the water's edge, intent on their recreation, indifferent to the drama at their backs. In what ways does this photograph comment on "About Suffering"?

15 We took an elevator to the cafeteria, had lunch, and I listened to Luke, the young Staff Sergeant. He recounted the whole story of that day in April, still a harrowing tale after many retellings. He told other stories, of the men he'd lost in previous roadside bombings, and of having to give orders to the youngest members of his unit, the stunned eighteen year olds, to scrape up the leftover flesh and other human tissue that remained after the bodies had been removed, and place the material in plastic bags. Graphic descriptions of the dead bodies of Iraqis left by the roadside, their heads swollen in the blazing sun to the size of basketballs. I listened to every story, and began to understand the meaning of the phrase "to bear witness."

16 I asked Luke what I should tell people when I went home, if he had any message. He said to say that he had not felt physically protected while he was in Iraq. He also said that he felt duped into going to Iraq for a second deployment under a program that our government calls, ironically, "Stop/Loss," a term lifted from stock market jargon. The program is, in effect, a draft foisted upon those military personnel who are about to finish their service but who receive orders for redeployment in the months or weeks before their expected release date. He also wanted me

to make sure that people knew that he is one of roughly twenty thousand men and women maimed by the war thus far. That Ward 57 is haunted by the phantoms of perhaps thirty thousand missing limbs.

On the way back to Luke's room after lunch we passed the entrance to Ward 58 marked by a sign that read "Neuroscience Unit." I hesitated at the double doors, ready for the rest of my "tour." I glanced at Luke. "NO-o-o-o, you don't want to go in there . . .," he said with eyebrows raised. I was about to say that I did want to go in, but I turned away from the doors, and followed the wheelchair down the hall. I could only imagine what he was preventing me from witnessing: the traumatically brain injured patients, their pain different from the amputees; the vacant eyes and "persistent vegetative states"; the families of those men and women. Why did I not insist upon going in? Why, after seeing all that I had seen did I turn away in fear at those who lie in the twilight between life and death? 17

Part Three: The Torturer's Horse

On the drive home from Walter Reed, tired and emotionally drained, 18 I wondered what had happened to Luke's amputated leg. A leg that I remembered as being muscular and tan, leg hair bleached white-blonde from the Florida sun. What had happened to the limbs of all those twenty thousand amputees? Was there some hapless soldier given the job of cremating young body parts? What had happened to the ashes? I imagined them being loaded into a plane, sprinkled over the White House lawn and dug into the rich soil of every suburban lawn in America.

It was at that moment that grief hit me. Thinking of Luke's once 19 beautiful leg, unrecognizable, being placed into a faraway crematorium with no one there to mourn, history repeating itself by another young man just doing his job.

Content

1. It's possible to understand this essay without reading W. H. Auden's poem, "Musee des Beaux Arts," on which it is based, since some of the poem's essential meaning—that, as Kennedy says, "people's suffering always takes place while we [ordinary people] are busy doing other things" (¶ 3), the ordinary activities of ordinary lives. It's also possible to understand the essay without looking at "The Fall of Icarus," the seventeenth century painting by Pieter Brueghel the Elder on which the poem is based, which Kennedy describes in ¶ 3—no one—not the farmer plowing his field, the shepherd tending his flock, nor the friar fishing—notices Icarus falling from the sky, his—as Auden says—"white legs disappearing into the green." Explain the introduction as you understand it (exclusively from Kennedy's essay).

2. **Second Look.** Now, read the Auden poem and view the Brueghel painting, both readily available through print and Internet sources. Then re-read the essay through this doubly new lens of poem and painting. "Musee des Beaux Arts," for

instance, was written in 1938, when Hitler's invasion of Europe was in process, leading to World War II; what is the relevance of this? What meanings come into focus that weren't apparent from your initial reading of Kennedy's essay? How do these specific works, juxtaposed with the example of the wounded soldier, concretize an abstraction—suffering?

3. Why does Kennedy devote a major section—Part One—of this essay to a monologue by the farmer in the painting, defending himself against Auden's charge of indifference to suffering? On what grounds does the farmer base his self-defense? Is his argument credible? Ethical? Does he become a sympathetic character in the course of his speech?

4. How do the introduction (Auden's poem and Brueghel's painting) and Part One (the farmer's monologue) prepare readers for Part Two: Luke's loss of his leg in the Iraq War? Why does Kennedy title this section "An Important Failure"?

5. What is the ultimate meaning of "About Suffering"? What are the underlying ethical issues in this essay?

Strategies/Structures/Language

6. This is a creative nonfiction essay, yet Part One, the monologue by the farmer in the painting, is clearly fictional. Justify the mixture of fact and fiction to make an ethical point, using both Kennedy's essay and Swift's "A Modest Proposal" (524–30) as examples.

7. Does Kennedy's creation of a fictitious example to discuss suffering interfere with or undercut the true example of suffering she presents in her visit to Luke in the Walter Reed Army Medical Center? Luke, as she presents him, actually seems to be making an excellent recovery: "I found Luke in good spirits and feeling strong" (¶ 14). In what ways, then, does his example reinforce her point? Would her argument have been more effective if her subject had appeared more devastated, more miserable?

8. The imagery of Luke's lost leg, "once beautiful," now "unrecognizable," dominates the conclusion—and makes what points? Given this, why title this section "The Torturer's Horse," a quotation from "Musee des Beaux Arts"—"Where the dogs go on with their doggy life and the torturer's horse/Scratches its innocent behind on a tree." Why use this quotation here, this literary allusion, instead of Auden's reference to "the white legs disappearing into the green/Water" or another reference in Auden to the "boy falling out of the sky"?

For Writing

9. Write an essay about an abstract concept ("good," "evil," "war," "peace," "love," "hate," among innumerable possibilities), using a poem as well as a personal example to provide a specific illustration of or commentary on your position.

10. Use an example of someone who has been a victim to make an ethical point about a larger issue. Avoid sentimentality, clichés, excessive emotion—and don't preach. Let the example speak for itself, as do the examples in this essay by Kennedy, Hockenberry's from *Moving Violations* (366–71), LaCasse's "Hegemony" (387–92), and Swift's "A Modest Proposal" (524–30).

Additional Topics for Writing Appealing to Emotion and Ethics

(For strategies for appealing to emotion and ethics, see 516.)

Multiple Strategies for Writing: Appealing to Emotion and Ethics

Implied arguments, appeals to emotion and ethics, commonly employ assorted strategies to make their points as compelling as possible, and to interpret their significance. Among these are the following:

- *definitions* of essential terms, component parts. These are likely to be subjective and favorable to the writer's point of view.
- a *narrative*, which may comprise the entire argument or an interrelated series of narrative examples. The *narrator* is likely to be the author, using characters or events to make the point, *dialogue, a time sequence*, evocative *setting(s)*, and *symbolism* to reinforce the implied point.
- *definitions, illustrations*, and *examples*, to show the meaning or significance of the key issues
- *process analysis*, to show either how the subject at hand arose and why it needs to be addressed or to show the process by which a remedy or solution can be effected
- *comparison* and *contrast* of the pro and con positions
- *division* and *classification* of the relevant subtopics and side issues
- *cause* and *effect*, to show the beneficial consequences of the arguer's point of view and the detrimental consequences of the opposition's stance

1. Write an essay that attempts to persuade one of the following audiences through a combination of appeals to reason, emotion, and ethics.

   a. To someone you'd like for a friend, lover, or spouse, or an enemy with whom you'd like a reconciliation: Love me.
   b. To an athlete, or to an athletic coach: Play according to the rules, even when the referee (umpire, or other judge) isn't looking.
   c. To a prospective employer: I'm the best person for the job. Hire me.
   d. To a police officer: I shouldn't receive this traffic ticket. Or, to a judge or jury: I am innocent of the crime of which I'm accused.
   e. To the voters: Vote for me (or for a candidate of my choice).
   f. To admissions officers of a particular college, university, or of a program within that institution (such as medical or law school, graduate program, or a division with a special undergraduate degree): Let me in.
   g. To the prospective buyer of something you want to sell or service you can perform: Buy this. Trust me.
   h. To an audience prejudiced against a particular group or simply to a majority audience: It is wrong to discriminate against X. (*X* may

be a minority, female, a member of a particular national or religious group, gay, disabled, elderly . . .)

i. To an antagonist on any issue: As Joan Didion says, *"Listen to me, see it my way, change your mind."*

j. To people engaging in behavior that threatens their lives or their health: Stop doing *X* (or stop doing *X* to excess)—smoking, drinking, overeating, undereating, or using drugs. Or: Start doing *X*—exercising regularly, using bike helmets or seatbelts, planning for the future by getting an education, a stable job, free of debt, an investment plan, a retirement plan . . .

2. Pick a work of fiction or nonfiction whose content intrigues you and whose style you admire, and write a brief parody (probably involving considerable exaggeration) of it to show your understanding of the content and your appreciation of the style.

3. Write a satire to argue implicity for a point, as Swift does in "A Modest Proposal" (524–30). Use whatever techniques seem appropriate, such as creating a character who does the talking for you; setting a scene (such as of pathos or misery) that helps make your point; using a tone involving understatement, irony, or exaggeration. Be sure to supply enough clues to enable your readers to understand what you really mean.

4. Write a humorous paper primarily for enjoyment—your own and your audience's—on a familiar topic that either shows its pleasant aspects to advantage (Twain, "Uncle John's Farm" 253–59) or parodies its subject (Verge, "The Habs" 107–11; Britt, "That Lean and Hungry Look" 281–83; Benedetto, "Home Away From Home" 436–38).

5. Write a worst-case scenario designed to frighten readers into accepting your argument on any of the above topics or those in Chapter 10 (511–12).

PART V: CONTROVERSY IN CONTEXT

Identity

Issues of identity permeate *The Essay Connection*, as they do throughout life. "Who am I?" we want to know, from childhood onward. "Where do I belong?" arrives early and remains throughout our lifetimes as we develop an understanding of family, friends, peers, nation, and wider world. What we initially take for granted—"I am an American"—or Hispanic American, African American, Asian American, or—fill in the blanks—becomes progressively more complicated as we understand more about our history, our heritage, our expectations. Changing the representations of one's identity, on *MySpace, Facebook, craigslist*, blogs, or other easily mutable locations is for some a daily, even an hourly, pastime. Responding to these requires a keen eye, a nimble imagination, an ability to improvise and reinvent oneself, as well as a sense of skepticism—do we really believe what we're reading or viewing? What we might have been inclined to trust in the days of cold print today becomes unstable in the twinkling of an eye. Reader, viewer, beware!

Some aspects of identity are highly conspicuous, such as one's name, skin color, body size and shape, or speech. Some are less visible, more ambiguous: one's ethnicity or nationality, physical or mental state, native intelligence or degree of education, or economic status. Other aspects of identity are more unobtrusive unless the individual—or society—chooses to emphasize them: individual beliefs and values, relationships with others, one's DNA, or the results of medical alteration. Some aspects of identity we consider intrinsic to our heritage: the "inalienable rights" addressed in "The Declaration of Independence"—"Life, Liberty, and the Pursuit of Happiness" (450–54) and a healthful environment of clean air and abundant water (though many, such as Diamond in "The World as a Polder" [472–83], say we can no longer take the latter for granted). Other aspects of identity we choose deliberately: whether or not to attend college, where to live after graduation, what friends to have, whom to marry, whether or not to have children. Yet because life is never static, whatever is incorporated into relationships, like whatever is embedded in society and in the natural world, is subject to change. The authors, in this chapter on identity and throughout the book, attempt to capture the transient as well as the more permanent aspects of identity and to interpret and analyze the causes and consequences of what makes us who we are. We can interpret identity, as well as other topics, from the following perspectives:

- political
- economic
- religious
- social
- intellectual
- aesthetic

(an easy way to remember these is that they spell P-E-R-S-I-A), though feel free to add other aspects as well.

It is possible to read every chapter of this book, every topic—growing up, family relationships, heritage, the natural world, science and technology, education, human and civil rights—through the lens of identity. But this chapter specifically focuses on two significant aspects of identity that affect every one on this earth: national identity and physical identity.

National Identity. E. B. White's two-paragraph definition of "Democracy" (558) was published in *The New Yorker*'s Fourth-of-July issue six months after the United States had entered World War II—on the side of democracy and in opposition of fascism. White's definition provides low-key, familiar illustrations of many of the principles addressed in the Bill of Rights: freedom of speech, press, religion, assembly, and the right to petition, granted to ordinary citizens. These citizens are, in White's encomium, people who, even in wartime, resent stuffed shirts and high hats; people who can appreciate baseball, the national pastime, and the hope for victory that exists (even) "at the beginning of the ninth"; people who can enjoy the small pleasures of life, "the mustard on the hotdog and the cream in the rationed coffee." Yet critics have pointed out the "whiteness" of the culture this definition represents. For in 1943 racial segregation persisted not only throughout the South, but in our nation's capital. In the South, many African Americans were not allowed to vote or to use the public libraries; how could they ever experience "the feeling of privacy in the voting booths, the feeling of communion in the libraries"? In 1943 major league baseball was lily-white; Jackie Robinson, the first African-American player, would not be hired until 1947; the notion of "national pastime" needed to expand, and has done so, dramatically, over time.

New Yorker readers, themselves predominantly white in 1943, might not have noticed the whiteness of the world that White (no pun intended) depicted. Twenty years later the Civil Rights movement profoundly challenged this orientation, as articulated in Martin Luther King, Jr.'s, eloquent "Letter from Birmingham Jail" (456–70), where he was confined after being arrested in a nonviolent civil rights protest. His rallying cry, "Injustice anywhere is a threat to justice everywhere. We are caught in an inescapable network of mutuality. . . . Whatever affects one directly, affects all indirectly" finds current resonance in the 2008 speech of then presidential candidate Barack Obama, "To Form a More Perfect Union" (559–69). Although throughout the campaign Obama himself did not emphasize his mixed-race ancestry, upon hearing or reading this speech voters would be reminded that he has a black father from Kenya and a white mother from Kansas. Obama further points with pride to the fact that he is "married to a black American who carries within her the blood of slaves and slaveowners" and that his immediate family includes people "of every race and every hue, scattered across three continents." Obama, a graduate of Harvard Law School, believes—as part of the fulfillment of the American dream—"that in no other country on Earth is my story even possible," for Obama's individual identity is intimately interwoven not only with his family but with America's national identity, which as President of the United States he now symbolizes.

A strong element of his campaign was Dr. King's sense of "mutuality," concern for—in Obama's words—the "future of black children and white children and Asian children and Hispanic children and Native American children." Both leaders reject the claim that "those kids who don't look like us are somebody else's problem," as Obama says. "The children of America are not those kids, they are our kids, and we will not let them fall. . . ." In this spirit, student Zara Rix, herself the child of Italian-Australian parents, addresses the positive consequences and the complexities of growing up in multi-ethnic America in "Corporality" (606–12).

The Essay Connection is, in fact, a testament to the wide spectrum of Americans of the diverse identities Obama identified who have not failed; people who have been highly successful as human beings in a variety of fields and activities and who have written about these topics. These include African Americans (Frederick Douglass and Dr. King), Hispanic Richard Rodriguez, Native Americans (Sherman Alexie and Linda Hogan), Asian Americans (Amy Tan and Lynda Barry), and survivors or children of survivors of the Holocaust (Elie Wiesel and Art Spiegelman). The American Dream is compressed into the expectation that regardless of one's origin, everyone in America has the "shining, golden opportunity" for self-fulfillment: "work hard and you'll succeed." That the American Dream may be a national myth, an overly simplistic vision of national identity, is posited by Sherman Alexie's satiric "What Sacagawea Means to Me" (85–87), and by the ethical questions raised by Robert Reich's "The Global Elite" (490–98) and Peter Singer's "The Singer Solution to World Poverty" (535–41). Moreover, in "Family Values" (321–28), Richard Rodriguez illustrates ways in which American beliefs about families are contradicted by the realities of American life and thus: "What immigrants know . . . is that when you come to this country, you risk losing your children."

In this chapter, Taiwanese American Eric Liu's "Notes of a Native Speaker" (589–99), from his autobiography, *The Accidental Asian*, deconstructs and disputes knee-jerk reactions to his Asian appearance. He begins with a list of the ways in which he is "white," which except for the fact that he "married a white woman" may be attributable more to a good education (this "Native Speaker" speaks "flawless, unaccented English") and upper-middle-class social status than to race. For he—like Obama—is "not too ethnic" (what Maxine Hong Kingston calls "fresh-off-the-boat-Chinese"). Moreover, like Obama, he is "wary of minority militants"—people like the Reverend Jeremiah Wright, Jr., who, in Obama's words, "use incendiary language to express views that have the potential . . . to widen the racial divide. . . ." Thus in *residence*, Liu is "a child of the suburbs" with Yuppie tastes in *furniture* (Crate & Barrel), *clothing* (khaki Dockers), *magazines (Foreign Affairs)*, and *radio programs* (National Public Radio). In *occupation*, he is involved in politics, "a producer of the culture" who expects his "voice to be heard." On *vacation*, he stays at "charming bed-and-breakfasts." Liu says he's "never once been the victim of blatant discrimination." Although he attributes this to being "white by acclamation," he may merely have been lucky—or unusually handsome or charming—for there are many types of discrimination not based on race, such as looks, age, gender, or disability status.

Genetic Identity. "Who am I," a question as old as the Greek philosophers, used to involve—on a physical and perhaps social level—more clear-cut answers than it does today. That biology is destiny (i.e., that women and African Americans, for example, have their lifelong fate predetermined from birth) has been challenged in a number of significant ways in the past century. With these challenges come the provocations, potential benefits and problems, ethical issues, and myriad of unforeseen consequences that are predicted to multiply in future years. No longer do large numbers of Americans accept what used to be considered inevitable: that gender, strength, intelligence, physical ability or disability, propensity for (or existence of) disease is determined at birth or through later injury and is essentially unchangeable throughout life. These stereotypes, however, provide the basis for much contemporary humor, including Roz Chast's "Men Are from Belgium, Women Are from New Brunswick" (409) and the Botox babes cartoon, "I never thought turning eighty would be so much fun!" (435).

Charles C. Mann's "Forever Young"—originally titled "The Coming Death Shortage" (422–33)—confronts the problems likely to occur when rich people cease to die according to their natural biological span of years. Fulfillment of the American Dream, says Mann, depends on old people dying on schedule so the young can take their places. This natural progression is altered when elderly people have enough money to buy costly medical procedures that can extend their lives indefinitely; if they beat the biological endgame young people won't have a chance.

Bill McKibben's "Designer Genes" (572–82) explores the ethical dimensions of human biological engineering, of modifying the genetic identity of human beings—as is currently being done with plants and animals—"to make them *better* in some way; to delete, modify, or add genes in developing embryos . . . [to] make them taller and more muscular, or smarter and less aggressive, maybe handsome and possibly straight." Even as early as 1993, 43 percent of Americans polled by the March of Dimes would willingly "engage in genetic engineering 'simply to enhance their children's looks or intelligence.'" Among families today dealing with—or trying to prevent—deafness, Down's syndrome, or Lou Gehrig's disease, powerful arguments erupt over whether prevention or eradication of these problems in future generations would diminish the resources given to current sufferers. Should tomorrow's children be improved if today's are neglected? Among more "normal" families—and what is "normal" in these days of in vitro fertilization, embryo transplants, and more—what would happen if genetic engineering could create new and improved models of superior children at, say, ten year intervals? Would this lead to a "biological arms race" in which each new generation would be superior to homegrown babies with natural, unmodified DNA, as well as to its genetically engineered predecessors? If parents could add "thirty points to their child's IQ," would failure to "soup up" the embryos amount to child abuse? If we disallow the opportunistic notions that those with the most money or the easiest access to the treatment should get what they want, what principles should be operative?

Beauty. That genetic engineering raises innumerable ethical questions and offers few if any clear-cut answers is echoed in Virginia Postrel's "The Truth About Beauty" (584–87). She argues that, "we know beauty when we see it, and our reactions are remarkably consistent" to "the centuries-old bust of Neferititi, the Venus de Milo, and the exquisite faces painted by Leonardo and Botticelli." Her comments hold true even though the Cupid's bow faces of the "It" girls of the silent movies gave way to the beach-blanket bimbos of the 1950s, who a half-century later gave way to the looks of Britney Spears and Paris Hilton and the ever self-inventing Madonna, adaptive to time and taste. Contrary to the new Dove ads, Postrel claims that "beauty is not just a social construct, and not every girl is beautiful just the way she is."

In response to physical beauty we could propose—as many have done throughout *The Essay Connection*, and elsewhere—additional dimensions of human identity:

- *Intelligence*, in all its infinite varieties: familial, social, political, physical, aesthetic, mechanical, and more (see Scott Russell Sanders, "The Inheritance of Tools" 143–50; Howard Gardner, "Who Owns Intelligence?" 351–61).

- *Temperament*, whether inborn or cultivated, that may include where one ranks on a continuum of extremes that range, for instance, from being highly goal-oriented to vague; being aggressive to laid-back; or being either tolerant or intolerant of risk, change, ambiguity, or uncertainty (see Natalie Angier, "Why Men Don't Last: Self-Destruction as a Way of Life" 302–05; Deborah Tannen, "Communication Styles" 403–07).
- *Holder/conveyor of a belief system or set of values*, formal or informal: religious, ethical, philosophical, political, aesthetic (see Elie Wiesel, "Why I Write: Making No Become Yes" 22–27; Brian Doyle, "Joyas Voladoras" 372–74).
- *Occupation or avocation or consuming passion*, initially defined in terms of one's parents' social or economic status, then by one's education, and eventually by one's type of job and one's stature therein (see Orhan Pamuk, "My Father's Suitcase" 42–47; Barack Obama, "To Form a More Perfect Union" 559–69).

Identity Creation, Identity Theft. That there are innumerable aspects of identity and innumerable possibilities for self-creation, re-creation, and interpretation is apparent, in part from Michael J. Bugeja's "Facing the Facebook" (601–04), which explores a topic that, on its face (oops), seems so obvious to today's generation of students that it scarcely needs discussion. Nevertheless, what may seem to be an innocent posting of photographs—candid or manipulated, serious or in jest—and information about oneself is fraught with possibilities for manipulation, fraud, theft, and other forms of abuse. Who reads what is broadcast to the wide world, or even to a restricted segment thereof? Where does this material reside—not only photographs but other vital personal information, such as Social Security number, medical history, credit record? Who owns these manifestations of oneself? Who can store them, alter them, transmit them, comment on them, buy and sell them? Use them for other transactions licit and illicit? These are questions that, before the ubiquitous presence of the Internet, might not have been asked or would certainly have been answered differently than they are today.

Indeed, all of the issues addressed in this chapter raise questions that may have different answers tomorrow than they do today. Identity, like life itself, is never static. Who we are, what we make of ourselves, what we become and may yet become again raises new questions, and in turn new answers. Welcome to the wide, wonderful world of knowledge and self-knowledge—at times full of roadblocks and fear, but nevertheless, as long as there is hope for the world (to be addressed in Chapter 13), full of challenge and inspiration as well.

JUDITH HALL

Judith Hall (born 1952) is the author of *To Put the Mouth To* (1992), selected for the National Poetry Series; *Anatomy, Errata* (1998); and *The Promised Folly* (2003). Her poems have appeared in numerous publications, including *The New Republic, Best American Poetry, Paris Review*, and *Yale Review*. She has served as poetry editor of the *Antioch Review* since 1995 and teaches at the California Institute of Technology and in the MFA program at New England College. "Perilous Riddle" interrogates the construction of gender through the cultural archetypes embodied in ancient Greek myth and drama.

Perilous Riddle

If I am a riddle, I am not a man.
Ain't that the truth. Ain't I a riddle?
If I am a man, I am not a riddle.

If I am a woman, am I a riddle?
Ain't I a woman?
If I am a riddle, I am not a man.

If I am Sophocles, I am not mad.
If I am mad,
If I am a man, I am not a riddle.

If I am tragic, I am proud, middling manly.
If I am proud, am I tragic?
If I am a riddle, I am not a man.

Not a warrior, nor an old man,
Nor an infant's versatile diddle.
If I am a man, I am not a riddle.

If I am a sphinx, my intellect
Unmans you. Ending choice? Chance?
If I am a riddle, I am not a man.
If I am a man, I am not a riddle.

E. B. WHITE

E. B. White (born in 1899 in Mount Vernon, New York) wrote for the *New Yorker* magazine for nearly six decades, from 1927 until the end of his career, including the "Talk of the Town" and "Notes and Comments" columns. He also wrote columns for *Harper's Magazine* from 1938 to 1943. He published essays, collected in *One Man's Meat* (1944), *The Second Tree from the Corner* (1954), and *The Points of My Compass* (1962); poetry, including *The Lady Is Cold* (1929); and, with James Thurbur, the satiric *Is Sex Necessary*? (1939). Famed for his children's books *Stuart Little* (1945), *Charlotte's Web* (1952), and *The Trumpet of the Swan* (1970), White is also renowned for his elegant style, the principles of which are set out in *The Elements of Style* (1959), his revision of William Strunk, Jr.'s, 1918 handbook for writers. White won many awards in the course of his career, including a special Pulitzer Prize in 1978 and a Presidential Medal of Freedom in 1963. "Democracy," which was first published in *The New Yorker* on July 3, 1943, and reprinted in *The Wild Flag* (1946), is notable for its metaphoric and concrete imagery, which conceals as much as it conveys.

Democracy

1 We received a letter from the Writers' War Board the other day asking for a statement on "The Meaning of Democracy." It is presumably our duty to comply with such a request, and it is certainly our pleasure.

2 Surely the Board knows what democracy is. It is the line that forms on the right. It is the don't in don't shove. It is the hole in the stuffed shirt through which the sawdust slowly trickles; the dent in the high hat. Democracy is the recurrent suspicion that more than half of the people are right more than half of the time. It is the feeling of privacy in the voting booths, the feeling of communion in the libraries, the feeling of vitality everywhere. Democracy is the letter to the editor. Democracy is the score at the beginning of the ninth. It is an idea which hasn't been disproved yet, a song the words of which have not gone bad. It's the mustard on the hot dog and the cream in the rationed coffee. Democracy is a request from a War Board, in the middle of the morning in the middle of a war, wanting to know what democracy is.

BARACK OBAMA

Barack Obama was born 1961 in Hawaii; his black father was from Kenya, his white mother from Kansas. His mother's second husband was Indonesian and his early schooling took place in Jakarta. Obama graduated from the prestigious Punahou Academy in Honolulu before attending Occidental College in Los Angeles, California, and earning a BA in political science from Columbia (1983). He graduated magna cum laude from Harvard Law School (1991), worked in Chicago as a community organizer and civil rights advocate. Obama was elected as a U.S. Senator from Illinois in 2004, and as President of the United States in November 2008. He has published a memoir, *Dreams From My Father: A Story of Race and Inheritance* (1995), the audio version of which won a Grammy. He also wrote *The Audacity of Hope: Thoughts on Reclaiming the American Dream* (2006), a political treatise and meditation on faith and values; and *It Takes a Nation: How Strangers Became Family in the Wake of Hurricane Katrina* (2006), a collection of stories about the volunteers and evacuees during and after the hurricane that devastated New Orleans and the Gulf coast in 2005. Obama, seeking to become the Democratic Party's first African American candidate for President, delivered "To Form a More Perfect Union" on March 18, 2008. This is Obama's extended public response to the history of incendiary racist remarks by his Chicago pastor, the Reverend Jeremiah Wright, Jr. In the spirit of "hate the sin but love the sinner," Obama explains his tolerance of the minister's right to hold these views, even though he himself had already repudiated such opinions. However, by April 30, 2008, the Associated Press reported that Obama "angrily disowned his former pastor and friend of 20 years," saying that Wright's recent comments about race, religion, and the U.S. government were "divisive and destructive" and that Wright was "not the person that I met 20 years ago." Obama called the pastor's appearance a "spectacle" and a "performance," and said it was a "show of disrespect to me" and "an insult to what we've been trying to do in this campaign," which was remarkably free of racism throughout.

To Form a More Perfect Union

"We the people, in order to form a more perfect union." 1

Two hundred and twenty one years ago, in a hall that still stands across the street, a group of men gathered and, with these simple words, launched America's improbable experiment in democracy. Farmers and scholars; statesmen and patriots who had traveled across an ocean to escape tyranny and persecution finally made real their declaration of independence at a Philadelphia convention that lasted through the spring of 1787. 2

The document they produced was eventually signed but ultimately unfinished. It was stained by this nation's original sin of slavery, a question 3

Emmanuel Dunand/Getty Images

This photo shows Senator Barack Obama, Democrat from Illinois and presidential hopeful, standing at his podium on March 18, 2008, delivering the speech, "To Form a More Perfect Union." Try reading this picture from a strictly visual perspective. Comment on body, clothing, grooming, posture, gesture, lights/shadows, flags. Now read it with what you know—about the candidate, about the presidential campaign in March 2008, and about its outcome. How do your own political preferences influence your interpretation of the photograph? Of the speech? Have subsequent events—the campaign, the election results—caused you to reinterpret your original reactions?

that divided the colonies and brought the convention to a stalemate until the founders chose to allow the slave trade to continue for at least twenty more years, and to leave any final resolution to future generations.

4 Of course, the answer to the slavery question was already embedded within our Constitution—a Constitution that had at its very core the ideal of equal citizenship under the law; a Constitution that promised its people liberty, and justice, and a union that could be and should be perfected over time.

5 And yet words on a parchment would not be enough to deliver slaves from bondage, or provide men and women of every color and creed their full rights and obligations as citizens of the United States. What would be needed were Americans in successive generations who were willing to do their part—through protests and struggle, on the streets and in the courts, through a civil war and civil disobedience and always at great risk—to narrow that gap between the promise of our ideals and the reality of their time.

This was one of the tasks we set forth at the beginning of this campaign—to continue the long march of those who came before us, a march for a more just, more equal, more free, more caring and more prosperous America. I chose to run for the presidency at this moment in history because I believe deeply that we cannot solve the challenges of our time unless we solve them together—unless we perfect our union by understanding that we may have different stories, but we hold common hopes; that we may not look the same and we may not have come from the same place, but we all want to move in the same direction—towards a better future for our children and our grandchildren. 6

This belief comes from my unyielding faith in the decency and generosity of the American people. But it also comes from my own American story. 7

I am the son of a black man from Kenya and a white woman from Kansas. I was raised with the help of a white grandfather who survived a Depression to serve in Patton's Army during World War II and a white grandmother who worked on a bomber assembly line at Fort Leavenworth while he was overseas. I've gone to some of the best schools in America and lived in one of the world's poorest nations. I am married to a black American who carries within her the blood of slaves and slaveowners—an inheritance we pass on to our two precious daughters. I have brothers, sisters, nieces, nephews, uncles and cousins, of every race and every hue, scattered across three continents, and for as long as I live, I will never forget that in no other country on Earth is my story even possible. 8

It's a story that hasn't made me the most conventional candidate. But it is a story that has seared into my genetic makeup the idea that this nation is more than the sum of its parts—that out of many, we are truly one. 9

Throughout the first year of this [2008 presidential] campaign, against all predictions to the contrary, we saw how hungry the American people were for this message of unity. Despite the temptation to view my candidacy through a purely racial lens, we won commanding victories in states with some of the whitest populations in the country. In South Carolina, where the Confederate Flag still flies, we built a powerful coalition of African Americans and white Americans. 10

This is not to say that race has not been an issue in the campaign. At various stages in the campaign, some commentators have deemed me either "too black" or "not black enough." We saw racial tensions bubble to the surface during the week before the South Carolina primary. The press has scoured every exit poll for the latest evidence of racial polarization, not just in terms of white and black, but black and brown as well. 11

And yet, it has only been in the last couple of weeks that the discussion of race in this campaign has taken a particularly divisive turn. 12

On one end of the spectrum, we've heard the implication that my candidacy is somehow an exercise in affirmative action; that it's based solely on the desire of wide-eyed liberals to purchase racial reconciliation on the 13 cheap. On the other end, we've heard my former pastor, Reverend Jeremiah Wright, use incendiary language to express views that have the potential not only to widen the racial divide, but views that denigrate both the greatness and the goodness of our nation; that rightly offend white and black alike.

14 I have already condemned, in unequivocal terms, the statements of Reverend Wright that have caused such controversy. For some, nagging questions remain. Did I know him to be an occasionally fierce critic of American domestic and foreign policy? Of course. Did I ever hear him make remarks that could be considered controversial while I sat in church? Yes. Did I strongly disagree with many of his political views? Absolutely—just as I'm sure many of you have heard remarks from your pastors, priests, or rabbis with which you strongly disagreed.

15 But the remarks that have caused this recent firestorm weren't simply controversial. They weren't simply a religious leader's effort to speak out against perceived injustice. Instead, they expressed a profoundly distorted view of this country—a view that sees white racism as endemic, and that elevates what is wrong with America above all that we know is right with America; a view that sees the conflicts in the Middle East as rooted primarily in the actions of stalwart allies like Israel, instead of emanating from the perverse and hateful ideologies of radical Islam.

16 As such, Reverend Wright's comments were not only wrong but divisive, divisive at a time when we need unity; racially charged at a time when we need to come together to solve a set of monumental problems—two wars, a terrorist threat, a falling economy, a chronic health care crisis and potentially devastating climate change; problems that are neither black or white or Latino or Asian, but rather problems that confront us all.

17 Given my background, my politics, and my professed values and ideals, there will no doubt be those for whom my statements of condemnation are not enough. Why associate myself with Reverend Wright in the first place, they may ask? Why not join another church? And I confess that if all that I knew of Reverend Wright were the snippets of those sermons that have run in an endless loop on the television and YouTube, or if Trinity United Church of Christ conformed to the caricatures being peddled by some commentators, there is no doubt that I would react in much the same way.

18 But the truth is, that isn't all that I know of the man. The man I met more than twenty years ago is a man who helped introduce me to my Christian faith, a man who spoke to me about our obligations to love one another; to care for the sick and lift up the poor. He is a man who served his country as a U.S. Marine; who has studied and lectured at some of the finest universities and seminaries in the country, and who for over thirty years led a church that serves the community by doing God's work here on Earth—by housing the homeless, ministering to the needy, providing day care services and scholarships and prison ministries, and reaching out to those suffering from HIV/AIDS.

In my first book, *Dreams From My Father*, I described the experience of my first service at Trinity: 19

> "People began to shout, to rise from their seats and clap and cry out, a forceful wind carrying the reverend's voice up into the rafters. . . . And in that single note—hope!—I heard something else; at the foot of that cross, inside the thousands of churches across the city, I imagined the stories of ordinary black people merging with the stories of David and Goliath, Moses and Pharaoh, the Christians in the lion's den, Ezekiel's field of dry bones. Those stories—of survival, and freedom, and hope—became our story, my story; the blood that had spilled was our blood, the tears our tears; until this black church, on this bright day, seemed once more a vessel carrying the story of a people into future generations and into a larger world. Our trials and triumphs became at once unique and universal, black and more than black; in chronicling our journey, the stories and songs gave us a means to reclaim memories that we didn't need to feel shame about . . . memories that all people might study and cherish—and with which we could start to rebuild."

That has been my experience at Trinity. Like other predominantly black churches across the country, Trinity embodies the black community in its entirety—the doctor and the welfare mom, the model student and the former gang-banger. Like other black churches, Trinity's services are full of raucous laughter and sometimes bawdy humor. They are full of dancing, clapping, screaming and shouting that may seem jarring to the untrained ear. The church contains in full the kindness and cruelty, the fierce intelligence and the shocking ignorance, the struggles and successes, the love and yes, the bitterness and bias that make up the black experience in America. 20

And this helps explain, perhaps, my relationship with Reverend Wright. As imperfect as he may be, he has been like family to me. He strengthened my faith, officiated my wedding, and baptized my children. Not once in my conversations with him have I heard him talk about any ethnic group in derogatory terms, or treat whites with whom he interacted with anything but courtesy and respect. He contains within him the contradictions—the good and the bad—of the community that he has served diligently for so many years. 21

I can no more disown him than I can disown the black community. I can no more disown him than I can my white grandmother—a woman who helped raise me, a woman who sacrificed again and again for me, a woman who loves me as much as she loves anything in this world, but a woman who once confessed her fear of black men who passed by her on the street, and who on more than one occasion has uttered racial or ethnic stereotypes that made me cringe. 22

23 These people are a part of me. And they are a part of America, this country that I love.

24 Some will see this as an attempt to justify or excuse comments that are simply inexcusable. I can assure you it is not. I suppose the politically safe thing would be to move on from this episode and just hope that it fades into the woodwork. We can dismiss Reverend Wright as a crank or a demagogue, just as some have dismissed Geraldine Ferraro, in the aftermath of her recent statements, as harboring some deep-seated racial bias.

25 But race is an issue that I believe this nation cannot afford to ignore right now. We would be making the same mistake that Reverend Wright made in his offending sermons about America—to simplify and stereotype and amplify the negative to the point that it distorts reality.

26 The fact is that the comments that have been made and the issues that have surfaced over the last few weeks reflect the complexities of race in this country that we've never really worked through—a part of our union that we have yet to perfect. And if we walk away now, if we simply retreat into our respective corners, we will never be able to come together and solve challenges like health care, or education, or the need to find good jobs for every American.

27 Understanding this reality requires a reminder of how we arrived at this point. As William Faulkner once wrote, "The past isn't dead and buried. In fact, it isn't even past." We do not need to recite here the history of racial injustice in this country. But we do need to remind ourselves that so many of the disparities that exist in the African-American community today can be directly traced to inequalities passed on from an earlier generation that suffered under the brutal legacy of slavery and Jim Crow.

28 Segregated schools were, and are, inferior schools; we still haven't fixed them, fifty years after Brown v. Board of Education, and the inferior education they provided, then and now, helps explain the pervasive achievement gap between today's black and white students.

29 Legalized discrimination—where blacks were prevented, often through violence, from owning property, or loans were not granted to African-American business owners, or black homeowners could not access FHA mortgages, or blacks were excluded from unions, or the police force, or fire departments—meant that black families could not amass any meaningful wealth to bequeath to future generations. That history helps explain the wealth and income gap between black and white, and the concentrated pockets of poverty that persist in so many of today's urban and rural communities.

30 A lack of economic opportunity among black men, and the shame and frustration that came from not being able to provide for one's family, contributed to the erosion of black families—a problem that welfare policies for many years may have worsened. And the lack of basic services in so many urban black neighborhoods—parks for kids to play in, police walking the beat, regular garbage pick-up and building code

enforcement—all helped create a cycle of violence, blight and neglect that continues to haunt us.

This is the reality in which Reverend Wright and other African-Americans of his generation grew up. They came of age in the late '50s and early '60s, a time when segregation was still the law of the land and opportunity was systematically constricted. What's remarkable is not how many failed in the face of discrimination, but rather how many men and women overcame the odds; how many were able to make a way out of no way for those like me who would come after them. 31

But for all those who scratched and clawed their way to get a piece of the American Dream, there were many who didn't make it—those who were ultimately defeated, in one way or another, by discrimination. That legacy of defeat was passed on to future generations—those young men and increasingly young women who we see standing on street corners or languishing in our prisons, without hope or prospects for the future. Even for those blacks who did make it, questions of race, and racism, continue to define their worldview in fundamental ways. For the men and women of Reverend Wright's generation, the memories of humiliation and doubt and fear have not gone away; nor has the anger and the bitterness of those years. That anger may not get expressed in public, in front of white co-workers or white friends. But it does find voice in the barbershop or around the kitchen table. At times, that anger is exploited by politicians, to gin up votes along racial lines, or to make up for a politician's own failings. 32

And occasionally it finds voice in the church on Sunday morning, in the pulpit and in the pews. The fact that so many people are surprised to hear that anger in some of Reverend Wright's sermons simply reminds us of the old truism that the most segregated hour in American life occurs on Sunday morning. That anger is not always productive; indeed, all too often it distracts attention from solving real problems; it keeps us from squarely facing our own complicity in our condition, and prevents the African-American community from forging the alliances it needs to bring about real change. But the anger is real; it is powerful; and to simply wish it away, to condemn it without understanding its roots, only serves to widen the chasm of misunderstanding that exists between the races. 33

In fact, a similar anger exists within segments of the white community. Most working- and middle-class white Americans don't feel that they have been particularly privileged by their race. Their experience is the immigrant experience—as far as they're concerned, no one's handed them anything, they've built it from scratch. They've worked hard all their lives, many times only to see their jobs shipped overseas or their pension dumped after a lifetime of labor. They are anxious about their futures, and feel their dreams slipping away; in an era of stagnant wages and global competition, opportunity comes to be seen as a zero sum game, in which your dreams come at my expense. So when they are told to bus their children to a school across town; when they hear that an 34

African-American is getting an advantage in landing a good job or a spot in a good college because of an injustice that they themselves never committed; when they're told that their fears about crime in urban neighborhoods are somehow prejudiced, resentment builds over time.

35 Like the anger within the black community, these resentments aren't always expressed in polite company. But they have helped shape the political landscape for at least a generation. Anger over welfare and affirmative action helped forge the Reagan Coalition. Politicians routinely exploited fears of crime for their own electoral ends. Talk show hosts and conservative commentators built entire careers unmasking bogus claims of racism while dismissing legitimate discussions of racial injustice and inequality as mere political correctness or reverse racism.

36 Just as black anger often proved counterproductive, so have these white resentments distracted attention from the real culprits of the middle class squeeze—a corporate culture rife with inside dealing, questionable accounting practices, and short-term greed; a Washington dominated by lobbyists and special interests; economic policies that favor the few over the many. And yet, to wish away the resentments of white Americans, to label them as misguided or even racist, without recognizing they are grounded in legitimate concerns—this too widens the racial divide and blocks the path to understanding.

37 This is where we are right now. It's a racial stalemate we've been stuck in for years. Contrary to the claims of some of my critics, black and white, I have never been so naive as to believe that we can get beyond our racial divisions in a single election cycle, or with a single candidacy—particularly a candidacy as imperfect as my own.

38 But I have asserted a firm conviction—a conviction rooted in my faith in God and my faith in the American people—that working together we can move beyond some of our old racial wounds, and that in fact we have no choice if we are to continue on the path of a more perfect union.

39 For the African-American community, that path means embracing the burdens of our past without becoming victims of our past. It means continuing to insist on a full measure of justice in every aspect of American life. But it also means binding our particular grievances—for better health care, and better schools, and better jobs—to the larger aspirations of all Americans—the white woman struggling to break the glass ceiling, the white man who's been laid off, the immigrant trying to feed his family. And it means taking full responsibility for our own lives—by demanding more from our fathers, and spending more time with our children, and reading to them, and teaching them that while they may face challenges and discrimination in their own lives, they must never succumb to despair or cynicism; they must always believe that they can write their own destiny.

40 Ironically, this quintessentially American—and yes, conservative—notion of self-help found frequent expression in Reverend Wright's

sermons. But what my former pastor too often failed to understand is that embarking on a program of self-help also requires a belief that society can change.

The profound mistake of Reverend Wright's sermons is not that he spoke about racism in our society. It's that he spoke as if our society was static; as if no progress has been made; as if this country—a country that has made it possible for one of his own members to run for the highest office in the land and build a coalition of white and black; Latino and Asian, rich and poor, young and old—is still irrevocably bound to a tragic past. But what we know—what we have seen—is that America can change. That is true genius of this nation. What we have already achieved gives us hope—the audacity to hope—for what we can and must achieve tomorrow. 41

In the white community, the path to a more perfect union means acknowledging that what ails the African-American community does not just exist in the minds of black people; that the legacy of discrimination—and current incidents of discrimination, while less overt than in the past—are real and must be addressed. Not just with words, but with deeds—by investing in our schools and our communities; by enforcing our civil rights laws and ensuring fairness in our criminal justice system; by providing this generation with ladders of opportunity that were unavailable for previous generations. It requires all Americans to realize that your dreams do not have to come at the expense of my dreams; that investing in the health, welfare, and education of black and brown and white children will ultimately help all of America prosper. 42

In the end, then, what is called for is nothing more, and nothing less, than what all the world's great religions demand—that we do unto others as we would have them do unto us. Let us be our brother's keeper, Scripture tells us. Let us be our sister's keeper. Let us find that common stake we all have in one another, and let our politics reflect that spirit as well. 43

For we have a choice in this country. We can accept a politics that breeds division, and conflict, and cynicism. We can tackle race only as spectacle—as we did in the O. J. trial—or in the wake of tragedy, as we did in the aftermath of Katrina, or as fodder for the nightly news. We can play Reverend Wright's sermons on every channel, every day and talk about them from now until the election, and make the only question in this campaign whether or not the American people think that I somehow believe or sympathize with his most offensive words. We can pounce on some gaffe by a Hillary supporter as evidence that she's playing the race card, or we can speculate on whether white men will all flock to John McCain in the general election regardless of his policies. 44

We can do that. 45

But if we do, I can tell you that in the next election, we'll be talking about some other distraction. And then another one. And then another one. And nothing will change. 46

47 That is one option. Or, at this moment, in this election, we can come together and say, "Not this time." This time we want to talk about the crumbling schools that are stealing the future of black children and white children and Asian children and Hispanic children and Native American children. This time we want to reject the cynicism that tells us that these kids can't learn; that those kids who don't look like us are somebody else's problem. The children of America are not those kids, they are our kids, and we will not let them fall behind in a 21st-century economy. Not this time.

48 This time we want to talk about how the lines in the emergency room are filled with whites and blacks and Hispanics who do not have health care; who don't have the power on their own to overcome the special interests in Washington, but who can take them on if we do it together.

49 This time we want to talk about the shuttered mills that once provided a decent life for men and women of every race, and the homes for sale that once belonged to Americans from every religion, every region, every walk of life. This time we want to talk about the fact that the real problem is not that someone who doesn't look like you might take your job; it's that the corporation you work for will ship it overseas for nothing more than a profit.

50 This time we want to talk about the men and women of every color and creed who serve together, and fight together, and bleed together under the same proud flag. We want to talk about how to bring them home from a war that never should've been authorized and never should've been waged, and we want to talk about how we'll show our patriotism by caring for them, and their families, and giving them the benefits they have earned.

51 I would not be running for president if I didn't believe with all my heart that this is what the vast majority of Americans want for this country. This union may never be perfect, but generation after generation has shown that it can always be perfected. And today, whenever I find myself feeling doubtful or cynical about this possibility, what gives me the most hope is the next generation—the young people whose attitudes and beliefs and openness to change have already made history in this election.

52 There is one story in particularly that I'd like to leave you with today—a story I told when I had the great honor of speaking on Dr. King's birthday at his home church, Ebenezer Baptist, in Atlanta.

53 There is a young, 23-year-old white woman named Ashley Baia who organized for our campaign in Florence, South Carolina. She had been working to organize a mostly African-American community since the beginning of this campaign, and one day she was at a roundtable discussion where everyone went around telling their story and why they were there.

54 And Ashley said that when she was nine years old, her mother got cancer. And because she had to miss days of work, she was let go and lost

her health care. They had to file for bankruptcy, and that's when Ashley decided that she had to do something to help her mom.

55 She knew that food was one of their most expensive costs, and so Ashley convinced her mother that what she really liked and really wanted to eat more than anything else was mustard and relish sandwiches. Because that was the cheapest way to eat.

56 She did this for a year until her mom got better, and she told everyone at the roundtable that the reason she joined our campaign was so that she could help the millions of other children in the country who want and need to help their parents too.

57 Now Ashley might have made a different choice. Perhaps somebody told her along the way that the source of her mother's problems were blacks who were on welfare and too lazy to work, or Hispanics who were coming into the country illegally. But she didn't. She sought out allies in her fight against injustice.

58 Anyway, Ashley finishes her story and then goes around the room and asks everyone else why they're supporting the campaign. They all have different stories and reasons. Many bring up a specific issue. And finally they come to this elderly black man who's been sitting there quietly the entire time. And Ashley asks him why he's there. And he does not bring up a specific issue. He does not say health care or the economy. He does not say education or the war. He does not say that he was there because of Barack Obama. He simply says to everyone in the room, "I am here because of Ashley."

59 "I'm here because of Ashley." By itself, that single moment of recognition between that young white girl and that old black man is not enough. It is not enough to give health care to the sick, or jobs to the jobless, or education to our children.

60 But it is where we start. It is where our union grows stronger. And as so many generations have come to realize over the course of the 221 years since a band of patriots signed that document in Philadelphia, that is where the perfection begins.

Content

1. What is the "gap between the promise of our ideals and the reality of their time" (¶ 5)? Why does Obama see this gap as the defining characteristic of American history and culture?
2. How does Obama characterize the media's role and activities during his campaign and more generally (¶s 11–17, 44)? Why does he compare the media's coverage of Reverend Wright's remarks with the "spectacle" of the O. J. Simpson trial and with the discussion of race following Hurricane Katrina (¶ 44)?
3. According to Obama, what role does the church play in the black community (¶s 19–20, 33)? How does his discussion explain his relationship with Reverend Wright (¶s 21–24)? Why does Obama compare his relationship with Wright to that with his white grandmother (¶ 22)?

4. What is, according to Obama, the "legacy of slavery and Jim Crow" (¶s 27–32)? How have segregation and discrimination impacted the African-American community?

5. What are the sources, in Obama's view, of racial hostility in the United States (¶s 33–35)? Which problems does he believe exacerbate racial tension (¶ 36)?

6. Obama refers to the Reagan Coalition (¶ 35), the name given to white, socially conservative voters who left the Democratic party to vote for Ronald Reagan in 1980 and 1984 and George H. W. Bush in 1988. How, according to Obama, has this part of American political history contributed to a "racial stalemate" (¶ 37)? Why does he mention "conservative commentators" at this point in his speech (¶ 35)?

7. How does Obama propose a way forward (¶s 39, 42)? What specific images and values does he allude to in his appeal for national unity (¶s 39–40, 43, 47)? What political issues does he raise in conjunction with that appeal (¶s 42, 47–50)?

8. E. B. White's "Democracy" (558) was written for the Writers' War Board, a government-subsidized organization established shortly after the bombing of Pearl Harbor on December 7, 1941. The WWB recruited writers to publish articles, cartoons, and poetry in newspapers across the country supporting the war effort. How does this knowledge influence your reading of "Democracy"? Why might White have been recruited (see his biographical headnote)? Can you identify an overriding principle in White's metaphorical expression of democracy? Why does White use the first person plural?

Strategies/Structures/Language

9. Obama opens his speech with a quote from the *Preamble* to *The United States Constitution* and his first paragraph looks back in time ("Two hundred and twenty one years ago") in a manner reminiscent of President Abraham Lincoln's "The Gettysburg Address" (519). How do these twin allusions set the stage for his discussion of the themes of diversity, commonality, and the ongoing struggle for justice? How do they support his argument that "out of many, we are truly one" (¶ 9)?

10. ***Mixed Modes.*** Obama's speech begins with the idea of unfinished democracy and ends with a narrative of interracial communion. Why might this structure appeal to his audience? How do other elements of his speech create a sense of conflict that he then resolves? How, for example, does Obama's self-portrait (¶s 7–9) imply that he is the "everyman" in an historical drama? Who, or what, are the sources of conflict hindering the story's resolution? How does his discussion of the media, Reverend Wright, the black church, and the history of racial discrimination build to a climax in paragraphs 37 and 38? Why does Obama end where he began, with "a band of patriots" in Philadelphia (¶ 60)?

11. Why does Obama summarize the controversy over Reverend Wright's "incendiary language" (¶ 13) in the form of questions which he then answers (¶s 14, 17)? How does this rhetorical device give the speech momentum? How do such questions allow him to control the terms of the debate?

For Writing

12. Obama characterizes American democracy as an "improbable experiment" (¶ 2) and a "path to a more perfect union" (¶ 42). Compare this metaphorical description with E. B. White's characterization of democracy. Which elements

of "Democracy" imply that change is fundamental to our system of government? What portrait of America's populace does White's description paint? What assumptions does he make about, for example, who can vote and use libraries (¶ 2)?

13. ***Journal Writing.*** What local, state, or national political issues—such as education, health care, global warming, genetic testing and gene manipulation, gay marriage, or America's relations with Iraq—do you believe will define your future and that of your children? Explore the reasons for your voting decisions. Did you vote in the last presidential election? If not, why not? If so, was your vote based on specific issues, the character of the candidate, party loyalty, and/or other reasons?

14. Based on your journal writing, choose an issue of national policy— concerning war, education, health care, the economy—that affects your life in some specific way. Write an essay on why the issue is important to you.

15. ***Dialogues.*** Obama argues that his campaign seeks "to continue the long march of those who came before us" (¶ 6). Find other examples of metaphors and imagery that link Obama to political activists such as Frederick Douglass (89–93), Martin Luther King, Jr. (456–70), and Sojourner Truth (521). How do such connections support the idea of a more just future? How do they allow Obama to acknowledge past injustices without intensifying racial antagonism?

BILL McKIBBEN

After graduating from Harvard in 1982, Bill McKibben (born 1960) started at the top, becoming a staff writer, and later an editor, for *The New Yorker*. Five years later he turned to writing full time, married, moved to upstate New York, and had a child. His books, such as *The End of Nature* (1989); *Hope, Human and Wild: True Stories of Living Lightly on the Earth* (1995); and *Maybe One: A Case for Smaller Families* (1998), concentrate on "the effects of rampant consumerism on the future of the global ecosystem." All of his books, says commentator Michael Coffey, "pursue the same theme . . . what do we consume, why do we consume it, and what are the consequences?" Answering his own question, McKibben replies, "What I've learned so far is that what is sound and elegant and civilized and respectful of community is also environmentally benign."

Enough: Staying Human in an Engineered Age (2003) is about the moral ramifications of biological engineering—the topic of "Designer Genes," as well. This essay, first published in *Orion* in 2003, was reprinted in the book *The Best American Spiritual Writing* in 2004. Here McKibben offers a chilling, clearheaded analysis of what could happen if aspiring (and wealthy) parents resort to genetic engineering to create new and ever-newer models of superior children, a "biological arms race." Each new model might seem better than its predecessor in intelligence, say, or appearance or strength, and every one might appear superior to the homegrown babies who receive their DNA naturally. Be careful what you wish for, warns McKibben. "'Suppose parents could add thirty points to their child's IQ? Wouldn't you want to do it?' . . . Deciding not to soup them up . . . well, it could come to seem like child abuse".

Designer Genes

1 I grew up in a household where we were very suspicious of dented cans. Dented cans were, according to my mother, a well-established gateway to botulism, and botulism was a bad thing, worse than swimming immediately after lunch. It was one of those bad things measured in extinctions, as in "three tablespoons of botulism toxin could theoretically kill every human on Earth." Or something like that.

2 So I refused to believe the early reports, a few years back, that socialites had begun injecting dilute strains of the toxin into their brows in an effort to temporarily remove the vertical furrow that appears between one's eyes as one ages. It sounded like a Monty Python routine, some clinic where they daubed your soles with plague germs to combat athlete's foot. But I was wrong to doubt. As the world now knows, Botox has become, in a few short years, a staple weapon in the cosmetic arsenal—so prevalent that, in the words of one writer, "it is now rare in certain social enclaves to see a woman over the age of thirty-five with the ability to look angry." With their facial muscles essentially paralyzed, actresses are having trouble acting; since the treatment requires periodic booster shots, doctors "warn that you could marry a woman (or a man) with a flawlessly even face and wind up with someone who four months later looks like a Shar-Pei." But never mind—now you can get Botoxed in strip mall storefronts and at cocktail parties.

3 People, in other words, will do fairly far out things for less than pressing causes. And more so all the time: public approval of "aesthetic surgery" has grown 50 percent in the United States in the last decade. But why stop there? Once you accept the idea that our bodies are essentially plastic and that it's okay to manipulate that plastic, there's no reason to think that consumers would balk because "genes" were involved instead of, say, "toxins." Especially since genetic engineering would not promote your own vanity, but instead be sold as a boon to your child.

4 The vision of genetic engineers is to do to humans what we have already done to salmon and wheat, pine trees and tomatoes. That is, to make them *better* in some way; to delete, modify, or add genes in developing embryos so that the cells of the resulting person will produce proteins that make them taller and more muscular, or smarter and less aggressive, maybe handsome and possibly straight. Even happy. As early as 1993, a March of Dimes poll found that 43 percent of Americans would engage in genetic engineering "simply to enhance their children's looks or intelligence."

5 Ethical guidelines promulgated by the scientific oversight boards so far prohibit actual attempts at human genetic engineering, but researchers have walked right to the line, maybe even stuck their toes a trifle over. In the spring of 2001, for instance, a fertility clinic in New Jersey

impregnated fifteen women with embryos fashioned from their own eggs, their partner's sperm, and a small portion of an egg donated by a second woman. The procedure was designed to work around defects in the would-be mother's egg—but in at least two of the cases, tests showed the resulting babies carried genetic material from all three "parents."

And so the genetic modification of humans is not only possible, 6
it's coming fast; a mix of technical progress and shifting mood means it could easily happen in the next few years. Consider what happened with plants. A decade ago, university research farms were growing small plots of genetically modified grain and vegetables. Sometimes activists who didn't like what they were doing would come and rip the plants up, one by one. Then, all of a sudden in the mid-1990s, before anyone had paid any real attention, farmers had planted half the corn and soybean fields in America with transgenic seed.

Every time you turn your back this technology creeps a little closer. 7
Gallops, actually, growing and spreading as fast as the internet. One moment you've sort of heard of it; the next moment it's everywhere. But we haven't done it yet. For the moment we remain, if barely, a fully human species. And so we have time yet to consider, to decide, to act. This is arguably the biggest decision humans will ever make.

Right up until this decade, the genes that humans carried in their bodies 8
were exclusively the result of chance—of how the genes of the sperm and the egg, the father and the mother, combined. The only way you could intervene in the process was by choosing who you would mate with—and that was as much wishful thinking as anything else, as generation upon generation of surprised parents have discovered.

But that is changing. We now know two different methods to change 9
human genes. The first, and less controversial, is called somatic gene therapy. Somatic gene therapy begins with an existing individual—someone with, say, cystic fibrosis. Researchers try to deliver new, modified genes to some of her cells, usually by putting the genes aboard viruses they inject into the patient, hoping that the viruses will infect the cells and thereby transmit the genes. Somatic gene therapy is, in other words, much like medicine. You take an existing patient with an existing condition, and you in essence try and convince her cells to manufacture the medicine she needs.

Germline genetic engineering, on the other hand, is something very 10
novel indeed. "Germ" here refers not to microbes, but to the egg and sperm cells, the germ cells of the human being. Scientists intent on genetic engineering would probably start with a fertilized embryo a week or so old. They would tease apart the cells of that embryo, and then, selecting one, they would add to, delete, or modify some of its genes. They could also insert artificial chromosomes containing predesigned genes. They would then take the cell, place it inside an egg whose nucleus had been removed, and implant the resulting new embryo inside a woman.

The embryo would, if all went according to plan, grow into a genetically engineered child. His genes would be pushing out proteins to meet the particular choices made by his parents and by the companies and clinicians they were buying the genes from. Instead of coming solely from the combination of his parents, and thus the combination of their parents, and so on back through time, those genes could come from any other person, or any other plant or animal, or out of the thin blue sky. And once implanted, they will pass to his children and on into time.

11 But all this work will require one large change in our current way of doing business. Instead of making babies by making love, we will have to move conception to the laboratory. You need to have the embryo out there where you can work on it—to make the necessary copies, try to add or delete genes, and then implant the one that seems likely to turn out best. Gregory Stock, a researcher at the University of California and an apostle of the new genetic technologies, says that "the union of egg and sperm from two individuals . . . would be too unpredictable with intercourse." And once you've got the embryo out on the lab bench, gravity disappears altogether. "Ultimately, says Michael West, CEO of Advanced Cell Technology, the firm furthest out on the cutting edge of these technologies, "the dream of biologists is to have the sequence of DNA, the programming code of life, and to be able to edit it the way you can a document on a word processor."

12 Does it sound far-fetched? We began doing it with animals (mice) in 1978, and we've managed the trick with most of the obvious mammals, except one. Some of the first germline interventions might be semimedical. You might, say some advocates, start by improving "visual and auditory acuity," first to eliminate nearsightedness or prevent deafness, then to "improve artistic potential." But why stop there? "If something has evolved elsewhere, then it is possible for us to determine its genetic basis and transfer it into the human genome," says Princeton geneticist Lee Silver—just as we have stuck flounder genes into strawberries to keep them from freezing, and jellyfish genes into rabbits and monkeys to make them glow in the dark.

13 But would we actually do this? Is there any real need to raise these questions as more than curiosities, or will the schemes simply fade away on their own, ignored by the parents who are their necessary consumers?

14 Anyone who has entered a baby supply store in the last few years knows that even the soberest parents can be counted on to spend virtually unlimited sums in pursuit of successful offspring. What if the "Baby Einstein" video series, which immerses "learning-enabled" babies in English, Spanish, Japanese, Hebrew, German, Russian, and French, could be bolstered with a little gene tweaking to improve memory? What if the Wombsongs prenatal music system, piping in Brahms to your waiting fetus, could be supplemented with an auditory upgrade? One sociologist told the *New York Times* we'd crossed the line from parenting to "product

development," and even if that remark is truer in Manhattan than elsewhere, it's not hard to imagine what such attitudes will mean across the affluent world.

15 Here's one small example. In the 1980s, two drug companies were awarded patents to market human growth hormone to the few thousand American children suffering from dwarfism. The PDA thought the market would be very small, so HGH was given "orphan drug status," a series of special market advantages designed to reward the manufacturers for taking on such an unattractive business. But within a few years, HGH had become one of the largest selling drugs in the country, with half a billion dollars in sales. This was not because there'd been a sharp increase in the number of dwarves, but because there'd been a sharp increase in the number of parents who wanted to make their slightly short children taller. Before long the drug companies were arguing that the children in the bottom 5 percent of their normal height range were in fact in need of three to five shots a week of HGH. Take eleven-year-old Marco Oriti. At four foot one, he was about four inches shorter than average, and projected to eventually top out at five foot four. This was enough to convince his parents to start on a six-day-a-week HGH regimen, which will cost them $150,000 over the next four years. "You want to give your child the edge no matter what," said his mother.

16 A few of the would-be parents out on the current cutting edge of the reproduction revolution—those who need to obtain sperm or eggs for in vitro fertilization—exhibit similar zeal. Ads started appearing in Ivy League college newspapers a few years ago: couples were willing to pay $50,000 for an egg, provided the donor was at least five feet, ten inches tall, white, and had scored 1400 on her SATs. There is, in other words, a market just waiting for the first clinic with a catalogue of germline modifications, a market that two California artists proved when they opened a small boutique, Gene Genies Worldwide, in a trendy part of Pasadena. Tran Kim-Trang and Karl Mihail wanted to get people thinking more deeply about these emerging technologies, so they outfitted their store with petrI dishes and models of the double helix and printed up brochures highlighting traits with genetic links: creativity, extroversion, thrill-seeking criminality. When they opened the doors, they found people ready to shell out for designer families (one man insisted he wanted the survival ability of a cockroach). The "store" was meant to be ironic, but the irony was lost on a culture so deeply consumeristic that this land of manipulation seems like the obvious next step. "Generally, people refused to believe this store was an art project," says Tran. And why not? The next store in the mall could easily have been a Botox salon.

17 But say you're not ready. Say you're perfectly happy with the prospect of a child who shares the unmodified genes of you and your partner. Say you think that manipulating the DNA of your child might be dangerous, or presumptuous, or icky? How long will you be able to

hold that line if the procedure begins to spread among your neighbors? Maybe not so long as you think. If germline manipulation actually does begin, it seems likely to set off a kind of biological arms race. "Suppose parents could add thirty points to their child's IQ?" asks MIT economist Lester Thurow. "Wouldn't you want to do it? And if you don't, your child will be the stupidest in the neighborhood." That's precisely what it might feel like to be the parent facing the choice. Individual competition more or less defines the society we've built, and in that context love can almost be defined as giving your kids what they need to make their way in the world. Deciding not to soup them up . . . well, it could come to seem like child abuse.

18 Of course, the problem about arms races is that you never really get anywhere. If everyone's adding thirty IQ points, then having an IQ of one hundred fifty won't get you any closer to Stanford than you were at the outset. The very first athlete engineered to use twice as much oxygen as the next guy will be unbeatable in the Tour de France—but in no time he'll merely be the new standard. You'll have to do what he did to be in the race, but your upgrades won't put you ahead, merely back on a level playing field. You might be able to argue that society as a whole was helped, because there was more total brainpower at work, but your kid won't be any closer to the top of the pack. All you'll be able to do is guarantee she won't be left hopelessly far behind.

19 In fact, the arms race problem has an extra ironic twist when it comes to genetic manipulation. The United States and the Soviet Union could, and did, keep adding new weapons to their arsenals over the decades. But with germline manipulation, you get only one shot; the extra chromosome you stick in your kid when he's born is the one he carries throughout his life. So let's say baby Sophie has a state-of-the-art gene job: her parents paid for the proteins discovered by, say, 2005 that on average yield ten extra IQ points. By the time Sophie is five, though, scientists will doubtless have discovered ten more genes linked to intelligence. Now anyone with a platinum card can get twenty IQ points, not to mention a memory boost and a permanent wrinkle-free brow. So by the time Sophie is twenty-five and in the job market, she's already more or less obsolete—the kids coming out of college plainly just have better hardware.

20 "For all his billions, Bill Gates could not have purchased a single genetic enhancement for his son Rory John," writes Gregory Stock at the University of California. "And you can bet that any enhancements a billion dollars can buy Rory's child in 2030 will seem crude alongside those available for modest sums in 2060." It's not, he adds, "so different from upgraded software. You'll want the new release."

21 The vision of one's child as a nearly useless copy of Windows 95 should make parents fight like hell to make sure we never get started down this path. But the vision gets lost easily in the gushing excitement about "improving" the opportunities for our kids.

Beginning the hour my daughter came home from the hospital, I spent 22
part of every day with her in the woods out back, showing her trees and ferns and chipmunks and frogs. One of her very first words was "birch," and you couldn't have asked for a prouder papa. She got her middle name from the mountain we see out the window; for her fifth birthday she got her own child-sized canoe; her school wardrobe may not be relentlessly up-to-date, but she's never lacked for hiking boots. As I write these words, she's spending her first summer at sleepaway camp, one we chose because the kids sleep in tents and spend days in the mountains. All of which is to say that I have done everything in my power to try to mold her into a lover of the natural world. That is where my deepest satisfactions lie, and I want the same for her. It seems benign enough, but it has its drawbacks; it means less time and money and energy for trips to the city and music lessons and so forth. As time goes on and she develops stronger opinions of her own, I yield more and more, but I keep trying to stack the deck, to nudge her in the direction that's meant something to me. On a Saturday morning, when the question comes up of what to do, the very first words out of my mouth always involve yet another hike. I can't help myself.

In other words, we already "engineer" our offspring in some sense 23
of the word: we do our best, and often our worst, to steer them in particular directions. And our worst can be pretty bad. We all know people whose lives were blighted trying to meet the expectations of their parents. We've all seen the crazed devotion to getting kids into the right schools, the right professions, the right income brackets. Parents try to pass down their prejudices, their politics, their attitude toward the world ("we've got to toughen that kid up—he's going to get walked all over"). There are fathers who start teaching the curveball at the age of four, and sons made to feel worthless if they don't make the Little League traveling team. People move house so that their kids can grow up with the right band of schoolmates. They threaten to disown them for marrying African Americans, or for not marrying African Americans. No dictator anywhere has ever tried to rule his subjects with as much attention to detail as the average modern parent.

Why not take this just one small step further? Why not engineer chil- 24
dren to up the odds that all that nudging will stick? In the words of Lee Silver, a Princeton geneticist, "Why not seize this power? Why not control what has been left to chance in the past? Indeed, we control all other aspects of our children's lives and identities through powerful social and environmental influences. . . . On what basis can we reject positive genetic influences on a person's essence when we accept the rights of parents to benefit their children in every other way?" If you can buy your kid three years at Deerfield, four at Harvard, and three more at Harvard Law, why shouldn't you be able to turbocharge his IQ a bit?

But most likely the answer has already occurred to you as well. 25
Because you know plenty of people who managed to rebel successfully

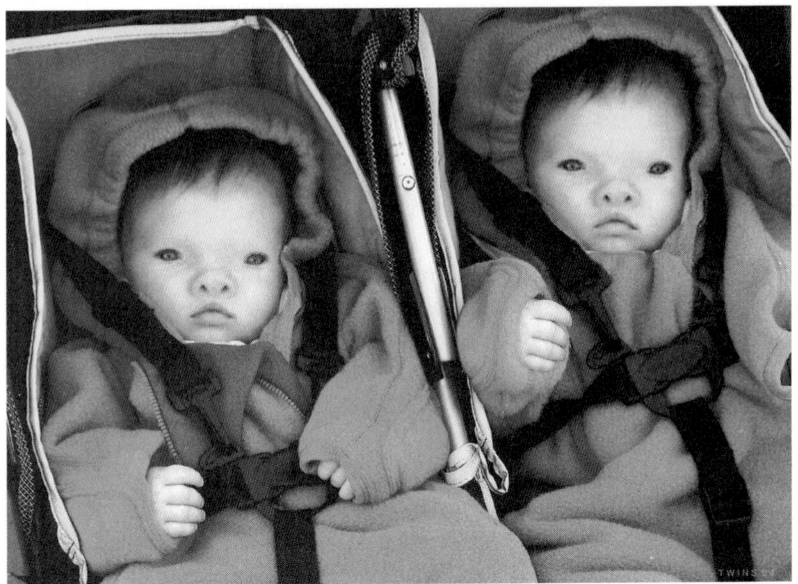

© Daniel Lee

Twins, particularly identical twins, are special, as Jenny Spinner reminds us in "Together in the Old Square Print, 1976" (300–01), capable of having a unique relationship and intimate understanding not shared with others who lack this common genetic heritage. Explain some of the advantages—and possible disadvantages—of such a relationship. If such twins were conceived as the result of in vitro fertilization or another method of artificial reproduction, does the method of conception affect your answer? What differences—ethical and relational—exist between natural-born twins and human clones? Now, look again at this picture, very closely. What do the twins resemble? If you sense a resemblance to animals, you are "reading" this photo accurately, for it is composed of manipulated animal images. Does this knowledge affect your answers to any of the above questions? What statement does the manipulated photo make about the subject, which is no longer twins, but cloning?

against whatever agenda their parents laid out for them, or who took that agenda and bent it to fit their own particular personality. In our society that's often what growing up is all about—the sometimes excruciatingly difficult, frequently liberating break with the expectations of your parents. The decision to join the Peace Corps (or, the decision to leave the commune where you grew up and go to business school). The discovery that you were happiest davening in an Orthodox shul three hours a day, much to the consternation of your good suburban parents who almost always made it to Yom Kippur services; the decision that, much as you respected the Southern Baptist piety of your parents, the Bible won't be your watchword.

26 Without the grounding offered by tradition, the search for the "authentic you" can be hard; our generations contain the first people who routinely shop religions, for instance. But the sometimes poignant

difficulty of finding yourself merely underscores how essential it is. Silver says the costs of germline engineering and a college education might be roughly comparable; in both cases, he goes on, the point is to "increase the chances the child will become wiser in some way, and better able to achieve success and happiness." But that's half the story, at best. College is where you go to be exposed to a thousand new influences, ideas that should be able to take you in almost any direction. It's where you go to get out from under your parents' thumb, to find out that you actually don't have to go to law school if you don't want to. As often as not, the harder parents try to wrench their kids in one direction, the harder those kids eventually fight to determine their own destiny. I am as prepared as I can be for the possibility—the probability—that Sophie will decide she wants to live her life in the concrete heart of Manhattan. It's her life (and perhaps her kids will have a secret desire to come wander in the woods with me).

We try to shape the lives of our kids—to "improve" their lives, as we would measure improvement—but our gravity is usually weak enough that kids can break out of it if and when they need to. (When it isn't, when parents manage to bend their children to the point of breaking, we think of them as monstrous.) "Many of the most creative and valuable human lives are the result of particularly difficult struggles" against expectation and influence, writes the legal scholar Martha Nussbaum. 27

That's not how a genetic engineer thinks of his product. He works to ensure absolute success. Last spring an IsraelI researcher announced that he had managed to produce a featherless chicken. This constituted an improvement, to his mind, because "it will be cheaper to produce since its lack of feathers means there is no need to pluck it before it hits the shelves." Also, poultry farmers would no longer have to ventilate their vast barns to keep their birds from overheating. "Feathers are a waste," the scientist explained. "The chickens are using feed to produce something that has to be dumped, and the farmers have to waste electricity to overcome that fact." Now, that engineer was not trying to influence his chickens to shed their feathers because they'd be happier and the farmer would be happier and everyone would be happier. He was inserting a gene that created a protein that made good and certain they would not be producing feathers. Just substitute, say, an even temperament for feathers, and you'll know what the human engineers envision. 28

"With reprogenetics," writes Lee Silver, "parents can gain *complete control* [emphasis mine] over their destiny, with the ability to guide and enhance the characteristics of their children, and their children's children as well." Such parents would not be calling their children on the phone at annoying frequent intervals to suggest that it's time to get a real job; instead, just like the chicken guy, they would be inserting genes that produced proteins that would make their child behave in certain ways throughout his life. You cannot rebel against the production of that protein. Perhaps you can still do everything in your power to defeat the wishes of 29 your parents, but that protein will nonetheless be pumped out relentlessly into your system, defining who you are. You won't grow feathers, no matter how much you want them. And maybe they can engineer your mood enough that your lack of plumage won't even cross your mind.

30 Such children will, in effect, be assigned a goal by their programmers: "intelligence," "even temper," "athleticism." (As with chickens, the market will doubtless lean in the direction of efficiency. It may be hard to find genes for, say, dreaminess.) Now two possibilities arise. Perhaps the programming doesn't work very well, and your lad spells poorly, or turns moody, or can't hit the inside fastball. In the present world, you just tell yourself that that's who he is. But in the coming world, he'll be, in essence, a defective product. Do you still accept *him* unconditionally? Why? If your new Jetta got thirty miles to the gallon instead of the forty it was designed to get, you'd take it back. You'd call it a lemon. If necessary, you'd sue.

31 Or what if the engineering worked pretty well, but you decided, too late, that you'd picked the wrong package, hadn't gotten the best features? Would you feel buyer's remorse if the kid next door had a better ear, a stronger arm?

32 Say the gene work went a little awry and left you with a kid who had some serious problems; what kind of guilt would that leave you with? Remember, this is not a child created by the random interaction of your genes with those of your partner, this is a child created with specific intent. Does *Consumer Reports* start rating the various biotech offerings?

33 What if you had a second child five years after the first, and by that time the upgrades were undeniably improved: how would you feel about the first kid? How would he feel about his new brother, the latest model?

34 The other outcome—that the genetic engineering works just as you had hoped—seems at least as bad. Now your child is a product. You can take precisely as much pride in her achievements as you take in the achievements of your dishwashing detergent. It was designed to produce streak-free glassware, and she was designed to be sweet-tempered, social, and smart. And what can she take pride in? Her good grades? She may have worked hard, but she'll always know that she was spec'ed for good grades. Her kindness to others? Well, yes, it's good to be kind—but perhaps it's not much of an accomplishment once the various genes with some link to sociability have been catalogued and manipulated. I have no doubt that these qualms would be one of the powerful psychological afflictions of the future—at least until someone figures out a fix that keeps the next generations from having such bad thoughts.

35 Britain's chief rabbi, Jonathan Sacks, was asked a few years ago about the announcement that Italian doctors were trying to clone humans. "If there is a mystery at the heart of human condition, it is otherness: the otherness of man and woman, parent and child. It is the space we make for otherness that makes love something other than narcissism."

The Environment: Save It or Lose It

© Chris Rogers/Corbis

Photograph 1: Grand Teton reflected in Jackson Lake, Grand Teton National Park, Wyoming
Although in the twenty-first century we Americans tend to take the existence of our national parks for granted, many of them have a contentious history, including Grand Teton National Park. The Teton Range is a stretch of the Rocky Mountains, 40 miles long and 7–9 miles wide, adjacent to Yellowstone National Park. Grand Teton, pictured here, is 13,770 feet high; eight other peaks are over 12,000 feet above sea level. The area was used for twelve thousand years by Native American hunters, with Jackson Hole (named after fur trapper David Jackson) a crossroads for trade and travel; the Lewis and Clark expedition and other explorers and surveyors mapped the area in the nineteenth century. In the early twentieth century, a proposal to make the site an extension of Yellowstone National Park aroused the wrath of various groups. Sheep and cattle ranchers (themselves enemies) wanted to continue grazing their herds; others lobbied for traditional hunting, grazing, and ranching activities. In 1927, philanthropist John D. Rockefeller, Jr. and others secretly bought the land and held it in trust for the National Park Service, but because of harassment and opposition from both local residents and the U.S. Senate, Grand Teton National Park was not signed into existence until 1950—requiring support and intervention from presidents Calvin Coolidge, Franklin Roosevelt, and Harry Truman.

Considering the Image

1. What makes this a picture-perfect photograph? What mood does it convey? What messages about the environment does it send? Does it disclose any of the disputes, bitterness, skullduggery, secrecy, and threats that comprise the history of the area up until 1950, and that bleed beyond even this border? To what extent might it be possible to generalize about the public image and history of other national parks, either existing or proposed?
2. This is a beautiful sight: the blue sky is full of puffy white clouds; the snowy mountains appear pristine, as does the clear lake that mirrors them. The evergreens in the foreground appear healthy, the surrounding snow white and untouched by human beings, the water pure. To what extent do these images reflect reality? Are there any people or animals in this picture? To your knowledge, is this environment threatened in any way? Check the accuracy of your evidence, concerning this or any other national park of your choice.
3. What do people mean by "Save our national parks"? Identify some of the ways this can be done.

© Rob Crandall/The Image Works

Photograph 2: Bison herd crossing road in Yellowstone National Park, August 2004 *Yellowstone National Park, mostly in Wyoming, is known for its geothermal activity—geysers, boiling springs (and consequently earthquakes)—and for its mountains, waterfalls, petrified wood, and varied terrain. Outside of Alaska, it is the largest surviving stretch of pristine land in the United States and the focal point of the 31,250 square-mile Greater Yellowstone ecosystem that includes Grand Teton National Park and the adjacent national forests and wilderness areas: home to 1,700 species of trees and 60 species of mammals. In addition to black bears, elk, moose, pronghorn and bighorn sheep, and mountain lions, endangered species—gray wolves and grizzly bears—have been reintroduced after years of deliberate slaughter and are thriving.*

Yet all is not tranquil in Eden. The area is subject to 35 natural fires per year, 29 an inevitable consequence of lightning, and 6 caused by humans. Before 1970, when the impact of fires on natural ecosystems was finally recognized, all fires were suppressed, leaving large areas of underbrush and dying forests ready for uncontrollable conflagration. Current policy allows natural fires to burn unless they endanger lives and property. Today's population of 3,000 bison has recently shrunk from nearly twice that due to slaughter at the urging of cattle ranchers who claimed that brucellosis would decimate their herds (although the disease could have been controlled through vaccinations). But the greatest damage to the park's environment is caused by humans. The number of visitors in 2006 (three million) was six times greater than the pre–World War II annual average. The park's users make enormous demands on water and sanitation: they drive polluting snowmobiles through wilderness areas, break off limestone structures, steal petrified wood, throw trash into the geysers—and yes, they feed the bears.

Considering the Image

1. Who has the right of way in this picture? Does it remind you of any other street scenes? Is this the ideal way for people to view wildlife—from their cars, in transit? What effect does proximity to people have on wildlife species that were accustomed to living in isolation?
2. Research and comment on one or another of the changes in wildlife, fire, and land management in Yellowstone National Park during the past hundred (or even fifty) years. What influences policy decisions on whether to reintroduce wild species that were once native (such as grizzlies and wolves), whether to declare them endangered, and what the optimum population of a given species is? To what extent should human visitors be restricted: in numbers, behavior, use of machinery (such as snowmobiles) and weapons? Who should make these decisions? Who should monitor them?

NASA Goddard Space Flight Center/AP Images

Photograph 3: Computer composite image of North America, August 10, 2001 *We have become accustomed to the beautiful, iconic photograph of Earth (the "Blue Marble") taken during the Apollo 17 space mission (1972) that shows large patches of snow in the Arctic, green in Greenland and the Eastern seaboard, deep blue oceans, and white clouds swirling over portions of South America and the Antarctic. All looks serene, and—from that vast distance of 125,000 miles—immortal, unassailable, clean.*

Compare the image shown here, a composite of multiple, Earth-observing satellite images taken on the night of August 10, 2001, during the annual Perseids, an awesome meteor shower—as many as sixty an hour visible from the Northern Hemisphere. But the lights here are not from meteors but from the brightest spots of human habitation: the greater the congestion, the brighter the lights. You can view comparable images, but closer, via Google Earth.

Considering the Image

1. Consider the levels of luminescence, the brightest spots illuminating both coasts of North America and the entire eastern seaboard. What is most striking about this picture? In what ways can you "read" it—visually? Intellectually? Ecologically? Compare and contrast this image with the image of Grand Teton National Park (Photograph 1).
2. What might the continent have looked like a hundred years ago? Fifty years ago? What would you predict seeing fifty years from now? With what consequences?

Michael Stevens/AP Images

Photograph 4: "Seven Million Londoners" *proclaim the banners streaming from the lampposts marching along Oxford Street in October 2005. Crowds throng this major shopping street, their turbans, hats, and beards representing people from all over the world—so many, packed so closely together, that they dwarf the cars and even the double-decker bus attempting to make its way along the congested thoroughfare.*

Might we interpret this as evidence of too many people? The crowds here could be replicated in many places in the world—subways and sidewalks bursting with commuters in New York, Beijing, and Tokyo, many wearing masks to filter polluted air; open-air markets seething with seas of shoppers in Lagos; traffic jams in Bangkok—and on the Long Island Expressway, "the world's longest parking lot"; jerry-built favelas *(slums) in Rio; pilgrims bathing, sari blending into sari, in the Ganges—simultaneously sacred and polluted; vacationers too close together while skiing, swimming, camping, hiking—you name it—in what was once wilderness.*

In Hot, Flat, and Crowded: Why We Need a Green Revolution—and How It Can Renew America *(2008), Thomas Friedman cites the 2007 United Nations Population Division report estimating that the world's population will increase 40% or more, from 6.7 billion in 2007 to 9.2 billion in 2050, mostly in the "less developed regions" ill equipped to provide people's basic needs: "food, housing, education, employment." In 1800, London—population 1 million—was the world's largest city. By 1960, there were 111 cities with more than a million; today that number has nearly tripled. There will be 26 "megacities" by 2015, with populations of over 10 million. Five key problems, says Friedman ("energy supply and demand, petropolitics, climate change, energy poverty, and biodiversity loss"), have been building for years, but the tipping point in destruction of quality of life occurred on January 1, 2000 (47). More than half the 2008 population lives in cities, the sites of particular congestion and stress on the infrastructure, including "loss of arable land, deforestation, overfishing, water shortages, and air and water pollution" (29–30). Although the developed regions' population is expected to remain static, at around 1.2 billion, these people use a disproportionate percentage of resources. Each of the United States' three million inhabitants, for example, consumes as much in a year as do 32 Kenyans. Since the U.S. population is ten times greater, the U.S. resource use is 320 times as large as in Kenya (65).*

Considering the Image

1. Look closely at the individuals in this crowd. Do they look purposeful, peaceful? Is the group orderly? What are they doing? Where are they going? Do they give any indication that they are bothered or inconvenienced by such large numbers—either in their immediate vicinity, or in the knowledge that there are "Seven Million Londoners"? Why or why not?
2. What, if anything, should cities do to make their inhabitants aware of their impact on the world's diminishing resources? Research the optimum city size and come up with some solutions on how city size might be related to conservation efforts in a specific area of the world.

Terje Rakke/Getty Images

Photograph 5: Car wrecks in Bærum, Norway, Summer 1997 *We could view this photograph as a work of art: colorful ribbons of a crumpled substance, full of irregularities and indentations. The colors range from blue and white to red, maroon, orange, yellow, and lime green; all are bright, as is the blue sky above. But we also recognize what we're looking at—wrecked cars—each of which may have been further compressed for more compact waste disposal. The story behind each wreck may tell of human loss—of judgment, of health and strength, of life. There is economic loss as well—not only in the medical costs of the accident, but of the car itself, which has little or no value if it is totaled. Or the car may simply have been considered obsolete or old and junked: how many years, how much mileage does it take to make a car old? Each replacement vehicle, of course, requires more raw materials, just as each junked car requires (in addition to money) either space to store the refuse, or energy to strip out the reusable parts and to recycle the steel.*

The same commentary could be made about all sorts of other manufactured items, large and small—refrigerators, air conditioners, computer monitors, cell phones, rechargers, batteries, dirty diapers, plastic bags, and bottles, to name only a few of millions. Add to this the accumulation of waste—industrial, human, and animal—all of which grows in proportion to the humans whose own population explosion affects every aspect of the problem. As Al Gore's An Inconvenient Truth *explains, "It took more than 10,000 generations for the human population to reach 2 billion. Then it began to rocket upward from 2 billion to 9 billion in the course of a single lifetime: ours" (216), each and every person generating waste from the moment of their birth until their last breath.*

Considering the Image

1. What are the costs of the accumulation of junk, detritus, refuse, and waste of all kinds—to a single municipality, state, nation? Who pays for the land, labor, and energy to dump this refuse? To what other uses might the space, money, and energy currently tied up in waste disposal be put? Are there any benefits to the generation of junk and garbage, or are there only costs? Explain.
2. Visit a local business or institution (such as a hospital or school, or your college residence or dining hall) and determine what sorts of waste are generated on a daily, weekly, and/or annual basis. What is done with it? At what cost? What would be the best ways to reduce or eliminate some of this waste?
3. Develop a plan by which you can conduct your daily life in a more environmentally friendly manner. What resources—electricity, water, heat, gasoline, paper, other—can you conserve? Identify three to four of these, explain your conservation plan, and identify its costs (including expenditures of time and effort) and benefits.

James P. Bair/National Geographic/Getty Images

Photograph 6: Border of Haiti and the Dominican Republic (south of Dajabon, Dominican Republic), 2001 *This photograph illustrates the effect of the environmental management policies of two different governments, those of Haiti (pop. 8,700,000) and the Dominican Republic (pop. 10,000,000). In the nineteenth century these two nations, occupying the Caribbean island of Hispaniola, 600 miles off the Florida coast, were blessed, as Jared Diamond observes in* Collapse, *with an "exuberance . . . of forests, full of trees and valuable wood." Haiti differed from the Dominican Republic in its higher population density, lower rainfall, and a colonial slave-plantation culture in which the "French ships that brought slaves to Haiti returned to Europe with cargoes of Haitian timber." By mid-nineteenth century, the land was largely stripped of trees. Haiti's ruthless "Papa Doc" and "Baby Doc" Duvalier followed an unstable series of presidents; none protected the environment, leaving only 1% of Haiti forested today. As Diamond points out, wherever deforestation occurs, its consequences "include loss of timber and other forest building materials, soil erosion, loss of soil fertility, sediment loads in the rivers, loss of watershed protection and hence of potential hydroelectric power, and decreased rainfall" (330).*

Diamond continues, in contrast is the Dominican Republic, with 28% forested land, rigorously and ruthlessly maintained. In the 1860s and 1870s the Dominican Republic appeared to be on the Haitian road to environmental ruin. People were clearing the forests for sugar plantations and burning trees to make charcoal for cooking fuel; as the twentieth century began, rapid urbanization and deforestation were occurring. However, in contrast to Haitian neglect, citizens in the Dominican Republic launched bottom-up conservation efforts, executed with rigor by that country's own ruthless, evil dictators, Trujillo and Balaguer. Although they maintained extensive logging operations, their management included natural reforestation and use of the army to expel squatters and rogue loggers. Among numerous environmental safeguards, they preserved "forested watersheds" in order to provide adequate hydroelectric power and water for the Republic's burgeoning industries and growing population (343); imported and subsidized gas as the preferred cooking fuel (over charcoal); and established 74 large national parks, in contrast to two threatened ones in Haiti. Whereas outsiders rule the roost in Haiti and think small, in the Dominican Republic, citizens' groups and NGOs promote environmental efforts on a large scale.

Considering the Image

1. Use the above information to interpret what you see in this photograph.
2. Propose an environmental policy—one feasible in a democracy rather than in a strong-arm dictatorship—that will both sustain natural resources and accommodate human needs.

Janduari Simoes/AP Images

Photograph 7: Fire caused by Brazilian farmers burning out of control in the Amazon state of Rondonia, Brazil, October 1998 *Subsistence farmers, often squatters—estimated to be between 200 and 500 million people worldwide—employ slash-and-burn agriculture, clearing forests to plant crops. Rainforest soil is a "wet desert" with so few nutrients that it becomes depleted within four years and is thereby made unfit for use, forever. The farmers then move to other parts of the forest where they continue this destructive cycle.*

The Amazon rainforest, sometimes called "the lungs of our planet," produces 20% of the world's oxygen and contains the largest diversity of plant and animal species in the world. Over 438,000 species of plants of economic and social interest have been registered, and many more are uncatalogued; one in five of the world's birds live there. Even a single hectare (2.47 acres) includes more than 750 types of trees and 1,500 other plants. Yet these are vanishing before our eyes. Although Brazil has one-third of the world's remaining rainforests, more than 2.7 million acres are burned or logged every year. Twenty percent of the Amazon rainforest has already been destroyed as the land is cleared there for the same enterprises for which the North American forests (and those in Haiti—see commentary on Photograph 6) were demolished: timber, ranching, grazing, hydroelectric power, subsistence, and more extensive agriculture.

Within forty years the entire Amazon rainforest could disappear entirely, and with it the last 200,000 indigenous tribespeople—a population decimated from the estimated ten million who lived there five centuries ago—in addition to a massive loss of biodiversity as plants and animals become extinct. Other profound, ugly consequences include less rain, less oxygen, and more carbon dioxide in the atmosphere; air and water pollution; soil erosion; the spread of malaria; and increased global warming. What would it take to save the rain forest: United Nations action?A strong-arm dictator (like the Dominican Republic's Balaguer) with an enlightened public policy? Scientists' reports, reinforced by local advocates? Subsidies to the subsistence farmers and squatters? Who will pay the costs? And where will the money come from?

Source: Leslie Taylor, The Healing Power of Rainforest Herbs (Garden City: Square One Publishers, Inc., 2004).

Considering the Image

1. How does knowledge of the above commentary influence your reading of this photograph? Could you imagine this forest burning occurring in other places in the world? With what consequences?
2. The rainforest's natural products—nuts, fruits, oil-producing and medicinal plants—could be harvested at a profit for the individual farmers. But would that be sufficient to bring about the massive changes in public policy, conservation practices, and individual attitudes necessary to save the rainforest? What can individuals do, anywhere, to conserve and preserve the environment—at home, and elsewhere in the world? What can private groups do? Will it take the concerted efforts of governments worldwide and international agencies, such as the UN, to effect long-term changes?

© Paul Souders/Corbis

Photograph 8: Water streaming from a melting iceberg carved from Kangerlua Glacier (Jakobshavn Icefjord) in Disko Bay, Ililussant, Greenland, July 31, 2006 *Melting glaciers of the Antarctic, and Greenland ice sheets, are a beautiful but ominous sight. Accompanied by booms and crashes, huge chunks of snow and ice—compacted for as long as 150,000 years—break off and fall into the warming Arctic Ocean. The world's temperature is expected to rise 3–8 degrees in the twenty-first century, largely due to greenhouse gases such as carbon dioxide and methane from smokestacks, vehicles, and burning forests. Glaciers are melting worldwide, from the Andes to the Alps to the snows of Kilimanjaro; many are expected to vanish entirely within thirty or forty years, and the oceans to rise several feet, according to the Intergovernmental Panel on Climate Change, representing a consensus of 2,000 scientists.*

But these aspects of global warming are truly only the tip of the iceberg. As the natural habitat of polar bears and other arctic animals shrinks, they will be forced to cling to icebergs in the open sea and to swim between increasingly distant ice floes to search for food; their population in the Hudson Bay south of Churchill has declined 20% in seventeen years. The impact may be felt far from the Arctic, too. Rising water levels in the oceans cause floods from Bangladesh to New Zealand to Cape Cod. Houses, whole villages, wash away, the process exacerbated by severe hurricanes that lash coastal areas. The result? Lost lives, billions of dollars of damage, destruction of coral reefs and marine habitats, salinated water unfit for humans or agriculture, and increases in malaria and other diseases. As the snow melts, the air temperatures rise and contribute to greater aridity worldwide, forcing indigenous peoples from the Andes to Africa to compete for ever-scarcer water. These are but a few of the numerous interrelated and devastating effects of global warming.

Considering the Image

1. How could melting glaciers have such worldwide effects? How could they produce such seemingly contradictory consequences, producing both flooding and drought?
2. In *An Inconvenient Truth,* Al Gore proposes several arguments to refute those who deny that global warming exists and that something needs to be done about it. These include challenging the "misconception that the scientific community is in a state of disagreement about whether global warming is real" (261); presenting evidence that changes are not happening gradually, as some people claim, but rather are accelerating to a crisis point at lightning speed (254–55); countering "the false belief that we have to choose between a healthy economy and a healthy environment" (270–71); and emphasizing that global warming is *not* too large a problem to reverse, as some argue, though this will require judicious intervention and extensive international cooperation (278). Pick one of Gore's positions, discuss it with a partner or with your class, and write a response, amplifying the points Gore makes.

Source: Al Gore, *An Inconvenient Truth: The Planetary Emergency of Global Warming and What We Can Do About It.* Emmaus, PA: Rodale, 2006.

I remember so well the feeling of walking into the maternity ward with Sue, and walking out with Sue and Sophie: where there had been two there were now, somehow, three, each of us our own person, but now commanded to make a family, a place where we all could thrive. She was so mysterious, that Sophie, and in many ways she still is. There are times when, like every parent, I see myself reflected in her, and times when I wonder if she's even related. She's ours to nurture and protect, but she is who *she is*. That's the mystery and the glory of any child.

Mystery, however, is not one of the words that thrills engineers. They try to deliver solid bridges, unyielding dams, reliable cars. We wouldn't want it any other way. The only question is if their product line should be expanded to include children. 36

Right now both the genes, and the limits that they set on us, connect us with every human that came before. Human beings can look at rock art carved into African cliffs and French caves thirty thousand years ago and feel an electric, immediate kinship. We've gone from digging sticks to combines, and from drum circles to symphony orchestras (and back again to drum circles), but we still hear in the same range and see in the same spectrum, still produce adrenaline and dopamine in the same ways, still think in many of the same patterns. We are, by and large, the same people, more closely genetically related to one another than we may be to our engineered grandchildren. 37

These new technologies show us that human meaning dangles by a far thinner thread than we had thought. If germline genetic engineering ever starts, it will accelerate endlessly and unstoppably into the future, as individuals make the calculation that they have no choice but to equip their kids for the world that's being made. The first child whose genes come in part from some corporate lab, the first child who has been "enhanced" from what came before—that's the first child who will glance back over his shoulder and see a gap between himself and human history. 38

These would be mere consumer decisions—but that also means that they would benefit the rich far more than the poor. They would take the gap in power, wealth, and education that currently divides both our society and the world at large, and write that division into our very biology. A sixth of the American population lacks health insurance of any kind—they can't afford to go to the doctor for a *check-up*. And much of the rest of the world is far worse off. If we can't afford the fifty cents per person it would take to buy bed nets to protect most of Africa from malaria, it is unlikely we will extend to anyone but the top tax bracket these latest forms of genetic technology. The injustice is so obvious that even the strongest proponents of genetic engineering make little attempt to deny it. "Anyone who accepts the right of affluent parents to provide their children with an expensive private school education cannot use 'unfairness' as a reason for rejecting the use of reprogenetic technologies," says Lee Silver. 39

40 These new technologies, however, are not yet inevitable. Unlike global warming, this genie is not yet out of the bottle. But if germline genetic engineering is going to be stopped, it will have to happen now, before it's quite begun. It will have to be a political choice, that is—one we make not as parents but as citizens, not as individuals but as a whole, thinking not only about our own offspring but about everyone.

41 So far the discussion has been confined to a few scientists, a few philosophers, a few ideologues. It needs to spread widely, and quickly, and loudly. The stakes are absurdly high, nothing less than the meaning of being human. And given the seductions that we've seen—the intuitively and culturally delicious prospect of a *better* child—the arguments against must be not only powerful but also deep. They'll need to resonate on the same intuitive and cultural level. We'll need to feel in our gut the reasons why, this time, we should tell Prometheus thanks, but no thanks.

Content

1. This essay is an excellent example of inductive reasoning that makes its major points in the conclusion (¶s 40–41), after presenting an escalating series of examples. What's the thesis? Is it ever explicitly stated? Explain, with examples, how it can be inferred from virtually every paragraph.
2. How close are humans to achieving "germline genetic engineering" that would enable scientists, or physicians, to construct DNA sequences, "the programming code of life," and "to be able to edit [them] the way you can a document on a word processor" (¶ 11)?
3. What does McKibben speculate the consequences might be of a "biological arms race" devoted to continually enhancing infants' IQ, physical strength, beauty, or other desirable features (¶s 17–20)? What evidence does he offer that people are already receptive to such genetic enhancements (consider, for instance, the current market for egg donors with specific characteristics of height, color, and SAT scores [¶ 16])?
4. Why is genetic engineering inherently unfair, and why would attempts to level the playing field at the high end inevitably have negative social consequences for the poor (¶s 39–41)?

Strategies/Structures/Language

5. Why does McKibben begin his essay with botulism toxin ("three tablespoons [of which] could theoretically kill every human on Earth") and quickly segue to Botox—a dilute strain of the same toxin and a "staple weapon in the cosmetic arsenal" (¶s 1–2)? What language in these first two paragraphs lets readers know where he stands on the issue?
6. Why does McKibben compare the consequences of germline genetic engineering to upgrading computer software: "The vision of one's child as a nearly useless copy of Windows 95 should make parents fight like hell to make sure we never get started down this path" (¶ 21)? Does McKibben's example of a genetically engineered "featherless chicken" (¶ 28) reinforce his argument? Explain.

For Writing

7. With a partner—preferably one who disagrees with you—explore the question, "On what basis can we reject positive genetic influences on a person's essence when we accept the rights of parents to benefit their children in every other way" (¶ 24)? Do you agree with McKibben that in our competitive and affluent society genetic engineering could lead to a "biological arms race" (¶ 17) among parents devoted to continually enhancing infants' IQ, physical strength, beauty, or other desirable features (¶s 17–20)? Together, write an essay on the social and cultural factors that influence parents in the "pursuit of successful offspring" (¶ 14). Present your positions on the topic of whether genetic enhancements should be left up to parents by analyzing how and why such a choice might be politically curtailed.

8. ***Journal Writing.*** Have you (or someone you know well) experienced a conflict between your family's and community's expectations and perceptions of you and your own quest for self-determination? How do you balance the need to develop your own intellect and character with your need to respect and be accepted within your family and community? Do you agree that rebelling is essential in the development of an "authentic" self (¶s 25–26)?

9. On the basis of your journal writing (see question 8), write an essay on whether we are defined by our genetic inheritance. If, as McKibben suggests, we could not "rebel against . . . that protein [which] will nonetheless be pumped out relentlessly into your system, defining who you are" (¶ 29), do we exert any free will over who we are?

10. ***Dialogues.*** What does Judith Hall's poem "Perilous Riddle" (557) suggest about the relationship between identity and gender? How much freedom do we have to decide who we are, given the genetic and social influences on our development as gendered beings? Or simply as human beings, given the range of potential genetic options that McKibben raises? What does Hall's poem imply about Western culture's definitions of woman, man, intellect, tragedy, pride, change, and choice?

VIRGINIA POSTREL

Virginia Postrel (born 1960) graduated from Princeton (1982) with a degree in English. A writer on cultural and economic topics for many publications, including the *Wall Street Journal*, she was an economics columnist for *The New York Times* (2000–2006) and is currently a contributing editor for the *Atlantic Monthly* and a columnist for *Forbes*. She has been a media fellow at the Hoover Institution at Stanford University and is the author of *The Future and Its Enemies: The Growing Conflict Over Creativity, Enterprise, and Progress* (1998) and *The Substance of Style: How the Rise of Aesthetic Value is Remaking Commerce, Culture, and Consciousness* (2004). In "The Truth About Beauty," first published in the *Atlantic Monthly* in 2007, Postrel argues that by selling the idea that all women are beautiful, Dove's "Campaign for Real Beauty" actually reinforces our culture's perception of beauty as the source and measure of a woman's value.

The Truth About Beauty

1 Cosmetics makers have always sold "hope in a jar"—creams and potions that promise youth, beauty, sex appeal, and even love for the women who use them. Over the last few years, the marketers at Dove have added some new-and-improved enticements. They're now promising self-esteem and cultural transformation. Dove's "Campaign for Real Beauty," declares a press release, is "a global effort that is intended to serve as a starting point for societal change and act as a catalyst for widening the definition and discussion of beauty." Along with its thigh-firming creams, self-tanners, and hair conditioners, Dove is peddling the crowd-pleasing notions that beauty is a media creation, that recognizing plural forms of beauty is the same as declaring every woman beautiful, and that self-esteem means ignoring imperfections.

2 Dove won widespread acclaim in June 2005 when it rolled out its thigh-firming cream with billboards of attractive but variously sized "real women" frolicking in their underwear. It advertised its hair-care products by showing hundreds of women in identical platinum-blonde wigs—described as "the kind of hair found in magazines"—tossing off those artificial manes and celebrating their real (perfectly styled, colored, and conditioned) hair. It ran print ads that featured atypical models, including a plump brunette and a ninety-five-year-old, and invited readers to choose between pejorative and complimentary adjectives: "Wrinkled or wonderful?" "Oversized or outstanding?" The public and press got the point, and Dove got attention. Oprah covered the story, and so did the *Today* show. Dove's campaign, wrote *Advertising Age*, "undermines the basic proposition of decades of beauty-care advertising by telling women—and young girls—they're beautiful just the way they are.

3 Last fall, Dove extended its image building with a successful bit of viral marketing: a seventy-five-second online video called *Evolution*. Created by Ogilvy & Mather, the video is a close-up of a seemingly ordinary woman, shot in harsh lighting that calls attention to her uneven skin tone, slightly lopsided eyes, and dull, flat hair. In twenty seconds of time-lapse video, makeup artists and hair stylists turn her into a wide-eyed, big-haired beauty with sculpted cheeks and perfect skin. It's *Extreme Makeover* without the surgical gore.

4 But that's only the beginning. Next comes the digital transformation, as a designer points-and-clicks on the model's photo, giving her a longer, slimmer neck, a slightly narrower upper face, fuller lips, bigger eyes, and more space between her eyebrows and eyes. The perfected image rises to fill a billboard advertising a fictitious line of makeup. Fade to black, with the message "No wonder our perception of beauty is distorted." The video has attracted more than 3 million YouTube views. It also appears on Dove's campaignforrealbeauty.com Web site, where it concludes, "Every girl deserves to feel beautiful just the way she is."

Courtesy of Unilever

In this composite of stills from Dove's viral-marketing video, the left half depicts the "evolution" of the face represented from the right half of the original photograph. What changes have been made: in eye; nose; lips—upper and lower; skin—color, texture, highlights; length of neck; hair—style, volume, highlights; clothing—color, design, exposure of shoulder and bone structure? What appeals does the altered half of the photograph contain that are absent from the original? Is beauty, and perhaps sexiness or other types of appeal, in the mind of the subject, the photo-manipulator/ad designer, the viewer, or all of these?

Every girl certainly wants to, which explains the popularity of 5
Dove's campaign. There's only one problem: Beauty exists, and it's unevenly distributed. Our eyes and brains pretty consistently like some human forms better than others. Shown photos of strangers, even babies look longer at the faces adults rank the best-looking. Whether you prefer Nicole Kidman to Angelina Jolie, Jennifer Lopez to Halle Berry, or Queen Latifah to Kate Moss may be a matter of taste, but rare is the beholder who would declare Holly Hunter or Whoopi Goldberg—neither of whom is homely—more beautiful than any of these women.

For similar reasons, we still thrill to the centuries-old bust of 6
Nefertiti, the Venus de Milo, and the exquisite faces painted by Leonardo and Botticelli. Greta Garbo's acting style seems stilted today, but her face transcends time. We know beauty when we see it, and our reactions are remarkably consistent. Beauty is not just a social construct, and not every girl is beautiful just the way she is.

7 Take Dove's *Evolution* video. The digital transformation is fascinating because it magically makes a beautiful woman more striking. Her face's new geometry triggers an immediate, visceral response—and the video's storytelling impact is dependent on that predictable reaction. The video makes its point about artifice only because most people find the manipulated face more beautiful than the natural one.

8 In *Survival of the Prettiest: The Science of Beauty*, Nancy Etcoff, a psychologist at Harvard Medical School, reported on experiments that let people rate faces and digitally "breed" ever-more-attractive composite generations. The results for female faces look a lot like the finished product in the Dove video: "thinner jaws, larger eyes relative to the size of their faces, and shorter distances between their mouths and chins" in one case, and "fuller lips, a less robust jaw, a smaller nose and smaller chin than the population average" in another. These features, wrote Etcoff, "exaggerate the ways that adult female faces differ from adult male faces. They also exaggerate the youthfulness of the face." More than youth, the full lips and small jaws of beautiful women reflect relatively high levels of female hormones and low levels of male hormones—indicating greater fertility—according to psychologist Victor Johnston, who did some of these experiments.

9 More generally, evolutionary psychologists suggest that the features we see as beautiful—including indicators of good health like smooth skin and symmetry—have been rewarded through countless generations of competition for mates. The same evolutionary pressures, this research suggests, have biologically programmed human minds to perceive these features as beautiful. "Some scientists believe that our beauty detectors are really detectors for the combination of youth and femininity," wrote Etcoff. Whether the beauty we detect arises from nature or artifice doesn't change that visceral reflex.

10 Perhaps surprisingly, Etcoff herself advised Dove on several rounds of survey research and helped the company create workshops for girls. Dove touts her involvement (and her doctorate and Harvard affiliation) in its publicity materials. She sees the campaign as a useful corrective. Media images, Etcoff notes in an e-mail, are often so rarefied that "they change our ideas about what people look like and what normal looks like . . . Our brains did not evolve with media, and many people see more media images of women than actual women. The contrast effect makes even the most beautiful non-model look less attractive; it produces a new 'normal.'"

11 Dove began its campaign by recognizing the diverse manifestations of universally beautiful patterns. The "real women" pictured in the thigh-cream billboards may not have looked like super-models, but they were all young, with symmetrical faces, feminine features, great skin, white teeth, and hourglass shapes. Even the most zaftig had relatively flat stomachs and clearly defined waists. These pretty women were not a random sample of the population. Dove diversified the portrait of beauty without abandoning the concept altogether.

But the campaign didn't stop there. Dove is defining itself as the brand that loves regular women—and regular women, by definition, are not extraordinarily beautiful. The company can't afford a precise definition of *real beauty* that might exclude half the population—not a good strategy for selling mass-market consumer products. So the campaign leaves *real beauty* ambiguous, enabling the viewers to fill in the concept with their own desires. Some take *real beauty* to mean "nature unretouched" and interpret the *Evolution* video as suggesting that uncannily beautiful faces are not merely rare but nonexistent. Others emphasize the importance of character and personality: Real beauty comes from the inside, not physical appearance. And *Advertising Age*'s interpretation is common: that Dove is reminding women that "they're beautiful just the way they are." 12

Another Dove ad, focusing on girls' insecurities about their looks, concludes, "Every girl deserves to feel good about herself and see how beautiful she really is." Here, Dove is encouraging the myth that physical beauty is a false concept, and, at the same time, falsely equating beauty with goodness and self-worth. If you don't see perfection in the mirror, it suggests, you've been duped by the media and suffer from low self-esteem. 13

But adult women have a more realistic view. "Only two percent of women describe themselves as beautiful" trumpets the headline of Dove's press release. Contrary to what the company wants readers to believe, however, that statistic doesn't necessarily represent a crisis of confidence; it may simply reflect the power of the word *beautiful*. Dove's surveys don't ask women if they think they're unattractive or ugly, so it's hard to differentiate between knowing you have flaws, believing you're acceptably but unimpressively plain, and feeling worthlessly hideous. In another Dove survey, 88 percent of the American women polled said they're at least somewhat satisfied with their face, while 76 percent said they're at least somewhat satisfied with their body. But dissatisfaction is not the same as unhappiness or insecurity. 14

Like the rest of the genetic lottery, beauty is unfair. Everyone falls short of perfection, but some are luckier than others. Real confidence requires self-knowledge, which includes recognizing one's shortcomings as well as one's strengths. At a recent conference on biological manipulations, I heard a philosopher declare during lunch that she'd never have plastic surgery or even dye her hair. But, she confessed, she'd pay just about anything for fifteen more IQ points. This woman is not insecure about her intelligence, which is far above average; she'd just like to be smarter. Asking women to say they're beautiful is like asking intellectuals to say they're geniuses. Most know they simply don't qualify. 15

Content

1. What is Postrel's thesis? Why does she consider a marketing campaign based on the idea that "beauty is a media creation" (¶ 1), an appealing, if disingenuous ploy? What evidence does she provide in support of the idea that "beauty exists"

(¶ 5)? If beauty does exist, why, according to Postrel, is Dove's message so appealing? Why does she suggest that Dove's professed goal of "widening the definition" of beauty (¶ 1) "falsely [equates] beauty with goodness and self-worth" (¶ 13)?

2. Postrel argues that "recognizing plural forms of beauty" is *not* the same "as declaring every woman beautiful" (¶ 1). How do the Dove advertisements Postrel describes in paragraph 2 make such an association? Why does Postel consider these ads misleading? Does her argument imply that beauty *doesn't* exist in plural forms?

Strategies/Structures/Language

3. Postrel's list of beauties in paragraphs 5 and 6 consists of film stars, singers, models, the Egyptian queen Nefertiti, an ancient Greek marble sculpture, and the creations of two Renaissance artists (Leonardo da Vinci and Sandro Botticelli). What do these beauties have in common? When Postrel writes that "our eyes and brains pretty consistently like some human forms better than others" (¶ 5), who does the plural pronoun "our" include? How has Postrel constructed her list to support her overall argument?

4. According to Postrel, what does the preference for one face over another indicate? Must the reader agree that Queen Latifah and Jennifer Lopez are more beautiful than Holly Hunter and Whoopi Goldberg (¶ 5) to agree with Postrel's argument? Might you find these women beautiful in different ways and still find Postrel's argument persuasive?

5. Postrel argues that beauty is rewarded "through countless generations of competition for mates" (¶ 9) and is an evolutionary device that signals "greater fertility" (¶ 8). Do you see a contradiction between this assertion and her observation that "regular women, by definition, are not extraordinarily beautiful" (¶ 12)? Explain.

For Writing

6. ***Journal Writing.*** Do you agree with Postrel that self-esteem does *not* come from "ignoring imperfections" (¶ 1), but rather, from "recognizing one's shortcomings as well as one's strengths" (¶ 15)? How do you define "shortcomings"? Is physical attractiveness, like the development of one's intelligence or talents, a matter of "the genetic lottery" (¶ 15), or a question of lifestyle, appropriate choices, attitude, and discipline? Must beauty necessarily be related to one's physical appearance?

7. ***Dialogues.*** "Introducing **new** GoValue!™ Service" (532) satirically redefines concepts such as freedom, convenience, and privacy. How, according to Postrel, does Dove redefine beauty? How would you create a cosmetic company's advertisement similar to "GoValue!™ Service"? For example, the ad copy might read "Overweight? Don't worry! Fat is the new thin!" or "Crows feet got you down? Remember, age is just a number—and we've got the anti-wrinkle cream to keep that number at bay." Alternatively, you might create a satiric narrative that explores concepts of beauty and self-esteem in the vein of Lynda Barry's "Common Scents" (376–85) or Suzanne Britt's "That Lean and Hungry Look" (281–83). Experiment with a variety of devices such as self-deprecation, exaggeration, irreverence, and slang to examine cultural ideas about beauty, age, race, and body type.

ERIC LIU

Eric Liu (born 1969) grew up in New York state, the child of Taiwanese immigrants who worked in the computer industry. A history major at Yale, Liu served a summer internship in the office of Senator Daniel Patrick Moynihan; he spent two subsequent summers at Marine Officer Candidates School in Quantico, Virginia, happy to have survived grueling drill sergeants and emerging with a "sense of common cause." After graduating in 1990, Liu worked as a legislative assistant to Senator David Boren and started a magazine of writings from people aged 24 to 32, *The Next Progressive,* with positive views of society and politics. The magazine was designed to contradict the negative stereotypes (compiled 1994 in *Next: Young American Writers on the New Generation*) of "Generation X" as self-centered hedonists. As a consequence, he became a speechwriter, first for Secretary of State Warren Christopher (1993), and then for President Clinton, whose deputy domestic policy adviser he became before entering Harvard Law School at age 25. He teaches at the University of Washington's Evans School of Public Affairs and writes *Slate's* "Teachings" column. He is the author of *Guiding Lights: The People Who Lead Us Toward Our Purpose in Life* (2005), which focuses on transformative mentors, leaders, and teachers.

In his autobiography, *The Accidental Asian* (1998), of which "Notes of a Native Speaker" is a chapter, Liu explores identity—in particular, the meaning of his own dual identity as American and Asian American: "I define my identity, then, in the simplest way possible: according to those with whom I identify. And I identify with whoever moves me." Should he, like other children of immigrants, embrace, resist, or redefine assimilation? Liu defines himself as an "accidental Asian," someone who has stumbled upon a sense of race and tries to describe it in order to define and live with it. This isn't always easy. "If Asians were shy and retiring," he says, "I'd try to be exuberant and jocular. If they were narrow-minded specialists, I'd be a well-rounded generalist." The irony is, he realizes, that in working so hard "to defy stereotype, I became a slave to it. . . . I could have spared myself a great deal of heartache had I understood . . . that the choice of race is not simply 'embrace or efface.'"

Notes of a Native Speaker

1.

Here are some of the ways you could say I am "white": 1

I listen to National Public Radio.
I wear khaki Dockers.
I own brown suede bucks.
I eat gourmet greens.
I have few close friends "of color."

I married a white woman.
I am a child of the suburbs.
I furnish my condo à la Crate & Barrel.
I vacation in charming bed-and-breakfasts.
I have never once been the victim of blatant discrimination.
I am a member of several exclusive institutions.
I have been in the inner sanctums of political power.
I have been there as something other than an attendant.
I have the ambition to return.
I am a producer of the culture.
I expect my voice to be heard.
I speak flawless, unaccented English.
I subscribe to *Foreign Affairs*.
I do not mind when editorialists write in the first person plural.
I do not mind how white television casts are.
I am not too ethnic.
I am wary of minority militants.
I consider myself neither in exile nor in opposition.
I am considered "a credit to my race."

I never asked to be white. I am not literally white. That is, I do not have white skin or white ancestors. I have yellow skin and yellow ancestors, hundreds of generations of them. But like so many other Asian Americans of the second generation, I find myself now the bearer of a strange new status: white, by acclamation. Thus it is that I have been described as an "honorary white," by other whites, and as a "banana," by other Asians. Both the honorific and the epithet take as a given this idea: to the extent that I have moved away from the periphery and toward the center of American life, I have become white inside. *Some are born white, others achieve whiteness, still others have whiteness thrust upon them*. This, supposedly, is what it means to assimilate.

2 There was a time when assimilation did quite strictly mean whitening. In fact, well into the first half of this century, mimicry of the stylized standards of the WASP gentry was the proper, dominant, perhaps even sole method of ensuring that your origins would not be held against you. You "made it" in society not only by putting on airs of anglitude, but also by assiduously bleaching out the marks of a darker, dirtier past. And this bargain, stifling as it was, was open to European immigrants almost exclusively; to blacks, only on the passing occasion; to Asians, hardly at all.

3 Times have changed, and I suppose you could call it progress that a Chinaman, too, may now aspire to whiteness. But precisely because the times have changed, that aspiration—and the *imputation* of the aspiration—now seems astonishingly outmoded. The meaning of "American" has undergone a revolution in the twenty-nine years I have been alive, a revolution of color, class, and culture. Yet the vocabulary of

"assimilation" has remained fixed all this time: fixed in whiteness, which is still our metonym for power; and fixed in shame, which is what the colored are expected to feel for embracing the power.

I have assimilated. I am of the mainstream. In many ways I fit the psychological profile of the so-called banana: imitative, impressionable, rootless, eager to please. As I will admit in this essay, I have at times gone to great lengths to downplay my difference, the better to penetrate the "establishment" of the moment. Yet I'm not sure that what I did was so cut-and-dried as "becoming white." I plead guilty to the charges above: achieving, learning the ways of the upper middle class, distancing myself from radicals of any hue. But having confessed, I still do not know my crime. 4

To be an accused banana is to stand at the ill-fated intersection of class and race. And because class is the only thing Americans have more trouble talking about than race, a minority's climb up the social ladder is often willfully misnamed and wrongly portrayed. There is usually, in the portrayal, a strong whiff of betrayal: the assimilist is a traitor to his kind, to his class, to his own family. He cannot gain the world without losing his soul. To be sure, something *is* lost in any migration, whether from place to place or from class to class. But something is gained as well. And the result is always more complicated than the monochrome language of "whiteness" and "authenticity" would suggest. 5

My own assimilation began long before I was born. It began with my parents, who came here with an appetite for Western ways already whetted by films and books and music and, in my mother's case, by a father who'd been to the West. My parents, who traded Chinese formality for the more laissez-faire stance of this country. Who made their way by hard work and quiet adaptation. Who fashioned a comfortable life in a quiet development in a second-tier suburb. Who, unlike your "typical" Chinese parents, were not pushy, status-obsessed, rigid, disciplined, or prepared. Who were haphazard about passing down ancestral traditions and "lessons" to their children. Who did pass down, however, the sense that their children were entitled to mix and match, as they saw fit, whatever aspects of whatever cultures they encountered. 6

I was raised, in short, to assimilate, to claim this place as mine. I don't mean that my parents told me to act like an American. That's partly the point: they didn't tell me to do anything except to be a good boy. They trusted I would find my way, and I did, following their example and navigating by the lights of the culture that encircled me like a dome. As a function of my parents' own half-conscious, half-finished acculturation, I grew up feeling that my life was Book II of an ongoing saga. Or that I was running the second leg of a relay race. *Slap*! I was out of the womb and sprinting, baton in hand. Gradually more sure of my stride, my breathing, the feel of the track beneath me. Eyes forward, never backward. 7

Library of Congress Prints and Photographs Division Washington DC, LC-A351-T01-3-M-38

This photograph by Ansel Adams is titled "Mr. and Mrs. Henry J. Tsurutani and Baby Bruce. Manzanar Relocation Center, California, 1943." What is "typically American" about this family portrait? What do you see, in clothing, furniture, toys, household artifacts that indicate the social class of these people? Of what ethnicity are they? Why is this family at the Manzanar Relocation Center? Why is it so important to know the date? Why was this picture taken? Does it matter that the boy in this picture, Bruce Tsurutani, is now an astrophysicist with the NASA Jet Propulsion Labs? What complex commentary on being an American does this picture make?

8 Today, nearly seven years after my father's death and two years after my marriage into a large white family, it is as if I have come round a bend and realized that I am no longer sure where I am running or why. My sprint slows to a trot. I scan the unfamiliar vista that is opening up. I am somewhere else now, somewhere far from the China that yielded my mother and father; far, as well, from the modest horizons I knew as a boy. I look at my limbs and realize I am no longer that boy; my gait and grasp exceed his by an order of magnitude. Now I want desperately to see my face, to see what time has marked and what it has erased. But I can find no mirror except the people who surround me. And they are mainly pale, powerful.

9 How did I end up here, standing in what seems the very seat of whiteness, gazing from the promontory of social privilege? How did I cover so much ground so quickly? What was it, in my blind journey, that I felt I should leave behind? And what *did* I leave behind? This, the jettisoning of one mode of life to send another aloft, is not only the immigrant's tale; it is the son's tale, too. By coming to America, my parents made themselves into citizens of a new country. By traveling the trajectory of an assimilist, so did I.

2.

As a child, I lived in a state of "amoebic bliss," to borrow the felicitous phrase of the author of *Nisei Daughter*, Monica Sone. The world was a gossamer web of wonder that began with life at home, extended to my friendships, and made the imaginary realm of daydream seem as immediate as the real. If something or someone was in my personal web of meaning, then color or station was irrelevant. I made no distinctions in fourth grade between my best friend, a black boy named Kimathi, and my next-best friend, a white boy named Charlie—other than the fact that one was number one, the other number two. I did not feel, or feel for, a seam that separated the textures of my Chinese life from those of my American life. I was not "bicultural" but omnicultural, and omnivorous, too. To my mind, I differed from others in only two ways that counted: I was a faster runner than most, and a better student. Thus did work blend happily with play, school with home, Western culture with Eastern: it was all the same to a self-confident boy who believed he'd always be at the center of his own universe. 10

As I approached adolescence, though, things shifted. Suddenly, I could no longer subsume the public world under my private concept of self. Suddenly, the public world was more complicated than just a parade of smiling teachers and a few affirming friends. Now I had to contend with the unstated, inchoate, but inescapable standards of *cool*. The essence of cool was the ability to conform. The essence of conformity was the ability to anticipate what was cool. And I wasn't so good at that. For the first time, I had found something that did not come effortlessly to me. No one had warned me about this transition from happy amoeboid to social animal; no one had prepared me for the great labors of fitting in. 11

And so in three adjoining arenas—my looks, my loves, my manners—I suffered a bruising adolescent education. I don't mean to overdramatize: there was, in these teenage banalities, usually something humorous and nothing particularly tragic. But in each of these realms, I came to feel I was not normal. And obtusely, I ascribed the difficulties of that age not to my age but to my color. I came to suspect that there was an order to things, an order that I, as someone Chinese, could perceive but not quite crack. I responded not by exploding in rebellion but by dedicating myself, quietly and sometimes angrily, to learning the order as best I could. I was never ashamed of being Chinese; I was, in fact, rather proud to be linked to a great civilization. But I was mad that my difference should matter now. And if it had to matter, I did not want it to defeat me. 12

Consider, if you will, my hair. For the first eleven years of my life, I sported what was essentially the same hairstyle: a tapered bowl cut, the handiwork of my mother. For those eleven joyful years, this low-maintenance do was entirely satisfactory. But in my twelfth year, as sixth grade got under way, I became aware—gradually at first, then urgently—that bangs were no 13 longer the look for boys. This was the year when certain early bloomers first made the height-weight-physique distribution in our class seem startlingly wide—and when I first realized that I was lingering near the bottom. It was essential that I compensate for my childlike mien by cultivating at least a patina of teenage style.

14 This is where my hair betrayed me. For some readers the words "Chinese hair" should suffice as explanation. For the rest, particularly those who have spent all your lives with the ability to comb back, style, and part your hair *at will*, what follows should make you count your blessings. As you may recall, 1980 was a vintage year for hair that was parted straight down the middle, then feathered on each side, feathered so immaculately that the ends would meet in the back like the closed wings of angels. I dreamed of such hair. I imagined tossing my head back casually, to ease into place the one or two strands that had drifted from their positions. I dreamed of wearing the fluffy, tailored locks of the blessed.

15 Instead, I was cursed. My hair was straight, rigid, and wiry. Not only did it fail to feather back; it would not even bend. Worse still, it grew the wrong way. That is, it all emanated from a single swirl near the rear edge of my scalp. Parting my hair in any direction except back to front, the way certain balding men stage their final retreat, was a physical impossibility. It should go without saying that this was a disaster. For the next three years, I experimented with a variety of hairstyles that ranged from the ridiculous to the sublimely bad. There was the stringy pothead look. The mushroom do. Helmet head. Bangs folded back like curtains. I enlisted a blow-dryer, a Conair set on high heat, to force my hair into stiff postures of submission. The results, though sometimes innovative, fell always far short of cool.

16 I feigned nonchalance, and no one ever said anything about it. But make no mistake: this was one of the most consuming crises of my inner life as a young teen. Though neither of my parents had ever had such troubles, I blamed this predicament squarely on my Chinese genes. And I could not abide my fate. At a time when homogeneity was the highest virtue, I felt I stood out like a pig-tailed Manchu.

17 My salvation didn't come until the end of junior high, when one of my buddies, in an epiphany as we walked past the Palace of Hair Design, dared me to get my head shaved. Without hesitation, I did it—to the tearful laughter of my friends and, soon afterward, the tearful horror of my mother. Of course, I had moments of doubt the next few days as I rubbed my peach-fuzzed skull. But what I liked was this: I had managed, without losing face, to rid myself of my greatest social burden. What's more, in the eyes of some classmates, I was now a bold (if bald) iconoclast. I've worn a crew cut ever since.

18 Well-styled hair was only one part of a much larger preoccupation during the ensuing years: wooing girls. In this realm I experienced a most

frustrating kind of success. I was the boy that girls always found "sweet" and "funny" and "smart" and "nice." Which, to my highly sensitive ear, sounded like "leprous." Time and again, I would charm a girl into deep friendship. Time and again, as the possibility of romance came within reach, I would smash into what I took to be a glass ceiling.

The girls were white, you see; such were the demographics of my school. I was Chinese. And I was convinced that this was the sole obstacle to my advancement. It made sense, did it not? I was, after all, sweet and funny and smart and nice. Hair notwithstanding, I was not unattractive, at least compared with some of the beasts who had started "going out" with girls. There was simply no other explanation. Yet I could never say this out loud: it would have been the whining of a loser. My response, then, was to secretly scorn the girls I coveted. It was *they* who were subpar, whose small-mindedness and veiled prejudice made them unworthy. 19

My response, too, was to take refuge in my talents. I made myself into a Renaissance boy, playing in the orchestra but also joining the wrestling team, winning science prizes but also editing the school paper. I thought I was defying the stereotype of the Asian American male as a one-dimensional nerd. But in the eyes of some, I suppose, I was simply another "Asian overachiever." 20

In hindsight, it's hard to know exactly how great a romantic penalty I paid for being Chinese. There may have been girls who would have had nothing to do with me on account of my race, but I never knew them. There were probably girls who, race aside simply didn't like me. And then there were girls who liked me well enough but who also shied from the prospect of being part of an interracial couple. With so many boys out there, they probably reasoned, why take the path of greater resistance? Why risk so many status points? Why not be "just friends" with this Chinese boy? 21

Maybe this stigma was more imagined than real. But being an ABC ("American-born Chinese," as our parents called us) certainly affected me another way. It made me feel like something of a greenhorn, a social immigrant. I wanted so greatly to be liked. And my earnestness, though endearing, was not the sort of demeanor that won girls' hearts. Though I was observant enough to notice how people talked when flirting, astute enough to mimic the forms, I was oblivious to the subterranean levels of courtship, blind to the more subtle rituals of "getting chicks" by spurning them. I held the view that if you were manifestly a good person, eventually someone of the opposite sex would do the rational thing and be smitten with you. I was clueless. Many years would pass before I'd wise up. 22

3.

I recently dug up a photograph of myself from freshman year of college that made me smile. I have on the wrong shoes, the wrong socks, the wrong checkered shirt tucked the wrong way into the wrong slacks. I look 23 like what I was: a boy sprung from a middle-brow burg who affected a secondhand preppiness. I look nervous. Compare that image to one from my senior-class dinner: now I am attired in a gray tweed jacket with a green plaid bow tie and a sensible button-down shirt, all purchased at the Yale Co-op. I look confident, and more than a bit contrived.

24 What happened in between those two photographs is that I experienced, then overcame, what the poet Meena Alexander has called "the shock of arrival." When I was deposited at the wrought-iron gates of my residential college as a freshman, I felt more like an outsider than I'd thought possible. It wasn't just that I was a small Chinese boy standing at a grand WASP temple; nor simply that I was a hayseed neophyte puzzled by the refinements of college style. It was *both*: color and class were all twisted together in a double helix of felt inadequacy.

25 For a while I coped with the shock by retreating to a group of my own kind—not fellow Asians, but fellow marginal public-school grads who resented the rah-rah Yalies to whom everything came so effortlessly. Aligning myself this way was bearable—I was hiding, but at least I could place myself in a long tradition of underdog exiles at Yale. Aligning myself by race, on the other hand, would have seemed too inhibiting.

26 I know this doesn't make much sense. I know also that college, in the multicultural era, is supposed to be where the deracinated minority youth discovers the "person of color" inside. To a point, I did. I studied Chinese, took an Asian American history course, a seminar on race politics. But ultimately, college was where the unconscious habits of my adolescent assimilation hardened into self-conscious strategy.

27 I still remember the moment, in the first week of school, when I came upon a table in Yale Station set up by the Asian American Student Association. The upperclassman staffing the table was pleasant enough. He certainly did not strike me as a fanatic. Yet, for some reason, I flashed immediately to a scene I'd witnessed days earlier, on the corner outside. Several Lubavitcher Jews, dressed in black, their faces bracketed by dangling side curls, were looking for fellow travelers at this busy crossroads. Their method was crude but memorable. As any vaguely Jewish-looking male walked past, the zealots would quickly approach, extend a pamphlet, and ask, "Excuse me, sir, are you Jewish?" Since most were not, and since those who were weren't about to stop, the result was a frantic, nervous, almost comical buzz all about the corner: Excuse me, are you Jewish? Are you Jewish? Excuse me. Are you Jewish?

28 I looked now at the clean-cut Korean boy at the AASA table (I think I can distinguish among Asian ethnicities as readily as those Hasidim thought they could tell Gentile from Jew), and though he had merely offered an introductory hello and was now smiling mutely at me, in the back of my mind I heard only this: *Excuse me, are you Asian? Are you Asian? Excuse me. Are you Asian*? I took one of the flyers on the table, even put my name on a mailing list, so as not to appear impolite. But I had

already resolved not to be active in any Asians-only group. I thought then: I would never *choose* to be so pigeonholed.

This allergic sensitivity to "pigeonholing" is one of the unhappy hallmarks of the banana mentality. What does the banana fear? That is, what did *I* fear? The possibility of being mistaken for someone more Chinese. The possibility of being known only, or even primarily, for being Asian. The possibility of being written off by whites as a self-segregating ethnic clumper. These were the threats—unseen and, frankly, unsubstantiated—that I felt I should keep at bay. 29

I didn't avoid making Asian friends in college or working with Asian classmates; I simply never went out of my way to do so. This distinction seemed important—it marked, to my mind, the difference between self-hate and self-respect. That the two should have been so proximate in the first place never struck me as odd, or telling. Nor did it ever occur to me that the reasons I gave myself for dissociating from Asians as a group—that I didn't want to be part of a clique, that I didn't want to get absorbed and lose my individuality—were the very developments that marked my own assimilation. I simply hewed to my ideology of race neutrality and self-reliance. I didn't need that crutch, I told myself nervously, that crutch of racial affinity. What's more, I was vaguely insulted by the presumption that I might. 30

But again: Who was making the presumption? Who more than I was taking the mere existence of Korean volleyball leagues or Taiwanese social sets or pan-Asian student clubs to mean that *all* people of Asian descent, myself included, needed such quasi-kinship groups? And who more than I interpreted this need as infirmity, as a failure to fit in? I resented the faintly sneering way that some whites regarded Asians as an undifferentiated mass. But whose sneer, really, did I resent more than my own? 31

I was keenly aware of the unflattering mythologies that attach to Asian Americans: that we are indelibly foreign, exotic, math and science geeks, numbers people rather than people people, followers and not leaders, physically frail but devious and sneaky, unknowable and potentially treacherous. These stereotypes of Asian otherness and inferiority were like immense blocks of ice sitting before me, challenging me to chip away at them. And I did, tirelessly. All the while, though, I was oblivious to rumors of my *own* otherness and inferiority, rumors that rose off those blocks like a fog, wafting into my consciousness and chilling my sense of self. 32

As I had done in high school, I combated the stereotypes in part by trying to disprove them. If Asians were reputed to be math and science geeks, I would be a student of history and politics. If Asians were supposed to be feeble subalterns, I'd lift weights and go to Marine officer candidate school. If Asians were alien, I'd be ardently patriotic. If Asians were shy and retiring, I'd try to be exuberant and jocular. If they were narrow-minded specialists, I'd be a well-rounded generalist. 33

If they were perpetual outsiders, I'd join every establishment outfit I could and show that I, too, could run with the swift.

34 I overstate, of course. It wasn't that I chose to do all these things with no other purpose than to cut against a supposed convention. I was neither so Pavlovian nor so calculating that I would simply remake myself into the opposite of what people expected. I actually *liked* history, and wasn't especially good at math. As the grandson of a military officer, I *wanted* to see what officer candidates school would be like, and I enjoyed it, at least once I'd finished. I am *by nature* enthusiastic and allegiant, a joiner, and a bit of a jingo.

35 At the same time, I was often aware, sometimes even hopeful, that others might think me "exceptional" for my race. I derived satisfaction from being the "atypical" Asian, the only Chinese face at OCS or in this club or that.

36 The irony is that in working so duteously to defy stereotype, I became a slave to it. For to act self-consciously against Asian "tendencies" is not to break loose from the cage of myth and legend; it is to turn the very key that locks you inside. What spontaneity is there when the value of every act is measured, at least in part, by its power to refute a presumption about why you act? The *typical Asian* I imagined, and the *atypical Asian* I imagined myself to be, were identical in this sense: neither was as much a creature of free will as a human being ought to be.

37 Let me say it plainly, then: I am not proud to have had this mentality. I believe I have outgrown it. And I expose it now not to justify it but to detoxify it, to prevent its further spread.

38 Yet it would be misleading, I think, to suggest that my education centered solely on the discomfort caused by race. The fact is, when I first got to college I felt deficient compared with people of *every* color. Part of why I believed it so necessary to achieve was that I lacked the connections, the wealth, the experience, the sophistication that so many of my classmates seemed to have. I didn't get the jokes or the intellectual references. I didn't have the canny attitude. So in addition to all my coursework, I began to puzzle over this, the culture of the influential class.

39 Over time, I suppose, I learned the culture. My interests and vocabulary became ever more worldly. I made my way onto what Calvin Trillin once described as the "magic escalator" of a Yale education. Extracurriculars opened the door to an alumni internship, which brought me to Capitol Hill, which led to a job and a life in Washington after commencement. Gradually, very gradually, I found that I was not so much of an outsider anymore. I found that by almost any standard, but particularly by the standards of my younger self, I was actually beginning to "make it."

40 It has taken me until now, however, to appraise the thoughts and acts of that younger self. I can see now that the straitening path I took was not the only or even the best path. For while it may be possible to transcend race, *it is not always necessary to try*. And while racial identity is

sometimes a shackle, it is not *only* a shackle. I could have spared myself a great deal of heartache had I understood this earlier, that the choice of race is not simply "embrace or efface."

I wonder sometimes how I would have turned out had I been, from the start, more comfortable in my own skin. What did I miss by distancing myself from race? What friendships did I forgo, what self-knowledge did I defer? Had certain accidents of privilege been accidents of privation or exclusion, I might well have developed a different view of the world. But I do not know just how my view would have differed. 41

What I know is that through all those years of shadow-dancing with my identity, something happened, something that had only partially to do with color. By the time I left Yale I was no longer the scared boy of that freshman photo. I had become more sure of myself and of my place—sure enough, indeed, to perceive the folly of my fears. And in the years since, I have assumed as sense of expectation, of access and *belonging*, that my younger self could scarcely have imagined. All this happened incrementally. There was no clear tipping point, no obvious moment of mutation. The shock of arrival, it would seem, is simply that I arrived. 42

Content

1. On what basis does Liu define himself as "white, by acclamation" (¶ 1)? Why is racial identification and definition so important to Liu? Why is he so concerned with defying Asian stereotypes?
2. Given the variability of white (or any) culture, to what aspects of "white" culture has Liu assimilated? Is his assimilation more a matter of class than race (see ¶s 6–7)?
3. Why did the adolescent Liu's "bad hair" present so many problems (¶s 13–17)? Why as an adult, after he's solved the hair problem, does he devote so much space to discussing it?
4. Liu refers to people having a "choice of race" (¶ 40) when he says "I could have spared myself a great deal of heartache had I understood . . . earlier, that the choice of race is not simply 'embrace or efface'" (¶ 40). Explain what he means by this. Does his essay compel you to agree with him? Why or why not?

Strategies/Structures/Language

5. Is Liu writing primarily for an audience of himself? White Americans? Asians? Other immigrants? How can you tell?
6. Why does Liu begin by describing his present self (¶s 1–9) before moving back, first to his childhood (¶ 10) and then to his adolescence (¶s 11–21) and college years (¶s 23–39)? Why does he spend so little space on his childhood in comparison with the other periods of his life?
7. Liu refers to himself as "Asian American" (¶ 1), "an honorary white" (¶ 1), "a banana" (¶ 1), "Asian" (¶ 2), "a Chinaman" (¶ 3), an "assimilist" (¶ 5). Do all these labels fit equally well? Or are some better than others and if so, for what

purposes? Which of these are labels that only Chinese can use in talking about themselves?

8. In what places is this essay humorous? In ironic self-mockery, does Liu (or any other author who uses this technique) invite readers to laugh with him or to laugh at him? Can readers take him seriously if he's laughing at himself?

For Writing

9. "How did I cover so much ground so quickly [in my quest for assimilation]," asks Liu. "What was it, in my blind journey, that I felt I should leave behind? And what *did* I leave behind? This, the jettisoning of one mode of life to send another aloft, is not only the immigrant's tale, it is the son's tale, too" (¶ 9). Identify a culture (of family, gender, race, class, occupation, nationality) that helped to shape you and which to an extent you have resisted. What did you take from it and what about it did you resist? If you have made deliberate choices, on what basis did you do so? If the shaping was unavoidable, explain why this was so. If stereotyping played any role in either your acceptance or resistance, identify the stereotype and the nature of its influence.

10. ***Second Look.*** Liu's list of the ways in which he is "white" (¶ 1) covers food, clothing, shelter, entertainment, affiliations, jobs, ambition, language, groups he identifies with and rejects, measures of self-esteem, and attitudes toward himself and his status. Why is he making this comparison? Make a list of the ways in which you are "white" that address these same topic areas, and other significant ones (note, for instance, that Liu omits a spiritual dimension) if you wish. Write a paper of self-description in which you compare your list with Liu's, and show how each list defines its author. In what ways is your self-description congruent with the ways that others would describe you? To what extent might their description depend on whether or not they share major aspects of your identity?

11. Apply the same considerations of identity to your viewing of Ansel Adams's photograph of Mr. and Mrs. Henry J. Tsurutani and baby Bruce at Manzanar Relocation Center in 1943.

MICHAEL J. BUGEJA

Michael Bugeja (pronounced "boo-shay-ah") (born 1952) earned graduate degrees at South Dakota State University (MS in Mass Communication, 1976) and Oklahoma State University (PhD English, 1985). Bugeja—ethicist, poet, and journalism professor—is director of the Greenlee School of Journalism and Communication at Iowa State University, where he also serves on the board of the Institute of Science and Society. He has published twenty books, including several volumes of poetry and *Academic Socialism: Merit and Moral in Higher Education* (1994), *Living Ethics: Developing Values in Mass Communication* (1996), and most recently *Interpersonal Divide: The Search for Community in a Technological Age* (2005), which documents how the Internet and other digital technologies have failed to deliver the hoped-for "global village." Indeed, claims Bugeja, we have fallen into the "interpersonal divide"—the void that develops when we spend too much time in virtual rather than real communities, neglecting our primary relationships, and with these, our sense of self.

He writes and lectures widely on ethical issues, including the dubious ethics of spending huge amounts of institutional (such as university) money on technology at the expense of fostering meaningful human relationships. It is from an ethical perspective that he wrote "Facing the Facebook," first published in the *Chronicle of Higher Education* (January 2006). *Facebook*'s virtual subculture absorbs thousands of student-hours, often to the students' detriment in terms of what they post and the ways it is used. He argues that professors, as well as students, need to develop "'interpersonal intelligence,' or the ability to discern when and where technology may be appropriate or inappropriate."

Facing the Facebook

Information technology in the classroom was supposed to bridge digital divides and enhance student research. Increasingly, however, our networks are being used to entertain members of "the Facebook Generation" who text-message during class, talk on their cellphones during labs, and listen to iPods rather than guest speakers in the wireless lecture hall. 1

That is true at my institution, Iowa State University. With a total enrollment of 25,741, Iowa State logs 20,247 registered users on Facebook (see http://www.facebook.com), which bills itself as "an online directory that connects people through social networks at schools." 2

While I'd venture to say that most of the students on any campus are regular visitors to Facebook, many professors and administrators have yet to hear about Facebook, let alone evaluate its impact. 3

On many levels, Facebook is fascinating—an interactive, image-laden directory featuring groups that share lifestyles or attitudes. Many students find it addictive, as evidenced by discussion groups with names like "Addicted to the Facebook," which boasts 330 members at Iowa State. Nationwide, Facebook tallies 250 million hits every day and ranks ninth in overall traffic on the Internet. 4

That kind of social networking affects all levels of academe: 5

- Institutions seeking to build enrollment learn that "technology" rates higher than "rigor" or "reputation" in high-school focus groups. That may pressure provosts to continue investing in technology rather than in tenure-track positions.
- Professors and librarians encounter improper use of technology by students, and some of those cases go to judiciary officials who enforce the student code.

- Career and academic advisers must deal with employers and parents who have screened Facebook and discovered what users have been up to in residence halls.
- Academics assessing learning outcomes often discover that technology is as much a distraction in the classroom as a tool.

6 To be sure, classroom distractions have plagued teachers in less technological times. In my era, there was the ubiquitous comic book hidden in a boring text. A comic book cannot compare with a computer, of course. Neither did it require university money at the expense of faculty jobs.

7 John W. Curtis, research director at the American Association of University Professors, believes that investment in technology is one of several factors responsible for the well-documented loss of tenure-track positions in the past decade.

8 Facebook is not the sole source of those woes. However, it is a Janus-faced symbol of the online habits of students and the traditional objectives of higher education, one of which is to inspire critical thinking in learners rather than multitasking. The situation will only get worse as freshmen enter our institutions weaned on high-school versions of Facebook and equipped with gaming devices, iPods, and other portable technologies.

9 Michael Tracey, a journalism professor at the University of Colorado, recounts a class discussion during which he asked how many people had seen the previous night's *NewsHour* on PBS or read that day's *New York Times*. "A couple of hands went up out of about 140 students who were present," he recalls. "One student chirped: 'Ask them how many use Facebook.' I did. Every hand in the room went up. She then said: 'Ask them how many used it today.' I did. Every hand in the room went up. I was amazed."

10 Christine Rosen, a fellow at the Ethics and Public Policy Center, in Washington, D.C., believes experiences like that are an example of what she calls "egocasting, the thoroughly personalized and extremly narrow pursuit of one's personal taste." Facebook "encourages egocasting even though it claims to further 'social networking' and build communities," she says. Unlike real communities, however, most interactions in online groups do not take place face-to-face. It's no surprise, she says, that "people who use networks like Facebook have a tendency to describe themselves like products."

11 To test that, I registered on the Iowa State Facebook and noticed that the discussion groups looked a lot like direct mailing lists. Some, in fact, were the same or barely distinguishable from mailing lists compiled in *The Lifestyle Market Analyst*, a reference book that looks at potential audiences for advertisers. For instance, "Baseball Addicts" and "Kick Ass Conservatives" are Facebook groups, while "Baseball Fanatics" and

"Iowa Conservatives" are the names of commercial mailing lists. You can find "PC Gamers," "Outdoor Enthusiasts," and advocates for and against gun control on both Facebook and in marketing directories. "It is ironic," Rosen says, "that the technologies we embrace and praise for the degree of control they give us individually also give marketers and advertisers the most direct window into our psyche and buying habits they've ever had."

Online networks like Facebook allow high levels of surveillance, 12 she adds, and not just for marketers. "College administrators are known to troll the profiles on Facebook for evidence of illegal behavior by students," she says. "Students might think they are merely crafting and surfing a vast network of peers, but because their Facebook profile is, in essence, a public diary, there is nothing to stop anyone else—from marketers, to parents, to college officials—from reading it."

Her comments bear out. For instance, a panel at the University of 13 Missouri at Columbia has been formed to educate students about Facebook content that may violate student-conduct policies or local laws. A Duquesne University student was asked to write a paper because the Facebook group he created was deemed homophobic. Students at Northern Kentucky University were charged with code violations when a keg was seen in a dorm-room picture online.

My concerns are mostly ethical. In my field, I know of students who 14 showcase inappropriate pictures of partners or use stereotypes to describe themselves and others on Facebook. What does that mean in terms of taste, sensitivity, and bias? I know of disclosures about substance abuse that have come back to haunt students under investigation for related offenses. I know of fictitious Facebook personae that masquerade as administrators, including college presidents.

Facebook forbids such fabrications. According to Chris Hughes, a 15 spokesman, misrepresentation is against the directory's "Terms of Service."

"In other words," he says, "you can't create a profile for Tom Cruise 16 using your account. When users report a profile, we take a look and decide if the content seems authentic. If not, we'll remove the user from the network."

Shortly after interviewing Hughes, I heard from Michael Tracey, the 17 Colorado journalism professor, who learned that an account had been opened in his name on MySpace (see http://www.myspace.com), another networking site, "with photos and all kinds of weird details." He suspects a student from the course he spoke with me about is behind the ruse.

Unless we reassess our high-tech priorities, issues associated with 18 insensitivity, indiscretion, bias, and fabrication will consume us in higher education.

Christine Rosen believes that college administrators "have 19 embraced technology as a means of furthering education, but they have failed to realize that the younger generation views technology largely as a means of delivering entertainment—be it music, video games, Internet access, or television—and secondarily, as a means of communicating."

20 What can we do in the short term about the misuse of technology, especially in wireless locales?

21 The Facebook's spokesman, Hughes, is not overly concerned. He notes that students who use computers in classrooms and labs routinely perform "a host of activities online while listening to lectures," like checking e-mail, sending instant messages, or reading the news.

22 "Usage of Facebook during class," he says, "doesn't strike me as being that different than usage of those other tools."

23 "If professors don't want their students to have access to the Internet during class," Hughes adds, "they can remove wireless installations or ask their students not to bring computers to class."

24 Some less-drastic measures include clauses in syllabi warning against using Facebook or other nonassigned Internet sites during class. Some professors punish students who violate such rules and reward those who visit the library. Others have stopped using technology in the classroom. A few institutions are assessing how to respond to Facebook and similar digital distractions. Last fall the University of New Mexico blocked access to Facebook because of security concerns. My preference is not to block content but to instill in students what I call "interpersonal intelligence," or the ability to discern when and where technology may be appropriate or inappropriate.

25 That, alas, requires critical thinking and suggests that we have reached a point where we must make hard decisions about our investment in technology and our tradition of high standards. Because the students already have.

Content

1. Why is *Facebook* "addictive"? What reasons does Bugeja give? What other reasons can you add from your own experience or that of others with *Facebook* or its equivalent?
2. What does *Facebook* have to do with ethical questions such as surveillance, illegal behavior, insensitivity, and homophobia, for example? Who uses the information (doctored or otherwise) they find there? To what extent do administrators have the right to use the *Facebook* as a surveillance tool? Are students' rights being violated in such cases? Why or why not?
3. In this essay and elsewhere, Bugeja argues that the ethical and educational consequences of that time spent online need more attention. Colleges invest heavily in technology, but technology could be undermining their educational goal, which is "to inspire critical thinking in learners rather than multitasking" (¶ 8). Do you agree that among college students technology, *Facebook* included, could be undermining the very qualities their educational institutions are seeking to foster?

Strategies/Structures/Language

4. This essay, published in the *Chronicle of Higher Education* (January 2006), has as its intended readers college faculty and administrators rather than students. How can you tell?

5. Do you agree with Christine Rosen's definition of "egocasting" as "the thoroughly personalized and extremely narrow pursuit of one's personal taste" (¶ 10), as manifested on *Facebook*? Explain. Invent some comparable terms to describe or explain heavy blogging or other personal Internet use.

6. In what ways is *Facebook* a reliable representation of any given posted identity? A "public diary"? Are students in fact "'merely crafting and surfing a vast network of peers" (¶ 12)? Although the *Facebook* management says it removes inauthentic subscribers and content (¶s 15, 16), does your own experience bear this out? What clues do you use in evaluating any given entry?

For Writing

7. ***Journal Writing.*** Are you a member of "the Facebook Generation," someone who text-messages during class, talks on the cell phone during labs, and listens "to iPods rather than guest speakers in the wireless lecture hall" (¶ 1)? If so, how did this behavior begin? Has it escalated or diminished since you came to college? With what consequences?

8. ***Dialogues.*** What are some major differences between "social networking" online and face-to-face? With a partner, try this out. Discuss a topic online; then discuss the same topic in person. Do this with several topics (and/or several partners) and write up your results. What disadvantages, and advantages, accompanied online communication? With face-to-face conversation? To what extent does the topic influence the nature of these communications? To what extent does your relationship with the other person make a significant difference in what you say and how you say it?

9. Do you have an online identity? In more than one venue or site? Did you craft this carefully? What comprises it? Do you ever change it? In what ways? How often? Whom do you expect to see it? Interact with it? Are these people you actually know in real life? If so, what percentage of your contacts are online versus face-to-face? Is this a matter of distance? Convenience? Other factors? Has your virtual identity/life had any significant impact on your "real" identity/life? Are you comfortable, pleased with your identity in either or both venues? If so, why? If not, what changes will you make? How will you make these? What consequences will you expect?

ZARA RIX

Zara Rix (born 1982) is a graduate student in English at the University of Connecticut. She is the oldest of four children from an Australian-Italian marriage; her mother moved to the United States with her family at 13, and her father stopped in the United States on his way back to Australia from Europe at 25. "He never intended to stay in the U.S.," says Rix, "and my mother was willing to move to Australia with him, but the timing (in the form of work, children, my maternal grandparents) never worked out. My mother says the marriage probably succeeded because they were in the U.S., on nobody's cultural home ground, when they began married life."

She wrote this essay when studying *corporalité* in a contemporary Francophone literature class. "It was an experiment, a game," she explains. "I wanted to see what I would read if I treated my body like a book. The results surprised me. Almost all my memories of significant events attached to my body involve other people, other nations, or both. For example, the scar on my right knee is from a car accident when I was two, the first time my father brought me to meet his family in Australia. Examples like that continued to crop up as I wrote. My body's story incorporated the stories of my family, my friends, places I've lived, and in the midst of those stories, places, and people, I tried to find me. If so much of my self is defined in contrast or in relation to others, then where am I? This isn't an abstract philosophical question; I cannot even talk about my body—my present, corporeal self—without referencing others. So it was both a surprise and not a surprise when the essay began circling around identity and issues of race and being a second-generation American, issues that interest me although I have no clear-cut answers to the questions they pose.

"As much as this essay deals with individual identity," she continues, "I was comforted by the corporate aspect of my *corporalité*. I focused a lot of the essay on my friends because we are similar more because of our differences than despite them. And while I know that for the most part my experience deals with a very specific social and educational class of people, I think that's all right. Questions regarding identity, race, and 'American-ness' occur across a spectrum of people, and so I can see my story as one part of that corporate search."

✧ Corporality

1 I use my body to map who I am. Perhaps "map" is the wrong word, since I know I'm more than the external SWF. Running my eyes down my body, I read stories upon each part of me. *Corporalité,* the French call it: reading the body in a text, reading the body as though it were a text. I like their word. *Corps* is the word for "body," but in English it sounds like "core." Reading me, I read my core, and I'm surprised how much of my *corps* is corporate; others' stories flow through me until parts of them are included in my body. All these stories, I realize, are layered. More than a map, I need a deep-water chart in order to navigate.

2 I (the SWF) am 5' 4". I range between 110 and 120 pounds, and I look like my friend Aliya. Not on the face, perhaps (she's Taiwanese), but our

bodies are almost mirror images. We can share clothes and shoes, and we both look good in red. She prefers a maroon shade but I like the bright red that brings out the color in my face: celebratory red, in Chinese.

Aliya and I started school together at the age of five. Both of our 3
parents moved to the Lexington suburbs for the school system and both of our parents (ambitious) enrolled us in first grade, skipping kindergarten. It didn't work. We got held back.

"My English wasn't good enough," Aliya says. She came from 4
Taiwan two years earlier.

Aliya went to special English classes, but I don't remember ever 5
having trouble understanding her. I consistently beat her at spelling, but that was only satisfying until she forbade me from drawing humans during free time. Aliya said she had a special magic where if she drew someone, she could tell if the person was good or evil by the number of lines in their hair. I tried to do the same thing, but she said I couldn't because I didn't have the special magic; I could only draw animals and objects.

I'm not sure when we became friends. I think I started thinking of 6
her as a friend by fifth grade, and by seventh grade the rest of our friends moved out of state or overseas. Aliya and I remained. Midway through middle school, Aliya described us as best friends and, once I adjusted to the idea, I realized it was true. We'd grown into a friendship.

Outwardly, I sometimes think we've also grown into each other, 7
although supposedly genetics governs that. Our Asian/Caucasian differences remain, but they're irrelevant to what's inside. I know her metabolism (Aliya needs to eat within two hours of a set mealtime or she'll grow cranky), and Aliya understands what I'm saying even with my mouth full. When we visit each other's homes, we translate our grandmothers' greetings: Chinese or Italian into English. Aliya calls me by my home name, Zarita, and I can almost pronounce "Xian-Yu." We travel together. She visited me at boarding school in Australia, and I visited her when she attended Oxford.

Two summers ago, after I finished working in France and after she 8
finished an internship in a hospital in Dehradun, we met up in India. We stayed with my college roommate and her family, and they arranged for us to tour northern India in a taxi. Aliya insisted on visiting McLeod Ganj; she wanted to bring her father a gift from the Dalai Lama's temple. While there, displaced Tibetans stopped to talk to us along the street. Aliya wore a red salwar (a bridal color in India) and they asked her if she was Tibetan. They asked me for money.

Driving home in the taxi, I watched out the window for tea planta- 9
tions, elephants, and eucalyptus trees. Aliya listened to music.

"Hey," I asked, "you know how we've spent so much time over- 10
seas—do you think that's made you different?"

She looked at me. 11

12 I repeated the question, in case she hadn't heard. "Do you think it's made you different? You know, as though you don't fit in anywhere?"

13 "No," she said, shortly, replacing her earpiece. "I always felt different. I looked different."

14 I was confused. Honestly, I don't remember ever thinking Aliya looked different. My memory of the Lexington school system is of lots of Asians. Or at least, most of our friends were Asians, I thought. Now, as I look at a photo of our group of friends from junior prom, I count 10 Asian-skinned people (if I include the dark-skinned Armenians, who are technically European) and 11 whites (if I include the Israelis, who look white but are technically Asian). If I undo my arbitrary skin-color count, sorting us into European vs. Asian ancestry, the numbers remain the same. But that only represented our group of friends. The populations of Lexington and wider New England as a whole are predominantly white, something I didn't notice until Aliya pointed it out to me.

15 At times like this, when Aliya forwards me "You Know You're Asian If . . ." emails or sits on my bed reading my brother's copy of *American Born Chinese,* I feel the difference between us. It lies like a jagged crack down the center of our friendship, marking the boundary of our individualities. It doesn't hurt, but it reminds me that no matter how similar we are, there are aspects of Aliya's experience that I will never comprehend.

16 I am white. Clearly, unmistakably white. Veins show blue through my skin. I can trace them like a roadmap over my feet, down my arms and into my hands, up my neck until they meet the blue of my eyes.

17 "So blue!"

18 Javier adored putting his hand under my chin, tilting my face as he examined my eyes. I dated him briefly while living in France, where we both taught English. He was Mexican, but there wasn't much call for a Spanish teacher.

19 I was captivated by his smooth hair, held back in a band, and his *conquistador* nose, but he made me uncomfortable when he exclaimed over my eyes and traced his fingers over my pale skin. He asked me to tell him frankly, what stereotypes of Mexicans are in the US. I said I didn't know because in my town there are more Asians than Mexicans. That in itself was an answer, I suppose, if he knew how to translate the social undercurrents of Massachusetts' suburbs.

20 Shortly after Javier and I stopped seeing each other, he moved in with a different blue-eyed girl. My roommate Beatriz, annoyed that he never returned the DVDs she brought with her from Mexico, snorted. "You were his first pick," she told me. "You have blonde hair *and* blue eyes."

21 I don't have blonde hair.

22 My hair is brown, neither dark nor light. It's nothing remarkable, and so I pay for blonde highlights. Sometimes, carried away by "adding summer warmth" or the fun of being blond(er), I make my hair very light.

After Javier, I dyed it back to brown. The dye sat on top of the blonde, making it orange when it faded. I dyed it again.

In New York, a few months after our trip to India, Aliya compli- 23
mented my hair. "It looks good," she said. "And it's so curly now you cut it."

It took Fahaad, the friend we were visiting, a full day to realize my 24
hair was brown again. He looked at me, frowned, and then looked closer. "Hey!" he said. "Why'd you dye it? It looked good!"

Fahaad is sort-of Indian. He joined Lexington High School right 25
before I moved back from Australia. Both of us were in eleventh grade, lost, and trying to understand how we fit in (or, in my case, re-fit in) to SATs, AP classes, and burgeoning life (read: college) decisions.

"I thought you were going to be another Indian Muslim," he told me 26
years later. "They kept talking about you moving back, and the only other Zaras I know are Muslim."

It took us a long time to figure out where Fahaad came from. His 27
family moved to Lexington from Malaysia, but he didn't look Malaysian and when we asked where he came from, he said, "I'm American." He is, too. He was born in California; more American than Aliya, if birthplace is a marker.

"I'm American, too," Aliya told him. "Naturalized. But we speak 28
Chinese at home and you sure weren't speaking English when your mom called."

Fahaad's family is from the northeast of India, closer to China than 29
the Ganges. "That's why I'm chinky-eyed," he explained.

Once, either at the end of high school or the beginning of college, 30
Aliya didn't talk to him for a week. "You know what he said?" Her voice over the phone was tight. "He said, 'Light matters to dark people.' And I don't care if—well, okay, it's true—but he shouldn't *say* it!"

Back in Lexington one summer after high school, Fahaad put his arm 31
beside mine. "I'm too dark," he said, "and you're too light." His nose wrinkled. I was shocked. My skin had been flippantly dismissed. I was used to being the only blue-eyed one in our group of friends, the only one who sunburned and got teased, but I'd never felt an aesthetic judgment on the color of my skin. "If we had kids," he added, "they'd be the right color."

It felt odd to look down at our arms, to look at my white-and-red 32
splotched hands and the brown into beige of his palms, and think he was right.

As a child, I once woke up and didn't recognize my arm. It lay 33
beside my face on the bed, but my arm had fallen asleep during the night and I couldn't feel it. I ordered the fingers to move and watched them wriggle without feeling the scratch of my sheets. It looked like a strange, alien thing.

That happened to me again, another time when my arm lay beside 34
Fahaad's. I woke early, when dawn was just starting to lighten the day,

leaving the world visible but colorless. Fahaad's warmth was behind me, and in front of me I saw two arms. I knew one of my arms was beneath me and that therefore only one of those two was mine, but the arms were so close, so entangled, I couldn't tell which belonged to me and which belonged to him.

35 *This isn't that hard*, I told myself. *He's a guy; his arm is bigger and it's got to be hairier.*

36 I studied our arm hairs, and as I did so, I realized that I hadn't thought of color. A thrill of excitement ran through me: I hadn't thought to look for color. It was as though, for the first time I could recall, skin and all it symbolized didn't matter.

37 If I told you I didn't sleep with Fahaad, would you still believe his body is written on mine?

38 Because what I read doesn't stop there. My delight at looking for the difference of sex and not of race made me wonder. If I felt that Javier dated my whiteness more than he dated me, if I sometimes suspected Fahaad enjoyed my blondeness more than I wanted him to, how was I different? I didn't think I was drawn to them because they were "exotic"—Javier spoke English while I was still floundering in French, and I'd known Fahaad for enough years to have no illusions—but perhaps I did have something to prove. If my joy at not thinking about color felt like a release, then—no less than them—wasn't I trapped by belonging to a family that was on the wrong side of colonization?

39 I think of it as my ugly underbelly: white and pasty, like something that emerges after you've poked at rotting wood.

40 Despite Australia's heat, the only time I saw my belly while at boarding school was over exeats. Exeat weekends shut down the boarding house, and I spent that time with my grandparents. That, after all, was the main purpose of my being in Australia: so that I could get to know my father's family.

41 For me, those were comfortable weekends, filled with sleeping in, reading the funnies, and feeling as though I belonged someplace. I could come out to breakfast whenever I liked, tucking my T-shirt up so my navel was bare and not having to worry about whether my shorts were in style.

42 Grandpa sat at the head of the kitchen table each morning, his back to the sliding doors so that the light fell on his newspaper. "All the troubles in the world," he told me, "were caused by colonization. My Godfather! The French, the Dutch, and the Portuguese—every one of them—and the British had to go in and sort it all out."

43 I sat next to him, eating my cornflakes. Grandpa didn't keep the air conditioner on in the morning, so the doors were open and warm Australian air, smelling of Grandpa's garden and sunshine, breezed across my bare legs.

When Grandpa was finished with the world, he usually turned to 44
the family. "Your cousin," he told me, "By Gor, she dates all of them. Black, brown, red, speckled, spotted, striped."

The real trouble, of course, started with his children. They didn't listen 45
to him. They married Dagos, Polacks, Dutch, and had the nerve to be happy.

My mother was the Dago. Her feet waggle at me from the end of my 46
legs. Humiliatingly, I was born with bunions. I imagine the knobby bones being like the warped trunks of vineyards along the hills of Gorizia.

The first time my mother brought me to Italy, I was eleven and 47
my ears played tricks on me. I sat by the side of the luggage claim and watched the Carabinieri. They looked like something out of a story book, with the red stripes down their trousers and gleaming badges on their caps. They were talking about lunch, or some other entirely mundane detail, and I frowned at them. Story book characters have no right to do commonplace things like eat lunch or lounge by the sliding doors.

"Are you understanding anything?" My mother looked concerned, 48
and it took me a moment to realize she'd addressed me in English. When I concentrated harder, I realized that the Carabinieri were speaking Italian. It hadn't sounded like either English or Italian to me; it had just been words about lunch. Many years later, after I'd lived and worked in France a while, I found the same thing occurring. If I didn't think about it, I couldn't tell whether I was hearing English or French. I thought in both languages, and could only remember which language a conversation occurred in by recalling who I'd been speaking to at the time.

It's always my tongue that exposes me. 49

"Ma non è italiana?" The waiter looked startled. Small wonder. 50
I look north Italian and speak simple sentences with my mother's accent. Anything more complex than "Yes, thank you," however, gives me away: I make the grammatical mistakes of a child.

"Se mettre à parler est plus difficile que de comprendre," my French 51
teacher told me. To put one's self to speaking is harder than to understand.

I want to understand, though, and I want to speak and be under- 52
stood. I see this, even now, back in the US again. I hear others talking and strain to understand what they're saying: the Spanish-speaking maintenance people, the Korean Bible study, Aliya's Taiwanese grandmother. My body leans forward, as though absorbing the words into me will erase the barrier, or as though if I correctly interpret facial expressions and posture, the words won't matter. This method hasn't worked yet, so I suppose I'll have to work to learn the language and understand the customs.

Trying to make myself understood is almost as hard. Here I am: a 53
SWF body that blends in. When I'm asked where I'm from, I say, "Boston." It's true. Thus far most years of my life have been spent in and around the Boston area. I'm a US citizen and consider myself American.

If I say "Boston," though, very few question me further. Unlike 54
Fahaad or Aliya—or even my parents, with their accented English—no

one expects me to elaborate. And often, that's okay. For day-to-day affairs, my story is as irrelevant as everyone else's, and for less usual situations, I'm saved a lot of trouble. I'm selfishly okay with that, too. In Chinese (or Italian) restaurants, no one expects me to place the orders. And unlike Fahaad, who faces airport security guards as a brown Muslim, I don't need to "dress like I expect to keep living."

55 "Boston" isn't my story, though. Neither is Lexington. They're parts of my story, parts of me, but so are Australia and Italy, France and India, Aliya and Fahaad.

56 So is Ghana. I studied at the university in Legon during college, and whenever I went to the market, vendors and children cried out, "Obruni!" It was entirely without malice, and they laughed if I answered, "Obibini."

57 "Obruni doesn't mean 'white person,'" a professor told me. "It just means 'foreigner.' Even people from North Africa, they are obruni."

58 The year after I was in Ghana, another group of American exchange students came back and had a T-shirt made. OBRUNI, it said. If the word hadn't been printed white on a black background, I may have asked for one. I could wear it over my body and advertise:

59 This is my country, but it's also not.

60 This is my home, but it's also not.

61 I'm not a foreigner, but I'm also not . . . Not quite locatable on a map.

Content

1. Explain why Rix views her body as "corporate" (¶ 1). Why does she need "a deep-water chart" to read her body (¶ 1)? How does she distinguish between "core" and a "corporate" *corps* (¶ 1)?
2. Rix writes that the "Asian/Caucasan" differences between herself and her friend Aliya are "irrelevant to what's inside" (¶ 7). Nevertheless, at times she senses the difference as "a jagged crack down the center of our friendship" (¶ 15). Explain this contradiction, if it is one. Considering their similarities and differences (¶s 2–5), their translations of their grandmothers' greetings, and their use of each other's ethnic names (¶ 7), are the girls' ethnic differences a source of their individuality or a metaphor for it—or both?
3. How does the girls' visit to northern India (¶s 8–13) change their relationship? Why hasn't Rix asked Aliya before their travels abroad whether she feels as if she doesn't "fit in" (¶s 12, 14)?
4. What does Rix's attitude toward her hair and her changes of color suggest about her feelings toward her ethnicity and identity? How do her relationships with Javier (¶s 17–22) and Fahaad (¶s 24–37) illustrate her feelings about her ethnic and national identity and "*corporalité*" (¶ 1)? What does she have to "prove" by dating Fahaad (¶ 38)?
5. As you get to know Rix through her narrative, why does "SWF" fail to describe her? Why is she "Not quite locatable on a map" (¶ 61)?

Strategies/Structures/Language

6. Trace the geographical "map" that Rix's narrative describes. How does she structure her narrative around her travels? What does she learn in each location? Does the "map" of the world she describes correspond to the "map" of her body? How does the "map" of her story organize its themes?

7. What role do foreign languages play in Rix's narrative? How does language expand and hinder her understanding of herself and others? Do language differences represent for Rix impenetrable cultural differences?

For Writing

8. ***Journal Writing.*** How do you define yourself? Make a list of defining characteristics such as age, ethnicity, gender, political affiliation, religious faith, sexual orientation, socioeconomic background, family (or other) values, and personality. Do these classifications fully express who you are? Does the identity you project to the world differ from who you *really* are?

9. Using your journal writing (question 8) and Rix's narrative, write an essay about how an individual constructs his or her own identity in the contemporary world. How does your definition of identity compare to Rix's? Does identity depend on time and place? What cultural norms play a major role in shaping our identities? How much individuality can a person express within one's peer group, family, or community?

10. ***Dialogues.*** In "Notes of a Native Speaker" (589–99), how does Eric Liu's description of his development compare to Rix's exploration of identity? Does Liu feel, like Rix, that his body is "corporate"? What elements of his identity does he experience as intrinsic and which does he experience as the result of the social and intellectual maturation that occurred gradually when he was in college? Compare Liu's feeling that "color and class were all twisted together in a double helix of felt inadequacy" (¶ 24) with Rix's question of whether she is "trapped by belonging to a family that was on the wrong side of colonization" (¶ 38) and her description of her whiteness as "my ugly underbelly" (¶ 39). How does each author live through, willingly or unwillingly, his or her history and ethnicity? How does each experience cultural displacement as an opportunity to gain self-knowledge?

11. Write a paper defining yourself according to the four or five most significant dimensions of personality, mind, character, body, interests, commitments, or passions that you'd like your readers to know about you. You may use photographs, drawings, icons, significant objects (clothing, your residence, car, favorite books) to augment your definition. In what ways does this definition resemble your *Facebook* self-portrait, if you have one? If you intend this to be for a specific readership—for instance, a prospective employer or scholarship donor—indicate the audience and show how you're shaping your self-presentation to this reader.

Additional Topics for Discussion and Writing

1. If you or people you know well, perhaps family members or good friends, are from another country, discuss with them their understanding of what national identity means to them. Take notes and write a paper on your findings. In what ways do the countries you're discussing resemble one another? In what ways do they differ? You can approach the topic from one or more of the perspectives below.

   - *Political level.* What are some conspicuous aspects of national politics, the relation of the government to the citizens? (For example, is the government totalitarian? Democratic? Communist? Socialist? Who holds power and how do they exercise it?)
   - *Individual level.* What does "the American Dream" mean to you? How likely are you or your family to fulfill it? Is going to college related to this fulfillment? Does the other country have an equivalent? If so, what is this? If not, according to what criteria do people feel contented, satisfied? If goals are limited in either culture, why is this so? What can an individual do to address, accommodate, or overcome these limitations?

2. Either in relation to question 1 or independent of it, write a paper on the nature of your own identity, with respect to "the good life." What, for you, is a "good life," and how would living such a life affect your identity? Either through reading about or in dialogue with someone whose life might serve as a role model, identify define, and analyze three or four components of the good life. You will need to explain the reasons for the choices you expect to make during the life you're anticipating. Possible dimensions might be:

   - *philosophical, spiritual, ethical.* According to what principles (the Golden Rule, for example) do I want to make decisions? Treat other people?
   - *educational.* What do I want to gain from my formal education? What have I already learned, informally, that I expect to remain of value throughout life? What am I not interested in learning? Why?
   - *relational.* How close do I expect to remain to my parents, grandparents, siblings? Do I want or need a lot of good friends? Do I expect to marry or to live for a long period with a significant other? Do I intend to have children? If so, how many? How will I integrate these relationships with the rest of my life?
   - *material.* What material goods do I currently need to function happily and well? In the future? Consider significant aspects of clothing, food, shelter, transportation, intellectual or artistic life, recreation, or whatever else is important to you.
   - *ecological.* How "green" will my future be? How big a "footprint" do I expect to leave on this earth? (For example, what means of transportation do I expect to use the most heavily?)

3. Research and write a paper on a changing identity, either a national or internationally known figure (you might get some ideas from Noble Prize-winners in various areas—see Chapter 13 and/or consult the Nobelprize.org website) or someone you know well, perhaps even yourself. What changes—physical, lifestyle, job, geographic, anything else—were or will be made? For what reasons? (Consider, for instance, Frederick Douglass's life change from slave to freedman ["Resurrection" 89–93] or Marisa Acocella Marchetto's life change from cancer victim to cancer survivor ["Why Haven't We Won the War on Cancer?" 488]. To provide desired physical or intellectual changes, would you use cosmetic surgery, chemicals, genetic engineering on yourself or loved ones? Under what circumstances? With what limitations?
4. To what extent is beauty and/or an attractive physique integral to your self-definition? To whether or not you find others appealing?
5. Define identity theft according to the experiences you or someone you know have had with it, consult prevention guidelines (see James Fallows's, "Tinfoil Underwear" 151–57), and write a paper on how to prevent identity theft. You may wish to consider the four categories of the Identity Theft Resource Center's definition:

   - financial (using another's identity to obtain goods and services)
   - criminal (posing as another when apprehended for a crime)
   - business/commercial (using another's business name to obtain credit)
   - identity cloning (using another's information to assume that identity in daily life)

World Peace: Nobel Peace Prize Speeches

In this final chapter, it is fitting to focus on world peace and on the significant contributions of individuals and organizations to the sustenance and survival of large numbers of people, animals, and the planet itself. To focus only on the negative (consider, for example, Jared Diamond's doomsday scenario in "The World as a Polder" 472–83 or the reports of William Collins and colleagues on global warming, 214–26; see also the photo insert on environmental issues) would be to ignore the best that is represented by the recipients of the Nobel Prize, whose acceptance speeches comprise this chapter. Goodness, selflessness, and adherence to high moral principles, as the lives and works of the Nobel Prize winners reveal, can emerge even in times of trauma—often, in responses to the challenges of trauma itself. Their talks, like their works, are beacons of faith, hope, and good will. If, as Franklin Roosevelt said, "the only thing we have to fear is fear itself," we need to reinforce a value system that will enable us to lead lives governed by principles and values that bring out the best rather than the worst of our common humanity. This is the message, implied and stated overtly, by every one of these Nobel Prize winners.

These Nobel winners form an international spectrum of the brave, the bold, the morally beautiful. Some of these Nobelists are people of high visibility and power—United Nations Secretary General Kofi Annan (Egypt); national leaders Al Gore (U.S.A.) and Frederik Willem de Klerk (South Africa); and organizational movers and shapers such as Wangari Maathai (Kenya), founder of the Green Belt Movement. Others are religious and political leaders who have suffered extensive privations for living their beliefs: the 14th Dalai Lama (Tibet), sentenced by the Chinese to lifetime exile as the embodiment of the Tibetan Buddhist nation; Nelson Mandela (South Africa), anti-apartheid head of the African National Congress under harsh imprisonment for a quarter century; and Aung San Suu Kyi (Myanmar), Burmese pro-democracy leader confined by the military junta to house arrest for over sixteen years. Still others include Guatemalan champion of indigenous rights and culture, Mayan Rigoberta Menchú Tum. Activist humanitarian organizations are represented by the U.N.'s Intergovernmental Panel on Climate Change, which shared the 2007 award with Al Gore.

All of these Nobel recipients, and others (like Martin Luther King, Jr.), are "witnesses to the truth of injustice," as Dr. James Orbinski, president of Médecins Sans Frontières 1998–2000 when the organization (Doctors Without Borders) received the 1999 Nobel Peace Prize, says, willing to lay their lives on the line—and to lose them, as Dr. King and others have done—for a moral cause. Each of these awards is enmeshed in a complex web of political, moral, and ethical issues in flux, which the prefatory notes attempt to address. (More detailed discussions may be found on the Nobel Prize website [nobelprize.org]—a good place to begin a long trail of investigation and analysis.) Like the lives of these inspiring leaders, the words in these stimulating speeches can guide us to some answers.

How we as individuals, family members, friends, and citizens can do our best not only to lead the good life but to make that life better for humankind is one of the aims of a liberal education and of this book. Following the readings in this chapter you will find suggestions for discussion and writing. The individual speeches presented here may be read in connection with or opposition to one another and in relation to other works throughout the book. Among others these include Collins's and Havel's essays on climate change (214–26 and 227–28) and Jared Diamond's chapter from *Collapse* (472–83); Pollan's (261–68) and Nestle's (270–79) analyses of the politics of food production; and essays on human rights and reconciliation: "The Declaration of Independence" (450–54), Martin Luther King Jr.'s "Letter From Birmingham Jail" (456–70), Lincoln's "The Gettysburg Address" (519), and Sojourner Truth's "Ain't I a Woman?" (521).

AL GORE

Albert Arnold "Al" Gore, Jr. (born 1948) shared the Nobel Peace Prize for 2007 with the Intergovernmental Panel on Climate Change (IPCC) for their efforts to inform the world about "man-made climate change" and their work to establish measures needed to counteract such change. Gore, says the Nobel press release, "is probably the single individual who has done most to create greater worldwide understanding of the measures that need to be adopted" to strengthen "the struggle against climate change." Representing Tennessee, Gore was elected to the U.S. House of Representatives in 1976–84 and to the U.S. Senate, 1985–93. Among Gore's notable contributions was the legislation developed to create a national information infrastructure, "The Information Superhighway." He then served eight years as Bill Clinton's Vice President. He won the popular vote for the presidency in 2000, but as a consequence of a Supreme Court decision lost the Florida election recount, and ultimately the presidency, to George W. Bush. His books on ecology have been bestsellers: *Earth in the Balance: Ecology and the Human Spirit* (1992) and *An Inconvenient Truth: The Planetary Emergency of Global Warming and What We Can Do About It* (2006); the movie won an Oscar for Best Documentary. Gore's mission is to warn people of the rapid climate changes that have thrown the world into crisis, to cause them to acknowledge these harsh environmental truths and acknowledge "a moral imperative to act." The following Nobel lecture was delivered in Oslo, Norway, on December 10, 2007.

A Planetary Emergency (2007)

1 Nobel Lecture, Oslo, 10 December 2007.

2 We, the human species, are confronting a planetary emergency—a threat to the survival of our civilization that is gathering ominous and destructive potential even as we gather here. But there is hopeful news as well: we have the ability to solve this crisis and avoid the worst—though not all—of its consequences, if we act boldly, decisively and quickly.

3 However, despite a growing number of honorable exceptions, too many of the world's leaders are still best described in the words Winston Churchill applied to those who ignored Adolf Hitler's threat: "They go on in strange paradox, decided only to be undecided, resolved to be irresolute, adamant for drift, solid for fluidity, all powerful to be impotent."

4 So today, we dumped another 70 million tons of global-warming pollution into the thin shell of atmosphere surrounding our planet, as if it were an open sewer. And tomorrow, we will dump a slightly larger amount, with the cumulative concentrations now trapping more and more heat from the sun.

As a result, the earth has a fever. And the fever is rising. The experts 5
have told us it is not a passing affliction that will heal by itself. We asked for a second opinion. And a third. And a fourth. And the consistent conclusion, restated with increasing alarm, is that something basic is wrong.

We are what is wrong, and we must make it right. 6

Last September 21, as the Northern Hemisphere tilted away from 7
the sun, scientists reported with unprecedented distress that the North Polar ice cap is "falling off a cliff." One study estimated that it could be completely gone during summer in less than 22 years. Another new study, to be presented by U.S. Navy researchers later this week, warns it could happen in as little as 7 years.

Seven years from now. 8

In the last few months, it has been harder and harder to misinterpret 9
the signs that our world is spinning out of kilter. Major cities in North and South America, Asia and Australia are nearly out of water due to massive droughts and melting glaciers. Desperate farmers are losing their livelihoods. Peoples in the frozen Arctic and on low-lying Pacific islands are planning evacuations of places they have long called home. Unprecedented wildfires have forced a half million people from their homes in one country and caused a national emergency that almost brought down the government in another. Climate refugees have migrated into areas already inhabited by people with different cultures, religions, and traditions, increasing the potential for conflict. Stronger storms in the Pacific and Atlantic have threatened whole cities. Millions have been displaced by massive flooding in South Asia, Mexico, and 18 countries in Africa. As temperature extremes have increased, tens of thousands have lost their lives. We are recklessly burning and clearing our forests and driving more and more species into extinction. The very web of life on which we depend is being ripped and frayed.

We never intended to cause all this destruction. . . . 10

But unlike most other forms of pollution, CO_2 is invisible, tasteless, 11
and odorless—which has helped keep the truth about what it is doing to our climate out of sight and out of mind. Moreover, the catastrophe now threatening us is unprecedented—and we often confuse the unprecedented with the improbable.

We also find it hard to imagine making the massive changes that are 12
now necessary to solve the crisis. And when large truths are genuinely inconvenient, whole societies can, at least for a time, ignore them. Yet as George Orwell reminds us: "Sooner or later a false belief bumps up against solid reality, usually on a battlefield."

In the years since this prize was first awarded, the entire relation- 13
ship between humankind and the earth has been radically transformed. And still, we have remained largely oblivious to the impact of our cumulative actions.

14 Indeed, without realizing it, we have begun to wage war on the earth itself. Now, we and the earth's climate are locked in a relationship familiar to war planners: "Mutually assured destruction."

15 More than two decades ago, scientists calculated that nuclear war could throw so much debris and smoke into the air that it would block life-giving sunlight from our atmosphere, causing a "nuclear winter." Their eloquent warnings here in Oslo helped galvanize the world's resolve to halt the nuclear arms race.

16 Now science is warning us that if we do not quickly reduce the global warming pollution that is trapping so much of the heat our planet normally radiates back out of the atmosphere, we are in danger of creating a permanent "carbon summer."

17 As the American poet Robert Frost wrote, "Some say the world will end in fire; some say in ice." Either, he notes, "would suffice."

18 But neither need be our fate. It is time to make peace with the planet. . . .

19 We must understand the connections between the climate crisis and the afflictions of poverty, hunger, HIV-AIDS and other pandemics. As these problems are linked, so too must be their solutions. We must begin by making the common rescue of the global environment the central organizing principle of the world community. . . .

20 The world needs an alliance—especially of those nations that weigh heaviest in the scales where earth is in the balance. I salute Europe and Japan for the steps they've taken in recent years to meet the challenge, and the new government in Australia, which has made solving the climate crisis its first priority.

21 But the outcome will be decisively influenced by two nations that are now failing to do enough: the United States and China. While India is also growing fast in importance, it should be absolutely clear that it is the two largest CO_2 emitters—most of all, my own country—that will need to make the boldest moves, or stand accountable before history for their failure to act.

22 Both countries should stop using the other's behavior as an excuse for stalemate and instead develop an agenda for mutual survival in a shared global environment. . . .

23 We have to expand the boundaries of what is possible. In the words of the Spanish poet, Antonio Machado, "Pathwalker, there is no path. You must make the path as you walk."

WANGARI MAATHAI

Wangari Maathai was born in Nyeri, Kenya (Africa) in 1940, earned a BS in biology from Mount St. Scholastica College in Atchison, Kansas (1964), a MS from University of Pittsburgh (1966), and after studying in Germany, obtained a PhD from the University of Nairobi. There

AFP/Getty Images

Wangari Maathai receiving the Nobel Peace Prize, December 10, 2004.

she chaired the Department of Veterinary Anatomy. During this time, while serving in the National Council of Women of Kenya, she introduced the idea of planting trees on farms and in school and church compounds. Trees would reforest the mountains and create an environment conducive to clean drinking water; they would provide firewood; fruit trees would help alleviate malnutrition. Over 30 million were planted in Kenya through the Green Belt Movement; this eventually developed into the Pan African Green Belt Network serving Tanzania, Uganda, Malawi, Lesotho, Ethiopia, Zimbabwe, and other countries. As a co-chair of the Jubilee 2000 Africa Campaign, she promoted cancellation of the unpayable backlog debts of the poor countries in Africa by the year 2000 and led a campaign against land grabbing and rapacious allocation of forest land. Beaten, harassed, and jailed for her efforts by Daniel arap Moi, Kenya's strongman president, she was elected to parliament in 2002 in Kenya's first free elections in a generation and soon thereafter was appointed Kenya's Assistant Minister of Environment, Natural Resources, and Wildlife. She has received innumerable awards, worldwide, for her visionary efforts.

The Green Belt Movement (2004)

1 . . . In this year's prize, the Norwegian Nobel Committee has placed the critical issue of environment and its linkage to democracy and peace before the world. For their visionary action, I am profoundly grateful. Recognizing that sustainable development, democracy and peace are indivisible is an idea whose time has come. Our work over the past 30 years has always appreciated and engaged these linkages.

2 My inspiration partly comes from my childhood experiences and observations of Nature in rural Kenya. It has been influenced and nurtured by the formal education I was privileged to receive in Kenya, the United States and Germany. As I was growing up, I witnessed forests being cleared and replaced by commercial plantations, which destroyed local biodiversity and the capacity of the forests to conserve water.

3 Excellencies, ladies and gentlemen,

4 In 1977, when we started the Green Belt Movement, I was partly responding to needs identified by rural women, namely lack of firewood, clean drinking water, balanced diets, shelter and income.

5 Throughout Africa, women are the primary caretakers, holding significant responsibility for tilling the land and feeding their families. As a result, they are often the first to become aware of environmental damage as resources become scarce and incapable of sustaining their families.

6 The women we worked with recounted that unlike in the past, they were unable to meet their basic needs. This was due to the degradation of their immediate environment as well as the introduction of commercial farming, which replaced the growing of household food crops. But international trade controlled the price of the exports from these small-scale farmers and a reasonable and just income could not be guaranteed. I came to understand that when the environment is destroyed, plundered or mismanaged, we undermine our quality of life and that of future generations.

7 Tree planting became a natural choice to address some of the initial basic needs identified by women. Also, tree planting is simple, attainable and guarantees quick, successful results within a reasonable amount time. This sustains interest and commitment.

8 So, together, we have planted over 30 million trees that provide fuel, food, shelter, and income to support their children's education and household needs. The activity also creates employment and improves soils and watersheds. Through their involvement, women gain some degree of power over their lives, especially their social and economic position and relevance in the family. This work continues.

9 Initially, the work was difficult because historically our people have been persuaded to believe that because they are poor, they lack not only capital, but also knowledge and skills to address their challenges. Instead

they are conditioned to believe that solutions to their problems must come from 'outside.' Further, women did not realize that meeting their needs depended on their environment being healthy and well managed. They were also unaware that a degraded environment leads to a scramble for scarce resources and may culminate in poverty and even conflict. They were also unaware of the injustices of international economic arrangements.

In order to assist communities to understand these linkages, we 10
developed a citizen education program, during which people identify their problems, the causes and possible solutions. They then make connections between their own personal actions and the problems they witness in the environment and in society. They learn that our world is confronted with a litany of woes: corruption, violence against women and children, disruption and breakdown of families, and disintegration of cultures and communities. They also identify the abuse of drugs and chemical substances, especially among young people. There are also devastating diseases that are defying cures or occurring in epidemic proportions. Of particular concern are HIV/AIDS, malaria and diseases associated with malnutrition.

On the environment front, they are exposed to many human activi- 11
ties that are devastating to the environment and societies. These include widespread destruction of ecosystems, especially through deforestation, climatic instability, and contamination in the soils and waters that all contribute to excruciating poverty.

In the process, the participants discover that they must be part of 12
the solutions. They realize their hidden potential and are empowered to overcome inertia and take action. They come to recognize that they are the primary custodians and beneficiaries of the environment that sustains them.

Entire communities also come to understand that while it is neces- 13
sary to hold their governments accountable, it is equally important that in their own relationships with each other, they exemplify the leadership values they wish to see in their own leaders, namely justice, integrity and trust.

Although initially the Green Belt Movement's tree planting 14
activities did not address issues of democracy and peace, it soon became clear that responsible governance of the environment was impossible without democratic space. Therefore, the tree became a symbol for the democratic struggle in Kenya. Citizens were mobilised to challenge widespread abuses of power, corruption and environmental mismanagement. In Nairobi's Uhuru Park, at Freedom Corner, and in many parts of the country, trees of peace were planted to demand the release of prisoners of conscience and a peaceful transition to democracy.

15 Through the Green Belt Movement, thousands of ordinary citizens were mobilized and empowered to take action and effect change. They learned to overcome fear and a sense of helplessness and moved to defend democratic rights.

16 In time, the tree also became a symbol for peace and conflict resolution, especially during ethnic conflicts in Kenya when the Green Belt Movement used peace trees to reconcile disputing communities. During the ongoing re-writing of the Kenyan constitution, similar trees of peace were planted in many parts of the country to promote a culture of peace. Using trees as a symbol of peace is in keeping with a widespread African tradition. For example, the elders of the Kikuyu carried a staff from the thigi tree that, when placed between two disputing sides, caused them to stop fighting and seek reconciliation. Many communities in Africa have these traditions.

17 Such practises are part of an extensive cultural heritage, which contributes both to the conservation of habitats and to cultures of peace. With the destruction of these cultures and the introduction of new values, local biodiversity is no longer valued or protected and as a result, it is quickly degraded and disappears. For this reason, The Green Belt Movement explores the concept of cultural biodiversity, especially with respect to indigenous seeds and medicinal plants.

18 As we progressively understood the cause of environmental degradation, we saw the need for good governance. Indeed, the state of any country's environment is a reflection of the kind of governance in place, and without good governance there can be no peace. Many countries, which have poor governance systems, are also likely to have conflicts and poor laws protecting the environment.

19 In 2002, the courage, resilience, patience and commitment of members of the Green Belt Movement, other civil society organizations, and the Kenyan public culminated in the peaceful transition to a democratic government and laid the foundation for a more stable society.

20 Excellencies, friends, ladies and gentlemen,

21 It is 30 years since we started this work. Activities that devastate the environment and societies continue unabated. Today we are faced with a challenge that calls for a shift in our thinking, so that humanity stops threatening its life-support system. We are called to assist the Earth to heal her wounds and in the process heal our own—indeed, to embrace the whole creation in all its diversity, beauty and wonder. This will happen if we see the need to revive our sense of belonging to a larger family of life, with which we have shared our evolutionary process.

22 In the course of history, there comes a time when humanity is called to shift to a new level of consciousness, to reach a higher moral ground. A time when we have to shed our fear and give hope to each other.

23 That time is now.

KOFI ANNAN

Kofi Annan spent his entire career in the United Nations. Born in 1938 in Kumasi, Ghana, Annan completed an undergraduate degree in economics at Macalester College in St. Paul, Minnesota, in 1961 and studied economics in Geneva from 1961 to 1962 before beginning work at the UN as a budget officer with the World Health Organization in Geneva. As a Sloan Fellow (1971–1972) he earned an MS in management from M.I.T. He later served with the UN Economic Commission for Africa in Addis Ababa; the UN Emergency Force in Ismailia; and the Office of the UN High Commissioner for Refugees in Geneva. At the UN in New York he held a variety of posts, including that of under secretary-general during a period of unprecedented growth in UN peacekeeping operations around the world (including Kuwait, Iraq, Bosnia, and Herzegovina) to, in 1995, 70,000 military and civilian personnel from seventy-seven countries. He was chosen as the seventh secretary-general of the UN in January of 1997 and served until his retirement in 2006. The 2001 Nobel Peace Prize was awarded to both the United Nations and to Kofi Annan for "their work for a better organized and more peaceful world. For one hundred years," says the citation, "the Norwegian Nobel Committee has sought to strengthen organized cooperation between states. The end of the cold war has at last made it possible for the UN to perform more fully the part it was originally intended to play. Today the organization is at the forefront of efforts to achieve peace and security in the world," and of international efforts to meet the world's economic, social, and environmental challenges. These include significant action on human rights and providing humanitarian aid to countries experiencing famine, drought, and medical epidemics such as HIV/AIDS.

Doug Kanter/AFP/Getty Images

Kofi Annan was United Nations Secretary General 1997–2006.

The United Nations in the 21st Century (2001)

1 We have entered the third millennium through a gate of fire. If today, after the horror of 11 September, we see better, and we see further—we will realize that humanity is indivisible. New threats make no distinction between races, nations or regions. A new insecurity has entered every mind, regardless of wealth or status. A deeper awareness of the bonds that bind us all—in pain as in prosperity—has gripped young and old.

2 In the early beginnings of the 21st century—a century already violently disabused of any hopes that progress towards global peace and prosperity is inevitable—this new reality can no longer be ignored. It must be confronted.

3 The 20th century was perhaps the deadliest in human history, devastated by innumerable conflicts, untold suffering, and unimaginable crimes. Time after time, a group or a nation inflicted extreme violence on another, often driven by irrational hatred and suspicion, or unbounded arrogance and thirst for power and resources. In response to these cataclysms, the leaders of the world came together at mid-century to unite the nations as never before.

4 A forum was created—the United Nations—where all nations could join forces to affirm the dignity and worth of every person, and to secure peace and development for all peoples. Here States could unite to strengthen the rule of law, recognize and address the needs of the poor, restrain man's brutality and greed, conserve the resources and beauty of nature, sustain the equal rights of men *and* women, and provide for the safety of future generations.

5 We thus inherit from the 20th century the political, as well as the scientific and technological power, which—if only we have the will to use them—give us the chance to vanquish poverty, ignorance and disease.

6 In the 21st century I believe the mission of the United Nations will be defined by a new, more profound, awareness of the sanctity and dignity of every human life, regardless of race or religion. This will require us to look beyond the framework of States, and beneath the surface of nations or communities. We must focus, as never before, on improving the conditions of the individual men and women who give the state or nation its richness and character. We must begin with the young Afghan girl [born in poverty], recognizing that saving that one life is to save humanity itself.

7 Over the past five years, I have often recalled that the United Nations' Charter begins with the words: "We the peoples." What is not always recognized is that "we the peoples" are made up of individuals whose claims to the most fundamental rights have too often been sacrificed in the supposed interests of the state or the nation.

A genocide begins with the killing of one man—not for what he has 8
done, but because of who he is. A campaign of "ethnic cleansing" begins with one neighbour turning on another. Poverty begins when even one child is denied his or her fundamental right to education. What begins with the failure to uphold the dignity of one life, all too often ends with a calamity for entire nations.

In this new century, we must start from the understanding that 9
peace belongs not only to states or peoples, but to each and every member of those communities. The sovereignty of States must no longer be used as a shield for gross violations of human rights. Peace must be made real and tangible in the daily existence of every individual in need. Peace must be sought, above all, because it is the condition for every member of the human family to live a life of dignity and security.

The rights of the individual are of no less importance to immigrants 10
and minorities in Europe and the Americas than to women in Afghanistan or children in Africa. They are as fundamental to the poor as to the rich; they are as necessary to the security of the developed world as to that of the developing world.

From this vision of the role of the United Nations in the next century 11
flow three key priorities for the future: eradicating poverty, preventing conflict, and promoting democracy. Only in a world that is rid of poverty can all men and women make the most of their abilities. Only where individual rights are respected can differences be channelled politically and resolved peacefully. Only in a democratic environment, based on respect for diversity and dialogue, can individual self-expression and self-government be secured, and freedom of association be upheld. . . .

The idea that there is one people in possession of the truth, one 12
answer to the world's ills, or one solution to humanity's needs, has done untold harm throughout history—especially in the last century. Today, however, even amidst continuing ethnic conflict around the world, there is a growing understanding that human diversity is both the reality that makes dialogue necessary, and the very basis for that dialogue.

We understand, as never before, that each of us is fully worthy of 13
the respect and dignity essential to our common humanity. We recognize that we are the products of many cultures, traditions and memories; that mutual respect allows us to study and learn from other cultures; and that we gain strength by combining the foreign with the familiar.

In every great faith and tradition one can find the values of toler- 14
ance and mutual understanding. The Qur'an, for example, tells us that "We created you from a single pair of male and female and made you into nations and tribes, that you may know each other." Confucius urged his followers: "when the good way prevails in the state, speak boldly and act boldly. When the state has lost the way, act boldly and speak softly." In the Jewish tradition, the injunction to "love thy neighbour as thyself," is considered to be the very essence of the Torah.

15 This thought is reflected in the Christian Gospel, which also teaches us to love our enemies and pray for those who wish to persecute us. Hindus are taught that "truth is one, the sages give it various names." And in the Buddhist tradition, individuals are urged to act with compassion in every facet of life.

16 Each of us has the right to take pride in our particular faith or heritage. But the notion that what is ours is necessarily in conflict with what is theirs is both false and dangerous. It has resulted in endless enmity and conflict, leading men to commit the greatest of crimes in the name of a higher power.

17 It need not be so. People of different religions and cultures live side by side in almost every part of the world, and most of us have overlapping identities which unite us with very different groups. We *can* love what we are, without hating what—and who—we are *not*. We can thrive in our own tradition, even as we learn from others, and come to respect their teachings.

18 This will not be possible, however, without freedom of religion, of expression, of assembly, and basic equality under the law. Indeed, the lesson of the past century has been that where the dignity of the individual has been trampled or threatened—where citizens have not enjoyed the basic right to choose their government, or the right to change it regularly—conflict has too often followed, with innocent civilians paying the price, in lives cut short and communities destroyed.

19 The obstacles to democracy have little to do with culture or religion, and much more to do with the desire of those in power to maintain their position at any cost. This is neither a new phenomenon nor one confined to any particular part of the world. People of all cultures value their freedom of choice, and feel the need to have a say in decisions affecting their lives.

20 The United Nations, whose membership comprises almost all the States in the world, is founded on the principle of the equal worth of every human being. It is the nearest thing we have to a representative institution that can address the interests of all states, and all peoples. Through this universal, indispensable instrument of human progress, States can serve the interests of their citizens by recognizing common interests and pursuing them in unity. No doubt, that is why the Nobel Committee says that it "wishes, in its centenary year, to proclaim that the only negotiable route to global peace and cooperation goes by way of the United Nations."

21 I believe the Committee also recognized that this era of global challenges leaves no choice but cooperation at the global level. When States undermine the rule of law and violate the rights of their individual citizens, they become a menace not only to their own people, but also to their neighbours, and indeed the world. What we need today is better governance—legitimate, democratic governance that allows each individual to flourish, and each State to thrive.

NELSON MANDELA AND FREDERIK WILLEM DE KLERK

Nelson Mandela and Frederik Willem de Klerk shared the Nobel Peace Prize in 1993 for "their work for the peaceful termination of the apartheid regime," the citation explains, "and for laying the foundations of a new democratic South Africa." For twenty-eight years Mandela (born in Transeki, South Africa, in 1918) was the imprisoned leader of the African National Congress and—as time went on—an internationally known symbol of determined resistance to apartheid. His autobiography, *Long Walk to Freedom* (1994), explains, in serenely charitable language, the great physical and psychological fortitude he needed to endure the hard labor (which included several oppressive years of breaking rocks), isolation, and other deprivations of this long and harsh time. De Klerk (born in Johannesburg in 1936, son of Senator Jan de Klerk), who had held a series of ministerial positions in the South African government from 1978 to 1989, "was not known to advocate reform" before his election as state president in September 1989. Nevertheless, says the Nobel Prize committee, "In his first speech after assuming the party leadership he called for a nonracist South Africa and for negotiations about the country's future. He lifted the ban on the ANC and released Nelson Mandela. He brought apartheid to an end and opened the way for the drafting of a new constitution for the country based on the principle of one person, one vote." Thus, coming from very different points of departure, Mandela and de Klerk looked "ahead to South African reconciliation instead of back at the deep wounds of the past," showing "great integrity and great political courage." Mandela served as South Africa's eleventh president from 1994 to 1999.

Nelson Mandela, The End of Apartheid (1993)

1 Because of their courage and persistence for many years, we can, today, even set the dates when all humanity will join together to celebrate one of the outstanding human victories of our century.

2 When that moment comes, we shall, together, rejoice in a common victory over racism, apartheid and white minority rule.

3 That triumph will finally bring to a close a history of five hundred years of African colonisation that began with the establishment of the Portuguese empire.

4 Thus, it will mark a great step forward in history and also serve as a common pledge of the peoples of the world to fight racism, wherever it occurs and whatever guise it assumes.

5 At the southern tip of the continent of Africa, a rich reward in the making, an invaluable gift is in the preparation for those who suffered in the name of all humanity when they sacrificed everything—for liberty, peace, human dignity and human fulfillment.

6 This reward will not be measured in money. Nor can it be reckoned in the collective price of the rare metals and precious stones that rest in the bowels of the African soil we tread in the footsteps of our ancestors.

7 It will and must be measured by the happiness and welfare of the children, at once the most vulnerable citizens in any society and the greatest of our treasures.

8 The children must, at last, play in the open veld, no longer tortured by the pangs of hunger or ravaged by disease or threatened with the scourge of ignorance, molestation and abuse, and no longer required to engage in deeds whose gravity exceeds the demands of their tender years.

9 In front of this distinguished audience, we commit the new South Africa to the relentless pursuit of the purposes defined in the World Declaration on the Survival, Protection and Development of Children.

10 The reward of which we have spoken will and must also be measured by the happiness and welfare of the mothers and fathers of these children, who must walk the earth without fear of being robbed, killed for political or material profit, or spat upon because they are beggars.

11 They too must be relieved of the heavy burden of despair which they carry in their hearts, born of hunger, homelessness and unemployment.

12 The value of that gift to all who have suffered will and must be measured by the happiness and welfare of all the people of our country, who will have torn down the inhuman walls that divide them.

13 These great masses will have turned their backs on the grave insult to human dignity which described some as masters and others as

servants, and transformed each into a predator whose survival depended on the destruction of the other.

The value of our shared reward will and must be measured by the 14
joyful peace which will triumph, because the common humanity that bonds both black and white into one human race, will have said to each one of us that we shall all live like the children of paradise.

Thus shall we live, because we will have created a society which rec- 15
ognises that all people are born equal, with each entitled in equal measure to life, liberty, prosperity, human rights and good governance.

Such a society should never allow again that there should be prison- 16
ers of conscience nor that any person's human right should be violated.

Neither should it ever happen that once more the avenues to peace- 17
ful change are blocked by usurpers who seek to take power away from the people, in pursuit of their own, ignoble purposes.

In relation to these matters, we appeal to those who govern Burma 18
that they release our fellow Nobel Peace Prize laureate, Aung San Suu Kyi, and engage her and those she represents in serious dialogue, for the benefit of all the people of Burma.

We pray that those who have the power to do so will, without fur- 19
ther delay, permit that she uses her talents and energies for the greater good of the people of her country and humanity as a whole.

© NTB/AP Images

South African President Nelson Mandela (on left) and South African Deputy President F. W. de Klerk (on right) holding their Nobel Peace Prize gold medals and diplomas on December 10, 1993. Interpret and comment on the significance of this photograph—historical, ethical, political, human.

20 Far from the rough and tumble of the politics of our own country. I would like to take this opportunity to join the Norwegian Nobel Committee and pay tribute to my joint laureate[,] Mr. F. W. de Klerk.

21 He had the courage to admit that a terrible wrong had been done to our country and people through the imposition of the system of apartheid.

22 He had the foresight to understand and accept that all the people of South Africa must through negotiations and as equal participants in the process, together determine what they want to make of their future.

23 But there are still some within our country who wrongly believe they can make a contribution to the cause of justice and peace by clinging to the shibboleths that have been proved to spell nothing but disaster.

24 It remains our hope that these, too, will be blessed with sufficient reason to realise that history will not be denied and that the new society cannot be created by reproducing the repugnant past, however refined or enticingly repackaged.

25 We would also like to take advantage of this occasion to pay tribute to the many formations of the democratic movement of our country, including the members of our Patriotic Front, who have themselves played a central role in bringing our country as close to the democratic transformation as it is today.

26 We are happy that many representatives of these formations, including people who have served or are serving in the "homeland" structures, came with us to Oslo. They too must share the accolade which the Nobel Peace Prize confers.

27 We live with the hope that as she battles to remake herself, South Africa will be like a microcosm of the new world that is striving to be born.

28 This must be a world of democracy and respect for human rights, a world freed from the horrors of poverty, hunger, deprivation and ignorance, relieved of the threat and the scourge of civil wars and external aggression and unburdened of the great tragedy of millions forced to become refugees.

29 The processes in which South Africa and Southern Africa as a whole are engaged, beckon and urge us all that we take this tide at the flood and make of this region as a living example of what all people of conscience would like the world to be.

30 We do not believe that this Nobel Peace Prize is intended as a commendation for matters that have happened and passed.

31 We hear the voices which say that it is an appeal from all those, throughout the universe, who sought an end to the system of apartheid.

32 We understand their call, that we devote what remains of our lives to the use of our country's unique and painful experience to demonstrate, in practice, that the normal condition for human existence is democracy, justice, peace, non-racism, non-sexism, prosperity for everybody, a healthy environment and equality and solidarity among the peoples.

Moved by that appeal and inspired by the eminence you have thrust 33
upon us, we undertake that we too will do what we can to contribute to the renewal of our world so that none should, in future, be described as the "wretched of the earth."

Let it never be said by future generations that indifference, cynicism 34
or selfishness made us fail to live up to the ideals of humanism which the Nobel Peace Prize encapsulates.

Let the strivings of us all prove Martin Luther King Jr. to have been 35
correct, when he said that humanity can no longer be tragically bound to the starless midnight of racism and war.

Let the efforts of us all prove that he was not a mere dreamer when 36
he spoke of the beauty of genuine brotherhood and peace being more precious than diamonds or silver or gold.

Let a new age dawn! 37

Frederik Willem de Klerk, Reformation and Reconciliation in South Africa (1993)

Five years ago people would have seriously questioned the sanity of 1
anyone who would have predicted that Mr. Mandela and I would be joint recipients of the 1993 Nobel Peace Prize.

And yet both of us are here before you today. 2

We are political opponents. 3

We disagree strongly on key issues and we will soon fight a strenu- 4
ous election campaign against one another. But we will do so, I believe, in the frame of mind and within the framework of peace which has already been established.

We will do it—and many other leaders will do it with us— 5
because there is no other road to peace and prosperity for the people of our country. In the conflicts of the past, there was no gain for anyone in our country. Through reconciliation all of us are now becoming winners.

The compromises we have reached demand sacrifices on all sides. It 6
was not easy for the supporters of Mr. Mandela or mine to relinquish the ideals they had cherished for many decades.

But we did it. And because we did it, there is hope. 7

The coming election will not be about the past. It will be about the 8
future. It will not be about Blacks or Whites, or Afrikaners and Xhosas. It will be about the best solutions for the future in the interests of all our

people. It will not be about apartheid or armed struggle. It will be about future peace and stability, about progress and prosperity, about nation-building.

9 In my first speech about becoming Leader of the National Party, I said on February the 8th, 1989:

10 Our goal is a new South Africa:
A totally changed South Africa;
a South Africa which has rid itself of the antagonism of the past;
a South Africa free of domination or oppression in whatever form;
a South Africa within which the democratic forces—all reasonable people—align themselves behind mutually acceptable goals and against radicalism, irrespective of where it comes from.

11 Since then we have made impressive progress, thanks to the cooperation of political, spiritual, business and community leaders over a wide spectrum. To Mr. Mandela I sincerely say: Congratulations. And in accepting this Peace Prize today I wish to pay tribute to all who are working for peace in our land. On behalf of all South Africans who supported me, directly or indirectly, I accept it in humility, deeply aware of my own shortcomings.

12 I thank those who decided to make the award for the recognition they have granted in doing so—recognition of a mighty deed of reformation and reconciliation that is taking place in South Africa. The road ahead is still full of obstacles and, therefore, dangerous. There is, however, no question of turning back.

AUNG SAN SUU KYI

Aung San Suu Kyi, the daughter of Burma's liberation leader Aung San, was born in Rangoon, then Burma, now Myanmar, in 1945. In 1991 she was awarded the Nobel Peace Prize, which her sons accepted on her behalf because she was under house arrest. Her father, General Aung San, then commander of the Burma Independence Army, was assassinated when Suu Kyi was two years old. Her mother, Daw Khin Kyi, continued to champion the cause, attaining prominence in social planning and social policy, and it was partly through her efforts that the Independent Union of Burma was established in 1948. In 1960 Daw Khin Kyi was appointed Burma's ambassador to India. Suu Kyi, who accompanied her mother, attended preparatory school in New Delhi,

David Van Der Veen/AFP/Getty Images

"Read" the speech that Aung San Suu Kyi is making. Who is her audience? What does she want to happen as a consequence of her speaking? How do her physical attractiveness, gender, and dress reinforce—or contradict—your interpretation?

followed by a BA in philosophy, politics, and economics at Oxford. Her background, marriage to Michael Aris, a scholar of Tibetan civilization, and friendships with high-ranking officials in England, the United States, Bhutan, Japan, and India, led to work at the UN, study at Oxford, and international visibility as she assumed leadership of the opposition party, the National League for Democracy, in Burma as her mother was dying in 1988.

Harassment of Suu Kyi and her nonviolent party began immediately, with brutal arrests and killings. After facing down troops with rifles aimed at her in April 1989, she was placed under house arrest in July 1989. Her heroic actions had already made her an important symbol in the struggle against oppression. In May 1990, despite Suu Kyi's continued detention, her party won 82 percent of the seats in parliament, but the military state voided the results. It was in this climate that the Nobel Prize committee awarded her the Peace Prize, "to honor her nonviolent struggle for democracy and human rights" and to show "support for the many people throughout the world who are striving to attain democracy, human rights, and ethnic conciliation by peaceful means." As of 2008, Aung San Suu Kyi had spent a total of sixteen years under house arrest, refusing offers of freedom and reunion with her husband (who died in 1999 without being allowed to visit her) and sons if she would leave the country and withdraw from politics. Like Nelson Mandela, she chose separation from her family as one of the personal sacrifices she had to make in order to work for a larger, more humanitarian cause—in this case, a free Burma.

The Revolution of Spirit (1991)

1 . . . I stand before you here today to accept on behalf of my mother, Aung San Suu Kyi, this greatest of prizes, the Nobel Prize for Peace. Because circumstances do not permit my mother to be here in person, I will do my best to convey the sentiments I believe she would express.

2 Firstly, I know that she would begin by saying that she accepts the Nobel Prize for Peace not in her own name but in the name of all the people of Burma. She would say that this prize belongs not to her but to all those men, women and children who, even as I speak, continue to sacrifice their well being, their freedom and their lives in pursuit of a democratic Burma. Theirs is the prize and theirs will be the eventual victory in Burma's long struggle for peace, freedom and democracy.

3 Speaking as her son, however, I would add that I personally believe that by her own dedication and personal sacrifice she has come to be a worthy symbol through whom the plight of all the people of Burma may be recognized.

4 And no one must underestimate that plight. The plight of those in the countryside and towns, living in poverty and destitution, those in prison, battered and tortured; the plight of the young people, the hope of Burma, dying of malaria in the jungles to which they have fled; that of the Buddhist monks, beaten and dishonoured. Nor should we forget the many senior and highly respected leaders besides my mother who are all incarcerated.

5 It is on their behalf that I thank you, from my heart, for this supreme honour. The Burmese people can today hold their heads a little higher in the knowledge that in this far distant land their suffering has been heard and heeded.

6 We must also remember that the lonely struggle taking place in a heavily guarded compound in Rangoon is part of the much larger struggle, worldwide, for the emancipation of the human spirit from political tyranny and psychological subjection. The Prize, I feel sure, is also intended to honour all those engaged in this struggle wherever they may be. It is not without reason that today's events in Oslo fall on the International Human Rights Day, celebrated throughout the world.

7 Mr Chairman, the whole international community has applauded the choice of your Committee. Just a few days ago, the United Nations passed a unanimous and historic resolution welcoming Secretary-General Javier Pérez de Cuéllar's statement on the significance of this award and endorsing his repeated appeals for my mother's early release from detention. Universal concern at the grave human rights situation in Burma was clearly expressed. Alone and isolated among the entire nations of the world a single dissenting voice was heard, from the military junta in Rangoon, too late and too weak.

This regime has through almost thirty years of misrule reduced the once prosperous "Golden Land" of Burma to one of the world's most economically destitute nations. In their heart of hearts even those in power now in Rangoon must know that their eventual fate will be that of all totalitarian regimes who seek to impose their authority through fear, repression, and hatred. When the present Burmese struggle for democracy erupted onto the streets in 1988 it was the first of what became an international tidal wave of such movements throughout Eastern Europe, Asia and Africa. Today, in 1991, Burma stands conspicuous in its continued suffering at the hands of a repressive, intransigent junta, the State Law and Order Restoration Council. However, the example of those nations which have successfully achieved democracy holds out an important message to the Burmese people: that, in the last resort, through the sheer economic unworkability of totalitarianism this present regime will be swept away. And today in the face of rising inflation, a mismanaged economy and near worthless Kyat, the Burmese Government is undoubtedly reaping as it has sown. 8

However, it is my deepest hope that it will not be in the face of complete economic collapse that the regime will fall, but that the ruling junta may yet heed such appeals to basic humanity as that which the Nobel Committee has expressed in its award of this year's Prize. I know that within the military government there *are* those to whom the present policies of fear and repression are abhorrent, violating as they do the most sacred principles of Burma's Buddhist heritage. This is no empty wishful thinking but a conviction my mother reached in the course of her dealings with those in positions of authority, illustrated by the election victories of her party in constituencies comprised almost exclusively of military personnel and their families. It is my profoundest wish that these elements for moderation and reconciliation among those now in authority may make their sentiments felt in Burma's hour of deepest need. 9

I know that if she were free today my mother would in thanking you also ask you to pray that the oppressors and the oppressed should throw down their weapons and join together to build a nation founded on humanity in the spirit of peace. 10

Although my mother is often described as a political dissident who strives by peaceful means for democratic change, we should remember that her quest is basically spiritual. As she has said, "The quintessential revolution is that of the spirit," and she has written of the "essential spiritual aims" of the struggle. The realization of this depends solely on human responsibility. At the root of that responsibility lies, and I quote, "the concept of perfection, the urge to achieve it, the intelligence to find a path towards it, and the will to follow that path if not to the end, at least the distance needed to rise above individual limitation. . . ." "To live the full life," she says, "one must have the courage to bear the responsibility of 11 the needs of others . . . one must *want* to bear this responsibility." And she links this firmly to her faith when she writes, " . . . Buddhism, the foundation of traditional Burmese culture, places the greatest value on man, who alone of all beings can achieve the supreme state of Buddhahood. Each man has in him the potential to realize the truth through his own will and endeavour and to help others to realize it." Finally she says, "The quest for democracy in Burma is the struggle of a people to live whole, meaningful lives as free and equal members of the world community. It is part of the unceasing human endeavour to prove that the spirit of man can transcend the flaws of his nature."

12 It only remains for me to thank you all from the bottom of my heart. Let us hope and pray that from today the wounds start to heal and that in the years to come the 1991 Nobel Prize for Peace will be seen as a historic step towards the achievement of true peace in Burma. The lessons of the past will not be forgotten, but it is our hope for the future that we celebrate today.

RIGOBERTA MENCHÚ TUM

Rigoberta Menchú Tum received the 1992 Nobel Peace Prize "in recognition of her work for social justice and ethno-cultural reconciliation based on respect for the rights of indigenous peoples." In the 1970s and 1980s Guatemala, like many other countries in South and Central America, was filled with tremendous tension between descendants of European immigrants and the native Indian peoples, who were brutally suppressed and persecuted. Menchú Tum, a social and political activist, said the Nobel committee, "stands out as a vivid symbol of peace and reconciliation across ethnic, cultural and social dividing lines," nationwide and worldwide.

Rigoberta Menchú Tum was born in 1959 to a poor Indian peasant family in Guatemala and raised in the Quiche branch of the Mayan culture. As a teenager she became involved in social reform activities through the Catholic Church, including becoming an advocate for women's rights—efforts that aroused opposition of those in power. The Menchú family was accused of guerilla activities; her father was imprisoned and tortured for allegedly having participated in the execution of a local plantation owner. After his release he became a member of the Committee of the Peasant Union (CUC), which Menchú Tum joined in 1979—the year her brother was tortured and killed by the army. The following year her father was killed by security forces, and her mother died after being arrested, raped, and tortured. In 1981 Menchú Tum's activities in educating the Indian peasant population to resist military oppression forced her to go into hiding in Guatemala and then flee to Mexico. She helped to found an opposition body, the United Representation of the Guatemalan Opposition (RUOG). In a week of recorded interviews with anthropologist Elisabeth Burgos-Debray, she told her life story. The book, *I, Rigoberta Menchú*, was published in 1983, translated into a dozen languages, and soon acquired incendiary international fame as the embodiment of the atrocities committed by the Guatemalan army in peasant villages during the civil war.

In 1999 David Stoll, though fully supportive of her Nobel Prize, published a critique of the book—*Menchú and the Story of All Poor Guatemalans* (1999)—demonstrating that parts of her own and her family history are in error, even when she speaks as an eyewitness. Stoll, an anthropologist who studied Mayan peasants, feels that "by inaccurately portraying the events in her own village as representative of what happened in all such indigenous villages in Guatemala, she gives a misleading interpretation of the relationship of the Mayan peasants to the revolutionary movement." The Nobel Prize committee defended its decision to award the prize to Menchú Tum, saying that this "was not based exclusively or primarily on the autobiography," and dismissed any suggestion that the Committee should consider revoking the prize. *The Rigoberta Menchú Controversy* (2002) is a superb collection of "primary documents—newspaper articles, interviews, and official statements" complemented by assessments by distinguished international scholars of the political, historical, and cultural implications of this debate.

Five Hundred Years of Mayan Oppression (1992)

Please allow me, ladies and gentlemen, to say some words about my country and the Civilization of the Mayas. The Maya people developed and spread geographically through some 300,000 square km; they occupied parts of the South of Mexico, Belize, Guatemala, as well as Honduras and El Salvador; they developed a very rich civilization in the area of political organization, as well as in social and economic fields; they were great scientists in the fields of mathematics, astronomy, agriculture, architecture and engineering; they were great artists in the fields of sculpture, painting, weaving and carving. . . . 1

Who can predict what other great scientific conquests and developments these people could have achieved, if they had not been conquered in blood and fire, and subjected to an ethnocide that affected nearly 50 million people in the course of 500 years. 2

I would describe the meaning of this Nobel Prize, in the first place as a tribute to the indian people who have been sacrificed and have disappeared because they aimed at a more dignified and just life with fraternity and understanding among the human beings. To those who are no longer alive to keep up the hope for a change in the situation in respect 3 of poverty and marginalization of the indians, of those who have been banished, of the helpless in Guatemala as well as in the entire American Continent.

4 This growing concern is comforting, even though it comes 500 years later, to the suffering, the discrimination, the oppression and the exploitation that our people has been exposed to, but who, thanks to their own cosmovision—and concept of life, have managed to withstand and finally see some promising prospects. How those roots, that were to be eradicated, now begin to grow with strength, hopes and visions for the future!

5 It also represents a sign of the growing international interest for, and understanding of the original Rights of the People, of the future of more than 60 million indians that live in our America, and their uproar because of the 500 years of oppression that they have endured. For the genocides beyond comparison that they have had to suffer all this time, and from which other countries and the elite of the Americas have profited and taken advantage.

6 Let there be freedom for the indians, wherever they may be in the American Continent or else in the world, because while they are alive, a glow of hope will be alive as well as the real concept of life.

7 The expressions of great happiness by the Indian Organizations in the entire Continent and the worldwide congratulations received for the award of the Nobel Peace Prize, clearly indicate the great importance of this decision. It is the recognition of the European debt to the American indigenous people; it is an appeal to the conscience of Humanity so that those conditions of marginalization that condemned them to colonialism and exploitation may be eradicated; it is a cry for life, peace, justice, equality and fraternity between human beings.

8 The peculiarities of the vision of the indian people are expressed according to the way in which they relate. First of all, between human being[s], through communication. Second, with the earth, as with our mother, because she gives us our lives and is not a mere merchandise. Third, with nature, because we are integral parts of it, and not its owners.

9 To us mother earth is not only a source of economic riches that give us the maize, which is our life, but she also provides so many other things that the privileged ones of today strive after. The earth is the root and the source of our culture. She keeps our memories, she receives our ancestors and she therefore demands that we honour her and return to her, with tenderness and respect, those goods that she gives us. We have to take care of her and look after mother earth so that our children and grandchildren may continue to benefit from her. If the world does not learn now to show respect to nature, what kind of future will the new generations have?

10 From these basic features derive behaviour, rights and obligations in the American Continent, for indians as well as for non-indians,

whether they be racially mixed, blacks, whites or Asian. The whole society has the obligation to show mutual respect, to learn from each other and to share material and scientific achievements, in the most convenient way. The indians have never had, and they do not have, the place that they should have occupied in the progress and benefits of science and technology, although they have represented an important basis.

If the indian civilizations and the European civilizations could have 11
made exchanges in a peaceful and harmonious manner, without destruction, exploitation, discrimination and poverty, they could, no doubt, have achieved greater and more valuable conquests for Humanity.

Let us not forget that when the Europeans came to America, there 12
were flourishing and strong civilizations there. One cannot talk about a discovery of America, because one discovers that which one does not know about, or that which is hidden. But America and its native civilizations had discovered themselves long before the fall of the Roman Empire and the Medieval Europe. The significance of its cultures form part of the heritage of humanity and continue to astonish the learned ones. . . .

We the indians are willing to combine tradition with modernism, but 13
not at all costs. We will not tolerate nor permit that our future be planned as possible guardians of ethno-touristic projects at continental level.

At a time when the commemoration of the Fifth Centenary of the 14
arrival of Columbus in America has repercussions all over the world, the revival of hopes for the indian people claims that we reassert to the world our existence and the value of our cultural identity. It demands that we endeavour to actively participate in the decisions that concern our destiny, in the building-up of our countries/nations. Should we, in spite of all, not be taken into consideration, there are factors that guarantee our future: struggle and endurance; courage; the decision to maintain our traditions that have been exposed to so many perils and sufferings; solidarity towards our struggle on the part of numerous countries, governments, organizations and citizens of the world.

That is why I dream of the day when the relationship between the 15
indigenous people and other people is strengthened; when they can join their potentialities and their capabilities and contribute to make life on this planet less unequal.

THE 14TH DALAI LAMA, TENZIN GYATSO

The 14th Dalai Lama, Tenzin Gyatso, born to a peasant family in Takster, Tibet, in 1935, was recognized at the age of two as the reincarnation of his predecessor, the 13th Dalai Lama. In the Buddhist faith, Dalai Lamas (the name means "Oceans of Wisdom") are believed to be manifestations

Tenzin Gyatso, 14th Dalai Lama, speaking in Seattle in April 2008, in advance of the Beijing Olympics, on peoples' right to peaceful demonstration.

of the Bodhisattva of Compassion, who chose to reincarnate to serve the people. His monastic education began at six and culminated in a Doctorate of Buddhist Philosophy awarded when he was twenty-five. His political education took place concurrently, for in 1950 he assumed full power as Head of State and Government when Tibet's autonomy was threatened by Communist China. His meetings with Mao Tse-Tung and Chou En-Lai were in vain, for in 1959 he was forced into exile in India by the Chinese military occupation of Tibet—events depicted in the popular film *Kundun* (meaning "The Presence").

Since then the Dalai Lama has conducted the Tibetan government-in-exile from Dharamsala, India, and—unlike many of his predecessors—traveled worldwide on diplomatic missions, in part aiming to preserve the integrity of the Tibetan national identity and cultural heritage. He proposed to the Congressional Human Rights Caucus in 1987 a Five-Point Peace Plan designed to ensure the integrity of Tibet: (1) designate Tibet as a zone of peace, (2) end the massive transfer of ethnic Chinese into Tibet, (3) restore to Tibet fundamental human rights and democratic freedoms, (4) abandon China's use of Tibet to produce nuclear weapons and as a dumping ground for nuclear waste, and (5) create a self-governing Tibet, in association with the People's Republic of China. The Tibetan people themselves, insists His Holiness, "must be the ultimate deciding authority." It was because of these "constructive and forward-looking proposals for the solution of international conflicts, human rights issues, and global environmental problems" that the 14th Dalai Lama was awarded the Nobel Peace Prize for 1989. Although none of these proposals has come to pass, the Dalai Lama remains a revered spiritual leader, internationally respected except by the government of the People's Republic of China.

Inner Peace and Human Rights (1989)

Peace, in the sense of the absence of war, is of little value to someone 1
who is dying of hunger or cold. It will not remove the pain of torture inflicted on a prisoner of conscience. It does not comfort those who have lost their loved ones in floods caused by senseless deforestation in a neighbouring country. Peace can only last where human rights are respected, where the people are fed, and where individuals and nations are free. True peace with oneself and with the world around us can only be achieved through the development of mental peace. The other phenomena mentioned above are similarly interrelated. Thus, for example, we see that a clean environment, wealth or democracy mean little in the face of war, especially nuclear war, and that material development is not sufficient to ensure human happiness.

Material progress is of course important for human advancement. 2
In Tibet, we paid much too little attention to technological and economic development, and today we realise that this was a mistake. At the same time, material development without spiritual development can also cause serious problems. In some countries too much attention is paid to external things and very little importance is given to inner development. I believe both are important and must be developed side by side so as to achieve a good balance between them. Tibetans are always described by foreign visitors as being a happy, jovial people. This is part of our national character, formed by cultural and religious values that stress the importance of mental peace through the generation of love and kindness to all other living sentient beings, both human and animal. Inner peace is the key: if you have inner peace, the external problems do not affect your deep sense of peace and tranquility. In that state of mind you can deal with situations with calmness and reason, while keeping your inner happiness. That is very important. Without this inner peace, no matter how comfortable your life is materially, you may still be worried, disturbed or unhappy because of circumstances.

Clearly, it is of great importance, therefore, to understand the inter- 3
relationship among these and other phenomena, and to approach and attempt to solve problems in a balanced way that takes these different aspects into consideration. Of course it is not easy. But it is of little benefit to try to solve one problem if doing so creates an equally serious new one. So really we have no alternative: we must develop a sense of universal responsibility not only in the geographic sense, but also in respect to the different issues that confront our planet.

Responsibility does not only lie with the leaders of our countries 4
or with those who have been appointed or elected to do a particular job. It lies with each one of us individually. Peace, for example, starts with each one of us. When we have inner peace, we can be at peace with those around us. When our community is in a state of peace, it can share that

peace with neighbouring communities, and so on. When we feel love and kindness towards others, it not only makes others feel loved and cared for, but it helps us also to develop inner happiness and peace. And there are ways in which we can consciously work to develop feelings of love and kindness. For some of us, the most effective way to do so is through religious practice. For others it may be non-religious practices. What is important is that we each make a sincere effort to take our responsibility for each other and for the natural environment we live in seriously.

5 I am very encouraged by the developments which are taking place around us. After the young people of many countries, particularly in northern Europe, have repeatedly called for an end to the dangerous destruction of the environment which was being conducted in the name of economic development, the world's political leaders are now starting to take meaningful steps to address this problem. The report to the United Nations Secretary-General by the World Commission on the Environment and Development (the Brundtland Report) was an important step in educating governments on the urgency of the issue. Serious efforts to bring peace to war-torn zones and to implement the right to self-determination of some people have resulted in the withdrawal of Soviet troops from Afghanistan and the establishment of independent Namibia. Through persistent nonviolent popular efforts dramatic changes, bringing many countries closer to real democracy, have occurred in many places, from Manila in the Philippines to Berlin in East Germany. With the Cold War era apparently drawing to a close, people everywhere live with renewed hope. Sadly, the courageous efforts of the Chinese people to bring similar change to their country was brutally crushed last June. But their efforts too are a source of hope. The military might has not extinguished the desire for freedom and the determination of the Chinese people to achieve it. I particularly admire the fact that these young people who have been taught that "power grows from the barrel of the gun," chose, instead, to use nonviolence as their weapon.

6 What these positive changes indicate, is that reason, courage, determination, and the inextinguishable desire for freedom can ultimately win. In the struggle between forces of war, violence and oppression on the one hand, and peace, reason and freedom on the other, the latter are gaining the upper hand. This realisation fills us Tibetans with hope that some day we too will once again be free.

7 The awarding of the Nobel Prize to me, a simple monk from faraway Tibet, here in Norway, also fills us Tibetans with hope. It means, despite the fact that we have not drawn attention to our plight by means of violence, we have not been forgotten. It also means that the values we cherish, in particular our respect for all forms of life and the belief in the power of truth, are today recognised and encouraged. It is also a tribute to my mentor, Mahatma Gandhi, whose example is an inspiration to so

many of us. This year's award is an indication that this sense of universal responsibility is developing. I am deeply touched by the sincere concern shown by so many people in this part of the world for the suffering of the people of Tibet. That is a source of hope not only for us Tibetans, but for all oppressed people.

As you know, Tibet has, for forty years, been under foreign occupa- 8
tion. Today, more than a quarter of a million Chinese troops are stationed in Tibet. Some sources estimate the occupation army to be twice this strength. During this time, Tibetans have been deprived of their most basic human rights, including the right to life, movement, speech, worship, only to mention a few. More than one sixth of Tibet's population of six million died as a direct result of the Chinese invasion and occupation. Even before the Cultural Revolution started, many of Tibet's monasteries, temples and historic buildings were destroyed. Almost everything that remained was destroyed during the Cultural Revolution. I do not wish to dwell on this point, which is well documented. What is important to realise, however, is that despite the limited freedom granted after 1979, to rebuild parts of some monasteries and other such tokens of liberalisation, the fundamental human rights of the Tibetan people are still today being systematically violated. In recent months this bad situation has become even worse.

If it were not for our community in exile, so generously sheltered 9
and supported by the government and people of India and helped by organisations and individuals from many parts of the world, our nation would today be little more than a shattered remnant of a people. Our culture, religion and national identity would have been effectively eliminated. As it is, we have built schools and monasteries in exile and have created democratic institutions to serve our people and preserve the seeds of our civilisation. With this experience, we intend to implement full democracy in a future free Tibet. Thus, as we develop our community in exile on modern lines, we also cherish and preserve our own identity and culture and bring hope to millions of our countrymen and -women in Tibet.

The issue of most urgent concern at this time, is the massive influx 10
of Chinese settlers into Tibet. Although in the first decades of occupation a considerable number of Chinese were transferred into the eastern parts of Tibet—in the Tibetan provinces of Amdo (Chinghai) and Kham (most of which has been annexed by neighboring Chinese provinces)—since 1983 an unprecedented number of Chinese have been encouraged by their government to migrate to all parts of Tibet, including central and western Tibet (which the People's Republic of China refers to as the so-called Tibet Autonomous Region). Tibetans are rapidly being reduced to an insignificant minority in their own country. This development, which threatens the very survival of the Tibetan nation, its culture and spiritual heritage, can still be stopped and reversed. But this must be done now, before it is too late.

For Discussion and Writing

Each of the issues identified below is complicated, for matters of war and peace are never simple, never static, particularly when negotiated in an international arena. Most can be seen not just from two points of view, but from many perspectives embedded in the political, economic, religious, ethical, and cultural values of a great variety of individuals, cultures, and countries. In discussing any of the topics identified below, or others stimulated by your reading and thinking, you will find it helpful to talk with your instructor, peers, and to consult reliable outside sources (determined, in part, according to the principles presented in How to Search . . . accessible at the companion website for this text, www.cengage.com/english/bloomEC9e). You will be aiming to write papers informed by accurate information, terms clearly defined, that avoid blanket generalizations and simplistic conclusions.

Rather than trying to cover the gigantic issues embedded in the overall subject, pick a small enough segment of the topic to handle in a well-developed paper. The complex nature of the issues embedded in these subjects—war, peace, maintenance of a healthful productive ecology and environment, national culture, economic survival, values, justice, security, civil liberties, social action, leadership, among others—lends itself to group projects. Each participant could be assigned to research a specific segment of a larger issue and the results could be combined in a co-authored paper. It is advisable, even when discussing issues on which you feel strongly, to avoid either/or thinking, stereotyping, and incendiary language. It is appropriate, however, to build your case on accurate information, principle, and passion—the principles of communication and of life—that have guided the Nobel Prize winners and established exemplary models for nations as well as individual citizens.

Because the events related to world peace and world survival occur in political, economic, and natural milieus that are constantly changing, you will need to update your information before discussing any of the topics or their implications or consequences. Be aware that all of them, like any other source of information on any subject—particularly those as incendiary as ethnic, tribal, religious, or national identity; ecology; global warming—contain opinions and other interpretations of fact that support the author's point of view, just as your own writing does. As every reading in *The Essay Connection* illustrates, every author who writes expresses biases; reliable authors also honor the obligation to be fair.

Ways to Think and Write about the Readings

1. Provide an extended definition of *peace*, using examples from the speeches or lives of two or three of the Nobel Peace Prize recipients and supplemented by your own understanding of the term. Is *peace* a constant term, or one that changes with changing interpretations of current events and past history? Why do war, imprisonment, torture, genocide, segregation, and other forms of evil figure so prominently in the struggle to find and maintain peace?

2. Should our first priority be survival of the planet? What can we do, as individuals, as nations, as international alliances, to promote a return to global health? Your discussion will need to acknowledge highly variable standards of living (and availability of resources) around the world, and competing priorities and agendas for allocations of effort, action, money, and other resources.

3. Is world peace possible? Is long-term prosperity possible without peace? Will our quest involve nation with (or against) nation; culture with (or against) culture; technology, economy, or ideology with (or against) its counterpart?

4. What are—or should be—the highest priorities for our private life in the United States? Security? Freedom? Peace and prosperity? A healthful environment? Truly equal opportunity for all (remember, for instance, that as of 2008 there are 2.3 million Americans in prison)? How do—or should—these coincide with our national priorities?

5. There are infinite possibilities for natural disasters (floods, fires, tornadoes, snowstorms) and terrorist attacks in the future. What changes, specific or vague, will these events make in the ways we live our lives, plan for our futures, look at our environment, our neighbors, our friends—and our enemies?

6. What civil liberties are indispensable to life as guaranteed by the Constitution of the United States? What can we, as individuals and as a nation, do to balance the free and open nature of our hospitable society against needs for protection and security?

7. Is it possible for our country to act unilaterally in attaining any of its aims? To what extent do we live in a world in which the interests of all countries are intimately intertwined? Is it even possible for our country to consider autonomy, in light of its global business interests, dependence on foreign oil, and a host of other products? You might pick a single area—medicine, oil or other natural resources, automobiles, the Internet—and focus your answer on that area.

8. How can we avoid suspicion and paranoia, dividing the world into "us" against "them," and nevertheless be on our guard? Against what must we be on guard?

9. What qualities does it take to become a nationally or internationally distinguished leader? What can the rest of us learn from the experiences of the Nobel Peace Prize winners?

10. What would you personally be willing to sacrifice your time and freedom to attain? Would you lay down your life for a cause? If so, what is that cause and why is it worth this degree of commitment?

Glossary

abstract refers to qualities, ideas, or states of being that exist but that our senses cannot perceive. What we perceive are the concrete by-products of abstract ideas. No single object or action can be labeled *love*, but a warm embrace or a passionate kiss is a visible, concrete token of the abstraction we call "love." In "What Sacagawea Means to Me" (85–87), Sherman Alexie treats Sacagawea as an iconic abstraction of Indian. In many instances abstract words such as *beauty, hatred, stupidity,* or *kindness* are more clearly understood if illustrated with **concrete** examples (*see* **concrete** *and* **general and specific**).

allusion is a writer's reference to a person, place, thing, literary character, photograph, image, or quotation that the reader is expected to recognize. Because the reader supplies the meaning and the original context, such references are economical; writers don't have to explain them. By alluding to a young man as a *Romeo* or *Don Juan,* a writer can present the subject's amorous nature without needing to say more. Visual artists and musicians can make comparable references in their chosen media.

analogy is a comparison made between two things, qualities, or ideas that have certain similarities although the items themselves may be very different. For example, Scott Russell Sanders characterizes his alcoholic father, "Like a torture victim who refuses to squeal, he would never admit that he had touched a drop, not even in his last year when he seemed to be dissolving in alcohol before our very eyes" ("Under the Influence: Paying the Price of My Father's Booze" 192–203). The emphasis is on the similarities between Mr. Sanders, drunk or sober, and the torture victim; dissimilarities would have weakened the analogy. **Metaphors** and **similes** are two figures of speech that are based on analogies, and such comparisons are often used in argumentation (*see* **figures of speech** *and* **argument**).

argument, in a specialized literary sense, is a prose summary of the plot, main idea, or subject of a prose or poetic work. For *argumentation,* see introductions to the chapters "Appealing to Reason: Deductive and Inductive Arguments" and "Appealing to Emotion and Ethics."

audience consists of the readers of a given writing. Writers may write some pieces solely for themselves; others for their peers, teachers, or supervisors; others for people with special knowledge of the subject. Writers adapt the level of their language and the details of their presentation to readers of different ages, backgrounds, interests, and education. (See Chapters 1, 2.) Gertrude Stein once observed, "I write for myself and strangers." Writers often aim to convert strangers into friends.

cliché is a commonplace expression that reveals the writer's lack of imagination to use fresher, more vivid language. If a person finds himself *between a rock and a hard place,* he might decide to use a cliché *come hell or high water,* but cliché is *as dead as a doornail.* Its excessive familiarity dulls the reader's responses. Avoid clichés *like the plague.*

coherence indicates an orderly relationship among the parts in a whole essay or other literary work. Writing is coherent when the interconnections among clauses, sentences, and paragraphs are clearly and logically related to the main subject under discussion. The writer may establish and maintain coherence through the use of transitional words or phrases (however; likewise), a consistent point of view, an ordered chronological or spatial presentation of information, appropriate pronoun references for nouns, or strategic repetition of important words or sentence structures.

colloquial expressions (*see* **diction**)

conclusion refers to sentences, paragraphs, or longer sections of an essay that bring the work to a logical or psychologically satisfying end. Although a conclusion may (**a**) summarize or restate the essay's main point, and thereby refresh the reader's memory, it may also end with (**b**) the most important point, or (**c**) a memorable example, anecdote, or quotation, or (**d**) identify the broader implications or ultimate development of the subject, or (**e**) offer a prediction. Stylistically, it's best to end with a bang, not a whimper; Lincoln's "The Gettysburg Address" (519) concludes with the impressive " . . . and that government of the people, by the people, for the people, shall not perish from the earth." A vigorous conclusion grows organically from the material that precedes it and is not simply tacked on to get the essay over with.

concrete terms give readers something specific to see, hear, touch, smell, or feel, while abstract terms are more general and intangible. Writers employ concrete words to show their subject or characters in action, rather than merely to tell about them. Yet a concrete word does not have to be hard, like cement; anything directly perceived by the senses is considered concrete, including an ostrich plume, the sound of a harp, a smile, or a cone of cotton candy (*see* **abstract** *and* **general and specific**).

connotation and denotation refer to two levels of interpreting the meanings of words. Denotation is the literal, explicit "core" meaning—the "dictionary" definition. Connotation refers to additional meanings implied or suggested by the word, or associated with it, depending on the user's or reader's personal experience, attitudes, and cultural conditioning. For example, the word *athlete* denotes a skilled participant in a sport. But to a sports enthusiast, *athlete* is likely to connote, as well, physical qualities, such as robust physical condition and well-coordinated movements. An idealist might also endow athletes with moral qualities, such as a wholesome character, and a concern with fair play. Those disenchanted with sports might regard an *athlete* as a marketable commodity, an overpaid exploiter of the public, a drug user, or someone who has developed every part of his anatomy but his brain—a "dumb jock."

creative nonfiction is writing that employs the techniques of fiction to tell a true story—and which readers regard as true. These techniques include a narrator or narrative voice, plot, characters, dialogue, setting, symbolism; they may be found in autobiography, descriptions of a place or experience, personal-sounding interpretations of phenomena, and social commentary with a human face, a human voice. *See* Amanda Cagle's "On the Banks of the Bogue Chitto" (245–49) and Meredith Hall's "Killing Chickens" (120–23).

diction is word choice. Hemingway was talking about diction when he explained that the reason he allegedly rewrote the last page of *A Farewell to Arms* thirty-nine times was because of problems in "getting the words right." Getting the words right means choosing, arranging, and using words appropriate to the purpose, audience, and sometimes the form of a particular piece of writing. Puns are fine in limericks and shaggy-dog stories ("I wouldn't send a knight out on a dog like this"), but they're out of place in technical reports and obituaries. Diction ranges on a continuum from highly formal (a *repast*) to informal writing and conversation (a *meal*) to slang (*eats*), as illustrated below:

formal English words and grammatical constructions used by educated native speakers of English in sermons, oratory, and in many serious books, scientific reports, and lectures. *See* Abraham Lincoln, "The Gettysburg Address" (519).

informal (conversational or colloquial) *English* the more relaxed but still standard usage in polite (but not stuffy) conversation or writing, as in much popular newspaper writing and in many of the essays in this book. In informal writing it's all right to use contractions ("I'll go to the wedding, but I won't wear tails") and some abbreviations, but not all. OK is generally acceptable in conversation, but it's not OK in most formal or informal writing.

slang highly informal (often figurative) word choice in speech or writing. It may be used by specialized groups (*pot, grass, uppers*) or more general speakers to add vividness and humor (often derogatory) to their language. Although some slang is old and sometimes even becomes respectable (*cab*), it often erupts quickly into the language and just as quickly disappears (*twenty-three skidoo*); it's better to avoid all slang than to use outmoded slang.

regionalisms expressions used by people of a certain region of the country, often derived from the native languages of earlier settlers, such as *arroyo* for *deep ditch* used in the Southwest, *frappe* for *milkshake* in New England.

dialect the spoken (and sometimes written) language of a group of people that reflects their social, educational, economic, and geographic status ("My mamma done tole me . . . "). Dialect may include regionalisms. In parts of the Northeast, *youse* is a dialect form of *you*, while its counterpart in the South is *y'all*. Even some educated Southerners say *ain't*, but they don't usually write it except to be humorous.

technical terms (jargon) words used by those in a particular trade, occupation, business, or specialized activity. For example, medical personnel use *stat* (immediately) and *NPO* (nothing by mouth); surfers' vocabularies include *shooting the curl, hotdogging*, and *hang ten; hardware* has different meanings for carpenters and computer users.

emphasis makes the most important ideas, characters, themes, or other elements stand out. The principal ways of achieving emphasis are through the use of the following:

proportion saying more about the major issues and less about the minor ones.

position placing important material in the key spots, the beginning or ends of paragraphs or larger units. Arrangement in climactic order, with the main point of an argument or the funniest joke last, can be particularly effective.

repetition of essential words, phrases, and ideas ("Ask not what your country can do for you; ask what you can do for your country.")

focus pruning of verbal underbrush and unnecessary detail to accentuate the main features.

mechanical devices such as capitalization, underlining (italics), and exclamation points, conveying enthusiasm, excitement, and emphasis, as advertisers and new journalists well know. Tom Wolfe's title *Las Vegas (What?) Las Vegas (Can't Hear You! Too Noisy) Las Vegas*!!!! illustrates this practice, as well as the fact that nothing exceeds like excess.

essay refers to a composition, usually or primarily nonfiction, on a central theme or subject, usually brief and written in prose. As the contents of this book reveal, essays come in varied modes—among them descriptive, narrative, analytic, argumentative—and moods, ranging from humorous to grim, whimsical to bitterly satiric. Essays are sometimes categorized as *formal* or *informal*, depending on the author's content, style, and organization. Formal essays, written in formal language, tend to focus on a single significant idea supported with evidence carefully chosen and arranged, such as Robert Reich's "The Global Elite" (490–98). Informal essays sometimes have a less obvious structure than formal essays; the subject may seem less significant, even ordinary; the manner of presentation casual, personal, or humorous. Yet these distinctions blur. Although Mark Twain's "Uncle John's Farm" (253–59) discusses a personal experience in conversation and humorous language, its apparently ordinary subject: the daily life of a boy, his companions, and his relatives on a Southern farm bursting with abundance and small pleasures, takes on universal, existential significance.

evidence is supporting information that explains or proves a point. General comments or personal opinions that are not substantiated with evidence usually aren't convincing. Skeptical readers require proof. Writers establish credibility by backing general statements with examples, facts, and figures that make evident their knowledge of the subject. We believe what Martin Luther King, Jr., says about racism and segregation in "Letter from Birmingham Jail" (456–70) because his specific examples show that he has experienced these events and has understood their context and implications.

exposition is a mode of discourse that, as its name indicates, exposes information, through explaining, defining, or interpreting its subject. Expository prose is to the realm of writing what the Ford automobile was historically to the auto industry—useful, versatile, accessible to the average person, and heavy duty—for it is the mode of the most research reports, critical analyses, examination answers, case histories, reviews, and term papers. In exposition, writers employ a variety of techniques, such as definition, illustration, classification, comparison and contrast, analogy, and cause-and-effect reasoning. Exposition is not an exclusive mode; it is often blended with **argumentation, description**, and **narration** to provide a more complete or convincing discussion of a subject.

figures of speech are used by writers who want to make their subject unique or memorable through vivid language. Literal language often lacks the connotations of figurative language. Instead of merely conveying information ("The car was messy"), a writer might use a figure of speech to attract attention ("The car was a Dumpster on wheels"). Figures of speech enable the writer to play with words and with the reader's imagination. Some of the most frequently used figures of speech include the following:

metaphor an implied comparison that equates two things or qualities. "No dictionary of synonyms for *drunk* would soften the anguish of watching our prince turn into a frog" (Scott Russell Sanders).

simile a direct comparison; usually with the connecting word *like* or *as*. " . . . inside [the sawed board] there was this smell waiting, as of something freshly baked" (Scott Russell Sanders).

personification humanization of inanimate or nonhuman objects or qualities, as in giving a car, a boat, or a plane a person's name, nickname, or label (The Katz Meow, The Enola Gay).

hyperbole an elaborate exaggeration, often intended to be humorous or ironic. "When I was younger I could remember anything, whether it had happened or not; but my faculties are decaying now, and soon I shall be so I cannot remember any but the things that never happened" (Mark Twain).

understatement a deliberate downplaying of the seriousness of something. As with the *hyperbole*, the antithesis of understatement, this is often done for the sake of humor or irony. [My "Modest Proposal"] is "innocent, cheap, easy, effectual" (Jonathan Swift).

paradox a contradiction that upon closer inspection is actually truthful. ("You never know what you've got until you lose it.")

rhetorical question a question that demands no answer, asked for dramatic impact. In "Letter from Birmingham Jail" (456–70) Martin Luther King, Jr., asks, "Will we be extremists for hate or for love? Will we be extremists for the preservation of injustice or for the extension of justice?"

metonomy the representation of an object, public office, or concept by something associated with it. ("Watergate brought down the White House, as Woodward and Bernstein explain in *All the President's Men*.")

dead metaphor a word or phrase, originally a figure of speech, that through constant use is treated literally (the *arm* of a chair, the *leg* of a table, the *head* of a bed).

focus represents the writer's control and limitation of a subject to a specific aspect or set of features, determined in part by the subject under discussion (*what* the writer is writing about), the audience (to *whom* the writer is writing), and the purpose (*why* the writer is writing). Thus, instead of writing about food in general, someone writing for college students on limited budgets might focus on imaginative but economical meals.

general and specific are the ends of a continuum that designates the relative degree of abstractness or concreteness of a word. General terms identify the class (*house*); specific terms restrict the class by naming its members (a *Georgian mansion*, a *Dutch colonial*, a *brick ranch*). To clarify relationships, words may be arranged in a series from general to specific: writers, twentieth-century authors, Southern novelists, William Faulkner (*see* **abstract** *and* **concrete**).

generalization (*see* **induction and deduction** *and* **logical fallacies**)

illustrations can be visual works—photographs (the photo essay that follows 580), drawings (Linda Villarosa, 250–51), cartoons (Istvan Banyai, 285), graphic narratives (Art Spiegelman, 96–97; Lynda Barry, 376–85; Evan Eisenberg, 486). All make a statement or combination of statements through lines and shapes, colors, light and shadow, presence and absence, that can be "read"—sometimes with the addition of captions, thought balloons, or other language. *See* Scott McCloud "Character Design" (135–42). Verbal illustrations, such as anecdotes, examples, analyses, and statistical evidence can work in similar ways to clarify, describe, explain, or argue.

induction and deduction refer to two different methods of arriving at a conclusion. Inductive reasoning relies on examining specific instances, examples, or facts in an effort to arrive at a general conclusion. Conversely, deductive reasoning involves examining general principles in order to arrive at a specific conclusion; *see* Chapter 10, "Appealing to Reason: Deductive and Inductive Arguments."

introduction is the beginning of a written work that is likely to present the author's subject, focus (perhaps including the thesis), attitude toward it, and possibly the plan for organizing supporting materials. The length of the introduction is usually proportionate to the length of what follows; short essays may be introduced by a sentence or two; a book may require an entire introductory chapter. In any case, an introduction should be sufficiently forceful and interesting to let readers know what is to be discussed and entice them to continue reading. An effective introduction might do one or more of the following:

1. state the thesis or topic;
2. present a controversial or startling focus on the topic;
3. offer a witty or dramatic quotation, statement, metaphor, or analogy;
4. provide background information to help readers understand the subject, its history, or significance;
5. give a compelling anecdote or illustration from real life;
6. refer to an authority on the subject.

irony is a technique that enables the writer to say one thing while meaning another, often with critical intention. Three types of irony are frequently used by writers: *verbal, dramatic*, and *situational*. Verbal irony is expressed with tongue in cheek, often implying the opposite of what is overtly stated. The verbal ironist maintains tight control over tone, counting on the alert reader (or listener) to recognize the discrepancy between words and meaning, as does Jonathan Swift in "A Modest Proposal" (524–30), where deadpan advocacy of cannibalism is really a monstrous proposal. Dramatic irony, found in plays, novels, and other forms of fiction, allows readers to see the wisdom or folly of characters' actions in light of information they have—the ace up their sleeve—that the characters lack. For example, readers know Desdemona is innocent of cheating on her husband, Othello, but his ignorance of the truth and of the behavior of virtuous women leads him to murder her in a jealous rage. Situational irony, life's joke on life, entails opposition between what would ordinarily occur and what actually happens in a particular instance. In O. Henry's "The Gift of the Magi," the husband sells his watch to buy his wife combs for her hair, only to find out she has sold her hair to buy him a watch chain.

jargon (*see* **diction**)

logical fallacies are errors in reasoning and often occur in arguments. *See* "Appealing to Reason: Deductive and Inductive Arguments," introduction (442–47).

metaphor (*see* **figures of speech**)

metonomy (*see* **figures of speech**)

modes of discourse are traditionally identified as narration, description, argumentation, and exposition. In writing they are often intermingled. The *narration* of Frederick Douglass's "Resurrection" (89–93), for instance, involves *description of characters* and settings, an explanation (*exposition*) of their motives, while the expression of its theme serves as an *argument*, direct and indirect. Through its characters, actions, and situations it argues powerfully against slavery.

nonfiction is writing based on fact but shaped by the writer's interpretations, point of view, style, and other literary techniques. Nonfiction writings in essay or book form include interviews, portraits, biographies and autobiographies, travel writings, direct arguments, implied arguments in the form of narratives or satires, investigative reporting, reviews, literary criticism, sports articles, historical accounts, how-to instructions, and scientific and technical reports, among other types. These vary greatly in purpose (to inform, argue, entertain . . .), form, length (from a paragraph to multiple volumes), intended audience (from general readers to specialists), mood (somber to joyous, straightforward to parody), and techniques, including those of fiction—scene setting, characterization, dialogue, and so forth. *The Essay Connection* gives examples of most of these.

non sequitur a conclusion that does not follow logically from the premises. In humorous writing, the *non sequitur* conclusion is illogical, unexpected, and perhaps ridiculous: the resulting surprise startles readers into laughter—as in Roz Chast's dialogue in "Men Are from Belgium, Women Are from New Brunswick" (409).

objective refers to the writer's presentation of material in a personally detached, unemotional way that emphasizes the topic, rather than the author's attitudes or feelings about it as would be the case in a **subjective** presentation. Some process analyses, such as many computer instruction manuals, are written objectively. Many other process writings combine objective information with the author's personal, and somewhat subjective, views on how or why to do something (*see* Chapter 5, "Cause and Effect," with essays by Zitkala-Sa (184–90), Scott Russell Sanders (192–203), Atul Gawande (206–12), William Collins and colleagues (224–26), and Vaclav Havel (227–28)). The more heavily emotional the writing, the more subjective it is.

oxymoron a contradiction in terms, such as "study date" or "airline food."

paradox (*see* **figures of speech**)

paragraph has a number of functions. Newspaper paragraphs, which are usually short and consist of a sentence or two, serve as punctuation—visual units to break up columns for ease of reading. A paragraph in most other prose is usually a single unified group of sentences that explain or illustrate a central idea, whether expressed overtly in a topic sentence, or merely implied. Paragraphs emphasize ideas; each new topic (or sometimes each important subtopic) demands a new paragraph. Short (sometimes even one-sentence) paragraphs can provide transitions from one major area of discussion to another, or indicate a change of speakers in dialogue.

parallelism is the arrangement of two or more equally important ideas in similar grammatical form ("I came, I saw, I conquered"). Not only is it an effective method of presenting more than one thought at a time, it also makes reading more understandable and memorable for the reader because of the almost rhythmic quality it produces. Within a sentence parallel structure can exist between words that are paired ("All work and no play made Jack a candidate for cardiac arrest"), items in a series ("His world revolved around debit, credit, cash flow, and profit"), phrases ("Reading books, preparing reports, and dictating interoffice memos—these were a few of his favorite things"), and clauses ("Most people work only to live; Jack lived only to work"). Parallelism can also be established between sentences in a paragraph and between paragraphs in a longer composition, often through the repetition of key words and phrases, as Lincoln does throughout "The Gettysburg Address" (519).

parallel structure (*see* **parallelism**)

paraphrase is putting someone else's ideas—usually the essential points or illustrations—into your own words, for your own purposes. Although a summary condenses the original material, a paraphrase is a restatement that may be short or as long as the original, even longer. Students writing research papers frequently find that paraphrasing information from their sources eliminates excessive lengthy quotations, and may clarify the originals. Be sure to acknowledge the source of either quoted or paraphrased material to avoid plagiarism.

parody exaggerates the subject matter, philosophy, characters, language, style, or other features of a given author or particular work. Such imitation calls attention to both versions; such scrutiny may show the original to be a masterpiece—or to be in need of improvement. Parody derives much of its humor from the double vision of the subject that writer and readers share, as in Jason Verge's double take on his love affair with the Montreal Canadiens in "The Habs" (107–11) or Alexander J. G. Schneider's awareness of and commentary on potential peer responses in "What I Really Wanted to Write in My Admissions Essays" (66–68).

person is a grammatical distinction made between the speaker (first person—*I, we*), the one spoken to (second person—*you*), and the one spoken about (third person—*he, she, it, they*). In an essay or fictional work the point of view is often identified by person. Eric Liu's "Notes of a Native Speaker" (589–99) is written in the first person, while Robert Reich's "The Global Elite" (490–98) is a third-person work (*see* **point of view**).

persona, literally a "mask," is a fictitious mouthpiece or an alter ego character devised by a writer for the purpose of telling a story or making comments that may or may not reflect the author's feelings and attitudes. The persona may be a narrator, as in Swift's "A Modest Proposal" (524–30), whose ostensibly humanitarian perspective advocates cannibalism and regards the poor as objects to be exploited. Swift as author emphatically rejects these views. In such cases the persona functions as a disguise for the highly critical author.

personification (*see* **figures of speech**)

plot is the cause-and-effect relationship among events that tell a story. Unlike narration, which is an ordering of events as they occur, a plot is a writer's plan for showing how the occurrence of these events actually brings about a certain effect. The plot lets the reader see how actions and events are integral parts of something much larger than themselves. See Tim O'Brien's "How to Tell a True War Story" (77–84).

poetry is a compact literary work of compressed meaning, held together by a dominant metrical and sound pattern, imagery, and sometimes rhyme. It is often sensual (Mary Oliver, 183); evocative (V. Penelope Pelizzon, 346–47); lyrical; or intended to provoke thought (Judith Hall, 557), pleasure (Mary Oliver), or other emotional reactions—including grief (Seamus Heaney, 517); sympathy (Spinner, 300–01), anger, and social protest (Marilyn Nelson, 449).

imagery may include symbols, similes, analogies, and metaphors—all aspects of figurative language whose meaning extends far beyond the literal language and requires the reader to supply many of its connotations. "Our flag," for instance, would mean different flags (or the countries they represent) with different connotations for citizens, friends, and foes of any given nation.

meter is a rhythmic pattern of unaccented [‿] and accented ['] syllables. The number of feet in a line determines the meter.

foot is the rhythmic unit within a line of poetry. Standard poetic feet in English are the: iamb (‿'), trochee ('‿), anapest, (‿‿'), dactyl ('‿‿), and spondee. (").

line The most common lines in English poetry are trimeter (three feet), tetrameter (four feet), pentameter (five feet), and hexameter (six feet). A sentence in poetry doesn't necessarily end at the end of a line; a sentence in poetry, as in prose, stops when the end punctuation—.,!,?— signals its end. Therefore, when you're reading poetry, let the punctuation—not the poem's shape—tell you where to pause.

point of view refers to the position—physical, mental, numerical—a writer takes when presenting information (*point*), and his attitude toward the subject (*view*). A writer sometimes adopts a point of view described as "limited," which restricts the inclusion of thoughts other than the narrator's, as Scott Russell Sanders does in "Under the Influence: Paying the Price of My Father's Booze"

(192–203). Conversely, the "omniscient" point of view allows the writer to know, see, and tell everything, not only about himself, but about others as well, as John Hockenberry does in *Moving Violations* (366–71).

prewriting is a writer's term for thinking about and planning what to say before the pen hits the legal pad. Reading, observing, reminiscing, and fantasizing can all be prewriting activities if they lead to writing something down. The most flexible stage in the writing process, prewriting enables writers to mentally formulate, compose, edit, and discard before they begin the physical act of firing up the computer. Peter Elbow discusses this in *Writing Without Teachers*.

purpose identifies the author's reasons for writing. The purposes of a writing are many and varied. One can write to *clarify an issue for oneself*, or to *obtain self-understanding* ("Why I Like to Eat"). One can write to *tell a story*, to *narrate* ("My 1000-Pound Weight Loss"), or to *analyze a process* (Michael Pollan's "The Meal" 261–68). Writing can explain *cause and effect* (Marion Nestle's, "Eating Made Simple" 270–79); it can also *describe* ("The Perfect Meal"), *define* ("Calories"), or *divide and classify* ("Fast Food, Slow Food, and Food That Just Sits There"). Writing can *illustrate* through examples ("McDonald's as a Symbol of American Culture"), and it can *compare and contrast* people, things, or ideas (Suzanne Britt's "That Lean and Hungry Look" 281–83). Writing can *argue, deductively* or *inductively* (Matt Nocton's "Harvest of Gold, Harvest of Shame" 286–90), sometimes appealing more to emotions than to reason ("Anorexia! Beware!"). Writing can also provide *entertainment*, sometimes through parody or satire.

revise, to revise is to make changes in focus, accommodation of audience, structure or organization, emphasis, development, style, mechanics, and spelling in order to bring the written work closer to one's ideal. For most writers, revising is the essence of writing. Donald M. Murray discusses the revising process in "The Maker's Eye" (58–62).

rhetoric, the art of using language effectively to serve the writer's purpose, originally referred to speech-making. Rhetoric now encompasses composition; its expanded definition includes a host of dynamic relationships between writer (or speaker), text (or message), and readers (or hearers). The information in this book is divided into rhetorical modes, such as exposition, narration, description, and argumentation.

rhetorical question (*see* **figures of speech**)

satire is humorous, witty criticism of people's foolish, thoughtless, or evil behavior. The satirist ridicules some aspect of human nature—or life in general—that should be changed. Depending on the subject and the severity of the author's attack, a satire can be mildly abrasive or ironic, as in Sherman Alexie's "What Sacagawea Means to Me" (85–87) and Evan Eisenberg's "Dialogue Boxes You Should Have Read More Carefully" (486), or viciously scathing, as is Swift in "A Modest Proposal" (524–30). Usually (although not always) the satirist seeks to bring about reform through criticism.

sentence, grammatically defined, is an independent clause containing a subject and verb, and may also include modifiers and related words. *Sentence structure* is another name for *syntax*, the arrangement of individual words in a sentence that shows their relationship to each other. Besides word choice (*diction*), writers pay special attention to the way their chosen words are arranged to form clauses, phrases, entire sentences. A *thesis sentence* (or *statement*) is the main idea in a written work that reflects the author's purpose. Some writings, notably parodies and satires, only imply a thesis; direct arguments frequently provide an explicitly stated thesis, usually near the beginning, and organize subsequent paragraphs around this central thought. A *topic sentence* clearly reflects the major idea and unifying thought of a given paragraph. When it is placed near the beginning of a paragraph, a topic sentence provides the basis for other sentences in the paragraph. When the topic sentence comes at the end of a paragraph or essay, it may function as the conclusion of a logical argument, or the climax of an escalating emotional progression.

short story is a fictional narrative, usually with a *plot* that has a beginning, middle and an end. A story may *emphasize character* or *character development, embody a theme* (Elizabeth Tallent's "No One's a Mystery" 400–02), *explore an idea* (Tim O'Brien's "How to Tell a True War Story" 77–84), or *express an abstract concept.* Readers accept the characters and events as fictional, even if they appear to be slightly changed versions of reality.

simile (*see* **figures of speech**)

style, the manner in which a writer says what s/he wants to say, as the result of the author's *diction* (word choice) and *syntax* (sentence structure), *arrangement of ideas, emphasis,* and *focus.* It is also a reflection of the author's *voice* (personality). Although Ntozake Shange, "What Is It We Really Harvestin' Here?" (158–63) and Matt Nocton, "Harvest of Gold, Harvest of Shame" (286–90) both describe farming, the writers' styles differ considerably.

symbol refers to a person, place, thing, idea, or action that represents something other than itself. A dove, for example, can be a symbol of peace or a peaceable person, or—by extension—an antiwar proponent (even a militant opponent). Sherman Alexie's "What Sacagawea Means to Me" (85–87) uses Sacagawea as a symbol to critique America's exploitation of its Indian population throughout history.

tone, the author's attitude toward a subject being discussed, can be serious (Tannen's "Fast Forward: Technologically Enhanced Aggression" (308–15)), critical (Charles Mann, "Forever Young" (422–33)), or loving (Scott Russell Sanders, "The Inheritance of Tools" (143–50)), among many possibilities. Tone lets readers know how they are expected to react to what the writer is saying.

topic sentence (*see* **sentence**)

transition is the writer's ability to move the reader smoothly along the course of ideas. Abrupt changes in topics confuse the reader, but transitional words and phrases help tie ideas together. Stylistically, transition serves another purpose by adding fullness and body to otherwise short, choppy sentences and paragraphs. Writers use transition to show how ideas, things, and events are arranged chronologically (*first, next, after, finally*), spatially (*here, there, next to, behind*), comparatively (*like, just as, similar to*), causally (*thus, because, therefore*), and in opposition to each other (*unlike, but, contrary to*). Pronouns, connectives, repetition, and parallel sentence structure are other transitional vehicles that move the reader along.

understatement (*see* **figures of speech**)

voice refers to the extent to which the writer's personality is expressed in his or her work. In *personal voice,* the writer appears to be on fairly intimate terms with the audience, referring to herself as "I" and the readers as "you." In *impersonal voice,* the writer may refer to himself as "one" or "we," or try to eliminate personal pronouns when possible. Formal writings, such as speeches, research papers, and sermons, are more likely to use an impersonal voice than are more informal writings, such as personal essays. In grammar, *voice* refers to the form of a verb: *active* ("I *mastered* the computer") or *passive* ("The computer *was mastered* by me").

Credits

AMY TAN, "Mother Tongue" copyright © 1990 by Amy Tan. First appeared in THE THREEPENNY REVIEW. Reprinted by permission of the author and the Sandra Dijkstra Literary Agency.

ELIE WIESEL, "WHY I WRITE" from FROM THE KINGDOM OF MEMORY: Reminiscences by Elie Wiesel. Copyright © 1990 by Elirion Associates, Inc. Appeared in THE NEW YORK TIMES BOOK REVIEW (April 14, 1985). Originally published in CONFRONTING THE HOLOCAUST: The Impact of Elie Wiesel, edited by Alvin Rosenfeld and Irving Greenberg, translated by Rosette C. Lamont (Indiana University Press, 1978). Reprinted by permission of Georges Borchardt, Inc., on behalf of the author.

JOAN DIDION, "LIFE CHANGES FAST" from THE YEAR OF MAGICAL THINKING by Joan Didion, copyright © 2005 by Joan Didion. Used by permission of Alfred A. Knopf, a division of Random House, Inc.

ORHAN PAMUK, "My Father's Suitcase." Excerpt from Nobel lecture for 2006 Nobel Prize in Literature. © The Nobel Foundation 2006. Reprinted with permission.

WILLIAM LEAST HEAT-MOON, "A List of Nothing in Particular" from BLUE HIGHWAYS. Copyright © 1982, 1999 by William Least Heat-Moon. By permission of Little, Brown and Company, Inc.

DONALD MURRAY, "The Maker's Eye: Revising Your Own Manuscripts." Reprinted by permission of the author from READ TO WRITE. Published by Holt, Rinehart & Winston. Copyright © 1986 by Donald M. Murray.

ALEXANDER J. G. SCHNEIDER, "What I Really Wanted to Write in My Admissions Essays," THE CHRONICLE OF HIGHER EDUCATION, April 27, 2007, B29. Reprinted by permission of The Chronicle of Higher Education.

RACHEL TOOR, "Which One of These Essay Questions in the Real Thing?" THE CHRONICLE OF HIGHER EDUCATION, April 27, 2007. Copyright © 2007 by Rachel Toor. Reprinted by permission of the author.

TIM O'BRIEN, Excerpt from "How To Tell a True War Story," from THE THINGS THEY CARRIED by Tim O'Brien. Copyright © 1990 by Tim O'Brien. Reprinted by permission of Houghton Mifflin Harcourt Publishing Company. All rights reserved.

SHERMAN ALEXIE, "What Sacagawea Means to Me," TIME, June 30, 2002. © 2002 TIME Inc. Reprinted by permission.

LINDA HOGAN, "Waking" from BEST AMERICAN SPIRITUAL WRITING 2006. Ed. Philip Zaleski. Houghton Mifflin, 2006, pp. 149–151. Reprinted by permission of Linda Hogan.

ANNE FADIMAN, "Under Water" by Anne Fadiman. Originally appeared in THE NEW YORKER. Copyright © 1999 Anne Fadiman. Reprinted by permission of Lescher & Lescher, Ltd. All rights reserved.

MEREDITH HALL, "Killing Chickens," CREATIVE NONFICTION #18: INTIMATE DETAILS, 2001. Reprinted with permission.

JOSEPH R. DiFRANZA, "Hooked from the First Cigarette," SCIENTIFIC AMERICAN, May 2008. Reprinted with permission. Copyright © 2008 by SCIENTIFIC AMERICAN, Inc. All rights reserved.

SCOTT RUSSELL SANDERS, "The Inheritance of Tools" from THE PARADISE OF BOMBS. Copyright © 1986 by Scott Russell Sanders. First appeared in THE NORTH AMERICAN REVIEW. Reprinted by permission of the author and the author's agent, Virginia Kidd Agency.

NTOZAKE SHANGE, "What Is It We Really Harvestin' Here?" from CREATIVE NONFICTION 9, pp. 6–12. Copyright © 1998 Creative Nonfiction Foundation. Reprinted with permission.

MARY OLIVER, "August" from AMERICAN PRIMITIVE by Mary Oliver. Copyright © 1978, 1979, 1980, 1981, 1982, 1983 by Mary Oliver. By permission of Little, Brown and Co., Inc.

ZITKALA-SA, from THE SCHOOL DAYS OF AN INDIAN GIRL, ATLANTIC MONTHLY, February, 1900. Copyright © 1900 Atlantic Monthly.

SCOTT RUSSELL SANDERS, "Under the Influence: Paying the Price of My Father's Booze." Copyright © 1989 by HARPER'S MAGAZINE. All rights reserved. Reproduced from the November issue by special permission.

ATUL GAWANDE, Excerpt from "On Washing Hands" from BETTER: A Surgeon's Notes on Performance by Atul Gawande. Copyright © 2007 by Atul Gawande. Reprinted by permission of Henry Holt and Company, LLC.

VACLAV HAVEL, "Our Moral Footprint," THE NEW YORK TIMES, September 27, 2007, translated by Gerald Turner. © 2007, THE NEW YORK TIMES. Reprinted by permission.

AMANDA CAGLE, "On the Banks of the Bogue Chitto" from THE ONTARIO REVIEW, Spring 2005. Reprinted by permission of the author.

MICHAEL POLLAN, "The Meal: Fast Food," from THE OMNIVORE'S DILEMMA by Michael Pollan, copyright © 2006 by Michael Pollan. Used by permission of The Penguin Press, a division of Penguin Group (USA) Inc.

SUZANNE BRITT, "That Lean and Hungry Look," NEWSWEEK 1978. Reprinted by permission of the author.

NATALIE ANGIER, "Why Men Don't Last: Self-Destruction as a Way of Life" THE NEW YORK TIMES, February 17, 1999. Copyright © 1999 Natalie Angier. Reprinted by permission of the author.

DEBORAH TANNEN, "Fast Forward: Technologically Enhanced Aggression" from THE ARGUMENT CULTURE by Deborah Tannen, copyright © 1997 by Deborah Tannen. Used by permission of Random House, Inc.

DAVID SEDARIS, "Make That a Double" from ME TALK PRETTY ONE DAY by David Sedaris. Copyright © 2000 by David Sedaris. By permission of Little, Brown and Co., Inc.

RICHARD RODRIGUEZ, "Family Values" by Richard Rodriguez. Copyright © 1992 by Richard Rodriguez. Reprinted by permission of Georges Borchardt, Inc. on behalf of the author.

GELAREH ASAYESH, "Shrouded in Contradiction." Copyright © 2001 by Gelareh Asayesh. First appeared in THE NEW YORK TIMES MAGAZINE, November 2, 2001. Reprinted by permission of the author.

SUMBUL KHAN, "Mirror, Mirror on the Wall, Who's the Fairest of them All?" Copyright © 2002 Sumbu Khan. Reprinted by permission of the author.

V. PENELOPE PELIZZON, "Clever and Poor" from NOSTOS, Ohio University Press. Reprinted with permission of Ohio University Press, Athens, Ohio. www.ohioswallow.com

HOWARD GARDNER, "Who Owns Intelligence?" Copyright © 1999 by Howard Gardner. Reprinted by permission of the author.

BRIAN DOYLE, "Joyas Voladoras," first appeared in THE AMERICAN SCHOLAR, included in BEST AMERICAN ESSAYS, 2005. Reprinted by permission of the author.

ELIZABETH TALLENT, "No One's a Mystery" from TIME WITH CHILDREN, Knopf, 1987. First appeared in THE NEW YORKER. Reprinted by permission of the author.

DEBORAH TANNEN, "Communication Styles" originally published as "Teacher's Classroom Strategies Should Recognize that Men and Women Use Language Differently," THE CHRONICLE OF HIGHER EDUCATION, June 19, 1991. Copyright © 1991 by Deborah Tannen. Reprinted by permission.

SHERRY TURKLE, "How Computers Change the Way We Think," CHRONICLE OF HIGHER EDUCATION 30, January 2004. Reprinted by permission of the author.

BEN STEIN, "Connected, Yes, but Hermetically Sealed" from THE NEW YORK TIMES, August 23, 2008. © 2008 THE NEW YORK TIMES. All rights reserved. Used by permission and protected by the Copyright Laws of the United States. The printing, copying, redistribution, or retransmission of the Material without express written permission is prohibited.

MARILYN NELSON, "Friends in the Klan" from CARVER: A LIFE IN POEMS by Marilyn Nelson. Front Street, an imprint of Boyds Mills Press, Inc. 2001. Reprinted with the permission of Boyds Mills Press, Inc. Copyright © 2001 by Marilyn Nelson.

MARTIN LUTHER KING, JR., "Letter from Birmingham Jail" is reprinted by arrangement with The Heirs to the Estate of Martin Luther King, Jr., c/o Writers House as agent for the proprietor New York, NY. Copyright © 1963 Martin Luther King, Jr., copyright renewed 1991 Coretta Scott King.

ROBERT REICH, "The Global Elite," THE NEW YORK TIMES MAGAZINE, January 20, 1991. © 1991, Robert Reich. Reprinted by permission.

SEAMUS HEANEY, "Horace and the Thunder" Odes 1, 34 from TIMES LITERARY SUPPLEMENT, Jan. 18, 2002. Copyright © 2002 by Seamus Heaney. Reprinted by permission of the author.

PETER SINGER, "The Singer Solution to World Poverty," THE NEW YORK TIMES MAGAZINE, September 5, 1999. Reprinted by permission of the author.

JUDITH HALL, "Perilous Riddle," from THE ATLANTIC MONTHLY, July/August 2007. Copyright © 2007 by Judith Hall. Reprinted by permission of the author.

ERIC LIU, "Notes of a Native Speaker," adapted from THE ACCIDENTAL ASIAN: Notes of a Native Speaker by Eric Liu, copyright © 1998 by Eric Liu. Used by permission of Random House, Inc.

BILL MCKIBBEN, "Designer Genes" from ORION. Reprinted in BEST AMERICAN SPIRITUAL WRITING 2004. Reprinted by permission of the author.

VIRGINIA POSTREL, "The Truth About Beauty." Copyright © 2007 by Virginia Postrel. This article was originally published in the March 2007 ATLANTIC MONTHLY. Reprinted by permission of the author.

MICHAEL J. BUGEJA, "Facing the Facebook," CHRONICLE OF HIGHER EDUCATION, January 27, 2006. Copyright © 2006 by Michael J. Bugeja. Reprinted by permission of the author.

AL GORE, excerpt from 2007 Nobel Peace Prize lecture. © The Nobel Foundation 2007. Reprinted with permission.

WANGARI MAATHAI, "Planting the Seeds of Peace." Excerpt from 2004 Nobel Peace Prize lecture. © The Nobel Foundation 2004. Reprinted with permission.

KOFI ANNAN, "The United States in the 21st Century," from Nobel Prize Speech, 2001. Copyright © The Nobel Foundation. Reprinted with permission.

NELSON MANDELA, "The End of Apartheid" from Nobel Prize Speech, 1993. Copyright © The Nobel Foundation. Reprinted with permission.

FREDERIK WILLEM DE KLERK, "The End of Apartheid" from Nobel Prize Speech, 1993. Copyright © The Nobel Foundation. Reprinted with permission.

AUNG SAN SUU KYI, "The Revolution of Spirit" from Nobel Prize Speech, 1991. Copyright © The Nobel Foundation. Reprinted with permission.

RIGOBERTO MENCHÚ TUM, "Five Hundred Years of Mayan Oppression" from Nobel Prize Speech, 1992. Copyright © The Nobel Foundation. Reprinted with permission.

14TH DALAI LAMA (Tenzin Gyatso), "Inner Peace and Human Rights" from Nobel Prize Speech, 1989. Copyright © The Nobel Foundation. Reprinted with permission.